Africa, I

And the Covid-19 Pandemic:

Mitigation Dynamics and their Implications for Human Rights, Freedoms and Civil Liberties

Editors

Fidelis Peter Thomas Duri,
James Hlongwana
& Munyaradzi Mawere

Langaa

Langaa Research & Publishing CIG
Mankon, Bamenda

Publisher:
Langaa RPCIG
Langaa Research & Publishing Common Initiative Group
P.O. Box 902 Mankon
Bamenda
North West Region
Cameroon
Langaagrp@gmail.com
www.langaa-rpcig.net

Distributed in and outside N. America by African Books Collective
orders@africanbookscollective.com
www.africanbookscollective.com

ISBN-10: 9956-552-47-x

ISBN-13: 978-9956-552-47-4

Notes on the Authors

Fidelis Peter Thomas Duri is a Full Professor of History in the Department of History, Archaeology and Development Studies at Great Zimbabwe University in Zimbabwe. Previously, he had started off his professional career as a History teacher at St David's Girls High School, Bonda, before becoming a History lecturer at Marymount and Mutare Teachers' Colleges, both in Zimbabwe. He was also a part-time lecturer in History and African Studies at Africa University in Zimbabwe during his full-time tenure at Marymount and Mutare Teachers' Colleges. Duri is a holder of a PhD in History from the University of the Witwatersrand in Johannesburg, South Africa (2012), where he was also a part-time History tutor while pursuing his studies. He also holds a Bachelor of Arts Honours degree in African Experience (1986), a Graduate Certificate in Education (1988), and a Master of Arts degree in African History (1999), all from the University of Zimbabwe. He has more than fifty publications, including academic books, book chapters and journal articles which focus on environmental history, socio-cultural dynamics, subaltern struggles, African border studies, and Zimbabwe's socio-economic and political landscape during the colonial and post-colonial periods. Among his most popular and best-selling books are: *The relentless governance by the sword: Situating Operation Murambatsvina in Zimbabwean history* (2010); *Resilience amid adversity: Informal coping mechanisms to the Zimbabwean crisis during the new millennium* (2016); *Contested spaces, restrictive mechanisms and corridors of opportunity: A social history of Zimbabwean borderlands and beyond since the colonial period* (2017); *The end of an era? Robert Mugabe and a conflicting legacy* (2018); *Violence, peace and everyday modes of justice and healing in post-colonial Africa* (2019); *Mugabeism after Mugabe? Rethinking legacies and the new dispensation in Zimbabwe's 'Second Republic'* (2019); *New millennium woes and livelihood struggles in Africa: Begging to survive by Zimbabwe's marginalised* (2021); and *Morgan Richard Tsvangirai's legacy: Opposition politics and the struggle for human rights, democracy and gender sensitivities* (2022). Duri is also reviewer of articles for international academic journals such as *International Migration: A Journal of the International Organisation for Migration; Third World Thematics*; and *Dzimbahwe: Journal of Humanities and Social Sciences.* In addition to reviewing scholarly articles of many local and international journals, he is also a member of the editorial boards of the *Zimbabwe Journal of Historical Studies* and the *International Journal of Developing Societies*. He has also been engaged on a number of occasions by the Zimbabwe Council for Higher Education (ZIMCHE) to review proposed regulations of History degree programmes offered at various Zimbabwean universities.

James Hlongwana is a Senior Lecturer of History in the Department of History, Archaeology and Development Studies at Great Zimbabwe University in Zimbabwe. He is a holder of a PhD in History from the North-West University in South Africa, a Master of Arts degree in History from the Midlands State University in Zimbabwe, a Bachelor of Arts Honours degree from the University of South Africa (UNISA), a Bachelor of Arts General degree from UNISA, and a Diploma in Education from the University of Zimbabwe. Hlongwana has published several peer-reviewed articles in internationally acclaimed journals. His research interests concern conflict and borderland issues. He has presented conference papers in Zimbabwe, South Africa, Finland and Italy.

Munyaradzi Mawere is Professor Extraordinarius of Interdisciplinary Research in the School of Interdisciplinary Research & Graduate Studies at the University of South Africa, and a Full Professor of African Studies and incumbent Research Chair in the Simon Muzenda School of Arts, Culture and Heritage Studies at Great Zimbabwe University in Zimbabwe. Prof Extraord. Mawere holds a PhD in Social Anthropology from the University of Cape Town, South Africa; three Masters Degrees namely: Master of Arts Degree in Social Anthropology (passed with Distinction); Master of Arts Degree in Development Studies (passed with University Book Prize); Master of Arts Degree in Philosophy; a BA (Hons) Degree in Philosophy, and several certificates across disciplines. He is an author and editor of more than 90 books and over 200 book chapters and peer-reviewed academic journals with internationally acclaimed publishers, with a focus on Africa straddling the following areas: poverty and development, African philosophy, society and culture, democracy, human rights, politics of food production, humanitarianism and civil society organisations, indigenous knowledge systems, urban anthropology, existential anthropology, cultural philosophy, environmental anthropology, society and politics, decoloniality and African studies. Professor Extraord. Mawere has also won several prestigious international honours such as the Wenner-Gren Research Fellowship (2011) and the much-coveted Association of African Studies (ASA) Presidential Fellowship Award (2017).

Ngonidzashe Marongwe is an Associate Professor in the History, Archaeology and Development Studies Department at Great Zimbabwe University. He holds a PhD in African History from the University of the Western Cape (UWC), South Africa. He is a past Andrew Mellon Foundation Doctoral Fellow at the Centre for Humanities Research, UWC (2009-2010 & 2012); and a SEPHIS fellow at the Centre for the Study of Culture and Society, Bangalore, India (2011). His research interests include African governance, political violence, gender, military history and terrorism. Marongwe has edited several books such as *Myths of peace and democracy: Towards building pillars of hope, unity and transformation in Africa* (2016); *Violence, politics and conflict management in Africa: Envisioning transformation, peace and unity in the twenty-first century* (2016); *Contested spaces, restrictive mechanisms and corridors of opportunity: A social history of Zimbabwean borderlands and beyond since the colonial period* (2018); *End of an era? Robert Mugabe and a conflicting legacy* (2018); and *Violence, peace and everyday modes of justice and healing in post-colonial Africa* (2019).

Nancy Mazuru is a lecturer in the Department of History, Archaeology and Development Studies at Great Zimbabwe University. She holds a PhD in Development Studies from the University of the Witwatersrand, Johannesburg, in South Africa; and a Master of Science degree in Development Studies from the Women's University in Africa in Zimbabwe.

Takavafira Masarira Zhou is an environmental historian, trade unionist and human rights defender. He is a holder of the following qualifications: Bachelor of Arts General, Bachelor of Arts Special Honours in History, Master of Arts in African History, Graduate Certificate in Education, and D.Phil. in Environmental History, all from the University of Zimbabwe. He was a Teaching Assistant in the History Department at the University of Zimbabwe (1991-1995), a History Lecturer at Mutare Teachers' College (2002-2004), and a part time History Lecturer at Africa University (2002-2004). As a History Lecturer at Great Zimbabwe University (2004-2008), he helped to transform the History subject area into the Department of History and Development Studies. He was a technical advisor (researcher) in the Zimbabwe Constitution Select Committee (2010-2011) that produced Zimbabwe's new Constitution in 2013. He was also a member of the National Education Advisory Board (2009-2013) that, among other things, helped the then Ministry of Education, Sports, Arts and Culture in strategic planning, resource mobilisation and policy formulation during the period of the Inclusive Government. Currently, Zhou is the President of the Progressive Teachers' Union of Zimbabwe, and Treasurer of the Non-Aligned Teachers' Unions of Southern Africa (ANTUSA). He has presented various papers at conferences in Zimbabwe, Africa, Europe and Asia. He has also published on African agriculture; white settler farming; environmental impact of mining in Zimbabwe; peace and security in Africa; History curricula changes in Zimbabwe; post-2016 Africa's development; teacher education; poverty, natural resources and underdevelopment in Africa; conflict and vulnerability in Africa; partition and impact of borders on African societies in colonial Zimbabwe; climate/environmental change in Africa, and general history and politics of Zimbabwe.

David Tobias is a Senior Lecturer of History in the Department of History, Archaeology and Development Studies at Great Zimbabwe University. He holds Master of Arts degree in History from Midlands State University in Zimbabwe. He is a PhD candidate registered with Great Zimbabwe University. He has published a number of articles and book chapters on land, elections in Africa, economic sanctions, human rights and democracy.

Tasara Muguti is a Senior Lecturer in the History, Archaeology and Development Studies Department at Great Zimbabwe University. He holds a Bachelor of Arts Honours degree in Economic History, a Master of Arts in African Economic History and a Graduate Certificate in Education, all obtained from the University of Zimbabwe. He is currently a registered PhD student with the University of South Africa (UNISA). He has several published book chapters and journal articles to his credit. His research interests are in Indigenous Knowledge Systems with special emphasis on African traditional medicine, land reform, human rights, democracy and many other topical issues on contemporary Southern African history.

Terence Tapiwa Muzorewa holds a PhD in Development Studies and is a Lecturer at the Midlands State University's Department of

Development Studies. Muzorewa has broad research interests in sustainable development, housing cooperatives, land and the economic history of rural and urban development. He has written and co-authored works including refereed journal publications on development issues in Zimbabwe. Muzorewa is a member of professional organisations which include the Zimbabwe Historical Association (ZHA) and Young Scholar Initiative (YSI).

Benice Farai Nkomo passed on 9 June 2022 while this book was undergoing review in preparation for publication. The late Nkomo was a holder of a Master of Arts degree in African History from the University of Zimbabwe. At the time of his death, Nkomo was a Lecturer in the Department of History, Heritage and International Studies at the Midlands State University, Zimbabwe. His lifelong academic, research and teaching interests included colonial and post-colonial socio-political developments, gender and human rights in Zimbabwe, and peace and conflict in Africa. May the soul of Benice Farai Nkomo rest in eternal peace.

Golden Maunganidze is a Lecturer in the Department of English and Media Studies at Great Zimbabwe University. He holds a Master of Arts degree in Media and Society Studies from Midlands State University in Zimbabwe. He also holds various mid-carrier journalism certificates from the International Institute of Journalism in Berlin, Germany. Maunganidze is a distinguished media practitioner. He is the founding and current Director of Great Zimbabwe University's Campus Radio, Zimbabwe's first university-run radio station. He has over 15 years of experience working in the Zimbabwean media industry. He worked as a journalist and editor with *The Masvingo Mirror* newspaper before establishing his own community newspaper, *TellZim News*, in 2015. He is also the national (Zimbabwe) and regional (Southern African Development Community) Board Chairperson for the Media Institute of Southern Africa (MISA). Maunganidze is a recipient of two prestigious American fellowship awards, namely the International Visitors Leadership Program (IVLP) Edward R. Murrow Fellow for Journalists (2011) as well as the 2016 Young African Leadership Initiative (YALI) under the Mandela-Washington Fellowship. He is also a receiver of other awards that include the UNICEF and Transparency International National Integrity Award for the Child Reporter of the year 2009.

Mudadirwa Mujuru is currently a part-time lecturer at the Catholic University of Zimbabwe since 2014. He has had a long history as a teacher and lecturer in Zimbabwe which started off with him teaching English and Political Economy at Charles Clack Secondary School. In 1996, he joined Mutare Teachers' College as a lecturer of Philosophy of Education. He was also a lecturer of Philosophy of Education and Curriculum Issues at the Africa University, initially on a part-time basis, and later as a full-time lecturer until 2004 when he retired on medical grounds. From 2007 to 2008, he was a lecturer of Philosophy of Technology Education at Chinhoyi University of Technology in Zimbabwe. Mujuru is a holder of a Master of Arts degree in Philosophy, Bachelor of Arts Honours degree in Philosophy, and a Graduate Certificate of Education (all from the University of Zimbabwe) as well as a Diploma in Philosophy from the Chishawasha Roman Catholic Seminary in Zimbabwe.

Innocent Rupoterera Madenga is presently a lecturer of various conflict transformation-related modules at the Bindura University of Science Education in Zimbabwe. He holds a PhD in Public Management and Peace Building from the Durban University of Technology, South Africa. He is also a holder of a Master of Science degree in Peace, Leadership and Governance from Africa University (Zimbabwe); a Master of Arts degree in African History, Bachelor of Arts Honours degree in History and a Graduate Certificate in Education, both from the University of Zimbabwe. Madenga's research interests lie in community-based challenges and initiatives as well as life-threatening and life-changing dynamics in the contemporary world.

Trust Makwinja Asima is a lecturer in the Department of History, Archaeology and Development Studies at Great Zimbabwe University. He is a holder of a Master of Arts degree in Development Studies, a Bachelor of Arts Honours degree in Economic History and a Post-Graduate Diploma in Higher and Tertiary Education, both from Great Zimbabwe University. He is currently a Development Studies PhD candidate at Great Zimbabwe University.

Lisa Mubaiwa is currently studying for a Master of Arts Degree in Development Studies at Great Zimbabwe University. She is a holder of a Bachelor of Arts Honours degree in Development Studies from Great Zimbabwe University. Presently employed as an Administrator at the Farm and City Centre in the city of Masvingo, Zimbabwe, Mubaiwa has keen research interests in topical issues such as peace, conflict, governance and gender dynamics.

Peter Machenjera is a holder of a Master of Arts degree in African History from the Midlands State University (MSU) in Zimbabwe. He also holds a Bachelor of Arts Fourth-Year Honours degree in History, a Bachelor of Arts General degree in History and Geography from Great Zimbabwe University (GZU), and a Post-Graduate Diploma in Education (PGDE) from the Zimbabwe Open University (ZOU). He is currently employed as a History teacher, and Head of the Humanities Department at Mazungunye Government High School under the Ministry of Primary and Secondary Education in Zimbabwe. Machenjera is also the incumbent Secretary for Information and Publicity of the Progressive Teachers' Union of Zimbabwe (PTUZ). He is interested in history-related research, especially environmental issues, labour dynamics, governance, poverty and development, among other contemporary topical issues. He has co-authored published book chapters and has made presentations at national and regional conferences.

Cuthbert Mavedzenge is a Roman Catholic priest in the Diocese of Masvingo, Zimbabwe. He is a holder of a Master of Arts degree in Development Studies from the Great Zimbabwe University. He also holds a Bachelor of Theology Honours degree from the Catholic University in Zimbabwe. Reverend Father Mavedzenge has diplomas in Philosophy (University of Zimbabwe), Religious Studies (University of Zimbabwe) and Theology (Chishawasha Seminary, Zimbabwe). He also has certificates from St. Augustine's Regional Seminary, Zimbabwe, in Seminary Formation and Computer Courses.

Costain Tandi is a Senior lecturer at Gweru Teachers' College in Zimbabwe. Prior to his current position, Tandi was a Graduate teacher of Advanced Level History and Sociology as well as Head of Department (Humanities) at Rufaro High School in Chatsworth, Zimbabwe. He is a holder of a Master of Arts degree in Development Studies from Midlands State University in Zimbabwe; Bachelor of Arts Fourth-Year Honours degree in History from Great Zimbabwe University; Bachelor of Arts General degree from the University of Zimbabwe; Graduate Certificate in Education from Great Zimbabwe

University; Executive Certificate in Project and Programme Monitoring and Evaluation from the University of Zimbabwe; and an Executive Certificate in Project Management from the University of Zimbabwe. With a number of publications to his credit, Tandi's research interests include, but not limited to, Indigenous Knowledge Systems, Climate Change and Variability, Rural Poverty, Human Rights, Agriculture and Community Development.

Constance Makuvise is a Project Field Officer at Care International-Zimbabwe, a non-governmental organisation, based in the Buhera District of Manicaland Province in Zimbabwe. She holds a Bachelor of Social Science Honours degree in Sociology from Great Zimbabwe University. She is currently pursuing a Master of Arts Degree in Development Studies at Great Zimbabwe University. Her research interests concern gender, livelihoods, and human rights.

Nicholas Govo is a lecturer in the Department of History, Heritage and International Studies at Midlands State University (MSU), Zimbabwe. He is a holder of a Bachelor of Arts General degree and a Bachelor of Arts Fourth Year Honours degree in History, both from Great Zimbabwe University; and a Master of Arts in African Studies from the University of Venda, South Africa. He is currently studying for a DPhil in History with the MSU. Govo has keen research interests in understanding the relationship between the state and traditional leaders in Zimbabwe, human rights, democracy, constitutionalism, leadership renewal, and electoral political transitioning in Africa.

Table of Contents

Chapter 1

Africa's Two Pandemics in the Name of Covid-19 and Human Rights Abuses

Fidelis Peter Thomas Duri James Hlongwana & Munyaradzi Mawere

Introduction

The beginning of the year 2020 saw the whole world being besieged by one of the most serious threats to human existence in the form of the Covid-19 pandemic. The pandemic rapidly spread across the globe like a veldfire, killing millions of people and instilling great fear and uncertainty in many survivors. Covid-19 (also known as the new Corona virus), became a pandemic of global dimensions with some analysts labelling it "the Third World War" (Martel, 14 April 2020). It was indeed a war as people grappled with infections, casualties, human rights abuses, and subsequent socio-economic hardships while governments battled to contain the spread of the pandemic, often clashing with citizens in the process.

Corona viruses are a broad category of several viruses, some of which cause common colds in human beings while others infect animals, including cattle, camels and bats (WebMD, August 2021). Research into the virus that was to be called Corona in the mid-1960s began in 1931 when it was discovered in animals by Schalk and Hawn (Aronson, 19 July 2020). In 1965, two scientists, David Tyrrell and Mark Bynoe (Aronson, 19 July 2020; Kahm and McIntosh, 2005), were the first to identify a human Corona virus which caused a common cold (WebMD, August 2021). Later during the decade, Tyrrell and a group of virologists found a group of similar human and animal viruses and named them 'Corona' since the surface projections of the virus appeared like those of a crown (Kahm and McIntosh, 2005; WebMD, August 2021).

Covid-19 was first reported in Wuhan City, China, in December 2019 (Odigbo *et al*, 2020). On 31 December 2019, Chinese authorities alerted the World Health Organisation about the outbreak of pneumonia cases, whose cause was not yet known, in Wuhan City in the country's Hubei Province. This mystery ailment was first referred to as 2019-nCoV and later renamed Covid-19 (Ravelo & Jerving, 31 December 2019). By mid-December 2020, according to the World Health Organisation (WHO), more than 68 million people had been infected with the virus while more than 1.5 million people had died (Muchena, 14 December 2020).

On 11 March 2020, as the virus spread across the world at an alarming rate, the World Health Organisation declared Covid-19 a global pandemic and requested governments across the world to put in place a raft of measures to contain it (Moyo & Phulu, 2021; Odigbo *et al,* 2020). The WHO declaration saw many governments around the world instituting securitised Covid-19 containment measures, most of which suspended constitutional processes through states of emergency (Moyo & Phulu, 2021). In many countries, the authorities restricted air, sea and land travel; isolated immigrants and returning citizens; ordered people to stay at home; imposed curfews; and locked down public places, educational institutions, services deemed non-essential as well as religious, sports and recreation centres (Ibid).

As highlighted above, the Corona virus pandemic proved to be not only a threat to human existence, but also to global economies, human freedoms and liberties. Indeed, a number of texts on Covid-19 have so far been written, most of which focus on the general challenges, opportunities and the future of global economies in the wake of Covid-19. Other texts have looked at Covid-19 from a multi-disciplinary perspective. So far, much of the academic literature hardly focuses exclusively and comprehensively on Covid-19 from a legal, democratic and human rights perspective, which makes this volume a timely and worthwhile text.

Covid-19 and discourses of human rights and civil liberties

It is prudent from the onset to get a clear understanding of the concepts of human rights and civil liberties. The Institutional Research Information Services Solution (2007: 1) provides insightful definitions of human rights and civil liberties and the technical distinction and connectedness between them:

> Human rights are those rights derived from natural law, regardless of local legal jurisdiction. They might include the right to life; freedom from torture; freedom from slavery; the right to move about freely; the right to food and shelter. Essentially, they are the rights that any human being should have in order to survive in the world. On a more basic

level, if someone is deprived of these rights, he or she may be deprived of the capacity to survive.

Civil liberties are those rights which are derived from the positive law, for example, legal statutes. They are rights which the state has contracted with its citizens and they are state-made or state-enforced rights - in other words, political rights. Examples might be the right to free elections (based on the idea of democracy); the right to vote; the right to silence; the right to a fair hearing. They are based on the western notion of democracy, but things are done differently in different democracies… So, in fact, civil liberties are contextual in that they reflect the society in which they are found.

The two concepts are inextricably linked. For example, if you are denied a fair trial by an independent, impartial tribunal, you are denied your civil rights as guaranteed by the state. If you are denied freedom of movement, you are being denied your civil as well as your human rights. Rights can also be categorised as: civil and political rights (those promised under the law and the constitution) and social and welfare rights (reflected in rising expectations of human beings).

While the world at large and Africa in particular were preoccupied with combatting the Covid-19 pandemic, the issue of human rights and civil rights in the context of this struggle increasingly came under close scrutiny. As Muchena (14 December 2020: 1) rightly observed: "While the world's attention has focused on the Covid-19 pandemic, there has been another pandemic that has spread in its shadow - human rights violations." Antonio Guterres, the Secretary General of the United Nations (22 February 2021) reverberated that owing to the Covid-19 pandemic, "our world is facing a pandemic of human rights abuses."

It should be noted that Covid-19 lockdown and quarantine provisions imposed by governments generally violated many clauses in the United Nations Universal Declaration of Human Rights adopted in 1948 such as liberty; and freedoms of movement, religion, peaceful assembly and association, and the right to education, work and protection against unemployment (Delvac, 25 May 2020). We acknowledge that governments can justifiably suspend some rights and freedoms for the common/public good or in the interest of the country when the nation is at risk. It is, however, crucial to note that *national* governments were obliged to justify the suspensions on a legal basis as strictly necessary (Odigbo *et al*, 2020). Furthermore, citizens had the right to be informed about the extent to which some rights and freedoms were compromised and/or suspended, as well as the timeframe in order to guard against excesses, abuses and prejudices (Ibid).

As far as the rights of women and girl children were concerned, stay-at-home orders in the form of nationwide lockdowns and curfews imposed by governments to curtail the spread of the virus meant that many women and girls were unable to escape from abusive partners and family members resulting in some of them being abused or even killed (Dersso, 9 September 2020; Muchena, 14 December 2020; Segun, 18 January 2021). Some women were also sexually abused by law-enforcement agents during Covid-19 containment operations. In Rwanda, for instance, five soldiers were charged in court in May 2020 for raping women under the pretext of enforcing the lockdown (Kuteesa, 2020). Thus, gender-based violence became a very topical issue in human rights debates during the Covid-19 period.

The rights [human] of men and the boy children were neither spared, as they endured beatings from law-enforcement agents who solely had the freedom to move around in the name of enforcing Covid-19 containment measures. In Zimbabwe, as elsewhere in Africa and beyond, most of the men who braved the curfew and other restrictions due to the urgent need to fend for their families suffered severe beatings and sometimes shootings. Some, even lost their lives from the brutalities perpetrated by the law-enforcement agents. It is in fact quite apparent that in many African countries, Covid-19 containment measures were "marred by abuse of power" (Sabiti, 19 April 2021; 1). The pandemic came as a blessing in disguise for some African dictators who utilised the subsequent lockdowns to "narrow the democratic space and muzzle political opponents" (Ibid) in an opportunistic attempt to "solidify autocracy" (Molloy, 1 May 2020: 1). In countries such as Egypt, Ethiopia, Niger and Nigeria, just to mention a few, the states of emergency imposed to control the pandemic were "repurposed for numerous agendas, including increasing social and political control of the population beyond public health concerns" (Moyo & Phulu, 2021: 50). Many African governments became accustomed to the "use of the disease as a pretext to curtail democratic freedoms and punish opposition" (Rivers & Ndlovu, 24 June 2020: 1). The political rights of many opposition political parties were often infringed. In a number of cases, the freedoms of assembly and movement suspended under lockdown regulations were manipulated and weaponised to limit the political space of opposition parties. Tanzania, for example, witnessed these experiences in 2020 (Muchena, 14 December 2020).

In some countries, Covid-19 related restrictions were capitalised to subvert electoral processes. In Zimbabwe during 2020, for example, by-elections were suspended citing Covid-19 fears in local government wards and parliamentary constituencies known to be strongholds of opposition parties thereby denying significant sections of the electorate political representation. In Ethiopia, Prime Minister Ahmed Abiy declared a state of emergency and indefinitely deferred the much-awaited August 2020 elections citing the Corona virus, much to the chagrin of many opposition political parties (Olewe, 9 April 2020). The hidden political hand in such restrictions was unmasked by examples of other African countries that successfully conducted national elections during the same Covid-19 period such as Malawi and Zambia in 2020 and 2021, respectively. Furthermore, some governments "weaponised the pandemic to quell popular protests and harass opposition politicians and their supporters," with Tanzania and Uganda being notable examples (Segun, 18 January 2021: 1).

Some governments tightened censorship rules to ensure considerable control over the content published by the local and foreign media thereby interfering with the right to freedom of expression (Muchena, 14 December 2020). In Zambia in 2020, for example, "the government's decision to suspend the license of a television station that criticised the government's handling of Covid-19 led to protests" (Okech, 2020: 551). In Tanzania, in 2020, the Communication Regulatory Authority (TCRA) imposed heavy fines on three television stations for broadcasting content that was said to be "misleading and untrue" about the government's strategy of combating Covid-19. The TCRA did not give details, but speculation was that it took great exception to a report which criticised the then President John Magufuli for declaring that churches should not be closed because "Corona virus cannot survive in a church" (Olewe, 9 April 2020). In Uganda in early 2020, 10 journalists covering the impact of that country's lockdown were severely assaulted by security officers (Ibid). Other African countries that gained notoriety for restricting and suppressing information during the Covid-19 period are Morocco, Ghana and Guinea-Bissau (Cascais, 2020).

The movement of independent journalists was sometimes restricted while some were arrested for breaching lockdown travel and curfew restrictions. On the contrary, journalists from the state media and others belonging to institutions sympathetic to incumbent governments were not subjected to the same treatment. On 24 June 2020, for instance, two freelance journalists who had just left their office in Harare's Warren Park 1 Suburb were severely beaten by security forces with truncheons and whips for violating the curfew restrictions despite having identified themselves as journalists by producing their press cards (International Federation of Journalists, 30 June 2020). A Human Rights Watch report published on 11 February 2021 narrated how more than 20 African governments, including Zimbabwe, were using the Covid-19 pandemic to suppress media freedom (Mavhunga, 11 February 2021).

In a number of cases, states of emergency instituted by African governments to control the spread of Covid-19 were used as cover for gross human rights abuses. As Molloy (1 May 2020: 1) avers: "Countries under states of emergency can be breeding grounds for human rights infringements." In Africa, as was the case in many other parts of the world, cases abound of peaceful anti-government demonstrations against deteriorating livelihoods and other genuine grievances that were banned or violently supressed using Covid-19 lockdown emergency regulations, a clear manifestation of how the pandemic "offers new opportunities for repression" (Rivers & Ndlovu, 24 June 2020: 1). In addition, the army and police details deployed to enforce Covid-19 preventive measures reportedly used excessive and unlawful force on civilians resulting in serious injuries (Dersso, 9 September 2020; Muchena, 14 December 2020). More often than not, soldiers and police details enforcing Covid-19 restrictions appeared "motivated by a desire to instil fear rather than to protect citizens from the potentially deadly virus" (Rivers & Ndlovu, 24 June 2020: 1). In countries such as Angola, Kenya, Nigeria, Rwanda and South Africa, arbitrary arrests, beatings and torture were quite common (Segun, 18 January 2021). This is in spite of the fact that Article 5 of the United Nations Universal Declaration of Human Rights stipulates that there is no excuse whatsoever for subjecting someone to torture or to cruel, inhumane, or degrading treatment or punishment (Delvac, 25 May 2020). In addition, Article 9 of the declaration specifically protects citizens from arbitrary arrests and detentions (Odigbo *et al*, 2020).

Extrajudicial killings were reported in many African countries as overzealous soldiers and police details enforced Covid-19 restrictions. Within just two weeks after the imposition of a lockdown in Nigeria, for example, the security forces who were enforcing it shot dead 18 people while Covid-19 killed only 12 people within the same period (Odigbo *et al*, 2020), which means security forces were more deadly than the virus itself. In Kenya, there were reports that six people were killed by the police during the first days of the Covid-19 dusk-to-dawn curfew imposed in that country (Ibid). As Dickens Olewe (9 April 2020: 1), a *British Broadcasting Corporation News* correspondent, lamented:

> Armed variously with guns, whips and tear gas canisters, security officers in several African countries have been beating, harassing and, in some cases, killing people as they enforce measures aimed at preventing the spread of Covid-19. The actions of the police and military are at the sharp end of a debate over the balance between personal freedoms and human rights on the one hand, and the need to protect society as a whole from Corona virus on the other…Rights groups have warned that if they are not reversed once the crisis is over, then these new measures could undermine basic freedoms. The authorities say the lockdowns, curfews, and other crowd control measures are aimed at saving lives, but overzealous enforcement has cost lives.

Given that many people in Africa earn livelihoods from the informal sector, national lockdowns and travel restrictions imposed by African governments had devastating effects on their livelihoods. In 2018, for instance, informal sector employment in Africa accounted for 76% of the labour market in the urban areas and 88% in the rural areas (International Labour Organisation, 2018: 30). Informal sector employment also accounted for 79% of the source of employment for women, which far exceeded that for men at 68% (Ibid). In many countries, the informal sector was closed after being classified as a non-essential service. As the pandemic spread across the continent, millions of people were threatened by hunger perhaps more than the virus since lockdowns prohibited them from going to work and accessing food. Such restrictions severely compromised the right of citizens to food, among other violations (Muchena, 14 December 2020). The International Covenant on Economic, Social and Cultural Rights, adopted by nearly all countries in the world, stipulates that everyone has the right to have the highest standards in health, be it emotional, physical or mental (Odigbo *et al*, 2020).

Digital (or Information Technology) rights also became a talk of the moment during Covid-19 era, having come to the limelight during the 21st century. However, as with infringements of other freedoms highlighted above, digital surveillance and mobile phone tracking by the authorities have increasingly been viewed by many activists as a violation of privacy rights (Okech *et al*, 2020; Olewe, 9 April 2020). From early 2020, for example, the authorities in Kenya were tracking mobile phones of people suspected to have Covid-19 in order to enforce a 14-day mandatory isolation period (Olewe, 9 April 2020). In South Africa, authorities also reportedly liaised with cell-phone companies to collect geo-location data from mobile phone towers to help follow up people who had contact with Covid-19 patients (Ibid). Digital authoritarianism also saw some governments using the internet to monitor and censor the flow of information and access the online correspondence of individuals and institutions without their knowledge or consent (Rivers & Ndlovu, 24 June 2020). This was not only unethical but also illegal before the law, at least, under normal circumstances.

From this background, it should be appreciated that the global struggle against Covid-19 was also very much a war for the respect of basic freedoms, human rights and civil liberties. Undoubtedly, the efforts by governments to contain the pandemic severely jeopardised people's liberties, freedoms and rights in the whole world at large and Africa in particular. The chapters in this volume interrogate, from different angles, these issues with dexterity through detailed analyses from across the African continent.

Summary of chapters

This volume contains 18 chapters, with the first one being introductory while most of the remaining ones focus on a broad range of infringements on human rights, civil liberties and freedoms across the African continent that were occasioned, directly or indirectly, by the Covid-19 pandemic. Chapters 2-14 dwell on abuses and vulnerabilities brought about by state policies and law-enforcement agencies in the process of implementing Covid-19 containment initiatives. In most cases, as these chapters show, the victims of abuse were the ordinary people seeking livelihoods, including workers in the formal and informal sectors, and vulnerable sections of the population such as women, people living with HIV-AIDS, and people living with disabilities. Furthermore, as some chapters ably demonstrate, human rights activists, journalists from the independent media, and opposition political leaders and supporters were also victimised, harassed and gagged in many

African countries during the Covid-19 period. Chapters 15, 16 and 17 focus on struggles waged against pandemic-related human rights abuses while the last chapter seeks to justify some heavy-handed strategies employed by [African] governments to contain the spread of the pandemic. What now follow are synopses of the contents of individual chapters in this volume.

In Chapter 2, Nancy Mazuru and Fidelis Peter Thomas Duri devote considerable attention to the brutal manner in which Zimbabwe's security operatives from the army, police and intelligence enforced Covid-19 containment regulations such as stay-at-home orders, travel bans and curfews. Mazuru and Duri note with concern how physical assaults, torture and arbitrary arrests became banal in the enforcement of Covid-19 mitigation measures by Zimbabwe's security officers. Basic human rights, civil liberties and freedoms were severely compromised in the generally brutal process of curtailing the pandemic. Lamentably, most of the so-called violators of Covid-19 lockdown protocols who suffered at the hands of law-enforcement agents were marginalised people who ventured out of their homes to salvage livelihoods in Zimbabwe's seemingly inexorable harsh socio-economic environment. Given the rampant abuse of power and the consequent gross violation of human rights during Zimbabwe's lockdown, Mazuru and Duri call for the police to be policed during times of emergencies in order to ensure adherence to the law by people who are mandated and salaried to enforce it. Overall, the two scholars assert that pandemic policing was another disaster in itself in which struggles against Covid-19 also became human rights crusades.

Security sector barbarity in the enforcement of Covid-19 curtailment measures prevailed not only in Zimbabwe but in many other countries across the African continent and the case study of Nigeria by Trust Makwinja Asima and Fidelis Peter Thomas Duri in Chapter 3 attests to this. In their fascinating chapter, Asima and Duri, examine the combative or warrior like approach taken by Nigerian security agents, largely comprising the army and the police, while enforcing public compliance to Covid-19 lockdown measures. Asima and Duri bemoan the fact that as of 13 April 2020, the security forces on lockdown enforcement duties in various parts of Nigeria had killed more people than the Corona virus itself! (Khalid, 16 April 2020; Mugabi, 20 April 2020; Ohajuruka, 16 November 2020). The chapter provides numerous examples of human rights infringements that were exhibited by government security agents through beatings, torture, arbitrary arrests, extra-judicial killings and general heavy-handedness, among other horrendous abuses. In their analysis, Asima and Duri note that the barbarity, arbitrariness and lawlessness displayed by Nigeria's so-called law-enforcement operatives exposed their ignorance of the symbiotic link between health and human rights issues in life. On the whole, the chapter laments the futile determination of Nigerian security agents to save human life by containing the spread of a disease at the expense of the right to life itself, including other critical rights, liberties and freedoms. It was indeed ironic, as Asima and Duri lay bare, that pandemic monitoring by security officers caused considerable insecurity among the citizenry; the so-called law-enforcement agents were generally lawless in their conduct to the extent that they overzealously fought and endangered the very lives they were meant to safeguard.

In Chapter 4, Takavafira Masarira Zhou and Costain Tandi illustrate how the Covid-19 pandemic was weaponised and instrumentalised for political currency by the ruling Zimbabwe African National Union Patriotic Front (ZANU-PF) party under the leadership of President Emmerson Mnangagwa. Given that many Zimbabweans were increasingly becoming restive owing to severe socio-economic hardships which the opposition Citizens' Coalition for Change (CCC) party fully capitalised on to expand its support base, Zhou and Tandi argue that the advent of the pandemic in early 2020 came as a political blessing for President Mnangagwa's ZANU-PF. In addition to diverting the people's attention from the failures of the government that had critically eroded their livelihoods, the virus provided the ruling party with a golden opportunity to silence opposition political parties and other critics under the pretext of combating the pandemic. Thus, as Zhou and Tandi noted, the political landscape in Zimbabwe during the Covid-19 period was heavily manipulated to fulfil ZANU-PF's hegemonic agenda. The chapter articulates how the pandemic was weaponised to suppress the right to vote, entitlement to political representation as well as freedoms of speech, expression and assembly. Broadly, Chapter 4 demonstrates how the ruling ZANU-PF government instrumentalised the Covid-19 pandemic to taper democratic space in Zimbabwe through entrenched authoritarian shenanigans which involved coercion, repression and selective application of the law in ways that grossly flouted people's rights, freedoms and liberties.

In Chapter 5, Fidelis Peter Thomas Duri and Golden Maunganidze illuminate the erosion of media freedom and freedom of speech and expression brought about by various crescendos related to the Covid-19 pandemic in Zimbabwe. The chapter details how state security agents tormented the media, particularly the independent press, as the government battled to contain the ravaging pandemic from early 2020. This period witnessed the criminalisation of many journalists, mostly from the private media institutions, for being critical of the government's handling of the Covid-19 pandemic. As Duri and Maunganidze observe, independent and critical journalists were often arbitrarily apprehended, unlawfully detained and brutally tortured on trumped-up charges of contravening lockdown regulations such as stay-at-home orders, travel bans and curfew. These savage tactics were meant to intimidate, harass and force independent and critical journalists into writing favourably about the government's Covid-19 response. For the most part, the chapter shows how the government instrumentalised pandemic lockdown regulations to sanitise press censorship and contraventions of the rights to freedom of expression and media freedom. Consequently, many journalists lived in constant fear of being harassed, tortured and even killed by the government and its security operatives. Additionally, the right to information on the part of ordinary citizens who usually depended on the media for news was severely compromised consequent to the harassment of journalists.

Chapter 6 by Nicholas Govo also critically examines the suppression of media freedom and other freedoms of expression by the Tanzanian government of the then President John Pombe Magufuli. As Govo notes, the Tanzanian Covid-19 experience was rather peculiar as compared to many countries around the world owing to the fact that President Magufuli denied the existence of the Corona virus disease, rejected Covid-19 vaccines and refused to impose a strict lockdown for the greater part of the pandemic period. Consequent upon his personal denialism, Magufuli ruthlessly descended on media houses, journalists, politicians, bloggers and ordinary citizens who dared to report, publish or share information on the dynamics of Covid-19 and measures to contain it at least in Tanzania. To this end, legislation in Tanzania was manipulated to curtail press freedom and other freedoms of expression; several media houses were suspended and fined while many journalists, bloggers, activists, politicians and ordinary citizens were accordingly arbitrarily arrested, unlawfully detained, tortured and penalised. Broadly, Govo castigates Magufuli's Covid-19 approach as parochially retrogressive as far as discourses of medical science, human rights and democracy are concerned. The unrestricted flow of information regarding Covid-19 was vital in raising public awareness on its dangers and preventive measures. Given this context, the government's efforts to clamp down on media freedom and freedom of expression were therefore homicidal. Predictably, as Govo accurately observes, Magufuli's repressive policies with regards to the monopolisation of information and expression were suicidal to himself (considering that he was widely believed to have died from Covid-19) and many Tanzanians, together with other people they came into contact with, who perished due to both misinformation campaigns and information embargoes.

In Chapter 7, Tasara Muguti laments the erosion of the right to health and other critical livelihood entitlements of ordinary Zimbabweans during the Covid-19 era. Interestingly, Muguti takes a historical approach and argues that the erosion of these rights and entitlements would not have been so profound had it not been the ZANU-PF government's longstanding political and socio-economic failures which had long made the lives of many citizens unbearable. It is Muguti's contention that the critical erosion of the right to health and other livelihood rights on the part of many Zimbabweans during the Covid-19 era can best be understood in the context of longstanding political and socio-economic dynamics in which the ruling ZANU-PF party was largely to blame for incompetence, corruption and mismanagement, among other shortcomings.

Muguti's chapter begins by submitting that the Zimbabwean government had long failed in its mandate to avail basic social services and other human needs for its people. The government's failures to fulfil various livelihood rights over the years tended to catalyse the spread of the pandemic. The economy had been on a free fall since 2000 when the government seized many farms belonging to commercial farmers for redistribution (Duri, 2014; Meredith, 2002; Moyo, 2000; Pilossof, 1 December 2010; Sachikonye, 2003). As property rights were violated, investors fled, companies closed down, workers were retrenched and widespread poverty set in (Chiriga, 16 April 2011; Hammar & Raftopoulos, 2003; Richardson, 2005). Deindustrialisation followed and the economy became highly informalised (Chiriga, 16 April 2011; Dube, 12 June 2013; Hammar & Raftopoulos, 2003). Disputed elections amid accusations of rigging and voter intimidation, and state-orchestrated political violence over the years did not help matters for the ruling ZANU-PF government as the country was ostracised from the greater part of the international community (Hammar & Raftopoulos, 2003; Hill, 2003; Meredith, 2002; Masunungure, 2004; Raftopoulos, 2003). Deindustrialisation and international isolation resulted in a drastic slump in export earnings. Foreign currency reserves became depleted and the government increasingly found it difficult to import critical medical facilities and drugs, among other things (Duri & Marongwe, 2021). The collapse of the agricultural sector, investor flight and deindustrialisation largely contributed to government bankruptcy as corporate tax remittances plummeted (Ibid; Butler, 1 July 2013). Consequently, the Zimbabwean government became bankrupt to the extent of failing to provide adequate social protection for its people (Duri & Marongwe, 2021).

Having traced this disastrous history of failure by the ZANU-PF government, Muguti notes that when the pandemic descended on Zimbabwe in early 2020, the majority of the population terribly lacked basic services and needs such as adequate healthcare, clean water, food, shelter, employment, and descent remuneration for workers. Given these historic failures that continued to haunt citizens in the present times, Muguti points out that the government was incapacitated to rescue its citizens from the ravages of the Covid-19 pandemic. Thus, these inadequacies, together with the government's incompetence and helplessness, forced many citizens to thumb their noses on lockdown provisions and venture out of their homes to seek livelihoods regardless of the danger of either being infected by Covid-19 or being arrested and prosecuted by the police.

Seemingly taking off from where Chapter 7 left, Chapter 8 by Ngonidzashe Marongwe and Tasara Muguti analyses in considerable detail the effects of the Covid-19 pandemic on the socio-economic and livelihood rights of informal sector traders and workers in Mashava, a mining settlement in Zimbabwe's Masvingo Province. When the lockdown was initially declared in the country, most informal sector participants in Mashava were adversely affected, particularly vegetable vendors, flea market operators and commercial sex workers. Bars, bottle stores, schools and the only university in the area, Great Zimbabwe University, were closed in line with Covid-19 lockdown provisions declared by the government. Some of the few enterprises that were classified as essential services and allowed to continue operating were retail businesses and artisanal mining. Marongwe and Muguti acknowledge that the livelihoods of many informal traders, such as vendors of vegetables and used clothes, were markedly jeopardised by the lockdown ban, forcing many of them to engage in cat-and-mouse encounters with the police.

An important observation made by Marongwe and Muguti in Chapter 8 is that the informal sector cannot viably operate in isolation but is largely dependent on the formal sector for customers and many other services. Thus, the closure of formal businesses and institutions in the Mashava area aggravated the plight of informal sector traders and workers. Commercial sex workers, for example, lost a lot of business as a result of the closure of bars from where they used to get most of their clients. The closure of Great Zimbabwe University, bars and bottle stores also saw food vendors falling on hard times. When lockdown restrictions were eventually relaxed, Marongwe and Muguti observe how it never rained but poured for most informal traders as the government imposed stringent conditions for resumption of business. Some of the requirements for resuming operations had financial implications which the already pauperised informal traders could not afford such as thermometers and hand sanitisers. Worse still, the government failed to provide informal traders with safety nets. By and large, Marongwe and Muguti argue that Covid-19 mitigation protocols violated the socio-economic rights and livelihood entitlements of informal sector participants to the extent of threatening their very existence.

As was the case with Marongwe and Muguti's Chapter 8, Chapter 9 by Constance Makuvise dwells on the impact of the Covid-19 pandemic on the informal sector but specifically focuses on rural traders in the Zaka District of Masvingo Province in Zimbabwe. These informal entrepreneurs include vendors of various wares such as fruits, vegetables, edible insects, and second-hand clothes; cross-border traders, small-scale farmers, unregistered beer-brewers and hair-dressers. Makuvise starts off the chapter by exploring the various ways in which the advent of the pandemic and the subsequent measures decreed by the government to curtail its spread frustrated many informal traders in the Zaka District and in fact elsewhere in Zimbabwe. Among other things, as Makuvise notes, the pandemic-induced lockdown criminalised informal sector trade during the early days. Later on, after the lockdown had been relaxed, travel prohibitions, the curfew and other restrictions continued to work against the resurgence of many informal traders. Drawing from many interviews with affected respondents, Makuvise discusses various responses taken by informal traders in the wake of the adversities brought about by the Covid-19-occasioned dynamics. While some informal traders were completely knocked out of business, many soldiered on by operating either within or against the Covid-19 restrictions, or both. The chapter winds up by urging governments and other stakeholders to put in place mechanisms that cushion vulnerable population groups in the event of calamities such as epidemics.

In Chapter 10, Benice Farai Nkomo conducts a wide-ranging discussion on the impact of the Covid-19 pandemic on political dynamics and democratic space in Zimbabwe. The chapter maintains that the implementation of Covid-19 alleviation measures assumed political undertones as the ruling ZANU-PF party sought to manipulate and censor the press, pacify human rights activists and other critical civil society organisations, and annihilate opposition parties, all under the pretext of managing a health emergency. Nkomo discusses how, pursuant to its self-seeking determination to monopolise political space, the ZANU-PF government took advantage of the Covid-19 pandemic to ban gatherings, defer electoral and parliamentary schedules, and arrest rival politicians, activists and journalists allegedly for breaching lockdown measures. Consequently, as Nkomo suggests, the politicisation of the Covid-19 pandemic by President Mnangagwa's government saw many citizens' rights and liberties, including freedom of political choice and participation, of assembly, of information and of movement, right to peaceful protest and legal or legislative representation being trampled upon as the ruling ZANU-PF party desperately sought political survival at any cost. Thus, Nkomo contends that the advent of the Covid-19 pandemic and its subsequent curtailment dynamics witnessed the emergence of a bitter contestation for political hegemony at the expense of many rights, freedoms and liberties; what was supposed to be the management of an otherwise purely health issue became a politically-charged affair in which many citizens, including the ordinary people, civic activists, as well as opposition political party leaders and their supporters suffered a broad range of abuses at the hands of the ZANU-PF government.

Chapter 11 by Aaron Rwodzi and Terence Tapiwa Muzorewa complements and augments the arguments raised in Chapter 10 on the political dimensions of the Covid-19 pandemic and their implications on human rights discourses. The chapter begins by establishing how the enforcement of Covid-19 preventive measures in Zimbabwe took place in the context of political tension. It then explores how political antagonism was heightened by the advent of the pandemic as the ruling ZANU-PF party instrumentalised it to close democratic space to its advantage. In addition, the chapter illustrates how the enforcement of pandemic mitigation regulations substantially negated various forms of human rights and human dignity thereby contravening many national, regional and international conventions to which Zimbabwe was a signatory. An interesting observation which Rwodzi and Muzorewa make in their chapter is that instead of using lockdown measures to ensure safety as far as the health and wellbeing of citizens were concerned, the ZANU-PF government actually manipulated the situation to provide safety guarantees to its hold on political power. They also decried that rather than deploying Covid-19 containment regulations to have people safe from infections, the government actually posed significant danger by exploiting the measures to create an unsafe political environment characterised by harassment, arbitrary arrests, torture and unlawful detentions, among other human rights abuses. On the whole, Rwodzi and Muzorewa avow that the lockdown declared by the government, supposedly to contain the spread of the pandemic, actually 'locked' democratic space against the citizenry and barred them from freely exercising their right to freedom of movement, association, assembly and expression with dignity, among other fundamental rights and freedoms.

While the Covid-19 pandemic and lockdown measures that were instituted by governments to diminish its threats adversely affected many sections of the population and severely compromised their rights, liberties and freedoms, Chapter 12 by Mudadirwa Mujuru and Innocent Rupoterera Madenga observes that persons living with disabilities, the elderly aged 65 years and above, people living with HIV/AIDS, beggars, and street children were worse off. Focusing on sub-Saharan Africa, Mujuru and Madenga examine how these vulnerable groups were threatened in socio-economic, physical, psycho-emotional and spiritual terms by the Covid-19 pandemic and the mitigation strategies rolled out by various governments. Having already been disadvantaged variously in physical, emotional and socio-economic terms, the plight of these marginalised people was exacerbated by pandemic-occasioned dynamics. Among other things, since these groups were often overlooked in terms of preventive and treatment facilities, they ran the highest risk of being infected and affected by the Corona virus, hence their right to health was grossly compromised. The same applied to their right to food as Covid-19 relief aid was often monopolised by those who were relatively able and privileged. Mujuru and Madenga further observe that many vulnerable persons lost considerable moral and material support from relatively privileged and abled sections of the society, most of who were not spared from pandemic ravages and subsequent lockdown measures which included job and income losses, among other things. In addition, many vulnerable persons were subjected to a broad range of abuses as people who were supposed to protect and support them vented their Covid-19 related frustrations on them. In the closing stages of the chapter, Mujuru and Madenga advise African governments to institute elaborate policies that effectively deal with pandemic or disaster outbreak preparedness in order to cushion vulnerable population groups in a manner that respects their dignity.

In Chapter 13, Takavafira Masarira Zhou and Peter Machenjera identify workers as one of the most vulnerable groups whose rights were largely expunged by Covid-19 dynamics in Zimbabwe. The chapter demonstrates how the advent of the Covid-19 pandemic and the strategies employed by the government to subdue it aggravated the already antagonistic employer-employee relations and compromised the right to fair labour practices in Zimbabwe. To start with, the closure of businesses and services deemed not essential under lockdown provisions resulted in many workers losing their jobs and incomes. With the outbreak of the pandemic, as Zhou and Machenjera note, labour and workers' rights were breached by both the government and the private sector using lockdowns as an excuse for paying meagre wages and failing to improve working conditions in the workplaces that were allowed to remain operational. To compound the situation, workers found it difficult to gather and organise industrial action in the form of demonstrations as Covid-19 lockdowns inhibited freedoms of movement and assembly. In effect, the right of workers to engage in lawful unionism were revoked. By implication, workers' rights to collective bargaining and collective job action were rescinded. In the final analysis, Zhou and Machenjera charge that employers, comprising both the government and the private sector, weaponised the pandemic against labour, leaving many workers disarticulated, marginalised, disempowered, and absolutely impoverished.

Written from a feministic perspective, Chapter 14 by Lisa Mubaiwa, singles out women as a marginalised section of the Zimbabwean population whose rights, liberties and freedoms were significantly annulled by Covid-19-related developments. The chapter generally examines the escalation of various forms of gender-based violence cases, most of which were perpetrated against women and girls during the Covid-19 pandemic. Mubaiwa divides the chapter into six sections in order to illustrate the manner in which pandemic dynamics caused a significant surge in cases of gender-based violence against women and girls. The first section discusses the victimhood of women to physical, emotional and sexual violence within households owing to the advent of Covid-19 and subsequent measures instituted by the government to thwart its spread. The second section dwells on the erosion of women's economic rights and other freedoms as a result of pandemic pressures which forced them to take up additional household responsibilities. The third section focuses on women as victims of economic violence and deprivation as a result of Covid-19-occasioned developments. The fourth section devotes attention to rising cases of violence against women and girls living with disabilities. The fifth section attends to the sexual abuse of girl children while the last one unravels the plight of female commercial sex workers, all being largely consequent upon the advent of the Covid-19 pandemic and related dynamics. All in all, Mubaiwa proves beyond reasonable doubt that cases of gender-based violence in which the majority of victims were women and girls skyrocketed during Covid-19 as a result of the pandemic and subsequent lockdown measures. Thus, Covid-19 exposed and amplified existing gender inequalities, with rising cases of gender-based violence, including domestic violence, child marriages, sexual exploitation, and harassment.

It is worth noting that most chapters in this book, particularly Chapters 2-14, dwell on the violation of human rights, freedoms and liberties as a result of Covid-19-related dynamics. Chapters 15 and 16 mark a significant departure by shifting focus to the role of the church and civic organisations in defending rights and other human entitlements that were abraded by pandemic-occasioned developments. In Chapter 15, for instance, Cuthbert Mavedzenge examines the church's involvement in struggles to safeguard human rights, liberties and freedoms during the Covid-19 period in Africa. The chapter notes that while most churches appreciated that lockdown provisions imposed in most African countries, despite interfering with freedoms of worship and assembly, were necessary on grounds of saving lives, they were always quick to urge governments to allow them to resume services whenever the pandemic subsided. Mavedzenge also examines the church's preoccupation with rights issues to do with the conduct of law-enforcement operatives, provision of food and health, and gender-based violence during Covid-19-induced lockdowns in Africa. The chapter cites numerous examples from across the African continent to illustrate the commendable role played by the church to defend the rights of ordinary people that were increasingly being flouted by state security and sometimes civilian perpetrators during the Covid-19 pandemic. Towards this end, as Mavedzenge explains, the church often advised governments to guarantee the safety and lives of citizens by enforcing Covid-19 curtailment measures necessarily and proportionately in ways that respected human rights and complied with the rule of law and international standards on emergency legislation. Undoubtedly, the chapter ably demonstrates how churches became the voice of the voiceless where governments and other perpetrators violated human rights, liberties and freedoms during the Covid-19 pandemic in Africa.

In Chapter 16, David Tobias considers the role played by the Zimbabwe Lawyers for Human Rights (ZLHR), a law-based civic organisation, in combating human rights abuses occasioned by the Covid-19 lockdown(s) in Zimbabwe. Among other strides, the chapter explores how the ZLHR worked to raise public awareness on constitutional rights issues during the Covid-19 pandemic by issuing media statements to challenge arbitrary arrests, unwarranted fines, abductions and torture of citizens on allegations of breaching Covid-19 stipulations. The organisation also represented victims of police brutality during the enforcement of lockdown measures to claim compensation in the courts. Generally, Tobias illuminates the multi-faceted nature of Covid-19 struggles which involved the government's determination to stem the spread of the pandemic, and the efforts of civic institutions to ensure that such measures were implemented with due regard for human rights, liberties, freedoms and the rule of law.

So far, the chapters in this book look at human rights violations associated with the Covid-19 pandemic and the efforts of churches and civic organisations to seek redress. Given this coverage, a critical questions arises: To what extent were the ordinary people passive victims of pandemic-related abuses whose salvation only lay in the intervention of human rights watchdogs such as churches and civic organisations? In Chapter 17, Trust Makwinja Asima and Fidelis Peter Thomas Duri grapple with this question and come up with what they think is a convincing answer. The chapter examines the agency of marginalised populations in defending and reclaiming their rights, liberties and freedoms that were being gnawed by the Covid-19 pandemic and measures instituted by governments across the African continent to curb its spread. Asima and Duri discuss at length, some of the informal strategies employed by the subaltern to seek redress. The chapter devotes particular attention to the circumvention of lockdown orders by informal sector participants, the looting of Covid-19 relief aid by hungry people, overt interventions and backlashes at security sector abuses, and the use of the social media as a weapon by the disadvantaged people. Thus, Asima and Duri establish that the downtrodden are not always docile victims of machination, marginalisation and subordination who sit idly watching those with privileges and power thumbing their noses on their rights, freedoms and liberties. Rather, they have the ability and capability to rise in defence of their entitlements as human beings in ways that are mostly informal owing to their resource limitations and inability to command significant influence beyond their immediate communities.

While discussion in all the chapters so far has centred on various human rights abuses and attempts at redressing the same by churches and civic organisations, Chapter 18 by James Hlongwana justifies most of the infringements on grounds of containing the pandemic and saving lives. Taking Zimbabwe as a case study, the chapter starts off by discussing the flaccidness and scepticism exhibited by the generality of the population towards the scientific principles and practices announced by the government to manage the virus. Given the slackness and indifference on the part of citizens, Hlongwana sees the desirability of the government's deployment of force to combat the spread of the virus. While acknowledging the suffering that was inflicted on the society by law-enforcement agents, Hlongwana insists that the draconian measures yielded remarkable achievements. Broadly, the chapter adopts a Hobbesian approach and argues that the deployment of force by the Zimbabwean government was a necessary evil meant to save lives from the perils posed by the Covid-19 pandemic.

Conclusion

This chapter has noted how the Covid-19 pandemic became a major talking point across the globe as far as discourses of human rights, civil liberties and freedoms are concerned. As most of the chapters in this volume note, the strategies instituted by various governments across the world in an effort to contain the spread of the pandemic triggered debate on the human rights implications of the measures and whether the infringements that took place were justifiable on health and moral grounds. This volume on Africa contributes to this debate. It is hoped that further studies will be conducted in Africa and other parts of the world in order to establish a sustainable interaction between pandemic dynamics and human rights.

References

Aronson, J.K. (19 July 2020) 'The history of Corona viruses since 1931,' Available at: https://www.bmj.com/content/369/bmj.m1547/rr-2, Accessed 25 September 2021.

Butler, D. (1 July 2013) 'Finance history: Zimbabwe economic collapse, 2000-2008,' Available at: www.db.financial.reports.blogspot.com, Accessed 16 November 2019.

Cascais, A. (8 April 2020) 'Is the Corona virus killing press freedom in Africa?' Available at: https://www.dw.com/en, Accessed 16 July 2021.

Chiriga, E. (16 April 2011) 'Unemployment still high in Zimbabwe,' Available at: www.dailynews.co.zw, Accessed 14 May 2019.

Delvac, K.S. (25 May 2020) 'Human rights abuses in the enforcement of Corona virus security measures,' in: *National Law Review*, Volume X, Number 146, Available at: www.natlawreview.com/article, Accessed 12 July 2021.

Dersso, S. (9 September 2020) 'The impact of Covid-19 on human and peoples' rights in Africa,' Available at: https://www.accord.org.za/analysis/, Accessed 23 September 2021.

Dube, G. (12 June 2013) 'Zimbabwe workers living below breadline,' Available at: www.voazimbabwe.com, Accessed 18 August 2018.

Duri, F.P.T. (2014) 'Linguistic innovations for survival: The case of illegal panning and smuggling of diamonds in Chiadzwa, Zimbabwe, 2006-2012', in: *Africana*, Volume 7, Number 1, pp.41-60.

Duri, F.P.T. & Marongwe, N. (2021) *New millennium woes and livelihood struggles in Africa: Begging to survive by Zimbabwe's marginalised*, Bamenda: Langaa Research and Publishing Common Initiative Group.

Guterres, A. (22 February 2021) 'The world faces a pandemic of human rights abuses in the wake of Covid-19,' Available at: https://www.theguardian.com/global-development/2021/feb/22/world, Accessed 27 September 2021.

Hammar, A. & Raftopoulos, B. (2003) 'Zimbabwe's unfinished business: Rethinking land, state and nation,' in: A. Hammar, B. Raftopoulos & S. Jensen (eds.) *Zimbabwe's unfinished business: Rethinking land, state and nation in the context of crisis*, Harare: Weaver Press.

Hill, G. (2003) *The battle for Zimbabwe: The final countdown*, Cape Town: Zebra Press.

International Labour Organisation (2018) *Women and men in the informal economy: A statistical picture,* Geneva: International Labour Organisation.

Institutional Research Information Services Solution (IRISS) (2007) 'Human rights and civil liberties distinguished,' Available at: https://content.iriss.org.uk/humanrights/rights_02.html, Accessed 1 August 2021.

International Federation of Journalists (30 June 2020) 'Zimbabwe: Journalists beaten and humiliated by security forces,' Available at: https://www.ifj.org/media-centre/news/detail/article/zimbabwe, Accessed 12 September 2021.

Kahm, J.S. & McIntosh, K. (2005) 'History and recent advances in Corona virus discovery,' in: *The Paediatric Infectious Disease Journal*, Volume 24, Issue 11, pp.223-227.

Khalid, I. (16 April 2020) 'Corona virus: Security forces kill more Nigerians than Covid-19,' Available at: https://www.bbc.com/news/world-africa-52317196, Accessed 26 February 2022.

Kuteesa, H. (11 May 2020) 'Five Rwanda Defence Forces soldiers court-martialled for assaulting Kangondo residents,' Available at: https://www.newtimes.co.rw/news, Accessed 12 June 2021.

Martel, F. (14 April 2020) 'Bolivia's Evo Morales on Corona virus: China won the Third World War,' Available at:

https://www.breitbart.com/asia/2020/04/14, Accessed 26 September 2021.

Masunungure, E. (2004) 'Travails of opposition politics in Zimbabwe since independence,' in: D. Harold-Barry (ed.) *Zimbabwe: The past is the future: Rethinking land, state and nation in the context of crisis*, Harare: Weaver Press.

Mavhunga, C. (11 February 2021) 'Zimbabwe among African countries using Covid-19 to crack down on journalists, report finds,' Available at: https://www.voanews.com/a/africa, Accessed 22 September 2021.

Meredith, M. (2002) *Mugabe: Power and plunder in Zimbabwe*, New York: Public Affairs.

Molloy, S. (1 May 2020) 'Human rights in Africa in the context of Covid-19,' Available at: https://www.iconnectblog.com/2020/04, Accessed 22 September 2021.

Moyo, G. & Phulu, K.I. (2021) 'The weaponisation of the Corona virus crisis in Zimbabwe: Legal and extra-legal instruments,' in: *iBusiness*, Volume 13, pp.48-66, Available at: https://doi.org/10.4236/ib.2021.131004, Accessed 26 September 2021.

Moyo, S. (2000) 'The interaction of market and compulsory land acquisition processes with social action in Zimbabwe's land reform,' Paper presented at the SAPES Trust Annual Colloquium, Harare.

Muchena, D. (14 December 2020) 'Pandemic of human rights abuses haunts governments in East and Southern Africa,' Available at: https://mg.co.za/africa/2020-12-14, Accessed 18 September 2021.

Mugabi, I. (20 April 2020) 'Covid-19: Security forces in Africa brutalising civilians under lockdown,' Available at: https://www.dw.com/en/covid-19-security-forces-in-africa-brutalizing-civilians-under-lockdown/a-53192163, Accessed 21 February 2022.

Odigbo, B. Eze, F. & Odigbo, R. (2020) 'Covid-19 lockdown controls and human rights abuses: The social marketing implications,' in: *Emerald Open Research*, Volume 2, Number 45, pp.1-18.

Ohajuruka, U. (16 November 2020) 'Police brutality and the girl child,' Available at: https://globalgirlsglow.org/police-brutality-and-the-girl-child/, Accessed 12 January 2022.

Okech, A. Mwambari, D. & Olonisakin, F. (2020) 'Covid-19 responses and human rights in selected African countries,' in: *Australian Journal of Human Rights*, Volume 26, Number 3, pp.549-555.

Olewe, D. (9 April 2020) 'Corona virus in Africa: Whipping, shooting and snooping,' Available at: https://www.bbc.com/news/world-africa-52214740,' Accessed 6 September 2021.

Pilossof, R. (1 December 2010) 'The Commercial Farmers Union of Zimbabwe and its policies after *jambanja*,' Available at: www.solidaritypeacetrust.org, Accessed 5 November 2018.

Raftopoulos, B. (2003) 'The state in crisis: Authoritarian nationalism, selective citizenship and distortions of democracy in Zimbabwe,' in: A. Hammar, B. Raftopoulos & S. Jensen (eds.) *Zimbabwe's unfinished business: Rethinking land, state and nation in the context of crisis*, Harare: Weaver Press.

Ravelo, J.L. & Jerving, S. (31 December 2019) 'Covid-19: A timeline of the Corona virus outbreak,' Available at: https://www.devex.com/news, Accessed 24 September 2021.

Richardson, C.J. (2005) 'The loss of property rights and the collapse of Zimbabwe,' in: *Cato Journal*, Volume 25, Number 3, pp.541-565.

Rivers, M. & Ndlovu, P. (24 June 2020) 'Covid-19 raises the stakes for Zimbabwe's civil society movement,' Available at: https://www.usip.org/publications/2020/06, Accessed 21 September 2021.

Sabiti, B. (19 April 2021) 'Africa's handling of Covid-19 marred by abuse of power,' Available at: https://ifex.org, Accessed 10 May 2021.

Sachikonye, L. (2003) 'The situation of commercial farm workers after land reform in Zimbabwe,' Report prepared for the Farm Community Trust of Zimbabwe, Harare: Farm Community Trust of Zimbabwe.

Segun, M. (18 January 2021) 'Human rights abuses escalate in Africa during the pandemic,' Available at: https://www.hrw.org/news/2021/01/18, Accessed 26 September 2021.

WebMD (August 2021) 'Corona virus history: Origin and evolution', Available at: https://www.webmd.com/lung/coronavirus-history, Accessed 24 September 2021.

Chapter 2

Covid-19 Terror and Human Rights Abuses: Civilians at the Mercy of Zimbabwe's State Security Apparatus

Nancy Mazuru & Fidelis Peter Thomas Duri

Introduction

Pandemics across the globe have several negative ramifications on the socio-economic well being of societies and Covid-19 is not an exception. The deadly Covid-19 pandemic saw different countries across the globe embracing various mitigation measures to curb its spread. Lockdowns were part of those measures and the aim was to restrict the movement of people within and across borders. While the concept of lockdowns was noble, the manner in which these restrictions were enforced in Zimbabwe was another disaster in itself as there was widespread abuse of power by state security forces namely: the Zimbabwe Republic Police (ZRP), the Zimbabwe National Army (ZNA) and the intelligence service fondly known as the Central Intelligence Organisation (CIO). The operations of these forces during lockdowns saw many civilians being assaulted, tortured, arbitrarily arrested or unlawfully detained, allegedly for flouting pandemic curtailment regulations.

There is, however, a methodological challenge pertaining to the exact numbers of the victims who were abused by law-enforcement agents for breaching lockdown provisions. It is a fact that many civilian victims suffered in silence as going out to report cases to Police Camps actually tantamounted to violating stay-at-home orders imposed during the different phases of the lockdown. Some victims also chose not to report the abuses for fear of retribution. However, some were bold enough to report these abuses to non-governmental organisations (Zenda, 24 April 2020: 1). As if that were not enough, some households relying on informal livelihoods saw their living standards rapidly deteriorating due to the harsh mitigation measures imposed by the government through state security forces. Thus, in many instances, security agents operated as if the travel and other lockdown restrictions had suspended all human rights, freedoms and liberties. In actual fact, the law-enforcement agents embarked on a combative approach based on warped logic that likens every remedy to a nail that needs a hammer. This chapter unpacks the terror and human rights abuses suffered by civilians at the hands of state security operatives in Zimbabwe.

Zimbabwe's early Covid-19 experiences and the government's response

The first Covid-19 case in Zimbabwe was announced on 21 March 2020 by the then Minister of Health and Child Care, Obadiah Moyo, during a press conference (Maulani *et al*, 2020; Mugari & Obioha, 2021). The patient had recently arrived in the country from England via South Africa (Gasa, 21 April 2020; Maulani *et al*, 2020; Mugari & Obioha, 2021). On 23 March 2020, the country recorded its first Covid-19 death after the patient who was admitted at Wilkins Hospital in Harare succumbed to the virus (Tshili, 23 March 2020). The fatality generated a panic mode among government officials and the general public. As time progressed, cases of Covid-19 infections and deaths increased. As of 22 July 2020, the country had officially recorded 1 800 confirmed cases and 26 deaths (Mavhunga, 22 July 2020). By 12 August 2020, the country had recorded 4 893 infections and 122 deaths (Maulani *et al*, 2020). As of 13 December 2020, Zimbabwe had recorded, at least officially, a total of 11 219 positive cases and 307 fatalities (Moyo & Phulu, 2021). In late April 2021, the country had 38 191 confirmed Covid-19 infections and 1 565 deaths (Mavhunga, 29 April 2021). By 31 December 2021, Zimbabwe had recorded 211 728 infections and 4 997 deaths (*Herald*, 31 December 2021). As of 14 February 2022, the country's cumulative Covid-19 cases stood at 231 337 and 5 374 deaths (*Newsday*, 15 February 2022).

On 19 March 2020, in an effort to curtail the spread of the pandemic, President Emmerson Mnangagwa used Statutory Instrument 76 of 2020 on Civil Protection (Declaration of State of Disaster: Rural and Urban Areas of Zimbabwe) to declare Covid-19 a national disaster (Maulani *et al*, 2020; Moyo & Phulu, 2021). He then announced a national lockdown that was to take effect from 30 March 2020 (Mugari & Obioha, 2021). The government went on to set up a National Covid-19 Response Taskforce headed by the then Second Vice President, Kembo Mohadi (Maulani *et al*, 2020; Moyo & Phulu, 2021). On 30 March 2020, the previously announced national lockdown took effect. The lockdown conditions, which were spelt out in Statutory Instrument 83 of 2020 on Public Health (Covid-19 Prevention, Containment and Treatment) (National Lockdown) Order of 2020, included compulsory wearing of face masks, banning of all gatherings, stay-at-home orders and the restriction of movement by the public except those providing essential services (Maulani *et al*, 2020; Moyo & Phulu, 2021). Under the lockdown conditions, services deemed non-essential were suspended indefinitely and these included most informal sector activities. Essential services that were authorised to continue operating during the lockdown include health and sanitation, government security, fire brigade and ambulances, water and electricity, humanitarian relief, money transfer and exchange, and communications service providers (Maulani *et al*, 2020). The government also closed its borders. Zimbabweans in the diaspora were, however, allowed to return but had to quarantine themselves for 14 days upon arrival. All learning institutions were closed and learners were told to go to their homes until further notice (Maulani *et al*, 2020; Moyo & Phulu, 2021).

The lockdown conditions also included movement restrictions such as inter-city travel prohibition except for those with exemption letters and a ban on informal vendors and private-owned commuter omnibuses (Centre for Innovation and Technology, 26 September 2020). The ban on private passenger transport operators left the state-run Zimbabwe United Passenger Company (ZUPCO) as the sole officially-recognised public transport service in the country (Mugari & Obioha, 2021). On 4 April 2020, the government deployed the army to help the police to enforce Covid-19 control measures (Moyo & Phulu, 2021; Ndoma, 21 July 2020). On 21 July 2020, President Mnangagwa tightened Covid-19 mitigation measures owing to a spike in infections by imposing a dusk to dawn curfew lasting from 6pm to 6am (Amnesty International, 7 April 2021; Amnesty International, 2021; Chidombwe, 18 August 2020; Mavhunga, 22 July 2020; Moyo & Phulu, 2021).

This section has presented the early Covid-19 experiences in Zimbabwe. It has also discussed the responses by the Zimbabwean government to the advent of this deadly pandemic. Among other things, the ruling Zimbabwe African National Union Patriotic Front (ZANU-PF) government of President Emmerson Mnangagwa imposed a national lockdown and deployed the police and the army to enforce its provisions which included stay-at-home orders, travel bans, shutdowns of some business sectors and the curfew. Given the poor human rights record of Zimbabwe's law-enforcement agents in dealing with civilians, it became inevitable that the government's administration of Covid-19 curtailment measures was going to be brutal. It is this history of violence by Zimbabwe's law-enforcement agents since independence that the next section briefly explores in order to historically contextualise this chapter.

Brief history of violence by Zimbabwe's law-enforcement agents since independence

In post-colonial Zimbabwe, brutality by the state's security forces can be traced back to the rule of Robert Mugabe since the dawn of independence in 1980. Historically, the military and police have largely played the role of safeguarding state power in Zimbabwe, sacrificing the rights of many ordinary citizens in the process (Rivers & Ndlovu, 24 June 2020). This was irrespective of the fact that Zimbabwe had ratified many human rights conventions and treaties such as the International Covenant on Economic, Social and Cultural Rights; International Covenant on Civil and Political Rights (ICESCR); Convention on the Elimination of all Forms of Discrimination Against Women (CEDAW); Convention on Children's Rights (CRC); and the African Charter on the Rights and Welfare of the Child (ACRWC), among others. Most of the provisions enshrined in these international instruments were also incorporated in the National Constitution of Zimbabwe. Unfortunately, the dictates of these conventions and treaties remained largely theoretical with no operationalisation or implementation in Zimbabwe.

The torture of civilians by state security forces began during Robert Mugabe's reign and continued to take place under Emmerson Mnangagwa. During Mugabe's rule, it was common practice for ZANU-PF to use intimidation and violence to sustain political power (Makwerere *et al,* 2012). The security forces would beat, torture, abduct or kill civilians, especially those perceived to be a threat to Mugabe's government. The Gukurahundi atrocities of the 1980s in the provinces of Matabeleland and parts of the Midlands remain "one of the worst forms of state-organised violence [or rather genocide] in the history of post-independence Zimbabwe" (Zengwa, 2 May 2020: 1). During this pogrom, it was the national army's Fifth Brigade that was used to annihilate ZANU-PF's opponents in these areas (Duri, 2010; Moyo, 9 April 2020a).

The brutality of security forces on civilians was also evidenced during various demonstrations and protests that took place in the country. Since the dawn of independence, the police and the army never tolerated demonstrations and protests. Since the reign of Mugabe, peaceful protests and demonstrations were always violently suppressed. In 1998, for instance, the state unleashed the riot police and the army on food rioters, which resulted in mass beatings, torture, and severe injuries on unarmed civilians (Zengwa, 2 May 2020). Although Section 208 (2) of the Zimbabwean Constitution forbids members of the security services from furthering the interests of any political party or violating the fundamental rights or freedoms of any person, the police and the army often deviated from their code of conduct to protect the interests of the ruling ZANU-PF elites.

The harassment of civilians by the security forces during Mugabe's era also extended to student activists. It was always the practice of the ZANU-PF government to descend on students and silence their voices through ferocious means and this often saw many of their representatives being arrested, abducted or tortured. In 2006, for example, Promise Mkwananzi, the then president of the Zimbabwe National Student Union (ZINASU), together with many other student leaders, were arrested, detained and tortured on several occasions for organising student demonstrations against fees hikes (*Zimbabwean*, 26 November 2006; Guma, 26 October 2006). While in detention, the students were often assaulted and denied access to food and lawyers (Ibid). Leaders and members of opposition political parties were also not spared from violence and torture by state security agents and the then opposition Movement for Democratic Change (MDC) party was always on the receiving end. A case in point was the brutal suppression of the 11 March 2007 MDC rally which saw the arrest and torture of Morgan Tsvangirai, its founding leader, as well as 49 other political activists (Masunungure, 2020; O'Doherty, 2017).

Security forces sometimes coerced civilians to vote for the ZANU-PF party during election times. Supporters of opposition political parties were always abducted or tortured by state security agents during election times. In 2008, for example, some Zimbabwe National Army (ZNA) soldiers savaged villagers in the Midlands and Mashonaland provinces after the ruling ZANU-PF party had lost the March 2008 elections (Moyo, 9 April 2020a). This exemplified how prejudice manifested itself in the operations of Zimbabwe's law-enforcement agents. Such acts contravened Section 208 (2a) of the

Zimbabwean Constitution which forbade security forces from exercising their duties in a partisan manner. Another vivid case in which the military exposed its partisan nature was in 2012 when Major General Martin Chedondo, the then Zimbabwe Defence Forces Chief of Staff, stated that soldiers should be involved in national politics because they are political beings. Chedondo uttered these sentiments while addressing 3 000 soldiers from 2 Brigade who were undergoing a battlefield training exercise in the small town of Mutoko (*Newsday*, 10 May 2012). Part of Chedondo's speech read:

> A national defence force the world over is there to protect the national politics, national integrity, and the Executive and other systems that form part of the Government. By virtue of this, defence forces automatically become a political animal…As soldiers, we will never be apologetic for supporting ZANU-PF because it is the only political party that has national interests at heart (Ibid).

It was, therefore, this kind of partisanship that often saw leaders and supporters of opposition political parties being tortured or assaulted by security forces. As Masunungure (2020) noted, ZANU-PF and the military were always two sides of the same coin because when ZANU-PF was in trouble, the military leapt to its rescue.

Sadly, the bestial conduct of Zimbabwe's security forces did not end with the demise of Mugabe's rule as Mnangagwa's regime also inherited the same tactics. One of the earliest incidents that revealed the brutal nature of state security agents during Mnangagwa's era was in August 2018 when soldiers who had been deployed in the streets of Harare to disperse unarmed protesters opened fire, killing six and injuring more than a dozen others (Zengwa, 2 May 2020). The protests were triggered by the delay of the Zimbabwe Electoral Commission (ZEC) to announce the results of the July 2018 presidential elections amid fears that they were being doctored in favour of the ruling ZANU-PF party (*Independent*, 1 August 2018). The use of live ammunition against unarmed civilians was condemned by the international community, including Amnesty International, which stated that the militarisation of the post-election environment was stifling freedoms of expression, association and assembly in Zimbabwe (Chingono, 3 August 2018). The violent suppression of protests by state security forces was also witnessed in January 2019 when the week-long anti-government protests against fuel price hikes resulted in 17 fatalities and hundreds of arrests (Rivers & Ndlovu, 24 June 2020; Zenda, 24 April 2020). During the security crackdown that ensued, "hundreds of people were brutalised in their homes, with some cases of women being raped by armed men in their homes" (Zenda, 24 April 2020: 1).

This section illuminated the unpopularity of Zimbabwe's law-enforcement agents that stemmed from their brutal handling of civilians since independence. All the cases discussed in this section illustrate the ruthless characterisation of Zimbabwe's state security forces and eloquently articulate how they stifled a broad range of human rights, civil liberties and freedoms for many decades. As will be noted in the following sections of this chapter, similar acts of brutality and gross human rights violations were also prevalent during the Covid-19 period as evidenced by assaults on the generality of the Zimbabwean population and some particular sections of the citizenry such as women, journalists, health workers, informal traders and political activists, just to mention a few. Furthermore, lockdown violators were often harassed, bribed, extorted and robbed by the so-called law-enforcement agents.

Assaults on the generality of Zimbabweans during the Covid-19 pandemic

The Covid-19 pandemic was a double tragedy to the general populace of Zimbabwe as people were terrorised by both the virus and state security forces. Although the law provided for security forces to apply lawful means to enforce the lockdowns, including arresting the violators and bringing them before a court of law, these duties were often conducted in a manner that violated human rights, civil liberties and freedoms. More often than not, the involvement of the army and the police in enforcing Covid-19 mitigation measures "harassed citizens and threatened communities, appearing motivated by a desire to instil fear rather than to protect citizens from the potentially deadly virus" (Rivers & Ndlovu, 24 June 2020: 1).

Within the first two days of the lockdown in Zimbabwe, the police reportedly assaulted 10 people in various parts of the country for flouting Covid-19 containment measures (Mutambasere, 2020). This prompted the Zimbabwe Human Rights NGO Forum in early April 2020, when the lockdown was just a week old, to express serious concern at the brutal force displayed by the uniformed forces while enforcing Covid-19 curtailment measures. In one of its updates, the Forum noted: "As violence against civilians increases, the Forum continues to call upon law-enforcement officers to respect human rights and to employ non-violent measures to enforce the national lockdown" (Zenda, 24 April 2020: 1). While Zimbabwean government officials often denied committing gross human rights abuses since the outbreak of the Covid-19 pandemic, human rights doctors revealed on 21 April 2020 that they had treated 31 victims of torture by state security agents deployed to enforce lockdown measures (*Africa News*, 21 April 2020).

The brutal enforcement of lockdown regulations was prevalent in urban areas compared to rural areas. On 6 April 2020, for example, soldiers allegedly violently dispersed people at Chigovanyika Business Centre in St Mary's Suburb of Chitungwiza Town a few hours before President Emmerson Mnangagwa's convoy passed through the busy shopping centre. Later at night, the soldiers reportedly returned to the suburb and indiscriminately assaulted the residents for booing Mnangagwa earlier in the day, but using the Covid-19 lockdown as a scapegoat (Mangirazi *et al*, 8 April 2020). In a similar case, in early April 2020, Homani Matamba, a 79-year-old man from the town of Kariba, was reportedly battered by police officers while seated at home with his two sons (Ibid). He narrated the terrifying experience as follows:

> I was seated outside around 8pm when I was assaulted by the police, who accused us of not staying indoors. When they hit me, I passed out and do not remember how I fell after they hit me all over the body and face. I was only attended to by my wife after the police had left (Ibid).

The incident invited sharp criticism from many human rights activists who felt that the rights of civilians were being trodden upon and violated by overzealously rancorous police and military officers. Jeremiah Bamu, a human rights lawyer, for example, complained:

> A lockdown is not a declaration of a state of emergency. People still have their rights and members of the security services have an obligation to respect, protect and promote these rights. Anyone whose rights have been violated has recourse in terms of the Constitution and law. They need to consult their lawyers on the available remedies they may have at law (*News dzeZimbabwe*, 8 April 2020: 1).

In a related case, in late April 2020, a man from the mining town of Bindura whose name was withheld for fear of victimisation had his arm fractured after being beaten up by rowdy soldiers, allegedly for defying lockdown stay-at-home orders. The man was reportedly assaulted by an iron bar in Bindura's Chipadze Suburb while he was going to the market place to buy food for his family. Local residents believed that the soldiers who were enforcing the lockdown in Bindura were generally pitiless to the civilian population as retribution for the murder of their colleague by artisanal miners in a dispute over a commercial sex worker in mid-April 2019 (*Zim Eye*, 1 May 2020).

In the city of Bulawayo on 25 April 2020, Sethukani Ncube, a male resident of Lobengula Suburb, was savagely attacked with booted feet by uniformed police at his home following a misunderstanding. As a result of the brutal assault, Ncube suffered serious injuries, including a dislocated left shoulder. Upon realising the gravity of the injuries, and in an effort to cover up their unlawful and unwarranted conduct, the police assailants dragged him into a truck and drove to Magwegwe Police Station where they detained him overnight. On the following day, he was set free after being forced to pay a fine on fabricated charges of violating lockdown regulations (*Zim Eye*, 15 May 2020).

On 30 April 2020, around 10am, Chief Trymore Nhari, a Zimbabwean traditional leader, and Shepard Moyo, his acquaintance, were severely assaulted twice within one day in the Gweru Central Business District by police details who were enforcing lockdown regulations (Zimbabwe Lawyers for Human Rights, 16 May 2020). They met a truckload of police officers who stopped their vehicle after which they were harassed and assaulted with baton sticks allegedly for defying stay-at-home orders. The chief reported the assault at Mutapa Police Station. At 3pm on the same day, the chief and his colleague came across another group of police officers who assaulted them again resulting in the traditional leader having his chieftaincy badge, three mobile phones, wrist watch and laptop being damaged. Having sustained a broken left arm from the assault, Chief Nhari filed a report at Gweru Central Police Station and also requested to be escorted to Gweru General Hospital for medical treatment. The Officer-in-Charge at Gweru Central Police Station turned down the chief's request and threatened to physically assault him further (*Zim Eye*, 15 May 2020). On 11 May 2020, the chief served a notice of intention to sue for payment of damages on Godwin Matanga, the Commissioner-General of the ZRP and the Home Affairs and Cultural Heritage Minister, Kazembe Kazembe. In the notice of intention to sue, Nhari demanded to be paid ZWL$300 000 in damages after ZRP officers damaged his Chief's badge, three mobile phone handsets, wrist watch and a laptop, and also broke his left arm (Ibid).

On 1 May 2020, Obvious Nkomo, a 35-year-old soldier based at Induna Barracks and employed as a corporal in the ZNA, and Dennis Maturi, a 45-year-old policeman employed as a sergeant by the ZRP, allegedly assaulted Weston Chandomba, a 33-year-old mechanic, in Bulawayo's Njube Suburb. Nkomo and Maturi were conducting lockdown duties that included routine checks and escorting a truck doing door-to-door selling of maize meal as a measure to prevent the spread of the Corona virus when they had a misunderstanding with Chandomba. Apparently, the delivery truck had blocked Chandomba who was driving a different vehicle. When he complained, the soldier and the policeman accused him of disorderly behaviour (Zimbabwe Lawyers for Human Rights, 3 July 2020). The police officer switched off Chandomba's car and removed keys from the ignition, dragged him out of the vehicle and severely assaulted him with open hands. Not to be outdone by the policeman, the soldier struck Chandomba with the butt of a gun (*Zim Eye*, 15 May 2020). They then handcuffed him together with other people they had arrested and ordered them to sit down on the tarmac before force-marching them to Njube Police Station. He was released without charge after being detained for several hours. Chandomba sustained numerous bodily injuries and a damaged ear that left him with a hearing impairment as a result of the assault (Ibid; Zimbabwe Lawyers for Human Rights, 3 July 2020).

In Bulawayo's Cowdray Park Suburb around 8pm on 23 July 2020, people living in the Empompini area "were ruthlessly clobbered by uniformed police officers for being outside after 6pm" (Centre for Innovation and Technology, 26 September 2020: 1). The police justified the beatings on the grounds that, "holding cells at Luveve Police Station were full, so they were administering instant justice" (Ibid). Given such barbarous incidents, it was not surprising that during the month of July 2020, the ZRP and the ZNA topped the list of the perpetrators of human rights violations in Zimbabwe with a combined 80.66%. During this period, the Zimbabwe Peace Project (ZPP) recorded 48 cases of unlawful detention, 68 cases of assault and 168 cases of harassment and intimidation, 15 cases of abduction and torture, with the majority of these cases being attributable to state security agents (ZPP, 30 July 2020).

On 1 August 2020, at a fuel station in the border town of Beitbridge, Edmund Zeyazeya and Benson Tawengwa were severely mauled by dogs unleashed on them by the police. Police officers on Covid-19 lockdown patrols arrested the two Beitbridge men to cover up for their negligence in handling the police dogs and charged them with disorderly conduct. Zeyazeya and Tawengwa were fined and released the same day but went on to file a lawsuit against the police in which they sued for damages amounting to Z$3 million and Z$500 000 respectively. In early November 2021, the court ordered the ZRP to pay Z$425 000 to Zeyazeya and Z$85 000 to Tawengwa as damages emanating from the unlawful conduct exhibited by the law-enforcement agents (Chikandiwa, 5 November 2021).

In Harare's Mabvuku Suburb on 5 August 2020, David Antony Mutendera, a 48-year-old male resident, was brutally assaulted by a group of soldiers for allegedly contravening the 12-hour curfew (Ndoro, 11 August 2020; *ZW News*, 10 August 2020). As Mutendera himself narrated his ordeal, he had finished work in town and failed to get home in time due to transport challenges. In fact, commuters across the country had begun facing serious transport blues after the government banned private transporters from servicing all urban centres and gave the state-owned ZUPCO the monopoly to ply these areas (Ndoro, 11 August 2020; *ZW News*, 10 August 2020). Mutendera eventually boarded a ZUPCO bus that had come much later and arrived in his neighbourhood after 7 pm, an hour after the 12-hour curfew had started. As he rushed home, he ran into a group of soldiers who brutally assaulted him despite his efforts to explain his situation. Mutendera suffered grievous injuries which also left his three front teeth shaking (Ndoro, 11 August 2020; *ZW News*, 10 August 2020).

In mid-September 2020, Njabulo Chikumira, a 23-year-old man from Bulawayo's Old Magwegwe Suburb, "suffered several lacerations and a sprained ankle after police descended upon him ostensibly for breaking the 6pm curfew" (Centre for Innovation and Technology, 26 September 2020: 1). As Chikumira narrated his horrendous encounter: "I was coming from visiting my sister who stays near Marisha (Magwegwe) when police pounced and beat me up. They said I was not supposed to be outside home at that time" (Ibid).

When Constantino Chiwenga, the Vice President and Health Minister, announced fresh lockdown measures on 2 January 2021 and the then Acting President Kembo Mohadi announced the following day that the army would continue to assist the police to ensure compliance, many citizens were deeply concerned (*New Zimbabwe*, 5

January 2021). Former liberation war combatants of the Zimbabwe People's Revolutionary Army (ZIPRA), for example, urged the authorities to ensure that army personnel on lockdown duties respect citizens' rights. In a strongly-worded statement, Job Ndlovu, ZIPRA Veterans Association Deputy Secretary General, said:

> We are appealing to the government, through Defence Minister Oppah Muchinguri and Commander Defence Forces, Philip Valerio Sibanda, to make sure that citizens are not harassed by the security forces. The security sector is there to protect the citizens of this country. They are not there to abuse and threaten people. People are afraid to see heavily armed soldiers wielding AKs in the streets. People should be more afraid of Covid-19 than soldiers who are peacekeepers. Zimbabwe is a democratic country where people should not be afraid of their army (Ibid: 1).

In early February 2021, a senior ZANU-PF official actually acknowledged that the army was committing various human rights abuses during the course of enforcing lockdown regulations. Maybe Mbowa, the ZANU-PF's Women's League National Commissar and the Senator for the Gokwe-Nembudziya Constituency, was heard in a video claiming that soldiers were on the rampage in the district, "harassing shoppers and forcing villagers to crawl in water" (Matenga, 4 February 2021: 1). In a statement that seemed to implicate the army in Covid-19 related violence than the police, Mbowa said:

> As Senator and Political Commissar of the Women's League, I am not happy with the reports. I can phone straight to the President because I suspect there is something happening behind the scenes. I do not know what it is, but I am even ready to engage their (soldiers') leader here. You can invite me to your meetings and I talk to them. I got several reports and I initially ignored them thinking people were lying. The recent report was about a former teacher who was harassed and was beaten up by soldiers who also forced him to crawl. Another victim was forced into the water. Imagine in these Covid-19 times, someone is forced into the water exposing them to the virus. We want to know what these soldiers stand for. Are they there for the government and are they there to see to it that government regulations have been followed? Where in town have you seen people running away from soldiers? Why is it only Nembudziya that is experiencing that?...We have a police force and the police force should be the one on the forefront of enforcing the

regulations and when they are overwhelmed, that is where the government said soldiers should come in to help and not for soldiers to be in the front (Matenga, 4 February 2021: 1).

At around 11pm on 27 October 2021, the police in the small farming town of Chivhu set dogs on Darlington Manjokota, a 28-year-old man, for disregarding the nation-wide Covid-19 lockdown curfew that began at 10pm. Manjokota suffered serious injuries and had to be admitted at Chivhu General Hospital where medical sources stated that his hand could be amputated (*News dzeZimbabwe*, 6 November 2021). Speaking from his hospital bed, Manjokota narrated his ordeal as follows:

> I was leaving the bar and suddenly people started fleeing in different directions. I ran away trying to find a place to hide but I did not realise that I was going in the direction of the police. They then let loose their dog and it attacked me. It dragged me eight metres towards the police officers. They picked me up and dumped me at the hospital (Ibid: 1).

The physical attacks on civilians by the police as a way of enforcing Covid-19 lockdown rules contravened human rights, particularly the right not to be subjected to torture and other cruel, inhumane or degrading treatment or punishment. These rights are clearly spelt out in Article 5 of the 1948 Universal Declaration of Human Rights and Section 53 of the 2013 Constitution of Zimbabwe. It is without doubt that many members of the public came to fear the army and the police as much as or more than they feared the Covid-19 pandemic.

Bribery and robbery of lockdown violators

Some military and police officers became notorious for corruption as they harassed, bribed and extorted money from alleged violators of lockdown regulations (*ZW News*, 8 May 2020). The victims of these corrupt activities included both pedestrians and motorists who were deemed to be moving around in contravention of stay-at-home orders and those that violated the curfew. Some journalists who visited Westlea Park near Epworth Suburb in Harare during the morning of 8 May 2020 witnessed altercations between motorists and security officers during which soldiers sometimes used catapults to threaten motorists who attempted to drive off to evade arrest for defying stay-at-home orders. After arresting a motorist, the police and the soldiers demanded between US$5 to US$10 and more. They threatened to take those who failed to pay the bribes to the nearby Domboramwari Police Station where official fines were more expensive and failure to pay could attract a prison term (Ibid). Such threats left many motorists in an unenviable predicament without freedom of choice but to pay the bribe. In these circumstances, the motorist became a hostage of the police and military officers while the bribe became the ransom to secure one's freedom! By July 2021, police corruption during Zimbabwe's Covid-19 lockdown period had become so endemic to the extent that citizens referred to the US$10 bill as "the national identity card to pass a roadblock" (Gwacha-Dube, 11 July 2021: 1). Consequently, the majority of Zimbabweans came to regard the police as "the most corrupt institution in the country" (Ibid).

There were reports of military and police officers on lockdown assignments robbing lockdown violators, sometimes at gunpoint. On 25 July 2020, for instance, Cloudy Tasukwa, a father of two from the town of Chitungwiza, reportedly committed suicide by drinking poison after soldiers and police enforcing lockdown regulations allegedly robbed him of US$1 200 (Mpofu, 28 July 2020). Lancelot Tasukwa, a spokesperson of the deceased's family, confirmed that his brother had taken his life after US$1 200 had been taken from him by soldiers at Huruyadzo Shopping Centre in Chitungwiza's St Mary's Suburb. Lancerot explained that his brother was so distressed by the loss of the money since he was unemployed and had sold his vehicle in order to start an informal business (Ibid).

As this section has demonstrated, many Zimbabweans came to live in fear during the lockdown period owing to the unscrupulous shenanigans of some members of the state security, especially the police and the army. A sense of vulnerability and insecurity gripped many Zimbabweans as some pachydermatous and avaricious members of the security service sector abrogated their mandate to safeguard the welfare of citizens by harassing, bribing and robbing them under the guise of enforcing lockdown provisions. The rights of many Zimbabweans to live as free citizens were, therefore, severely compromised as they were no longer guaranteed of protection from people who were mandated and remunerated to safeguard their welfare.

Physical assault of women

Women suffered a double tragedy involving the pandemic and violence, both of which culminated in the gross violation of their [human] rights and dignity during Zimbabwe's Covid-19 period. Violence against women became widespread during this period with the major instigators and perpetrators being the government's law-enforcement agents (Dube, 7 April 2021).

On 1 April 2020 in the city of Bulawayo, for example, Lydia Chapalapata, a 63-year-old female resident of Nkulumane Suburb, was allegedly assaulted by Assistant Inspector Brighton Muchingami while she was queuing to purchase maize meal at Sekusile Shopping Centre. According to Chapalapata, Muchingami flogged her on allegations of breaching lockdown regulations. As a result of the assault, Chapalapata claimed that she had sustained serious injuries on her back, thighs, head and knees and had to be admitted at Mpilo Central Hospital for treatment. Muchingambi reportedly told Chapalapata that it was futile for her to seek legal recourse as he was empowered by the lockdown regulations to beat her up (Nkala, 12 June 2021). In early June 2021, Chapalapata approached the Zimbabwe Lawyers for Human Rights for legal assistance to sue Muchingami. The lawsuit which was subsequently submitted to the court demanded Z$3 million from the Zimbabwe Republic Police Commissioner-General, Godwin Matanga, and the Minister of Home Affairs and Cultural Heritage as compensation "for pain and suffering, trauma and nervous shock ... (and) for future medical expenses" (Ibid: 1). In a related incident in mid-April 2020, the police reportedly whipped an old woman who was queueing for maize meal outside a shop in Harare. After they failed to get maize meal, the police ordered them to disperse in line with Covid-19 lockdown restrictions which banned public gatherings and imposed social distancing. The stony-hearted police went on to brutally assault the old woman after accusing her of not moving fast enough (Gasa, 21 April 2020).

In the city of Bulawayo on 16 April 2020, two blood sisters were "brutally assaulted for hours with batons on their backs, hips and legs by police officers who accused them of violating the ongoing national lockdown" (Tshili, 8 May 2020: 1). On the day in question, two marauding police officers pounced on two sisters, Nokuthula and Ntombizodwa Mpofu, who had gone to the shops to buy food stuff for their children (Catholic Commission for Justice and Peace, 2020;

Dube, 7 April 2021; Kudzayi, 7 April 2021; Tshili, 8 May 2020). The police officers are said to have followed the two women into a supermarket in Cowdray Park Suburb, pulled them out of the queue and accused them of loitering instead of staying at home (Catholic Commission for Justice and Peace, 2020; Tshili, 8 May 2020), and "breaching social distancing rules on a supermarket queue" (Gukurume, 22 May 2020: 1). The sisters were handcuffed behind their backs and allegedly force-marched through a bush to the Cowdray Park Police Base (Tshili, 8 May 2020). Along the way to the police base, the officers made frequent stops during which they forced them to sit down and took turns to beat them with batons while verbally assaulting them as prostitutes, among other demeaning things (Catholic Commission for Justice and Peace, 2020; Tshili, 8 May 2020). Upon arrival at the police base, the women were forced to sit behind a parked vehicle and two police officers continued to lash them with batons while verbally abusing them (Tshili, 8 May 2020). As one of the sisters recounted:

> They told us they would teach us a lesson. They said they wanted to show us that they had better women than us at their homes. They said our being 'yellow-boned' (light-skinned) did not exempt us from the stay-at-home order. We asked them why they were beating us and they said we were rude (Ibid: 1).

The women further charged that the police refused to allow their relatives to pay fines for them. They were also detained overnight even though their family members wanted to take them out to hospital for treatment since their buttocks and hips were swollen. They were eventually fined Z$200 the following afternoon and released after which their relatives rushed them to Mpilo Central Hospital for treatment (Ibid). The two female victims later approached the National Peace and Reconciliation Commission (NPRC) for assistance to make a formal report to the police with a view to having the matter taken to the courts of law. Leslie Ncube, an investigator of the NPRC responsible for the three Matabeleland provinces, expressed grave concern at the way the two women had been brutalised by the police:

> They were brutally attacked by male police officers who beat them on the thighs and buttocks while insulting them. We are told that the officers insulted them using derogatory language which also fuels ethnic hatred. The victims told us that the officers were telling them that there

is nothing special with their hips and they also have wives with bigger hips. So, clearly, the police officers became too personal instead of executing their police duties. The police are supposed to protect the lives of the vulnerable in our society. We condemn the behaviour of the said police officers. The victims were allegedly insulted. Such actions are not expected from the police officers, especially in an independent Zimbabwe (Ibid).

Police Assistant Commissioner Paul Nyathi weighed in and also condemned the heavy-handed nature of law-enforcement exhibited by the police details. He added:

> They should not get carried away when they perform their duties. They should stick to the mandate which the police have in terms of the constitution of the country, in terms of deployment which would have been done by their commanders. So, anyone who goes outside the deployment order and does their own things will face the full wrath of the law (Ibid).

In another thick-skinned show of force on 3 April 2020, some over-enthusiastic members of the ZRP and the ZNA severely assaulted Lucia Masvondo, a 26-year-old woman, for violating lockdown regulations while she was cooking food in her yard using wood on an open fire outside her house in the Chikangwe Suburb of the small farming town of Karoi in Mashonaland West Province (Mangirazi *et al*, 8 April 2020; Mavhunga, 10 April 2020; Ndebele, 15 April 2020; Zimbabwe Lawyers for Human Rights, 14 April 2020). It was reported that the assailants barged Masvondo's homestead, unleashed dogs and then flogged her (Chirimambowa, 11 July 2020; Ndebele, 15 April 2020; Zimbabwe Lawyers for Human Rights, 14 April 2020). Masvondo complained bitterly that the law-enforcement agents had overstepped their bounds, adding: "I am worried that this lockdown is forcing us to be indoors at 8pm. Are we not allowed to prepare supper? Is it what the President has told these officers?" (Mangirazi *et al*, 8 April 2020: 1). She sought legal assistance from the Zimbabwe Lawyers for Human Rights who went on to present her case to the courts (Mavhunga, 10 April 2020; Ndebele, 15 April 2020).

On 14 April 2020, following the presentation of Masvondo's case by the Zimbabwe Lawyers for Human Rights, the High Court granted an interim order that the police, soldiers and other state security agents should respect human rights, dignity and fundamental freedoms of persons while enforcing Covid-19 lockdown provisions (Chingarande, 15 April 2020; Ndebele, 15 April 2020; Zimbabwe Lawyers for Human Rights, 14 April 2020). In addition, the court ordered that the police and the army on lockdown assignments should desist from treating people in any degrading manner. Such demeaning acts, the court stated, included "ordering any person to sing meaningless or offensive songs about Corona virus, ordering any person to jump up and down in one spot while carrying heavy items of personal property such as bicycles or with their hands locked behind their heads and ordering any person to lie prone on the ground with their hands spread out or locked at the back of their heads" (Chingarande, 15 April 2020: 1).

Lamentably, the High Court ruling fell on deaf ears! On 13 May 2020, three female activists and members of the opposition Movement for Democratic Change Alliance (MDC-A), Joanna Mamombe, a Member of Parliament, Cecilia Chimbiri and Netsai Marova, who were leading a demonstration against the rise of Covid-19-related socio-economic hardships on the poor people were arrested at a police roadblock in Harare (Dube, 7 April 2021; Mafundikwa, 21 September 2020). Later during the day, they were abducted from Harare Central Police Station by a group of men believed to be intelligence operatives and went missing for two days (Dube, 7 April 2021; Rivers & Ndlovu, 24 June 2020). According to eye witnesses, masked assailants forced the three women into an unmarked Toyota mini-van and sped away (Burke & Chingono, 17 May 2020). They were later found by a local man dumped on a rural roadside near the town of Bindura (Human Rights Watch, 2020), 87 kilometres from their homes in Harare, critically injured from beatings (Burke & Chingono, 17 May 2020; Dube, 7 April 2021). They reported having been abducted, flogged and sexually abused by armed security details (Dube, 7 April 2021; Rivers & Ndlovu, 24 June 2020).

Among the abuses the three women were subjected to were being "beaten, stripped naked, forced to drink each other's urine and sexually assaulted with firearms" (Mafundikwa, 21 September 2020: 1). As the then 33-year-old Chimbiri later told reporters from her hospital bed: "They were taking a very big gun … they were putting it inside my anal passage and then the other guy was sucking my breasts" (Ibid). She added:

> They beat me on my back, all over the body using sticks. They used a gun to beat us, then molested me. They pushed us out of the truck on

> to the road. They left us there. They said, "We will be watching you … What is so special about you that you want to turn against the government?" (Burke & Chingono, 17 May 2020: 1).

The 36-year-old Joana Mamombe, then one of the youngest Zimbabwean Members of Parliament, narrated how they were force-marched in a thickly-wooded area and made to sing protest songs: "They were pouring water on us. They beat us if we stopped. They made us drink each other's urine. They were fondling Cecilia (Chimbiri)" (Ibid: 1). Henry Chimbiri, the father of Cecilia Chimbiri, complained about the ordeal which his daughter and her colleagues had experienced and lamented: "They (police and state agents) are not humane. They are killers. The girls are in bad shape. They are in pain. One cannot talk. She is just crying. The police is no longer our police" (Ibid: 1). The Zimbabwe Lawyers for Human Rights condemned the abduction and torture of the three political activists. Their official statement read: "The Zimbabwe Lawyers for Human Rights strongly condemns such wanton disregard of human rights and the constitution. Enforced disappearances, torture, cruel, inhumane and degrading treatment can never be justified. All perpetrators must be held accountable" (Ibid: 1).

A month later in June 2020, the government instituted legal proceedings on the three activists, charging them with faking their abductions and tarnishing the image of the country (Dube, 7 April 2021; Mafundikwa, 21 September 2020). They were then remanded in custody for 14 days after which the court granted them bail. The judge ordered them to surrender their passports and report thrice a week at a police station. Furthermore, the judge warned them against communicating with the media in relation to the issue (Mafundikwa, 21 September 2020). On 31 July, they were re-arrested at a roadblock during which a soldier whipped Cecilia Chimbiri on allegations of insulting him (Dube, 7 April 2021).

As violence against women continued unabated, Noxolo Maphosa, a 23-year-old woman resident in the city of Bulawayo, was also brutally by security forces who were enforcing Covid-19 regulations (Mafundikwa, 21 September 2020). On 7 August 2020, four state security agents abducted her in public in Bulawayo's Central Business District. She was bundled into a truck and driven to a house where she was allegedly assaulted, both physically and sexually, to reveal the whereabouts of her uncle, Josphat Ngulube, an MDC-Alliance supporter who was being accused of issuing out Covid-19 face masks bearing the slogan 'ZANU-PF must go' (Dube,

7 April 2021). After expressing ignorance on the whereabouts of Ngulube, Maphosa was allegedly flogged while "one of the men pulled out a knife and cut through her clothing and underclothing" (Mafundikwa, 21 September 2020:1). Surprisingly, the government spokesperson, Nick Mangwana, justified the bestiality of the state security agents on grounds that Maphosa had been "obstructing the police from enforcing the law" (Ibid).

On 28 December 2020, three women, Naomi Burayimu (a street vendor aged 42), Sabina Jiri (50 years) and Eunice Muchenje (52 years) were severely assaulted by more than 10 police officers in the Lion's Den area of Makonde District in Mashonaland West Province for allegedly contravening Covid-19 lockdown stay-at-home orders. The three women had intended to vote in the ruling party's by-elections in the district but had been told to return to the polling station later after technical issues had been resolved. While the women were sitting on the veranda at Jiri's home waiting to go back to the polling station, the police showed up and beat them up before following them into the house to mete out further punishment. After the assault, the police details went on the rampage, indiscriminately attacking people in the area. As a result of the unsparing assault, Burayimu suffered a broken hand while Jiri and Muchenje were left nursing serious injuries after being beaten on their backs, chests, feet and buttocks (Zwinoira, 8 March 2021).

The three injured women visited the nearby Murereka Police Station to file a complaint against the officers so that they could use the police report to get treatment at a clinic. Instead, they were reportedly chased away by the Officer-in-Charge. As they were returning to Jiri's house, some of the officers who had beaten them earlier followed them and threatened to assault them again if they left the house. Some well-wishers later took the three women to a nearby clinic where they received limited treatment due to a shortage of medical supplies, forcing them to return to Jiri's house in pain. The women sought assistance from the ruling party's District Coordinating Committee Chairman front-runner and Member of Parliament, Kindness Paradza, who was in Chinhoyi, the province's capital. After Paradza arrived and the women told him what had happened, he accompanied them to the police station and convinced officers to allow them to make their report so that they could get treatment at a government hospital. While making their police report, however, the three women were arrested by the same officers who had initially chased them. They were detained on trumped-up charges of launching an assault on the police station two days earlier that the women knew nothing about. At that point, Paradza stopped assisting them. The women were later released on 31 December 2020 after paying bail equivalent to US$115 each at the Provincial Magistrates Court (Ibid).

As discussed in this section, the physical assault of women by the police violated human rights in general and women's rights and dignity in particular. The physical and sexual harassment experienced by some of these women are clear examples of gender-based violence perpetrated by law-enforcement agents, who instead should be seen protecting and upholding human and women's rights. Thus, instead of upholding the law, these so-called law-enforcement agents acted otherwise and became the chief perpetrators of violence as well as being gross violators of human rights, freedoms and civil liberties.

Assault of journalists

Journalists were not spared from the brutal attacks of Zimbabwe's security forces during the Covid-19 period. During the first week of the lockdown, nine journalists reported being manhandled by the army and the police while undertaking their duties (Zenda, 24 April 2020). On 11 April 2020, Terence Sipuma, a freelance journalist, was assaulted by police officers and soldiers while on his way to Chegutu to report on the Covid-19 lockdown in the town (Media Institute of Southern Africa, 12 April 2020). Sipuma recalled the harrowing experience: "They asked where I was going and the moment I showed them my journalism identity card, I was asked to lie down and was beaten, being accused of exposing them" (Zenda, 24 April 2020: 1).

On 20 July 2020, the police violently arrested investigative journalist Hopewell Chin'ono at his home and charged him with "incitement to participate in public violence" (*Newsday*, 21 July 2020: 1). This came after Chin'ono allegedly covered a case involving the fraudulent procurement of Covid-19 preventive materials by the Ministry of Health which led to the arrest and sacking of the then Health Minister, Obadiah Moyo. In May 2020, the Zimbabwean government, through the Ministry of Health, had authorised the payment of US$987 720 for a consignment of Covid-19 equipment at an inflated cost from a company called Drax International, owned by controversial businessman, Delish Nguwaya (*Newsday*, 29 May 2020). The items in the consignment included 5 040 N95 masks, which were supposed to be procured at a cost of US$28 per unit, 15 000 Covid-19 test kits at US$34 each and 3 740 coveralls for US$90 each. However, the prices for the items were too high in the sense that the masks charged at a cost of US$28 each often cost about US$5 per unit, coveralls cost an average of US$30 and rapid tests cost US$15 (Ibid). Basing on the prices, Drax International was going to make a profit of about US$500 000 from the consignment and this triggered a debate in parliament on 28 May 2020 about the inflated pricing (Ibid). Although Delish Nguwaya and Obadiah Moyo were arrested over the Drax International deal, this did not clear President Mnangagwa from this scandal as his son, Collins Mnangagwa, was alleged to be Nguwaya's business partner in the aforementioned deal (Ibid). Although Mnangagwa's family tried to distance itself from Nguwaya and his company, these damage-control efforts were contradicted by several photos of Nguwaya having friendly moments with the first family that began to circulate on social media. Since Chino'no had covered this corruption case that implicated the first family, his arrest was perceived by many human rights groups and the general public as a way of silencing him or punishing him for exposing this deal. On 24 July 2020, while leaving the court, Chin'ono told journalists that his arrest and detention entailed that journalism was being criminalised in Zimbabwe (*Guardian*, 24 July 2020). The Committee to protect Journalism (2020) complained that instead of detaining those responsible for stealing public funds, the government employed strong-arm tactics to silence the messenger.

From this section, it is quite apparent that many journalists, particularly freelancers and those from the independent media, were subjected to various forms of harassment and abuse by Zimbabwe's law-enforcement agents on lockdown assignments. The journalists, especially freelancers, were particularly targeted for harassment by police, military and intelligence details as retribution for exposing the shortcomings of the government and law-enforcement agents in handling the Covid-19 pandemic and the administration of the national lockdown. The vindictive and hard-handed actions of the law-enforcement agents severely curtailed media freedom, deprived many members of the public of the right to information and subjected many journalists to physical harm and emotional stress.

Arbitrary arrest of political activists

The arbitrary arrests and torture of political activists who spoke against Covid-19 corruption were also other forms of human rights abuse witnessed in Zimbabwe during the pandemic. Most of these activists were protesting against high levels of corruption by top government officials who were misusing public funds at the expense of the general populace in the country. On 20 July 2020, for example, the police arrested Jacob Ngarivhume, a political activist, after he had organised a nationwide protest against corruption. The anti-corruption protest, which was scheduled for 31 July 2020, received massive support from the then MDC-A and some civil society organisations but it did not get approval from the ZANU-PF government as it was considered as a demonstration sponsored by Western nations to destabilise peace, unity and harmony in the country (*Chronicle*, 14 July 2020; *New Zimbabwe*, 13 July 2020). The government also criminalised the protest on grounds that it was a violation of the national lockdown whose regulations included a ban on gatherings of large numbers of people to prevent the transmission and spread of Covid-19 (*Chronicle*, 14 July 2020).

The arbitrary arrest of civilians during the Covid-19 period did not end with the detention of Ngarivhume. Despite the fact that Ngarivhume had been arrested and charged for inciting violence, some activists proceeded with the anti-corruption protest on 31 July 2020. Among them was the MDC-A spokesperson, Fadzai Mahere, renowned author Tsitsi Dangarembga, and nine other protestors (*Newsday*, 1 August 2020). They were charged with incitement to commit violence and breaching Covid-19 health regulations. Challenging their arrest, Mahere, a lawyer by profession, argued that during the protests, they did not violate any Covid-19 regulation as they were wearing masks as well as observing social distancing (Ibid). As mentioned earlier in this chapter, while observance of Covid-19 regulations was essential in preventing the spread of the pandemic, the Zimbabwean government was now manipulating and instrumentalising them to supress peaceful protests against corruption and bad governance, thereby exacerbating the political crisis bedevilling the country. Mahere stated that their arrest was illegal, citing Section 59 of Zimbabwe's 2013 Constitution which guaranteed the right to demonstrate and present petitions peacefully (Ibid).

The harassment of political activists discussed in this section illustrates the manner in which the police and other law-enforcement agents violated human rights in the name of enforcing Covid-19 containment measures. It can therefore be argued that while the implementation of lockdown rules was crucial in order to curb the spread of the Covid-19 pandemic, the government, through the police and the military, weaponised these regulations to suppress protests and political opponents, acts which had negative implications on the citizens' human rights, freedoms and liberties.

Harassment and pauperisation of informal sector workers

Even though the majority of Zimbabweans worked in the informal economy, the authorities never treated informal traders kindly during the Covid-19 lockdown period. In mid-2020, according to Hilal Elver, a United Nations researcher on global food security, 60% of Zimbabwe's economy was informal and a similar percentage of its people were not able to obtain enough food to meet basic needs owing to challenges such as hyperinflation (Rivers & Ndlovu, 24 June 2020). The arrest and confiscation of vendors' goods became routine as the government unleashed law-enforcement agents on several occasions to penalise and eliminate informal economy participants as they were accused of spreading Covid-19. Police and army patrols enforcing lockdown measures often targeted street vendors and hawkers, some of whom were brutally assaulted. Many of these informal sector workers remained adamant as they had no option other than to seek livelihoods though they had to contend with the great risk of being detected and battered by marauding police officers and soldiers (Zenda, 24 April 2020). On 3 April 2020, as shown in Pictures 1 and 2 below, the police confiscated and burnt three tones of vegetables that small-scale farmers had supplied to vendors at the Sakubva Vegetable Market in the city of Mutare (*Herald*, 3 April 2020). The vegetables that were confiscated include tomatoes and cabbages, among others (Ibid). The seizure of the vegetables laid bare the take-no-prisoner, inconsiderate and insensitive attitude of the police and the government towards the people's right to food and livelihoods, given the harsh economic conditions that were being experienced by many ordinary people in the country in general and families that were surviving on the informal economy in particular. Thus, amid a deteriorating economy, Covid-19 added greatly to the challenges that afflicted many ordinary Zimbabweans (United Nations High Commissioner for Human Rights, 2020).

Picture 1: Mutare police loading confiscated vegetables onto a truck (*Herald*, 3 April 2020)

Picture 2: A Mutare municipal worker burning confiscated vegetables (*Herald*, 3 April 2020)

From early April 2020, informal traders in the town of Chiredzi, some of whom worked late into the night, were reportedly living in fear of army brutality as soldiers patrolling the streets earned notoriety for beating up curfew violators and sometimes taking them to unknown destinations (Bhebhe, 13 April 2020; Mafirakurewa, 12 April 2020). These developments were disclosed by Jonathan Mupamombe, the Chairperson of the Chiredzi Residents and

Ratepayers Association. As Mupamombe stated, the soldiers targeted mostly tuck-shop owners who operated during the late hours and vegetable vendors who went to the markets in the early hours of the day (Bhebhe, 13 April 2020; Mafirakureva, 12 April 2020). "Soldiers are beating up people at night," said Mupamombe, "We have one tuck-shop owner whose whereabouts are not yet known after she was taken by soldiers around 10pm…Some vegetable vendors are still nursing their injuries after they were severely beaten in the early hours of the day" (Mafirakureva, 12 April 2020: 1).

An operation against informal traders was launched at Jambanja Market in the town of Chitungwiza on 5 July 2020. When the police raided the market to arrest traders and confiscate their goods, Samson Chamunorwa Zharare, an informal trader, immediately tried to escape by driving off in his car. Police officers fired two shots, one of which hit Samson on the leg, causing a large wound. As news of the shooting spread and the civil society started to condemn the situation, the police quickly re-adjusted the story: Samson was accused of attempted murder and resisting arrest for allegedly trying to run over police officers, and he was to be subjected to a trial as he recovered in hospital (Teixeira, 29 July 2020).

Following this incident, the Zimbabwe Chamber of Informal Economy Associations (ZCIEA) issued a statement denouncing police high-handedness against informal traders as follows:

> ZCIEA represents the informal economy workers in Zimbabwe and by such, we cannot ignore this bad incident. The unfortunate incident shows that the police are not carrying out their mandate to protect the public but instead are now brutalising innocent traders trying to earn a living. Using live gunshots on civilians is uncalled for. This action by the Zimbabwe Republic Police is not new as they are ever at loggerheads with the informal economy workers, raiding their wares and confiscating their goods. The informal economy in Zimbabwe cannot breathe due to police brutality. Such militant acts on the informal economy workers and traders must stop forthwith…It is a shame to realise that the state security agents are using the Covid-19 lockdown to prey on informal traders or put up an operation on the poor, innocent citizens of Zimbabwe who equally have a right to life and employment without any stakeholders' consultations. Such characters are a threat to societal development. We all want a happy, healthy, friendly, and peaceful country full of accountability and human rights respect. Our collective effort should be to fight Covid-19 and not the vendors (Ibid: 1).

Street-Net International, another civil organisation, threw its weight behind the ZCIEA and argued:

> Street-Net International stands with ZCIEA stating that informal traders' lives matter and denounce this horrifying situation to the world. Street-Net International once again reiterates the calls made to the Zimbabwe government in 2019. We urge the Zimbabwean government to adopt a more inclusive way of dealing with street vendors in Zimbabwe through negotiations with organisations of street vendors…We further urge the Zimbabwean government to release jailed civil society activists and trade unionists, and let the law take its course in accordance with internationally accepted standards and respect for human rights.

Neither Samson nor any other informal trader trying to make a living during these difficult times belongs in prison. This kind of harassment and violence are intolerable and are in complete violation of the ILO Convention 190 (C190), which recognises, among other things, "the right of everyone to a world of work free from violence and harassment, including gender-based violence and harassment" and "that violence and harassment in the world of work can constitute a human rights violation or abuse, and that violence and harassment is a threat to equal opportunities, is unacceptable and incompatible with decent work." Informal economy workers deserve to be heard, supported and assisted; they should never be brutalised for trying to survive! The situation for informal traders in many countries is still critical. Now, more than ever, their essential contribution to social and economic development must be recognised. Street-Net International is mobilising all their affiliates and supporters to promote the rights of street vendors, hawkers, and cross-border traders during the Covid-19 pandemic crisis (Ibid: 1).

The unleashing of dogs on Enerty Chimedza, a female vendor in the town of Chivhu, by the police on 22 August 2021 is another clear evidence of police barbarity and gross violation of human rights that constituted a real threat to human life. The police set dogs on Chimedza for remaining at her vending stall after the 3.30pm cut-off time for businesses as prescribed in the country's lockdown stipulations. In her defence, Chimedza argued that vendors at the local market closed at 3.30pm as ordered by lockdown rules but they left one person to guard their wares until 6pm when a security guard came for the night shift. When the police came on this particular day, Chimedza was on duty to guard the wares until the guard came. They accused her of flouting Covid-19 regulations by doing business after 3.30pm. Chimedza was assaulted before dogs were unleashed on her. She was arrested and taken to Chivhu Police Station where she was fined RTGS1 000 even though she had explained her cause, besides having been injured. When she sought treatment at Chivhu General Hospital, the institution had no drugs and she was given a prescription for medication amounting to US$140 (Mubaiwa, 25 August 2021). Even if Chimedza had been guilty of violating lockdown orders, the police simply needed to effect an arrest and have her prosecuted in accordance with the laws of the land. There was absolutely no need to beat her up and unleash dogs upon her. This case is a classic example of the abuse of power by Zimbabwe's ruthless security operatives, especially the Zimbabwe Republic Police, during the enforcement of Covid-19 preventive measures.

Christopher Muchenje, the local Ward Councillor in Chivhu, criticised the brutal action and lamented the failure of the police to exhibit remorse for their heavy-handedness: "This was just a defenceless woman. She is not a criminal; she is a mother; she is not armed; she is a poor vendor. Why use police dogs on her? What touched us more is that police got her mauled by the dogs, arrested her and then fined her. Now she is faced with a medical bill" (Ibid: 1). Kumbirai Mafunda, the Spokesperson of the Zimbabwe Lawyers for Human Rights, also condemned the bestiality of the police that severely compromised the real mandate of the Zimbabwe Republic Police and basic human rights: "We condemn this kind of brutality by the police on this poor woman. We are concerned by increasing cases across the country where the police are not executing their duty professionally. They should not take the law in their hands and they should respect human rights" (*Zim Eye*, 26 August 2021: 1).

Admittedly, informal traders and workers were unenviably perched between the devil and the deepest sea during the Covid-19 lockdown period in Zimbabwe. While the pandemic posed a real threat to their health and existence, it came at a time when poverty was already an endemic feature in their lives. As if these life-threatening challenges were not enough, the government's lockdown orders criminalised their operations. Security officers pounced on them, destroying their stalls and confiscating their wares while subjecting most of them to inhumane and degrading treatment in the form of beatings, torture, arbitrary arrests and unlawful detentions, among other abuses.

Arbitrary arrest and torture of health workers

The arbitrary arrest and torture of civilians such as informal sector participants discussed in the previous section also extended to health workers. On 6 July 2020, for instance, 13 nurses at Harare Central Hospital were arrested by the Zimbabwe Republic Police after they had protested against poor remuneration and lack of protective clothing to ensure their safety during Covid-19 assignments (*Daily News*, 7 July 2020). Picture 3 below shows police officers chasing some of the nurses who were protesting.

Picture 3: Police chasing protesting nurses at Harare Central Hospital (Source: *Nehanda Radio*, 6 July 2020)

After their arrest, the nurses were bundled into a truck and taken to Mbare Police Station where they were detained overnight and charged for violating Covid-19 regulations, particularly failing to practise social distancing (Ibid). The bundling of protestors into police trucks was in itself a violation of Covid-19 regulations as people were squashed, leaving no space for social distancing thereby exposing them to infections. Sadly, because justice during Covid-19 was selective, no one could police the Zimbabwe Republic Police for violating the same regulations on social distancing. The arrest and detention of nurses saw the Zimbabwe Nurses' Association and non-governmental organisations such as the Crisis in Zimbabwe Coalition (CiZC) criticising the government for suppressing workers' rights

(*Zimbabwe Situation*, 6 July 2020). While denouncing the arrest of the nurses, the CiZC said:

> The Crisis in Zimbabwe Coalition (CiZC) condemns the arrest of striking nurses at Harare Hospital…We are not surprised by this action of the government of Zimbabwe; we know too well it is in the DNA of the Zimbabwean administration to behave in this manner… Nurses, like any other public servants, are facing hunger and starvation in this Covid-19 lockdown and are expected to be at the forefront in the fight against this global pandemic. How can they take such a huge risk to serve the nation while their own families are starving *and their own health at risk*? (Ibid: 1).

Thus, the arrest and detention of nurses was another vivid example of failure by law-enforcement agents to promote and protect workers' rights in particular and human rights in general during the Covid-19 period. Police brutality on civilians during the period of the Covid-19 pandemic was partially explained by the wage disparities between the security forces and the rest of civil servants. It is important to note that just before the 31 July 2020 protests, the police and soldiers got a salary increment of Z$5 000 and Z$8 000 respectively while other civil servants including nurses and teachers received only Z$1 200 (*Newsday*, 9 July 2020). These wage disparities were perceived by the general public as a ploy by the government to bribe the security sector workers ahead of the protests (Ibid).

Deaths of alleged lockdown violators from police and army brutality

Given that some people were actually killed for thumbing their noses at Covid-19 containment measures, Gukurume (22 May 2020: 1) accurately observed that many Zimbabweans feared the brutality of the security forces in enforcing lockdown regulations than the pandemic itself. He argued:

> While fear and anxiety about Covid-19 has gripped people in the country, many seem to be more afraid of something different. Since the lockdown and subsequent deployment of the police and army, it is common to hear people say, 'In this country we are more afraid of hunger and the state security than the Corona virus itself.' For many people, the state and its repressive apparatus represent an immediate and serious threat to their lives and livelihoods (Ibid: 1).

There was a disturbing report of an incident that took place on 4 January 2021 in which an overzealous police officer who was on patrol enforcing Covid-19 regulations allegedly hit and killed a nine-month-old baby strapped on the back of its mother in Harare. The incident reportedly took place at a popular bus stop for commuters to Mashonaland Central Province near the intersection of Second Street and Fife Avenue. The police are reported to have arrived at the bus stop claiming to be enforcing Covid-19 lockdown regulations and ordered people to disperse. They allegedly assaulted and chased the travellers with baton sticks. The woman was unable to sprint to safety because of the baby that she had on her back. Social media accounts stated that, as the policeman tried to strike the mother, he mistakenly hit the baby who died on the spot (Munemo, 5 January 2021). In their official response, the police stated that the baby was alive and that a medical examination had established that the injuries sustained by the infant were not a threat to life (*Global Voices sub-Saharan Africa*, 25 January 2021). What can be derived from this disturbing event is that even though the baby may not have been killed, as no further details were provided, violence that sometimes caused serious bodily harm on civilians was part of the inhumane strategies employed by the security officers to enforce compliance to Covid-19 restrictions. Thus, in this incident, the police were actually admitting that the minor was injured in a cross-fire by a strike that was directed at its mother by a ZRP officer.

A report published by Amnesty International, the London-based international human rights watchdog, on 7 April 2021 accused the government of condoning murders perpetrated on people alleged to have breached Covid-19 lockdown regulations by the police and the army (Kudzayi, 7 April 2021). During the year 2020, according to the report, Zimbabwe's security forces killed at least 10 people as President Emmerson Mnangagwa took advantage of the Covid-19 pandemic to escalate human rights infringements through deploying ZANU PF supporters, intelligence agents, the police and army to abduct and torture critics (Dube, 7 April 2021; Kudzayi, 7 April 2021). Included among those who were killed for contravening Covid-19 lockdown restrictions, among other issues, are Levison Moyo from Bulawayo and Mazwi Ndlovu "who was murdered by suspected ZANU-PF supporters in Plumtree for asking why opposition supporters were being denied access to Covid-19 aid" (Kudzayi, 7 April 2021). A man suspected of killing Ndlovu was later apprehended but freed without appearing in court or applying for bail (Dube, 7 April 2021).

On 30 March 2020, Levison Moyo, a 25-year-old man, was beaten by police in Bulawayo, Zimbabwe's second largest city, for allegedly breaching lockdown regulations (Amnesty International, 2021; Dube, 7 April 2021; Ndebele, 18 May 2020). Moyo died four days later from what a post-mortem report conducted by a government pathologist at the local United Bulawayo Hospitals termed 'subarachnoid haemorrhage and head trauma' (Ndebele, 18 May 2020). On the tragic day in question, Moyo and his pregnant girlfriend were on their way to the shops to buy basic commodities in Mabuthweni, a low-income suburb in Bulawayo, when the police reprimanded them for disregarding lockdown regulations (Ibid). In May 2020, Moyo's family engaged the Zimbabwe Lawyers for Human Rights and filed a notice of intent to sue Godwin Matanga, the Commissioner-General of the Zimbabwe Republic Police. Citing Levison Moyo's post-mortem, the Zimbabwe Lawyers for Human Rights filed a lawsuit claiming reparations for medical and funeral costs, general damages for loss of support and any other ancillary liabilities incurred due to the death (Ibid).

It is ironical that some people were actually killed as law-enforcement agents in Zimbabwe purportedly sought to curb the spread of the Covid-19 pandemic. It is an absurdity to kill people on grounds of saving their lives! How can one save people's lives by killing the very same people that are meant to be protected from a deadly virus? The right to life is always sacrosanct and there is no justification whatsoever for terminating someone's life in the name of enforcing Covid-19 curtailment measures.

Conclusion

This chapter has proved beyond doubt that in Zimbabwe, "the fights against Covid-19 have equally been a fight for human rights" (Zengwa, 2 May 2020: 1) and freedom. Several human rights and freedoms were infringed by state security forces as they were enforcing lockdown regulations. The enforcement of the lockdown in Zimbabwe was largely done with little or no consideration of the prevailing socio-economic circumstances in the country and the rights, freedoms and liberties of the majority of the population. The harsh economic environment in Zimbabwe saw many people forced by circumstances to breach the Covid-19 regulations in a bid to make ends meet thereby leaving them at the mercy of state security agents. Many civilians lost their lives from security agents' brutality while others were severely assaulted and tortured; more others were denied access to basic services. In other circumstances, the pandemic was used as a ploy to settle scores with political opponents as many political activists were arrested and tortured for violating Covid-19 regulations. While the so-called law-enforcement agents were policing civilians to ensure compliance to lockdown regulations, a question remains on who was supposed to police the police and other security personnel to ensure that basic human rights, freedoms and civil liberties were religiously respected and upheld.

References

Africa News (21 April 2020) 'Doctors expose lockdown brutality,' Available at: https://www.africa-press.net/zimbabwe/all-news, Accessed 29 September 2021.

Amnesty International (7 April 2021) 'Document #2048795: Amnesty International Report 2020/21; The state of the world's human rights; Zimbabwe 2020,' Available at: https://www.ecoi.net/en/document/2048795.html, Accessed 5 November 2021.

Amnesty International (2021) 'Zimbabwe 2020', Available at: https://www.amnesty.org/en/location/africa/southern-africa/zimbabwe/report-zimbabwe/, Accessed 5 November 2021.

Bhebhe, N. (13 April 2020) 'Covid-19 lockdown: Soldiers mercilessly beat up residents, abduct woman from her tuckshop at 10pm,' Available at: https://www.myzimbabwe.co.zw/news/63005.html, Accessed 5 November 2021.

Burke, J. & Chingono, N. (17 May 2020) 'Zimbabwean MDC activists abducted and sexually assaulted,' Available at: https://www.theguardian.com/world/2020/may/17, Accessed 29 September 2021.

Catholic Commission for Justice and Peace (2020) 'Two Zimbabwean journalists charged with violating Covid-19 lockdown,' Available at: https://cpj.org/2020/06, Accessed 30 September 2021.

Centre for Innovation and Technology (CITE) (26 September 2020) 'Human rights violations escalate as police enforce lockdown,' Available at: https://kubatana.net/2020/09/26/human-rights-violations-escalate-as-police-enforce-lockdown, Accessed 19 August 2021.

Chidombwe, N. (18 August 2020) 'Covid-19 and a clampdown on fundamental freedoms to quell dissent,' Available at: https://www.humanrightspulse.com/mastercontentblog, Accessed 27 July 2021.

Chikandiwa, H. (5 November 2021) 'Court orders $500K compensation for police brutality,' Available at: https://www.zimfocus.co.zw/index.php/2021/11/05/court-orders-500k-compensation-for-police-brutality-newsday/, Accessed 7 November 2021.

Chingarande, D. (15 April 2020) 'Do not beat up civilians: Court,' Available at: https://www.newsday.co.zw/2020/04, Accessed 5 November 2021.

Chingono, N. (3 August 2018) 'World condemns brutality' in: *The Zimbabwe Independent*, Available at: https://www.theindependent.co.zw/2018/08/03/world-condemns-brutality/, Accessed 28 September 2021.

Chronicle (14 July 2020) 'Government will not allow anarchy- July 31 illegal demos plot exposed,' Available at: https://www.chronicle.co.zw, Accessed 20 October 2021.

Daily News (13 June 2020) 'MDC trio in court for alleged fake abduction,' Available at: https://dailynews.co.zw, Accessed 17 October 2021.

Daily News (21 July 2020) 'Planned protests organiser arrested,' Available at: https://dailynews.co.zw/planned-protests-organiser-arrested/, Accessed 20 November 2021.

Dube, G. (7 April 2021) 'Amnesty International: Zimbabwe security forces killed 10 people under nation's Covid-19 lockdown,' Available at: https://www.voazimbabwe.com, Accessed 29 September 2021.

Duri, F.P.T. (2010) *The relentless governance by the sword: Situating Operation Murambatsvina in Zimbabwean history*, Saarbrucken: VDM Verlag Dr. Muller.

Gasa, S. (21 April 2020) 'Zimbabwe: The perils of reporting on the pandemic,' Available at: https://www.dailymaverick.co.za/article/2020-04-21-zimbabwe-the-perils-of-reporting-on-the-pandemic/, Accessed 1 October 2021.

Global Voices sub-Saharan Africa (25 January 2021) 'A Zimbabwean journalist, two opposition politicians jailed for tweets about police brutality,' Available at: https://advox.globalvoices.org/2021/01/25/a-zimbabwean-journalist-two-opposition-, Accessed 4 October 2021.

Guardian (24 July 2020) 'Journalism has been criminalised: Zimbabwean reporter denied bail,' Available at: https://www.theguardian.com/world/2020/jul/24/, Accessed 25 November 2021.

Gukurume, S. (22 May 2020) 'Abductions, brutality, and demolitions: When the state becomes more harmful than Covid-19,' Available at: http://democracyinafrica.org, Accessed 30 September 2021.

Guma, L. (27 October 2006) 'ZINASU leader arrested as over 12 students receive expulsion letters,' Available at: http://www.swradioafrica.com/News_archives/files, Accessed 27 September 2021.

Gwacha-Dube, B. (11 July 2021) 'Zimbabwe: Police corruption now a threat to economy,' Available at: https://allafrica.com/stories/202107110128.html, Accessed 6 November 2021.

Herald (3 April 2020) 'Lockdown: Police confiscate vegetables,' Available at: https://www.herald.co.zw, Accessed 25 October 2021.

Herald (31 December 2021) 'Daily Covid-19 cases remain above 2000,' Available at: https://www.herald.co.zw, Accessed 4 February 2022.

Human Rights Watch (2021) 'World Report 2021: Zimbabwe,' Available at: https://www.hrw.org/world-report/2021/country-chapters/zimbabwe, Accessed 1 October 2021.

Independent (1 August 2018) 'Zimbabwe election: Three dead in violent Harare protests as security forces battle demonstrators after ZANU-PF win in parliament vote,' Available at: www.zimbabweindependent.com, Accessed 4 November 2021.

Kudzayi, F. (7 April 2021) 'At least 10 killed as Mnangagwa dialled up rights abuses in 2020: Amnesty,' Available at: https://www.zimlive.com/2021/04/07, Accessed 22 September 2021.

Mafirakureva, G. (12 April 2020) 'Residents squeal over army torture,' Available at: https://www.zimbabwesituation.com/news/residents-squeal-over-army-torture/, Accessed 6 November 2021.

Mafundikwa, T. (21 September 2020) 'Critics: Zimbabwe stepping up arrests and assaults against female protesters,' Available at: https://www.zenger.news/2020/09/21/zimbabwe-steps-up-arrests-and-assaults-against-female-protesters/, Accessed 29 September 2021.

Makwerere, D. Chinzete, G.T. & Musorowegomo, C. (2012) 'Human rights and policing: A case study of Zimbabwe,' in: *International Journal of Humanities and Social Science,* Volume 2, Number 17, pp.129-138.

Mangirazi, N. Chingarande, D. & Matenga, M. (8 April 2020) 'Residents fume over lockdown brutality', Available at: https://www.newsday.co.zw/2020/04, Accessed 26 September 2021.

Masunungure, E.V. (2020) 'Zimbabwe's fragile independence, 1980-2020,' in: E.V. Masunungure (ed.) *Zimbabwe's trajectory: Stepping forward or sliding back,* Harare: Weaver Press.

Matenga, M. (4 February 2021) 'ZANU-PF chef exposes army brutality,' Available at: https://www.newsday.co.zw/2021/02/zanu-pf-chef-exposes-army-brutality/, Accessed 1 October 2021.

Maulani, N. Nyaburi, I. & Wandekha, B. (2020) 'The generals and the war against Covid-19: The case of Zimbabwe,' Available at: www.jogh.org, Accessed 28 September 2021.

Mavhunga, C. (10 April 2020) 'Zimbabwean sues government to end lockdown over alleged abuse,' Available at: https://www.voanews.com/a/science-health_coronavirus-outbreak, Accessed 22 August 2021.

Mavhunga, C. (22 July 2020) 'Zimbabwe's new 12-hour curfew hotly debated,' Available at: https://www.voanews.com/a/africa, Accessed 2 August 2021.

Mavhunga, C. (29 April 2021) 'Zimbabweans take stock of abuses during Covid-19 lockdowns,' Available at: https://www.voanews.com/a/africa, Accessed 20 August 2021.

Media Institute of Southern Africa (12 April 2020) 'Police assault freelance journalist,' Available at: https://zimbabwe.misa.org/2020/04/12, Accessed 12 September 2021.

Moyo, G. & Phulu, K.I. (2021) 'The weaponisation of the Corona virus crisis in Zimbabwe: Legal and extra-legal instruments,' in: *iBusiness*, Volume 13, pp.48-66, Available at: https://doi.org/10.4236/ib.2021.131004, Accessed 26 September 2021.

Mpofu, M. (28 July 2020) 'So sad: Man drinks poison and dies after evil soldiers and police officers robbed him of US$1 200,' Available at: https://www.myzimbabwe.co.zw/news/68030.html, Accessed 5 November 2021.

Mubaiwa, S. (25 August 2021) 'Vendor pays RTGS$1 000 fine after being mauled by police dogs,' Available at: https://masvingomirror.com/vendor-pays-rtgs1-000-fine-after-being-mauled-by-police-dogs/, Accessed 6 November 2021.

Mugari, I. & Obioha, E.E. (2021) 'Covid-19 and the restrictive measures: The national security conundrum for Zimbabwe,' in: *African Security Review*, pp1-14, Available at: https://doi.org/10.1080/10246029.2021.1972015, Accessed 30 September 2021.

Munemo, D. (5 January 2021) 'Covid-19 lockdown cop "kills" nine-month-old baby in bus stop rampage,' Available at: https://www.zimlive.com/2021/01/05/covid-19-lockdown-cop-kills-9-month-old-baby-in-bus-stop-rampage/, Accessed 3 October 2021.

Mutambasere, S.C. (2020) 'Constitutionalism in the time of Covid-19: The Zimbabwe experience,' Available at: https://ancl-radc.org.za/node/641, Accessed 27 September 2021.

Ndebele, L. (15 April 2020) 'Do not beat people up, court tells Zimbabwe's soldiers and police,' Available at: https://www.timeslive.co.za/news/africa/2020-04-15, Accessed 27 September 2021.

Ndebele, L. (18 May 2020) 'Zimbabwe police sued over Bulawayo man's lockdown death,' Available at: www.timeslive.co.za/news/africa/2020, Accessed 30 September 2021.

Ndoma, S. (21 July 2020) 'Covid-19 lockdown: Zimbabweans trust police and military, but not enough to criticise them,' in: *Afrobarometer Dispatch*, Number 375, 2020.

Ndoro, T.E. (11 August 2020) 'Man brutally assaulted by soldiers for violating curfew after ZUPCO transport woes,' Available at: https://iharare.com/pics, Accessed 26 July 2021.

Nehanda Radio (6 June 2020) 'Nurses in Zimbabwe arrested as they protest over pay,' Available at: https://nehandaradio.com/2020/07/06/nurses-in-zimbabwe-arrested-as-they-protest-over-pay-pictures, Accessed 22 July 2021.

New Zimbabwe (5 January 2021) 'Ex-fighters urge security forces restraint in enforcement of lockdown measures,' Available at: https://www.newzimbabwe.com/ex-fighters-urge-security-forces-restraint-in-enforcement-of-lockdown-measures/, Accessed 5 November 2021.

Newsday (10 May 2012) 'Army General threatens coup,' Available at: https://www.newsday.co.zw/2012/05/2012-05-10-army-general-threatens-coup/, Accessed 20 December 2021.

Newsday (29 May 2020) 'ED's son in USD$1m Covid-19 tender scam,' Available at: https://www.newsday.co.zw/2020/05/eds-son-in-us1m-covid-19-tender-scam/, Accessed 27 October 2021.

Newsday (21 July 2020) 'Protests: ED goes after critics,' Available at: https://www.newsday.co.zw/2020/07/protests-ed-goes-after-critics/, Accessed 28 November 2021.

Newsday (1 August 2020) '13 arrests as army, police quash demo,' Available at: https://www.newsday.co.zw/2020/08/13-arrests-as-army-police-quash-demo/, Accessed 27 October 2021.

Newsday (15 February 2022) 'First post-cabinet press briefing,' Available at: https://www.newsday.co.zw/2022/02/first-post-cabinet-press-briefing-february-15-2022/, Accessed 17 February 2022.

News dzeZimbabwe (8 April 2020) 'Lockdown brutality angers residents,' Available at: http://www.newsdzezimbabwe.co.uk/2020/04/lockdown-brutality-angers-residents.html, Accessed 6 November 2021.

News dzeZimbabwe (6 November 2021) 'Cops set dogs on Chivhu man,' Available at: http://www.newsdzezimbabwe.co.uk/2021/11/cops-set-dogs-on-chivhu-man.html, Accessed 6 November 2021.

Nkala, S. (12 June 2021) 'Bulawayo resident sue police, minister over lockdown brutality,' Available at: https://www.newsday.co.zw/2021/06/byo-resident-sue-police-minister-over-lockdown-brutality, Accessed 30 September 2021.

O'Doherty, M. (2017) *Healing Zimbabwe: Improving human rights, equality and education in the Republic of Zimbabwe,* Berlin: Crystal Grooves Books.

Teixeira, M. (29 July 2020) 'Informal traders are not criminals; stop police violence in Zimbabwe!' Available at: https://streetnet.org.za/2020/07/29/informal-traders-are-not-criminals-stop-police-violence-in-zimbabwe/, Accessed 1 October 2021.

Tshili, N. (23 March 2020) 'Corona virus: Zimbabwe records first death,' Available at: https://www.chronicle.co.zw/coronavirus-zimbabwe-records-first-death/, Accessed 18 November 2021.

Tshili, N. (8 May 2020) 'Police "brutality": Women battered for lockdown defiance,' Available at: https://www.chronicle.co.zw/coronavirus-zimbabwe-records-first-death/, Accessed 29 September 2021.

United Nations High Commissioner for Human Rights (2019) *Ensuring respect for human rights in regional military operations*, Brussels: United Nations.

United Nations High Commissioner for Human Rights (24 July 2020) 'Press briefing on Zimbabwe,' Available at: www.covid19africawatch.org, Accessed 12 September 2021.

Zenda, C. (24 April 2020) 'Army and police brutality keeps starving Zimbabweans indoors,' Available at: https://www.fairplanet.org/story, Accessed 27 September 2021.

Zengwa, F.R. (2 May 2020) 'Rule of law and accountability for security forces,' Available at: https://www.zimrights.org.zw/rule-of-law-and-accountability-for-security-forces/, Accessed 1 October 2021.

Zim Eye (1 May 2020) 'Soldiers beat up and break man's arm for defying lockdown regulations,' Available at: https://www.zimeye.net/2020/05/01/soldiers-beat-up-and-break-mans-arm-for defying-lockdown-regulations/, Accessed 5 November 2021.

Zim Eye (15 May 2020) 'Police, army hauled to court for assaulting chief during lockdown,' Available at: https://www.zimeye.net/2020/05/15/police-army-hauled-to-court-for-assaulting-chief-during-lockdown/, Accessed 6 November 2021.

Zim Eye (26 August 2021) 'Vendor mauled by police dogs fined ZW$1 000,' Available at: https://www.zimeye.net/2021/08/26/vendor-mauled-by-police-dogs-fined-zw1-000/, Accessed 6 November 2021.

Zimbabwean (23 November 2006) '80% of tertiary students cannot afford fees,' Available at:

https://www.thezimbabwean.co/2006/11/, Accessed 20 September 2021.

Zimbabwe Lawyers for Human Rights (14 April 2020) 'Zimbabwe court censures soldiers and police conduct during Covid-19 national lockdown violations,' Available at: https://www.zlhr.org.zw/?p=2001, Accessed 3 September 2021.

Zimbabwe Lawyers for Human Rights (16 May 2020) 'Brutality backfires as chief, residents sue police and soldiers for assault during national lockdown period,' Available at: https://www.zlhr.org.zw/?p=2037, Accessed 28 September 2021.

Zimbabwe Lawyers for Human Rights (3 July 2020) 'Soldier, police officer arrested as lockdown assault backfires,' Available at: https://kubatana.net/2020/07/03/soldier-police-officer-arrested-as-lockdown-assault-backfires/, Accessed 6 November 2021.

Zimbabwe Peace Project (30 July 2020) 'Who shall protect the people? When the state unleashes violence on people it is supposed to protect, who shall protect the people?' Available at: https://reliefweb.int/sites/reliefweb.int/files/resources, Accessed 6 November 2021.

Zimbabwe Situation (6 July 2020) 'CiZC statement condemns the arrest of nurses in Zimbabwe,' Available at: https://www.zimbabwesituation.com/news/cizc-statement-condemns-the-arrest-of-nurses-in-zimbabwe/, Accessed 20 November 2021.

Zwinoira, T.R. (8 March 2021) 'Police violence against women in Zimbabwe increases with impunity during pandemic: Three female street vendors tell of brutal assault at home,' https://www.zenger.news/2021/03/08/police-violence-against-women-in-zimbabwe-increases-with-impunity-during-pandemic/, Accessed 1 October 2021.

ZW News (8 May 2020) 'Corrupt military and police officers cash in on lockdown regulations violators,' Available at: https://zwnews.com/corrupt-military-and-police-officers-cash-in-on-lockdown-regulations-violators/, Accessed 6 November 2021.

ZW News (10 August 2020) 'Harare: Mabvuku man nearly killed by Zimbabwe soldiers over lockdown curfew,' Available at: https://zwnews.com/harare, Accessed 11 August 2021.

Chapter 3

Security Officers on the Rampage: The Covid-19 Pandemic and Human Rights Infractions in Nigeria

Trust Makwinja Asima & Fidelis Peter Thomas Duri

Introduction

This chapter explores the various ways in which a broad range of human rights, liberties and freedoms of many Nigerian citizens were blatantly violated by security officials or law-enforcement agents during the process of implementing Covid-19 curtailment regulations. Specifically, these security officials largely comprised personnel from the police and the army. In some isolated cases, however, officers from the correctional service and local Covid-19 lockdown enforcement committees were involved in violating civilians' human rights.

In Nigeria, as in many other countries in Africa, the mobilisation of law-enforcement agents to assist health authorities and other stakeholders to implement Covid-19 containment regulations sent shock waves across the public domain owing the bad reputation of the army and the police in their interactions with civilians. A report published on 6 December 2021 by the Centre for Democracy and Development (CDD), a pro-democracy group, revealed that Nigerian security operatives had killed more than 13 000 people extra-judicially during the 10 years spanning from 2011 to 2021, adding that "unlawful killings have become a common place in the country since 1999" (Ejekwonyilo, 6 December 2021: 1). Khalid (16 April 2020: 1) weighed in: "Nigerian security forces have a reputation for brutality," adding that their image was already soiled owing to "brutality, extortion and harassment even before the…Corona virus pandemic and the lockdown imposed to contain the virus." Thus, in Nigeria, "it is common knowledge among citizens that the reputation of the police has been synonymised with brutality" (Arimie *et al*, 2021: 1).

The Special Anti-Robbery Squad (SARS), a controversial police unit that was disbanded on 11 October 2020 (Human Rights Watch, 19 October 2021), for example, became unpopular for its brutality that resulted in the death of many people (Oyebanji, 30 October 2020). Having been formed in 1992 to combat armed robbery and other violent crimes, SARS became notorious for harassing and brutalising citizens. The police unit was often accused of committing the crimes it was created to curb and its members were implicated in widespread human rights infringements, including extrajudicial killings, torture, arbitrary arrests, unlawful detention, extortion, and sexual violence (Human Rights Watch, 19 October 2021). Thus, as Izobo and Abiodun (23 June 2020: 1) aptly observed, history shows that Nigerian law-enforcement officials were "perpetually locked in an aggressive mode whenever they [were] called upon to enforce and or defend national interests at the detriment of the people they [were] supposed to protect."

The abusive modus operandi of the police in Nigeria's recent history was also exemplified by their conduct during an operation against the presence of commercial sex workers in the nightclubs of Abuja in April 2019. During the blitz, more than 65 women were arrested and taken to a police station "where bribes were demanded in exchange for their release. When a few of the women could not pay the money, they were allegedly raped by the police officers using empty plastic bags, often used to sell water, instead of condoms" (Obaji, 9 September 2020: 1).

Given the bad reputation of violence by Nigeria's law-enforcement agents, many civilians were not off the mark when they foresaw the advent of the Corona virus being complemented by a brutality virus in due course. As Sister Eucharia Madueke, a nun with the Sisters of Notre Dame de Namur, stated:

> The first time I heard they would be using the police to implement and enforce the lockdown in Nigeria, I was so scared, and my fear came from the history of the police service in the country. The police is never for the people but for institutions that created it. I knew it was going to be very brutal because the security agents who are going to be implementing this are not interested in the people (Egwu, 25 June 2020: 1).

The Federal Government's announcement in late March 2020 that the army would also be involved in the enforcement of Covid-19 lockdown regulations also sent shivers down the spines of many people and drew sharp criticism from several quarters. In a statement issued on 1 April 2020, the Socio-Economic Rights and Accountability Project (SERAP), for example, complained:

> Covid-19 does not mean suspension of the Nigerian Constitution. The president's plan to use the military to police any public security challenges in the context of the Covid-19 lockdown in some parts of the country is wrong and unconstitutional. Deploying the military in this context will lead to widespread human rights violations (Odita *et al*, 2 April 2020: 1).

When the Covid-19 pandemic struck and the Nigerian authorities instituted measures to contain its spread, the police and the army often came to the spotlight for savaging the very civilians they were mandated by law to protect. Nigerian security agents, like those in other African countries, particularly South Africa, Uganda, Zimbabwe and Kenya, earned notoriety for employing brutal means to force civilians off the streets during the Covid-19 period (Mugabi, 20 April 2020). For the greater part of October 2020, as the nation was grappling with the Covid-19 pandemic, many young Nigerians were taking to the streets in various parts of the country to protest against police brutality. In many instances, the peaceful demonstrators were repulsed violently by the police and the army (Oyebanji, 30 October 2020).

Indeed, there is overwhelming evidence that Nigerian law-enforcement officers adopted "a muscular approach" epitomised by "forceful and violent means" to deal with alleged violators of lockdown regulations (Izobo & Abiodun, 23 June 2020: 1). Between 30 March 2020, when the lockdown commenced, and 4 April 2020, for example, the National Human Rights Commission of Nigeria (NHRC), a government agency, reported receiving 105 complaints of human rights infringements against law-enforcement agents from 24 of Nigeria's 36 states (Aborisade, 2021; *Aljazeera*, 16 April 2020). The states, including the Federal Capital Territory of Abuja, from which the abuses were reported are: Abia, Adamawa, Akwa Ibom, Bayelsa, Benue, Cross Rivers, Ebonyi, Edo, Enugu, Ekiti, Delta, Gombe, Imo, Kaduna, Katsina, Kogi, Kwara, Lagos, Nasarawa, Niger, Ogun, Osun, Plateau, and Rivers (Government of the Federal Republic of Nigeria, 2021). While it is a fact that lockdown violators deserved punishment, it was the responsibility of the courts of law and not the police and the army to mete out justice.

This chapter unravels one of the sad realities or dimensions of Covid-19 experiences in Africa in which the very law-enforcement personnel statutorily deployed and empowered to ensure that civilians enjoyed peace, security and good health came to constitute one of the greatest threats to human existence through numerous forms of harassment and gross human rights abuses. Thus, the threats posed by the Corona virus to people's health and life came to be accompanied by the abusive and belligerent law-enforcement agents who caused significant bodily harm, psychological stress and, at times, loss of life, in the fight to stop the spread of the virus.

Advent of the Covid-19 pandemic in Nigeria and official responses

This section traces the origins and spread of the Covid-19 pandemic in Nigeria. It also examines the various measures instituted by the Federal Government of Nigeria, and adopted by State Governments, to curb the spread of the deadly pandemic. The section provides a very useful background or context against which human rights abuses by law-enforcement officials were premised.

Nigeria's first Covid-19 case was reported in the Lagos State where it was confirmed by the Federal Ministry of Health on 27 February 2020 (Friedrich Ebert Stiftung Foundation: Nigeria Office, September 2020). This case was of an Italian citizen who was working in Nigeria and had returned to Lagos from Milan in Italy on 25 February 2020. His Covid-19 infection was confirmed by the Lagos University Teaching Hospital's Virology Laboratory (Ezeigwe, 2021). The country then recorded its first Covid-19 death on 23 March 2020 (Mercy Corps, 2021).

Broadly, there were two distinct waves of Covid-19 infections across Nigeria. The first wave commenced in March/April 2020 and reached its peak in late June and early July 2020. The second wave started in early December 2020 and peaked in late January 2021 (Ibid). In mid-April 2020, Nigeria, with a population of about 200 million people, had recorded 407 cases of Corona virus infections (Khalid, 16 April 2020). In the region of West Africa, Nigeria recorded the highest number of Corona virus cases (Egwu, 25 June 2020). As of 19 June 2020, the country had 19 147 confirmed cases with 6 581 recoveries and 487 deaths (Ibid). By 26 June 2020, Nigeria had recorded 1 083 deaths from Covid-19 (Ezeigwe, 2021). As of 1 June 2021, the country had 166 518 officially-reported Covid-19 cases and 2 099 deaths (Mercy Corps, 2021).

The Nigerian Federal and State Governments invoked a raft of restrictions in an effort to curb the spread of the pandemic. On 30 March 2020, the Federal Government announced a lockdown in the Federal Capital Territory, Abuja, Lagos and Ogun States largely because of the rapid spread of the pandemic in these areas (Ezeigwe, 2021; Government of the Federal Republic of Nigeria, 2021; Igbekoyi, 11 April 2020). The content of the announcement, which was made by President Muhammadu Buhari, included a total lockdown on the Federal Capital Territory (Abuja), Lagos and Ogun states; prohibition of interstate movements; night curfew; stay-at-home orders except for essential service workers; ban on mass gatherings; and closure of national borders, airspace, schools, places of worship and other public places (Ojedokun, 2021). These provisions were all meant for an initial period of 14 days but on 13 April 2020, the lockdown was extended by another two weeks, and many more times thereafter (African Centre for Media and Information Literacy *et al*, 1 May 2020).

Nigeria's 36 state governments followed suit and imposed more-or-less similar forms of stay-at-home orders and curfews on their residents (Igbekoyi, 11 April 2020). In the Delta State, for example, an announcement by Governor lfeanyi Okowa on 31 March 2020 declared a lockdown that would take effect from 1 April 2020. The Delta lockdown provisions included the following: the movement of people, goods and services into, within, and out of all parts of the State was prohibited; and that all residents not on essential duty or providing essential services were to stay home until further notice (Ibid). Those exempted from movement restrictions included transporters of critical supplies such as food, water, petroleum products, and medical and pharmaceutical goods. Some of the essential services allowed to continue operating included banks for limited service, livestock farming (poultry, piggery) and fishery. All people who were exempted were obliged to carry with them valid identity tags to ensure easy identification and passage at check-points (Ibid). The restrictions also banned gatherings for conferences, meetings, religious worship, festivals, private events, public visits, burials, weddings, marriages and other social functions. Public places such as event centres, bars, night clubs, cinemas, markets, supermarkets, malls, shops, restaurants and canteens were temporarily closed. Street football and all other sporting activities on the streets or neighbourhoods were also banned (Ibid). Foodstuff sellers were allowed to operate from their homes being closely monitored to ensure their compliance to social distancing and hygienic regulations. Markets were permitted to sell food items and water in designated primary and secondary schools in each Local Government Area of the Delta State under the supervision of Local

Government Chairmen and their teams to ensure adherence to social distancing and other rules (Ibid).

In the Kaduna State, Governor Mallam Nasir El Rufai announced a series of measures including an instruction to civil servants to stay home for 30 days. He also banned gatherings, and limited the operations of markets only to traders who sold food and medicine. The Governor stated that the army would assist the police to enforce Covid-19 containment measures (African Centre for Media and Information Literacy *et al,* 1 May 2020).

The Lagos State also imposed similar provisions, including the compulsory use of the face mask and social distancing stipulations. The number of passengers carried by commercial vehicles was reduced to ensure social distancing. Non-essential inter-state movement was prohibited. Social and religious gatherings were banned and schools were closed. A curfew was also declared between 8pm and 6am (Akpan, 5 May 2020).

The lockdowns and restrictions introduced by the Federal Government and implemented by State Governments were in four phases that generally corresponded to major trends in the spread of the pandemic. The first phase of the restrictions, which was from late March to early May 2020, coincided with the global declaration of Covid-19 as a pandemic and the first fatalities of the virus in the country. The second phase of restrictions from June 2020 was in response to the increasing number of infections. The third round of restrictions from November 2020 corresponded to the second wave of increasing cases. The fourth phase from May 2021 was largely influenced by concerns about the spread of new variants of the virus (Mercy Corps, 2021).

In all Nigerian states, the security agencies (basically the army and the police) were called upon to enforce lockdown provisions (Government of the Federal Republic of Nigeria, 2021; Khalid, 16 April 2020). The law-enforcement authorities employed a number of operational strategies and tactics to ensure that civilians complied with the restrictions imposed by the government on movement and other forms of interactions. These included day and night patrols; mounting of road-blocks and check-points on major roads, border areas and strategic points in major urban centres; arresting violators; and impounding vehicles of offenders (Ojedokun, 2021). By 5 May 2020, in the Lagos State, for example, 2 310 lockdown violators had been arrested mostly in clubs, group exercises and at organised festivities. Out of the 2 310 who were apprehended, 2 185 suspects were charged in court while 125 minors were warned and released. A total of 2 092 vehicles, 1 535 motorcycles and 369 tricycles whose owners had breached Covid-19 containment regulations were impounded. From the 2 092 vehicles that were impounded, 800 were private while 1 292 were for commercial use (Akpan, 5 May 2020). Similarly, in the Sokoto State on 14 May 2020, Muhammad Sadiq, the State's Police Command's Public Relations Officer, announced that 155 people had been arrested between 8pm and 6am the previous night for violating the curfew imposed to curb the spread of the Covid-19 pandemic. Sadiq added that during the operation from 5 May to 14 May, the police had impounded more than 63 vehicles and motorcycles whose owners had breached lockdown provisions in the Sokoto State (*Premium Times*, 14 May 2020).

As noted in this section, the security service sector was heavily involved in enforcing Covid-19 containment provisions such as the lockdowns, curfews and stay-at-home orders across Nigeria. During their execution of duty, the law-enforcement officials on lockdown assignments became unpopular for grossly violating human rights, freedoms and civil liberties of many citizens through various abuses such as physical assaults, harassment and torture. The next sections of this chapter examine a broad range of such abuses which many civilians were subjected to by security officers in the name of curtailing the spread of the Covid-19 pandemic.

Excessive use of force through beatings, harassment and torture

Police brutality in the form of physical assaults, harassment and torture inflicted bodily harm, caused mental stress and at worst, killed people. Shehu Sani, a human rights activist and former Federal Legislator, criticised law-enforcement agents on lockdown duties for brutalising civilians.

> Our security apparatuses cannot differentiate between coup curfew and Corona virus lockdown. If it is justifiable to brutalise and abuse people to enforce the lockdown, then the moral aspect of its necessity is lost. Enlightenment and civility should continue to be used to enforce the lockdown rather than force and fear (*Sahara Reporters*, 25 April 2020: 1).

In April 2020, Tony Ojukwu, the Head of the NHRC, lamented the "disproportionate use of force and the abuse of power, corruption, and non-adherence to international and national human rights laws…by the security agents" (Mugabi, 20 April 2020: 1). As Adiele (29 April 2020: 1) also noted, the Nigerian security agents generally displayed a violent conduct towards civilians during the Covid-19 period thus:

> For some members of the police and the military, torturing, slapping, and whipping ordinary, defenceless citizens appear to be a birth right that must be morbidly lived out. Some officers of the police and the military seem to be in informal competition to bludgeon fellow citizens to damnation… In Nigeria, while the populace struggle and battle with Corona virus and hunger virus, there is another kind of virus presently plaguing the people, brutality virus enunciated by our security outfits…All over Nigeria, there are reported cases of manhandling and brutality by these overzealous officers who relish any opportunity to inflict pain and agony on their fellow citizens.

On 1 April 2020, just a day after the lockdown had been declared, a video went viral on social media showing a man who reportedly went out to buy food for his pregnant wife being beaten mercilessly and to death by policemen in Abuja, the Nigerian capital. The video showed the police officers and the man engaged in a heated argument over the breach of lockdown stay-at-home orders. As the altercation raged on, angry police officers beat up the man until he collapsed and died (Odita *et al*, 2 April 2020). Commenting on this incident, Inibehe Effiong, a human rights lawyer, advised that it was unconstitutional for security officers to assault or treat citizens in such a degrading and life-terminating manner. He argued:

> Section 34 of the Constitution of the Federal Republic of Nigeria, 1999 (as amended), guarantees the fundamental right to dignity of the human person. It states that no person shall be subjected to torture or to inhuman or degrading treatment. The Anti-Torture Act of 2017 makes it a criminal offence for the police and others to subject any person to torture or to inhuman or degrading treatment. We should not tolerate barbaric and abusive conduct and actions by law-enforcement agencies because of the Covid-19 pandemic (Ibid).

By 2 April 2020, when the lockdown was only two days old, many people in the Lagos State were already complaining about being harassed, assaulted and tortured by security elements for violating Covid-19 preventive measures. In the Lagos Metropolis, for instance, several residents "expressed dissatisfaction with the actions of some of the military security outfits. The residents said the military officials harassed and beat up some of them up. One man was reported to have sustained an injury on the head while trying to flee for his life" (Odita *et al*, 2 April 2020: 1).

On 8 April 2020, the police reportedly manhandled and brutally assaulted people in the Delta State while enforcing stay-at-home orders "as if someone cannot come out of his or her environment and take a walk around" (Igbekoyi, 11 April 2020: 1). One such victim was Asupa Forteta Peter, a member of the Delta State House of Assembly representing Burutu North Constituency, who was abused by the Delta Police Officers at his own premises (Igbekoyi, 1 April 2020). Besides subjecting citizens to physical and mental torture, which constituted infringements of basic rights such as freedom from torture, such police abuses also compromised the freedom of movement by innocent civilians outdoors but within their own premises. As Paul Akpowaide, the National President of the Ijaw Political Watchdog, complained:

> The Covid-19 lockdown does not mean we are prisoners. It only restricts movement from one border to another and also to avoid crowded places to stop the spread of the Covid-19 pandemic. It is disgusting; how could a Nigerian police claim that he cannot identify a lawmaker, despite several introductions and a flash of his identification card as a member of the Delta State House of Assembly Burutu North Constituency? (Ibid).

Police savagery in the Delta State heightened on 9 April 2020 when a medical doctor who was rushing to Okpanam for an emergency was stopped and physically assaulted for disregarding stay-at-home orders. Some of the doctor's colleagues who sought to intervene in order to rescue him were allegedly sprayed with teargas. Following this incident, members of the Association of Resident Doctors (ARD) at the Federal Medical Centre (FMC) in Asaba in the Delta State withdrew their services indefinitely as protest over the alleged harassment by security operatives enforcing lockdown directives (Igbekoyi, 11 April 2020; Ojedokun, 2021).

The death of Praise God John on 15 April 2020 also attests to Nigerian police brutality and torture during the lockdown period (Ezeigwe, 2021). On 10 April 2020, John, a tricycle (*Keke*) driver, was arrested and detained at the Estate Police Station in the Woji, Obi/Akpor Local Government Area of Rivers State for flouting stay-at-home orders. He was detained until 13 April 2020 when the police released him on condition that he returned with N30 000 to secure the release of his tricycle. After his release, John was hospitalised after telling his sister that he had been starved and tortured while in police custody. Despite denials from official sources, many human rights activists and relatives insisted that Praise God John lost his right to live at the hands of overzealous police officers who were enforcing lockdown stipulations (Sanction, 29 April 2020).

In a report released on 15 April 2020, the very day Praise God John was killed, the National Human Rights Commission lambasted the security officers enforcing Covid-19 preventive measures for "excessive or disproportionate use of force, abuse of power, corruption and non-adherence to national and international laws, best practices and rules of engagement" (*Aljazeera*, 16 April 2020: 1). Ahmed Idris, a journalist with *Aljazeera News Agency*, concurred:

> Security forces in Nigeria have been accused severally by individuals of harassment during the lockdown in several states. We have seen security officers mounting roadblocks, checking cars, identities and there are reports from various parts of the country alleging that several abuses have been carried out by these security officers. Apart from the usual demand for bribes, people were harassed (Ibid).

These abuses, which usually comprised assaults, torture and general harassment, severely compromised the rights, freedoms and liberties of many citizens. Personal freedoms and liberties were significantly curtailed as many people lived in fear of the menacing security operatives on lockdown engagements, in as much as they also dreaded the deadly Covid-19 pandemic. A sense of insecurity therefore prevailed in many citizens across the country. Added to this, beatings and other forms of physical molestation humiliated many innocent Nigerians and deprived them of their right to be treated in a dignified and humane manner. Above all, brutalities meted out by law-enforcement agents on Covid-19 assignments caused a great deal of physical and psychological harm that sometimes robbed many victims of their inalienable right to life. It was, therefore, quite alarming that by 1 May 2020, the NHRC had recorded 33 incidents of torture, and inhumane and degrading treatment by security officers engaged in lockdown duties in Nigeria (African Centre for Media and Information Literacy *et al*, 1 May 2020).

The nationwide demonstrations against police brutality that rocked the country in October 2020 did not help much to improve the human rights record of security service operations. During demonstrations in Abuja on 11 October 2020, for example, the Human Rights Watch interviewed three people who either participated in or were in the vicinity of the protests and had been severely flogged by police officers (Human Rights Watch, 19 October 2021). In the immediate aftermath of the two-week countrywide protests held in October 2020 against the brutalities of law-enforcement agents, the police arrested dozens of demonstrators and subjected them to torturous experiences. The rights of the protesters to fair trial were severely compromised by their detention incommunicado for many hours or days and being denied access to lawyers. In many cases, trumped-up charges were brought up against those who had been arrested after the police had failed to raise strong cases against them for either violating lockdown protocols or participating in demonstrations. These developments motivated two young lawyers, Adetola Onayemi and Modupe Odele, to set up the End-SARS Legal Aid Programme for people who had been arbitrarily arrested, detained and harassed in the aftermath of the October 2020 protests (Human Rights Watch, 19 October 2021). To this end, the lawyers acknowledged receiving reports of the arrest of 352 protesters during the October 2020 demonstrations and that they had helped to secure the release of 337 protesters in 13 Nigerian states (Ibid). As Odele, one of the lawyers said:

> We saw from the cases we handled that the police commanders are so powerful and there is no central accountability system, so the police officers can do whatever they want to people they arrest - they can transfer them anywhere or even kill them. That is why we tried to deploy lawyers as quickly as we could. Those first few minutes are crucial or else people can get lost or disappear in the system (Ibid: 1).

The Federal Government of Nigeria considered some of the concerns and in 2021, it strongly advised law-enforcement agents in all states across the country to ensure speedy trials of lockdown violators and avoid detentions at all costs in an effort curtail the spread of the pandemic. In this regard, the Federal Government made the following recommendations:

> Law-enforcement agencies should ensure that persons who are arrested on account of flouting the lockdown orders are promptly

brought before a court of competent jurisdiction and not unduly detained in flagrant disregard to constitutional provisions. In this regard, it is advised that such persons be immediately released on bail and promptly arraigned in court. Detention or incarceration should not be an option during Covid-19 law-enforcement no matter the circumstance. Admission of any new inmates to any correctional service or police detention facility could introduce Covid-19 into such facility and complicate the already precarious situation of our detention facilities (Government of the Federal Republic of Nigeria, 2021: 4-5).

The numerous human rights abuses committed by Nigeria's law-enforcement agents during the Covid-19 lockdown period saw civil society organisations rising up to the challenge. A good example was the CLEEN Foundation, an organisation that had become a reputable watchdog of police conduct over the years. The foundation gathered evidence to back up its advocacy through the Covid-19 Public Safety Support Virtual Centre. The CLEEN Foundation provided many Nigerians with information on public safety and security and went on to establish the Covid-19 Nigeria Security Support Group (CNSSG) that was made up of state coordinators and observers in the 774 local government areas across the 36 states and Abuja. Among other things, CNSSG members used an electronic media platform to record and report human rights infringements by the police and the army during the lockdown period (Ojewale, 23 September 2021).

Excessive use of force through the use of heavy-handed military paraphernalia

During protests against the brutality of the state security agents in handling civilians in general and in the enforcement of Covid-19 regulations in particular, the police and the army often deployed heavy-handed military hardware to disperse crowds. In most cases, the force and machinery used were disproportionate given that people were demonstrating peacefully. During the protests that took place in many states, including Ogun, Oyo, and Lagos, and in Abuja against state brutalities in law-enforcement between 7 and 20 October 2020, the security forces repeatedly used excessive force which involved the use of gunfire, water cannons, and teargas fired at close range (Human Rights Watch, 19 October 2021).

In the capital, Abuja, on 11 October 2020, for instance, the police used tear smoke and water cannons to disperse protesters who were marching towards the police headquarters. The Human Rights Watch also analysed several videos posted on social media by protesters or filmed by journalists documenting the demonstrations. One video obtained and verified by Human Rights Watch showed a police water cannon truck "projecting a strong force of water on dozens of protesters, some of whom were on the ground, kneeling, or standing and holding hands with others while struggling to maintain their balance" (Human Rights Watch, 19 October 2021: 1). Furthermore, the police "used water cannon trucks to chase protesters on foot and in their cars, projecting forceful bouts of water on them at close range. Some protesters clung to moving vehicles in an effort to escape. In one video …three protesters fell from moving vehicles which were being closely pursued by the police water cannon truck, and narrowly missed being crushed when the truck came to a stop right in front of them" (Ibid).

Peaceful demonstrations were often greeted with brute and heavy-handed force under the guise of enforcing Covid-19 curtailment measures pertaining to stay-at-home orders, social distancing stipulations and the prohibition of public gatherings. On Democracy Day, 12 June 2021, Nigerian demonstrators who protested against the erosion of democracy, human rights, liberties and freedoms "were once again met with the deployment of security forces spraying tear gas and firing live bullets into the air" (Ejekwonyilo, 6 December 2021: 1).

The deployment of disproportionate use of force by law-enforcement authorities undertaking lockdown duties was a blatant disregard for basic human rights by the Nigerian government. As Izobo & Abiodun (23 June 2020: 1) advised:

> While law-enforcement officials are allowed to use force in the performance of their duties, they must comply with the national and international standards of necessity and proportionality in the use of force. Breaching the law does not necessitate arbitrary force in return from law-enforcement officials. There is the need to strike a balance between protecting human rights and the public health interest that the restriction regulations seek to protect…Reasonable and proportionate force may be used in ensuring compliance without having to violate human rights in the process.

From the foregoing, it becomes quite apparent that the concept of squashing an ant with a boulder was very popular among Nigerian law-enforcement operatives on Covid-19 lockdown engagements.

Peaceful and unarmed demonstrators were often dispersed violently by security officers through the use of heavy-handed paraphernalia such as teargas and high pressure water cannons. In addition to causing serious injuries, such blatant strategies of handling civilian protests sometimes led to unwarranted loss of life.

Trigger-happiness in the execution of Covid-19 assignments

The excessive use of force by Nigeria's law-enforcement agents was also demonstrated by their frequent resort to the use of firearms on civilians as a way of enforcing compliance to Covid-19 lockdown regulations. The wanton discharge of firearms by security officers on lockdown assignments defied international human rights conventions to which Nigeria was a signatory. Under the United Nations Basic Principles on the Use of Force and Firearms by Law Enforcement Personnel, for instance, law-enforcement officials are obliged to employ non-violent means before opting for force. In addition, they are urged to desist from using coercive means to disperse non-violent demonstrations even when the authorities consider them to be unlawful. Furthermore, any justified use of force must be preceded by clear warnings and should only be resorted to if other means to address a real threat have proved ineffective or are not likely to accomplish the desired outcome. Again, law-enforcement operatives are advised to exercise restraint and act proportionately when dealing with problematic situations involving civilians (African Centre for Media and Information Literacy *et al*, 1 May 2020; Human Rights Watch, 19 October 2021).

On 1 April 2020, a young man was reportedly killed at the intersection of Ayorinde Street and Tolu Road in the Olodi-Apapa area of Lagos when soldiers on lockdown patrol used firearms to disperse a crowd fighting over a soccer match. The trigger mongers shot into the air and a stray bullet hit the man, killing him instantly (Odita *et al*, 2 April 2020). From this event, it cannot be doubted that the trigger-happiness and recklessness of the soldiers resulted in someone's right to life being lost. Undoubtedly, there was no need to use firearms to disperse the crowd as it is quite clear that the lives of the soldiers were not in danger because the civilians were fighting among themselves.

The next day, 2 April 2020, in the oil city of Warri in the southern state of Delta, Joseph Pessu was shot dead by a soldier on lockdown assignment for breaching stay-at-home orders and the curfew. The fatal shooting immediately triggered demonstrations by nettled youths in various parts of the city with many protestors lighting fires along the streets before the police restored calm (*Associated Press*, 3 April 2020). In condemning the heavy-handedness of security officers and calling for the perpetrators to be prosecuted, Senator Ovie Omo-Agege, the legislator who represented the area, said:

> Those who are authorised to bear arms in defence of the nation ought to understand that this comes with responsibility, especially when human life is sacrosanct. The killing in Warri ... is one too many, as the issue should not have led to what, in my opinion, amounted to extrajudicial killing (Ibid: 1).

Similarly, on 15 April 2020, Amobi Igwe, a commercial truck driver, was shot dead by Eke Richard, an officer of the Nigeria Security and Civil Defence Corps, near the tollgate on the Umuahia-Aba Expressway in Umuikea, Isialangwa South Local Government Area of Abia State (Ezeigwe, 2021). Igwe met his fate while transporting food items to Aba when the officer stopped him and demanded a bribe to enable him to proceed since the roads were blocked owing to the Covid-19 lockdown. When the driver refused, the police officer shot him dead (Sanction, 29 April 2020). This act of brutality by law-enforcement agents that resulted in the death of an innocent driver provoked violent reactions from youths in Ebem. Enraged youths went on the rampage, burning down a police station and releasing detainees who had been detained there (African Centre for Media and Information Literacy *et al*, 1 May 2020).

In a related incident on 14 April 2020, the police in Anambra State gunned down two people while enforcing lockdown orders (Ezeigwe, 2021). During the incident, which took place at the New Tyre Market of Nkpor in the Idemili North Local Government Area of Anambra State, two young men were reportedly shot dead outside their home as a police officer sought to implement the stay at home order. An argument had arisen after the two men had insisted that since they were in front of their residences, the police had no right to force them into their rooms (Sanction, 29 April 2020). Such incidents bring to light the need to synergise human rights observance and policing during pandemic lockdowns. Even if the two young men had been uncooperative, a question that arises is whether the excessive force deployed in the form of firearms that ultimately obliterated their right to life was justified both legally and morally.

On 5 April 2020, Stanley Azu, a Police Inspector who was on lockdown duties, fatally shot Chibuisi Okameme, a 29-year-old filling station attendant at Greenmac Energy Limited, located along Umuaka Street in the Obingwa Local Government Area of Abia State (Busari, 8 March 2021). The lethal shot left Okameme's wife and three children without a breadwinner (Adiele, 29 April 2020). At about 1pm on the fateful day, Okameme was at work when he saw policemen flogging a man, who happened to be one of his customers, for violating stay-at-home orders. The customer had reportedly left his home to buy some medicines for his diabetic condition but on his way back, he was stopped by the police along the New Umuahia Road in Aba. An argument ensued during which the police officers began assaulting the man. Okameme and his colleague, Anthony Nnam, were relaxing at the car wash section of the filling station when they heard the customer yelling for help as he was being badly beaten by the security details. Okameme rushed to the scene to plead with the police officers to let him free as he was a regular customer at the fuel station. As he begged the police officers to stop flogging the customer, Inspector Azu shot Okameme dead (Busari, 8 March 2021). Ndubuisi Nwabeke, the manager of the filling station who also witnessed the incident, said Azu shot and killed Okameme without provocation. He explained:

> When he went there, he was begging the policemen to leave him (the customer). Unfortunately, one Inspector Stanley Azu by that time was inside the minibus that brought them. So, as Chibuisi was pleading [with] them, that inspector just jumped down from that bus, pointed that gun. The gun was at his shoulder [level] when he jumped down; he brought the gun down, lowered it and shot him [Chibuisi]. The boy fell, blood covered everywhere. Then, the police wanted to run away (Ibid).

As the perpetrators fled the scene, well-wishers were assisted to track them down by a soldier attached to the Ohuru-Isimiri Police Divisional Headquarters who happened to be at the service station at the time. Upon catching up with them, the tracking team demanded that the assailants take Okameme to the Abia State Teaching Hospital, Aba, for treatment but he died before admission (Ibid). This event shows the callousness of some Nigerian security officers in the manner they enforced lockdown regulations. It is unimaginable that a person lost the right to life for pleading with a police officer to stop brutalising an innocent civilian who was on his way from seeking medication for a critical diabetic condition. Again, this incident illustrates that while security sector brutalities became banal during the enforcement of Covid-19 curtailment measures, it is unfair to paint all operatives with one brush. In this case, and a few others recorded in this chapter, a soldier actually helped to chase other security officers who had shot a civilian in cold blood.

In mid-April 2020, again in the Abia State, a Police Sergeant gunned down Chukwubuike Onuoha, a 21-year-old man, for moving about in the vicinity of his compound, an act which was interpreted as a violation of stay-at-home orders prescribed under the Covid-19 preventive regulations (Adiele, 29 April 2020). Incidents such as these irked Enyinnaya Abaribe, the Senate Minority Leader, who condemned what he referred to as "the frightening rate of extra-judicial killing of innocent Nigerians, particularly in the South East by policemen in the guise of enforcing the Covid-19 lockdown" (Jimoh, 19 April 2020: 1). Abaribe reported cases of more than six Igbo youths who had been gunned down for failing to obey lockdown orders in the South East. He cited an incident on 17 April 2020 at the Uratta Junction in Abia State during which "one youth was allegedly gunned down, while another was heavily brutalised with gun butts to the point of coma. This came a day after another young man was killed at Umuikaa Junction…" (Ibid).

In the Delta State in late May 2020, a man who was on his way to buy drugs for his pregnant wife was gunned down by a law-enforcement agent for violating Covid-19 stay-at-home orders despite the fact that such travel was permitted by lockdown protocols (Izobo & Abiodun, 23 June 2020). While lockdown measures obliged people to stay at home, essential travel was allowed. In this case, the deceased victim was murdered in cold blood as he was out to purchase medicine for his pregnant wife. In any case, even if he could have been guilty, would the deprivation of the right to life be the fitting penalty for simply venturing outdoors with the intention to save life and without posing danger to anyone? Thus, as the Government of the Federal Republic of Nigeria (2021: 5) itself advised, "Law-enforcement agents and members of Task Force Teams on Covid-19 tasked with the responsibilities of enforcing the stay-at-home order should exercise restraint and exhibit high sense of professionalism in enforcing lockdown orders. [A] human rights-based approach should be adopted in interacting and managing civilian populations."

On 28 June 2020, a trigger-happy police officer shot and accidentally killed two people as he tried to arrest a bus driver for violating the nationwide curfew. The incident took place at the Iyana-Oworo Bus Stop in the city of Lagos (Oyemolan, 29 May 2020). The two deceased persons who were caught up in the crossfire were the bus conductor as well as Tina, a 16-year-old girl who was standing by the roadside (*Opera News*, 29 May 2020; Oyemolan, 29 May 2020).

At times, trigger-happy security officers caught their own colleagues in crossfire while brutalising civilians during the course of enforcing lockdown measures. On 23 April 2020, for example, Lavender Elekwachi, a policewoman attached to the Eneka Division in the Obio/Akpora area of Rivers State who was posted to the Eneka roundabout on traffic duties, was shot dead by a colleague, Sergeant Bitrus Osaiah, a member of the Rivers State Task Force on Decongestion (Sanction, 29 April 2020). Osiah shot the female police officer while trying to enforce movement restrictions imposed by the Rivers State Government to prevent the spread of the Covid-19 pandemic. The incident took place when the policewoman tried to prevent Sergeant Bitrus Osaiah and members of the Rivers State Decongestion Task Force from destroying commodities and property belonging to some informal traders who had created makeshift vending stalls in the area (Ibid; Ebisi, 2021; Ojedokun, 2021). This incident illustrates the unprofessional, reckless and barbaric conduct of some members of Nigeria's police force during the enforcement of Covid-19 lockdown regulations. In this incident, the liberal resort to the use of force in the form of dangerous weapons such as firearms by Nigeria's security agents to enforce obedience to lockdown protocols is quite evident. Undeniably, this heavy-handedness severely compromised the rights of many Nigerians, the right to life being an example in this case.

Given the brutalities of Nigeria's law-enforcement agents during lockdown assignments, Adiele (29 April 2020: 1) posed these rhetoric questions: "What exactly is the rationale for arming officers with AK-47 rifles just to enforce lockdown? Are these officers promoted on account of the number of fellow citizens they maim or kill daily?" Commenting on the brutality of security officers and the consequent loss of life during the lockdown period, Sister Eucharia Madueke, a nun with the Sisters of Notre Dame de Namur, reiterated:

> In Nigeria, they say police is your friend, but that is not the case. With the number of people they have killed during the lockdown, how will I trust the police again? When you are not trained for human rights, the chances of violating human rights will be high. I think there is

something wrong with the way security agents are trained in the world, including Nigeria (Egwu, 25 June 2020: 1).

In concurrence with the above concerns, Father Martin Anusi, the Communications Director at the Catholic Diocese in Awka, Nigeria's south-east region, observed that Nigerian law-enforcement agents needed retraining that would enable them to handle crisis situations in a non-belligerent manner. He argued: "Police training is also important so they can learn how to be compassionate…because every problem is not solved by shooting a rifle or use of force" (Ibid: 1). Father Aniedi Okure, the Executive Director of the Africa Faith and Justice Network (AFJN), a non-profit Catholic organisation, expressed similar sentiments and stressed that the police needed to be trained and retrained, particularly in the use of arms, to ensure that civilians were not killed extra-judicially:

> They need to be retrained to understand that their mission is to protect the people and ensure law and order because right now, they are antagonistic to the people. Just look at the basic human rights violation of the police during this lockdown. It is incredible in a country that is meant to be democratic (Ibid).

Despite these concerns from religious leaders, Nigeria's security operatives remained adamant and continued to use firearms to ensure compliance to Covid-19 preventive measures by civilians. On 3 October 2020, for example, a video that was distributed widely on social media showed a SARS police officer shooting a young Nigerian in front of a hotel in Ughelli, in the Delta State. This incident sparked peaceful protests in the country's major cities, including Lagos, Abuja, Port-Harcourt and Kano (Human Rights Watch, 19 October 2021; Oyebanji, 30 October 2020). From 7 to 20 October, demonstrations took place against the brutalities of the police and the army in many parts of Nigeria (Human Rights Watch, 19 October 2021; Oyebanji, 30 October 2020).

Perhaps the most brutal crackdown against the protests was the 'Lekki Massacre' in Lagos during the night of 20 October 2020. Precisely, the incident took place at the toll gate that connects Lekki, a Lagos suburb, with the city's Central Business District (Human Rights Watch, 19 October 2021). During the incident, soldiers arrived in about five trucks and encircled large groups of protesters who were holding a peaceful sit-in demonstration while singing the Nigerian national anthem to protest against police brutality (Ibid;

Olukoya & Oyekanmi, 21 October 2020). The soldiers accused the demonstrators, who had camped at the toll gate for two weeks (Olukoya & Oyekanmi, 21 October 2020), of defying lockdown stipulations, particularly the curfew and the ban on public gatherings, and without warning, fired indiscriminately into two large gatherings (Human Rights Watch, 19 October 2021; Olukoya & Oyekanmi, 21 October 2020). It was about 45 minutes to an hour after the soldiers had left that 15 police details from Maroko Police Station arrived in about three trucks and opened fire at protesters who had not managed to escape (Human Rights Watch, 19 October 2021). Even though Amnesty International reported the death of 12 people (Olukoya & Oyekanmi, 21 October 2020), witnesses claimed that more than 15 people were killed during the incident (Human Rights Watch, 19 October 2021). Commenting on the conduct of security officers in this incident, Michelle Bachelet, the United Nations High Commissioner for Human Rights, said: "There is little doubt that this was a case of excessive use of force, resulting in unlawful killings with live ammunition by Nigerian armed forces" (Olukoya & Oyekanmi, 21 October 2020).

Many relatives of demonstrators who either died or went missing during the Lekki Massacre criticised the government for being insensitive to their plight and failing to reign in on abusive state security agents. For instance, the brother of an 18-year-old man who died during the protests said:

> We feel bad but there is nothing we can do because we cannot fight the government. We tried to make a report at the police station after he died but they [the police] did not allow anybody near their stations, not even close to the gate, talk less of [reaching] the counter [inside the station] to make a report (Human Rights Watch, 19 October 2021: 1).

Peace Okon, the sister of the missing 18-year-old man reiterated:

> …My mom has developed high blood pressure; she calls me weeping, asking for her son… I am helpless and I feel responsible because I brought him to Lagos [from our village]. This, our country, is not fair. There is no justice for the ordinary man. The government has forgotten about those people who were killed or missing from the Lekki Toll Gate (Ibid).

Following the Lekki brutal clampdown, Osai Ojigho, the Country Director of Amnesty International Nigeria, protested bitterly against the gross violation of human rights that was occasioned by the high-handedness of Nigeria's security agents while enforcing Covid-19 lockdown regulations. He complained:

> Opening fire on peaceful protesters is a blatant violation of people's rights to life, dignity, freedom of expression and peaceful assembly. Soldiers clearly had one intention - to kill without consequences…These shootings clearly amount to extrajudicial executions. There must be an immediate investigation and suspected perpetrators must be held accountable through fair trials (Ibid).

In the immediate aftermath of the Lekki Massacre, Antonio Guterres, the United Nations Secretary-General, added his voice to the global outcry and noted with concern during an interview that the right of Nigerians "to protest peacefully needs to be guaranteed," adding that "police brutality needs to stop, and those responsible for acts of such dramatic violence are made accountable" (Ibid: 1). Furthermore, Guterres reported he had contacted President Buhari and was optimistic that he would be "able to bring things into a normal way to respect the rights of assembly of people, and to make sure that those that misbehaved are held accountable" (Ibid). As the United Nations Secretary General alluded to, the heinous clampdown on demonstrators which led to many people losing their lives in October 2020 was primarily motivated by the determination of overzealously bloodthirsty and trigger-happy security officers to suppress the people's right to freedoms of expression and peaceful assembly in the name of enforcing Covid-19 preventive directives. It should be noted that people had the right to express themselves and assemble to protest against pressing injustices as long as they did so non-violently and in a way that adhered to lockdown measures. Even if the demonstrators had flouted some Covid-19 containment protocols, the deployment of disproportionately excessive force to ensure compliance would still be unwarranted and unjustified.

In view of the October 2020 nationwide protests, the brutal crackdown by security officers and the subsequent public outcry at home and abroad, the Lagos State Governor set up the Lagos State Judicial Panel of Inquiry alongside other State Judicial Panels to gather and assess public misgivings over police brutality, including extrajudicial killings; identify operatives who were liable for prosecution; and suggest compensation for victims. The panel's mandate also included investigations into the shooting at civilian demonstrators by army and police officers at the Lekki Toll Gate in Lagos on 20 October 2020. The panel recorded testimonies from many informants, including victims and representatives of key agencies involved such as the operators of the Lekki Toll Gate, the army, the police, the Lagos State Government, and hospital staff who treated the injured victims (Human Rights Watch, 19 November 2021).

On 15 November 2021, the Judicial Panel of Inquiry submitted its 309-page report to the Lagos State Governor. The contents of the report largely confirmed the findings that had previously been made and circulated by Human Rights Watch to the effect that army and police officers shot, injured, and killed unarmed demonstrators at the Lekki Toll Gate in Lagos. While the army had denied reports from Human Rights Watch that its officers had shot and killed protesters, the judicial panel's findings confirmed that soldiers surrounded protesters at the toll gate and opened fire at them after which the police also came to inflict more harm. While the panel was unable to determine the total number of fatalities, it provided a list of 48 casualties, including 11 dead, four missing and presumed dead, and 21 injured by gunshots. The panel discovered that while many people were injured at the Lekki Toll Gate, the army blocked ambulances from rescuing wounded protesters thereby contributing to causing many deaths (Ibid).

This section has discussed human rights violations perpetuated through the use of lethal and offensive weapons, firearms in particular, by Nigerian security personnel, to enforce Covid-19 containment measures. It has illuminated that firearms were sometimes discharged on innocent civilians who were on genuine errands such as travelling to procure medicines for themselves and sick relatives. Even if one had breached some provisions of the lockdown, shots were often fired regardless of the violator being unarmed and posing no danger to the lives of other people. The section has also articulated how live shots were sometimes fired indiscriminately, and without warning, at peaceful and unarmed demonstrators by vicious security agents in the name of ensuring compliance to Covid-19 lockdown provisions. While several people lost their right to life as a result of the trigger-happiness of over-enthusiastic security details on lockdown duties, many of those who survived suffered life-threatening injuries; their rights, liberties and freedoms were severely compromised as they now lived in fear, and without meaningful guarantees of security and dignity.

Abuse of women

Having looked at the generally abusive and combative nature of Nigeria's security operatives in the enforcement of lockdown regulations, it is worth noting that women were not exempted from such hostile treatment. The police and other security officers sometimes took advantage of their responsibilities to enforce Covid-19 containment measures such as lockdowns, sit-at-home orders, travel bans and the curfew to abuse women in various ways that included physical, verbal and sexual assaults Furthermore, pregnant women were not spared as they were sometimes harassed by inconsiderate security details.

Some security officers sexually abused women and girls as punishment for violating lockdown regulations. Women who violated the curfew sometimes fell prey to some law-enforcement agents on patrol who raped them under the cover of darkness in return for freedom. Female informal traders, mostly market women and vendors, whose operations were prohibited under lockdown regulations and had retreated to dark corners to continue with their business often risked being sexually abused by marauding security operatives in these secluded locations (Ebisi, 2021). On 11 April 2020, for example, a 21-year-old woman was reportedly raped by a vigilante group that was enforcing Covid-19 preventive measures in Port Harcourt. Commenting on the incident, the Police Public Relations Officer acknowledged the existence of a mutual working relationship with vigilantes in enforcing lockdown protocols but stated that the sexual abuse case would be investigated and the culprits prosecuted (Ibid).

In mid-April 2020, two weeks into the lockdown in Nigeria, police brutality in the enforcement of Covid-19 containment measures was publicised in a video that went viral on social media showing them clobbering a woman. The video exposed two police officers, Inspector Iku Esan Taiwo and Corporal Abass Ibrahim, flogging a woman with long canes at the Odo Ori Market, Iwo, Osun State, in south-western Nigeria on 18 April 2020. Tola Azeez, the female victim, was reportedly to have been on her way to buy drugs for a relative and other household needs at the Odo Ori Market in Iwo when she was arrested by the overzealous officers who accused her of breaching stay-at-home orders (Aborisade, 2021; Kabir, 25 April 2020). The video of the assault, which the victim confirmed, was first published online by Rugged Man, a Nigerian musician, on his Twitter account (Kabir, 19 April 2020: 1).

On 22 April 2020, Tola Azeez spoke to the press for the first time since her ordeal. She revealed that police brutality had caused her severe bodily injuries and trauma to the extent that she was receiving medication and counselling (Ibid). She explained her plight as follows: "I am still under medical and psychological examination as the damage done to me physically, emotionally and psychologically is unquantifiable. I only pray to overcome the pains and the trauma in no distant time" (Ibid). From the foregoing, it can be noted that the beatings caused the innocent woman considerable physical and mental harm. Furthermore, the brutality of the two officers severely compromised the dignity and right to safety of the female victim.

The barbaric and pugnacious conduct of the police officers was roundly condemned by some police authorities, the Osun State Government and the *Oluwo* (King) of Iwo, the kingdom and ethnic group to which the female victim belonged. The Osun State Police Commissioner for Information, Funke Egbemode, a policewoman, for example, urged security judicial authorities to consider psychiatric evaluation in the disciplinary proceedings of the two accused officers. She fumed:

> This is public display of shame and bad upbringing…How can men in uniform do this to any woman? I am so totally angry. Like I have always said, a man who beats a woman is a sick man; a man who needs psychiatric attention. I implore the Inspector-General of Police to include psychiatric evaluation in the process of discipline of those two human beings in police uniform (Kabir, 19 April 2020: 1).

The *Oluwo* of Iwo, Abdulrosheed Akanbi, also expressed displeasure at the belligerent disposition exhibited by the two security operatives:

> The act and action of the police against an Iwo woman, Tola Azeez, is condemned. It is [an] unacceptable and barbaric display. Iwo is civilised beyond such incivility. The palace has time immemorial devised necessary machinery to ensure the community and the police cohabit peacefully for effective security. I have intervened; the police have gone to her place with the Divisional Police Officer (DPO) of the affected division to tender their apology formally (Ibid).

Consequent upon this horrendous assault of an innocent woman, the two overzealous police officers were dismissed (Adiele, 29 April 2020). This development was disclosed in a verified police Twitter handle on 24 April 2020 which read: "Inspector Ikuesan Taiwo and Police Constable Abass Ibrahim, captured in a viral video assaulting a woman in Osun, have been tried and found guilty. They have been dismissed from the force and they will be arraigned in court for prosecution" (Ibid).

In another incident of harassment on 28 July 2020, a 23-year-old widow and mother of two children from the city of Bori was sexually assaulted after being arrested by four policemen in Port-Harcourt, Rivers State, for breaching lockdown protocols (Aborisade, 2020; Obaji, 9 September 2020). On the day in question, the woman was on a public bus on her way to Port Harcourt, the capital of south-central Rivers State, about 45 kilometres west of Bori. When they reached a check-point in the town of Sakpenwa, 25 kilometres outside Bori, at 6.30pm, the four policemen arrested her for not putting on a face mask (Obaji, 9 September 2020). The police details force-marched her to their vehicle after which they drove her to a guest house where one of the officers "raped her till dawn after threatening to kill her if she did not cooperate" (Ibid: 1). After raping her, the policeman reportedly demanded the bank details of the female victim and later deposited N2 000 ($US5) into her account as compensation (Aborisade, 2020). The woman was left traumatised by the assault. She explained: "I have not been myself and have fainted twice since the rape incident. Because of my deteriorating health, I had to move…to live with my mother so I can be cared for" (Obaji, 9 September 2020: 1). Her older cousin reiterated: "She is terribly traumatised. It has been difficult for her to get a good sleep since the incident" (Ibid). This sexual assault was just one of many that took place in the context of Covid-19 lockdown enforcement by Nigeria's security officers. This incident clearly demonstrates how some Nigerian police details abused their power to harass innocent women under the pretext of implementing Covid-19 curtailment measures. Besides causing physical and psychological harm, the sexual assault violated many personal freedoms of the female victim such as freedom of choice and her entitlement to dignity.

Pregnant women were not spared from the overzealously abusive and unscrupulous shenanigans of law-enforcement agents on Covid-19 containment assignments. In Port Harcourt, in mid 2020, for instance, "a pregnant woman…miscarried on her way to hospital to see a doctor after policemen detained her for being out during lockdown" (Obaji, 9 September 2020: 1). Similarly, again in Port Harcourt, as Kofi Bartels, a journalist, told *Al Jazeera*: "There is even another pregnant woman who was arrested and detained by policemen for stepping out to buy food. The very sad thing about this is that some of those who were arrested by policemen were taken to an isolation centre, where Corona virus patients are kept" (Ibid).

In a related incident on 21 May 2020, Waidat Adedeji, a married pregnant woman who was experiencing early labour, died after she was reportedly delayed by some police officers at a check-point for not putting on a face mask in the Ogun Waterside Local Government Area of Ogun State (Kabir, 22 May 2020; Sylvester, 21 May 2020). One witness said on the day in question, Mrs Adedeji, who was seven months pregnant, woke up around 6am bleeding. While her husband could have taken her to hospital with his motorcycle, the lockdown in the state would not permit him. Instead, he requested a neighbour who was known to many police officers to whisk his wife to the Ita-Otu General Hospital in Ibiade (Kabir, 22 May 2020). They were stopped at the Sore River check-point by officers who asked them why they ventured out of their homes in defiance of lockdown orders, worse still without face masks. They were delayed for hours while the woman continued to bleed profusely and later died (Ibid). Thus, the woman's right to life was terminated at the roadblock by insensitive police officers.

The death of the woman at the Sore River check-point incensed surrounding communities. A group of agitated youths from Ibiade, for example, reportedly took the corpse of the woman to the Abigi Divisional Police Headquarters and dumped it there while accusing the police of having been responsible for her death (Oludare, 21 May 2020; Sylvester, 21 May 2020). As one of the protesting youths said: "When we got to the police station, we dropped the remains of the woman on their counter and some of the officers ran away" (Kabir, 22 May 2020: 1). The situation threatened to degenerate into violence had the peeved youths not been calmed down by local community leaders (Oludare, 21 May 2020; Sylvester, 21 May 2020). It was only after the intervention of the local community leaders that "the corpse was taken out of the police station by her families for burial" (Kabir, 22 May 2020: 1).

Among other things, this incident illustrates how the heartless conduct of some law-enforcement operatives on lockdown duties sometimes cost the right to life of some innocent women. A fact of life that also emerges from this case is that the ordinary people are not always passive or hapless victims of police brutality. As this incident showed, they can confront the authorities in an effort to reassert their rights as human beings with the inalienable right to life and who should be treated with dignity. It should, therefore, be noted that the subaltern should never be taken for granted because they have the potential to become defiant whenever their rights are trampled upon. Thus, the police themselves failed to restrain the agitated Ibiade youths and had to be assisted by the intervention of local community leaders.

On 31 August 2020, officers of the Nigeria Police Force enforcing the Covid-19 curfew in Lagos State allegedly caused the death of Mistura, a pregnant woman, and her unborn baby by delaying a female surgeon who was supposed to operate her. It was reported that the woman died in pain at the Lagos University Teaching Hospital while waiting for the doctor who was delayed for about an hour on Airport Road, Ikeja, Lagos State, for allegedly violating the Covid-19 curfew. The doctor's pleas to the policemen that she was on an emergency call fell on deaf ears for quite some time. Even though she was finally released after about an hour, it was too late to save the pregnant woman's life together with that of her unborn baby. In fact, the patient and her unborn baby died before the doctor's arrival at the hospital (Ogunsile, 7 September 2020). A witness narrated what transpired as follows:

> The doctor is a woman. In fact, she was also ill and was placed on a drip at home when she was called for the emergency. Because her car was bad, she got a cab-man to take her to the hospital. She left her house around past 9pm. [At] around 10.15pm, they got to the under-bridge around Airport Road where they met the policemen. They had been stopped by other policemen before they got to that spot. But when she showed them her [identity] card, they allowed her to pass. But these ones refused. After she showed one of them her [identity] card and said she was on an emergency to see a patient who was between life and death, the policeman ordered the driver to park. He took her [identity] card and asked her to prove she was on an emergency. She went to meet another member of the team and begged him that she needed to leave immediately and that the life of her patient was at risk. She was in a night-gown; she could not even change when she got the call. But the second policeman shunned her. The policeman said she was foolish and she was a prostitute because a doctor would never dress the way she was dressed. She begged them and explained the circumstances but they refused to listen and demanded the emergency letter. There were four policemen on duty that night. Only one was on mufti. Their tags were not visible because they wore overalls. They saw the drip in the doctor's

hand; she was risking her life to save another person but they never allowed her (Ibid: 1).

This very unfortunate case clearly shows how women received a raw deal at the hands of security operatives enforcing Covid-19 preventive orders. The female surgeon's freedom of movement was unnecessarily breached as the lockdown regulations exempted her as an essential service worker. This humiliating treatment, together with the derogatory reference to her as a prostitute, which constituted grievous verbal assault, denied the innocent and caring female doctor the right to be treated with dignity. Ultimately, another innocent woman, a pregnant mother, and her unborn baby lost their right to life.

Such incidents seem to have prompted the Federal Government to advise law-enforcement agents on lockdown mission to avoid inconveniencing pregnant women and treat them with due care. This recommendation was made in a report published by the Federal Government, part of which read: "The Government of Nigeria at all levels should categorise pregnant women and persons in need of medical care as essential persons to facilitate their unrestricted movements to hospitals and health care centres" (Government of the Federal Republic of Nigeria, 2021: 5).

This section has unravelled the gender dimensions of policing and their implications on human rights, freedoms and liberties in the context of Covid-19 containment measures and enforcement in Nigeria. Broadly, women's entitlement to dignity and equal treatment was deeply eroded by patriarchal chauvinism on the part of some arrogantly confrontational male security officers. As the section has ably articulated, the subordination and marginalisation of women was perpetuated during the enforcement of Covid-19 preventive protocols by rogue security operatives who subjected them to a multiplicity of physical, verbal and sexual assaults as well as various forms of harassment that triggered mental stress. The section has also shown how some innocent women lost their right to life owing to a broad range of abuses committed by law-enforcement agents on lockdown duties.

Death toll emanating from security sector brutality during lockdown enforcement

As already noted in the preceding sections, the brutalities of the security officers on lockdown engagements sometimes led to loss of life on the part of innocent citizens. It is a fact that the exact number of people killed by security details for breaching Covid-19 preventive orders can never be ascertained as the perpetrators sometimes concealed evidence. It is also beyond reasonable doubt that some incidents in which civilians lost their lives owing to brutalities committed by officers on lockdown assignments went unrecorded, especially those that took place in remote areas that were not covered by rights groups and the press, among other stakeholders, at those times.

It is common knowledge, needing no reminder, that the right to life is fundamental and inalienable. Chapter IV (Fundamental Rights) of Nigeria's 1999 Constitution recognises the right to life as follows: "Everyone has the right to life and no one shall be intentionally deprived of his life except in the execution of the sentence of a court for a criminal offence of which he has been convicted in Nigeria" (African Centre for Media and Information Literacy *et al*, 1 May 2020: 1). In addition, Nigeria also ratified international treaties which guarantee these rights. The International Covenant on Civil and Political Rights (ICCPR), for instance, provides that "every human being has the inherent right to life. This right shall be protected by law. No one shall be arbitrarily deprived of his life" (Ibid). Furthermore, the ICCPR states that governments cannot derogate from their obligations under this provision, even "in time of public emergency which threatens the life of the nation" (Ibid). Similarly, the African Charter on Human and Peoples' Rights (ACHPR) provides for the right to security and life of a person (Ibid).

It was quite alarming that as of 13 April 2020, the security forces on lockdown enforcement duties in various parts of Nigeria had killed more people than the Corona virus itself. At this time, when the lockdown was just two weeks old, as the NHRC noted, the law-enforcement agents had killed 18 people while Covid-19 had only claimed the lives of 12 Nigerians (Khalid, 16 April 2020; Mugabi, 20 April 2020; Ohajuruka, 16 November 2020). In terms of the perpetrators, the 18 fatalities can be analysed as follows: eight were committed by correctional service officers in the Kaduna State, seven by the police, two by the army, and one by a local committee enforcing the lockdown in the south-eastern part of the country (*Aljazeera*, 16 April 2020; Government of the Federal Republic of Nigeria, 2021). As far as the states where the killings took place: 12 were recorded in Kaduna, two in Abia while Delta, Niger, Ebonyi and Katsina recorded one death each (Government of the Federal Republic of Nigeria, 2021).

As of 19 April 2020, Nigeria's South East Region had recorded less than three Covid-19 deaths, yet the police had killed more than six people in an effort to enforce compliance to orders put in place to control the spread of the pandemic (Jimoh, 19 April 2020). By 25 April 2020, more than 22 people had "lost their lives to police and military brutality, a figure almost matching the death toll of the pandemic itself in the country" (*Sahara Reporters*, 25 April 2020: 1). Within five weeks of the lockdown, the number of extrajudicial civilian deaths had risen to 29 (Ohajuruka, 16 November 2020). These developments prompted Ojukwu (17 April 2020: 1) to assert that in Nigeria, "police brutality is more lethal than Covid-19." Similarly, Ojewale (23 September 2021: 1), a scholar with the Institute for Security Studies, wondered whether Nigerians "were…more at risk from security and law-enforcement agents enforcing the lockdown than the virus itself."

During the lockdown period spanning from 30 March to mid-April 2020, the NHRC reported eight separate incidents of extrajudicial killings by the law-enforcement details that culminated in the deaths of 18 civilians (Khalid, 16 April 2020; Mugabi, 20 April 2020). In mid-April 2020, Auwal Musa Rafsanjani, an official of the Abuja Civil Society Legislative Advocacy, a civic group, expressed grave concern at extra-judicial killings of civilians by the police and army enforcing lockdown duties: "There are so many reported cases of human rights abuses, including outright murder and killing of Nigerians in the name of keeping them at home. We think this is a shame and outrageous that Corona virus did not kill Nigerians, but security agents are killing Nigerians" (Mugabi, 20 April 2020: 1).

By 1 May 2020, 21 Nigerians had been killed by law-enforcement agents on lockdown duties (Izobo & Abiodun, 23 June 2020). The killings provoked sharp criticism from many civil and human rights organisations. The African Centre for Media and Information Literacy (AFRICMIL), the Rule of Law and Accountability Advocacy Centre (RULAAC), and the Human Environment Development Agenda Resource Centre (HEDA), in a joint statement issued on 1 May 2020, for example, urged the Federal Government of Nigeria to investigate the allegations of unlawful killings of at least 21 persons, and other acts of violence and intimidation that took place in the context of the Covid-19 lockdown (AFRICMIL *et al*, 1 May 2020). They reminded the government that "emergency measures to reduce the spread of Covid-19 should not be used to violate the right to life, as guaranteed under the Nigerian Constitution, the African Charter on Human and Peoples' rights and the International Covenant on Civil and Political Rights" (Ibid). Part of the statement from the civil organisations read:

> We are profoundly outraged and deeply saddened by the deadly crackdown that resulted in the deaths of 21 people and other human rights abuses across Nigeria. We express our concern at the continuing violence and deaths in the various states. We condemn all forms of violence, inhuman and degrading treatment reported. The law-enforcement agencies responsible for the security of the people must fulfil their duty by protecting citizens and not turning against them in these difficult times. They must refrain from any excessive or unlawful use of force. The allegations must be quickly investigated and those responsible prosecuted (Ibid).

On 21 October 2020, Amnesty International reported that during the two weeks of widespread protests against police bestiality in October 2020, 56 people had been killed as marauding trigger-happy security operatives sought to break up gatherings and enforce the curfew as prescribed by the Covid-19 lockdown regulations (Olukoya & Oyekanmi, 21 October 2020). Given the rising figures of Nigerians who were killed by security officials on lockdown duties, human rights activists lamented that the families of the victims of extra-judicial killings were left without support and languishing in poverty in many cases because they were oblivious of their right to compensation. Inibehe Effiong, a human rights lawyer, advised dependents of the victims of police and military brutality to seek redress as follows:

> The first step is to file an action in court because the court has to make determination that the infringement is a violation of the fundamental right of the victim. In furtherance of that, an order of compensation will be made. If there is an order of court, first compensation will usually arise from a judgment of court mostly when an action for enforcement of fundamental rights has commenced and has been successfully concluded. After the court determines that the rights or dignity of the applicant have been violated, an order of public apology or compensation will be issued. It is a conditional right, the right to public apology, and compensation is guaranteed under the constitution specifically Section 34 and 35 on the right to personal liberty and the right to dignity of the human person. Under Section 35, the condition allows for compensation and public apology but that has

to be when the court has made a determination that the right of a citizen has been violated. The challenge is how to recover the compensation because you will have to go to court by way of enforcement of judgment to garnish the account of the police because it is an agency of government. The order will then be used to scan the accounts of the law-enforcement agency and a directive of payment will be made to the complainant. Garnishing proceedings is when you search for the accounts of the police in the bank where they have funds, mostly now in the Central Bank of Nigeria (CBN) because of the Single Treasury Account. So, for police funds that are domiciled in the CBN, it is possible to garnish that account and the court will then order the bank to remit the judgment sum. Under the National Human Rights Commission Amendment Act, the commissioner has power to also award damages and compensation to victims of rights violation (*Sahara Reporters*, 25 April 2020: 1).

From the foregoing, it can be noted that the Nigerian government, through its law-enforcement agents, severely infringed the people's rights to life in the name of containing the Covid-19 pandemic. Such measures also went against the African Charter on Human and Peoples' Rights (ACHPR) and the International Convention on Civil and Political Rights (ICCPR), which guarantee the right to life for all, both of which were ratified by the Nigerian government (Human Rights Watch, 19 October 2021).

Conclusion

This chapter has shown how the conduct of Nigeria's so-called law-enforcement agents was often characterised by brutality, arbitrariness and lawlessness during the Covid-19 lockdown period. It has demonstrated beyond doubt that the Nigerian police and the army, together with their functionaries, had a "warrior mind-set" which negated community relationships (Ezeigwe, 2021: 167) and grossly violated basic human rights, civil liberties and freedoms of many innocent citizens under the excuse of containing the Covid-19 pandemic. As this chapter illustrated, the Nigerian Covid-19 experience witnessed a dissonant relationship between preventative measures and fundamental freedoms. In an effort to thwart the spread of the pandemic, the government instituted containment measures and deployed the law-enforcement agents to ensure compliance by the generality of the population. The enforcement of the Covid-19 containment measures blatantly undermined national and international laws and severely compromised a broad range of basic human rights, freedoms and civil liberties.

In closing this chapter, it is prudent to note that while security sector brutalities and related human rights infringements were rampant during the enforcement of Covid-19 lockdown measures in Nigeria, there is no compelling evidence to suggest that they were institutionalised. The fact that they were not institutionalised is attested, among other things, by the work of the NHRC, a government agent that regularly monitored the operations of security officers on lockdown engagements and disclosed their human rights abuses. The fact that ordinary security officers sometimes criticised each over the brutal handling of civilians during the enforcement of Covid-19 preventive regulations, as noted in the chapter, also constitutes ample testament that the abuses were not engineered and instituted from the top. Rather, the barbarities were largely committed by heartless individuals or small groups in localised settings beyond the radar of senior security authorities. Some senior police and military officers should, however, shoulder part of the blame for sometimes attempting to play down or cover up some incidents of security sector brutality as fake news. Furthermore, some blame should also be apportioned to law-enforcement administrators for failing to adequately integrate human rights discourses in the process of inducting junior officers for lockdown assignments

References

Aborisade, R.A. (2021) 'Accounts of unlawful use of force and misconduct of the Nigerian police in the enforcement of Covid-19 measures,' in: *Journal of Police and Criminal Psychology*, Volume 36, pp.450-462.

Adiele, P. (29 April 2020) 'Covid-19: Police and military brutality,' Available at: https://www.sunnewsonline.com/covid-19-police-and-military-brutality, Accessed 3 March 2022.

African Centre for Media and Information Literacy (AFRICMIL), Rule of Law and Accountability Advocacy Centre (RULAAC) & Human Environment Development Agenda Resource Centre (HEDA) (1 May 2020) 'Nigeria: Covid-19 response should not be used to violate the right to life and intimidate journalists,' Available at: https://www.article19.org/resources/nigeria-covid-

19-response-should-not-be-used-to-violate-the-right-to-life-and-intimidate-journalists/, Accessed 21 April 2022.

Akpan, R. (5 May 2020) 'Covid-19 curfew: We will breathe down the neck of violators, Commissioner of Police, Odumosu, warns, says 2 310 violators, 2 092 vehicles, 1 535 motorcycles, 369 tricycles impounded in lockdown enforcement,' Available at: http://crimeworld.com.ng/2020/05/05/covid-19-curfew-we-will-breathe-down-the-neck-of-violators-cp-odumosu-warnssays-2310-violators-2092-vehicles-1535-motorcycles-369-tricycles-impounded-in-lockdown-enforcement/, Accessed 21 April 2022.

Aljazeera (16 April 2020) 'Nigerian security forces kill 18 during curfew enforcement,' Available at: https://www.aljazeera.com/news/2020/4/16/nigerian-security-forces-kill-18-during-curfew-enforcement, Accessed 21 April 2022.

Arimie, C.J. Eghaghe, A. & Omage, I. (2021) 'Policing and human rights violation in the Covid-19 lockdown in Nigeria: The role of the police in crisis intervention,' in: *Journal of the Management Sciences*, Volume 57, Number 1, pp.1-15.

Associated Press (3 April 2020) 'African man shot dead for breaking virus curfew,' Available at: https://www.courthousenews.com/african-man-shot-dead-for-breaking-virus-curfew/, Accessed 24 April 2022.

Busari, K. (8 March 2021) 'Blood on uniforms: In Nigeria's south-east, no justice for people killed during Covid-19 lockdown,' Available at: https://www.premiumtimesng.com/news/headlines/447496-blood-on-uniforms-3-in-nigerias-south-east-no-justice-for-people-killed-during-covid-19-lockdown.html, Accessed 24 April 2022.

Ebisi, N. (2021) 'Abuse of women in Port Harcourt City by security operates during Covid-19 pandemic lockdown,' Available at: https://healthasset.org/women-speak-for-themselves-abuse-of-women-in-port-harcourt-city-by-security-operates-during-covid-19-pandemic-lockdown/, Accessed 24 April 2022.

Egwu, P. (25 June 2020) 'Nigerian priests condemn police brutality during lockdown, offer solutions,' Available at: https://www.catholicworldreport.com/2020/06/25/nigerian-priests-condemn-police-brutality-during-lockdown-offer-solutions/, Accessed 27 February 2022.

Ejekwonyilo, A. (6 December 2021) 'Nigeria: How Nigerian security operatives extra-judicially killed 13 241 in 10 years - Centre for Democracy and Development,' Available at: https://allafrica.com/stories/202112070075.html, Accessed 22 April 2022.

Ezeigwe, A.C. (2021) 'Addressing the human rights abuses occasioned by the Corona virus lockdown,' in: *Nnamdi Azikiwe University Journal of International Law and Jurisprudence*, Volume 12, Number 2, pp.160-176.

Friedrich Ebert Stiftung Foundation: Nigeria Office (September 2020) *The impacts of current global pandemic on peace and security in Nigeria*, Friedrich Ebert Stiftung Foundation: Nigeria Office: Policy Brief for Nigeria.

Global Human Rights (1 December 2020) 'Where breaking curfew can mean being beaten by police,' Available at: https://globalhumanrights.org/stories/where-breaking-curfew-can-mean-being-beaten-by-police/, Accessed 1 March 2022.

Government of the Federal Republic of Nigeria (2021) 'Report on human rights violations following the implementation of Covid-19 regulations of 2020 and directives issued by Federal and State Governments from 31st March to 13th April 2020,' Available at: www.nigeriarights.gov.ng/files/publications, Accessed 22 April 2022.

Human Rights Watch (19 October 2021) 'Nigeria: A year on, no justice for #EndSARS crackdown - Prosecute those responsible for abusing protesters,' Available at: https://www.hrw.org/news/2021/10/19/nigeria-year-no-justice-endsars-crackdown, Accessed 16 February 2022.

Human Rights Watch (19 November 2021) Nigeria: Officials indicted in abuses of protesters,' Available at: https://www.hrw.org/news/2021/11/19/nigeria-officials-indicted-abuses-protesters, Accessed 23 April 2022.

Igbekoyi, F. (11 April 2020) 'Police brutality: Panic by doctors, lawmakers in Delta over Covid-19 lockdown,' Available at: https://independent.ng/police-brutality-panic-by-doctors-lawmakers-in-delta-over-covid-19-lockdown/, Accessed 8 March 2022.

Izobo, M. & Abiodun, F. (23 June 2020) 'Enforcement of lockdown regulations and law-enforcement brutality in Nigeria and South Africa,' Available at: https://africlaw.com/2020/06/23/enforcement-of-lockdown-regulations-and-law-enforcement-brutality-in-nigeria-and-south-africa/, Accessed 28 January 2022.

Jimoh, A.M. (19 April 2020) 'Covid-19: Abaribe kicks against police brutality, killings in South East,' Available at: https://guardian.ng/news/covid-19-abaribe-kicks-against-police-brutality-killings-in-south-east/, Accessed 12 March 2022.

Kabir, A. (19 April 2020) 'Lockdown: Police officers caught on camera assaulting woman,' Available at: https://www.premiumtimesng.com/news/more-news/388697-lockdown-police-officers-caught-on-camera-assaulting-woman.html, Accessed 24 April 2022.

Kabir, A. (25 April 2020) 'Lockdown: Police dismiss officers who assaulted woman in Osun,' Available at: https://www.premiumtimesng.com/regional/ssouth-west/389720-lockdown-police-dismiss-officers-who-assaulted-woman-in-osun.html, Accessed 20 April 2022.

Kabir, A. (22 May 2020) 'Covid-19: Pregnant woman dies in Ogun after police check-point delay,' Available at: www.premiumtimesng.com/regional/ssouth-west/394053, Accessed 22 April 2022.

Khalid, I. (16 April 2020) 'Corona virus: Security forces kill more Nigerians than Covid-19,' Available at: https://www.bbc.com/news/world-africa-52317196, Accessed 26 February 2022.

Mercy Corps (2021) *A clash of contagions: The impact of Covid-19 on conflict in Nigeria, Colombia, and Afghanistan*, Portland, Oregon: Mercy Corps.

Mugabi, I. (20 April 2020) 'Covid-19: Security forces in Africa brutalising civilians under lockdown,' Available at: https://www.dw.com/en/covid-19-security-forces-in-africa-brutalizing-civilians-under-lockdown/a-53192163, Accessed 21 February 2022.

Obaji, P. (9 September 2020) 'Women 'abused' by police enforcing Covid-19 rules in Nigeria,' Available at: https://www.aljazeera.com/features/2020/9/9/women-abused-by-police-enforcing-covid-19-rules-in-nigeria, Accessed 20 April 2022.

Odita, S. Olatunji, K. & Aikulola, S. (2 April 2020) 'Police, health workers bicker over alleged harassment on movement restrictions,' Available at: https://guardian.ng/news/police-

health-workers-bicker-over-alleged-harassment-on-movement-restrictions/, Accessed 22 April 2022.
Ohajuruka, U. (16 November 2020) 'Police brutality and the girl child,' Available at: https://globalgirlsglow.org/police-brutality-and-the-girl-child/, Accessed 12 January 2022.
Ogunsile, R. (7 September 2020) 'Pregnant mother, baby dies after police delayed doctor at check-point,' Available at: https://www.naijanews.com/2020/09/07/pregnant-mother-baby-dies-after-police-delayed-doctor-at-checking/, Accessed 22 April 2022.
Ojedokun, U.A. (2021) 'Covid-19 pandemic lockdown enforcement: Strategies of the Nigeria Police Force and lessons for the future,' in: *Salus Journal*, Volume 9, Number 2, pp.16-26.
Ojewale, O. (23 September 2021) 'Pandemic watchdog: How vigilant Nigerian civil society organisations tracked graft, discrimination and human rights abuses,' Available at: https://blogs.lse.ac.uk/covid19/2021/09/23/pandemic watchdog-how-vigilant-nigerian-civil-society-organisations-tracked-graft-discrimination-and-human-rights-abuses/, Accessed 6 February 2022.
Ojukwu, T. (17 April 2020) 'Nigeria: Police brutality is more lethal than Covid-19,' Available at: https://www.telesurenglish.net/news/nigeria-police-brutality-is-more-lethal-than-covid19-20200417-0001.html, Accessed 3 February 2022.
Oludare, I. (21 May 2020) 'Covid-19 lockdown: Crisis in Ogun as pregnant woman allegedly dies at police check-point,' Available at: https://dailypost.ng/2020/05/21/covid-19-lockdown-crisis-in-ogun-as-pregnant-woman-allegedly-dies-at-police-checkpoint/, Accessed 22 April 2022.
Olukoya, S. & Oyekanmi, L. (21 October 2020) 'Nigerian forces killed 12 peaceful protesters, Amnesty says,' Available at: https://apnews.com/article/police-violence-police-brutality-lagos-nigeria-98ee3550fb576d561d84b372a65cc95f, Accessed 21 April 2022.
Opera News (29 May 2020) 'Nigerian police shot and killed a 16 year-old girl,' Available at: https://ng.opera.news/ng/en/crime/7f9f3ac37d69e7f58778493064a21fbc, Accessed 25 April 2022.
Oyebanji, O. (30 October 2020) 'Two cases of SARS: Fighting police brutality and Covid-19 in Nigeria,' Available at:

https://blogs.bmj.com/bmjgh/2020/10/30/two-cases-of-sars-fighting-police-brutality-and-covid-19-in-nigeria/, Accessed 11 January 2022.

Oyemolan, J. (29 May 2020) 'Justice for Tina: Police officer arrested for killing 16-year-old girl in Lagos,' Available at: https://allnews.ng/news/justicefortina-police-officer-arrested-for-killing-16-year-old-girl-in-lagos, Accessed 25 April 2022.

Premium Times (14 May 2020) 'Covid-19: Police arrest 155 curfew violators in Sokoto,' Available at: https://www.premiumtimesng.com/coronavirus/392802-covid-19-police-arrest-155-curfew-violators-in-sokoto.html, Accessed 21 April 2022.

Sahara Reporters (25 April 2020) 'Victims of law-enforcement brutality during Covid-19 lockdown should seek compensation, rights activists say,' Available at: http://saharareporters.com/2020/04/25/victims-law-enforcement-brutality-during-covid-19-lockdown-should-seek-compensation, Accessed 17 February 2022.

Sanction (29 April 2020) 'Human rights violations during the Covid-19 lockdown in Nigeria,' Available at: https://saction.org/human-rights-violations-during-covid-19-lockdown-in-nigeria/, Accessed 2 March 2022.

Sylvester, T. (21 May 2020) 'Covid-19: Pregnant woman in labour dies while being delayed at police check-point in Ogun State,' Available at: https://www.kanyidaily.com/2020/05/covid-19-pregnant-woman-in-labour-dies-while-being-delayed-at-police-checkpoint-in-ogun-state.html, Accessed 22 April 2022.

Chapter 4

Weaponisation of the Covid-19 Pandemic and the Suppression of Political Rights and Freedoms in Zimbabwe

Takavafira Masarira Zhou & Costain Tandi

Introduction

This chapter examines how Covid-19 pandemic was weaponised for political expediency in Zimbabwe from early 2020 when the first case of Covid-19 was reported in the country. The honeymoon for President Mnangagwa's so-called Second Republic that came into power through a coup in November 2017 had by the end of 2019 distinctly come to an end. A growing contestation over presidential legitimacy raged on, while neo-liberal policies dubbed 'austerity measures for prosperity' aggravated a decades-long economic crisis. There was, therefore, growing disillusionment with threats of mass action by the opposition Movement for Democratic Change Alliance (MDC Alliance), now Citizens' Coalition for Change (CCC), and strikes by civil servants, particularly in the health and education sectors, becoming more frequent. We acknowledge that the challenges posed by the deadly Covid-19 pandemic called for extraordinary measures to contain its spread, including the use of security forces. It is, however, our argument that the advent of the Covid-19 pandemic provided the parasitic and predatory militarised political elites in Zimbabwe, aided by a bureaucratic bourgeoisie, a God-given opportunity to contain the political threats and challenges using security apparatus under the *alibi* of combating the deadly virus. Political coercion and repression continued to replace democracy, right to representation, freedom of speech, and expression as the country came to depend more on presidential proclamations under Covid-19 lockdowns and not parliamentary democracy with the consequent suspension of both local council and National Assembly by-elections.

Above all, the lockdown regulations were selectively applied with the ruling Zimbabwe African National Union-Patriotic Front (ZANU-PF) party members enjoying an unfettered right to assemblies, holding district elections, conferences, anti-sanctions demonstrations, just to mention a few, while the opposition (as well as the church) was constrained from any gatherings, and therefore limiting its democratic space, rights to access to its supporters, assembly or holding campaign rallies. These shenanigans by the ZANU-PF government were classical indicators of the effective weaponisation of the Covid-19 pandemic for political survival and attempts to decimate the opposition MDC Alliance party in Zimbabwe. The Covid-19 pandemic also exacerbated the conflation of the state and the ruling party as evidenced by the clamping down on opposition parties, muzzling critics, containing the restive population, ultimately entrenching ZANU-PF's totalising hegemonic power and seriously limiting democratic pluralism in Zimbabwe.

Historical background

Emmerson Mnangagwa ascended the presidency on 24 November 2017, thus formally ending Robert Mugabe's 37-year rule in Zimbabwe. He enunciated a new political dispensation predicated, among other things, on good governance and deep-rooted democracy; peace and tranquillity, economic expansion and sustainable development grounded on agricultural growth, tapping and harnessing of natural and human resources for the "benefit of the general populace, and an end to corruption; infrastructural development, reconciliation, compensation of white farmers for the seizure of their land during Mugabe's regime, engagement and trade with the international world" (Zhou, 2019: 75). The coup however only substituted the state driver (Mugabe) with his conductor (Mnangagwa who was then Vice President), but the autocratic trajectory, speed, and direction remained the same with minor differences in degree rather than kind. Mnangagwa's administration continued to perpetuate the conflation of the state and party in a way evocative of his predecessor, Mugabe. After the coup and the 2018 controversial election victory (tainted by vote-rigging and voter intimidation), Mnangagwa rewarded the military and war veterans in a fashion reminiscent of Mugabe's period. The consequent appointments of former military officers to the posts of Vice President (General Constantino Chiwenga), Minister of Agriculture (Air Marshal Perence Shiri), and Minister of Foreign Affairs (Major General Sibusiso Moyo) – among other positions – indisputably marked the coming back of the generals to the hub of governance.

Zimbabwe's economy continued to degenerate under the presidency of Mnangagwa. Sanguinity after the demise of Mugabe in 2017 gave way to pessimism as the 'new dispensation' failed to follow on promises they made to improve the business environment. Endemic corruption and looting by elite leaders throughout government ministries remained a serious challenge and continued to cripple production and export (Ndlovu-Gatsheni and Ruhanya, 2020; Zhou, 2021). Above all, the enforcement of anti-corruption statutes was discriminatory, often targeting political opponents. This made some critical scholars like Zhou (2019: 75) to argue that under Mnangagwa's regime "Zimbabwe has become a country run by parasitic and predatory militarised political elites aided by a bureaucratic bourgeoisie who raid and empty state coffers while speaking the neo-liberal economic language." Conversely, Mnangagwa's promised veritable paradise had, by the beginning of 2020, turned out to be hell on earth premised on bad governance, arbitrary detention, defilement of human rights, increased joblessness, and a diet of starvation.

Arguably, under a quantum leap of public agitation and the threat of mass protest by the opposition MDC Alliance, Mnangagwa's regime increasingly turned to security apparatus to suppress dissent. The government frequently responded to periodic street protests over economic mismanagement and violations of human rights through violence, unlawful arrests and arbitrary detentions. Six people, for instance, were gunned down with scores injured in August 2018. Again, in January 2019, 17 people were killed, hundreds suffered gunshot wounds and numerous females were raped by security forces, while more than 1 000 people were arbitrarily detained by security forces following one of the most ruthless clampdowns on protests in urban residential areas (Zhou, 2021).

The Covid-19 pandemic landed on the shores of Zimbabwe in 2020 on the back of a country whose government was battling political legitimacy, the worst economic turmoil in recent years, and a politically restive population. The virus was seen by the predatory regime as a golden opportunity to deal with its political problems under the pretext of combating the deadly pandemic. As much as there was a reasonable basis for the inclusion of the security sector in response to public health emergencies (Adayaalam Centre for Policy Research, 2020), it is important to scrutinise its actions given its entrenched historical role in the power structures of the country.

Weaponisation of Covid-19 in Zimbabwe

The view that the Second Republic weaponised the Covid-19 pandemic to achieve some political objectives beyond the public health concerns in Zimbabwe is very accurate. Yet, it is important to note that the human rights violation record in the country was already considered problematic before the onset of the virus. What cannot be denied is that the pandemic aggravated human rights violations in Zimbabwe. The country recorded the first case of Covid-19 on 21 March 2020 and by 13 April 2020, the record stood at 14 cases with three deaths (Rahman & Shaban, 2020). By 11 June 2020, Covid-19 cases in Zimbabwe had soared to 279 with infections being recorded among the Zimbabwean citizens who were returning from South Africa. According to Jokwiro (2020), South Africa during that time had the highest levels of recorded infections in Africa. Some infections of Covid-19 were also associated with inbound travellers, mainly from the United Kingdom, United States of America, Dubai, and contact cases of people who had travelled (Salcedo & Cherelus, 2020; Sawlani, 2020). More than one year since the pandemic landed in Zimbabwe, an estimated 40 318 infections and 1 637 fatalities were recorded countrywide (US Embassy, 2021). By 15 March 2022, Zimbabwe had recorded 243 365 cases, 232 787 recoveries and 5 417 deaths (Ministry of Health, 15 March 2022).

Admittedly, the response to the Corona virus pandemic adopted an exceedingly securitised *modus operandi* in most countries across the globe. The World Health Organisation provided the 'securitised speech' on 11 March 2020 when it declared the Covid-19 pandemic a universal health epidemic and requested countries across the world to take measures against it (Moyo & Phulu, 2021; World Health Organisation, 2020). In view of this exceptional situation and to preserve life, many countries in general, and Zimbabwe in particular, had no choice but to adopt extraordinary measures. According to Alonso-Zaldiva *et al* (2020), lockdown measures were the most common response adopted by many countries including Zimbabwe. Extensive lockdowns and fortnightly quarantines adapted to slow transmission of the virus restricted, by necessity, freedom of movement, and in the process, freedom to enjoy many other human rights (Ibid). Policy measures taken to mitigate any such unintended consequences included, but were not limited to: the Civil Protection (Declaration of State of Disaster: Rural and Urban Areas of Zimbabwe) (Covid-19) Notice, 2020 (Statutory Instrument 76 of

2020) that declared the Corona virus an infectious disease and a state of disaster; the Public Health (Covid-19 Prevention, Containment and Treatment) Regulations of 2020 published as Statutory Instrument 77 of 2020 that declared the disease a formidable epidemic; and the Covid-19 (Prevention, Containment and Treatment) (National Lockdown) Order of 2020 contained in Statutory Instrument 83 of 2020 that declared a period of 21 days of lockdown except for essential services and exempted cases (Harris, 2020; Gora, 2021). Regardless of the measures taken to combat the spread of Covid-19 in the early days, the pandemic continued to spread across the globe and that led to extended lockdowns and closure of national borders.

By definition, the weaponisation of Covid-19 in this chapter is perceived as the reutilisation of the fight against the Corona virus crisis for goals other than public health and preservation of human life. In the wake of the Covid-19 pandemic, wider restrictions on movement, assembly, expression, information and privacy were introduced – justified as measures to prevent the spread of the virus. While some restrictions on civil rights may be acceptable during serious public health emergencies under international human rights law, such measures must meet certain conditions (Human Rights Watch, 2020). Most countries that severely violated democratic standards during Covid-19 were already autocratic, while most democracies implemented emergency responses without undermining liberal-democratic standards (Lachapellel *et al*, 2020). Therefore, some specific regime characteristics and the nature of political leadership are important in understanding political decisions around Covid-19 responses, such as preference for 'cronyism', erosion of democratic institutions and systems of accountability, and willingness to use potentially violent political narratives around ethnic nationalism and 'toxic masculinity' (Cooper & Aitchison, 2020). For example, emergency restrictions must be based on scientific evidence and proportionality, must not be arbitrary or discriminatory, and should be instituted for a fixed duration (Ibid). Otherwise, they can lead to human rights violations and have long-term repressive impacts on civic freedoms, citizen voice, participation and accountability. Increasing reports and examples of abuses emerged of restrictive and emergency measures that were applied arbitrarily, discriminately, or for political gain (Civicus, 2020; Human Rights Watch, 2020; Sceats, 2020).

It is worth noting that, even though a disease does not discriminate, the responsive measures instituted by the Zimbabwean government were often discriminatory, both in the way they were developed, formulated, implemented, and measured. Zimbabwe, like many other countries, announced its first 21-day lockdown measures starting on 30 March 2020 (Makurumidze, 2020). Additional measures were covered in statutory instruments further promulgated and passed. Some of the extraordinary measures introduced to combat Covid-19 were drastic as they infringed on basic human rights (Mavhinga, 2020). These include rights such as freedom of movement and assembly, and halting various religious and cultural activities. However, in most cases, lockdown measures were used by the Zimbabwean government to target dissenting voices, especially members of the opposition and civic society. Harris (2020) opines that the lockdown regulations were supposed to be proportionate and reasonable.

It is the contention of this chapter that the dictatorial and predatory Zimbabwean state weaponised the fight against the Corona virus pandemic through deploying state security services backed by a battery of legal and extra-legal instruments as arsenal for sterilising political dissent, side-lining of parliament and the judicial services, arresting and detaining journalists, student leaders and civil society leaders among others (Beiber, 2020). Whereas the military had always been significant in Zimbabwe, there is no doubt that it expanded its domain in the economy, parastatals, state enterprises, parliament, and cabinet after the departure of Robert Mugabe more than at any other time in the history of Zimbabwe. Not surprisingly, the Zimbabwean government, which had more soldiers and police officers than professional health workers, deployed armed security forces to enforce the Covid-19 lockdown measures (Global Firepower, 2020; Moyo & Phulu, 2021). Above all, Mnangagwa's regime soon earned the reputation of being ultra-insensitive to criticism and public dissent (Ndimande & Moyo, 2018). The regime came to regard its critics, opposition leaders and human rights defenders as security threats that had to be eliminated together with the Corona virus pathogens.

The militarised government of Zimbabwe was more concerned with the opposition's challenge to its legitimacy since the 2018 disputed presidential elections. There had always been a realistic threat of mass protest against the 'new dispensation' which always kept the security services sector on high alert. Additionally, the advent of the Corona virus coincided with the country's worst economic blizzard in recent years. The virus also landed on the back of Cyclone Idai in 2019 which left over 270 000 people homeless, a devastating drought that saw 8.5 million people being food insecure in a population of 16 million, and an unsustainable sovereign debt burden of over US$20 billion (Moyo, 2020; Moyo & Phulu, 2021). Furthermore, over 80% of Zimbabweans were in the informal sector and had their access to livelihoods, health care, food, and water severely restricted by the lockdown measures (ZIMCODD, 2020). It was within this framework that Mnangagwa's regime sought to capitalise on the context of the Corona virus crisis to manage its political, economic, and social glitches. As such, the regime weaponised a battery of legal and extra-legal instruments, limited democratic space and freedoms in the name of combating the Covid-19 pandemic to clamp down on opposition members, journalists and civil society activists, and to muzzle the restive population in Zimbabwe.

Suffocation of democracy though the appropriation and manipulation of legal instruments

The institutional framework for combating the Corona virus pandemic was put in place on 19 March 2020 with the government declaration of a State of National Disaster in terms of the Civil Protection Act of 1989. Consequent to the declaration, the Public Health Order (Covid-19 Prevention, Containment and Treatment) (National Lockdown) Order, 2020, was issued by the Minister of Health and Child Care (Government of Zimbabwe, 2020). Between the first wave of Covid-19 in March 2020 and the fourth wave triggered by a new variant called Omicron from November 2021 and to February 2022 (*VOA News*, 30 November 2021; Bill Watch 4/2022), the government also issued a myriad of other Statutory Instruments as part of the restraint measures. It is noteworthy that all these instruments were furnished by the executive arm of the state without consulting the legislative arm and other stakeholders. At any rate, Mnangagwa's government issued more institutional instruments since 2017 than Mugabe in his entire 37 years of reign (Moyo & Phulu, 2021). Mnangagwa's militarised regime arrogated to itself the power to legislate by announcements. As much as some such powers were necessary to combat the Covid-19 pandemic and reflected those adopted in democratic countries, the challenge was their unrestrained use in Zimbabwe, which lacked legislative checks and balances. Criticising the loony decisions made by the government in November 2021, the head of the Zimbabwe Association of Doctors for Human Rights, Dr Norman Matara, remarked: "We are worried by the restrictions, especially the decision to quarantine returning residents, citizens, and travellers who test negative for Covid-19 with two PCR results. We think these restrictions are nothing more than punishment" (*VOA News*, 30 November 2021). Indeed, many Statutory Instruments were just knee-jerk decisions based on emotion rather than scientific evidence or common sense. Many such measures destroyed the tourism sector and business in general in Zimbabwe. The late constitutional law expert, Alex Magaisa (2020), posited that the powers contained in some of the Statutory Instruments exceeded the parameters of a declaration of a State of National Disaster as they infringed on the constitutionally-provided social, economic, and cultural rights as well as political and civil liberties of Zimbabweans.

Though the Constitution of Zimbabwe authorises the government to issue Statutory Instruments in cases of urgency and emergency, the same Constitution provides for the role of parliament for the sake of checks and balances as well as accountability and democratic governance. It is significant to note that the Zimbabwe government did not lawfully raise a state of emergency in the country as stipulated in Section 87 (1) of the Constitution (2013). Yet sound as this may appear, the government's behaviour as well as that of the security forces was tantamount to a state of emergency. Evidently, the predatory militarised regime appropriated and exploited the Statutory Instruments to evade the state of the emergency route. Arguably, while the regime dodged declaring a state of emergency, in practice it exercised powers reminiscent of emergency situations, without the arduous checks and balances. In short, Zimbabwe was in a de facto state of emergency.

From the onset of the Covid-19 pandemic in March 2020, democratic freedoms came under renewed strain in many countries in general and Zimbabwe in particular. The context was one of shrinking civic space in Zimbabwe, with attacks by the state on the key civic freedoms, of association, peaceful assembly, and expression, on which civil society relied. The state used the pandemic as a pretext to introduce new restrictions that had nothing to do with fighting the virus by extending state powers and reducing the space for accountability, dialogue, and dissent (Gora, 2021). In most cases, the government of Zimbabwe upped its powers by increasing censorship and extending surveillance in the name of controlling the virus. Furthermore, the state ramped up the power of security forces to criminalise and violently deal with breaches of pandemic regulations (Mukeredzi, 2020). The authorities also used Section 14 of Statutory Instrument 83 of 2020 on Public Health to prohibit demonstrations during the lockdown. By 31 July 2020, the state's paranoia had reached unprecedented levels, and dozens had been arrested, hundreds brutalised, and Zimbabwe was in a state of fear, with the state security agents deployed in every part of the country, both rural and urban (Makurumidze, 2020). The mass arrests, abductions, and assaults mostly targeted journalists, human rights defenders, opposition activists, and anyone who was courageous enough to utilise their constitutional right to self-expression including the international award-winning author, Tsitsi Dangarembga (Zimbabwe Peace Project, 2020).

In total contempt of the Constitution, an overnight curfew that ran from 6 o'clock in the evening to 6 o'clock in the morning was imposed on 21 July 2020, ostensibly to prevent the spread of Covid-19 infection, but critics interpreted the move as a clampdown on protests (Moyo & Phulu, 2021). The failure by the government to put in place sustenance options prior to affirming a curfew unduly affected the economically disarticulate and marginalised sections of the population who survived through vending. Above all, the declaration of the curfew coincided with the call by civil society and opposition parties for a demonstration against the deteriorating economic conditions and endemic corruption that even extended its tentacles to Covid-19 resources. Undoubtedly, the additional lockdown enforcement measures announced by President Mnangagwa some 10 days before the planned day of the demonstration scheduled for 31 July 2020 were also intended to pre-empt the demonstration apart from attempting to flatten the rising Corona virus infection curve. It is also noteworthy that one of the architects of the demonstrations, Pastor Jacob Ngarivhume, was arbitrarily detained a few days after the enunciation of the lockdown curfew (Ibid; *Pindula News*, 2020).

On 27 July 2020, a ZANU-PF spokesperson called on supporters to use all necessary means to defend themselves ahead of the nationwide demonstrations (Human Rights Watch, 2020; Jeewa, 2021). When the protests went ahead, the police arrested at least 20 people and charged them with various offences including 'public nuisance', 'intention to incite public violence', and breaking Covid-19 regulations (Mavhinga, 2020). They were later released on bail. On 4 August, the President said the protestors were "bad apples" who would be "flushed out" (Ibid). Conversely, the government had weaponised the fight to combat Covid-19 and used it to defensively dent the constitutional right of the people of Zimbabwe to peacefully demonstrate against corruption in the country. Put succinctly, the ruling predatory elite approached the Corona virus crisis with security lenses and manipulated the legal instruments as weapons to handle its political opponents over and above combating the global pandemic. Not surprisingly, it preferred exercising special executive powers than following the normal parliamentary process. The imposition of restrictive measures, even for the right reason, but without backing from the law, set a precedent where the executive was inspired to impose its will upon the people thereby side-stepping the constitution.

Abuse of human rights and freedoms

Admittedly, the government's response to the Covid-19 pandemic led to gross human rights abuses and limited freedoms. In continuation with infamous impunity of Mugabe's First Republic, Mnangagwa's security forces deployed to enforce the lockdown measures blatantly violated the right to personal liberty, human dignity, and personal security. In addition, the freedoms from torture, cruel inhuman or degrading treatment were also breached. The same can be said about the freedom of assembly and association, the right to demonstrate and petition, freedom of conscience, freedom of expression and freedom of the media. The right to administrative justice, and right to a fair hearing, guaranteed under Sections 68 and 69 of the Constitution (2013), were also flouted with impunity from the infancy of the Covid-19 pandemic.

A long list of activists and opposition members who were arrested on spurious grounds include Joanah Mamombe, Netsai Marova and Cecilia Chimbiri (Human Rights Watch, 2020). The trio were arrested at a police roadblock in the capital, Harare, while they were leading a demonstration against inadequate protection for the poor during the Covid-19 period. They were abducted the same day from Harare Central Police Station by a group of men believed to be intelligence agents, who physically and sexually assaulted them and dumped them 87 kilometres from their homes in Harare, three days later

(Kagurume, 2020; Roth, 2020). In June 2020, the state charged the women with faking their abductions and "tarnishing the country's image" (Zimbabwe Peace Project, 2020). On 31 July, they were re-arrested at a checkpoint. While they were being held, a soldier whipped Cecilia Chimbiri for allegedly insulting him. In December, in the case relating to the charges connected to their abduction in May, a Harare Regional Magistrate ordered that Joana Mamombe be tried separately from Cecilia Chimbiri and Netsai Marova on grounds that she had been declared medically unfit to stand trial (Kagurume, 2020). That their case had not reached finality by 2022 is a clear case of the violation of their rights to administrative justice and fair trial.

Similarly, the MDC Alliance youth leader, Godfrey Kurauone, indicated his intention to sue the police for delayed justice and wrongful arrest. He had spent 45 days in remand prison after his arrest on 31 July 2020 for criminal nuisance. The arrest came after he allegedly circulated a video on social media while singing a song with the words: '*Ichava nhoroondo kana ndatenderwa nababa kubvisa Mnangagwa… Ichava nhoroondo*', translated from Shona to English as: 'It will be history when I get a directive from my father to dethrone President Emmerson Mnangagwa' (Jeewa, 2021). The prolonged pre-trial detention, which was justified by the government on grounds that courts of law had scaled down operations as a Covid-19 preventive measure, was undoubtedly and increasingly used as tools of repression in Zimbabwe (Mavhinga, 2020). With threats to his rights to personal liberty and personal security, Kurauone fled to the United Kingdom in 2021. This abuse of the criminal law not only punished the legitimate assertion of freedom of expression but was often done in violation of basic fair trial and pre-trial rights protected under Zimbabwean and international law and fundamental to the fair administration of justice.

In most of these cases, Zimbabwe's Magistrate Courts appeared to have misapplied the law, possibly owing to them being biased in favour of the state (Ibid). This is evidenced by the fact that where bail appeals were lodged before the High Court, they were successful. A case in point was that of the Vice Chairperson of the then main opposition party, MDC Alliance, Job Sikhala, who was arrested on 21 August 2020 for allegedly posting videos on social media inciting the public to revolt against the government (Zimbabwe Peace Project, 2020). He was denied bail by the Magistrate's Court, but on appeal at the High Court after 31 days in remand prison, he succeeded. In actual fact, the High Court found that the Magistrate's

Court had not indicated any offence which they believed he was likely to commit if released on bail (Harris 2020).

The conjoined effect of the measures preferred by the government through the statutory instruments was the challenge to democratic principles (Human Rights Watch, 2020). While it is possible to justify restrictions to basic civil rights, such as freedom of movement, association or the right to privacy in times of emergency, it is important that these be limited to the necessary minimum. Restrictions of movement, and even a general lockdown, were necessary steps taken in many countries around the world, including Western democracies, to contain the pandemic but a semblance of democracy had to be maintained throughout the enforcement period. The excesses in the form of harassment and flogging of citizens by some members of the Zimbabwe Republic Police were reported (Zimbabwe Peace Project, 2020), thus indicating the extent to which the lockdowns opened yet other windows for human rights abuse. It was imperative for the security forces to strike a balance between law enforcement and respect for inalienable rights.

On 11 January 2021, the MDC Alliance spokesperson, Fadzayi Mahere, was arrested on trumped-up charges relating to "publishing or communicating false statements prejudicial to the State" in contravention of Section 31(a) (iii) of the Criminal Law Code (Gora, 2021). Mahere was released on bail a week later on 18 January. Statutory instruments were used to suspend constitutional rights. For example, Covid-19 restrictions led to courts closing early, ostensibly to allow staff to get home before the curfew. Consequently, hearings were repeatedly adjourned, and critics and activists were unable to get bail and were kept in prolonged pre-trial detention (Ibid). This explains why, for instance, Jacob Ngarivhume, spent around six weeks in pre-trial detention, having been denied bail three times.

Security forces frequently used excessive force to crack down on peaceful protests under the guise of enforcing lockdown restrictions. They reportedly killed at least 10 people in different parts of the country for violating the lockdown rules within two days of the announcement of the lockdown (Mutambasere, 2020; Moyo & Phulu, 2021). Security forces also arbitrarily arrested and detained protesters and others under the pretext of enforcing Covid-19 measures (Roth, 2020). In the first four months of the lockdown, 116 000 people were arrested allegedly for violating Covid-19 regulations (Amnesty International, 2020). The 'Ferret Team', a joint unit comprising agents from the police, military, the Central Intelligence

Organisation, terrorised government critics, opposition leaders and activists, and their family members. Many, including several members of the main opposition party, the MDC Alliance, were abducted from police custody, tortured and dumped far away from their homes (Ibid).

In the days running up to the 31 July 2020 protests, security forces raided the homes of those suspected of supporting the initiative, in some cases vandalising property. On 30 July, Tawanda Muchehiwa was arrested by police in a shop in Bulawayo (*Africa News*, 2020). On the way to the police station, the officers handed him over to the Ferret Team, who tortured him to reveal the whereabouts of his uncle, Mduduzi Mathuthu, the editor of an online newspaper *ZimLive* (Ibid). They dumped him far away from his home four days later. The same day, security forces raided Mduduzi Mathuthu's home, and when they failed to find him, took away his sister and two of his nephews who were later released after the Media Institute of Southern Africa intervened. The violence continued after July, and on 7 August, four unidentified men abducted Noxolo Maphosa in the street (Roth, 2020). According to the *Africa News* (2020), she was sexually assaulted in an effort to force her to reveal the whereabouts of her uncle, Josphat Ngulube, an MDC Alliance member, who had been accused of distributing face masks bearing the slogan '#ZANU-PF Must Go'. On 12 August, Tamuka Denhere, another member of the MDC Alliance, was abducted from his home in the city of Gweru by unidentified men and tortured over several hours after which they handed him over to the Harare Central Police Station. Police also arrested his wife when she came to report his abduction (Ibid). It is a fact that the government, through its security agencies, used the Covid-19 pandemic to violate rights to personal liberty, human dignity, and personal security, and flout freedom from torture or cruel, inhuman or degrading treatment of real and imagined critics, let alone the general citizens of Zimbabwe.

At least 10 lawyers were harassed in connection with cases they represented, with some of them facing prosecution on trumped-up charges (Mavhinga, 2020). What is clear is that defective decisions were made in courts cognisant of Covid-19 restrictions on demonstrations and movement by the general populace. In June 2020, Thabani Mpofu was arrested and bailed, on allegations of obstructing justice by filing an affidavit allegedly from a fictitious person in a case which challenged the appointment of the Prosecutor General (Human Rights Watch, 2020). The author of the affidavit later presented himself to the police, but the case against Thabani Mpofu continued at the end of the year. In July 2020, the Chief Justice directed that all court judgements be 'approved' by the head of the court or division before being handed down. The directive was withdrawn following strong objections from lawyers and civil society activists. In August 2021, a magistrate barred Beatrice Mtetwa, a human rights lawyer, from representing her client and recommended that her licence be revoked after she was falsely accused of running a Facebook page that criticised the justice system (Ibid).

Police and military officers used the Covid-19 restrictions as a pretext to justify the harassment and intimidation of journalists and other media workers, at least 25 of whom were assaulted, arbitrarily arrested and detained while working, or on their way to and from work (Roth, 2020; Tsunga *et al*, 2020). They were accused of lockdown violations, disorderly conduct or using expired accreditation documents which, under the Covid-19 regulations, should have been considered valid during the lockdown. Journalists were frequently ordered by security details to delete their videos or photographs without a valid reason. The arrest and detention of journalist Hopewell Chin'ono show how the Mnangagwa regime used Covid-19 regulations to justify severe restrictions on the rights to freedom of expression (Catholic Commission for Justice and Peace, 2020; Moyo & Phulu, 2021). The government deployed security forces to abduct, assault and torture perceived critics, and opposition members and leaders. Chin'ono was arrested on charges of incitement to participate in public violence - having allegedly contravened Section 187(1) (a) as read with Section 37(1) (a) (i) of the Criminal Law (Codification and Reform) Act. He was accused of calling for the removal of a constitutionally-elected government through an uprising, using his Twitter account (Ibid). In fact, in June 2020, Chin'ono had done nothing more than investigative work which exposed corruption in the Corona virus-related contracts awarded by Zimbabwe's Ministry of Health and Child Welfare to Drax International and tweeted that uniformed police had been questioning his staff (Jeewa, 2021). Having been denied bail, Chin'ono spent 45 days in pre-trial detention during which time he was held at Harare's notorious Chikurubi Maximum Security Prison (Chin'ono, 2 October 2020).

On 3 November 2020, Chin'ono was arrested again for allegedly violating his bail conditions and obstructing justice by posting a tweet relating to his possession of confidential information from the

National Prosecuting Authority relating to the denial of bail to the president of the Zimbabwe Miners' Federation, Henrietta Rushwaya (Jeewa, 2021). After being denied bail again, Chin'ono remained at the Chikurubi Maximum Security Prison until 20 November 2020. On 8 January 2021, he was again arrested, this time on charges of "communicating falsehoods" for allegedly sharing a video he claimed showed a police officer beating a baby to death (Ibid). He was only granted bail after 20 days in remand detention. In the effort to clamp down on the independent and social media, the authoritarian Mnangagwa regime passed a decree that allowed the police to fine or imprison those deemed to be spreading 'fake news' critical of official management of the pandemic. On 3 December 2021, the Zimbabwe government gazetted the Data Protection Act (No. 5/21) which empowered it to perform unlimited surveillance on all communication among citizens while banning the distribution of any information it chose. Conversely, the dictatorial Mnangagwa regime affirmed its power over the media and other information and accountability institutions under the cover of fighting the Corona virus pandemic, thereby undermining freedoms of speech and expression, let alone the operations of the media as the fourth estate.

2020 will go down in history as a year when life, work and study came to a virtual standstill. Zimbabwean students will remember hastily how they struggled for their academic freedom. The students' attempts to raise their voices about the conditions during the pandemic resulted in the arrest and detention of more than 30 of their leaders since June 2020, sparking reprobation from human rights and civil society organisations (Gora, 2021). There was growing concern about the 'weaponisation' of the judiciary by the state to persecute opposition and civil society activists. Alan Moyo, a student leader, spent 72 days in remand detention, after being denied bail (*Africa News*, 2020). Moyo was arrested on 7 December 2020 on charges of inciting public violence and for allegedly participating in the organisation of the 31 July 2020 peaceful anti-corruption protests (Ibid). The lengthy pre-trial detention was one of the numerous cases witnessed in recent years in Zimbabwe, targeting those perceived to be critical of the government's policies. As can be seen from the cases of Moyo and other activists, human rights defenders and members of opposition parties, the government of Zimbabwe displayed a pattern of abusing its criminal justice processes to stifle and intimidate critics under the veil of enforcing lockdown measures.

Makomborero Haruzivishe, a student activist who was at the forefront of the solidarity efforts to free Alan Moyo, was thrown behind bars (Civicus, 2020). On 3 March 2021, Haruzivishe had his bail revoked. Another student leader, Ngadziore, was assaulted by unknown assailants in 'unregistered' vehicles before being taken away by the police. He then spent more than 30 days in prison before being released on bail. His freedom was short-lived as he was arrested a third time after addressing a press conference against Muchehiwa's abduction on 18 September 2020. Tawanda Muchehiwa claims to have been abducted at gunpoint by five security force members on 30 July 2020 and tortured for at least three days (Kagurume, 2020). After a *habeas corpus* application was made before the courts to determine whether the detention was lawful, he was dumped near the house of his uncle, Mduduzi Mathuthu, barely able to walk. Muchehiwa's abduction, including the number plates of one of the vehicles used (which was later traced to Impala Car Rental), was reportedly captured by CCTV cameras. The prolonged incarceration of Ngadziore and the refusal of Impala Car Rental to follow a High Court order that they release the information of Muchehiwa's abductors prompted students to launch two campaigns dubbed *'#Free Taku'* and *'#Justice for Tawanda'*. These campaigns led to the arrest of even more students, including Arnold Mazonde, Nancy Njenge, Talent Jinga, Mitchel Liyeto, Takudzwa Gwaze, Takudzwa Mukono, Donald Marevanhema, John Ncobo, Youngerson Matete and Zvikomborero Mumbirimi (Gora, 2021). On 23 June 2020, eight Chinhoyi University of Technology students were also arrested for allegedly protesting the clampdown on human rights defenders in Zimbabwe and rising incidents of police brutality. The eight were the Zimbabwe National Students Union (ZINASU) Vice-President, Faustina Madava, together with Lionel Shayahama, Shamiso Whide, Nicola Makasu, Melody Madalamete, Ignatius Lochombo, Brian Mushakwe and Norman Makamanzi (Ibid). It was alleged that on 22 June 2020, during a lecture, the eight raised and distributed placards with messages calling for the release of the three MDC Alliance youth leaders: Joanah Mamombe, Netsai Marova and Cecilia Chimbiri. In addition to this misapplication of the law, there also appeared to be a selective and inconsistent application of the law by the Mnangagwa government. By comparison to the cases above, a few apparently politically-favoured persons were treated preferentially. On 19 June 2020, the then Minister of Health, Obadiah Moyo, was arrested on corruption charges. The prosecution did not oppose bail, which he was granted by the Magistrates' Court the following day (*Aljazeera News*, 20 June 2020). Similarly, on 7 February 2021, the former Zimbabwe Labour and Social Welfare Minister, Petronella Kagonye, was arrested on allegations of corruption and was also granted bail after two days (Chingarande, 10 February 2021).

This preferential treatment of 'others' raised questions as to whether activists like Alan Moyo, Chin'ono, Sikhala, Kurauone, and Ngarivhume were being denied their rights to equal protection of the law, both under national and international law (Beiber, 2020). Despite facing equally serious charges, Obadiah Moyo and Kagonye were granted bail while Alan Moyo, Chin'ono, Ngarivhume and Sikhala were not and remained on remand for at least 45 days (Ibid). It was also worrying that many of the accused were not provided with or allowed to wear adequate personal protective equipment in prison or had their prison cells sanitised, despite the broad extent of the Covid-19 infections in the country and in the prisons at the time.

It is within the above framework that in January 2022, member states, including South Africa, at a United Nations Human Rights Council Universal Periodic Review Working Group meeting in Geneva, Switzerland, accused Zimbabwe of using Covid-19 lockdown restrictions to undermine the freedoms of its people. They called for human rights violators in Zimbabwe to be held accountable. The United States Permanent Mission Charg'e d'Affaires to the United Nations, Benjamin Moeling, stated that Zimbabwe should "establish an independent complaints mechanism to investigate and hold accountable members of the security who … engaged in human rights violations and abuses" (Matenga & Gumbodete, 2022). Furthermore, he urged Zimbabwe to enforce security and process laws under the Constitution (2013) that prohibited arbitrary arrests and prolonged detentions. It was only by doing so, he argued, that the practice of constitutionally guaranteed freedoms of expression, peaceful assembly, and association for all could be guaranteed (Ibid).

There were also calls for the separation of powers to ensure independence of the judiciary and impartial decision-making. South Africa called on Zimbabwe to ensure alignment of the Zimbabwe Human Rights Council Act with the Paris Principles, and the Constitution (2013) and provide funding for the protection and promotion of human rights. The United Nations Human Rights Council office in Zimbabwe stated that, irrespective of the imposed unilateral Covid-19 restrictive measures, Zimbabwe had a duty to fulfil its human rights obligations. Despite attempts to defend Zimbabwe's human rights record by the Justice Minister, Ziyambi Ziyambi, who represented Zimbabwe alongside Permanent Secretary, Virgina Mabhiza, the United Nations recommended that allegations of excessive use of force should be promptly, thoroughly and independently investigated, and perpetrators prosecuted, and adequate remedy provided to the victims (Ibid). By and large, the state weaponised Covid-19 for political expediency with the consequent arbitrary arrests and politically-motivated violence, among many other violations of human rights and freedoms, as unravelled above.

Castration of the legislature and suspension of elections

Covid-19 lockdown measures also castrated the legislature, with the suspension of regular sessions on 5 May 2020 (Parliament of Zimbabwe, 2020). This was conveniently done without putting in place any regulations or standing orders to allow for its operations during the lockdown period in direct contravention of Section 139 of the Constitution (2013). It is important to note that Statutory Instrument 77 of 2020 which provided for the Covid-19 Prevention, Containment and Treatment Regulations and all its subsequent amendments, did not include parliament among the institutions that were exempted from the movement restrictions it imposed (Moyo & Phulu, 2021). In practical terms, this meant that parliament was technically hamstrung from performing its oversight duties during the initial phase of the lockdown. Considering parliament's lack of independence and the strangle-hold that the executive has on parliament, it is conceivable that there was a gag imposed on parliament during this period to fulfil political ends (Veritas, 2020a).

Surprisingly, parliament leaped into action on 5 March 2020 to deliver an assault on the MDC Alliance by being complicit in the recalling of its four Members of Parliament following a Supreme Court Judgement on the case involving the opposition party's internal squabbles. The Speaker of Parliament announced the expulsion of nine more MDC Alliance Members of Parliament in terms of Section 129 (1) (k) of the Constitution (2013), which expulsion was believed to have been engineered by ZANU-PF to fulfil its hegemonic projects (Veritas, 2020b). Ultimately, 27 legislators (21 Members of Parliament and 6 Senators) were recalled. The expulsion of the MDC Alliance Members of Parliament must be clearly comprehended within the context of questioning the legitimacy of President Mnangagwa and the heavy-handedness of the executive. Arguably, the legislature's inability to swiftly offer devices to address the oversight gap during the Covid-19 lockdown, while being able to intrude in the opposition MDC Alliance's intra-party matters, was an indication of its vulnerability to being employed as a political weapon for executive agendas.

The suspension of by-elections in 2020, and the lifting of the suspension on 24 December 2021 were not far detached from the political manoeuvres prosecuted under the veil of containing the public health crisis and alleged subsidence of the health pandemic, respectively. The Zimbabwe Electoral Commission (ZEC) deferred all electoral activities including council and parliamentary polls on 25 March 2020, allegedly in line with the lockdown orders. Munorinyana and Chambwera (2020) argue that the deferment of by-elections on the pretext of the Corona virus pandemic was an assault on the central precept of democracy. Veritas (2020c) posits that the suspension of the elections was unlawful as there was nothing in the Constitution (2013) permitting the electoral management body to suspend elections of its own accord. Above all, elections could not, in terms of the Constitution (2013), be suspended based on the Covid-19 measures which consisted of regulations passed by the executive without the involvement of parliament which was constitutionally charged with the responsibility of making laws in Zimbabwe. Section 13 (1) (a) of the Constitution (2013) did not tolerate the usurpation of parliament's main law-making power by the executive. Its domination by former military personnel compromised its independence and even legitimacy, and its proclamations reflected the mind of the executive rather than that of the electoral body.

Though ZEC's decision could be justified based on the 'doctrine of necessity', there is no doubt that it flouted democratic freedoms: not only people's ability to have their vote count in bye-elections emanating from recalls, deaths or dismissals but also their ability to express dissent, question and even criticise those in power and advance political alternatives. It is important to note that the announcement to suspend elections was not followed up with an official notice in the Gazette or a newspaper (Veritas, 2020c). Arguably, it was a typical boardroom decision not suitable for an important issue as national elections. Whereas it was logical that given the lockdown and the massive public health scare, suspension of elections could be justifiable, it is a historical fact that there was no consultation with the stakeholders leaving the move prone to being perceived as the ruling party taking advantage of the lockdown measures to tilt the electoral landscape to its advantage thereby flouting multi-party democracy. Even the police were converted into little more than a ZANU-PF militia, harassing and detaining opposition supporters at will while refusing to touch ZANU-PF supporters engaged in criminal violence and abuse of human rights.

The fact that Members of Parliament could be expelled without providing mechanisms of allowing the filling in of the vacancies so created (Zimbabwe Election Support Network, 2020) gives credence to the claim that the suspension of the electoral processes was part of the weaponisation of the fight against Covid-19. That parliament, in the interim, did not in the same vein put a moratorium on creating more vacancies by recalling members, is further testimony of the weaponisation process. It is conceivable that the suspension of elections by ZANU-PF was an expedient mechanism of decimating opposition voices challenging the legitimacy of the 'President' in parliament. In Malawi, the then incumbent President, Peter Mutharika, tried to stop the then imminent elections by putting in place a 21-day lockdown. The opposition, as well as civil society, resisted the weaponisation of Covid-19 to keep the incumbent in power by launching a court case that cancelled the lockdown restrictions and paved the way for elections in which Mutharika lost to the opposition leader, Lazarus Chakwera (Ellena, 2020). Zambia also held elections during the Covid-19 pandemic in August 2021 in which the incumbent, President Edgar Lungu, lost to opposition leader Hakainde Hichilema (Mfula, 16 August 2021). South Africa also held municipal elections during the Covid-19 period in November 2021 (Roodt, 2021). These examples are indicative of the need for the government to have balanced the pros and cons of the Covid-19 responses against the integrity of the Constitution and democracy.

It is noteworthy that while Covid-19 restrictions conveniently emasculated opposition parties from meetings with grassroots supporters, and therefore restrained their freedom of movement, association and gatherings, ZANU-PF had an open cheque of movement, conducting rallies and campaigns even as the Covid-19 virus was raging on, as if they were immune to the pandemic. ZANU-PF was able to conduct party district elections in 2021, and provincial elections in January 2022 (Mpofu, 2022). Having weaponised Covid-

19 to buttress ZANU-PF structures through unfettered campaigns and weaken the opposition, Mnangagwa went on to proclaim 26 March 2022 as the date for holding by-elections for both parliamentary and council seats. At this time, Zimbabwe had a total of 150 elective vacancies, which comprised 28 parliamentary seats and 122 council seats (Factsheet, 19 March 2022).

ZEC also suspended voter registration in 2020, meaning that many people who qualified to vote since 2018 had been disenfranchised thereby violating their political rights to vote and to be voted into public office in line with Section 67 (3) (a) and (b) of the Constitution (2013). ZEC's operations were therefore incompatible with the practice of democracy. Even the rebranding of the MDC Alliance into the Citizens' Coalition for Change (CCC) failed to curb the weaponisation of Covid-19 against the opposition. Whereas Mnangagwa's ZANU-PF and its Mwonzora-led proxy of MDC-T were allowed to bus their supporters to the venues of their by-election launches on 12 February 2022 and police did not force them to observe any stringent conditions, the Chamisa-led CCC was warned against busing people from other constituencies outside Highfields Constituency, chanting slogans, and constrained to observing Covid-19 protocols, among other restrictions for their star rally held on 20 February 2022 (Magwaya & Buwerimwe, 2022). Despite getting the green light from the High Court, the CCC Marondera rally was blocked by police on 12 March 2022, while the CCC Masvingo rally that the police also tried to block only proceeded on 20 March after a High court ruling (Chitagu, 2022; Kawadza & Saunyama, 2022).

Judicial capture and weaponisation

Unlike parliament, the judiciary was able to internally regulate its operations during the lockdowns. Up until the relaxation of restriction orders in February 2022, the judiciary was able to regulate its own response to the Covid-19 crisis by making its own directives that allowed limited movement of its members, including legal practitioners as well as the operations of its courts (Malaba, 2020). Order Number 12 (Statutory Instrument 153 of 2020) recognised the judiciary as an essential service. Yet sound as this appeared, it did not escape the radar and appendages of executive influence either directly or indirectly. The handing down of the Supreme Court Judgement in the case of Mashavira vs MDC and Others (2020) on 31 March 2020 referred to above, is a case in point as the court passed a judgement tailor-made to politically weaken the opposition and strengthen the ruling party at the height of the Covid-19 lockdown. In July 2015, the High Court dismissed the application by Kudakwashe Bhasikiti, the former Masvingo Provincial Minister, to outlaw ZANU-PF on grounds that he should have exhausted internal remedies before rushing to the courts (Chiripasi, 2015). Yet, in a case where Mashavira never sought any internal remedy, the court conveniently entertained the case, and during a period when the opposition could not demonstrate against the judgement given lockdown restrictions on movement, demonstrations and gatherings. Not surprisingly, the judgement came to be sarcastically referred to as the 'Corona virus Judgement' by some members of the public.

Faced with a legitimacy challenge from the Nelson Chamisa-led MDC Alliance emanating from the 2018 elections, President Mnangagwa used his judicial capture to deflate pressure by causing a legitimacy challenge within the opposition party and weakening its voice in parliament. This reality became more cogent taking cognisance of the fact that on 30 May 2020, the High Court ruled that the MDC Alliance was not a political party. This ruling was made despite the transformation of the MDC Alliance into a political party after the 2018 elections and its holding of an elective Congress in Gweru in 2019. Above all, on 4 June 2020, armed soldiers and police officers assisted 20 youths loyal to the Thokozani Khupe-led MDC-T in taking over the MDC Alliance party headquarters, Morgan Richard Tsvangirai House (Harvest House), in the centre of the capital, Harare (*Nehanda Radio*, 5 June 2020). That all these judgements and the jettisoning of the MDC Alliance from Morgan Richard Tsvangirai House happened during the Covid-19 period is a clear indicator of weaponisation of the pandemic to emasculate the opposition through skilful planning and extension of executive powers through the courts and security forces.

Despite the gravity of the Corona virus crisis, the Mnangagwa administration took advantage of the lockdown to change the way top judges were appointed in Zimbabwe. The procedure to appoint the judges involved the appointment powers of the President being subject to interviews by the Judicial Services Commission and picking from a list provided by the Judicial Services Commission (Veritas, 2020c). However, through the Constitutional Amendment (Number 2) Act of May 2021, the President now directly appointed the Constitutional Court judges, thus entrenching his executive powers while weakening the judiciary in the process. The public consultation process for Constitutional Amendment Number 2 was rushed through even though members of the public were under lockdown and could not participate effectively in this important process. The extension of the term of Chief Justice, Luke Malaba, despite the initial ruling by a panel of High Court judges of its illegality on an incumbent who occupied office and had reached retirement age, was viewed by critics as executive interference with the judiciary and payback for Malaba's ruling in favour of Mnangagwa over the disputed 2018 elections (Biti, 2022).

By and large, the executive used lockdown legal and extra-legal instruments to further its influence over the judiciary and legislative branches of the state. Therefore, while the government was profoundly engaged in managing the Corona virus crisis, it also sent contradictory messages through its political actions that further intensified political polarisation at a time when unity in diversity and social cohesion were critical factors in battling the lethal pandemic. Above all, the legal and extra-legal instruments espoused by the ZANU-PF-led government violated human rights and basic freedoms, including the right to liberty, freedom of association, and freedom of movement as reflected above.

Conclusion

This chapter has demonstrated that by and large, Mnangagwa's authoritarian and predatory regime weaponised the Covid-19 pandemic to entrench its totalising hegemonic agenda. In the process, the regime flouted the right to free, fair and credible regular elections; the right to make political choices freely; the right to join and participate in the activities of a political party or organisation of their choice; the right to campaign freely and peacefully for a political party or cause; the right to participate in peaceful political activity; and the right to participate, individually or collectively, in gatherings or groups or in any other manner, in peaceful activities to influence, challenge or support the policies of the government or any political or whatever cause. Other rights defied include personal liberty, human dignity, personal security, administrative justice, fair hearing, and voting.

Additionally, the Covid-19 pandemic was used by Mnangagwa's regime to suppress freedom from torture or cruel, inhumane or degrading treatment; freedom of assembly and association; freedom of conscience; freedom of expression and freedom of the media, among many others. Arguably, lockdown measures were used by the ZANU-PF government as a warhead to blow up political opposition, silence critics, contain the restive population, and entrench its power and control over some key accountability institutions, including the legislature, the judiciary, and the media. Consequently, the legislature was side-lined, journalists were arrested and harassed, and the opposition leaders, human rights defenders, and the general populace were treated with disgrace. The criminal justice system was effectively captured and weaponised to intimidate and suppress critics. The fight against the Covid-19 pandemic provided a perfect opportunity for the Second Republic to further its own political objectives through instrumentalising the lockdown measures to quash dissent, silence human rights defenders and opposition political actors. The extensive power exercised by the government underscored the importance of maintaining effective oversight of its actions and ensuring that it was subject to the rule of law.

References

Adayaalam Centre for Policy Research (ACPR) (2020) 'Sri Lanka's militarised response poses grave threats to human rights, situation brief No. 3,' Available at: http://adayaalam.org, Accessed 1 January 2022.

Africa News (2020) 'Zimbabwe arrests 100 000 for flouting lockdown rules - police,' Available at: https://www.africanews.com/2020/07/20/zimbabwe-arrests-100000-for-flouting-lockdown -rules-police, Accessed 21 December 2021.

Aljazeera News (20 June 2020) 'Zimbabwe health minister granted bail in $60m corruption case,' Available at: https://www.aljazeera.com › news › 2020 › 20 › zimba, Accessed 14 March 2022.

Alonso-Zaldivar, R. Burns, R. & Fox, B. (2020) 'State demands ventilators as feds ration limited supply,' Available at: https://www.google.com/amp/s/www.usnews.com/news/health-news/articles/, Accessed 4 December 2021.

Amnesty International (2020) 'Zimbabwe 2020,' Available at: www.amnesty.org, Accessed 15 January 2022.

Beiber, F. (2020) 'Authoritarianism in the time of the Corona virus: The pandemic offers dictators and democracies alike an opportunity for abuse,' Available at: https://www.everycrs report.com/reports/R46336.html, Accessed 11 December 2021.

Bill Watch 4/2022. (8 February 2022) 'Public Health Lock-down Order: Relaxation of restrictions,' Available at: https://www.veritaszim.net/billwatch, Accessed 17 March 2022.

Biti, T. (20 January 2022) Interview, Harare: Zimbabwe.

Catholic Commission for Justice and Peace (2020) 'Two Zimbabwean journalists charged with violating Covid-19 lockdown,' Available at: https://cpj.org/2020/06/two-zimbabwean-journalists-charged-with-violating-COVID-19-loc, Accessed 17 December 2021.

Chingarade, D. (10 February 2021) 'Kagonye granted $30 000 bail,' in: *Newsday*, Harare: Zimbabwe.

Chingono, N. (2 October 2020) 'Journalist Hopewell Chin'ono speaks out over brutal Zimbabwe prison conditions,' Available at: www.theguardian.com, Accessed 13 January 2022.

Chiripasi, T. (9 July 2015) 'High Court dismisses Bhasikiti's application to block ZANU-PF expulsion,' Available at: https://www.voazimbabwe.com, Accessed 14 February 2022.

Chitagu, T. (20 March 2022) 'Court gives CCC nod to hold Masvingo rally,' in: *The Standard*, Harare: Zimbabwe.

Civicus (2020) 'Civic freedoms and the Covid-19 pandemic: A snapshot of restrictions,' Available at: https:// www.civicus.org/index.php/media-resources/reports-publications/4396-civic-freedoms-and-thecovid19-pandemic-a-snapshot-of-restrictions, Accessed 2 December 2021.

Cooper, L. & Aitchison, G. (2020) *The dangers ahead: Covid-19, authoritarianism and democracy*, London: Conflict and Civil Society Research Unit, London School of Economics (LSE).

Ellena, K. (2020) 'Legal quagmire of postponing or modifying elections,' Available at: https://www.ifes.org/news/legal-quagmire-postponing-or-modifying-elections, Accessed 13 December 2021.

Global Firepower (2020) 'Active military manpower, 2020: Total available active military manpower by nation. Zimbabwe,' Available at: https://www.globalfirepower.com/active-military-manpower .asp, Accessed 5 February 2022.

Gora, P. (2021) 'Has Covid-19 become a weapon to gag student activists?' Available at:

www.universityworldnews.com/post.php?story=2021021515381786, Accessed 13 December 2021.

Government of Zimbabwe (2013) *Constitution of Zimbabwe Amendment (No.20) Act 2013*, Harare: Government of Zimbabwe.

Government of Zimbabwe (2020) *Statutory Instrument 83 of 2020*, Harare: Government of Zimbabwe.

Government of Zimbabwe (2021) *Data Protection Act [chapter 11:12], No. 5/21*, Harare: Government of Zimbabwe.

Harris, L.B. (2020) 'Jail time for breaking Covid-19 regulations,' Available at: https://www.cite.org.zw/jail-time-for-breaking-covid-19-regulations/, Accessed 4 November 2021.

Human Rights Watch (2020) 'Human rights dimensions of Covid-19 response,' Available at: https://www.hrw.org/sites/default/files/news_attachments/202003covid_report.pdf, Accessed 23 January 2022.

Jeewa, T. (2021) 'The weaponisation of the criminal law in Zimbabwe,' Available at: www.opinionjuris.org/2021/03/12/the-weponisation-of-the-criminal-law-in-zimbabwe, Accessed 13 December 2021.

Jokwiro, A. (2020) 'Covid-19: Which way for Zimbabwe,' Available at: https://www.herald.co.zw/covid-19-which-way-for-zimbabwe/, Accessed 11 January 2022.

Kagurume, S. (2020) 'Abductions, brutality, and demolitions: When the state becomes more harmful than Covid-19,' Available at: http://democracyinafrica.org/abductions-brutality-demolitions-state-becomes-harmful -COVID-19, Accessed 11 December 2021.

Kawadza, S. & Saunyama, J. (13 March 2022) 'Chamisa's CCC under siege as police block Marondera campaign rally,' in: *The Standard*, Harare: Zimbabwe.

Lachapelle, L Luhrmann, A. & Maerz, S.F.M. (2020) 'An update on pandemic backsliding: Democracy four months after the beginning of the Covid-19 pandemic,' Available at: https://www.vdem.net/media/filer public/b9/2e/b92e59da-2a06-4d2e-82a1-b0a8dece4af7/vdem_policybrief-24_update-pandemic-backsliding_200702.pdf, Accessed 4 December 2021.

Magaisa, A. (2020) 'BSR: What exactly did the Supreme Court order?' Available at: https://www.bigsr.co.uk/single-post/2020/05/20/BSR-What-exactly-did-the-Supreme-Court-order, Accessed 4 February 2022.

Magwaya, M. & Buwerimwe, S. (18 February 2022) 'Police set tough conditions for Chamisa rally,' in: *Newsday*, Harare: Zimbabwe.
Makurumidze, R. (2020) 'Corona virus-19 disease (Covid-19): A case series of early suspects reported and the implications towards the response to the pandemic in Zimbabwe', in: *Journal of Microbiology, Immunology and Infection*, Volume 53, Number 5, pp.493-498.
Malaba, L. (2020) 'Chief Justice, Practice Directive No. 1, 2020; Chief Justice, Practice Directive No. 2, 2020; Chief Justice, Practice Directive No. 3, 2020; Chief Justice, Practice Directive No. 4, 2020,' Available at: https://:zimlii.org/zw/legislation/si/2020/1, Accessed 3 December 2021.
Matenga, M. & Gumbodete, P. (27 January 2022) 'UN red-flags Zim on human rights,' in: *Newsday*, Harare: Zimbabwe.
Mavhinga, D. (3 April 2020) 'Lockdown laws draconian, excessive,' Available at: https://www.theindependent.co.zw/2020/04/03/lockdown-laws-draconian-excessive/, Accessed 4 January 2020.
Mfula, C. (16 August 2021) 'Hichilema faces task of reviving Zambian economy after landslide win,' Available at: www.Reuters.com, Accessed 10 January 2022.
Ministry of Health, Zimbabwe (15 March 2022) 'Covid-19 update as at 15 March 2022,' Available at: https://www.twitter.com/mohcczim?lang=en, Accessed 16 March 2022.
Moyo, G. (2020) 'Obstacles and opportunities for financing the fight against Covid-19 pandemic in a debt-trapped Zimbabwe,' Available at: https://www.researchgate.net/publication/342356779, Accessed 4 November 2021.
Moyo, G. & Phulu, K.I. (2021) 'The weaponisation of the Corona virus crisis in Zimbabwe: Legal and extra-legal instruments,' in: *iBusiness*, Volume 13, pp.48-66.
Moyo, T. (2020) 'A Covid-19 outbreak will devastate Zimbabwe,' Available at: https://www. dailymaverick.co.za/article/2020-03-28-a-covid19outbreak-will-devastate-zimbabwe-which-has-several ongoing crises to deal, Accessed 11 January 2022.
Mpofu, O. (9 January 2022) 'ZANU-PF provincial elections democratic,' in: *The Sunday Mail*: Harare: Zimbabwe.
Mukeredzi, T. (9 April 2020) 'Zimbabwe's triple threat: Corona virus, food shortages, and an economy in meltdown,' Available

at: https://www.thenewhumanitarian.org/news/2020/04/09/, Accessed 23 December 2021.

Munoriyarwa, A. & Chambwera, C. (2020) 'Tweeting the July 2018 elections in Zimbabwe', in: M.N. Ndlela & W. Mano (eds.) *Social media and elections in Africa*, Cham: Palgrave Macmillan.

Muronzi, C. (2020) 'In Zimbabwe, lack of tests sparks fear Covid-19 goes undetected, Aljazeera,' Available at: https://www.aljazeera.com/news/2020/04/zimbabwelack-tests-sparks -fearcovid-19-undetected-200409173206798.html, Accessed 25 January 2022.

Mutambasere, S.C. (2020) 'Constitutionalism in the time of Covid-19: The Zimbabwe experience,' Available at: https://ancl-radc.org.za/node/641, Accessed 4 January 2022.

Ndimande, J. & Moyo, K.G. (2018) 'Zimbabwe is open for business: Zimbabwe's foreign policy trajectory under Emmerson Mnangagwa,' in: *Afro-Asian Journal of Social Sciences*, Volume XI, Number 9, pp.1-25.

Ndlovu-Gatsheni, S. & Ruhanya, P. (eds.) (2020) *The history and political transition of Zimbabwe: From Mugabe to Mnangagwa*, London: Palgrave Macmillan.

Nehanda Radio (5 June 2020) 'Armed soldiers and police help Khupe/Mwonzora youths capture opposition HQ,' https://nehandaradio.com ›news, Accessed 14 January 2022.

Rahman, A. & Shaban, A. (2020) 'Corona virus in Africa: Close to 8000 cases, 334 deaths, 702 recoveries, Available at: https://www.africanews.com/2020/04/04/coronavirus-in-africa-breakdown-of-infected-virus-free-countries/, Accessed 4 January 2020.

Roodt, M. (2021) 'What did we learn from South Africa's local elections?' Available at: https://africanarguments.org/2021/11/what-did-we-learn-from-south-africa-local-elections/, Accessed 15 January 2022.

Roth, K. (2020) 'How authoritarians are exploiting the Covid-19 crisis to grab power,' Available at: https://www.hrw.org/news/2020/04/03/, Accessed 4 January 2021.

Salcedo, A. & Cherelus, G. (2020) 'Corona virus travel restrictions across the globe,' Available at: https://www.nytimes.com/article/coronavirus-travel-restrictions.html, Accessed 24 December 2020.

Sawlani, S. (2020) 'Covid-19: Africa told to prepare for worst. What's the response? Aljazeera,' Available at: https://www.aljazeera.com, Accessed 21 December 2021.

Sceats, S. (2020) 'Covid-19 brings human rights into focus,' Available at: https://www. chathamhouse.org/expert/comment, Accessed 26 January 2022.

Tsunga, A. Mazarura, T. & Heywood, M. (2020) 'Democracy in lockdown: Authorities clamp down on pro-democrats and civilians under cover of Covid-19 restrictions,' Available at: https://www.dailymaverick.co.za/article/2020-05-22, Accessed 25 January 2022.

United States Embassy in Zimbabwe (2021) 'Covid-19 questions: Country-specific information,' Available at: https://zw.usembassy.gov/covid-19-information-2/, Accessed 16 January 2021.

Veritas (2020a) 'Election Watch 1: Suspension of election activities,' Available at: http://www.veritaszim.net/node/416, Accessed 2 December 2021.

Veritas (2020b) 'Bill Watch 42/2020: More MDC-T recalls and two more Bills sent to Senate,' Available at: http://www.veritaszim.net/node/4278, Accessed 2 December 2021.

Veritas (2020c) 'Court Watch 9/2020,' Available at: http://www.veritaszim.net/courtwatch, Accessed 11 December 2021.

World Health Organisation (2020) 'WHO Director-General's opening remarks at the media briefing on Covid-19,' Available at: https://www.who.int/dg/speeches/detail/, Accessed 12 December 2021.

Zhou, T.M. (2018) 'Poverty, conflict and vulnerability in Africa', in M. Mawere (ed.) *Jostling between mere talk and blame game? Beyond Africa's poverty and underdevelopment game talk*, Bamenda: Langaa, pp. 83-138.

Zhou, T.M. (2021) 'Labour in Zimbabwe, 1980-2020', in: C. Chidoko and P. Mupa (eds.), *Social policy and development matrix in Zimbabwe: Where is the missing link?* Gweru: Dream Discoveries Publishers, pp.15-46.

Zimbabwe Election Support Network (2020) 'How to conduct elections,' Available at: http://kubatana.net/source/zesn, Accessed 15 December 2021.

Zimbabwe Peace Project. (2020) 'Human rights in the midst of the Covid-19 global pandemic,' Available at: http://kubatana.net/2020/04/03/human-rights-in-the-midst-of-the-covid-19- global-pandemic-zim-in-stateof-neglect-march-2020-monthly-report/, Accessed 4 December 2021.

Zimfact (19 March 2022) 'March 26 by-elections,' Available at: https://zimfact.org/factsheet-march-26-by-elections/, Accessed 19 February 2022.

Chapter 5

Media Under Siege? The Covid-19 Pandemic and the Violation of Press Freedom in Zimbabwe

Fidelis Peter Thomas Duri & Golden Maunganidze

Introduction

Journalists, especially freelancers and those from the independent media, had a raw deal at the hands of the Zimbabwean government and its agencies during the Covid-19 lockdown period that took effect from 30 March 2020. Within the first seven days of the lockdown, nine journalists were allegedly physically assaulted by law-enforcement officers while carrying out their work (Zenda, 24 April 2020). In a statement issued on 10 April 2020, the Media Institute of Southern Africa (MISA) confirmed receiving nine disturbing accounts involving the arrest, harassment or assault of journalists and newspaper vendors in different parts of Zimbabwe during the lockdown that was just about a week old. Five of the incidents pertained to journalists while four related to newspaper vendors (Gasa, 21 April 2020). Mkhululi Thobela, a Zimbabwe-born freelance photo-journalist, noted in mid-April 2020:

> If you are a freelance journalist or if you do not work for a government or a state newspaper or publication, it becomes very difficult. The police actually told me that if I do not work for Zimbabwe newspapers or for any state publication, I should not cover anything; I should leave. So, it is very difficult to work in Zimbabwe right now (Ibid. 1).

In May 2020, Reporters Sans Frontières, a Paris-based press freedom organisation, expressed concern at the rising number of journalists arrested in Zimbabwe under Covid-19 restrictions and noted that the country had the largest number of press freedom infringements in sub-Saharan Africa (Rivers & Ndlovu, 24 June 2020). In the year 2020 alone, MISA reported violations against 52 media workers, including journalists, vendors and media students by the Zimbabwean government's agents, mostly the police and the army. This number of infringements more than doubled that of 2019 (Maukonen & Sanomat, 17 May 2021).

The mistreatment of journalists, particularly freelancers and those from the independent media, continued in 2021 and beyond. A Human Rights Watch report published on 11 February 2021 chronicled how more than 20 African governments were capitalising on the Covid-19 pandemic to clamp down on media freedom (Mavhunga, 11 February 2021). In March 2021, according to the International Press Institute's Covid-19 tracker, Zimbabwe came first in the list of African countries with highest number of pandemic-related press freedom violations (Maukonen & Sanomat, 17 May 2021).

This chapter examines some of the strategies employed by the Zimbabwean government and its agencies to besiege the media, particularly the private press institutions and their workers, during the Covid-19 period. It is a fact that this period marked a tumultuous and forgettable era in Zimbabwean history as far as media freedom and freedom of expression are concerned. The lockdown imposed by the government in an effort to curtail the spread of the pandemic was accompanied by rampant violations of media freedom and free speech. In many instances, the authorities instrumentalised Covid-19 lockdown regulations to justify press censorship and severe curtailments on the rights to freedom of expression and media freedom. This chapter argues that press freedom and freedom of expression were severely compromised during Zimbabwe's Covid-19 period as the ruling Zimbabwe African National Union Patriotic Front (ZANU-PF) government of President Emmerson Mnangagwa weaponised lockdown regulations for selfish political ends. The arbitrary arrest and detention of journalists; the government's spirited efforts to silence critical reporting; and the harassment of media personnel for allegedly contravening lockdown regulations, among other things, attest to this as shall be discussed in this chapter.

The state's attempts to silence critical reporting and arbitrary detentions

Journalists were often tormented, harangued, tortured and detained by law-enforcement agents as the government desperately sought to prevent sensitive information related to the Covid-19 pandemic from being accessed by the public. This information included statistics of people infected and mortality rates, independent evaluation of the government's responses to rising numbers of people who either contracted or died from the pandemic, and the heavy-handedness of the police and the army in enforcing lockdown measures.

The very first day of the national lockdown in Zimbabwe on 30 March 2020 saw the arrest of two journalists in different parts of the country. Tatenda Julius, a reporter for the *New Ziana*, a local news agency, was arrested in the eastern city of Mutare on accusations of using an expired accreditation card (*Reporters Sans Frontières,* 10 April 2020). Similarly, Kudzanai Musengi, a freelancer, was arrested in the Gweru Central Business District where he was investigating the implications of the recently imposed Covid-19 national lockdown. The police again charged Musengi for operating without valid accreditation (Maukonen & Sanomat, 17 May 2021). The accusations of using expired press cards was a deliberate attempt to frustrate journalists who were not affiliated with the state. In actual fact, the Zimbabwe Media Commission, a government agency that accredited journalists, had issued a statement that journalists could continue operating with their 2019 press cards until new cards for 2020 were prepared (Chirimambowa, 11 July 2020; *Reporters Sans Frontières,* 10 April 2020).

On 2 April 2020, Nunurai Jena, a reporter with the *Newsday*, a Zimbabwean daily newspaper, and the *Voice of America*, was arrested while filming a police roadblock in the northern town of Chinhoyi. He was charged for 'disorderly conduct' and having an out-of-date press card (*Reporters Sans Frontières*, 10 April 2020). Following the arrest of many journalists on charges of using 2019 press cards, Arnaud Froger, the head of *Reporters Sans Frontières* Africa desk issued a statement that blamed the government for harassing journalists and prioritising insignificant issues at a time when the pandemic was wreaking havoc. He argued:

> Ever since the start of the epidemic, Zimbabwe has been at the forefront of those African countries that are restricting the freedom to inform in an arbitrary and extremely disproportionate manner. Arresting journalists does not stop the epidemic. These press freedom violations also run counter to government directives authorising journalists to work during the lockdown and to use their 2019 press cards, of which the validity has been extended. The government must give the police clear instructions to stop preventing journalists from doing their job of informing the public, which helps to combat the epidemic (Ibid: 1).

Having noted the ever-increasing number of journalists being victimised for using expired press cards, the Zimbabwean chapter of MISA approached the High Court in April 2020 seeking an order to stop the police from further harassing journalists doing their work. On 21 April 2020, the court ordered the police to immediately refrain from assaulting, harassing and arresting journalists providing coverage during the Corona virus lockdown. According to MISA Zimbabwe, several journalists in the country had raised concerns over harassment by the police. The journalists had argued that reporting during Covid-19 pandemic was proving to be the worst nightmare for media practitioners. MISA Zimbabwe then issued a strongly worded statement highlighting that "Covid-19 is the enemy and elephant in the room, not the media", adding: "It should, therefore, be: All hands on deck against Covid-19 and hands off the media, in the fight against this global pandemic of which the media is a critical component (MISA Zimbabwe, 9 April 2020: 1).

The arrest of Tatenda Julius, a student journalist attached to *Pungwe News*, on 30 March 2020 demonstrates how Zimbabwe's law-enforcement agents demonised media practitioners by viewing them as spies. Julius was arrested in Dangamvura Suburb in the city of Mutare while taking pictures of the police enforcing the Covid-19 lockdown. The police accused him of practising journalism without a press card. Attempts by the management of *Pungwe News* to prove that Julius worked for the newspaper hit a brick wall as the police insisted that the reporter could only be freed by the courts of law (MISA Zimbabwe, 30 March 2020). Julius spent the night in prison and was released after paying a fine of Z$500 for "criminal nuisance" (Moyo, 9 April 2020b: 1).

On 4 April 2020, Panashe Makufa, a freelance journalist, was detained and beaten up by four police officers who accused him of interfering with their duties. Makufa was arrested in Harare's Kuwadzana Suburb when he was photographing the police beating up people as they sought to disperse them in accordance with the lockdown stay-at-home orders (*Reporters Sans Frontières*, 10 April 2020). A large crowd had gathered at a local shopping centre around 1700 hours to buy maize meal whose supplies had dwindled considerably across the country (*Infosplusgabon*, 9 April 2020). He was bundled into a police truck, assaulted and forced to delete the pictures he had taken before being dropped off (*News 24*, 6 April 2020). In addition to sustaining injuries that required urgent medical attention, Makufa also lost a day's worth of media coverage as a result of the forced deletion of material from his photographic device (Ibid).

In a related incident on 11 April 2020, Terence Sipuma, a freelance journalist and member of the Young Journalists Association (YOJA), was assaulted by police details and soldiers while on his way from Harare to the town of Chegutu to report on the Covid-19 lockdown (Mabhiza, 25 June 2020; MISA, 12 April 2020). Sipuma narrated his ordeal as follows: "They asked where I was going and the moment I showed them my journalism identity card, I was asked to lie down and was beaten, being accused of exposing them" (Zenda, 24 April 2020: 1). He added: "They took my phone and as they were searching through the phone they promised me that they were going to do more if I had videos or pictures of that operation" (MISA, 12 April 2020: 1).

It is now quite apparent that for many Zimbabwean journalists, "reporting on heavy-handed policing could earn them a beating and time in jail" (Gasa, 21 April 2020: 1) thereby raising questions on who should be policing the police. In mid-April 2020, Mkhululi Thobela, a Zimbabwe-born freelance photo-journalist who covered stories in Zimbabwe and South Africa, was harassed by the law-enforcement agents for exposing their brute force in dealing with civilians during the Covid-19 lockdown period. Thobela wrote:

> I was actually arrested for photographing a story where police were brutally beating an old lady. She had gone to queue for mealie-meal but then because she did not get the mealie-meal they were told to leave. She was beaten for not moving quickly. And when I saw that I moved swiftly to cover that story, but I was arrested and held without charge in a cell for eight hours (Ibid: 1).

Thobela was only released by the police after paying a fine equivalent to 400 South African Rands (Ibid). What this incident demonstrates is the gross violation of human rights as evidenced by the arrest and harassment of a journalist and the subsequent unlawful detention in a desperate endeavour by the state to suppress media freedom and also to hinder unfettered access to information by the general public.

Mduduzi Mathuthu, the editor of the independent online newspaper, *Zim-Live*, was also targeted by the ZANU-PF government (Kudzayi, 7 April 2021). On 30 July 2020, Tawanda Muchehiwa, a civil rights activist, was arrested by police in a Bulawayo shop and on the way to the police station they tortured him to disclose the whereabouts of his uncle, Mduduzi Mathuthu. They released him four days later in a remote area far away from his home (Ibid). Muchehiwa sustained "serious injuries, including extensive bruises and an acute kidney injury" (Human Rights Watch, 2021: 1). On the day of Muchehiwa's release, a group of soldiers raided Mathuthu's home and upon failing to find him, took with them his sister and two of his nephews. The hostages were later set free after the intervention of the Media Institute of Southern Africa (Dube, 7 April 2021).

The Zimbabwe Republic Police (ZRP), the national police force, sometimes teamed up with the municipal police in various urban centres to brutalise media practitioners during the Covid-19 lockdown period. During the morning of 17 July 2020, in an operation that can be likened to an unholy alliance, officers from the Harare Municipality and the ZRP teamed up to brutally assault a Zimbabwe Peace Project officer, Tinashe Njodzi, as he attempted to rescue Tapiwa Zivira, the organisation's Media and Communications Officer, an accredited journalist, who was filming an incident in which they were enforcing lockdown provisions near the flyover on Lytton Road in Harare (Zimbabwe Peace Project, 30 July 2020). During the incident, about six municipal police officers and two ZRP details ran towards Zivira and asked him why he was filming them. Zivira introduced himself as a media practitioner and produced his media accreditation card. All this fell on deaf ears as the officers punched him with fists and open palms, and dragged him all over the place. In addition, one of the assailants confiscated Zivira's mobile phone. He was bundled into a municipal vehicle and driven off to Harare Central Police Station (Ibid). As they approached the Central Business District, the municipal officers began dropping off and by the time they arrived at the Harare Central Police Station, only two ZRP officers and three municipal police details remained in the truck. The ZRP members asked him to disembark and apologised for what they had done to him while everyone else disappeared (Ibid). This incident illustrates how media practitioners were abused by state security agents. This was deliberately done to silence professional journalism, indeed a violation of journalistic rights, and censor information available to the public thereby infringing people's right to information. As will be noted in the next section, such incidents increased as the lockdown progressed during which the police harassed many journalists in the name of enforcing lockdown regulations and protocols.

Independent or freelance journalists who critically evaluated the government's Covid-19 curtailment measures were often subjected to gross physical and emotional abuse. On 20 July 2020, for example, Hopewell Chin'ono, a freelance journalist who had publicly condemned corruption in the handling of Covid-19 relief funds and other resources, particularly at the Ministry of Health, was arrested (Maulani *et al*, 2020). Chin'ono was abducted from his home in Harare by eight police officers who charged him with inciting public violence after he had openly supported the planned nationwide protests scheduled for 31 July the same month against government corruption and deteriorating socio-economic conditions (MISA, 12 April 2020). It should be noted, however, that Chin'ono had written a story about corrupt activities in Covid-19 programmes which implicated President Mnangagwa's family and other high-profile people (Mazarura, 25 May 2021; Moyo & Phulu, 2021). In actual fact, Chin'ono's investigative journalism into corrupt activities in Covid-19 mitigation activities resulted in the implication, arrest and expulsion from cabinet of Obadiah Moyo, the then Minister of Health and Child Care (Moyo & Phulu, 2021). Despite the fact that Chin'ono had professionally executed his journalistic mandate of reporting on corruption in the Covid-19 alleviation programmes, he became a wanted man for exposing the ZANU-PF government and its leader, Emmerson Mnangagwa. As Moyo & Phulu (2021: 49) remarked:

> …the Covid-19 crisis has offered a convenient cover for the ruling elite to clamp down on political opposition, silence critics, contain the restive population, and entrench its power and control over some of the key accountability institutions including the legislature, the judiciary, independent media, and civil society among others.

After being arrested on 20 July 2020, Chin'ono was detained behind bars for six weeks, only to be granted bail in September 2020 (Maukonen & Sanomat, 17 May 2021). As if to keep him away from public reach and prevent him from conducting more investigations that could further expose more corruption cases within the government, Chin'ono was detained at various periods for a total of nine weeks between July and November 2020 (Mavhunga, 11 February 2021).

The arrests and detentions of Hopewell Chin'ono ignited criticism from media stakeholders who expressed concern at the government's criminalisation of the freedom of the press. Kholwani Nyathi, the editor of the local weekly newspaper, *The Standard*, complained:

> There is a climate of fear in the Zimbabwean media industry caused by the frequent arrests of prominent journalists such as Hopewell Chin'ono. While certain repressive legal instruments have been repealed in the last three years, senior government officials continue to use threats of arrests and unspecified actions against journalists to curtail press freedom. This affects the morale of reporters and the quality of their journalism (Maukonen & Sanomat, 17 May 2021: 1).

Despite such concerns, the government's pursuit of Chin'ono was relentless. On 8 January 2021, Chin'ono was arrested on charges of sharing falsehoods on social media with Job Sikhala and Fadzai Mahere, two officials of the opposition Movement for Democratic Change (MDC) Alliance. Sikhala and Mahere were also arrested on 9 and 11 January respectively. The three were being accused of tweeting about an incident that allegedly took place at a Harare taxi rank where a police officer who intended to hit a woman with a baton stick for violating Covid-19 restrictions accidentally struck to death an infant who was on its mother's back (*Global Voices sub-Saharan Africa*, 25 January 2021). The police later issued a statement dismissing the claims about the baby's death and pointed out that a medical examination had ascertained that the minor had no life-threatening injuries (Ibid). What emerges from this incident is that even though the baby may not have died, police details sometimes enforced Covid-19 regulations violently. Thus, in this case, the police themselves were admitting that the baby was injured accidentally by a whip that was intended for the mother. Furthermore, the police went on to harass Chin'ono for covering the story, a clear violation of media freedom and the right to information. Despite the admission by the police, veiled though, the three were charged for publishing or communicating false information that had the potential to prejudice the state. They were then charged for contravening Section 31(a) (iii) of the Criminal Law Code, which read:

> Any person, whether inside or outside Zimbabwe, publishes or communicates to any other person a statement which is wholly or materially false…realising there is a real risk or possibility of undermining public confidence in a law enforcement agency…or the Defence Forces of Zimbabwe…shall whether or not the publication or communication results in a consequence referred to (above), be guilty

> of publishing or communicating a false statement prejudicial to the state and liable to a fine…or imprisonment for a period not exceeding twenty years or both (Ibid: 1).

On 18 January 2021, Mahere was released on bail by a Harare magistrate after spending a week in state custody. Chin'ono and Sikhala were denied bail and remained in police custody (Ibid). On 27 January 2021, Chin'ono was released on bail (Maukonen & Sanomat, 17 May 2021). In the end, however, the state failed to get overwhelming evidence to prosecute the trio (Ibid). These events clearly showed the determination of the Zimbabwean government to curtail press freedom and regulate the flow of information by inflicting physical and emotional harm on journalists and their informants.

The state's onslaught on the media was also witnessed in February 2021 when freelance journalists, Godfrey Mtimba and Tonderai Sharo, were allegedly barred from covering the government-administered rollout of the Covid-19 vaccination programme near the city of Masvingo (Ibid). It is most likely that the newsmen were barred because the independent press had previously been very critical on issues to do with the way the government awarded contracts for vaccines and personal protective equipment (Ibid).

On 17 August 2021, Elizabeth Mashiri, an Assistant Editor and Bureau Chief of the Midlands Province for the *Mirror*, a privately-owned daily newspaper, was arrested by the police in the city of Gweru. Apparently, Mashiri had been arrested while taking pictures and videos of a physical altercation in the Gweru Central Business District between vendors and the police. Despite the fact that Mashiri identified herself as a journalist and produced her press card, one of the police details grabbed her by the jacket and dragged her to a municipal truck. Another police officer grabbed Mashiri and lifted her dress as she tried to force the journalist into the car. For taking videos of the police harassing civilians in the name of enforcing lockdown provisions, Mashiri was charged with disorderly conduct and "thrown in a disgusting cell" whose toilet "was full of human waste" (Committee to Protect Journalists, 30 August 2021: 1). She was detained for about four hours at the Gweru Central Police Station. Commenting on Mashiri's arrest, Angela Quintal, Africa's Programme Coordinator of the Committee to Protect Journalists (CPJ), lamented:

> The unprovoked arrest and humiliating detention of journalist Elizabeth Mashiri in Gweru is the latest example of the Zimbabwean police's contempt for basic human rights, including media freedom. Police should be protecting members of the press, not arresting them. Prosecutors must drop the baseless charges against Elizabeth Mashiri immediately (Ibid: 1).

The government also used legislation to gag the independent and social media in an effort to suppress criticism of its handling of the Covid-19 pandemic. An example is Section 14 of a decree that was passed on 12 June 2020 known as Statutory Instrument 83 of 2020 on Public Health (Covid-19 Prevention, Containment and Treatment) Regulations (Amnesty International, 2021). This statute empowered the police to fine or imprison people deemed to be spreading 'fake news' that was critical of the way the Covid-19 lockdown issues were being administered (Ibid, 2021; Moyo & Phulu, 2021). Part of the Covid-19 regulations issued by the Ministry of Health and Child Care (12 June 2020) and enunciated in Statutory Instrument 77 of 2020 read:

> For the avoidance of doubt any person who publishes or communicates false news about any public officer, official or enforcement involved with enforcing or implementing the national lockdown in his or her capacity as such, or about any private individual that has the effect of prejudicing the State's enforcement of the national lockdown, shall be liable for prosecution under Section 31 of the Criminal Law Code and liable to the penalty there provided, that is to say a fine of up to or exceeding level fourteen or imprisonment for a period not exceeding twenty years or both.

A report released by the Human Rights Watch on 11 February 2021 noted that the Zimbabwean government was one of the chief culprits and worst offenders in the world for exploiting the Covid-19 pandemic to interfere with the freedom of the press (Mavhunga, 11 February 2021). In April 2020, Lovemore Zvokusekwa from the town of Chitungwiza on the outskirts of Harare was arrested on accusations of circulating a fabricated press statement purporting to be from the President, announcing an extension of the lockdown. Later that month, President Mnangagwa interfered with the functions of the judiciary by declaring that Zvokusekwa should be imprisoned for 20 years in order to deter others from spreading fake news. On 30 April 2020, however, he was released from detention on remand and the court stated that he could be called by way of summons in future if necessary (Amnesty International, 2021).

Zimbabwe's senior military officials also interfered with press freedom during the lockdown period. In March 2021, for instance, Valerio Sibanda, the Commander of the Zimbabwe National Army, in an effort to influence media content during the Covid-19 lockdown period, warned that social media was proving to be a threat to national security and that the military would place private electronic communications under surveillance to "guard against subversion" (Amnesty International, 2021). In April 2021, Christian Rambu was arrested in the town of Chipinge for distributing a WhatsApp message accusing President Mnangagwa of incompetence (Ibid). Similarly, in August 2021, Rujeko Hither Mpambwa from the town of Kariba was arrested for using the social media to criticise President Mnangagwa's address to the nation (Ibid).

The harassment of journalists as a silencing mechanism to stop them from critical reporting during the Covid-19 lockdown in Zimbabwe became common to the extent that the then ZRP Officer Commanding Masvingo Province, Assistant Commissioner Taoneyi Nyazema, summoned two journalists in Masvingo on 11 April 2020 and threatened them openly with unspecified actions for a satirical article that had been published in *TellZim News* seemingly mocking the police for being unprofessional during the Covid-19 lockdown period. The two journalists, Golden Maunganidze and Passmore Kuzipa, instructed their lawyer, Dereck Charamba, to engage MISA Zimbabwe to petition the Police Commissioner General, Godwin Matanga, to restrain his subordinates who were harassing journalists across the country (MISA Zimbabwe, 13 April 2020).

This section has illustrated how journalists, particularly freelancers and those from the independent media, were subjected to physical and emotional abuse by law enforcement agents as the government desperately sought to conceal both its weaknesses and excesses in handling the Covid 19 pandemic. Zimbabwe's human rights record remained poor as many media practitioners were harassed, threatened, tortured, assaulted and detained for reporting the government's shortcomings in combatting the pandemic and exposing the brutalities of law enforcement agents in implementing lockdown measures, among other things. Thus, as Rivers & Ndlovu (24 June 2020: 1) rightly observed, "the pandemic [offered] new opportunities for repression" by security details, especially the police.

Harassment of journalists for allegedly violating lockdown regulations

Journalists, particularly those who were freelance and those from independent media institutions, were often harassed in spite of Covid-19 lockdown regulations that were proclaimed on 30 March 2020 in which communications workers such as journalists were designated as essential service workers and were not restricted in terms of movement (Burke & Chingono, 17 May 2020). On 19 April 2020, the essential worker category was broadened to encompass all media workers, including newspaper vendors (Ibid). Despite these developments, freelance journalists and those who did not belong to the state-owned media houses were often subjected to various forms of abuses.

Some journalists were arrested for violating the Covid-19 lockdown's stay-at-home orders. On 2 April 2020, for example, the Zimbabwe Republic Police arrested and charged Nunurai Jena, a 55-year-old freelance journalist, allegedly for contravening Covid-19 lockdown regulations that compelled people to stay at home. He was arrested while recording video footage of some police details who were manning a checkpoint along the Chinhoyi-Chegutu Highway in Mashonaland West Province. Jena was charged for violating Section 11(a) (b) of the Public Health (Covid-19), Prevention, Containment and Treatment (National Lockdown) Order of 2020. For recording video footage of a police roadblock, he was also charged for disorderly conduct as defined in Section 41(b) of the Criminal Law (Codification and Reform) Act (*Infosplusgabon*, 9 April 2020).

Similarly, on 8 April 2020, Beatific Gumbwanda, a reporter for *TellZim News*, a Zimbabwean weekly newspaper, was arrested for violating lockdown regulations in the south-eastern town of Chiredzi even though he had showed the police his press card confirming that he was a registered journalist. He was released after being detained for close to two hours (*Infosplusgabon*, 9 April 2020; *Reporters Sans Frontières*, 10 April 2020). Gumbwanda was in Chiredzi taking pictures of the police manning different checkpoints that were set up in line with national lockdown regulations (Ibid). In addition, the journalist had also visited Chiredzi General Hospital to investigate a Covid-19 death amid allegations that nurses at the institution had refused to treat the patient because they did not have protective clothing (Bhebhe, 13 April 2020; Mafirakureva, 12 April 2020). The harassment of journalists on allegations of violating lockdown stipulations fuelled criticism from a number of media organisations who felt that, besides causing physical and mental stress on the persons of the media practitioners, these acts were blatant violations of media freedom and the right to information by the general public. In early April 2020, for instance, the Zimbabwe Union of Journalists (ZUJ) issued a statement reminding the police and other law-enforcement agents that journalists were some of the essential service workers in the country that were authorised to continue operating during the national lockdown period. The ZUJ also advised both the government and its law-enforcement agents to fight Covid-19, not journalists (*Reporters Sans Frontières,* 10 April 2020).

ZUJ's concerns were largely ignored. On 10 April 2020, Mary Taruvinga, a journalist with the New Zimbabwe media company, was reportedly harassed by members of the army and police while on her way to work in Harare's Central Business District. Two soldiers and one police officer stopped Taruwinga and asked her where she was heading to. She produced her press accreditation card and informed them that she was a journalist going to her place of work at Causeway Building. The officers allegedly insisted that she was not supposed to be in the city centre due to the Covid-19 lockdown enforcement measures. She was delayed at the roadside for more than 30 minutes before the police officers allowed her to proceed to her place of work (MISA Zimbabwe, 10 April 2020). Meanwhile, she was given contradictory instructions on which direction to take, "with some of the officers telling her to go in one direction while others insisted that she should follow their instructions. Taruvinga found herself having to walk up and down the street at the command of the officers" (Ibid: 1). MISA Zimbabwe immediately castigated the action of the police and the army:

> MISA Zimbabwe is concerned with the manner with which security personnel are treating journalists, particularly during this lockdown period. The several cases involving the harassment, arrest and assault of journalists that have been recorded are uncalled for and unjustified. These actions directly contradict the statement by the Zimbabwe Republic Police on its Twitter account on 30 March 2020 in which the police pledged its commitment to promote cordial relations with media practitioners. MISA Zimbabwe calls on the Zimbabwe Media Commission to conduct investigations and inquiries into these media freedom violations which also impact on the citizens' right to access to information. As highlighted in our recent statement, MISA Zimbabwe reiterates that the enemy we are fighting at this critical time is Covid-19

and not the media. The media should thus be allowed to conduct its professional duties without hindrance as provided for in the Constitution (Ibid: 1).

Following the harassment and arbitrary arrests of many journalists, the Zimbabwean Chapter of the Media Institute of Southern Africa sought the intervention of the courts of law. On 20 April 2020, the High Court ordered the police to immediately refrain from assaulting, harassing and arresting journalists carrying out their lawful duties during the Covid-19 lockdown period (Cassim, 21 April 2020).

Some media practitioners who were investigating politically sensitive issues that had the potential of putting the ZANU-PF government into disrepute were often arrested on the pretext of violating Covid-19 lockdown regulations. This was the case of two journalists who were probing the abduction, torture and subsequent arrest by the state's law-enforcement agents of Joanna Mamombe, an opposition Member of Parliament, Cecilia Chimbiri, and Netsai Marova who were demonstrating against corruption in Harare. Two investigative journalists who had visited Parktown Hospital in Harare's Waterfalls Suburb on 22 May 2020 where the three opposition activists had been admitted for treatment of injuries they allegedly sustained from being tortured by state security agents, were apprehended and charged with contravening lockdown regulations (Committee to Protect Journalists, 23 June 2020; Kagurume, 2020; *Reporters Sans Frontières*, 2 June 2020; Rivers & Ndlovu, 24 June 2020). The two journalists who were arrested are Samuel Takawira, who worked for *263Chat*, a Zimbabwean online media outlet (Committee to Protect Journalists, 23 June 2020; Mavhunga, 11 February 2021), and Frank Chikowore, a freelance newsman (Committee to Protect Journalists, 23 June 2020; *Reporters Sans Frontières*, 2 June 2020). According to the police, the two journalists were arrested on the grounds that "they had violated social distancing rules and a lockdown ban preventing them from entering the hospital" (*Reporters Sans Frontières*, 2 June 2020: 1). Takawira explained that their arrest showed the government's determination to censor the media, and argued:

> Our arrest served as a reminder to all other journalists and media people not to pursue the story. Obviously, this was a ploy to silence people. This was a ploy by government to hinder its citizens from knowing the truth, what transpired to these ladies. No wonder why in

their bail conditions, they were not supposed to speak to the media (Mavhunga, 11 February 2021: 1).

Arnaud Froger, the head of *Reporters Sans Frontières* Africa desk, immediately issued a statement condemning the arrest of the two journalists:

> Arresting journalists in the course of their work and using Corona virus lockdown measures to prevent them from investigating a troubling story are methods that recall those of the Mugabe (Zimbabwe's former president) era. The Corona virus crisis is not just putting Zimbabwe's public health system and economy to the test. It is also exposing the state of fundamental freedoms in the wake of the dictator's removal in 2017. By arresting and attacking journalists since the start of the epidemic, the authorities are demonstrating that predatory attitudes to the media are an oppressive legacy that is hard to shake off. These journalists must be released at once (*Reporters Sans Frontières*, 2 June 2020: 1).

The government's harsh treatment of journalists continued despite numerous complaints from various media stakeholders. On 24 June 2020, Munashe Chokodza and Leopold Munhende, both journalists working for *263 Chat* and *New Zimbabwe* online news platforms respectively, had just left their office in Harare's Warren Park 1 Suburb at around 6.40pm when they were approached by a group of seven armed soldiers on patrol who accused them of violating the curfew that had been imposed by the government as one of the Covid-19 curtailment measures. Being essential workers, as stated in the lockdown regulations, the two journalists identified themselves by producing their press accreditation cards (International Federation of Journalists, 30 June 2020; Mabhiza, 25 June 2020; Maukonen & Sanomat, 17 May 2021; *Zim Live*, 25 June 2020). It was at this point that one of the soldiers chided them and exclaimed: "You journalists think you are special in this country" (Maukonen & Sanomat, 17 May 2021: 1). Munhende reported that a soldier clapped him twice before tripping him, while another group also assaulted Chokodza in a similar manner. As they lay on the ground, the soldiers and the two police officers took turns to kick and assault them with truncheons and sjamboks all over the body (International Federation of Journalists, 30 June 2020; *Zim Live*, 25 June 2020). Munhende added: "After about three minutes, they ordered us to get up and run. As I got up, my wallet fell out of my pocket and when I tried to retrieve it, one soldier kept kicking it away, and whenever I tried to pick it up he would kick or whip me. The cruelty was some kind of sport to them" (*Zim Live*, 25 June 2020: 1). The two journalists sustained injuries and had to seek medical attention (International Federation of Journalists, 30 June 2020; *Zim Live*, 25 June 2020).

The brutal treatment of the two journalists by the security forces drew sharp criticism from the media fraternity and many human rights activists. Forster Dongozi, the then Secretary General of the Zimbabwe Union of Journalists, for example, noted with concern:

> The admission that journalists are a special target explains the huge body count of journalists who have been beaten, arrested or harassed by the Zimbabwean security forces since the Covid-19 lockdown. This is totally unacceptable as Zimbabwean journalists are equally entitled to protection and safety which should be provided by the state and its different organs (International Federation of Journalists, 30 June 2020: 1).

The Zimbabwe Editors Forum (ZINEF) also anathematised the assault on the journalists: "ZINEF strongly condemns the assault of the journalists by security forces and expresses its disgust at the escalation of repression by state actors against media professionals" (*Zim Live*, 25 June 2020: 1). Antony Bellanger, the then General Secretary of the International Federation of Journalists, reiterated that the security forces "had deliberately overstepped their bounds" and acted in "total hatred and dislike and meted out brutal hostility to the two journalists resulting in such dehumanising treatments" (Ibid). He added: "This deliberate act of naked aggression by the security forces against two journalists who posed no threat to them whatsoever is a travesty of justice and a serious violation of human rights" (Ibid).

In a terrifying confrontation on 21 July 2020 in the city of Masvingo, a police officer reportedly threatened to shoot a *TellZim News* journalist, Upenyu Chaota. The overzealous officer had barred Chaota from passing through a police traffic checkpoint, arguing that no one, including journalists, was allowed to get into town in line with the Covid-19 lockdown stay-at-home orders that had been imposed by the government. He identified himself by displaying his valid press card but the officer remained adamant. Instead, the police officer went on to pull an assault rifle and threatened to shoot Chaota. On 22 July 2020, MISA Zimbabwe issued a statement execrating the actions of the ZRP officer: "We…reiterate our incessant calls for these cases to be investigated and ensure the perpetrators are brought to account for their criminal acts which seriously undermine the lawful and professional duties of the media, and ultimately citizens' right to access to information" (MISA Zimbabwe, 22 July 2020: 1).

This incident clearly showed how media practitioners were abused by Zimbabwe's law-enforcement agents under the guise of enforcing lockdown measures. Among other things, media freedom was severely jeopardised as the freedom of movement of journalists was unlawfully restricted. This also compromised the right of access to information by the generality of the Zimbabwean population. Furthermore, the pointing of a gun at someone is a threat to life and causes serious emotional stress on the part of the victim who in this case was a newsman executing his professional duties.

On 4 September 2021, in another case that manifested the Zimbabwe government's contempt for journalistic rights, Gilbert Munetsi, the editor of *The Courier*, a community newspaper, was arrested and detained overnight at St Mary's Police Station in the town of Chitungwiza on allegations of breaching Covid-19 curfew measures (Muonwa, 6 September 2021). In response, MISA-Zimbabwe deployed a lawyer to attend to the matter, resulting in the release of Munetsi on 5 September 2021. Munetsi was summoned to the police station on 6 September 2021 for purposes of recording his warned and cautioned statement. In his submissions, Munetsi denied the allegations on grounds that he was coming from work when he was apprehended. The MISA-Zimbabwe once more reminded the Zimbabwe Republic Police and other law-enforcement agents enforcing the Covid-19 lockdown regulations that journalists were declared as essential service workers and were not supposed to be unjustifiably arrested, detained or disturbed while executing their lawful professional duties (MISA Zimbabwe, 7 September 2021).

On 11 September 2021, Pamenus Tuso, a senior journalist and MISA Zimbabwe board member, and Brenda Lulu Harris, a freelance journalist, were detained by members of the military police and forced to delete their footage. The two journalists were covering the opposition Movement for Democratic Change (MDC) Alliance's 22nd anniversary commemorations in Bulawayo, Zimbabwe's second largest city. They were approached by a plain-clothed police officer who asked them why they were taking pictures before taking them to his superior who identified himself as a member of the military police. They were detained for over 30 minutes at the venue, despite having identified themselves as journalists and produced accreditation cards (MISA Zimbabwe, 11 September 2021). MISA Zimbabwe immediately expressed displeasure over the action of the police and the army when enforcing lockdown measures:

> MISA Zimbabwe wishes to remind the security personnel enforcing the lockdown regulations that journalists were declared essential services and should therefore not be unjustifiably detained but instead be allowed to undertake their professional duties without fear. MISA-Zimbabwe urges the security forces in Zimbabwe and all other stakeholders to respect media freedom as envisaged in Section 61 of the Constitution which provides the right to seek, receive and impart information. The journalists have a duty to receive and impart information without fear or favour. Hence our reminder: journalism is not a crime! (Ibid: 1).

The arrest of 10 journalists on 30 September 2021 clearly showed the government's disregard for media freedom on the pretext of enforcing lockdown provisions. While demonstrations were banned in Zimbabwe in line with Covid-19 curtailment measures, there was no reason to arrest journalists covering such events. The event in question was a demonstration organised by the opposition MDC Alliance (MDC-A) outside the offices of the Zimbabwe Electoral Commission's (ZEC) offices in Harare to censure its exclusion from the 2023 election preparation process (International Federation of Journalists, 1 October 2021; *New Zimbabwe*, 30 September 2021). The journalists who were apprehended and detained are Leopold Munhende from *New Zimbabwe*, Thomas Madhuku (*263 Chat*), Nyashadzashe Ndoro (*Nehanda Radio*), Robert Tapfumaneyi (*Sly Media*), Desmond Munemo and Marshal Bwanya (*Zim Live*), Gaddaffi Wells and Adrian Maratu (*Newsday*), and Tongai Mwenje and Tinashe Muringai (*Tech Mag*) (*New Zimbabwe*, 30 September 2021). Interestingly, all the arrested journalists were from independent media institutions and did not belong to the state media. This clearly shows that freedom of expression was only accorded to state journalists while denied to independent media practitioners. It is without doubt that the arrest of these independent media practitioners constituted a backlash by the ZANU-PF government during which they were being victimised for covering and publicising a demonstration organised by an opposition political party.

The media practitioners were released without charge following the intervention of the Media Institute of Southern Africa and the Zimbabwe Lawyers for Human Rights (ZLHR) after being detained for two hours (International Federation of Journalists, 1 October 2021; *New Zimbabwe*, 30 September 2021). The Zimbabwe Union of Journalists criticised the action of the police as "highly unacceptable" and deliberately designed at "foiling the journalists' coverage of the ZEC proceedings and thus stifling truth, which is fundamental to national development" (Ibid: 1). The General Secretary of the International Federation of Journalists reiterated: "There seems to be no basis for the arrest of our colleagues and their arbitrary detention is a clear attempt to prevent them from doing their job and informing the public. This is blatant intimidation and harassment against journalists who are simply doing their job" (Ibid: 1).

This section has illuminated beyond doubt how Zimbabwe's law-enforcement agents took advantage of the Covid-19 pandemic and the subsequent lockdown regulations to clamp down on media institutions and journalists who threatened to put the ZANU-PF government into disrepute by exposing its administrative weaknesses and other shortcomings. As this section has illustrated, lockdown regulations were often invoked to restrict the movement of journalists. In some instances, journalists were assaulted, arrested and detained allegedly for violating lockdown orders, most of which they were exempted from since they had been classified as essential service workers by the very government that was executing them.

Conclusion

This chapter illustrated how, throughout the Covid-19 period, the government was "a serial abuser of media freedom" (Mazarura, 25 May 2021: 1). The chapter also showed how Zimbabwean authorities, the police and military officers used the Covid-19 restrictions as a pretext to justify the harassment and intimidation of critical journalists and other media workers. This was seen through the increasing number of journalists who were attacked, criminalised, intimidated, threatened, assaulted, arrested, fined and jailed for doing their job. As noted in this chapter, most of the journalists who fell victim worked for independent media organisations while others worked as freelancers. Although some journalists from the public media were sometimes caught up during government-sponsored clampdowns, they were fairly safer as compared to their counterparts who were generally treated with suspicion by state security agents. In fact, more journalists could have fallen victim to abuse if civic organisations had not regularly intervened by engaging the government to ensure an enabling working environment for media practitioners. Consequently, many journalists lived in fear of being brutalised by the government and its law-enforcement agents. Furthermore, as this chapter has ably articulated, violations of the right of people's access to information as enshrined in Zimbabwe's Constitution under Sections 61 and 62 were on the rise. Ordinary citizens who usually relied on the media for news were greatly deprived of their right to information as a result of the harassment of journalists.

References

Bhebhe, N. (13 April 2020) 'Covid-19 lockdown: Soldiers mercilessly beat up residents, abduct woman from her tuckshop at 10pm,' Available at: https://www.myzimbabwe.co.zw/news/63005-covid-19-lockdown-soldiers-mercilessly-beat-up-residents-abduct-woman-from-her-tuckshop-at-10pm.html, Accessed 5 November 2021.

Cassim, J. (21 April 2020) 'Zimbabwe court orders police not to harass journalists,' Available at: https://www.aa.com.tr/en/africa/zimbabwe, Accessed 2 October 2021.

Chirimambowa, T.C. (11 July 2020) 'Covid-19 and the future of democracy in Zimbabwe,' Available at: https://www.theelephant.info/features/2020/07/11/covid-19-and-the-future-of-democracy-in-zimbabwe/, Accessed 1 October 2021.

Committee to Protect Journalists (23 June 2020) 'Two Zimbabwean journalists charged with violating Covid-19 lockdown,' Available at: https://cpj.org/2020/06, Accessed 28 September 2021.

Committee to Protect Journalists (30 August 2021) 'Zimbabwe journalist Elizabeth Mashiri detained, charged for filming police clash with vendors,' Available at: https://cpj.org/2021/08/zimbabwe-journalist-elizabeth-mashiri-detained-charged-for-filming-police-clash-with-vendors/, Accessed 13 November 2021.

Gasa, S. (21 April 2020) 'Zimbabwe: The perils of reporting on the pandemic,' Available at: https://www.dailymaverick.co.za/article/2020-04-21-zimbabwe-the-perils-of-reporting-on-the-pandemic/, Accessed 1 October 2021.

Global Voices sub-Saharan Africa (25 January 2021) 'A Zimbabwean journalist, two opposition politicians jailed for tweets about police brutality,' Available at: https://advox.globalvoices.org/2021/01/25, Accessed 4 October 2021.

Human Rights Watch (2021) 'World Report 2021: Zimbabwe,' Available at: https://www.hrw.org/world-report/2021/country-chapters/zimbabwe, Accessed 1 October 2021.

Infosplusgabon (9 April 2020) 'Corona virus: Amid lockdown, Zimbabwean journalists face prosecution,' Available at: https://www.infosplusgabon.com/a-la-une/23731, Accessed 3 October 2021.

International Federation of Journalists (30 June 2020) 'Zimbabwe: Journalists beaten and humiliated by security forces,' Available at: https://www.ifj.org/media-centre/news/detail/article/zimbabwe, Accessed 12 September 2021.

International Federation of Journalists (1 October 2021) 'Zimbabwe: At least nine journalists detained for two hours for covering a public demonstration,' Available at: https://www.ifj.org/media-centre/news/detail/category/press-releases/article, Accessed 7 November 2021.

Kagurume, S. (2020) 'Abductions, brutality and demolitions: When the state becomes more harmful than Covid-19,' Available at: http://democracyinafrica.org, Accessed 29 September 2021.

Kudzayi, E. (7 April 2021) 'At least 10 killed as Mnangagwa dialled up rights abuses in 2020: Amnesty,' Available at: https://www.zimlive.com/2021/04/07, Accessed 22 September 2021.

Mabhiza, L. (25 June 2020) 'Armed soldiers assault two journalists in Warren Park,' Available at: https://mbaretimes.com/2020/06/armed-soldiersrk/, Accessed 12 November 2021.

Mafirakureva, G. (12 April 2020) 'Residents squeal over army torture,' Available at:

https://www.zimbabwesituation.com/news/residents-squeal-over-army-torture/, Accessed 6 November 2021.
Maukonen, R. & Sanomat, H. (17 May 2021) 'In Zimbabwe, one year of Covid-19 saw surge in harassment of free press,' Available at: https://ipi.media/in-zimbabwe-one-year-of-covid-19-saw-surge-in-harassment-of-free-press, Accessed 29 September 2021.
Maulani, N. Nyaburi, I. & Wandekha, B. (2020) 'The generals and the war against Covid-19: The case of Zimbabwe,' Available at: www.jogh.org, Accessed 28 September 2021.
Mavhunga, C. (11 February 2021) 'Zimbabwe among African countries using Covid-19 to crack down on journalists, report finds,' Available at: https://www.voanews.com/a/africa, Accessed 22 September 2021.
Mazarura, T. (25 May 2021) 'Covid-19 and the escalating assault on press freedom across Southern Africa,' Available at: https://www.dailymaverick.co.za/article/2021-05-25-covid-19-and-the-escalating-assault-on-press-freedom-across-southern-africa/, Accessed 5 November 2021.
Media Institute of Southern Africa (12 April 2020) 'Police assault freelance journalist,' Available at: https://zimbabwe.misa.org/2020/04/12, Accessed 12 September 2021.
Media Institute for Southern Africa Zimbabwe (30 March 2020) 'Zimbabwe police arrest journalist in Mutare,' Available at: https://kubatana.net/2020/03/30/zimbabwe-police-arrest-journalist-in-mutare/, Accessed 8 November 2021.
Media Institute of Southern Africa Zimbabwe (10 April 2020) 'Zimbabwe: Journalist harassed by the army and police in Harare,' Available at: https://allafrica.com/stories/202004130621.html, Accessed 11 November 2021.
Media Institute of Southern Africa Zimbabwe (7 September 2021) 'Zimbabwe journalist arrested and detained for violating curfew regulations,' Available at: https://kubatana.net/2021/09/07, Accessed 1 October 2021.
Media Institute for Southern Africa Zimbabwe (11 September 2021) 'Journalists detained and forced to delete footage,' Available at: https://kubatana.net/2021/09/11/journalists-detained-and-forced-to-delete-footage/, Accessed 4 November 2021.

Ministry of Health and Child Care (2020) 'Statutory Instrument - The Public Health (Covid-19 Prevention, Containment and Treatment) Regulations. Published as Statutory Instrument 77 of 2020, Consolidated as at 12 June 2020,' Available at: https://www.tralac.org/documents/resources/COVID-19/countries/3734-zimbabwe-si-2020-136-public-health-COVID-19-national-lockdown-amendment-order-2020-no-10-12-june-2020/file.htm, Accessed 21 September 2021.

Moyo, G. & Phulu, K.I. (2021) 'The weaponisation of the Corona virus crisis in Zimbabwe: Legal and extra-legal instruments,' in: *iBusiness*, Volume 13, pp.48-66, Available at: https://doi.org/10.4236/ib.2021.131004, Accessed 26 September 2021.

Moyo, T. (9 April 2020a) 'Fighting dual infections of Covid-19 and corruption: Part 1,' Available at: https://www.dailymaverick.co.za/article/2020-04-09-fighting-dual-infections-of-covid-19-and-corruption-part-one/, Accessed 8 November 2021.

Moyo, T. (9 April 2020b) 'Covid-19 and the suppression of freedom of expression: Part 2', Available at: https://www.dailymaverick.co.za/article/2020-04-09-covid-19-and-the-suppression-of-freedom-of-expression-part-two/, Accessed 8 November 2021.

Muonwa, J. (6 September 2021) 'Zimbabwe: Journalist arrested for breaching Covid-19 curfew,' Available at: https://allafrica.com/stories/202109060269.html, Accessed 7 November 2021.

New Zimbabwe (30 September 2021) 'Chamisa's youths, 10 journalists arrested over ZEC meeting,' Available at: https://www.newzimbabwe.com/chamisas-youths-10-journalists-arrested-over-zec-meeting/, Accessed 8 November 2021.

News 24 (6 April 2020) 'Zimbabwe police accused of assaulting journalists during lockdown,' Available at: https://www.news24.com/news24/africa/news/zimbabwe-police-accused-assaulting-journalists-during-lockdown-20200406, Accessed 1 October 2021.

Reporters Sans Frontières (RSF) (10 April 2020) 'Five Zimbabwean reporters arrested while covering Corona virus lockdown,' Available at: https://rsf.org/en/news, Accessed 29 September 2021.

Reporters Sans Frontières (2 June 2020) 'Two Zimbabwean journalists arrested under Covid-19 lockdown regulations,' Available at: https://ifex.org/two-zimbabwean-journalists-arrested-under-covid-19-lockdown-regulations/, Accessed 5 November 2021.

Rivers, M. & Ndlovu, P. (24 June 2020) 'Covid-19 raises the stakes for Zimbabwe's civil society movement,' Available at: https://www.usip.org/publications/2020/06, Accessed 21 September 2021.

Zenda, C. (24 April 2020) 'Army and police brutality keeps starving Zimbabweans indoors,' Available at: https://www.fairplanet.org/story, Accessed 27 September 2021.

Zim Live (25 June 2020) 'Journalists brutally assaulted by soldiers, police in Harare suburb,' Available at: https://www.zimlive.com/2020/06/25/journalists-brutally-assaulted-by-soldiers-police-in-harare-suburb/, Accessed 5 November 2021.

Zimbabwe Peace Project (30 July 2020) 'Who shall protect the people? When the state unleashes violence on people it is supposed to protect, who shall protect the people?' Available at: https://reliefweb.int/sites/reliefweb.int/files/resources, Accessed 6 November 2021.

Chapter 6

Shut Up or Perish! John Pombe Magufuli's Covid-19 Denialism and the Violation of Information and Media Freedom in Tanzania

Nicholas Govo

Introduction

This chapter explores the response of President John Pombe Magufuli's government to the outbreak of the Corona virus disease (Covid-19) in Tanzania within the discourse of human rights. It focuses more on the freedom of expression, given that it is a basic human right to freely express and disseminate information in the public interest, especially in times of pandemics. The chapter underscores that the government of Tanzania under President Magufuli curtailed a broad range of human rights in the country as he sought to regulate the publication of information regarding the Covid-19 pandemic. His denial of the existence of Covid-19 was followed by a massive crackdown on the freedom of expression, media and access to information. By doing so, he sought to ensure that both government officials and independent media houses either toed his wayward line of thought or faced drastic punitive measures once they reported on Covid-19 in the country. The study makes use of qualitative evidence obtained from official statements of the government, and pertinent reports from media houses, media watchdogs, legal analysts and journalists' unions on violations of human rights and freedom of expression during the Covid-19 period in Tanzania.

Covid-19 presented a sudden shock to almost every political system in the world as it brought about unprecedented and turbulent mixtures of political and socio-economic forces that systematically challenged how states were governed (Greener, King & Fonseca, 2021; Jarman, 2021, Lipscy, 2020). The alarming spread of the Covid-19 virus across the world prompted the World Health Organisation (WHO) to declare it a global pandemic on 11 March 2020 and to request governments across the world to put in place a raft of measures to contain it (Moyo & Phulu, 2021; Odigbo *et al*, 2020). As such, leaders of governments were expected to provide their citizens with guidance as far as the containment of the pandemic was concerned (Jarman, 2021). In the case of Tanzania, when Covid-19 hit the nation in March 2020, President Magufuli denied its existence and downplayed its risks. Consequently, on 29 April 2020, the government stopped updating the public on levels of Covid-19 infections and deaths (Global Expression, 2021). On this last day when official data was last released, there were 509 cases, with 21 deaths in Tanzania (Odula, 22 May 2022). Six weeks later, Magufuli declared that citizens' prayers had eliminated the virus in Tanzania (Ibid). To conceal Covid-19 cases and deaths, Magufuli's government restricted press freedoms and made sure that journalists could not report on a pandemic that he believed to be non-existent (Ibid). This policy of denialism during the first year of the pandemic had far-reaching implications for journalists, most of who could not accurately report on Covid-19 either due to lack of correct information or fear of arrest.

For the purposes of analysis, notions of presidentialism, paternalism, populism, nationalism and Tanzania's founding discourse of self-reliance have been tapped in to explain Magufuli's response to Covid-19, particularly the motives behind the suppression of freedom of expression and the government's deliberate misinformation that dominated the society during the time of the pandemic. The response of the Tanzanian government to the Covid-19 shocks highlighted presidentialism because of the concentration of governance in a single person, the President, at a time of crisis. Presidentialism in Tanzania was largely rooted in nationalism, which tended to revolve around notions of familyhood and paternalism as well. The ruling party, Chama Cha Mapinduzi (CCM), was often perceived by its officials and supporters as a "political family" (Phillips, 2018: 20). This 'family' had a moral matrix in which the president was the father figure who presided over, administered, decided, and adjudicated; and also disciplined, punished, forgave, and pardoned the 'children' who challenged him (Schatzberg, 2001). Paternalistic discourses as portrayed in Tanzania's response to Covid-19 led to assumptions that state officials, led by the president, were acting in the population's interests, a narrative that was further amplified by Magufuli's elite plebeianism. Given these dynamics, claims of legitimacy enabled the Tanzanian ruling elite to act in ways that countered global norms and expectations as evidenced, among other things, by the government's refusal to implement most of the WHO measures to curb the spread of Covid-19 (Patterson, 2022).

By blending presidentialism and paternalism with nationalism and populism, Magufuli obliged the party elite to stand for the people and protect them from a widespread, predatory middle stratum of state officials and domestic and foreign business leaders. He further excavated anti-Western rhetoric, explained mainly through the lenses of continued economic and political marginalisation of the continent, and framed his response to the Covid-19 pandemic as a revolutionary confrontation against neo-imperialism. Furthermore, the discourse of self-reliance, interwoven in the nationalist rhetoric also informed the government's approach, particularly on the treatment of Covid-19. Instead of 'conventional' treatment, Magufuli encouraged traditional remedies in Tanzania, arguing that they would foster self-sufficiency and 'reduce dependency' on Western imports, themes that echoed Nyerere's ideas of self-reliance (Richey *et al*, 2021). The aforementioned adoption of Covid-Organics also stressed both self-reliance and the country's long history of supporting pan-Africanist solidarity.

Advent of the Covid-19 pandemic and the government's denialism

Following the World Health Organisation's declaration of Covid-19 as a global pandemic on 11 March 2020, many governments around the world instituted securitised Covid-19 containment measures, most of which suspended constitutional processes through states of emergency (Moyo & Phulu, 2021). In many countries, the authorities restricted air, sea and land travel; isolated immigrants and returning citizens; ordered people to stay at home; imposed curfews; and locked down public places, educational institutions, services deemed non-essential as well as religious, sports and recreation centres (Ibid). In Tanzania, the first imported case of Covid-19 was reported on 16 March 2020 and the government immediately issued instructions to limit the spread of the virus in the country, including capacity building of test facilities and health workers, limiting/prohibiting public meetings and international travel, while raising awareness on preventive measures such as hand washing and social distancing (*Citizen*, 10 May 2020). To protect people's livelihoods and the country's economy, no restrictions on economic activities were imposed. On 23 March 2020, the government mandated that international travellers undergo 14 days of quarantine in specific hotels (Taylor, 2020). For a brief period, Tanzania limited travel from other countries, but such restrictions had been lifted by mid-May 2020 when President Magufuli took the path of denialism by ridiculing Covid-19 testing and claiming that the virus had been "removed by the powers of God" (Hale *et al*, 2020). A series of photographs on social media showed Magufuli, a devout Catholic, at mass on Sunday 21 February 2020 during which he and his security details were not wearing masks while many in the congregation, including priests, were all masked (Rickard, 24 February 2021).

Magufuli increasingly became arrogant and parochial as he held onto his denialist position and advanced his claim that Covid-19 did not exist. His official statements since the first case of Covid-19 in Tanzania in March 2020 until his death in March 2021 initially insisted that Covid-19 did not exist, and later on that it was just a disease like any other. He stressed that prayers and God, not lockdowns and other measures like wearing masks and social distancing, would save the people, and that vaccinations were not important but only represented Western imperialist antics. As such, Magufuli believed that the WHO-sanctioned anti-Covid-19 interventions, including social distancing and the wearing of masks, were forms of economic, political and intellectual control that were tantamount to sabotage, and had to be rejected (Ogola, 2021). These sentiments became the cardinal features in Tanzania's policy towards Covid-19. In order to successfully push his claims, Magufuli deliberately censored the media through drastic legislation that curtailed the freedom of expression and access to information. It is common sense that the protection of media freedom becomes even more relevant during a pandemic as accurate data informs critical measures and steps that can be taken to save lives. On the contrary, various changes pertaining to laws and regulations in Tanzania during the first year of Covid-19 violated the fundamental right to freedom of expression and access to information. Such legislative changes also put media freedom and journalists' safety at grave risk (Global Expression, 2021; Jarman, 2021).

From the end of April 2020, Magufuli's government officials actively discouraged the use of masks, disputed the existence of Covid-19 and censored reports on the pandemic (Rickard, 24 February 2021). Magufuli also made it clear that Tanzania would not be ordering vaccines for the people of that country on grounds that he did not want his people to be "used as guinea pigs" (Ibid).

Addressing parishioners on 17 May 2020, Magufuli reported a drastic decrease in Covid-19 cases and called for another three days of national prayer to give thanks for this 'miracle' (Kamazima & Kakoko, 2020). A few days later, on 22 May, President Magufuli declared that Tanzania was Covid-19-free. This was not true as Covid-19 cases were rising in the world at an alarming rate. The desire by most authoritarian governments to suppress potentially politically-damaging information also explains the Tanzanian government's hesitancy to release official statistics on the number of confirmed Covid-19 cases and deaths. Such obfuscation was in keeping with the Magufuli administration's broader efforts to obstruct access to public information (Carlitz & McLellan, 2020).

Magufuli's Covid-19 denialism and rejection of vaccines put millions of Tanzanians at risk. To some, the Tanzanian President had become more dangerous than Covid-19 because even as hospitals filled up and funerals proliferated, he and his government continued to behave as if the country had been untouched by the pandemic (Chutel, 17 February 2021). On 28 January 2021, while addressing a large gathering at his home village of Chato, an event that was beamed live on national television, Magufuli urged people to stand firm and avoid using vaccinations from other countries. He argued: "Vaccinations are dangerous. If the white man was able to come up with vaccines, he should have found a vaccine for AIDS by now" (Buguzi, 28 July 2021; Kombe, 28 January 2022). Up until his death, Magufuli had not backed down from this stance; while vaccines had become available on the continent, his government explicitly rejected them (Makoni, 2021). The only moment he came close to admitting that Covid-19 existed was at the funeral of the country's head of the civil service. He admitted that the cause of death was a respiratory disease. In clear denial, he never associated the respiratory disease to Covid-19 complications. Media reports from Tanzania said that during the funeral, the president reiterated his earlier claims that prayer had saved the country from "this respiratory disease" (Rickard, 24 February 2021). He added that "this time round" - a phrase that seemed to concede that Covid-19 did exist, at least at the moment - prayer would again win out (Ibid). However, Magufuli made it clear that no lockdown or other steps would be introduced by the government, and that people of all faiths should pray more instead (Ibid).

Denialism and misinformation had devastating effects on the people of Tanzania as many subscribed to Magufuli's claim that

Covid-19 did not exist. The misinformation he disseminated as a Head of State became part of fake news which led many people astray and therefore exposed in the face of a deadly pandemic. When senior politicians, let alone the Head of State become the disseminators of fake news, as Farkas & Schou (2018: 300) argue, such misinformation becomes "an important component in contemporary political struggles" that is "utilised by different positions within the social space as means of discrediting, attacking and delegitimising political opponents." Such misinformation by a Head of State is what the WHO referred to as 'infodemics,' or the overabundance of false stories that made it difficult for people to make sense of the Covid-19 pandemic (Ogola, 2021).

A study by Baguzi (28 January 2021) revealed that many Tanzanians were convinced by the statements broadcast by their President to the effect that Covid-19 did not exist, and that international pronouncements of its existence were mere propaganda from Western countries. Dr. Deus Kitapondya, an emergency medical specialist based in Dar es Salaam, cited by Baguzi (28 January 2021), noted that it was very difficult to prove the people wrong about the existence of Covid-19 and the usefulness of vaccines when the authorities had already misinformed them. Another medical doctor who asked for anonymity for fear that speaking out could provoke government reprisals that would cost him his job had this to say: "The obvious truth is that the general public is still deeply divided about vaccines, even among some pro-government scientists. For a long time, people were officially made to believe that vaccines are not safe" (Ibid). The medical doctor added that doctors in Tanzania did not have the platform and the freedom to publicly fact-check what the government was telling the public: "Misinformation [about Covid-19 vaccines] is widespread, and unfortunately it came from official sources" (Ibid). It can be noted that the government wilfully denied reality, cast doubt on vaccines and testing, and punished those who reported facts relating to the global pandemic inside the country (Rickard, 24 February 2021).

When explaining the behaviour of government officials regarding their relentless support of President Magufuli's convictions over Covid-19, it is also important to appreciate the regime type in Tanzania and how party bureaucrats were perceived as threats to state power. Tanzania was understood to be a 'hegemonic party regime' since the same revolutionary CCM political party had been in power since independence in 1961, despite the legalisation of multiparty politics in 1992. Like in other African countries, the revolutionary CCM party had a slant towards authoritarianism. To borrow from Little (2017) and Wallace (2016), authoritarian regimes have problems of information flow that shape their politics with a strong belief that the regime should lie to the public. Again, in authoritarian states, incumbent leaders constantly watch for signs of disloyalty among government officials. This creates incentives for senior officials to exaggerate their degree of loyalty and hide instances of policy failures, lest they are perceived by the leaders a being disloyal. Another threat to regimes stems from large-scale uprisings, so authoritarian regimes generally try to weaken the incentive to rise up by suppressing information about bad policy outcomes and information about the pervasiveness of popular dissatisfaction (Greitens, 2016). Along with paternalist tendencies in most authoritarian regimes, officials tend to under-report negative events such as epidemics or famines, or in the worst cases, they blame outsiders for calamities. This is because failure to meet the moral obligation to care for citizen-children is both shameful and delegitimising (Philips, 2018).

Consequently, government officials and health personnel in Tanzania were always toeing the party line with extremely limited choices. Said (29 May 2020) observed that people within Magufuli's administration were ousted if their position or information contradicted the positive image of Tanzania as wanted by the CCM main leaders. As a result, officials at all levels of government repeatedly misinformed the public about the existence of Covid-19 and issues of vaccination. Taking a leaf from their leader, Magufuli's cabinet members reportedly mocked mask-wearing and criticised neighbouring countries for imposing lockdown measures (Chutel, 17 February 2021). In February 2021, the Permanent Secretary of the Ministry of Health, Mabula Mchembe, took to the ministry's official Twitter account to proclaim that "it is not true that hospitals are full of Corona patients," blaming "some people with bad intentions on social media" (*Wizaraya Afya Tanzania* , 3 February 2021).

In May 2020, state officials announced research plans for Covid-19, including projects on how traditional medicines and Tanzanian lifestyles could be protective and/or curative (*Citizen*, 10 May 2020). In early 2021, the Health Minister, Dorothy Gwajima, urged citizens to use steam baths and to drink mixtures of ginger, lemon, pepper, and onion to ward off illness (*BBC News*, 6 February 2021). In an embarrassing televised display, the Health Minister gave a demonstration on how to mix a smoothie of natural ingredients to boost the immune system and avoid diseases like Covid-19 (Chutel, 17 February 2021). Wrapping a scarf over her head, she demonstrated how Tanzanians could use herbal steaming as a remedy for respiratory infections. She also told the press that the government had no plans to procure vaccines (Ibid). This was despite the fact that the United States Embassy had already raised alarm over overwhelmed hospitals in Tanzania and claimed that the risk of getting infected by Covid-19 in Dar es Salaam was "extremely high" (*Monitor Civicus*, 8 September 2020).

A study by Carlitz *et al* (2021) showed how street-level bureaucrats adapted and responded to Covid-19 in Tanzania and further revealed how government workers praised Magufuli's denialism as a way of protecting their jobs. The Health Secretary in one CCM-led district, for instance, noted: "We learned from our top leaders like President John Pombe Magufuli that fear can bring greater impacts than the disease itself" (Ibid). A street-level officer in another CCM-controlled district echoed similar sentiments and went on to say that treating Covid-19 as a 'normal' disease meant that "we avoided economic threats like hunger and stagnation of other developmental activities" (Ibid). Beyond praising President Magufuli, local officials in both the ruling-party strongholds and opposition-led districts, expressed support for traditional remedies in line with Magufuli's advice on disease management. As one ward officer in the Morogoro District explained: "We can be independent when dealing with pandemics like Corona by using traditional ways, prayers and alternative treatments such as *kujifukiza* (steam inhalation), the use of lemons, and drinking *tangawizi* (ginger)" (Ibid). Similarly, in rural settings like Arusha, one ward officer articulated support for Magufuli's notion of self-reliance as follows: "We should also strive to have innovative solutions for treatment and vaccines designed for Covid-19 using our local remedies instead of depending on everything from other countries" (Ibid). This resonated with Magufuli's characterisation of Western public officials and donors as 'imperialists' in calling for Tanzania to follow the WHO guidelines and international best practices (Patterson & Balogun, 2021).

Magufuli further deployed global discourses of inequality along the lines of race to cast doubt on Covid-19 vaccinations, arguing: "[If] the white man was able to come up with vaccinations, then vaccinations for AIDS would have been brought" (Carlitz *et al*, 2021). Alleged laboratory problems were not attributed to low state capacity, but rather to potential problems with "imported reagents and swaps [sic] used in the testing processes" (Ibid). Magufuli cautioned about foreign donations that could be "used to transmit the virus" (*BBC News*, 18 March 2021). He insisted: "I want to urge you Tanzanians not to accept donations of masks. Instead, tell the donors to go and use them with their wives and children" (Ibid). In addition, Magufuli appropriated the language of de-colonial struggles to cast suspicion on international critics. He accused international health officials of exaggerating the crisis and suggested that some health workers "may have been put on the payroll of imperialists" (Beaumont, 19 May 2020). This escapist approach adopted by Magufuli was not new in the operations of revolutionary parties across Africa. His denialism took him to some imagined status of Africa's anti-imperialist 'champion.' The way he castigated the West and all locals who dared to consider Covid-19 seriously by propagating correct information shows that he had created some imagined opponents for political expediency as the nation was due for elections in October 2020.

Magufuli's Covid-19 denialism did not go unchallenged at local and international levels. A major international law firm, Amsterdam and Partners, for example, wrote to the Commonwealth Secretariat suggesting that the organisation considers expelling Tanzania from its membership. This was because, due to the policies of its president, John Magufuli, Tanzania was not living up to its undertakings as a member of the Commonwealth. They also argued that Magufuli's denialism and subsequent policies regarding the Covid-19 pandemic were endangering the lives of people in Tanzania and other Commonwealth countries (Rickard, 24 February 2021). Amsterdam and Partners warned of a "mounting human rights and humanitarian crisis" in the country as "the government under Mr. Magufuli is endangering the health of its citizens and depriving them of the right to accurate health information and essential treatments" (Ibid). In doing so, the government of Tanzania was also "endangering citizens of [other] members of the Commonwealth including Kenya, Uganda, Zambia, and Malawi" (Ibid). These concerns were shared by other organisations. The Human Rights Watch and the World Health Organisation also raised alarm about the effect of government policies on the health of Tanzanians (WHO, 20 February 2021). In another reaction to Tanzania's strategy on Covid-19, the Director-General of the World Health Organisation, Tedros Ghebreyesus lamented the failure by the government to provide statistics and other data on the pandemic in the country (Ibid).

Government's censorship of the press in the wake of the Covid-19 pandemic

As already alluded to, the government of Tanzania, under the influence of President Magufuli, was overzealously committed to the censorship of the press to make sure that Covid-19 information was concealed. A raft of measures were made to facilitate the suppression of freedom of expression. Legal instruments that were already in place to constrict press freedom were rejuvenated to make sure that the information on Covid-19 cases and deaths remained under tight government control. The Cybercrime Act of 2015, which was meant to protect sensitive infrastructure, reduce vulnerability and cyberbullying, and minimise any damage that cyber-attacks could cause, was re-energised to make sure that it applied to Covid-19 (Global Expression, 2021). The Act also made it an offence for anyone to hold any unauthorised information, and gave sweeping powers to investigate anyone in possession of so-called unauthorised or 'false' information, as well as to conduct investigations without obtaining court orders (Ibid). The police were empowered to use the Act to arrest and charge Haidary Hakam and Alona Tarimo from the *Mwananchi* newspaper for disseminating 'false' information about Covid-19 victims on WhatsApp (Ibid). In the same vein, Sections 37 (4) and (5) of the Statistics Act of 2015 made it an offence for a radio station, television station, newspaper or magazine, website or any other media to publish "false statistical information," or for an agency or person to publish "official statistical information which may result in the distortion of facts." Given the broad definition of 'official statistical information,' this would mean that the publication of all statistics, regardless of their source, which was deemed 'false' was considered a "distortion of facts," and punishable by a "fine not less than two million shillings (US$ 1 200) or imprisonment for a term of not less than six months or both" (Ibid). Despite the key role of statistics to public-health policy on Covid-19, the government of Tanzania tightly controlled statistical data, making it difficult for transparent public health policies to suffice. As a result of this and other legislations, little information got through to Tanzanian citizens and the wider world about the Covid-19 situation in the country. This was a clear abrogation of the freedom to access valuable information.

More so, the Electronic and Postal Communications (Online Content) Regulations of 2020, which came into force on 17 July 2020, became an affront to press freedom. It introduced licensing and taxation for bloggers, online discussion forums, and radio and television webcasters, and repressed online speeches, privacy, and access to information (Ibid). The accompanying regulations imposed numerous restrictions, including unrealistic time limits on content and licenses and prohibiting many categories of content. This regulation was used to charge journalists and suspend media outlets' licenses as punishment for their reporting in relation to Covid-19 (Ibid). The ostensible purpose of licensing schemes is usually to ensure that the task of informing the public is reserved for competent persons of high moral integrity. In practice, however, as shown by the aforementioned suspension of *Mwananchi* and *Kwanza Online* TV licenses, it became more than clear that the issuance of licenses became politicised and was often used to prevent critical or independent journalists from publishing accurate Covid-19 statistics that had the potential of putting President Magufuli and the ruling party into disrepute.

To operationalise the legal instruments and regulations, government officials in relevant line ministries made pronouncements that effectively made it difficult for journalists and media houses, especially the independent ones, to freely disseminate Covid-19 data. On 22 May 2020, for example, Prime Minister Kassim Majaliwa issued a directive restricting access to, and dissemination of information on Covid-19. From that point on, only the Health Minister could provide information on the virus and, if necessary, the Prime Minister himself. Even as late as February 2021, Health Minister Dorothy Gwajima was warning journalists against reporting unofficial statistics (Ibid). On 21 March 2020, the Prime Minister gave a stern warning as follows: "I am warning everyone against spreading baseless rumours and falsehood through mobile phones and social media platforms, which can create unnecessary panic and hardship to all around, they must all be monitored and measures taken against them" (Ibid).

On 10 August 2020, new online content regulations concerning the posting of information on social media were signed into law. This was done through the Electronic and Postal Communications (Online Content) Regulations of 2020 which tightened state control over the internet and social media by criminalising the posting of 'rumours' or messages that "ridicule, abuse or harm the reputation, prestige or status of the United Republic of Tanzania" (*Monitor Civicus*, 8 September 2020). In addition to that, the regulations also banned content on "the outbreak of deadly or contagious diseases in the country or elsewhere without the approval of the respective authorities" (Ibid), which definitely included Covid-19. The regulations also served to further restrict the media by banning local media outlets from broadcasting foreign content without government permission. All these measures were meant to affect local stations that aired content from international media outlets such as *British Broadcasting Corporation*, *Radio France Internationale*, and *Deutsche Welle*, amongst others (Ibid).

On 11 August 2020, the Tanzania Communication Regulatory Authority (TCRA) introduced new rules that forced local media stations to seek government approval before broadcasting foreign content. Press freedom activists and opposition leaders protested against the rules, which they saw as an attempt to prevent Tanzanians from freely receiving any information whatsoever about Covid-19 (Global Expression, 2021). This was a clumsy attempt to suppress critical voices and independent information. These developments signalled the creeping in of unimagined forms of state censorship at a time when a vibrant and free press was desperately needed to raise people's awareness of the deadly Covid-19 pandemic. The TCRA imposed heavy fines on three television stations for broadcasting content that was "misleading and untrue" about the government's strategy of combating Covid-19. Surprisingly, these media houses had accurately criticised Magufuli for declaring that churches should not be closed because "Corona virus cannot survive in a church" (Olewe, 2020). Thus, the continued approach of denialism when some sectors of society realised the negative effects of the policy squarely made the Tanzanian government under Magufuli responsible for serious violations of freedom of expression, a key aspect of human survival and the exercise of human rights.

Arrest and harassment of journalists and penalties against media houses

The censorship of the media through various pieces of legislation that trampled on free press and the transparent dissemination of Covid-19 information is well illustrated by the measures taken by the Tanzanian government to harass and silence journalists as well as human rights defenders and political activists. Many journalists and human rights activists were subjected to many forms of ill-treatment as the government sought to conceal Covid-19-related information. This section examines several cases that prove how widespread censorship made Tanzania one of the worst countries in the suppression of freedom of expression during the Magufuli-induced Covid-19 denialism.

On 21 March 2020, Prime Minister Kassim Majaliwa directed the TCRA to monitor and apprehend persons disseminating 'fake news' about Covid-19. A few weeks later on 17 April, the TCRA suspended the *Mwananchi* daily newspaper's licence for six months and fined them 5 million Tanzanian shillings (approximately US$2 155) for allegedly violating the Electronic and Postal (Online Content) Regulations of 2018 (Global Expression, 2021). This happened shortly after the *Mwananchi* posted a photo of President Magufuli shopping in a crowd of people, in an apparent violation of the government's social distancing rules, which sparked an online discussion about Tanzania's approach to Covid-19 (Ibid). The authorities claimed that the photo was taken prior to the pandemic, while *Mwananchi* quickly took it down and apologized (Ibid).

On 6 April 2020, Afrikana Mlay, the editor of the Kiswahili language publication *Kasheshe*, was arrested in the Kilimanjaro region for allegedly spreading 'false information' on social media. His post indicated that Tanzania was withholding the actual number of Covid-19 infections. The police charged Mlay for spreading information that was likely to create panic and undermine state security. This echoed the Prime Minister's warning to the public just a few weeks earlier (Ibid). The journalist was trying to expose the government's unwarranted restrictions on the free circulation of information for public consumption. It is prudent to note that throughout the Covid-19 experience across the globe, information from medical experts and other sectors would circulate, and people had the chance to scrutinise it and do the right things to prevent the spread of the deadly virus. While governments had to impose certain degrees of force, individuals had space to exercise their rights, but for the good of the society. Journalists played the critical role of publicising international standards stipulated by the WHO to prevent the spread of Covid-19 and it became worrisome to witness them being arrested and harassed in countries such as Tanzania.

The same week that Mlay was arrested, blogger Awadhi Lugoya was accused of "wrongful use of social media" and was arrested for allegedly creating a Facebook account called 'Corona virus Tanzania' to disseminate information which the Morogoro Regional Police Commander dismissed as misleading as far as the Covid-19 pandemic was concerned (Ibid). The offence was punishable by a minimum fine of 5 million Tanzanian shillings (approximately US$2 160) and/or a minimum 12-month jail sentence under the Electronic and Postal Communication (Online Content) Regulations of 2018 (Ibid). This case clearly shows how journalists were ordered to shut up at a time when they had a critical role to play in serving the nation during the Covid-19 period.

In its relentless efforts to thwart media freedom, the government arrested Talib Ussi Hamad, a reporter with the *Tanzania Daima* newspaper, on 20 April 2020 and suspended him for six months for making reference to a Covid-19 patient without consent. Hamad later disclosed that he was pressured to apologise but refused on the grounds that the information he reported was in the public interest. He was accused of flouting professional ethics and was charged under the Registration of News Agents, Newspapers, and Books Act Number 5 of 1988 and its amendment, Number 8 of 1997 (Ibid). This case shows how Magufuli's government was determined to curtail the freedom of expression to the extent of revisiting draconian laws that were passed before the country embraced multi-party democracy.

On 26 April 2020, *Star Media, Multichoice Tanzania*, and *Azam Digital Broadcast* were each fined 5 million Tanzanian shillings (approximately US$2 200) for allegedly flouting the rules on Covid-19 communication. The stations had aired content from Kenya's *Citizen* TV that described President Magufuli as stubborn for refusing to impose a lockdown. The stations were also compelled to broadcast an apology to President Magufuli for seven consecutive days. *Citizen* TV and Radio were asked to broadcast a similar apology (Ibid). In the process, media reporting was stifled and access to information was grossly restricted.

As social media dominated in the cross-pollination of information in almost all societies, Magufuli's government made sure that the Tanzanian social space was placed under close surveillance to prevent journalists and bloggers from freely sharing Covid-19 information. On 30 April 2020, for instance, two members of staff of the *Mwananchi* newspaper, Haidary Hakam and Alona Tarimo, were arrested and charged for disseminating 'false' information about Covid-19 victims on WhatsApp. They were charged under the Cybercrime Act of 2015. The Kinondani SACP Police Commander, Edward Bukombe, took the opportunity to remind Tanzanians to stop sharing information on social media that government authorities had not verified (Ibid). On 9 July 2020, Freeman Mbowe, the

Chairman of the Chadema opposition party, was assaulted and hospitalised in what his party regarded as a politically-motivated attack. Mbowe was attacked by armed men in Dodoma who broke his leg and warned him against speaking out. Mbowe had accused President Magufuli of being in a "state of denial" about the scale of Covid-19 in the country (*Monitor Civicus*, 8 September 2020). Thus, it became apparent that posting information about the Corona virus pandemic was considered unpatriotic as President Magufuli's government continued its relentless assault on the independent media and the freedom of expression in Tanzania.

On 10 July 2020, *Kwanza Online TV*'s licence was suspended for 11 months for sharing a health alert on Instagram that had been issued by the United States Embassy warning that Tanzania's Covid-19 cases were rising. Joseph Mapunda, the Vice-Chair of the TCRA's Content Committee, told journalists that *Kwanza Online TV* had published an unbalanced story that was designed to cause panic and damage the country's economy, and that this was against the Electronic and Postal Communications (Online Content) Regulations of 2018. *Kwanza Online TV* made a public statement indicating that the right of the journalists to be heard was not being adhered to as they were given less than 24 hours to respond to the initial summons and that the media house was not guilty of any offence (Global Expression, 2021).

It becomes quite apparent that in Magufuli's Tanzania, accurate reporting about the Covid-19 pandemic was deliberately rubbished as falsehoods by the government. There is no doubt that access to information was an essential part in the fight against Covid-19, yet the Tanzanian government chose to censor journalists and media outlets who were reporting on the disease. As noted by Muchena (14 December 2020), these reprisals were clearly politically motivated as the Tanzanian government's insensitivity to criticism was costing journalists their rights and livelihoods. Such levels of harassment and arrests of journalists and all those who wanted to inform society about the pandemic are a clear testimony that Tanzania was facing two tragedies: the Covid-19 pandemic and human rights abuse.

Tanzania's case and other African countries

Perhaps, it is important to note that Tanzania under Magufuli's Covid-19 approach was different from many other African countries, except for Burundi, Madagascar and Eretria. However, the reactionary nature of the Tanzanian government was beyond any other African country. Admittedly, it is important to note that media censorship and other forms of human rights abuses also took place in Africa, although with varying degrees from one country to another. Indeed, many African governments became accustomed to the "use of diseases as a pretext to curtail democratic freedoms and punish opposition" (Rivers & Ndlovu, 24 June 2020: 1). The political rights of many opposition political parties were often infringed. In a number of cases, the freedoms of assembly and movement suspended under lockdown regulations were weaponised to limit the political reach of opposition parties. It is quite apparent that in many African countries, Covid-19 containment measures were "marred by abuse of power" (Sabiti, 19 April 2021: 1). It is without doubt that the pandemic came as a blessing in disguise for some African dictators who utilised the subsequent lockdowns to "narrow the democratic space and muzzle political opponents" (Ibid: 1) in an opportunistic attempt to "solidify autocracy" (Molloy, 1 May 2020: 1).

Some governments "weaponised the pandemic to quell popular protests and harass opposition politicians and their supporters," with Uganda and Zimbabwe being notable examples (Nkomo & Mangiza, 2021; Segun, 18 January 2021). The securitised nature of Covid-19 lockdowns made it easier for security agents who were accustomed to using force to exaggerate their role in stultifying human freedoms in the name of Covid-19 restrictions. As Muchena (14 December 2020: 1) observed: "While the world's attention has focused on the Covid-19 pandemic, there has been another pandemic that has spread in its shadow - human rights violations." Antonio Guterres, the Secretary General of the United Nations, reiterated that owing to the Covid-19 pandemic, "our world is facing a pandemic of human rights abuses" (Guterres, 22 February 2021). It therefore evident that human rights abuses associated with Covid-19 were an ongoing issue in Africa but Tanzania scored very highly in the negative, considering the government's relentless torment of journalists and media houses that were supposed to play a key role in fighting the spread of the virus.

Conclusion

In concluding this chapter, it is important to briefly interrogate circumstances surrounding President John Pombe Magufuli's death in the context of the Covid-19 pandemic and human rights. The announcement of Magufuli's death was made on 17 March 2021. Officially, Magufuli was said to have died from heart problems at the age of 62 years. In the public domain, however, the 'heart problem' was widely believed to be connected to Covid-19 (Ogola, 2021). Having tried his best to muzzle the press and suppress media freedom on issues surrounding the Covid-19 pandemic and many others, Magufuli seemed to have stuck to these antics until death given that his ill-health was secretly handled by government officials (Ibid).

It is regrettable that Magufuli's approach to Covid-19 was largely punctuated by denialism and exposed Tanzanians and other people to the deadly pandemic. His determination to disregard people's freedoms, censor the media and suppress various forms of expression earned Tanzania a negative reputation on the international arena, as far as human rights are concerned. As the chapter has shown, paternalistic and populist tendencies rooted in African nationalism largely accounted for Magufuli's aversion to freedom of expression. Thus, he forced many sections of the Tanzanian population to shut up and comply with his dictates of denialism. In fact, Magufuli overzealously invested his energies in forging an anti-imperialist narrative within the pandemic, instead of living up to the expectations and realities of science. He will be remembered in history for unceremoniously destroying a legacy he started well by missing the virtues of science for political engineering. After Magufuli's demise, there was some light at the end of the tunnel as Samia Siluhu Hassan, his successor as CCM leader and Tanzanian President, started well by reversing her predecessor's authoritarian policies, in addition to pledging to form a scientific advisory committee on Covid-19, and opening up space for press freedom (Buguzi *et al*, 7 April 2021).

References

Afrobarometer (2016/2018) 'The online data analysis tool,' Available at: https://afrobarometer.org/online-data-analysis/analyse-online, Accessed 15 June 2022.

Aljazeera (12 March 2021) 'Tanzania officials deny Magufuli sick with Covid-19,' Available at:

https://www.aljazeera.com/news/2021/3/12/hes-ok-tanzania-denies-magufuli-sick-with-covid-19, Accessed 3 June 2022).

BBC News (30 October 2019) 'John Magufuli -Tanzania's "bulldozer" president in profile,' Available at: www.bbc.com/news/world-africa-34670983, Accessed 15 June 2022.

BBC News (6 February 2021) 'Corona virus in Tanzania: The country that is rejecting the vaccine,' Available at: https://www.bbc.com/news/world-africa-55900680, Accessed 17 June 2022.

BBC News (18 March 2021) 'John Magufuli: Tanzania's late president in his own words,' Available at: https://www.bbc.com/news/world-africa-56441421, Accessed 21 June 2021.

BBC News (8 June 2020) 'Corona virus: John Magufuli declares Tanzania free of Covid-19,' Available at: https://www.bbc.com/news/world-africa-52966016, Accessed 13 June 2022.

Beaumont, P. (19 May 2020) 'Tanzania's president shrugs off Covid-19 risk after sending fruit for "tests,"' Available at: https://www.theguardian.com/global-development/2020/may/19/, Accessed 8 June 2022.

Boniphace, E. (5 November 2020) 'Tanzanian media unable to cover Covid-19 epidemic,' Available at: https://rsf.org/en/tanzanian-media-unable-cover-covid-19-epidemic, Accessed 10 June 2022.

Buguzi, S. (28 July 2021) 'Tanzania's dilemma: It is not so easy to go from vaccine denier to vaccine embracer,' Available at: https://www.npr.org/sections/goatsandsoda, Accessed 11 June 2022.

Buguzi, S. (2021) 'Covid-19: Counting the cost of denial in Tanzania,' in: *BMJ,* Volume 373, Number 1052, pp.1-2.

Buguzi, S. Broom, F. Adriano, J. & Rueda, A. (7 April 2021) 'Covid-19, lies and statistics: corruption and the pandemic,' Available at: https://www.scidev.net/sub-saharan-africa/scidev-net-investigates/covid-19-lies-and-statistics-corruption-and-the-pandemic/, Accessed 11 June 2022.

Carlitz, R.D. & McLellan, R. (2020) 'Open data from authoritarian regimes: New opportunities, new challenges,' in: *Perspectives on Politics*, pp.1-11.

Carlitz, R. Yamanis, T. & Mollel, H. (2021) 'Coping with denialism: How street-level bureaucrats adapted and responded to Covid-19 in Tanzania,' in: *Journal of Health Politics, Policy and Law,* Volume 46, Number 6, pp.989-1017.

Cara, A. (29 January 2021) 'Tanzania's leader denies Covid-19, and countrymen push back,' Available at: https://apnews.com/article/tanzaniacoronavirus-pandemic-east-africa-africa-kenya43f232ee0e82cd0ee381e53d8aeb98d6, Accessed 18 June 2022.

Chutel, L. (17 February 2021) 'Africa's Covid-19 denialist-in-chief,' Available at: https://foreignpolicy.com/2021/02/17/tanzania-president-magufuli-coronavirus-pandemic-denial/, Accessed 6 June 2022.

Citizen (17 March 2020) 'Tanzania bans all public gatherings, closes schools, suspends the Premier League over Corona virus,' Available at: allafrica.com/stories/202003171108.html, Accessed 15 June 2022.

Citizen (10 May 2020) 'Tanzania lays down research priorities for Covid-19,' Available at: https://www.thecitizen.co.tz/tanzania/news/-tanzania-lays-down-research-priorities-for-covid-192708982, Accessed 15 June 2020.

Devermont, J. & Harris, M. (26 May 2020) 'Implications of Tanzania's bungled response to Covid-19,' Available at: https://www.csis.org/analysis/implications-tanzanias-bungled-response-covid-19, Accessed 9 June 2022.

Egorov, G & Sonin, K. (2011) 'Dictators and their viziers: Endogenising the loyalty-competence trade-of,' in: *Journal of the European Economic Association,* Volume 9, Number 5, pp.903-930.

Farkas, J. & Jannick S. (2018) 'Fake news as a floating signifier: Hegemony, antagonism and the politics of falsehood,' in: *Javnost - The Public*, Volume 25, Number 3, pp.298-314.

Global Expression (2021) 'Tanzania: Briefing on attacks against journalists, March 2020-July 2021,' Available at: https://www.article19.org/wp-content/uploads/2021/11/Covid-Response-Africa-Tanzania.pdf, Accessed 13 June 2022.

Greitens, S.C. (2016) *Dictators and their secret police: Coercive institutions and state violence,* Cambridge: Cambridge University Press.

Guterres, A. (22 February 2021) 'The world faces a pandemic of human rights abuses in the wake of Covid-19,' Available at:

https://www.theguardian.com/global-development/2021/feb/22/world, Accessed 27 September 2021.

Hale, T. N.A Emily, L. Kira, K, S. Petherick, A. Phillips, T. Tatlow, & S. Webster (2020) 'Covid-19 Government Response Tracker,' University of Oxford, Blavatnik School of Government, Available at: www.bsg.ox.ac.uk/research/research-projects/covid-19-government-response-tracker, Accessed 15 June 2022.

International Peace Information Service (2 December 2020) 'Briefing on "Business & Human Rights in Tanzania" 2020 Quarter 2: April-June,' Available at: https://ipisresearch.be/weekly-briefing/briefing-on-business-human-rights-in-tanzania-2020-quarter-2-april-june/, Accessed 10 June 2022.

Jarman, H. (2021) 'State responses to Covid-19 pandemic: Governance, surveillance, coercion and social policy,' in: S.L. Greener, E.J. King & E. Massard da Fonseca (eds.) *Corona virus politics: The comparative politics and policy of Covid-19*, Michigan: Michigan University Press.

Kamazima, S.R. & D.C.V. Kakoko (2020) 'Manifold tactics are used to control and prevent pandemics in contemporary Africa: A case of Tanzania's fight against Covid-19,' in: *International Journal of Advanced Scientific Research and Management,* Volume 5, Number 11, pp.20-33.

Kombe, C. (28 January 2022) 'Tanzania's president criticised for dismissing Covid-19 vaccines,' Available at: https://www.voanews.com/a/covid-19-pandemic_tanzanias-president-criticized-dismissing-covid-19-vaccines/6201338.html, Accessed 4 June 2022.

Kell, F. (21 May 2020) 'Tanzania evades Covid-19 lockdown, but restrictions persist,' Available at: https://www.chathamhouse.org/2020/05/tanzania-evades-covid-19-lockdown-restrictions-persist, Accessed 29 May 2022.

Langwick, S. (2011) *Bodies, politics and African healing: The matter of maladies in Tanzania,* Bloomington: Indiana University Press.

Lipscy, P.Y. (2020) 'Covid-19 and the politics of crisis,' in: *International Organisation,* pp.1-30.

Little, A.T. (2017) 'Propaganda and credulity,' in: *Games and Economic Behavior,* Volume 102, pp.224-232.

Makoni, M. (2021) 'Tanzania refuses Covid-19 vaccines,' in: *Lancet*, Volume 397, Number 10274, p.566.

Monitor Civicus (8 September 2020) 'Authorities embark on major crackdown on expression amid Covid-19 and ahead of elections,' Available at: https://monitor.civicus.org/updates/2020/09/08/authorities-embark-major-crackdown-expression-amid-covid-19-and-ahead-elections/, Accessed 7 June 2022.

Moyo, G. & Phulu, K.I. (2021) 'The weaponisation of the Corona virus crisis in Zimbabwe: Legal and extra-legal instruments,' in: *iBusiness*, Volume 13, pp.48-66, Available at: https://doi.org/10.4236/ib.2021.131004, Accessed 16 June 2021.

Muchena, D. (14 December 2020) 'Pandemic of human rights abuses haunts governments in East and Southern Africa,' Available at: https://mg.co.za/africa/2020-12-14, Accessed 18 September 2021.

Odula, T. (22 May 2022) 'Tanzania says virus defeated through prayer, but fears grow,' Available at: https://apnews.com/article/ap-top-news-international-news-pandemics-east-africa-virus-outbreak-9a0304b6798e8b0f63563258d29c888e, Accessed 6 June 2022.

Nkomo, B.F & Mangiza, O. (2021) 'Civil disobedience and images of war: The military and police in the face of the Covid-19 pandemic in Zimbabwe,' in: *The Dyke*, Volume 15, Number 1, pp.131-149.

Ogola, G. (2021) 'Covid-19, knowledge production and the (un)making of truths and fakes,' in: *Journal of African Cultural Studies*, Volume 33, Number 3, pp.305-311.

Olewe, D. (9 April 2020) 'Corona virus in Africa: Whipping, shooting and snooping,' Available at: https://www.bbc.com/news/world-africa-52214740,' Accessed 16 June 2022.

Patterson, A.S. (2022) 'The Tanzanian state response to Covid-19: Why low capacity, discursive legitimacy, and twilight authority matter,' WIDER Working Paper, No. 2022/34, The United Nations University World Institute for Development Economics Research (UNU-WIDER), Helsinki, Available at: https://doi.org/10.35188/UNU-WIDER/2022/165-5, Accessed 17 June 2022.

Patterson, A.S & Balogun, E. (2021) 'African responses to Covid-19: The reckoning of agency?' in: *African Studies Review*, Volume 64, Number 1, pp.1-24.

Phillips, K. (2018) *An ethnography of hunger*, Bloomington: Indiana University Press.

Richardson, H.C. (2022) 'Elephants in the room: Covid-19 pandemic political ecologies of tourism in Tanzania', in: *Theses and Dissertations: Geography*, Volume 88, Available at: https://uknowledge.uky.edu/geography_etds/88, Accessed 12 June 2022.

Richey, L.A., L.E. Gissel, O. Kweka, P. Baerendtsen, P. Kragelund, H.Q. Hambati & A. Mwamfupe. (2021) 'South-South humanitarianism: The case of Covid organics in Tanzania', in: *World Development*, Volume 141. Available at: https://doi.org/10.1016/j.worlddev.2020.105375, Accessed 12 June 2022.

Rickard, C. (24 February 2021) 'Law firm suggests expelling Tanzania from Commonwealth over Covid denialism,' Available at: https://africanlii.org/article/20210224/intl-law-firm-suggests-expelling-tanzania-commonwealth-over-covid-denialism, Accessed 12 June 2022.

Rivers, M. & Ndlovu, P. (24 June 2020) 'Covid-19 raises the stakes for Zimbabwe's civil society movement,' Available at: https://www.usip.org/publications/2020/06, Accessed 21 September 2021.

Said, K. (29 May 2020) 'A problem of denial: Why Tanzania could lose the war against Covid-19,' Available at: https://www.theelephant.info/features/2020/05/29/aproblem-of-denial-why-tanzania-could-lose-the-war-against-covid-19/, Accessed 12 June 2022.

Schatzberg, M. (2001) *Political legitimacy in Middle Africa: Father, family, food*. Bloomington: Indiana University Press.

Shivji, I.G. (2012) 'Nationalism and Pan-Africanism: Decisive moments in Nyerere's intellectual and political thought', in: *Review of African Political Economy,* Volume 39, Number 131, pp.103-116.

Svolik, M.W. (2009) 'Power-sharing and leadership dynamics in authoritarian regimes', in: *American Journal of Political Science,* Volume 53, Number 2, pp.477-494.

Taylor, B. (1 May 2020) 'Covid-19 hits Tanzania', in: *Tanzanian Affairs*, Available at: www.tzaffairs.org/2020/05/covid-19-hits-tanzania/, Accessed 18 June 2022.

Wallace, J.L. (2016) 'Juking the stats? Authoritarian information problems in China', in: *British Journal of Political Science*, Volume 46, Number 1, pp.11-29.

WHO (20 February 2021). 'WHO Director-General's statement on Tanzania and Covid-19,' Available at: www.who.int/news/item/20-02-2021-who-director-general-s-statement-on-tanzania-and-covid-19, Accessed 16 June 2022.

Wizaraya Afya Tanzania (3 February 2021) 'Twitter', Available at: twitter.com/wizara_afyatz/status/1356994906296897540, Accessed 16 June 2022.

Wintrobe, R. (2000) *The political economy of dictatorship,* Cambridge: Cambridge University Press.

Chapter 7

Battling a Pandemic in a Warped Economy: Contravention of Socio-Economic Rights during the Covid-19 Period in Zimbabwe

Tasara Muguti

Introduction

The Covid-19 pandemic sent shock waves across the globe. There are several unsubstantiated conspiracy theories that are associated with the origins of the Corona virus. These include the claim that the virus escaped or was manufactured in a laboratory in Wuhan City in China (Beaumont, 2020). Nonetheless, what is certain though is that the virus, which causes the disease Covid-19, was first diagnosed in the Wuhan Province of China in December 2019 (*Tehran Times*, 15 April 2020). The Corona virus quickly spread across the world with devastating human, social and economic impacts. World economies were destroyed, deaths were widespread, and health facilities became overstretched globally. Zimbabwe was not spared either. This chapter examines the challenges faced by people in countries with dysfunctional economies such as Zimbabwe as the government struggled to contain the pandemic. The challenges resulted in many people struggling to enjoy some basic livelihood rights such as the right to life and other rights that make life worth living.

The chapter explores how the government's failure in its obligation to provide basic social services and other human needs, aggravated the impact of the pandemic on many ordinary Zimbabweans. The government had long since failed to provide adequate healthcare, satisfactory remuneration for its workers, shelter, clean water, food and work, among many other failures. While the study will largely focus on the healthcare system, reference will also be made to the need to fulfil other livelihood rights that forced citizens to move out of their homes despite the threat of contracting Covid-19. These rights, which are indivisible, are inherent to every living being irrespective of "nationality, sex, origin, colour, religion, language, or any other status" (UNICEF, 2015). This is notwithstanding the restrictive mechanisms that were put in place by the state to contain the spread of the pandemic which, in some instances, were an infringement to the enjoyment of these livelihood rights.

The qualitative research methodology was deployed in undertaking this study. From the outset, it should be appreciated that conducting research under the Covid-19 pandemic's restrictive conditions was a daunting task as some tools which are ordinarily used in carrying out a research of this nature were difficult to deploy. When the study was carried out, movement and face-to-face contact were restricted and discouraged in order to contain the spread of the virus. As such, the study heavily relied on desktop literature, observations, online interviews and, where possible, intermittent face-to-face interviews. Since some of the people who participated in this study seemed uncomfortable in having their true identity revealed for various reasons, pseudonyms were used.

This study departs from the conventionally accepted Eurocentric norm of underpinning a study on a theoretical framework and instead, makes use of a contextual framework. The use of theories has been relentlessly drilled upon scholars by social scientists since the 19th century. Departure from using a theoretical framework is in sync with what one may refer to as 'the Southern Approach' in decolonising research (Keikelame & Swartz, 2019). This resonates with decolonial concerns that theoretical frameworks have resulted in the overrepresentation of Eurocentric thought in knowledge production processes. Thus, as Ndlovu-Gatsheni (2013) rightly argues, there is need to undo and re-do thinking itself. In this regard, the challenges faced in Zimbabwe in grappling with the Covid-19 pandemic will be firmly located within the context of the socio-economic and political fragility that bedevilled the country from the onset of the new millennium.

It is prudent to note that the challenges that were faced in battling the Covid-19 pandemic were borne out of a specific context, a context in which the socio-economic and political challenges confronting the country evolved. In Zimbabwe, particularly after 2000, the hotly contested political terrain which persistently failed to come up with conclusive election outcomes was at the epicentre of the country's perennial problems. Indeed, it may not be an overstatement to say that contested election outcomes, principally after 2000, were the 'mother of all crises' in Zimbabwe. This undoubtedly resulted in the fragility of all other activities in the country: a dysfunctional health-delivery system, a turbulent political environment and a comatose economy that increasingly became informalised. This fragility across many sectors has had a negative impact on individuals enjoying socio-economic rights and freedoms in the country.

As such, this study is anchored within the fragile situations context. Fragility is generally perceived as the dismal failure by a state to provide essential services to its citizens as a result of weak capacity, lack of political will, or both (Menocal & Othieno, 2008). Fragility normally results in unwarranted and harmful outcomes such as breakdown of institutions, violence, displacement and humanitarian crises or other emergencies (States of Fragility Report, 2016). The fragile situations contextual framework may be very useful in addressing issues pertaining to challenges that can be faced in dealing with a fatal epidemic such as Covid-19 in a compromised socio-economic and political environment. The fragile situations indicated above are consistent with the Zimbabwean crises in which the Covid-19 pandemic evolved.

The crises that prevailed in Zimbabwe include issues of political legitimacy and polarisation, governance, constitutionality, fragile economy, fragile health delivery system, fragile energy sector, rampant unemployment, and runaway inflation which made it very difficult for the majority of the citizenry to access basic essential services and goods, among others (Besada & Moyo, 2008). All these are typical examples of fragility which have a direct impact on how a state can deal with an epidemic. Hence, it is within this context of socio-economic and political fragility that the challenges faced in dealing with the Covid-19 epidemic will be analysed. As alluded to earlier on, the challenges had a direct bearing on the ability of the ordinary people to enjoy basic human and fundamental rights as expounded in the Constitution of Zimbabwe and other international conventions.

Human rights and people's livelihoods

To begin this section, it should be acknowledged that the Universal Declaration of Human Rights of 1948 and other human rights treaties play a critical role in contemporary struggles for decent livelihoods. Human rights have received increasing attention since the end of the Second World War in 1945. The atrocities committed by different belligerents during the war galvanised countries across the world to come up with elaborate international instruments to protect human rights of every citizen (UNICEF, 2015). Human rights depict rights innate to all human beings in spite of one's race, nationality, language, religion, ethnicity or any other standing without discrimination. They are principles that recognise and guard against the dignity of all human beings. The rights consist of the right to life, freedom from enslavement and torture, freedom of opinion and expression, the right to education and work, among others (Ibid). These rights are universal and inalienable, indivisible, interdependent and interrelated (UNFPA, 2005). As stated by UNICEF (2015), "The realisation of one right often depends, wholly or in part, upon the realisation of others. For instance, the realisation of the right to health may depend on the realisation of the right to education or of the right to information".

The United Nations Charter (1945) and its Universal Declaration of Human Rights of 1948 respectively, came up with a comprehensive list of internationally accepted rights that encompass civil, cultural, economic, social and political rights. These rights are documented in two protocols which are the International Convention on Civil and Political Rights and the International Covenant on Economic, Social and Cultural Rights, which both came into effect in 1976 and constitute the International Bill of Human Rights (Darrow & and Arbour, 2009). Since then, other human rights treaties and instruments have been adopted all with the intention to expand the body of international human rights law. These include the Convention on the Prevention and Punishment of the Crime of Genocide (1948), the International Convention on the Elimination of All Forms of Racial Discrimination (1965), the International Convention on the Elimination of All Forms of Racial Discrimination against Women (1979), the Convention on the Rights of the Child (1989) and the Convention of the Rights of Persons with Disabilities (2006) (UNICEF, 2015).

It is worthwhile to note that it is the responsibility of governments worldwide to act or abstain from certain acts so as to promote and protect human rights and fundamental freedoms of persons or groups within their jurisdictions. This is in line with the United Nations Human-based Approach to Development Coordination (2003) which stipulates that all developmental programmes and policies should be implemented within a context which furthers the realisation of human rights as stipulated in the UDHR and other human rights instruments (United Nations, 23 April 2020). Recognition of socio-economic rights is critical in the enjoyment of adequate standards of living. These rights include the right to medical care, food, shelter and necessary social services, among others (Zimbabwe Peace Project, February 2021). Socio-economic rights are also acknowledged in regional instruments such as the Rights and Welfare of the Child (1999) and the African Charter on Human and Peoples' Rights of Women in Africa (2003) (Evans & Murray, 2008). In the same vein, the Constitution of Zimbabwe fully captures the socio-economic rights as articulated in regional and international instruments as it has an expanded Constitutional Bill of Rights which guarantees diverse socio-economic rights such the right to health, the right to work, the right to adequate food and water, the right to adequate housing and sanitation, and the right to education (Constitution of Zimbabwe, Amendment Act, Number 20: 2013).

While this study does not in any way try to interrogate all the mentioned human rights protocols, it is within this framework that the rights of people to decent livelihoods during the Covid-19 pandemic in Zimbabwe is examined. This is done within the context of an economy which was threatened with virtual collapse after several decades of mismanagement, corruption and disputed electoral outcomes (Rwodzi, 2017). Though the definition of livelihoods is complex and often difficult to describe with precision (Moser & Norton, 2001), in this study, the rights to livelihoods will be confined to the peoples' rights in accessing healthcare, realistic living wages, reasonable shelter, safe drinking water, food, freedom of movement and education. Livelihoods are pre-fixed with specific socio-economic and political contexts. The alterations of these contexts also create new livelihood opportunities or obstacles (UNDP, 2005).

Situating the Covid-19 pandemic in Zimbabwe's socio-economic and political dynamics

Zimbabwe attained independence from the British in 1980 after having been colonised for close to a century from 1890 (Nyawo & Rich, 1980). At independence, the ruling Zimbabwe African National Union Patriotic Front (ZANU-PF) leadership inherited one of the most powerful economies in Southern Africa. The country's infrastructure, for example, roads, railways, bridges, schools and hospitals, was in a reasonable state although it was meant to largely benefit the small settler minority population (Lessing, 2003). In order to redress the colonial imbalances, the 1980s witnessed massive reconstruction and infrastructural development by the new government that included the construction of schools, hospitals, clinics, boreholes, bridges and roads to cater for the majority Zimbabweans (Dansereau & Zamponi, 2005; Riddell, 1984). More than 40 years after independence, the country, which founding presidents of Mozambique and Tanzania, Samora Machel and Julius Nyerere respectively once described as the 'jewel of Africa' struggled to extricate its citizenry from the jaws of poverty (Lessing, 2003).

By the early 1990s, the Zimbabwean economy was beginning to show serious signs of distress due to the failure of the government-adapted socialist ideological thrust to deliver, corruption and mismanagement (Muguti, 2016). Since then, the economy went on a steady decline with catastrophic consequences on the peoples' livelihoods. This was in spite of the fact that the country always enjoyed an abundance of natural resources and talented human capital. Faced with a deteriorating socio-economic situation since the late 1980s, the ZANU-PF government was forced to adopt the International Monetary Fund (IMF) and World Bank -prescribed Economic Structural Adjustment Programme (ESAP) in 1991 which was meant to revive the economy (Mlambo, 1997).

While ESAP resulted in the liberalisation of the economy, it proved to be a wrong prescription for the ailing Zimbabwean economy as it resulted in company closures which triggered massive retrenchments of workers countrywide. The removal of subsidies on basic goods and services was an enormous blow to many ordinary citizens. It became very difficult for people to access essential goods and services which had a negative impact on the ordinary peoples' livelihoods (Raftopoulos & Sachikonye, 2001). What is telling is that the Zimbabwean economy never recovered from the shocks brought about by the ESAP. Indeed, towards the end of the 1990s, the already bad situation was further exacerbated by the unbudgeted payment of gratuities to the country's former liberation war veterans and the country's involvement in the Democratic People's Republic of Congo civil war (Bond & Manyanya, 2001). These developments resulted in the collapse of the Zimbabwean dollar. The socio-economic and political challenges facing the country then resulted in the formation of the Zimbabwe Congress of Trade Unions (ZCTU)-backed political party, the Movement for Democratic Change (MDC), led by the late Morgan Tsvangirai, in 1999 (Raftopoulos & Sachikonye, 2001).

The formation of the labour-backed political party changed Zimbabwe's political landscape. Since then, the ZANU-PF regime faced serious opposition from the newly-formed movement which enjoyed widespread support among the workers, academics, white community, churches, non-governmental organisations, and even abroad by the Western countries which were fed up with ZANU-PF misrule (Ibid). Faced with the prospects of losing the pending presidential elections then, the ruling ZANU-PF was forced to embark on the Fast Track Land Reform Programme (FTLRP) in 2000 in order to regain its dwindling support base. The land reform programme was accompanied by unbridled human rights violations that were perpetrated by the war veterans on the 4 000 white commercial farmers and their workers (Bond & Manyanya, 2001). These included violence, rape and murder that were committed against white farmers and their workers during displacement from the farms (Ibid).

In response to these human rights violations, Western countries and the United States imposed sanctions on Zimbabwe. These sanctions, which heavily impacted on the country's capacity to access bilateral and multilateral financial and other forms of assistance from abroad, negatively impacted on the Zimbabwean economy (*Business Times*, 9-15 July 2020). The situation that unfolded in the country after 2000 has been aptly termed as 'the Zimbabwean crises'. Undoubtedly, a great deal of ink has already been spilled over the Zimbabwean crisis by several scholars across the academic divide (Hammar & Raftopoulos, 2003; Chiumbu & Musemwa, 2012). Perhaps, what can be added is that by 2022, the crises were so multi-layered to constitute a convergence of economic collapse, food insecurity, deepening poverty, hyperinflation, health service delivery collapse, power shortages, corruption and widespread human rights abuses perpetrated against human rights defenders, lawyers, journalists and anyone who dared speak against the regime (Human Rights Watch, 4 September 2020; *Newsday*, 14 January 2022; *Newsday*, 24 January 2022). The regime's motto seemed to be centred on hearing no evil, speaking no evil and seeing no evil'.

Since the onset of the new millennium, the struggle in Zimbabwe appeared to be between those who were determined to maintain the status quo and those who were 'on the march' as they were convinced that change should come (Machedu Trust, 20 December 2021). This struggle undoubtedly resulted in a multi-layered crisis as outlined above. While the Zimbabwean leadership perpetually attributed the country's dismal economic performance to the sanctions imposed by the West and the United States, it was apparent that corruption, failure to implement economic and political reforms, *discriminatory justice* and inconsistent policies were also at the root of the economic malaise (Moyo-Nyede, 29 October 2021).

Since the imposition of sanctions, the country failed to settle its international arrears and access long term capital from the IMF, the World Bank and the Paris Club. Financial support from these organisations usually compelled the recipient country to implement substantial and sustainable political and economic reforms as well as the respect for human rights, particularly the freedoms of assembly and expression (*Business Times*, 9-15 July 2020). However, it appeared Zimbabwe's 'New Dispensation' under President Emmerson Mnangagwa was reluctant to implement such reforms and as a result, the country continued to rely on costly loans from its allies and some regional financiers. At the end of January 2022, Zimbabwe was red-flagged at the UN Human Rights Council Universal Periodic Review working group meeting in Geneva, Switzerland, for gross human rights violations. At the meeting, Benjamin Moeling, the United States Permanent Mission Charge d'Affaires to the United Nations categorically stated that:

> Zimbabwe must enforce security and due process laws adopted under the 2013 Constitution that prohibit arbitrary arrests and prolonged detentions and allow the practice of constitutionally guaranteed freedoms of expression, peaceful assembly, and association for all (*Pindula News*, 27 January 2022).

The above sentiments were widely shared by delegates from other UN member states such as Australia, Canada, India and Sweden who also urged the Zimbabwean government to desist from using the Covid-19 lockdown restrictions to undermine peoples' freedoms. Even South Africa, which had always stood by Zimbabwe through thick and thin, also encouraged its neighbour to ensure the alignment of the Zimbabwe Human Rights Council Act with the Paris Principles and the Constitution, and avail funding for the protection and promotion of human rights (Ibid).

While the government's propaganda machinery was busy painting a false narrative of economic recovery at the beginning of 2022, the socio-economic crisis manifested itself in "mass starvation, over taxation, corruption, hyperinflation, 49% extreme poverty, joblessness, wage erosion, poor earnings by civil servants and poor remuneration crisis in the education sector" (*Pindula News*, 12 January 2022: 1). Such had been the situation since the onset of the new millennium to the extent that everything seemed to have come to a standstill. Furthermore, the political polarisation in the country rendered all productive economic enterprise impossible and life becoming unbearable for the majority of the country's citizens. As the Zimbabwean dollar continued to depreciate against the major currencies, basic commodities and services became unaffordable for many as inflation exceeded 800% by the end of July 2020 (ZimStat, August 2020).

It was in such a situation that the country found itself faced with a pandemic which even the most developed countries with very stable social and economic systems were struggling to manage. The coming of the Covid-19 pandemic, which inevitably required substantial resources to manage, was like adding fuel to an already burning house. As observed in a United Nations report on Zimbabwe, the pandemic presented:

> …an additional challenge to Zimbabwe's existing political and socio-economic dynamics, including a development trajectory beleaguered by deep-rooted historical conflicts that flare up at the slightest trigger, with women and girls often most affected. Deep polarisation has created a culture of mistrust and fear. This is further exacerbated by incidences of excessive use of force by security forces (Ribeiro, 2020).

In the same vein, a World Bank report on Zimbabwe highlighted that the loss of access to basic services by households and the deepening of negative coping strategies undermined the country's ability to deal with the pandemic (World Bank, 10 June 2021). The economic challenges, the drought and Cyclone Idai in 2019, coupled with the extraordinary shocks triggered by the pandemic, demanded that the government comes up with bold interventions in order to protect people's lives and livelihoods within a framework that was consistent with international human rights norms. As Stella llieva, a World Bank Senior Economist, opined:

> Preserving lives during this unprecedented pandemic in this challenging economic environment will require a strategic approach to addressing underlying problems in the health sector...Such a strategy needs to recognise and simultaneously attend to the Covid-19 and non-Covid-19 health burden in coordinating and allocating sector resources (Ibid).

As the pandemic raged on, new statistical records were being set on an almost weekly basis across the world. Since the outbreak of the pandemic, the virus continued to mutate from one variant to the other in unpredictable and dangerous ways resulting in shifting intensity levels of fatalities. Nonetheless, there is no doubt that the pandemic was among the worst to hit the world in recent times. Over the centuries, the world had also experienced pandemics and epidemics such as the Black Death, Bubonic Plague and Spanish Influenza (Taubenberger & Morens, 2006).

The Covid-19 pandemic was declared a Public Health Emergency of International Concern by the Director General of WHO on 30 January 2020 (United Nations Zimbabwe, 2020). Following the WHO declaration, the Zimbabwean government declared Covid-19 as a state of disaster on 20 March 2020 when the first case was recorded in the country. This was immediately followed by the imposition of a national lockdown for a 21-day period from 30 March 2020. Since then, the lockdowns were periodically reviewed and revised to allow for the gradual return to normal life (KPMG, 20 August 2020). Besides the lockdowns, sensitisation, banning of mass gatherings, social distancing, closure of borders, testing, contact tracing, the use of face masks and vaccination were some of the methods used by many countries to contain the spread of the virus.

The major objective was to flatten the curve and halt exponential growth in order to reduce pressure on medical facilities (Altimier & Seiver, 2020). The number of new infections had been fluctuating from time to time and the number of deaths had been steadily rising in Zimbabwe. What was disturbing was that during the pandemic, people were not only dying from Covid-19 infections but from how the lockdown measures were enforced which violated certain socio-economic rights such as the right to health and free movement. Between March and June 2020, for instance, 106 maternal deaths were recorded, mainly due to restrictions in movements which militated against many pregnant women accessing maternal services. By the end of January 2022, figures released by the Ministry of Health and Child Care showed that Zimbabwe had recorded 229 460 confirmed Covid-19 cases, 5 337 deaths and 218 325 recoveries since the outbreak of the pandemic (*Kubatana.net*, 31 January 2022).

With regards to lockdowns, countries with weak economies such as Zimbabwe generally implemented partial lockdowns to fight the pandemic. While this study does not intend to document the human rights abuses that were perpetrated by the security forces in detail, it is worth mentioning that the lockdowns were accompanied by many human rights abuses against civilians as had always happened in the country in the past (Makombe, 2021; Zimbabwe Human Rights Forum, 26 January 2022). The police and the army killed 10 people who were accused of violating Covid-19 lockdowns measures between March and June 2020 (Amnesty International, 2020). Furthermore, several incidences of violence against women and girls in and outside homes were recorded during the Covid-19 pandemic (Zimbabwe Peace Project, 2021). On 14 April 2020, following an urgent chamber application, the High Court ruled that security forces had an obligation to respect human rights when enforcing lockdown measures (Ribeiro, 2020).

As the pandemic unfolded, there were several instances in which statutory instruments were deployed to suspend various constitutional rights in Zimbabwe (Amnesty International, 2020). This clearly demonstrates that at times the enforcement of restrictive measures put in place by the government to contain the spread of Covid-19 clashed with human rights. Thus, adherence to the dictates of international human rights norms was critical in enforcing lockdowns. As the UN Secretary General once stated: "Human rights norms embed ethical dimensions of doing no harm" (United Nations, 23 April 2020: 3).

By early 2021, while it was taking time for a vaccine to control the spread of the pandemic to be found, a number of drugs had gone through the pre-trial and clinical stages and had been approved for human use by the WHO. In Zimbabwe, five vaccines had been approved for use by mid-February 2021. These were Sinopharm, Sinovac, Janssen (Johnson & Johnson), Sputnik V and Covaxin (Vaccine Tracker, 11 February 2021). Zimbabwe started a campaign to vaccinate its citizens as soon the country had acquired donated vaccines from China. The programme kicked off with the televised vaccination of high profile political figures such as the President and his two deputies. This was immediately followed by the inoculation of frontline workers such as medical personnel, teachers, university lecturers, uniformed forces, the elderly and people living with chronic ailments (*World Press*, 15 March 2021).

The government's expectation was that the pandemic would have been brought under control by the end of 2021 after about 60% of the population, involving about 10 million people in the country, had been vaccinated (*Xinhuanet*, 24 April 2021). As the then Minister of Health and Childcare stated in early 2021: "Our target is to reach what we call herd immunity by year-end as we seek to get back to normal life after the devastating effects of the Covid-19" (Ibid). Nonetheless, all set deadlines were missed as the country struggled to acquire enough vaccines for its citizens. Besides, there was reluctance to take the vaccines by some people due to various fears (Scoones, 10 May 2021). Thus, while it was envisaged that about 60% of the population would have been vaccinated by the end of 2021, only 4 267 550 people had received their first dose while the number of second jab recipients stood at 3 296 368 by the end of January 2022 (*Kubatana.net*, 31 January 2022). Due to the poor state of their economies, countries such as Zimbabwe had difficulty in accessing these vaccines and largely relied on donations from countries such as China, India and Russia (*Xinhuanet*, 24 April 2021). This left their populations exposed to the Covid-19 pandemic.

Health delivery challenges in dealing with Covid-19

Perhaps it is significant to acknowledge that there were several challenges that the government confronted in dealing with the pandemic. These challenges had a huge bearing on the government's capacity to fulfil people's livelihood needs as the Covid-19 pandemic unfolded. Due to misgovernance and elite corruption over the years, Zimbabwe was characterised by dilapidated infrastructure which made the fight against a pandemic such as Covid-19 an insurmountable task. The healthcare system, water supply, electricity and the transport infrastructure were in a sorry state when the pandemic crept in. The country's foreign debt, which was in excess of US$15 billion, remained a big albatross on its capacity to access developmental capital and/or credit facilities (Capital, 2019). In this regard, the Zimbabwean government had restricted legroom available to effectively respond to the pandemic as it was inadequately resourced in terms of infrastructural, social, human and financial capital when the pandemic broke out.

Zimbabwe's health delivery system was, and remained, fragile and ill-prepared to manage the pandemic. The right to health for all citizens in the country was severely impacted upon during the Covid-19 pandemic as the health delivery system was underfunded and dilapidated due to several decades of neglect (Zimbabwe Peace Project, 2021). Section 29 of the Constitution specifies that the government should guarantee access to health by taking all practical measures that ensure provision of basic, accessible and adequate health facilities countrywide. Furthermore, Section 76(1) of the Zimbabwean Constitution clearly states that "every citizen and permanent resident of Zimbabwe has the right to have access to basic healthcare services, including reproductive healthcare services" (Constitution of Zimbabwe Amendment Act, Number 20, 2013: 37). Thus, while it is a basic human rights requirement that all citizens should have access to reasonable healthcare, the health delivery system in Zimbabwe was found wanting at the most critical time as it had been in shambles for over two decades. The situation in the healthcare system continued to deteriorate for various reasons over the years: no drugs, no basic equipment such as ultrasound machines, ventilators and a decaying infrastructure (Muguti, 2016).

The Covid-19 pandemic exposed the government's failure to adequately invest in social infrastructure to meet the basic needs of a growing population. The multi-layered socio-economic and political crises that the country was facing made compliance to the Covid-19 guidelines as stipulated by WHO a colossal task. Coupled with all this was the government's failure to address rampant corruption involving its senior officials in the awarding of Covid-19 supply tenders (*Guardian*, 9 July 2020). There were several instances in which tenders were corruptly awarded, essential PPE kits overpriced and failure to fulfil tenders that had already been paid (Zimbabwe Peace Project, 2021). These challenges, no doubt, militated against the country's ability to effectively deal with the Covid-19 pandemic. As will be demonstrated below, the public health facilities were characterised by shortage of equipment, lack of PPEs, limited Intensive Care Unit beds and ventilators, shortage of staff, perennial strike action by medical health personnel due to unconducive working conditions and poor remuneration (*Lancet*, 15 August 2020). These challenges severely compromised the ordinary citizens' right to access health services and exacerbated the negative impact of the pandemic.

While the WHO blueprint for fighting the pandemic was very clear, it proved to be difficult to adhere to for countries like Zimbabwe with extremely weak and underperforming economies. The WHO clearly stipulated that specific conditions had to be met first before a country lifted the Covid-19 lockdown restrictions. A country's healthcare system was expected to be able to detect, test, isolate and treat every case and trace every contact. It was further stated that disease transmission should be under control; that hotspot risks were minimised in vulnerable places, and that schools, workplaces and other essential places established preventive measures. As the WHO Director General, Tedros Adhanom Ghebreyesus, stated in mid-April 2020: "One of the main things we learned in the past months about Covid-19 is that the faster all cases are found, tested, isolated and cared for, the harder we make it for the virus to spread" (WHO, 14 April 2020).

Nonetheless, it was always going to be difficult for Zimbabwe to fulfil all the WHO requirements as the country was experiencing some of its worst socio-economic and political challenges in years. Zimbabwe was among the world's most vulnerable countries as the Covid-19 pandemic surged through the continents due its decades-long economic implosion, a crippled healthcare system that had witnessed flight of qualified medical personnel for better opportunities outside the country, high fees for care and perennial industrial action by health workers (*Global Press Journal*, 29 March 2020). A 2018 study carried out on Zimbabwe's healthcare system by *Global Health Action*, a healthcare journal, revealed that poor working conditions forced 20% of health professionals to leave the country for better opportunities abroad (Masiyiwa, 29 March 2020). At the end of 2021, the Health Services Board confirmed that several health professional were leaving the country for greener pastures (*Newsday*, 17 December 2021; *Zimbabwe Independent*, 1 October 2021).

Undeniably, there was no right to fair wages in the public health sector as in other sectors in Zimbabwe. The poor remuneration and working conditions of the health personnel meant that the health workers did not enjoy the right to adequate living standards as stipulated in Article 25 of the UNDHR and also expounded in Section 65(1) of the Constitution of Zimbabwe (Constitution of Zimbabwe Amendment, No. 20, Act, 2013). Section 65(1) of the Constitution explicitly states that "every person has the right to fair and safe labour practices and standards and to be paid a fair and reasonable wage" (Ibid: 32). This is in line with UNDHR Articles 23 and 25 which focus on workers' rights. Article 23 specifies that "everyone has the right...to favourable conditions of work...Everyone who works has the right to just and favourable remuneration ensuring for himself and his family an existence worthy of human dignity, and supplemented, if necessary, by other means of social protection" (UNICEF, 2015). Article 25 states that "everyone has the right to a standard of living adequate for the health and well-being of himself, including food, clothing, housing and medical care and necessary social services" (Ibid).

Doctors and nurses started leaving the country especially from 2000 when the Zimbabwean crises commenced. Many healthcare professionals headed for Europe while others went to African countries such as South Africa, Namibia and Botswana (Mbiba *et al*, 2020). This created a work experience vacuum which inevitably contributed to the crumbling of a once vibrant healthcare system that had been highly regarded across the continent (International Organisation for Migration, 2010). Furthermore, doctors and nurses went on strike for over three months stretching to early September 2020 when the country was struggling to contain the spread of Covid-19. These challenges exposed the sheer unpreparedness of Zimbabwean hospitals to deal with Covid-19. There were genuine fears among progressive Zimbabweans that the consequences could be catastrophic if the Corona virus was to spread across the country. An informant, John Matizha, aptly put it this way: "With our collapsed health delivery system, my fear is that the Corona virus will spread like wildfire if nothing is done to address the challenges in the system" (Matizha, Interview: 20 April 2020).

Just before the outbreak of the Covid-19 pandemic in Zimbabwe in early 2020, doctors had gone on strike in September 2019 against low wages and poor working conditions. Between then and January 2020 when the strike came to an end after the intervention of a non-governmental organisation which had promised to augment the doctors' salaries, government hospitals, which were the most accessible to the impoverished Zimbabwean majority, only handled emergencies (World Bank, 10 June 2021). But morale remained very low among the health personnel for a very long time. Instead of addressing the workers' grievances, the government was preoccupied with coming up with pieces of legislation such as the Health Services Bill which sought to bar health professionals from engaging in strikes (*New Zimbabwe*, 28 December 2018; *Newsday*, 17 December 2021).

Some of the medical personnel who were interviewed but preferred anonymity for fear of retribution highlighted that they had lost all interest and were just going to work because they had limited options of survival. In order to cut down on transport costs, nurses worked for two days a week in a setup referred to as "flexi-hours" to ensure the continuity of nursing at the hospitals. As one nurse at Masvingo General Hospital lamented:

> We continue to come to work for two days in a week but our hearts are no longer in this profession. Our salaries are pathetic and we are

failing to make ends meet. The doctors are rarely at work and some just come for a few hours and depart (Murove, Interview: 15 April 2020).

On their part, some doctors also expressed disillusionment with their working conditions. For those who had been following developments in the healthcare system in Zimbabwe with keen interest, there was no doubt that the doctors' concerns were legitimate and that they had expressed these concerns to the authorities at various forums in vain. While the rate of Covid-19 infections continued to escalate and change from one variant to the other since end of March 2020, some doctors and nurses were refusing to go to work until they had received adequate protective equipment and their issues regarding remuneration had been resolved. As alluded to earlier on, it is a basic human right that workers should be given adequate clothing and equipment at the workplace.

Dr. Fortune Nyamande, the Chairperson of the Zimbabwe Association of Doctors for Human Rights, correctly observed: "More needs to be done....We need to look at the isolation facilities we have in Zimbabwe. We need well-equipped and high-level infection control facilities" (*Global Press Journal*, 29 March, 2020). Zimbabwe was inadequately prepared to deal with the pandemic. For instance, Harare, the capital city of Zimbabwe, had just two infectious disease hospitals, Wilkins and Beatrice, with compromised infrastructure. Wilkins Hospital had only 35 beds per ward and the Director of Health Services for Harare indicated that when they became full, tents were set up in the yard to attend to the overflow (Ibid).

The situation was pretty much the same in other healthcare facilities scattered countrywide. While hospitals were supposed to have at least 100 beds in their Intensive Care Units, according to international standards, Linda Mujuru, the Clinical Director for Sally Mugabe Central Hospital, one of the country's biggest referral hospitals, indicated that the hospital had just one (Ibid). A medical doctor at the institution stated that they had one ultra-sound unit and an X-ray machine that seldom functioned. He added that at times, the institution ran out of basic drugs such as painkillers and did not have enough machines to even check blood pressure. An orthopedic surgeon at the same institution indicated that lack of resources was a huge threat to healthcare. He further stated: "When we are in a situation that we are in, where there is only a single theatre room left aside for emergencies, this means all emergencies from various disciplines are put in a queue" (Masiyiwa, 29 March 2020).

While the government went overdrive in trying to convince the citizenry that it was adequately prepared and doing everything in its power to deal with the Covid-19 pandemic, the situation on the ground did not attest to that. To make matters worse, some hospitals around the country were shut down after Covid-19 infections had been reported. For instance, one of the biggest referral centres in the country, the Mpilo Central Hospital's National Tuberculosis Reference Laboratory in Bulawayo, was closed down after it ran out of consumables (*Kubatana.net*, 13 May 2020). This made it difficult for many people to access critical health services such as life-saving support in case of emergencies, access to medication by chronic patients suffering from tuberculosis and HIV/AIDS, and maternity services to pregnant women (Zimbabwe Peace Project, February 2021). This, undoubtedly, was in direct contravention to Section 25 of the Constitution which specified that it was the state's responsibility to take appropriate, fair and reasonable steps to ensure that no one was denied emergency medical treatment at any health facility (Constitution of Zimbabwe, 2013).

The challenges in the healthcare system made it difficult for the authorities to come up with accurate data on Covid-19. However, informed economic development policies and effective social interventions are only possible when and where accurate data can easily be accessed (*Zimbabwe Independent*, 22 May 2020). Among many Zimbabweans, the general consensus was that there were a lot of people with Covid-19 in the country but the government was just reluctant to admit this due to the poor health facilities (Chamunorwa, Interview: 12 December 2021). The authorities were not prepared to cause unnecessary panic and anxiety among the restive Zimbabwean populace. As the situation unfolded, there was no doubt that the government was not adequately prepared for the challenges posed by the Covid-19 pandemic. Besides, the fees charged by many hospitals were beyond the reach of many. Several respondents indicated that they now shunned hospitals and preferred the use of indigenous medicines which were readily available and easily accessible to ordinary Zimbabweans. Some informants showed a lot of concern and were scared about the implications of trying to contain a fatal pandemic in an environment with a dying healthcare system.

The shortage of test kits was a huge challenge in the fight against Covid-19. In May 2020, some health officials pointed out that there was a real danger of Covid-19 infections escalating due to undetected cases. Reliable sources highlighted that the Micro-Biology Centre at Sally Mugabe Referral Hospital in Harare was struggling with mounting samples from all over the country which had not been tested as the country ran out of Covid-19 test kits (*Zimbabwe Independent*, 22 May 2020). As another source rightly observed:

> What this means is that all these people are freely roaming the streets and in the event that some of them are infected, they could be spreading the virus. Remember that as of now, the country is only testing those who develop symptoms similar to Covid-19 who want to know their status. There is very little proactive testing going on (Zimbabwe Peace Project, February 2021).

These views aptly summarised the Covid-19 response in Zimbabwe as very little mandatory testing was carried out countrywide due to limited availability of appropriate resources to deal with the pandemic. In spite of the lack of reagent in the country, the government was already easing the lockdown measures by May 2020. This was despite the fact that it had not yet satisfied the minimum requirements as stipulated by WHO as already outlined elsewhere above. The government could not continue to enforce hard lockdowns and shutdowns in a situation where it was failing to provide adequate safety nets for the majority of the people whose livelihoods largely depended on informal activities.

In the former asbestos mining settlement of Mashava in Masvingo Province, for example, no Covid-19 testing had been done in the area by the end of September 2020. This was in spite of the fact that there were a lot of artisanal mining activities going on within and around the settlement with little regard to government and WHO guidelines on Covid-19. A nurse at the Great Zimbabwe University Mashava Campus Clinic confirmed that since the first case of Covid-19 was recorded in March 2020 in the country, no testing had been done at the university clinic since they did not have testing kits (Munyaka, Interview: 20 October 2020). Informants at Bere Clinic, which catered for the health needs of the majority of the residents of the former mining settlement and surrounding areas, also confirmed the same. This situation was reminiscent of what was happening in the rest of the province and probably beyond as confirmed by several health professionals consulted during this research.

The fight against the epidemic required the government to invest substantial resources in the health delivery system. There was need for the authorities to avail adequate testing kits and ventilators. As one nurse in Mashava retorted: "How can you effectively deal with critical Covid-19 cases without oxygen in hospitals?" (Ibid). Testing was critical in that reliable data could be generated and be used as an effective intervention strategy. Furthermore, the lack of adequate testing capacity also made it difficult for the authorities to test travellers from countries such as China (which is one of Zimbabwe's closest trading partners), the United Kingdom and the United States which had witnessed very high infection rates at some stage (Ministry of Health and Childcare, 6 April 2020). The socio-economic challenges in the country made significant testing difficult. Indeed, testing rates in Zimbabwe, like in some other parts of the continent, were extremely low which inevitably distorted official estimates of how the Corona virus was spreading.

A number of informants indicated that with a collapsed healthcare system, fighting a fatal pandemic such as Covid-19 was a mammoth task. During an interview, a medical specialist, who requested anonymity, indicated that under normal circumstances, up-to-date medical centres were supposed to be equipped with Level 3 laboratories which could offer the best precautions to safely run tests on the Corona virus. Nonetheless, as of March 2020, the country was only equipped with Level 1 and 2 laboratories which lacked effective safety facilities. While the medical specialist acknowledged that efforts were then underway to upgrade some laboratories to Level 3 with a containment area comprising double-door entries, a sealable room for decontamination and isolated ventilation systems, that required a lot of time and substantial financial resources (*Zimbabwe Independent*, 22 May 2020). That this was not in existence made the fight against Covid-19 a monumental task which undoubtedly increased the chances of the disease spreading.

In its forecast, the government had initially planned to test 1 000 people per day but was only able to conduct an average of 443 Polymerase Chain Reaction (PCR) diagnostic tests, which was less than half the set target (Ministry of Health and Childcare Updates, 2 April 2020). The target was to have tested about 40 000 people by the end of April 2020. The plan involved broadening the testing programme to include all returning citizens, admitted patients over 60 years of age, all the people who had been in contact with a positive case, and all patients with fever, among other conditions (Ibid). In addition, all businesses that wished to resume operations were directed to test, sanitise and monitor the temperatures of employees.

Unfortunately, this requirement was beyond the reach of most businesses which could not afford the high costs of test kits as they were also struggling to find their feet in the harsh hyperinflationary environment (Business and Human Resource Centre, 6 May 2020).

As the government heavily relied on the donor community for test kits and other Covid-19 equipment, it effectively abrogated its responsibilities to private sector players. What this meant was that the government had abdicated its mandate to ensure that all people enjoyed the right to reasonable healthcare. There was also the suspicion that the government was deliberately under-testing out of embarrassment to expose the crumbling health system to outside scrutiny. Interviews with some health workers around the country revealed a scarcity of reliable Covid-19 statistics and that it initially took too long for the test results to be released. Furthermore, there were several reported cases in which some people were tested Covid-19 positive posthumously. At one stage, the *Standard* newspaper reported that at least 13 bodies that had been taken to Parerenyatwa Hospital tested positive posthumously (*Standard*, 26 July 2020).

Deplorable conditions in quarantine and isolation centres

In another dimension, the quarantine and isolation centres that were established for returning residents from the other countries in the region and beyond lacked basic facilities and services as they did not receive meaningful support from the government. This was a gross violation of people's socio-economic rights. Some of the quarantine centres were largely uninhabitable as they offered sub-standard accommodation, had shortage of PPEs and had no running water which was critical in the fight against the pandemic. People were overcrowded and did not receive adequate food rations in these quarantine centres (Zimbabwe Peace Project, February 2021). Food shortages and overcrowding conditions often threatened the stay of inmates and exposed to the fast-spreading virus. Many, particularly those who tested negative to Covid-19, became hostile as they wanted to leave these facilities (Ibid). In the end, these quarantine and isolation centres turned out to be fertile breeding grounds for the spread of the Corona virus as the government failed to fulfil basic human needs such as supply of reasonable accommodation, food and running water as enshrined in the country's constitution and other international treaties. Section 77 of the Constitution of Zimbabwe, for instance, clearly states that "every person has the right to (a) safe, clean and potable water (b) sufficient food; and the State must take reasonable legislative and other measures... to achieve the progressive realisation of this right" (Constitution of Zimbabwe Amendment (No. 20) Act, 2013: 38).

The poor living conditions forced many people to escape from these holding centres. Security agents, whose salaries were also pathetic just like other civil servants, were routinely accused of taking bribes and allowing people to leave the quarantine centres (Mutero, Interview: 10 December 2021). As such, the authorities in Zimbabwe were having a torrid time in dealing with returnees who evaded quarantine centres. By mid-July 2020, the Zimbabwe Republic Police confirmed that it could not account for 215 returnees who had bolted from quarantine centres around the country (*Southern Times*, 17 July 2020). Many escaped returnees often reunited with their families and relatives without being tested and this posed further threats to the government's efforts to curb the spread of the deadly Corona virus.

There are numerous examples across the country which illustrate the challenges that were encountered in quarantine centres. In early August 2020, for instance, there was pandemonium at Masvingo Teachers' College quarantine centre when 12 returnees from South Africa and Botswana tested positive for Corona virus (*Pindula News*, 10 August 2020). A Ministry of Health and Child Care official who preferred anonymity commented: 'There is nothing right at Masvingo Teachers' College Covid-19 quarantine centre. Quarantined returnees from neighbouring South Africa and Botswana go about without personal protective equipment, not even masks" (Shumba, Online Interview: 20 July 2020). The health official further stated that nothing was being done to ensure that the 12 returnees who had tested positive to the Corona virus were being treated as inadequate attention was being given to the virus (Ibid). Some residents from the Rujeko Suburb in the city of Masvingo queried how people at the Masvingo Teachers' College Covid 19 isolation centre were allowed to move around without putting on masks. As consistently reported in the Zimbabwean newspapers and *Studio 7*, the same challenges were encountered at other quarantine centres in other cities, for example, Hillside and United College of Education Teachers' Colleges, Bulawayo Polytechnic (Bulawayo), Mkoba Teachers' College (Gweru), and Belvedere Teachers' College (Harare), among others (*Kubatana.net*, 28 May 2020). Furthermore, some health officials at Masvingo General Hospital also indicated that the government seemed to be deliberately under-testing and downplaying the Covid-19 statistics for the same reasons already outlined (Mutero, Interview: 10 December 2021).

While the returnees were supposed to be subjected to a 14-day quarantine period, some were accused of bribing their way out or escaped from the centres following delays in testing. Besides, due to inadequate resources to look after patients in isolation for two weeks as recommended by WHO, Zimbabwe, like other African countries, reduced the mandated quarantine period to one week (Mavhunga, 2020). Tracing the escapees was sometimes difficult because some of the quarantined people lacked proper documentation while others falsified information about their identities. Interestingly, the inability of the relevant authorities to test for the Corona virus, even in situations where potential cases had been tracked down, was a big challenge. Additionally, once a person tested positive at a quarantine centre, they were immediately sent home to self-quarantine. However, some of these people were sometimes seen going about their usual business in their localities, and in the process spread the virus (Dandara, Interview: 20 November 2021).

As corroborated by Doctor Agnes Mahomva, the Chief Covid-19 Co-ordinator in the Office of the President and Cabinet, there was a significant rise in infections when returnees started to leave quarantine facilities without permission. She indicated:

> We have actually managed to link a very large percentage of the cases to those who escaped from quarantine facilities. We are worried more about possible cases of irregular migration. These are people who are highly mobile (border jumpers) and meet a lot of people you cannot even trace...At this point, the masses need to learn what to do. Returnees from abroad have a right to their soils. So, returning home is unstoppable, but adherence to quarantine is very important and we should strengthen it (*Southern Times*, 17 July 2020: 1).

This section has examined the squalid and difficult conditions in Zimbabwe's Covid-19 quarantine and isolation centres. It has noted how adherence to the quarantine environment was difficult since the conditions in the centres were not conducive for decent human habitation. This left many people with little option but to find their way out of the quarantine centres as their rights to food, clean water and adequate shelter were trampled upon. Consequently, the risk of the pandemic spreading across the general population became higher.

Struggle for livelihoods in an informalised economy

The informalisation of the economy over the years made it difficult for ordinary Zimbabweans to enjoy some basic socio-economic rights during the pandemic. While the country had been under a 21-day total lockdown since 30 March 2020, the government was eventually forced to gradually ease conditions to revive an ailing economy that was characterised by severe shortages of foreign currency, electricity, food and medicines, among others. The government was forced to make very difficult choices between maintaining sustained lockdowns and opening up the economy in an environment in which there were no meaningful social security nets for the vulnerable people. Given that the government was unable to provide adequate social safety support, the continuation of lockdown measures was tantamount to completely annihilating peoples' livelihood rights through disruption of their sources of income. This inevitably rendered the lockdown measures ineffective as people defied them with impunity in an effort to make ends meet. As one vendor from the mining settlement of Mashava in Masvingo Province asked rhetorically: "If a government with a well-defined budget cannot provide basic care for people in isolation and quarantine centres, what hope would vulnerable people like the elderly, youth, women and people with disabilities who depend on the informal sector for their daily incomes have?" (Mukaro, Interview: 20 December 2021).

In Zimbabwe during the lockdown period, over 90% of people worked in the informal economy and could not afford to stay at home. The informal economy, including artisanal mining, contributed significantly to the country's economy, household welfare as well as filling the social protection gaps created by the socio-economic meltdown (Zimbabwe Congress of Trade Unions, 31 March 2020). People in the informal economy could not afford a day's loss in income in a collapsed economy without any other form of livelihood support from the government or any other source of income. The challenges brought about by Covid-19 in accessing livelihoods seemed to push the vulnerable groups even more and more into the open.

In the former mining settlement of Mashava, for instance, while the informal market stalls remained closed in accordance with government Covid-19 guidelines, there was "a gold and chrome rush" by people from all walks of life including civil servants (Govo,

Interview: 15 December 2021). In these places, no social distancing and sanitisation were practised in accordance with WHO guidelines on Covid-19. Lockdown fatigue also forced people to operate illegal businesses including shebeens in low-income settlements across the country. At times, no social distancing and face masking were practised in these places which could operate throughout the night. The situation was aggravated by the corrupt law-enforcement agencies that collected bribes from shebeen owners and left them to operate as they wished instead of enforcing curfew and other lockdown measures (Makura, Interview: 13 December 2021). As highlighted by some informants, the corrupt activities at times involved very high-ranking police officials.

At the inception of the first Covid-19-induced lockdown in Zimbabwe, the government was very clear on what was to be done to curb the spread of the pandemic. While social distancing, regularly washing hands with clean running water, and using sanitisers were deemed integral in containing the spread of the pandemic, there were structural challenges within the Zimbabwean set-up that made realisation of some of these requirements a mirage. In an economy characterised by hyperinflation, skyrocketing prices of basic commodities and shortage of other essentials, many people found it difficult to stay at home; thus, they were forced to occasionally venture out of their homes to sustain their livelihoods. Most people could not keep adequate stocks of basic necessities in their homes and had to replenish them from time to time.

It was during the search for basic livelihood necessities such as water, healthcare and food that most people found it difficult to socially distance as they went about their business. Indeed, it was pretty difficult for many urbanites that lived in close quarters without running water to meet some of these requirements. In some cities such as Harare, Bulawayo, Mutare, Bindura, Gweru and Masvingo, residents in high-density areas did not have regular supply and access to running water. They would spend hours on end queuing for water at boreholes where social distancing and sanitisation were difficult to practise (Muzvarirwofa & Moyo, 2020). In addition, shortage of basic commodities, such as mealie-meal, in the high-density suburbs across the country exacerbated the situation (Makombe, 2021). While people were encouraged to stay at home, the hand-to-mouth type of life they were accustomed to would not permit that. People were seen in long winding queues waiting for their turn to get mealie-meal with no social distancing being practised which was also a recipe for the spread of the Corona virus (Ibid).

Though it was initially envisaged that the pandemic would have little impact on rural areas, it was soon discovered that these spaces were also affected considerably as they did not operate in isolation. It is a fact that rural livelihoods and economies are intricately linked to urban and national economies through a complex network of production, migration, trade and remittance flows (*Economist*, 2020; Josephson *et al*, 2020). These intricate linkages made rural economies and livelihoods severely susceptible to undesirable impacts of the Covid-19 pandemic. Like urban dwellers, rural communities were regularly forced to rummage around in crowded places in search of livelihood necessities such as mealie-meal and other food items that were donated by non-governmental organisations (Ibid).

Overcrowding in the state-contracted Zimbabwe United Passenger Company (ZUPCO) buses and the few public taxis which operated illegally against lockdown measures also made the containment of Covid-19 difficult. At police checkpoints, the hungry and underpaid security agents often took bribes and allowed the overcrowded public taxis to pass through instead of enforcing the lockdown regulations. Security guards at supermarkets across the country had a torrid time in trying to enforce social distancing measures as people waited for their turn to enter into supermarkets. Some guards at different supermarkets confirmed that they were frequently abused by customers who deliberately and negligently ignored social distancing measures. A security guard at Pick-and-Pay Supermarket in Masvingo had this to say:

> I have been constantly reminded by some customers in these queues that the fact that I have a thermometer, surgical spirit or sanitiser does not qualify me to be a nurse or doctor and I should mind my business. Mob psychology plays a big role as other customers will join in and dress you down as you do your job. So, in the end, we end up failing to execute our duties in spite of the looming danger of the Corona virus spreading if people do not sanitise and maintain social distancing (Mototi, Interview: 15 April 2020).

These sentiments were corroborated by another guard at OK Supermarket in Masvingo who pointed out that customers were not concerned about social distancing and were easily offended if you asked them to step back. This situation was also rampant at banks countrywide where some people even had the audacity to borrow pens from strangers which was not safe as sharing of objects was discouraged in containing the spread of the Corona virus. Thus, the search for livelihood rights such as access to medicines, staple foods and other daily necessities in a contrived economy exposed the people to the virus. It also made the enforcement of the government's restrictive measures difficult.

Poverty and food shortages

The Covid-19 epidemic drove many people into hunger and poverty in Zimbabwe. A report by the Zimbabwe National Statistics Agency (ZimStat) in 2020 revealed that due to the economic contraction triggered by the pandemic and a swell in the prices of basic commodities, 50% of the Zimbabwean population faced extreme poverty (ZimStat, 23 July 2021). At the same time, humanitarian assistance and social protection programmes were reportedly limited. While the plight of many people across the globe had been the fear of contracting the virus, many vulnerable people, particularly in rural Zimbabwe, were primarily concerned with the struggle to put at least a meal a day on the table in a challenged economic environment. As Josephson *et al* (2020) observed, food insecurity was disproportionally experienced by households that were already impoverished before the pandemic.

The African Union, in its findings on the socio-economic effects of Covid-19 on the continent, exposed that international prices for key food commodities such as wheat and rice had a significant impact on countries such as Zimbabwe that were net importers of these (Ordu, 2021). In the challenging economic environment, the attainment of Sustainable Development Goals (SDGs) of zero hunger and poverty set up by the United Nations as part of Agenda 2030 remained a pipe dream. Some children in the rural Zimbiri Village of Mashonaland East Province who had been left behind by their father who had gone to work in the mines and were looked after by their grandparents innocently confessed that they survived by eating guava fruits. They had completely lost contact with their father since the imposition of the Covid-19-induced lockdown in March 2020. The father had not returned or contacted anyone since he did not have a mobile phone and the children had to fend for themselves (*Business Times*, 9-20 July 2020). This, in essence, was against moral and constitutional governance. How then would such people be able to deal with the challenges posed by the Covid-19 pandemic?

Obviously, if they could not afford at least a decent meal a day, they could not also be in a position to afford to buy the sanitisers, masks or even soap which were basic necessities in the fight against the pandemic. This situation was reminiscent of the experiences of many families across the country who survived on donor food handouts in the collapsed economic environment exacerbated by Covid-19.

In winding up this section, it can be observed that the Covid-19 pandemic brought about a number of challenges which made it difficult for people to fulfil certain socio-economic rights in an economy which was highly informal. The people were forced to make very difficult choices, that is, to stay at home and die of hunger or venture out of their homes and risk contracting the Corona virus. In the end, for most people especially those in rural Zimbabwe, Covid-19 ended up as being the least of their worries as they had pressing bread and butter issues to attend to. As they ventured out of their homes in search of livelihood rights, many did not even take the message about the risks of Covid-19 seriously as for some, it was an epidemic that affected those in the cities or the white people. As such, many did not even bother to put on masks. Indeed, it appeared the generality of the population in both rural and urban areas put on the masks for fear of being arrested by the law-enforcement agents rather than to protect themselves and others from contracting the Corona virus. These views are based on the author's personal experiences, observations and interactions with some people in the Chivi District of Masvingo Province.

Porosity of borders

One of the greatest challenges in the fight against the pandemic involved preventing it from entering the country. Among other factors, the porosity of the country's borders made it very difficult for the officials to effectively monitor the movement of travellers, even those from countries with known high numbers of infections. This was true with regards to travellers and returnees from neighbouring countries such as Mozambique, South Africa, Botswana, Namibia and Zambia. As a result, up to around July 2020, most of the people who tested positive to Covid-19 were returnees. The porosity of Zimbabwean borders made it very easy for people to move in and out of the country in search of livelihoods rights (Zimbabwe Peace Project, February 2021).

Many people from neighbouring countries took advantage of the porous borders and used undesignated entry points into the country. For some border communities, especially between Zimbabwe and Mozambique, the border only existed artificially in their minds as they were effectively 'a people of two worlds' (Hlongwana, 2018). Border porosity was also complicated by the complicity of the Zimbabwean underpaid security officials who accepted bribes from border jumpers. The underpaid border officials at the designated points of entry also routinely took bribes from people who were desperate to avoid the screening process (Makura, Interview: 25 November 2021). As a result, the unrestricted movement of people between Zimbabwe and its neighbours was a big catalyst in the spread of the pandemic. As the then Health and Child Care Minister, Obadiah Moyo, highlighted:

> We discovered that trucks from South Africa would stop before the border and people would alight and cross the Limpopo on foot and then get back onto the truck after it crosses the border. Police also intercepted illegal immigrants from Malawi and some of them tested positive. They will be sent home (*Herald*, 26 July 2021: 1).

In this way, the immigrants avoided immigration and quarantine formalities thereby posing the greatest risk for Covid-19 transmission in the country. Some of these returnees were coming from the continent's hot spots such as South Africa, Mozambique and Zambia which had over 20 000 confirmed Covid-19 cases by the end of May 2020. By May 2021, around 234 000 Zimbabwean migrants had returned from neighbouring countries since the outbreak of Covid-19 (European Commission, 2021). These statistics clearly demonstrate that fighting an epidemic in a struggling economy is no easy task. Coupled with that was corruption by public officials who were themselves deprived of their right to fair wages, hence their resort to unorthodox ways of survival.

Education

While access to education is a basic human right, it proved difficult for many children to continue learning during the Covid-19 pandemic due to the restrictive measures that were put in place by the government. Section 75 of the Constitution of Zimbabwe specifies that "every citizen and permanent resident of Zimbabwe has a right to basic state-funded education, including adult education, and that the state must take reasonable legislative and other measures, within the limits of the resources to it, to achieve the realisation of this right" (Constitution of Zimbabwe, Amendment (No 2) Act 2013: 37). This is reinforced in Article 26 of the UDHR which states that everyone has the right to education (UNICEF, 2015).

In late March 2020, with inadequate warning and nothing put in place to facilitate distance learning, schools were closed across the country, triggering a lot of fear and anxiety especially among pupils (*Newsday*, 20 March 2020). The lockdown measures that were put in place were in sync with the WHO guidelines on how to combat the spread of the pandemic. Thereafter, learning institutions were regularly closed each time the government announced a lockdown. During the extended closure of schools, the government struggled to ensure that all children had access to remote learning. The majority of children, especially those in remote parts of the country, could not cope with distance and online learning due to lack of electronic equipment and adequate support structures. This had far-reaching consequences on the children's right to education and social well-being (ZimStat Report, 2020). As demonstrated in the table below, most children, particularly those in rural areas, were unable to engage in distance or online learning. The statistics in the table clearly demonstrate that access to education during the pandemic was skewed. In the end, this threatened to exacerbate disproportion in education outcomes, poverty diminution and human development.

Table: Indicators of Zimbabwean households and individuals able to access education and supporting gadgets in percentage terms

Access to education	National	Urban	Rural	Male Head	Female Head
Completed assignments from teachers	15	21	11	17	13
Listened to educational radio programmes	2	2	1	2	1
Watched educational TV programmes	1	3	0	1	2
Used mobile learning applications	2	6	0	2	2

Source: ZimStat, 'Monitoring Covid-19 impacts on households in Zimbabwe,' Report Number 3, 30 June 2021

Although the government eventually launched educational programmes on radio and television, these were only accessed by people with these electronic gadgets. Likewise, online learning could only be enjoyed by those with internet access. The situation was particularly dire in rural areas with limited access to electricity and airwaves which rendered connectivity to radio, television and the internet a big challenge. A 2020 report by the United Nations on Zimbabwe noted: "It is predominantly urban and middle-class households who are able to access this e-learning, with many in low-income rural and high-density urban and peri-urban areas being currently left behind due to lack of digital equipment and support structures" (United Nations, 2000).

Similarly, another report by the Women's Academy for Leadership and Political Excellence (WALPE, 2020) also highlighted that about 15% of the surveyed school-going pupils could access e-learning platforms while the rest could not. The World Bank (2021) also indicated that when schools were closed during the lockdowns, there was limited accessibility to remote learning in rural areas, particularly among poor households. It concluded that only 9% of school-going children in rural areas had access to mobile applications during the Covid-19-related school closures compared with 40% for children in urban areas (Ibid).

Furthermore, some school heads in Masvingo Province confirmed that due to limited resources including electricity, they were not even able to set up e-learning platforms at their institutions. The situation could have been pretty much the same in other public and council-run schools dotted around the country. Thus, there is no doubt that students from poor backgrounds and those in remote areas were at great risk of missing out on education during the pandemic (Shumba, 2020). These students neither had access to smart phones with learning applications nor mobile data to access the applications. As a result, they were disenfranchised from the educational system.

Universities were left on their own and their Covid-19 responses varied from institution to institution depending on the available resources and resourcefulness (*Hub EdTech eLearning Africa*, 2020). At Great Zimbabwe University in Masvingo Province, for example, both students and lecturers were initially given mobile data by the institution in order to facilitate e-learning. This was eventually stopped in mid-2021 as the institution realised that this was not sustainable due to limited financial resources. A lecturer at Midlands

State University in the Midlands Province confirmed that the situation was pretty much the same at their institution (Govo, Interview: 24 January 2022). He further indicated that not all students were able to access e-learning platforms due to limited connectivity challenges in some remote areas or lack of appropriate internet-enabled gadgets (Ibid).

It is also important to note that in many learning institutions across all levels, the majority of students and tutors lacked experience in distance teaching and learning. The teachers were deficient in suitable training to design and manage remote learning programmes. The learners found it difficult to study enough content through distance learning. Thus, the teachers were ill-equipped to deal with this 'new normal' as well as their students (Hub, 2020). Besides, the underpaid teachers and lecturers lacked enough zeal to engage in remote learning. The treatment of civil servants was in direct contravention of Section 65 of the Constitution of Zimbabwe which stipulates that every person has "the right to fair labour practices and standards and to be paid fair and reasonable wage" (Constitution of Zimbabwe, 2013: 32). This is in line with the International Covenant on Economic, Social and Cultural Rights which seeks to promote and protect "the right to work in just and favourable conditions, the right to social protection, to an adequate standard of living and to the highest attainable standards of physical and mental well-being" (UNICEF, 2015).

Some children were more vulnerable to the impact of the closure of schools than others depending on the extent to which their home environments were suitable for learning. For instance, children living with disabilities were among the worst affected by the disruptions to the education sector during the pandemic. A UNESCO report indicated that pupils with disabilities were disenfranchised during the lockdown as some of the teaching modalities introduced were not suitable for all students (UNESCO Rapid Assessment Report, November 2020). While alternative learning platforms such as radio and television were eventually introduced in June 2020, these were not accessible to children with hearing and visual impairments (Muchanga *et al*, 2020). As such, they did not benefit much from these platforms and were deprived of their right to education. In this regard, home schooling raised fundamental questions on educational quality and equity issues which emanated from discrepancies by children in accessing digital devices to work and learn online. Furthermore, girls were also severely affected as most of them spent much time engaged in family chores at the expense of home-based learning (Moyo, 2020). This was a clear demonstration of the gendered effects of the Covid-19 pandemic on the children's right to education.

Conclusion

This chapter has explored the challenges faced in the fight against the spread of the Covid-19 pandemic in Zimbabwe's collapsed economy and their human rights implications. The chapter demonstrated that while the government was cognisant of its responsibility and obligations to facilitate the fulfilment of certain individual livelihood rights as enshrined in the country's constitution, the African Charter of Human Rights (ACHR), UDHR and other international conventions, the fulfilment of these rights remained a distant thought in Zimbabwe. This was due to the multiple socio-economic and political challenges that faced the country through decades of corruption and mismanagement, among other economic ills. As a result of these multi-layered challenges, containing the spread of the Corona virus remained a remote prospect as the ordinary citizens also failed to adhere to the restrictive measures put in place by the government to contain its spread as they continued to exercise their basic livelihood rights.

As outlined in this chapter, the government struggled to come up with effective intervention strategies due to a number of challenges. It has also been established that the government failed to provide adequate safety nets for most vulnerable groups which was a direct violation of basic human rights. Weakened social protection nets in Zimbabwe left the poorest unprotected, with little or no safeguards at all to weather the storm. As a result, basic livelihood rights were trampled upon as the government struggled to provide safety nets for the people. Lamentably, the majority of citizens were made to choose between dying of hunger in their homes and venturing out with all the attendant risks of contracting the Corona virus. For the most food-insecure households, Covid-19 was the least of their worries. This inevitably made the containment of the Covid-19 pandemic in the country a huge challenge, if not a monumental task.

References

Akedu, T. (2021) 'Addressing the impacts of Covid-19 in food crises', FAO: Global Covid-19 Humanitarian Response Plan.

Altimier, L. and Seiver, A. (2020) 'The 2020 Covid-19 pandemic', in: *Journal of Neonatal Nursing*, Volume 26, Number 4, pp.183-191.

Beaumont. P. (1 May 2020) 'Where did Covid-19 come from? What we know about its origins', in: *Guardian*, Available at: https://www.theguardian.com/world/2020/may/01/, Accessed 15 December 2021.

Besada, H. & Moyo, N. (2008) 'Zimbabwe in crisis: Mugabe's policies and failures', Working Paper Number 38, Centre for International Governance and Innovation, Available at: https://www.eldis.org/document/A40189, Accessed 12 April 2022.

Bond, P. & Manyanya, M. (2002) *Zimbabwe's plunge: Exhausted nationalism, neoliberalism and the search for social justice*, Asmara: Africa World Press.

Business and Human Resource Centre (6 May 2020) 'Zimbabwe: Employees' rights during the Covid-19 and national lockdown', Harare: Business and Human Resource Centre.

Business Times (9-15 July 2020) 'In Africa, lack of Corona virus data raises fears of 'silent epidemic', Available at: http:www.businesstimes.co.zw, Accessed 9 July 2020.

Business Times, (9-15 July 2020) 'Impact of Covid-19 on rural children', Available at: http:ww.business.co.zw, Accessed 9 July 2020.

Capital, E. (2019) 'Zimbabwe', in: *Exotix: Developing Markets Guide*, Cham: Palgrave Macmillan, pp.829-841.

Chamunorwa, C. (12 December 2021) Interview: Masvingo General Hospital, Zimbabwe.

Chiumbu, S. & Musemwa, M. (eds.) (2012) *Crisis! What crisis? The multiple dimensions of the Zimbabwe crisis*, Cape Town: Human Sciences Research Council.

Dandara, E. (20 November 2021) Interview: Masvingo, Zimbabwe.

Dansereau, S. & Zamponi, M. (2005) *Zimbabwe: The political economy of decline*, Uppsala: Nordic Africa Institute.

Darrow, M. & Arbour, L. (2009) 'The pillar of glass: Human rights in the development operations of the United Nations,' in: *American Journal of International Law*, Volume 103, Number 3, pp.446-501.

Duri, F.P.T. (ed.) (2016) *Resilience amid adversity: Informal coping mechanisms to the Zimbabwean crisis during the new millennium*, Gweru: Booklove Publishers.

Economist (26 September 2020) 'From plague to penury: The pandemic is lunging millions back into extreme poverty', Available at: https://blog.naver.com/PostView.nhn?blogId=7littlegiant&logNo=222103598391, Accessed 22 December 2021.

European Commission (16 February 2022) 'Zimbabwe Fact Sheet,' Available at: https://www.ec.europa.eu/echo/where/africa/zimbabwe_en, Accessed 19 February 2022.

Evans, M. & Murray, R. (2008) *The African Charter on human and peoples' rights: The system in practice, 1986-2006,* Cambridge: Cambridge University Press.

Government of Zimbabwe (2013) *Zimbabwe Act No. 1: Constitution of Zimbabwe Amendment (No. 20)*, Harare: Government of Zimbabwe.

Govo, N. (24 January 2022) Interview: Midlands State University, Zimbabwe.

Guardian (9 July 2020) 'Zimbabwe health minister facing Corona virus corruption charge sacked', Available at: https://www.theguardian.com/global-development/, Accessed 21 December 2021.

Hammer, A. & Raftopoulos, B. (2003) 'Zimbabwe's unfinished business: Rethinking land, state and nation', in: A. Hammar, B. Raftopoulos & S. Jensen (eds.) *Zimbabwe's unfinished business: Rethinking land, state and nation in the context of the crisis*, Harare: Weaver Press.

Herald (26 July 2021) 'Covid-19 immigrants escape from isolation', Harare: Zimbabwe.

Hlongwana, J. (2018) 'A people of two worlds? Reflections on the role of cross-border ethnicity in sustaining a partitioned Ndau community between Mozambique and Zimbabwe (1975-2014)', in: F.P.T. Duri & N. Marongwe (eds.) *Contested spaces, restrictive mechanisms and corridors of opportunity: A social history of Zimbabwean borderlands and beyond since colonial period.* Gweru: Booklove Publishers, 2018.

Hub, E. (2020) 'The effect of Covid-19 on education in Africa and its implications for the use of technology: A survey of the experience and opinions of educators and technology specialists',

Available at: https://www.edtechhub.org/wp-content/uploads/2020/09/, Accessed 10 January 2022.
International Labour Organisation (2020) 'Covid-19 crisis and the informal economy, immediate responses and policy challenges', Available at: https://www.ilo.org/global/topics, Accessed 8 February 2022.
International Organisation for Migration. (2010) 'The Impact of the brain drain on health service delivery in Zimbabwe: A response analysis', Available at: https://www.iomzimbabwe/org/zw , Accessed 12 December 2021.
Josephson, A. Kilic, T. & Michler, J.D. (2020) 'Socio-economic impacts of Covid-19 in four African countries', Policy Research Working Papers, Available at: https://www.doi.org/10.1596/1813-9450-9466, Accessed 10 January 2022.
Karombo, T. (9-15 July 2020) 'Behold, Zimbabwe's new economic sheriff in town', in: *Business Times*, Available at: http:www.businesstimes.co.zw, Accessed 9 July 2020.
Keikelame, M.J. & Swartz, L. (2019) 'Decolonising research methodologies: Lessons from a qualitative research project', in: *Global Health Action*, Volume 12, Number 1, pp1-8.
Klynveld Peat Marwick Goerdele (KPMG) International (2020) 'Government response on a global landscape', Available at: https://www.home.kpmg/xx/en/home/insights/2020/o4/, Accessed 11 January 2022.
Kubatana.net (13 May 2020) 'Mpilo Covid-19 lab runs out of consumables', Available at: https://www.kubatana.net/2020/05/13/mpilo-covid-19-lab-runs-out-of-consumables, Accessed 12 December 2021.
Kubatana.net (28 May 2020) 'Quarantine centres a cause for concern,' Available at: https://www.kubatana.net/2020/05/28, Accessed 10 January 2022.
Kubatana.net (26 January 2022) 'ZimRights statement on the Universal Periodic Review of Zimbabwe on 26 January 2022 at the United Nations', Available at: http://www.kubatana.net/source/hrforum, Accessed 28 January 2022.
Kubatana.net (31 January 2022) 'Zimbabwe lockdown: Day 673-WCOZ Situation Report', Available at: https://kubatana.net/22/01/31, Accessed 23 February 2022.

Kudejira, D. (2020) 'Covid-19 and the plight of informal cross-border traders in Zimbabwe', Working paper, Social Sciences and Humanities: Research Council of Canada.

Kulkarni, P. (29 April 2020) 'Small vendors hard hit by government-ordered demolitions in Zimbabwe', Available at: https://peoplesdispatch.org/2020/04/29 /small-vendors-hard-hit-by-government-ordered-demolitions-in-zimbabwe/, Accessed 29 December 2022.

Lancet (15 August 2020) 'Covid-19 worsens Zimbabwe's health crisis', Available at: https://www.thelancet.com/journals/lancet/article/, Accessed 18 December 2021.

Lessing. D. (10 April 2003) 'The jewel of Africa', in: *The New York Review*, Available at: https://www.nybooks.com/articles/2003/04/10/the-jewel-of-africa, Accessed 10 February 2022.

Makombe, E.K. (2021) 'Between a rock and a hard place: The Corona virus, livelihoods, and socio-economic upheaval in Harare's high-density areas of Zimbabwe', in: *Journal of Developing Societies*, Number 37, Volume 3, pp.275-301.

Makura, J. (13 December 2021) Interview: King Mine, Mashava, Zimbabwe.

Maru, M.T. (24 March 2020) 'Covid-19: Why it is so difficult for Africa to flatten the curve', Available at: https://mg.co.za/article/2020-03-24-covid-19-why-it-is-so-difficult-for-africa-toflatten-the-curve/, Accessed 21 August 2021.

Masiyiwa, G (29 March 2020) 'Corona virus looms over Zimbabwe's fragile health care system', in: *Global Press Journal*, Available at: mailto:info@globalpressjournal.com, Accessed 28 July 2020.

Matizha, J. (20 April 2020) Interview: Gaths Mine, Mashava, Zimbabwe.

Matore, J. (20 July 2020) Online Interview: Masvingo, Zimbabwe.

Mavhinga, D. (4 September 2020) 'Mnangagwa's broken human rights promises two years on', Available at: https://www.theindependent.co.zw/2020/09/04, Accessed 10 January 2022.

Mazvarirwofa, K. & Moyo, F. (16 August 2020) 'Zimbabwe's crowded cities struggle to defend against Corona virus', Available at:

https://www.bignewsnetwork.com/news/266114164, Accessed 20 January 2022.

Mbiba, B. Chireka B. Kunonga, E. Gezi, K. Matsvai, P. & Manatse, Z. (2020) 'At the deep end: Covid-19 experiences of Zimbabwean health and care workers in the United Kingdom', in: *Journal of Migration and Health*, Volumes 1-2, pp.1-9.

Menocal, A.R. & Othieno, T. (12-13 July 2008) 'The World Bank in fragile situations: An Issue Paper', Paper prepared for a Conference on 'An Eye on the future: The World Bank Group Changing World,' Amsterdam, Available at: https://odi.org/en/publications/the-world-bank-in, Accessed 18 December 2021.

Ministry of Health and Child Care, Zimbabwe (2 April 2020) 'Zimbabwe guidelines on the management of Covid-19,' Harare: Ministry of Health and Child Care, Republic of Zimbabwe.

Mlambo, A.S. (1997) *The economic structural adjustment programme: The case of Zimbabwe, 1990-1995*, Harare: University of Zimbabwe Publications.

Moser, C. & Norton, A. (2001) *To claim our rights: Livelihood security, human rights and sustainable development*, London: Overseas Development Institute.

Mototi, J. (15 April 2020) Interview: Masvingo City, Zimbabwe.

Moyo, N. (2020) 'Covid-19 and the future of practicum in teacher education in Zimbabwe: Rethinking the 'new normal' in quality assurance for teacher certification', in: *Journal of Education for Teaching*, Volume 46, Number 4, pp.536-545.

Moyo-Nyede, S. (29 October 2021) 'Zimbabweans blame government, not sanctions, for country's economic meltdown', in: *Afrobarometer*, Dispatch Number 485, 29 October 2021.

Muchanga, M. (2020) 'Exploring educational lives of the excluded youth under Covid-19 in the SADC region', Randburg: Jet Education Services.

Muguti. T. (2016) 'Accounting for the rising popularity of African Traditional Medicine as a panacea to the Zimbabwean crises since 2000', in: F.P.T. Duri (ed.) *Resilience amid adversity: Informal coping mechanisms to the Zimbabwean crisis during the new millennium*, Gweru: Booklove Publishers, pp.99-116.

Mukaro, J. (20 December 2021) Interview: Balmain Shopping Centre, Mashava, Zimbabwe.

Mumbengegwi, C. (ed.) (2002) *Macroeconomic and structural adjustment policies in Zimbabwe*, New York: Palgrave-Macmillan.

Munyaka, J. (20 October 2020) Interview: Great Zimbabwe University Mashava Campus Clinic, Zimbabwe.

Mutero, C. (10 December 2021) Interview: Gaths Mine, Mashava, Zimbabwe.

Ndlovu-Gatsheni, S.J. (2013) *Empire, global coloniality and African subjectivity*, New York: Berghahn Books.

Nelson P.J. (2007) 'Human rights, the Millennium Development Goals, and the future of development cooperation', in: *World Development*, Volume 35, Number 12, pp.2041-2055.

New Zimbabwe (28 December 2018) 'Government moves to block doctors' strike; VP says junior doctors not qualified- still students', Available at: https://www.newzimbabwe.com, Accessed 21 January 2022.

Newsday (20 March 2020) 'ED orders schools, varsities closure', Harare: Zimbabwe.

Newsday (17 December 2021) 'Mass exodus of health staff cause for concern,' Harare: Zimbabwe.

Newsday (14 January 2022) 'Zimbabwe's human rights record under spotlight', Harare: Zimbabwe.

Newsday (24 January 2022) 'Come clean on abuses, government told', Harare: Zimbabwe.

Nolan, A. (2015) 'Not fit for purpose? Human rights in times of financial and economic crisis', Available at: https://www:ssrn.com.abstract=2662881, Accessed 20 December 2021.

Nyawo, C. & Rich, T. (1980) 'Zimbabwe after independence,' in: *Review of African Political Economy: Special Issue on Zimbabwe*, Number 18, pp.89-93.

Ordu, A.U. (2021) 'Foresight Africa top priorities for the continent in 2022', Available at: https://www.africaportal.org/publications, Accessed 18 December 2021.

Pindula News (27 May 2020) 'Chaos at Masvingo Quarantine Centre after 12 returnees test positive for Corona', Available at: https://news.pindula,co.zw/p=166806, Accessed 10 August 2020.

Pindula News (12 January 2022) 'MDC Alliance demands urgent action on the deepening national crisis', Available at: https://news.pindula.co.zw/2022/01/11/, Accessed 10 February 2022.

Pindula News (27 January 2022) 'UN member states say human rights violators in Zimbabwe must be held accountable', Available at: https://news.pindula.co.zw/2022/01/27/un-member, Accessed 10 February, 2022.

Raftopoulos, B. & Sachikonye, L. (eds.) (2001) *Striking back: The labour movement and the post-colonial state in Zimbabwe, 1980-2000*, Harare: Weaver Press.

Ribeiro, M. (2020) 'Immediate socio-economic response to Covid-19 in Zimbabwe: A framework for integrated policy analysis and support', Available at: https://www.academia.edu/71497869, Accessed 11 February 2022.

Riddell, R.C. (1984) 'Zimbabwe: The economy four years after independence', in: *African Affairs*, Volume 83, Number, 333, pp.463-476.

Rwodzi, A. (2019) 'Democracy, governance and legitimacy in Zimbabwe since the November 2017 military coup', in: *Cadernos de Estudos Africanos*, Volume 38, pp.193-213.

Scoones, I. (10 May 2021) 'Rural livelihoods in the pandemic: Notes from Zimbabwe', Available at: https://www.zimbabweland.worldpress.com/2021/05/10/rural-livelihoods-in-the-pandemic-notes-from-zimbabwe, Accessed 15 January 2022.

Shumba, S. (20 July 2020) Online Interview: Bere Township, Mashava, Zimbabwe.

Southern Times (17 July 2020) 'Hundreds flee quarantine centres', Available at: https://www.facebook.com/southernafricanews/posts/3218975121458548, Accessed 15 February 2022.

Taubenberger, J.K. & Morens, D.M. (2006) '1918 Influenza: The mother of all pandemics', in: *Emerging Diseases*, Volume12, Number 1, pp.15 22.

Tehran Times (15 April 2020) 'Theories on origins of Covid-19 disease', Available at: https://www.tehrantimes.com/news/446831, Accessed 10 May 2021.

UNDP (17 July 2020) 'Contextualising the UN Global Framework in Zimbabwe: Preliminary impact of Covid-19 in Zimbabwe', Available at: https://zimbabwe.un.org/en/download/13451/50201, Accessed 20 December 2021.

UNESCO (November 2020) 'Rapid Assessment Report', Available at: https://en.unesco.org/news/rapid-assessment, Accessed 20 December 2021.

UNFPA (2005) 'Human Rights Principles', Available at: https://www.unfpa.org/resources/human-rights-principles, Accessed 20 December 2021.

UNICEF (2015) 'What are human rights?' Available at: https://www.unicef.org/media/press-centre, Accessed 7 January 2022.

United Nations (2020) 'Immediate socio-economic response to Covid-19 in Zimbabwe', Available at: https://zimbabwe.un.org/en/50201, Accessed 21 December 2021.

United Nations Committee for the Coordination of Statistical Activities (CCSA) (15 May 2020) 'How Covid-19 is changing the world: A statistical perspective,' Available at: https://unstats.un.org/unsd/ccsa/principles_stat_activities, Accessed 10 August 2021.

Vaccine Tracker (11 February 2021) 'Five vaccines approved for use in Zimbabwe', Available at: https://www.covid19.trackvaccines.org, Accessed 21 February 2022.

Women's Academy for Leadership and Political Excellence (2020) 'Report by the Women's Academy for Leadership and Political Excellence,' Harare: WALPE.

World Bank (10 June 2021) 'Zimbabwe economic update: Covid-19 further complicates Zimbabwe's economic and social conditions', Available at: https://www.worldbank/org/en/region/africa, Accessed 10 January 2022.

World Health Organisation (2020) 'Covid-19 updates', Available at: https://covid19.who.int, Accessed 21 December 2021.

World Press (15 March 2021) 'Vaccine politics in Zimbabwe', Available at: https://www.zimbabweland.worldpress.com/2021/3/15/vaccine-politics-zimbabwe, Accessed 15 January 2022.

Xinhuanet (24 April 2021) 'Zimbabwe aims to attain herd immunity by year-end: VP Chiwenga', Available at: http://www.xinhuanet.com/english/2021-04/24/c_139903301.htm, Accessed 8 February 2022.

Zimbabwe Congress of Trade Unions (31 March 2020) 'ZCTU response to the impact of Covid-19 (Corona virus) pandemic on workers and the Zimbabwean economy', Available at: https://cwc.ituc-csi.org/IMG/pdf/zctu, Accessed 22 December 2021.

Zimbabwe Independent (22 May 2020) 'Covid-19 bombshell - Zim test kits run out', Harare: Zimbabwe.

Zimbabwe Independent (1 October 2021) 'Health personnel exodus hits public hospitals', Harare, Zimbabwe.

Zimbabwe Peace Project (February 2021) *The impact of Covid-19 on socio-economic rights in Zimbabwe*, Harare: Zimbabwe Peace Project.

Zimbabwe Standard (26 July 2020) '70 Parirenyatwa workers test positive to Covid-19', Harare: Zimbabwe.

Zimbabwe Statistical Agency (2020) *Rapid Poverty, Income, Consumption and Expenditure Surveys (PICES), Telephone Monitoring Survey Report*, 2020, Harare: Zimbabwe Statistical Agency.

Zimstat (23 July 2021) 'Half of Zimbabweans faced extreme poverty in 2020 due to Covid-19: Rapid Poverty Income Consumption and Expenditure Survey (PICES)', Available at: https://worldbank.org/en/country/zimbabwe, Accessed 9 January 2021.

Chapter 8

Between a Rock and a Hard Surface: Reflecting on the Experiences of Informal Sector Participants During the Covid-19-Induced Lockdowns in Mashava, Zimbabwe

Ngonidzashe Marongwe & Tasara Muguti

Introduction

This chapter analyses the challenges faced by Zimbabweans involved in the informal sector in the Mashava area of Masvingo Province in the face of Covid-19-induced lockdowns that were meant to curb the spread of the highly infectious disease from 2020. As has become common-sense, the start of the year 2020 saw the world being engulfed by one of the worst epidemics in recent times, the Covid-19 (also known as Corona virus) pandemic. The last epidemic of similar magnitude to hit the world, often referred to as 'the mother of all epidemics' because of its devastating impact, was the Spanish influenza of 1918 to 1919 (Taubenberger & Morens, 2006). The Covid-19 pandemic, which spread across the globe with disquieting speed, had cumulatively recorded 255 324 963 confirmed infections and 5 127 696 deaths of people by 17 November 2021 (World Health Organisation, 17 November 2021). At this point in time, Zimbabwe had recorded 133 647 infections, 4 699 deaths and 128 437 recoveries from the same pandemic (*Worldometer*, 22 November 2021).

The exponential spreading of Covid-19 resulted in almost all countries of the world imposing stiff restrictions and lockdowns to proscribe the movement of people, whether locally or across their borders, to contain the lethal and mutating virus. Resultantly, many economic, social and political activities across the globe were put in intensive care units and brought to a near-standstill. For Zimbabwe, restrictions on the movement of people began with the imposition of the 21-day highly securitised lockdown from the 30th of March 2020 to the 19th of April 2020 (Statutory Instrument 83 of 2020). Subsequently, this lockdown was extended and followed up by many other lockdowns that curtailed domestic travel. Also, between the 30th of March 2020 up to the end of February 2022, international travel by road remained circumscribed, with only, at least officially, the countries' land borders restricted only to the conveyancing of commercial cargo, returning residents and those Zimbabweans with work or living permits in other countries (Statutory Instrument 83 of 2020; Statutory Instrument 18 of 2022). Air travel to and from international destinations, however, remained operational without many restrictions. On the whole, since March 2020, the national lockdown measures in Zimbabwe were systematically reviewed with certain restrictions either being eased or tightened depending on the situation on the ground pertaining to the infection, death and recovery rates as well as vaccination statistics.

The restrictions on the movement of people, especially those that were not classified as providing essential services by the various Statutory Instruments, which provided the decrees of the lockdowns with some legal force, resulted in a number of challenges for many sectors of the Zimbabwean economy. The informal sector, which was Zimbabwe's largest sector by employment figures, potential contribution to the sustenance of the economy and the upholding of livelihoods in the country, was one of the areas that were hardest hit. Among others, the imposition of the lockdowns criminalised the pursuance of some ventures in this sector, resulting in varying forms of cat-and-mouse encounters with the police. Additionally, some formal businesses, for example, bars and nightclubs, upon which some informal traders depended on, remained shut up to the beginning of October 2021 (*Herald*, 6 October 2021). Furthermore, the state imposed relatively harsh conditions for the resumption of business by the informal sector, including the compulsory requirement that every business had to have thermometer/s to check on incoming clients' body temperatures, and hand sanitising equipment. These requirements were, however, made without the Zimbabwean government attempting to help the struggling members to install these. This failure to assist has to be considered alongside the fact that ordinarily, informal traders are characterised by minimal or zero savings and restricted access to finance. Furthermore, the challenges posed by the Covid-19 lockdowns should be examined in the context that informal sector traders lack the privilege or means to social distance or work from home.

It is the contention of this chapter that the challenges the different members of the informal sector faced during the extended periods of the lockdowns, as much threatened the very existence of the sector and its participants as they also violated many of their rights as citizens whose livelihoods depended on informal activities in a toxic economic environment that was worsened by the outbreak of the Covid-19 pandemic. This is notwithstanding the fact that at the time this study was carried out, the epidemic's full impact had not been ascertained since it had not yet been brought under control as a cure had not been found. What cannot be denied, however, is that the Covid-19 pandemic was going to leave permanent scars on Zimbabwe's informal sector which would take long to erase.

Using a historical approach, the study is predominantly qualitative in nature, heavily relying on observations, online interviews and intermittent face-to-face interviews under the strict World Health Organisation (WHO) and Zimbabwe's Inter-Ministerial Taskforce guidelines on Covid-19, as well as desktop review. It is, however, significant to acknowledge that undertaking research during a pandemic such as Covid-19 when there were restrictions on movement was never an easy task. Linking up with potential respondents was a daunting task. As such, the study was largely based on observations and the involvement of a limited number of carefully selected participants. These partakers were largely informal sector actors scattered around Mashava whose livelihoods had been negatively affected by the inception of the government-imposed lockdown.

The population of Mashava is made up of both people of local and foreign origin. The foreigners, who are predominantly of Malawian origin, also include others from Mozambique and Zambia, who worked in colonial Shabanie and Mashaba Mines as migrant labourers or their descendants since the country was colonised in 1890. It is from these segments of the population that the participants were drawn from since they were the ones who were involved in informal sector activities since their forced retrenchment following the closure of formal mining activities in the area. Limited oral interviews afforded the researchers a window of opportunity to closely interact and effectively probe participants. Interviews were held with 50 people working full time in the informal sector and 20 working in the formal sector but also doubling in the informal sector to supplement their incomes. The areas covered during the study included Balmain Shopping Centre, Temaraire, Gaths Mine, King Mine, Boss Mine and Bere as these were the main sites for informal economic activities in Mashava. Desktop review, which augmented primary research, involved appropriate government and public documents on the informal sector. It also involved secondary data on the unfolding of the Zimbabwean crises, which have been a major impetus for the informalisation of the country's economy.

While it has been a generally accepted Eurocentric principle that studies should be premised within specific theories, this study is context-grounded. The researchers believe that the challenges faced in the informal economy in the country are borne out of a specific context, a context in which the socio-economic challenges facing the country evolved. The contested political terrain, characterised by disputed election outcomes, was always at the centre of problems facing Zimbabwe. This resulted in a fragile political set up, a fragile health delivery system and a fragile economic environment resulting in the informalisation of the economy which the country found itself in as people tried to make ends meet. As such, the study is underpinned on the 'fragile situations' contextual framework. This contextual framework is critical in addressing high level issues pertaining to the challenges posed by the Covid-19 epidemic on people whose livelihoods were largely dependent on an informal economy. While there may be a lack of consensus on what constitutes fragile situations, donor agencies such as the Department of Foreign and International Development (DFID), Canadian International Development Agency (CIDA), European Union (EU), United Nations Development Programme (UNDP) and United States Agency for International Development (USAID) perceive fragility as the failure by states to provide essential services to their people due to weak capacity, lack of political will or both (Menocal & Othieno, 2008). As rightly highlighted in the States of Fragility Report (2008), fragility can trigger negative outcomes such as breakdown of institutions, violence, displacement and humanitarian crises and/or other emergencies (States of Fragility Report, 2016).

The indicators above are consistent with the Zimbabwean situation in which the informal sector players found themselves in as the Covid-19 epidemic spread. As highlighted above, the concept of crises reverberates across the Zimbabwe socio-economic and political gamut. The crisis dimensions in the Zimbabwean context included crisis of legitimacy, political polarisation, governance, constitutionality, fragile economy, among others. All these are typical examples of fragility which had a direct bearing on the state of the Zimbabwean economy which largely became informal. The country plunged into a state of complete socio-economic collapse characterised by dilapidated health services, lack of clean water and unaffordable basic commodities. The ability of the government to deliver essential services remained in doubt as poor health services, unemployment and denial of opposition supporters food handouts at critical moments when the people were faced with starvation remained the order of the day.

The use of a contextual instead of a theoretical framework as a tool of analysis makes this study unique. Among other things, a contextual framework has the potential to be informed by the evidence from the research findings. This resonates with decolonial thinking which emphasises that anchoring research on theoretical frameworks has resulted in the overrepresentation of Eurocentric thought in knowledge production. Thus, as Ndlovu-Gatsheni (2013) rightly argues in his several works, there is need to unpack knowledge and repack it in African designs or re-do thinking itself. It is in this context that this chapter is rooted in local circumstances. Hence, it is within the context of the social, economic and political fragility that obtained in the country that the impact of Covid-19 on the informal economy in Mashava will be examined. The next section conceptualises Covid-19. A deep understanding of Covid-19 is germane and helps to situate the discussion of its influences on the informal sector into proper context.

Covid-19 and related restrictions in Zimbabwe

Corona viruses belong to a large family of viruses that may result in respiratory infections ranging from common to more serious diseases. As already intimated in the introduction of this chapter, Covid-19 was first diagnosed in Wuhan City in China in December 2019 but quickly spread around the world in the first months of 2020. The virus spreads primarily through droplets of saliva or discharge from the nose when an infected person coughs or sneezes. Covid-19 symptoms include: dry cough, fever, headache, fatigue, nausea, sore throat, breathing difficulties, muscle and body aches, vomiting, and a congested or running nose. The Corona virus can also be spread from person to person or through contact with infected surfaces. Many people infected by the virus may experience mild to moderate respiratory illness but may recover without undergoing special treatment. In some cases, Covid-19 can result in severe respiratory problems, kidney failure and/or even death. Older people and those living with underlying medical conditions such as diabetes, cardiovascular disease and cancer can easily develop serious illness if exposed to the virus (World health Organisation (WHO), 2020).

Health authorities emphasised that hand-washing using soap or an alcohol-based sanitiser for about 20 seconds, practising personal hygiene, social distancing, coughing into a flexed elbow, avoiding touching one's face, wearing of masks and dissemination of information were critical in curbing the spread of the Corona virus. Practising good hygiene was essential in that the virus was believed to survive on surfaces for about nine hours (Ibid).

By the end of February 2022, while numerous clinical trials to evaluate potential treatment were going on, no known specific remedy for Covid-19 had been found. However, there were numerous vaccines that had been developed to try to inoculate the world's population. These injectable vaccines included Sputnik, Sinovac, Sinopharm, Johnson and Johnson, Pfizer and Moderna (Vaccine Tracker, 11 February 2021). Added to the immunisations, physical distancing as well as masking up were believed to be effective in preventing the spread since the droplets did not normally travel more than a few feet and tended to fall to the ground or onto surfaces after a few seconds (Lauren & Sauer, 2020). As such, close contact with people who were unwell was discouraged. Self-isolation until one had recovered was also encouraged if someone had contracted the Corona virus. Touching one's mouth, eyes and nose was also discouraged. It should be noted that the Covid-19 pandemic followed in the long list of other disease outbreaks and pandemics recorded in history, such as the Spanish Flu, Hong Kong Flu, SARS, H7N9, Ebola and Zika (WHO, 2011), which all claimed millions of lives around the world.

Covid-19 proved to be an arduous threat to humanity in different aspects of life in a very short space of time. It impacted on how people live and interact, and also how they work, move around and travel. It resulted in the death of many people and destruction of national economies across the globe. Indeed, the epidemic had a huge impact on humanity through the disruption of lives and livelihoods. After its discovery in Wuhan in December 2019, Covid-19 had spread to 20 countries by the end of January 2020. By the end of February 2020, 54 countries had reported cases of Covid-19 and the number of countries affected by the pandemic continued to rise significantly thereafter. The number swiftly rose from 202 countries by the end of March 2020 to 212 in April 2020 (Committee for the Coordination of Statistical Activities, 2020). At the same time, in the first four months of 2020, the world recorded more than 3 million confirmed infections and more than 210 000 deaths (Shemin &

Dailey, 2020). By the 20th of July 2020, there were more than 14 348 858 confirmed cases in 188 countries and more than 603 691 deaths from Covid-19, primarily in China, Europe and North America (World Health Organisation, 19-20 July 2020).

As of mid-July 2020, as the world experienced a resurgence of infections, the number of Covid-19 cases and deaths among the most affected countries stood as follows: the United States of America: 3 773 260 infections, 140 543 deaths; Brazil: 2 098 389 infections, 79 488 deaths; India: 1 118 206 infections, 27 497 deaths; Russia: 777 311 infections, 12 323 deaths; South Africa: 364 328 infections, 5 033 deaths; Peru: 353 590 infections, 13 187 deaths; and Mexico: 344 224 infections and 39 184 deaths (Elflein, 2020).

Regarding Africa, the John Hopkins University and the Africa Centre for Disease Control on Covid-19 revealed that by the 13th of May 2020, all countries on the continent had recorded infections. The infections and deaths continued to escalate such that by 21st of July 2020, the Covid-19 statistics in Africa stood as follows: 736 587 active cases, 15 425 deaths and 389 314 recoveries with South Africa and Egypt the worst affected countries on the continent. The spread of the Covid-19 pandemic resulted in many African countries intensifying preventive and containment measures (Rahman & Shaban, 2020).

In Zimbabwe, the first case of Covid-19 was recorded in March 2020. While the rate at which the spread of Covid-19 in the country was retarded during the first four months of 2020, there was a considerable increase in infections from June. By the end of July 2020, the rate of daily infections in comparative terms, was becoming frightening. By the end of July 2020, with Harare and Bulawayo, the country's two biggest cities, being the epicentres of the pandemic, 2579 active cases and 69 confirmed Covid-19 deaths had been recorded (Ministry of Health and Child Care Covid-19 Update, 1 August 2020).

It should be highlighted that even before the June-July 2020 spike in the rate of Covid-19 infections, the government of Zimbabwe introduced national lockdowns to proscribe the movement of people in an effort to curtail the diffusion of the disease. As mentioned in the introduction, the government first proclaimed a total lockdown on 30 March 2020, initially for a period of three weeks (Statutory Instrument 83 of 2020). This completely restricted movement as people were made to stay at home with only those classified as providing essential services allowed to move. The restrictions were slightly relaxed between May and June 2020 as the government allowed for the partial opening of the economy and people were allowed limited movement; some people were allowed to go to work; colleges and universities were allowed to open for examinations, and some so-called essential service industries resumed operations (*Zimbabwean Mail*, 25 May 2020). However, most informal economic activities officially remained closed with the exception of those involved in the agricultural and mining sectors.

As Covid-19 infection rates continued to escalate, the Zimbabwean President, Emmerson Dambudzo Mnangagwa, announced a raft of new measures on 21 July 2020, christened Level 2 lockdown, in order to contain its spread. Under the new Covid-19 regulations, a dusk-to-dawn curfew was introduced and it was also directed that only those civil servants authorised by the Public Service Commission (PSC) were expected to report for work and the rest were to stay at home. The restrictions were extended to other sectors as workers were made to obtain letters of exemption from their employers that indicated that they would be providing critical services to be able to pass through police roadblocks. The rest of the citizenry was to stay at home or had to get clearance from the police to be able to travel in search of essential goods and services. Inter-city travel remained restricted except for essential services, funerals and work (*Zimbabwe Situation*, 21 July 2020).

It is important to acknowledge that the lockdowns were introduced at a time when 85% of employment in Africa was in the informal economy (Shemin & Dailey, 2020). In Zimbabwe, the informal sector accounted for 90% employment by 2020 (Dudzai & Wamara, 2021). Thus, the informal economy in Africa is not just a marginal phenomenon but relatively the space where the majority of people sustain themselves, sometimes precariously. In 2020, the informal economy contributed between 25% and 65% of the Gross Domestic Product (GDP) for all African states (Kiaga, Lapeyre & Marcadent, 2020). It is also worrying that ordinarily, informal traders are characterised by minimal or zero savings, limited access to finance and reside in overcrowded slum dwellings. Furthermore, the challenges posed by the Covid-19 lockdowns should be examined in the context that informal sector traders lack the privilege or means to social distance or work from home. It is noteworthy that it was under these adverse conditions of the precipitous spreading of the pandemic and a highly informalised economy that Covid-19 restrictions were introduced in Mashava as in the other parts of Zimbabwe.

Conceptualising the informal economy in Mashava

This section deals with the working framework for an informal economy in general and what it constituted in Mashava during the Covid-19 lockdown period. Informal economy can be defined as "all economic activities by workers and economic units that are – in law or in practice – not covered or insufficiently covered by formal arrangements" (International Labour Organisation, 2002). In addition, as Shinder (1998: 72) states, "most often the informal economy refers to owner/operator businesses of urban poor, unskilled or semi-skilled workers and the chronically unemployed" who make use of indigenous resources and unregulated markets. Another significant characteristic of the informal sector is that skills are not necessarily obtained from formal education (Morris & Pitt, 1995). Rather, these skills are learnt and passed internally and informally, usually from parents to their children.

Furthermore, the informal sector can be defined as an economic activity not included in a country's data on domestic product, and is not normally subjected to formal contracts, licensing and taxation (Labour and Economic Development Research Institute of Zimbabwe (LEDRIZ), 2015: 1). As such, informal business operations largely occur below the radar of state control with most classifiable as illegal whilst some border on criminal undertakings. Because these businesses sometimes exist beyond the purview of the economic regulatory frameworks, including "social security schemes and safety and health, maternity and other labour protection legislation" (Ibid: 1), they exist precariously. This perilousness occurs because the informalisation of the economy happens in the "context of high unemployment, underemployment, poverty, gender inequality and precarious work" (Ibid: 1). Thus, one's entrance into the informal sector almost always happens under adversity or duress and also as a means to eke survival.

The main advantages of the informal sector include: "…the relative ease of entry and low requirements for education, skills, technology and capital" (Ibid: 1). Furthermore, the informal sector may be the only avenue of survival, requires low start-up capital, may help to horn entrepreneurial skills, provides social capital connections, could also be a way to raise financial capital needed to establish economic activities, and affords economic buffering for those who cannot participate in the formal sector (Mbiriri, 2010). Thus, the informal sector is vital as it facilitates "in moderating economic hardships, reducing poverty and enhancing welfare and human development in the country" (Ibid).

Notwithstanding these advantages to an economy under duress, informalisation also contains inherent drawbacks. Besides the fact that "most people enter the informal economy by necessity rather than by choice", other demerits include:

> ...acute decent work deficits and a disproportionate share of the working poor. Workers in the informal economy face higher risks of poverty than those in the formal economy. Although some activities offer reasonable livelihoods and incomes, most people engaged in the informal economy are exposed to inadequate and unsafe working conditions. Illiteracy levels are high, skill levels are low and training opportunities are inadequate. Incomes are also lower, less certain and less regular and working hours are longer. There are no opportunities for collective bargaining and representation rights and their employment status is usually ambiguous or disguised. These workers are also physically and financially more vulnerable (LEDRIZ, 2015: 1).

The International Labour Organisation (ILO) sums up best the disadvantages by pointing out that:

> Work in the informal economy is often characterised by small or undefined work places, unsafe and unhealthy working conditions, low levels of skills and productivity, low or irregular incomes, long working hours and lack of access to information, markets, finance, training and technology. Workers in the informal economy are not recognised, registered, regulated or protected under labour legislation and social protection (ILO, Not Dated: Not Paged).

Added to the above, the informal economic sector in Zimbabwe was further disparaged as a sector meant for the uneducated, the unskilled, failures in life, the retired and those who had never been formally employed (Mbiriri, 2010). As well, it was regarded by many as an economy that catered for those who could not compete with the others for the dwindling jobs in the ever-shrinking post-colonial formal sector (Ibid). However, a critical scrutiny of the participants in the informal sector does not always attest to that since even some well-educated and skilled people are also involved.

There are various categories of individuals that fell in the category of informal sector workers in Mashava. These included food and vegetable vendors, street clothing sellers, gold panners, pirate taxi operators, cross-border traders, fire-wood sellers, backyard steel manufacturers, carpenters, tyre repairers, cobblers, stone and wood carvers, illegal money changers and commercial sex workers. Furthermore, most retail businesses in Mashava, including bottle stores, bars, night clubs, grocery and clothing stores, butcheries, barber shops, hair salons, bakeries, hardware shops as well as electronic sales and repair stores, also belong to the category of the regulated informal sector. This latter category had ventures that had been formalised through "registration, taxation, organisation and representation" and sometimes enjoyed "legal and social protection" as well as "business incentives and support" (LEDRIZ, 2015: 1). The formalisation of such informal business ventures led to some entrepreneurs accruing advantages of accessing funding for their operations, training and legal protection (Ibid). In the end, it should be noted, as Becker (2004) cited in Mbiriri (2010: 16) avers, that the informal sector must not only be considered alongside illegality and criminality but also with legality where there is the provision of "... goods and services whose production and distribution are perfectly legal."

Following the conceptualisation of the informal sector, the next section presents the history of the informalisation of the Zimbabwean economy. This affords the break for a discussion of the historical making(s) of the informal sector in the country. Of note is that this informal sector takes root from the colonial era but explodes from the post-colonial epoch.

Historicisation of the growth of Zimbabwe's informal sector

In terms of the historicisation of the post colonial development of the informal sector in Zimbabwe, it can be argued that it grew in strength and significance in terms of its contribution to the country's employment, the fiscal earnings and more generally to the economy over the years following the gaining of independence in 1980. This effectively positioned the informal sector as the bedrock of the Zimbabwean economy. In 1980, when the country attained independence, the sector contributed only 10% of the labour force due in part to a strong state-led economy and strict racial laws that proscribed the settlement of black people in urban areas (LEDRIZ,

2015). The informal sector's contribution to employment rose to about 27% in 1991 largely due to the upswing of rural-to-urban migration following the deregulation of entry into urban areas (1bid).

The decade of the 1990s saw a massive expansion of the informal sector in the country. This exponential rise of informal sector activities from the 1990s was driven by the twin combination of the negative effects of the Economic Structural Adjustment Programme (ESAP) that was adopted in the early 1990s and the advent of a multi-layered economic-cum-political crisis that ravaged the country from the end of the last millennium (Ibid; Mumbengegwi, 2002). ESAP was meant to arrest economic decline, correct dwindling tax revenues, cut government spending and promote economic growth (Mlambo, 2014). These aims, however, were not realised as the effects of the introduction of ESAP were catastrophic for the country leading to heavy job losses in the formal sector due to deindustrialisation, huge layoffs in government/public sector and other formal sectors and the consequent rise in urban poverty (Duri & Marongwe, 2021). Thus, ESAP dismally failed to stir the country to sustainable growth as it resulted in the massive retrenchment of workers and left a legacy of poverty and marginalisation, particularly among the urban poor. This gave the informal economy the opportunity to significantly expand as many workers lost their formal jobs and had to resort to unregulated survival routes.

Furthermore, and as a result of the failures of ESAP, the government was forced to institute a raft of measures to give impetus to the development of the informal economy as a measure to deal with rising unemployment (ILO, 2017). Among other strides, regulatory bottlenecks that prevented the entry of new players into production and distribution of goods and services were removed. As well, the government supported the development of small enterprises and black empowerment and relaxed physical planning requirements. In the latter vein, Statutory Instrument 216 of 1994 of the Regional Town and Country Planning Act permitted the pursuance of non-residential informal economic pursuits in residential areas (Ibid). Through these measures, the government had made clear to local authorities of its desire to see the promotion of the informal economy in residential areas and this allowed the sector to expand as more players participated. It was not only the people who had lost their jobs who were attracted to the informal economy but even those who were formally employed whose real incomes were diminishing and needed to maintain their standard of living. Overall, the desire by the state to promote the growth of the informal sector resonated with the evolutionist argument by Hosier (1987) that the informal economy is a reality, would continue to grow and as such, governments have the responsibility to support its growth as this sector is useful in alleviating poverty.

On the other hand, Zimbabwe's multi-layered crisis from the late 1990s (Raftopoulos, 2009), rooted in contested electoral outcomes and the controversial land reform programme (Duri, 2016; Guzura, 2016; Makumbe, 2012; Masunungure, 2006; Muzondidya, 2010; Raftopoulos & Mlambo, 2010; Sachikonye, 2011), spurred the informalisation of the economy. The combination of the disputed electoral processes and the unconventional land redistribution exercise between 2000 and 2003 placed the country in a quagmire regarding the observance of human rights and protection of private property, both of which scuttled the country's ability to attract foreign investment, foreign aid and foreign economic-political support. Zimbabwe, in the eyes of many in the international community, became a pariah state that nobody, especially in the global West, was willing to assist. Broadly, the crisis, which further accelerated the rate of deindustrialisation and the near collapse of the commercial agricultural sector, led to greater famishment, underemployment and unemployment. As a consequence, many people, both in urban and rural settings, came to resort more to hustling or getting by in their pursuits of survival.

The growth in significance of the informal sector remained steadfast in the new millennium. To this extent, in 2008, the informal sector accounted for up to 80% employment (Ibid). The phenomenal climb of this sphere further continued such that in 2011, it was responsible for 84% employment (Ibid). The trend to further informalise the economy proceeded in the post-2009-2013 Government of National Unity such that by 2014 the sector accounted for up to 94.5% employment (Kanyenze, Chitambara & Tyson, 2017). This growth was due in part to continued deindustrialisation and reduced capacity utilisation in manufacturing industries in the country (Ibid). In 2020, the informal sector accounted for a whopping 90% employment in Zimbabwe (Dudzai & Wamara, 2021).

From the foregoing, what emerges is that indeed, from the late 1990s to around 2020, the Zimbabwean economy was on a downward spiral with the formal sector shrinking, resulting in a decline in the total economic production. And, as the formal sector shrunk, it was replaced by the informal sector. As the World Bank (2020), cited in Dudzai & Wamara (2021) posited, this prodigious growth of the informal sector placed Zimbabwe in the unenviable second position in the world, only after Bolivia, in percentage terms of the informalisation of the economy. What was worse was that at the start of the Covid-19 pandemic, Zimbabwe was plagued by hyperinflation that resulted in the prices of basic commodities escalating beyond the reach of many, a comatose economy, dilapidated infrastructure, dysfunctional health delivery system, erratic energy supplies and a hotly contested political terrain. By extension, the economy of Mashava, a former bustling commercial asbestos and gold mining area was also dominated by a retail-led informal economy by 2020.

Impact of the Covid-19 lockdown on the informal economy in Mashava

This section turns to a discussion of the impacts of the Covid-19 pandemic and associated lockdown measures on the informal survival pursuits of Mashava communities. The Covid-19-induced lockdowns declared by the government to contain the spread of the virus had a broad range of devastating impacts on various sectors of the informal economy in Mashava. When the Covid-19-induced total lockdown was first introduced on the 30th of March 2020, all formal and informal business activities were brought to an abrupt halt in Mashava and other parts of the country (Statutory Instrument 83 of 2020). Retail shops, tuck shops, bottle stores and bars were either partially or completely closed. Although not completely stopped, artisanal mining was greatly affected. Between March and July 2020, the national lockdown was systematically reviewed and modified with certain restrictions either eased or tightened depending on the circumstances on the ground. This had far-reaching impacts on many sections of the Mashava community whose livelihoods mostly depended on these informal economic activities. There is no doubt that the restrictive measures that accompanied the lockdown to curb the spread of the Covid-19 pandemic had short term and long-lasting physical and psychological effects on many informal sector workers in Mashava.

As was the case across the breadth of Zimbabwe, all public places in Mashava, including market places, were closed. Gatherings of more than 50 people were prohibited countrywide. The lockdown also led to the closure of Great Zimbabwe University (GZU) which consequently deprived the local informal sector of a market of almost 10 000 people comprising staff and students (Moyo, Interview: 12 December 2021). The closure of the Great Zimbabwe University Mashava Campus, which was a source of livelihoods for many people in and around Mashava, had significant effects. At the Great Zimbabwe University's Main Teaching and Learning Centre as well as Chemberi Students' Residence, there were thriving open air/space food canteens. Tuck shops and formal shops were also forced to close. Flea markets, shebeens, hair salons, barber shops, photocopying and stationery shops, and computer and cell phone repair shops were not spared either. The situation was compounded by the closure of schools in the Mashava area which had also been a market for traders who sold different types of merchandise such as foodstuffs, groceries and other non-food items to both pupils and teachers, particularly during break times (Ncube, Interview: 15 December 2021).

Some informal food vendors at the Great Zimbabwe University's Main Teaching and Learning Centre and Chemberi Students' Residence bemoaned the missed income opportunities brought about by the immediate freeze in business activities at the introduction of the Covid-19-induced lockdown in March 2020. Since the announcement of the first lockdown coincided with the beginning of the semester, some vendors claimed that they suffered severe economic losses from goods that remained unsold or even gone to waste because of their perishable nature. This was further compounded by the fact that they also suffered from loss of pending payments by some customers who had received goods or services before the crisis set in. As their economic situation deteriorated while their livelihoods increasingly became threatened, most informal traders were forced to use whatever capital they had in their possession for survival. However, this significantly diminished their capacity to respond, recover and resume operations in the event that the situation was to normalise or permit. The case of Mary Gudo (Interview: 15 May 2020) illuminates this predicament:

> When the first lockdown was announced, I had done my input purchases including soft drinks such as Dragon and Switch energy drinks, Pepsi varieties and cokes; potatoes, rice and many others, which were supposed to last me through the semester. I had also raised 100 chickens that I had just slaughtered for my business. Once the lockdown measures were announced, it meant that I could not go ahead with my

> business. I ended up selling most of the chickens on credit and using the other food stuffs for the upkeep of the family, which meant that I ate into the capital for the business. I do not know how I will pick myself up once the university reopens or when the lockdown measures permit us to conduct operations.

A follow up on her situation in December 2021 revealed that she failed to recover and had to relocate to her rural home in the neighbouring Chirumhanzu District. The retreat to her rural home demonstrated her failure, like many others, to recover from the shock closure of their operations that came with the announcement of the first lockdown.

While the informal traders were accustomed to the cyclical and seasonal nature of business at the university and surrounding schools, they did not anticipate the abrupt and prolonged closure of the learning institutions, particularly the GZU Mashava Campus since the semester was just commencing. The closure of the university and schools in Mashava proved to be a double-edged sword for women in particular in that they were then finding it difficult to protect themselves and their children from the fatal Covid-19 pandemic, and looking for food and other essential primary needs for their families. Besides, the informal traders were also affected in that they were accustomed to a situation whereby when the conventional students at the university were on vacation, the business void left was filled by block/ part-time students who came to attend lectures during that period. The block students provided a very viable food market as the majority of them were gainfully employed, well-resourced and preferred to buy their lunch and supper from the vendors than cook on their own or purchase from the university canteens. Most of the informal traders had established very good rapport with some of the students to the extent that they had developed a stable, reliable and regular source of income. For most of the informal traders, vending was their only source of income and the lockdown obviously had deep effects on their livelihoods.

Several informants who were contacted largely through telephonic interaction lamented how the lockdown had negatively impacted on their businesses and hence their livelihoods. Mavis Mukato (Interview: 9 June 2021), a vendor who had been operating at the GZU Learning Centre food market since the establishment of the campus in 2013, for example, indicated that she had decided to relocate to her rural home until the situation improved. While she appreciated the challenges she was facing in the rural areas, she insisted that this was a better option since she did not pay rent and electricity bills there. Some informal sector players, particularly women, were also forced to make very difficult decisions on how to find alternative sources of livelihoods and better still, how to use their meagre resources in sustaining their families.

When the initial 21-day total lockdown period was reviewed in mid-April 2020, mining activities, which were then classified under essential services, were allowed to resume operations under strict health guidelines. Perhaps, it is worth acknowledging that as the lockdown was maintained, artisanal mining in and around Mashava became the source of livelihoods for many people. The resumption of artisanal mining in and around Mashava witnessed a rush by many people who included unemployed youths, civil servants (mostly teachers), and other informal sector workers who had been negatively affected by the lockdown. In particular, women who had been accustomed to earning livelihoods from other informal activities became the most vulnerable as they were even forced to resort to risk mechanisms such as engaging in transactional sex in the artisanal mining zones as the abrupt cut of income avenues they were used to had dried up. As one woman, Mary Jonasi (Interview: 15 July 2020), bemoaned:

The Covid-19 pandemic has seriously impacted on our lives. Before, we survived by selling foodstuffs to students and staff at Great Zimbabwe University. We could feed our families. We could send our children to school. We could pay our rentals. Now, we are forced to do anything that comes our way including prostitution to sustain our livelihoods.

At other shopping centres such as Balmain, Bere and Temaraire, all vegetable market stalls were also closed. What was most disturbing was that as these informal activities were temporally closed down, there appeared to be a new development in which formal shops and supermarkets now provided the goods and services that were previously supplied by the informal economy. Judith Macheka (Interview: 20 June 2020), a vendor who used to operate at the main Balmain fresh vegetable market, expressed fear that even after the Covid 19 pandemic, it would be difficult for them to recapture their previously lucrative fresh vegetable business from the formal shops. Thus, the challenge was that the pandemic had the potential to push the informal traders out of their usual business forever with wider negative spill-over effects, including the difficulty to pay rent, feed their families and meet their health bills in the event of illness. By early 2022, as this study was being finalised, there were no indications that the informal traders were likely to convalesce the fresh vegetable market at Balmain and other shopping centres as their former customers had become accustomed to purchasing perishables from shops and supermarkets.

Indeed, the restrictions brought about by Covid-19 triggered a radical shift from informal activities in the townships to the informal mining settlements within and around Mashava where even married women, girls, and sex workers found business attractive. In Mashava, the Covid-19 pandemic lockdown provided an enabling environment that exacerbated the sexual exploitation of vulnerable groups such as women. The vulnerability emanated from the lack of basic necessities such as food, soap and sanitisers. Undeniably, the poverty resulting from the Covid-19-induced lockdown drove some women who previously survived on the informal economy to resort to transactional sex in order to meet their basic needs. This, in the immediate and long term, put these women at risk of contracting the Human Immuno-deficiency Virus (HIV) and the Acquired Immune Deficiency Syndrome (AIDS). In addition, such women, particularly those who had been accustomed to earning livelihoods through 'honest' means, also lost self-esteem and plunged into psychological depression, resulting in many of them engaging into drug and alcohol abuse.

During the lockdown period in Mashava, many women sold virtually everything including foodstuffs, water and their bodies. Recently-used condoms were a common feature in the artisanal mining areas. Tuck shop owners and other business operators who found the going tough due to lockdown restrictions also found the artisanal mining settlements, popularly referred to as pits (*makomba*), attractive as business was carried out round the clock. Grocery items, beer and drugs were also sold at these premises (Mugodzwa, Interview: 16 June 2020). Commenting on the above developments, Nicholas Govo (Interview: 1 June 2020) rightly observed that Covid-19 certainly contributed to bringing about a sharp rise in HIV and AIDS infections in Mashava as young girls and countless women who had seen their livelihoods disappearing as a result of Covid-19 resorted to prostitution. As Dzingirayi & Munyeza (2020) reiterated, such developments obviously resulted in disastrous consequences that include Sexually Transmitted Infections (STIs), miscarriages and even unintended pregnancies.

Bars and nightclubs were a segment of the informal sector that was also negatively affected by the Covid-19-induced lockdowns. These businesses remained closed between 30 March 2020 and 5 October 2021 as a result of the government's Covid-19 statutory decrees (*Herald*, 6 October 2021). Thus, the owners and workers of these enterprises remained without a regular source of income for nearly two years. Most were pushed to the margins of survival and became poverty stricken. Several of these outlets were caught with huge stocks they intended to sell, most of which expired during the long period of closure. This meant huge losses for such outlets, which resulted in many people failing to survive the shock. What aggravated the situation for the bars and night clubs was that they continued to pay their liquor licenses to the Liquor Licensing Board, as well as rentals and council levies despite them remaining closed during the lockdown period. This forced those involved in these businesses to look for exterior sources of money or to resort to prior savings to pay their workers and/ or service their legal obligations and local government requirements (Marongwe, Interview: 23 December 2021). Broadly, in a crippling economy that was characterised by rising inflation and currency fluctuations, the resuscitation of the business operations that had been closed down was no mean feat.

The closure of bars and night clubs, such as Legends Sports Bar, Club Legacy, Upper Deck Nite Club and Highway Club, saw the mushrooming of a lot of shebeens and illegal alcohol-selling points. Our research showed that shebeens were opened in all the main townships of Bere, Lennox Mine, King Mine and Gaths Mine. In addition, illegal alcohol-selling points, some of which were owned and/or operated by police officers or their proxies, opened at the business centres, including Balmain where the main police station was located (Matuzura, Interview: 9 June 2021). These illegal liquor sales operated from grocery shops, hardware stores, saloons and butcheries. The mushrooming of these shebeens and unlicensed liquor sales not only undercut the bars and night clubs but also undermined the very call for the closing of the licensed joints. The national newspaper, *The Herald* (6 October 2021), also acknowledged this illegality and cited it as part of the reasons why the government decided to re-open the bars and clubs in late 2021.

In an effort to circumvent the harsh realities of closing down, which has already mentioned, meant lack of income, some operators resorted to cat-and-mouse games with the law-enforcement agencies, especially the police force. To this end, some entrepreneurs illegally operated through opening their doors to their patrons or selling alcohol through windows, which placed them in the direct line of fire from the police. And, indeed, many who adopted the above route had their fingers literally burnt as they were often extorted and made to pay protection fees or huge bribes to avoid prosecution (Nzou, Interview: 12 December 2021).

Oftentimes, members of the police service demanded free beer, meat or fake donations from the bar and night club operators, ostensibly for their superiors, as part of the extortion and protection fees. Those operators who refused to pay were either threatened, victimised, brutalised and/or arrested. Sometimes, in collusion with prosecutors and magistrates, hefty fines were imposed on some of them. In late June 2021, for example, one bar owner at Balmain Shopping Centre was arrested and made to pay a princely sum of ZWL$100 000, which then converted to more than USD$1 000-00 at both the official and parallel market rates (Nzou, Interview: 12 December 2021). This hefty fine in lieu of three months in prison was out of the norm as the others who had committed similar offences were made to pay only ZWL$20 000. Literally, the police officers, who had become virtual semi-gods, determined who would open their bars/night clubs and up to what time depending on the returns that accrued to them as individuals through corruption, bribery and extortion. To this end, there were some joints that "operated as if there was no lockdown because they were allowed to operate up to the wee hours of the days as the big chefs drank from them or they had shares" (Banda, Interview: 19 December 2021).

Informal cross-border traders in Mashava were also among the hardest hit by the Covid-19-induced lockdown. Before the lockdown, informal traders from Mashava would cross the borders to neighbouring countries such as Botswana and South Africa to purchase their wares. However, due to the closure of the borders between Zimbabwe and the neighbouring countries, this was no longer possible and the informal traders were forced to look for alternative ways of survival. According to one female informal cross-border trader who resided in Gaths Mine, life had become unbearable as this had been her only source of survival for a long time (Mapiye, Interview: 16 June 2020). She lamented:

> I have been in this type of business for a long time and this has been my only source of income. I am a single mother with three school-going children. I live in rented accommodation where I am supposed to pay US$ 30 per month. Rent is charged in United States dollars. Before the

lockdown, I could afford to pay my rentals, buy food for my children, send them to school, clothe them and foot our medical bills. Now I am trapped and do not even know where to start from (Ibid).

Another cross-border trader from Gaths Mine who specialised in selling various imported commodities such as perfume, and alcoholic and drug substances, including the highly-abused Broncleer cough mix, popularly known as *Bronco*, to university students had this to say:

> These university students provide me with a very lucrative market for my merchandise. They are my regular customers and have sustained my livelihood since the opening of the Mashava campus here. I cannot imagine what my life is going to be if this pandemic persists (Ngoro, Interview: 16 July 2021).

There is little doubt that the Covid-19-induced lockdowns resulted in the gross infringement of the socio-economic rights of informal traders in Mashava. As already alluded to, the lockdowns were spiced with numerous restrictions which exacerbated the informal traders' vulnerability as economic activities were diminished. The caprices and perils of the lockdown measures significantly contributed to many people abandoning their economic ways of life. The huge income losses for informal traders in Mashava directly impacted on food security and access to other basic necessities of life. Indeed, as has been demonstrated by several scholars, human rights are indivisible, interchangeable and are dependent on one another (Darrow & Arbour, 2009; Evans & Murray, 2008). As such, the infringement of one right may trigger the violation of several other basic rights. These rights are well defined and articulated in the 'Bill of Rights' of the Constitution of Zimbabwe, the African Charter of Human Rights (ACHR), the United Nations Declaration of Human Rights (UNDHR) and other international rights conventions (Constitution of Zimbabwe, Amendment Act, Number 20: 2013; Darrow & Arbour, 2009; Evans & Murray, 2008; UNICEF, 2015).

As the effects of the Covid-19 pandemic continued to play out in Mashava, some informal traders were forced to relocate to their rural homes. This was particularly true of the informal traders who hailed from areas around Mashava such as Madamombe, Masunda, Befura and Bwanya, among others. However, as indicated earlier on, some of the people in Mashava are descendants of migrant labourers from Malawi, Zambia and Mozambique who worked and resided in

Mashava since the early 20th century. To these people, Mashava was their only known home. Our interviews revealed that due to limited choices, these people of foreign origin were forced to engage in any livelihood activities that could result in short to medium term or to long term physiological and traumatic effects (Chirwa, Interview: 13 December 2021).

The challenges faced by informal traders in Mashava were not unique as they were characteristic of what was obtaining in other parts of the country and indeed in other African countries that could not provide adequate social nets for the vulnerable people. By early July 2020, for example, the government promised to pay an individual monthly cushion of ZWL$180 (US$1.63) for 202 000 vulnerable people out of a targeted one million (*Daily News*, 9 July 2020). This was eventually revised to ZWL$300 towards the end of July 2020. Needless to say, that even the revised cushioning allowance was insignificant as the consumer basket for an average family of five was way past ZWL$9 500 by the end of June 2020 (Marufu, 2020). It is also worth noting that the Covid-19 pandemic occurred at a time when the country was in the midst of its worst inflationary crisis since dollarisation in 2009 as the local currency continued to plunge against the United States dollar.

In winding up this section, it is significant to stress that when this study was conducted between March and December 2021, all the vending sites in the areas under study were still not operational. This was in line with the health standards and guidelines of the Ministry of Health and Child Care, and the Inter-Ministerial Taskforce on Covid-19. However, by the end of July 2020, lockdown fatigue in Mashava was gradually forcing people to operate shebeens and other informal businesses in their backyards. The 'gold rush' within and in the vicinity of Mashava was threatening to explode into another shadow pandemic as almost everyone saw a window of opportunity in that enterprise. In this emerging trend, lockdown measures such as social distancing, sanitisation and hand-washing were largely disregarded. Furthermore, the sector was also characterised by a lot of social ills and negative environmental implications. While it was difficult to really quantify the impact of the lockdown on informal activities in the area under study as the researchers' movements were also limited due lockdown restrictions, there was no doubt that the majority of informal traders suffered complete or partial loss of incomes due to the lockdown. As Luke *et al* (2020) argue: "For businesses that require daily activity to earn an income, even a few-days hiatus from work can translate to financial peril". As Linda Musekiwa (Interview: 13 July 2021), a food market vendor who used to operate at the Great Zimbabwe University Mashava Campus, highlighted:

> We continue to leave our homes despite the lockdown because we still have to fend for our families. How do we get the money to buy the sanitisers and extra soap for hand washing if we stay at home? We suffered complete loss of income and though we are skipping meals, we still cannot make ends meet.

This was a clear testimony that most informal traders in Mashava were faced with very difficult choices to make which involved risking their lives to Covid-19 or hunger. Indeed, for the people engaged in the informal economy in Mashava, loss of income induced by the Covid-19 lockdown translated to failure to putting a meal on the table. As some informants insinuated, they basically survived on one meal a day, either in the afternoon or evening. For many, breakfast became a luxury.

Conclusion

The chapter has examined the challenges faced by informal traders in Mashava since the imposition of the Covid-19 lockdown in March 2020 up to December 2021 when it was significantly relaxed. It has been highlighted that the lockdown had immediate short, medium and long term effects on the informal economy in Mashava. It was amplified that the different lockdowns had negative social, economic and psychological effects on the informal sector players which amounted to a considerable violation of their socio-economic rights. It was further observed that while most sectors of the informal economy in Mashava were negatively impacted upon by the Covid-19-induced lockdown, artisanal mining, which was classified as an essential sector, continued to thrive. It became a corridor of opportunity for many other informal traders and civil servants, particularly teachers, who had been negatively affected by the lockdown.

References

Committee for the Coordination of Statistical Activities (2020) 'How Covid-19 is changing the world: A statistical perspective', Available at: https://unstats.un.org/unsd/ccsa/principles_stat_activities/ , Accessed 15 July 2020.

Daily News (25 March 2020) Harare: Zimbabwe.

Daily News (9 July 2020) Harare: Zimbabwe.

Darrow, M., & Arbour, L., (2009) 'The pillar of glass: Human rights in the development operations of the United Nations,' in: *American Journal of International Law*, Volume 103, Number 3, pp.446-501.

Dudzai, C., & Wamara, C.K., (2021) 'Covid-19 pandemic and the informal sector in Zimbabwe', in: *African Journal of Social Work*, Volume 11, Number 4, pp.201-208, Available at: https://www.ajol.info/index.php/ajsw/article/view/215257, Accessed 18 March 2022.

Duri, F.P.T & Marongwe, N., (2021) *New millennium woes and livelihood struggles in Africa: Begging to survive by Zimbabwe's marginalised*, Bamenda: Langaa Research and Publishing Common Initiative Group.

Duri, F.P.T., (ed.) (2016) *Resilience amid adversity: Informal coping mechanisms to the Zimbabwean crisis during the new millennium*, Gweru: Booklove Publishers.

Dzingirayi, P. & Munyeza, N., (9-15 July 2020) 'Covid-19 lockdown and the abuse of women', in: *Business Times*, Available at: www.businesstimes,co.zw, Accessed 21 July 2020.

Elflein, J., (2020) 'Covid-19 cases and deaths among hardest hit countries worldwide as of July 20', Available at: https://www.statista.com/aboutus/our-research-commitment/1013/john-elflein, Accessed 5 July 2020.

Evans, M. & Murray, R., (2008) *The African Charter on human and peoples' rights: The system in practice, 1986-2006*, Cambridge: Cambridge University Press.

Government of Zimbabwe (2013) *Zimbabwe Act No. 1: Constitution of Zimbabwe Amendment (No. 20)*, Harare: Government of Zimbabwe.

Government of Zimbabwe (2022) *Statutory Instrument 18 of 2022: Public Health (Covid-19 Prevention, Containment, and Treatment) Amendment Order, 2022 (No. 40)*, Harare: Government of Zimbabwe.

Government of Zimbabwe (2020) *Statutory Instrument 83 of 2020: Public Health (Covid-19 Prevention, Containment and Treatment) (National Lockdown) Order, 2020*, Harare: Government of Zimbabwe.

Guzura. T., (2016) 'Are we there yet? A relook at SADC's role in the Zimbabwe conflict', in: *International Journal of Politics and Good Governance*, Volume 7, Number 3, pp.1-25.

Hammar, A. McGregor, J. & Landau, L., (2010) 'Introduction: Displacing Zimbabwe: Crisis and construction in Southern Africa', in: *Journal of Southern African Studies*, Volume 36, Number 2, pp.263-283.

Herald (6 October 2021) 'Bars, night clubs allowed to re-open', Harare: Zimbabwe.

Hosier, R.H., (1987) 'The informal sector in Kenya: Spatial variation and development alternatives', in: *The Journal of Developing Areas*, Volume 21, Number 4, pp.383-402.

International Labour Organisation (ND) 'Informal economy', Available at: https://www.ilo.org/global/topics/dw4sd/themes/informal-economy/lang--en/index.htm, Accessed 12 March 2022.

Kanyenze, G., Chitambara, P. & Tyson, J., (2017) 'The outlook for the Zimbabwean economy', Available at: https://set.odi.org/wp-content/uploads/2017/08/SET-Outlook-for-Zimbabwe-Economy_Sep2017.pdf, Accessed 10 March 2022.

Labour and Economic Development Research Institute of Zimbabwe (2015) 'Strategies for transitioning the informal economy to formalisation in Zimbabwe', Available at: https://library.fes.de/pdf-files/bueros/simbabwe/13714.pdf, Accessed 12 February 2022.

Lauren, M. & Sauer, M.S., (ND) 'What is Corona virus?', Available at: http://www.hopkinsmedicines.org/profiles/results/directory/10002278/lauren-sauer, Accessed 15 July 2020.

Makumbe, J., (2012) 'Zimbabwe: Political context study', in: B.A. Andreassen & G. Crawford (eds.) *Human rights, power and civil action: Comparative analysis of struggle for rights in developing societies*, London: Routledge.

Masunungure, E.V., (2011) 'Zimbabwe's militarised electoral authoritarianism', in: *Journal of International Affairs*, Volume 65, Number 1, pp.47-64.

Menocal, A.R. & Othieno, T., (2008) 'The World Bank in fragile situations: An issue paper', Paper prepared for a Conference on 'An eye on the future: The World Bank Group changing world,' Amsterdam, 12-13 July 2008, p.1.

Mugodzwa, D.M., (2017) 'Black economic empowerment, employment creation and resilience: The economic and social contribution of Lennox Mine to the development of Zimbabwe, 1970-2016', in: *International Journal of Management and Social Sciences*, Volume 6, Number 3, pp.390-410.

Mumbengegwi, C. (ed.) (2002) *Macroeconomic and structural adjustment policies in Zimbabwe*, New York: Palgrave-Macmillan.

Muzondidya, J., (2010) 'The Zimbabwean crisis and the unresolved conundrum of race in the post-colonial period', Available at: https://dol.org/10.1177/0169796x1002600102, Accessed 25 July 2020.

Ndlovu-Gatsheni. S.J., (2013) 'Why decoloniality in the 21st century?' in: *The Thinker: Journal of Progressive Thought*, Volume 48, pp.10-15.

Rahman, A. & Shaban, A., (2020) 'Africa news', Available at: http://twitter.com/alfaafrican, Accessed 22 July 2020.

Sachikonye, L., (2011) *When a state turns on its citizens: Institutionalised violence and political culture*, Sunnyside Auckland Park 2092: Jacana Media (Pvt) Ltd.

Shinder, L., (1998) 'Zimbabwe's informal sector: International Report', in: *Monthly Labour Review*, pp.72-73.

Taubenberger, J.K. & Morens, D.M., (2006) '1918 Influenza: The mother of all pandemics', in: *Emerging Diseases*, Volume 12, Number 1, pp.15-22.

UNICEF (2015) 'What are human rights?' Available at: https://www.unicef.org/media/press-centre, Accessed 7 January 2022.

Vaccine Tracker (11 February 2021) 'Five vaccines approved for use in Zimbabwe,' Available at: https://www.covid19.trackvaccines.org, Accessed 21 February 2022.

World Health Organisation (19-20 July 2020) 'Corona virus disease (Covid-19): Situation Report 182', Available at: https://www.who.int/docs/default-source/coronaviruse/situation-reports/20200720-covid-19-sitrep-182.pdf, Accessed 21 February 2022.

World Health Organisation (2021) 'WHO Corona virus (Covid-19) Dashboard', Available at: https://covid19.who.int/, Accessed 22 November 2021.

Worldometer (22 November 2021) 'Zimbabwe: Corona virus cases', Available at: https://www.worldometers.info/coronavirus/country/zimbabwe/, Accessed 22 November 2021.

Zimbabwean Mail (12 June 2020) 'Zimbabwe relaxes virus lockdown', Available at: https://zimbabwerelaxesviruslockdown/, Accessed 21 April 2022.

Zimbabwe Situation (21 July 2020) 'Covid-19 monitoring report, 19-21 July 2020', www.zimbabwesituation.com.news, Accessed 21 April 2022.

Chapter 9

Covid-19 Restrictions and the Woes of Informal Traders in the Zaka District, Zimbabwe

Constance Makuvise

Introduction

In Zimbabwe, the informal sector contributes significantly to the country's Gross Domestic Product (GDP). In 2008, for example, it was estimated that the informal sector contributed to over 60% of Zimbabwe's GDP and accounted for slightly over 80% of the country's total employment figure (African Union, 2008). Thus, the sector has always been a critical entrepreneurial component in terms of Zimbabwe's economic growth and job creation. In 2020, the International Monetary Fund indicated that 90% of Zimbabwean workers were employed in the informal sector. This goes to show the informal sector's pivotal role in sustaining the livelihoods of the majority of the population through job creation and poverty reduction (International Monetary Fund, 2020).

Prior to the Covid-19 pandemic, Zimbabwe's economy had become highly informalised and informal traders largely earned livelihoods by creating a market environment in which various necessities were accessed in an affordable and convenient manner (Mukeredzi, 2020). Many informal traders had a regular source of income through selling many commodities such as agricultural produce, fruits and vegetables, second-hand clothes, traditional medicine, pottery and beer to mention but a few. The Covid-19 pandemic and the subsequent responses by the Zimbabwean government to contain its spread caused catastrophic disruptions on the operations of the informal sector, most of whose participants were the poor and marginalised sections of the society (Mashapure, 2021). Indeed, Covid-19-induced restrictive measures disturbed and sometimes halted most informal sector activities thereby robbing many poor people of their livelihood options. Thus, the public health catastrophe deprived many impoverished people of their rights to do business and severely threatened their rights to food and livelihoods (Mhlanga & Ndhlovu, 2020).

To illustrate these observations, this chapter undertakes a case study of the rural Zaka District in the Masvingo Province of Zimbabwe located about 86 kilometres southeast of the city of Masvingo. According to the Zimbabwe Statistics Agency (2012), Zaka District had a population of 181 301 during the 2012 population census. The district is in Climatic Region 4 where informal trading is a major source of livelihood for the majority of the people. Jerera Growth Point is the major business centre within the district and is surrounded by other centres such as Ndanga, Chinorumba, Makuvaza, Chivamba, Gumbo and Rudhanda, among others. The major informal economic activities in the district prior to the Covid-19 pandemic included cross-border trade, food vending, beer-brewing, firewood sales and trading in second-hand clothes (Mugove, Interview: 20 March 2022). The district also has three dams: Manjerenje, Siya and Bangala where many communities derive their livelihoods through fishing and irrigation. The Fuve and Panganai Irrigation Schemes, for example, utilised water from these dams (Ibid).

In terms of the composition of informal sector participants, it should be noted that most of them were women and the youths. It is also prudent to note that women suffered most from Covid-19 lockdown measures given that many households were sustained by their daily chores and informal sector activities (Shaikh, 2020). Most of the measures introduced to combat Covid-19 negatively impacted on the human rights of informal sector participants (Mavhinga, 2020). The rights that were particularly violated include those pertaining to free movement and entitlements to food and livelihoods. The lockdown regulations were supposed to be proportionate and reasonable by taking into consideration the needs of the marginalised and the poor (Harris, 2020). Informal traders in the Zaka District were not spared by these Covid-19 lockdown restrictions and most of them put in place various mitigation and coping mechanisms in an effort to salvage sustenance.

Figure 1: Zaka District Map (Source: *OCHA 2010 District Atlas Admin*)

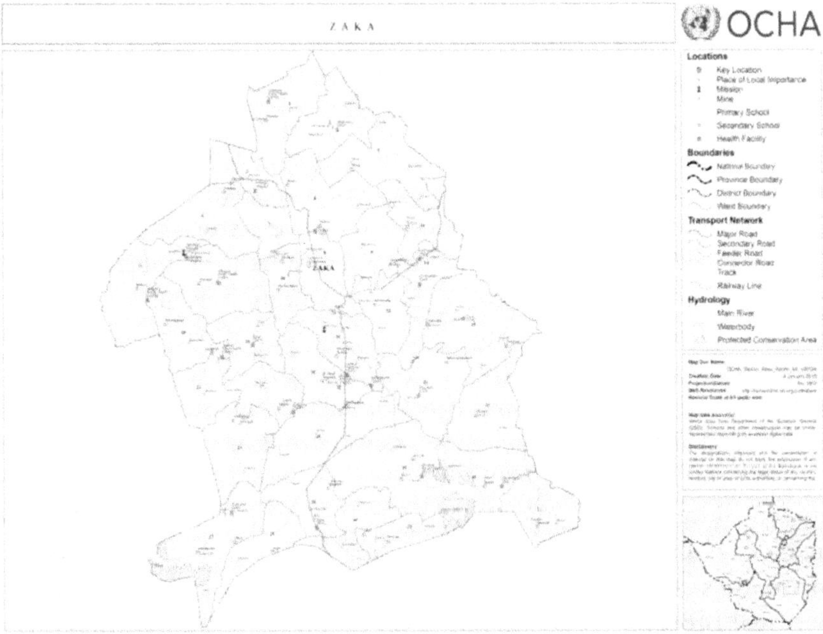

Advent of Covid-19 and government responses

Statutory Instrument 76 of 2020 declared the Corona virus an infectious disease and a state of disaster. Statutory Instrument 77 of 2020 proclaimed Covid-19 as a formidable epidemic disease. Zimbabwe's national lockdown was enforced through the issuance of Statutory Instrument 83 on 28 March 2020. Statutory Instrument 83 of 2020 declared a period of 21 days of lockdown except for essential services and exempted cases (Zimbabwe Human Rights NGO Forum, 17 April 2020). The announcement was immediately followed by the issuance of Statutory Instrument 93 of 2020 (Makombe, 2021). The government further introduced several policies, as well as institutional and operational measures to combat the pandemic and ameliorate its effects, especially on the poor and vulnerable members of the society (Zimbabwe Ministry of Health and Child Care, 2020). In addition, the government announced that all arrivals into the country were subject to strict screening procedures, including rigorous enforcement of a 21-day self-quarantine. The measures were meant to curtail the spread of Covid-

19 and required public activities to stop and informal markets to close (Makombe, 2021).

As part of the enforcement of Covid-19 regulations, the Zimbabwe Republic Police mounted several roadblocks on roads leading to Jerera Growth Point, barring unauthorised motorists and pedestrians from entering the business centre. Vending sites were totally closed and market stalls were destroyed to ensure that no activity would be carried out. Police and council officials moved around confiscating vendors' stock. Some of the stock was discarded or burnt after vendors failed to pay fines. When the lockdown was eased in May and June of 2020, there was some relaxation in terms of some informal sector activities even though most of them were still prohibited under the Covid-19 regulations. Informal traders were later allowed to operate only if they managed to observe Covid-19 health regulations that included provision of sanitisers, hand-washing facilities and maintaining social distance. These conditions meant that limited numbers of informal traders resumed business due to financial constraints. Given their miserable, unreliable, and insecure incomes, street vendors could not easily access proper Covid-19 personal protective equipment, sanitisers, masks and thermometers (Chigudu, 2021).

Social distancing was also problematic for most informal sector participants. One vegetable vendor highlighted that only 20 people were accommodated in the fruit and vegetable market at Jerera Growth Point due to the observation of social distancing rules. All other informal traders who conducted business in shop verandas and informal stalls were not allowed to resume business. John Mutewo narrated that he was left with no option but to sell his wardrobe to rent a corner in a certain shop. Informal traders of second-hand clothing were not allowed to operate as used clothes were regarded as prime carriers of Covid-19 (John Mutewo, Interview: 23 February 2022). Mavis Muchemwa, who traded in second-hand clothes, highlighted that she resorted to mobile vending during which she carried her stock comprising trousers and shorts to the customers' homes (Mavis Muchena, Interview: 13 April 2022).

Roadside vendors at business centres like Ndanga and Gumbo were prohibited from operating on grounds that there was no formal marketplace available, and that it was deemed difficult to observe Covid-19 measures in such a set up. Informal traders at these centres capitalised on open spaces and then spread their stock. In their quest to survive, these roadside vendors had to hide their stock in nearby bushes and look for customers. It was indeed very hard for street vendors to put food on the table for their families in such a difficult situation posed by the pandemic, and police raids also worsened their plight. In explaining the predicament of informal traders during the Covid-19 period, Mlambo (2021) noted that they experienced an array of abuses which included arbitrary arrests, harassment and confiscation of the wares, among other woes.

From the interviews conducted during this study, most of the respondents identified travel prohibitions, ban on public gatherings, closure of businesses considered to be non-essential, and forced leave and layoffs as the main restrictive measures enacted by government that greatly disrupted their pursuit of livelihoods. The restrictive measures were analysed in relationship to their impact on three major livelihood sources namely: workplace, marketplace, and shopping centres. As shown in Figure 2 below, the majority of respondents (99%) reported adhering to the government's lockdown provisions pertaining to travel restrictions to workplaces, ahead of marketplaces (95%) and shopping centres (90%) in their community. The closure of non-essential businesses was reported to be highly observed in workplaces (99%), followed by marketplaces (97.3%) and shopping centres (95.6%). Some 99% of the respondents also indicated they were observed the ban on marketplaces as compared to shopping centres (94.3%) and workplaces (90.8%).

Most of the lockdown measures, some of which are indicated in Figure 2, curtailed operations and activities in the informal sector thereby violating economic rights, and the rights to food and free movement. Under normal circumstances prior to the advent of Covid-19, informal sector participants used to capitalise on the movement of people and gatherings to make profits. In particular, food vendors depended on the operations of other business because most of their clients were employees. Maud Doka, a single mother, narrated that she used to sell samosas and edible bugs (*harurwa*) to workers in saloons and shops at Jerera Growth Point before most of them were closed in line with Covid-19 lockdown provisions (Maud Doka, Interview: 6 January 2022). It becomes apparent that despite their important contribution to the economy, street vendors remained overlooked by state authorities. Overall, informal workers were often misunderstood, underestimated, abused and negatively stereotyped.

Figure 2: Covid-19 restrictive measures directed at business centres (Source: Compiled by self from research data gathered in 2021)

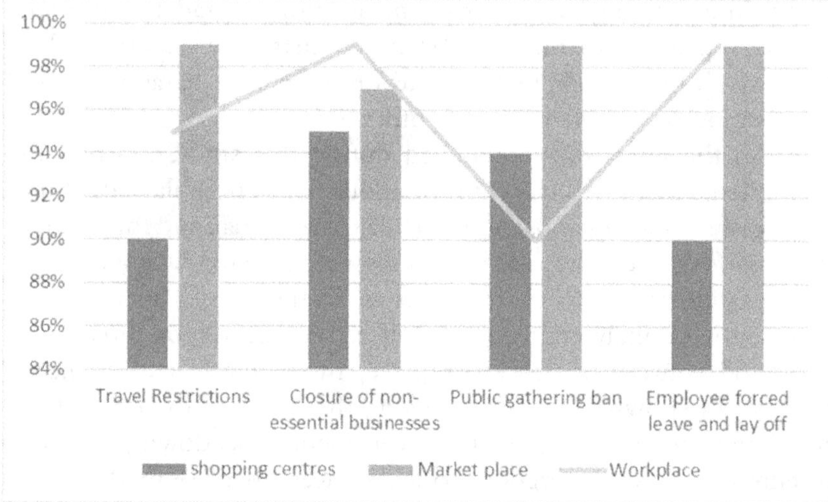

Impact of the suspension of informal sector activities on livelihoods

Covid-19 lockdown regulations led to closure of informal economy businesses and marketplaces. In some cities and towns, market stalls or vending sites deemed illegal and/or unsafe were demolished by the local authorities. Trading on street side pavements was also banned (Dzobo *et al*, 2020). This meant a loss of livelihood sources of income for households that were dependent on the informal economy for their daily survival. The government imposed lockdown regulations that required people who travelled within cities and towns to have exemption letters stamped by their employers. This requirement only applied to workers considered essential who included health personnel, security forces, NGO employees, and others designated as providing critical and essential services (Zimbabwe Peace Project Report, 2021). Vendors and many other informal sector participants were not considered and recognised as essential service providers. Furthermore, they could not have the letters of employment because they were not formally employed. This proved to be very difficult for vendors and other informal traders to access their suppliers and customers. Small-scale farmers from Fuve and Panganai Irrigation Schemes also faced challenges to market their produce at Jerera Growth Point owing to the travel prohibitions and the ban on informal sector activities such as vending. Survival for most informal sector participants became an uphill task as alternative sources of income shrunk owing to Covid-19 lockdown provisions. The unfortunate result was the depletion of household earnings and savings which prompted many to sell off movable properties and livestock in order to salvage sustenance.

There were frequent clashes between vendors and council authorities during the enforcement of lockdown regulations. Economic constraints and the need to earn livelihoods pushed many informal sector players into violating the lockdown regulations although they were very cognisant of the dangers of the pandemic to their health and lives (Malik & Naeem, 2020). Informal traders were left with virtually no other choice to survive than to engage in hide-and-seek encounters with law-enforcement agencies. The International Labour Organisation (2020) rightly noted that the disregard of informal sector participants by most governments during the Covid-19 lockdown period, which included the forced removal of street vendors and their exclusion from the economy, was life-threatening as it undermined and destroyed livelihoods without much hope of recovery.

The government's Covid-19 lockdown restrictions on the movement of goods and people had significant socio-economic repercussions on people's livelihoods. While these restrictions were necessary to limit the spread of the virus, they often disrupted market chains and trade of agricultural and non-agricultural products, with significant potential impacts on the populations that depended on them for consumption, nutrition and livelihoods (Mashapure, 2021). With limited resources and virtually no access to social protection or safety nets, most households that depended on the informal sector were plunged into poverty owing to lockdown prohibitions. During interviews conducted in the Zaka District, many respondents who had been involved in vending, tuck-shop grocery retail, and beer-brewing lamented that their working hours had decreased significantly with 90% of them completely suspending operations since the advent of Covid 19. Furthermore, 73% of those who were relying on agricultural activities such as horticulture, crop farming, fruit production, and poultry rearing indicated that their working hours had increased significantly but the challenge was the difficulty of accessing markets and customers owing to the Covid-19 lockdown travel bans and market prohibitions. Given these challenges, most informal businesses recorded considerable losses with very slim chances of recovery.

The plight of informal sector traders was exacerbated by a national crackdown in which the police and municipal authorities targeted vendors. During the blitz, many vegetable markets were raided and sometimes destroyed while produce was confiscated and disposed of (Ndebele & Matimaire, 2020). Evelyn Tonde, a vendor at Jerera Growth Point, stated that police officers seized her stock and later shared it among themselves. She failed to bounce back into business because she had invested all her profits in the stock that was looted by the merciless police officers (Evelyn Tonde, Interview: 12 March 2022). Like Evelyne, many other informal traders lost their stock through seizure by law-enforcement agents. Mary Tada, another vendor at Jerera Growth Point, pointed out that her tomatoes were taken away by Jerera Rural District Council police officers. The produce was dumped and left to perish in the backyard of council premises. For Mary, vending was her only source and means to put food on the table for herself and her two children (Mary Tada, Interview: 14 March 2022). Johannes Chingozha, a disabled airtime vendor, was left dumb-founded after the police took his airtime cards during a raid at Jerera Growth Point in May 2020 (Johannes Chingozha, Interview: 3 April 2022). What these incidents show is that the law-enforcement agents on Covid-19 lockdown assignments did not take into consideration the plight of informal sector participants, most of who were wallowing in poverty. In actual fact, informal trading was criminalised yet it was a major source of livelihoods for the majority of Zimbabweans.

Cross-border traders from the Zaka District were also affected negatively by the Covid-19 pandemic and the subsequent lockdown provisions imposed by the governments of Zimbabwe and neighbouring countries to curb its spread. Border closures shut out cross-border traders from their source of commodities and customers abroad. Border closures meant that more cross-border traders came to use undesignated entry and exit points during their travels to and from abroad. Some cross-border traders from Ndanga Business Centre who were interviewed stated that they were often prone to abuse and torture when crossing Limpopo River to and from South Africa after avoiding the border post that had been closed as a Covid-19 containment mechanism (Joseph Ndomene, Cleopas Chimera & Thandiwe Chando, Focus Group Discussion: 12 March 2022).

Those who smuggled their goods into the country had to take the risks and foot the exorbitant expenses after which they had to contend with the ban on flea market trade in the country. Memory Chasi, a cross-border trader and vendor at Jerera Growth Point, painfully narrated how her stock comprising shoes and clothes worth R5 000 which she intended to smuggle into the country from South Africa was seized by immigration officials at the Beitbridge Border Post. The loss made her to collapse from hypertension resulting in her being admitted at Ndanga Hospital in the Zaka District (Memory Chasi, Interview: 28 March 2022).

In the Zaka District, most informal sector participants generally defied lockdown measures and continued with their activities, clandestinely though, as they sought to survive under very difficult conditions. Many vendors, for example, relied on daily wages and most of them disregarded lockdown restrictions and continued hustling for a living. Social distancing policies and stay-at-home orders did not work for them given that their mode of operation involved going out and interacting closely with their customers. Indeed, FAO (2020) found out that the lockdown caused an income shock that negatively affected livelihoods of the poorest sections of the society.

It is lamentable that Zimbabwe's national lockdown was decreed without meaningful interventions on how to protect the livelihoods of marginalised informal traders, the majority of who were impoverished and surviving from hand to mouth. No stimulus packages were provided by the government as a way of cushioning informal operators' livelihoods (Dudzai & Wamara, 2021; Kulkarni, 2020). Thus, the Covid-19 lockdown measures plunged many informal sector operators into socio-economic vulnerability. By destroying informal market stalls and preventing informal traders from operating during the lockdown without providing them with any alternative solution, the government promoted an increase in illegal activities, as the traders were desperate to provide for their families within the context of a collapsing economy and a raging pandemic (International Labour Organisation, 2020). It is without doubt that the Covid-19 pandemic and the measures decreed by the government to contain its spread exacerbated poverty and increased vulnerabilities on the part of many participants in the informal economy.

Harassment of informal sector participants by law-enforcement agents

Zimbabwe implemented Covid-19 preventive and mitigation measures which ranged from national lockdowns to stay at home orders and curfews. While the implementation of these measures resulted in untold socio-economic hardships for informal business participants, the Zimbabwe Republic Police (ZRP) and the Zimbabwe National Army (ZNA) aggravated the situation by their unpalatable appetite for excessive and brute force as a way of ensuring compliance from the ordinary people (Ozili, 2020). The 21-day national lockdown period was marked by the menacing presence of marauding security forces in the streets and neighbourhoods to enforce the presidential directive (Zimbabwe Human Rights NGO Forum, 17 April 2020).

From March to September 2020, during a government-mandated Covid-19 lockdown, uniformed and plainclothes soldiers and police officers systematically harassed civilians and often used clubs to liberally beat up civilians in public places such as business centres for violating curfews, not wearing masks, or failing to exercise social distancing (United States Embassy, 2020). The majority of the victims of this brutality were the vulnerable people who had been left with little choice but to leave their homes in search of alternative ways to survive. Informal traders suffered most of the human rights and economic rights violations at the hands of law-enforcement operatives. During interviews conducted for this study, one respondent stated that he was handcuffed and then detained overnight in cold cells on 30 March 2020 after being arrested by the police for selling groceries behind closed doors at Jerera Growth Point (Malvin Chinhengo, Interview: 17 April 2022). A vegetable vendor also explained that she ran away leaving her stock behind at her stall at Jerera Growth Point when the police arrived. When she returned, she realised that her stall had been destroyed by the police (Dorothy Tapera, Interview: 21 March 2022). By destroying vending stalls of impoverished informal traders who were struggling to eke livelihoods during challenging Covid-19 times, the law-enforcement officers exhibited indiscriminate cruelty of unimaginable proportions. It is lamentable that instead of protecting poor and suffering civilians, the security operatives actually aggravated their predicament by subjecting them to a broad range of abuses (Bhebhe, 2020).

During the period spanning from late March 2020, when the national lockdown began, until August later during year, the Zimbabwe Peace Project (2020) managed to document at least 1 498 human rights violations perpetrated by the police and the army. Informal traders were often caught up as they sought sustenance outside their homes and sometimes during curfew hours. It became common practice for informal traders caught violating lockdown provisions to be manhandled, roughed up, bristly handcuffed and beaten up before being bundled into waiting police trucks without sanitisation and social distancing. They were then often detained in overcrowded holding cells which exposed them to greater risks of contracting and spreading Covid-19 (CITE, 2020). Law-enforcement agents were supposed to be the custodians of the law and protect vulnerable groups, but they were the greatest culprits in orchestrating and perpetrating violence and abuse on the very people whose security they were mandated to safeguard.

Coping mechanisms employed by informal traders during the Covid-19 period

Rural economies have limited livelihood diversity and cash reserves. Consequently, such economies, as was the case with most people in the Zaka District, were less prepared to resist shocks and livelihood disruptions caused by the Covid-19 pandemic. The Zimbabwean government unveiled ZWL$18 billion, equivalent to US$225 million at the November 2020 exchange rate (OECD, 2020), in an effort to cushion the ordinary people from the ravages of Covid-19. This was part of the Economic Recovery and Stimulus Package which was aimed at revitalising the economy and providing relief to individuals, families, small businesses, and industries negatively impacted by the economic slowdown caused by the Covid-19 pandemic (Government of Zimbabwe, 2020). The government promised a once-off cushioning allowance of ZWL$200 for each vulnerable person but more than four months into the lockdown, only 202 000 of the 1 million households targeted for assistance had received it (Mpofu, 2020). Even the targeted number of beneficiaries was a drop in the ocean considering the population of vulnerable people in Zimbabwe. Worse still, the relief fund was received by few individuals, especially those who had strong links to the ruling Zimbabwe African National Union Patriotic Front (ZANU-PF) party (Johnson Mutonzi, Christopher Gambo & Josam Ngano,

Separate Interviews: 18 April 2022). In actual fact, many people came to know about the fund when the registration of potential beneficiaries had been closed (John Ngoro, Samson Mutombo, Joel Shonga, Rabson Gudo & Knowledge Charindi, Separate Interviews: 19 April 2022). From the 40 interviews conducted for this study, only six respondents acknowledged receiving the cushion allowance from the government cushion. Many respondents from Ndanga, Chivamba, Chinorumba and Chekenyere areas of the Zaka District did not receive anything at all.

Some informal traders revealed during interviews that they devised a number of strategies to survive after their business operations had been disrupted by the advent of the Covid-19 pandemic and related developments. Most of the strategies involved surviving both within and against lockdown restrictions. From the interviews conducted for this study, most informal traders indicated that they played cat-and-mouse with the police during the day, 10% acknowledged resorting to night operations to sell their stock while 5% of the informants abandoned their businesses altogether. Many food vendors, grocery tuckshop owners and traditional beer-brewers in the Zaka District ceased operations altogether owing to the intensity of police raids and hefty fines. Itinerant vending became a major livelihood activity for most informal traders during which they had to travel over long distances to contact customers at a time when undesignated food markets were banned as a Covid-19 containment measure. During these travels, they often played hide-and-seek with the police, sometimes paying bribes in the process in an effort to avoid arrest and exorbitant fines. Chipo Matashu, a fruit and vegetable vendor, for example, stated during an interview that she had to walk from Muchavhutwi to Jerera Growth Point around 4am every day to be able to sell her stock before the police went out on patrols (Chipo Matashu, Interview: 11 April 2022).

Many informal traders who were involved in styling and dressing hairpieces, extensions and wigs, hair colouring and texturing highlighted that at the start of the total lockdown, they had to shut down their businesses completely as they were not considered essential service workers. During the first phase of the lockdown, some of them tried to continue their trade from their homes or travel to clients' homes, but this was difficult. Their clients were also hard-hit by income challenges owing to the Covid-19 lockdown and could not afford to spend scarce money on luxuries such hair-dressing. One hair-dresser commented that most of their female customers trimmed their hair to reduce expenditure and this meant a significant loss of business (Mercy Kondo, Interview: 4 February 2022). When the restrictions were relaxed, many hair-dressers struggled to get to Jerera Growth Point as they had no official letters to permit them to travel. Worse still, business was very low since most of their clients were also unable to travel and that most of them were cash-strapped owing to the Covid-19-induced lockdown (Joyce Chadzingwa, Mary Nyanyiwa & Josephine Jeresa, Focus Group Discussion, 7 April 2022).

Figure 3: Sources of income accessed by informal traders at six business centres in Zaka District during the lockdown (Source: Compiled by self from data gathered in 2021)

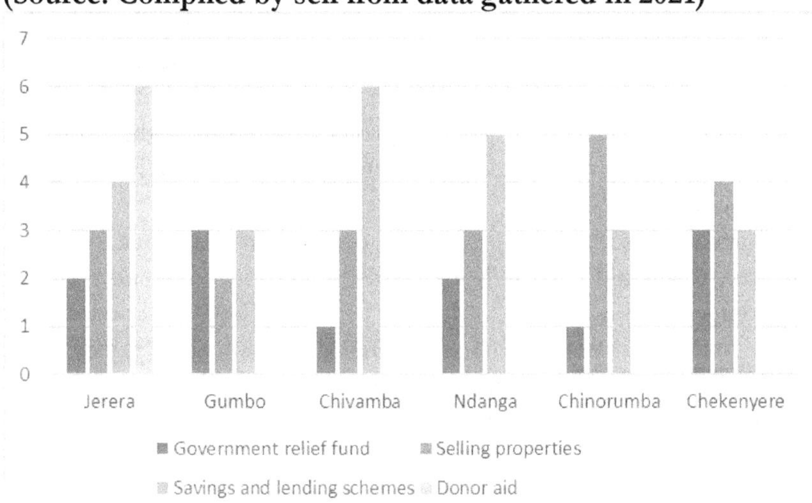

As mentioned earlier on in this chapter, the Covid-19 pandemic and government measures that were introduced to contain its spread increased the difficulties faced by the poor and marginalised people, most of who lacked the resources to respond to the disruptions that had been caused. Some vendors who had been knocked out of business by Covid-19 dynamics turned to the social media to ask for money and food donations (Ignatius Chari, Solomon Nharo & Numerous Tawonga, Separate Interviews: 27 April 2022). Some informal traders stated during focus group discussions that they either sold their properties or borrowed money from relatives and friends to bounce back into business, promising to pay back after the situation had normalised (Rumbidzai Chenjedzo, Lynette Gadzanga

& Grace Shanduko, Focus Group Discussion: 23 April 2022). Village savings and lending schemes (*mukando*) greatly assisted many informal traders to restart their business after the relaxation of lockdown restrictions. Savings from *mukando* were used to restock but such funds were accessed only by those who had joined these groups (Ibid; Ignatius Chari, Solomon Nharo & Numerous Tawonga, Separate Interviews: 27 April 2022).

Some informal traders at Jerera Growth Point were lucky enough to receive aid from Care International, a non-governmental organisation, under its Emergency Early Recovery Project that was launched as the Covid-19 pandemic subsided. Under this project, a household was entitled US$20 per head. Some informants testified during interviews that they managed to bounce back into business after utilising the funds donated by Care International under its Emergency Early Recovery Project (Rumbidzai Chenjedzo, Lynette Gadzanga & Grace Shanduko, Focus Group Discussion: 23 April 2022). The beneficiaries from this project highlighted that aid was only given to those vendors who were registered with the Jerera Rural District Council (Ibid).

Informal cross-border traders at privately-owned flea markets indicated that they had to borrow money to purchase new stock. They crossed the border illegally after bribing officials in most cases. They also relied on the help of unregistered cross-border transporters (*malaicha*) who acted as intermediaries between them and police officers. A respondent pointed out during an interview that some police officers and soldiers demanded sexual favours from female cross-border traders they would have arrested in exchange for their freedom, a move which was illegal, immoral and a violation of their rights (Janet Godzi, Interview: 10 April 2022). To compound the plight of informal cross-border traders, some *malaicha* were deceitful. As one cross-border trader indicated during an interview, most people were duped by the *malaicha*. Some *malaicha* delivered half the stock after converting the difference for their own use (Victoria Mhango, Interview: 11 April 2022).

Figure 4: Informal traders' coping mechanisms during the lockdown in Zaka District (Source: Compiled by self from research data gathered in 2021)

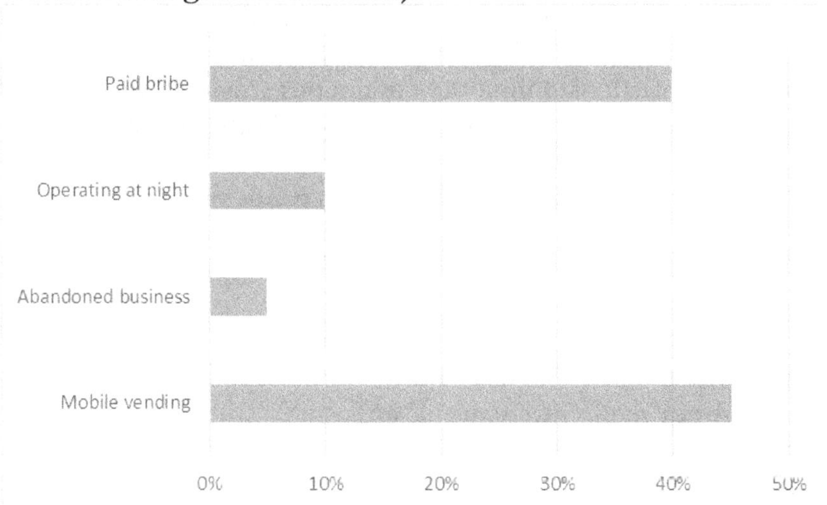

Interestingly, all these adversities experienced by informal traders in the Zaka District sometimes bred creativity and resilience. One respondent from Chinorumba Business Centre testified that she began to sew and sell cheaper cloth masks that had a ready market after the trade in second-hand clothes which she used to do was banned as a Covid-19 preventive measure (Cecilia Mukato, Interview: 25 April 2022). The closure of beer halls and bottle stores in the Zaka District during the lockdown saw a beer-brewer at Ndanga Business Centre managing to scoop the opportunity by converting one of his rooms into a shebeen. He explained that for the smooth operation of his shebeen, he had to pay a bribe of US$10 after every three days to the local police (Johannes Todyei, Interview: 16 April 2022).

Conclusion

The negative effects of the measures that were put in place by the government to curb the spread of the Covid-19 pandemic were felt by many sections of the population across the length and breadth of Zimbabwe including informal traders in the rural Zaka District of Masvingo Province. The closure of businesses that were deemed unessential had significant socio-economic repercussions on the livelihoods of rural informal traders and condemned many of them to poverty. The Covid-19 lockdown's travel restrictions constrained movements of informal traders and made it very difficult for them to access producers, manufacturers, retailers and customers. Despite these hardships, this chapter has demonstrated that the impoverished informal traders from many parts of the Zaka District devised an array of strategies to salvage livelihoods within and against the lockdown restrictions during the tumultuous Covid-19 period. The chapter winds up by urging governments and other stakeholders to put in place social assistance and protection mechanisms that prepare vulnerable groups for emergencies such as pandemics.

References

African Union (2020) 'Impact of the Corona virus (Covid-19) on the African economy,' Available at: https://au.int/sites/default/files/documents/, Accessed 26 May 2022.

Bhebhe, N. (13 April 2020) 'Covid-19 lockdown: Soldiers mercilessly beat up residents, abduct woman from her tuckshop at 10pm,' Available at: https://www.myzimbabwe.co.zw/news/63005-covid-19-lockdown-soldiers-mercilessly-beat-up-residents-abduct-woman-from-her-tuckshop-at-10pm.html, Accessed 27 May 2022.

Carreras, M. Saha, A. and Thompson, J. (2020) 'Rapid assessment of the impact of Covid-19 on food system and rural livelihoods in sub-Saharan Africa,' Available at: https://opendocs.ids.ac.uk/opendocs/handle/20.500.12413/15715. Accessed 25 May 2022.

Chigudu, D. (2021) 'Street entrepreneurship in the wake of Covid-19: The dilemma of street vending and strategies for endurance,' in: *International Journal of Economics and Business Administration,* Volume 6, Number 1, 2021. Available at: https://www.google.com/search? Accessed on 15 May 2022.

Dzobo, M. Chitungo, I. & Dzinamarira, T. (2020) 'Letter to the editors: Covid-19: A perspective for lifting lockdown in Zimbabwe', Available at: https://www.researchgate.net/publication/345323250, Accessed 27 May 2022.

Dudzai, C. & Wamara, C.K. (2021) 'The Covid-19 pandemic and the informal sector in Zimbabwe,' in: *African Journal of Social Work*, Volume 11, Number 4, pp.201-208. Available at:

https://africasocialwork.net/current-and-past-issues/, Accessed 25 May 2022.
Food and Agriculture Organisation (2020) 'Addressing the impacts of Covid-19 in food crises, April–December 2020: FAO's component of the Global Covid-19 Humanitarian Response Plan,' Rome: Food and Agriculture Organisation.
Government of Zimbabwe (2020) 'Public Health (Covid-19 Prevention, Containment and Treatment) (National Lockdown) (Amendment) Order, 2020 (No. 5). Statutory Instrument 99 of 2020 [CAP. 15:17]', Harare: Government Printer. Available at: https://www.smeaz.org.zw/media/com_acymailing/upload/, Accessed 24 May 2022.
International Labour Organisation (2020) 'Covid-19 crisis and the informal economy immediate responses and policy challenges,' ILO Brief, May 2020. Available at: https://www.ilo.org/wcmsp5/groups/public/ed_protect/protrav/travail/documents/briefingnote/wcms_743623.pdf, Accessed 25 May 2022.
Jaka, H. & Shava, E. (2018) 'Resilient rural women's livelihoods for poverty alleviation and economic empowerment in semi-arid regions of Zimbabwe,' Available at: https://www.researchgate.net/publication/327593997, Accessed 27 May 2022.
Kulkarni, P. (2020) 'Small vendors hard hit by government-ordered demolitions in Zimbabwe,' Available at: https://peoplesdispatch.org/2020/04/29/, Accessed 27 May 2022.
Malik, S. & Naeem, K. (2020) 'Impact of the Covid-19 pandemic on women's health, livelihoods and domestic violence,' Available at: https://www.iassw-aiets.org/wp content/uploads/2021/01/, Accessed 27 May 2022.
Makombe, E.K. (2021) 'Between a rock and a hard place. The Corona virus, livelihoods, and socio-economic upheaval in Harare's high-density areas of Zimbabwe,' in: *Journal of Developing Societies*, Volume 37, Number 3, pp.275-301, Available at: https://journals.sagepub.com/doi/full/10.1177/0169796X211030062t, Accessed on 14 May 2022.
Mashapure, R. (2021) 'Socio-economic implications of the Covid-19 pandemic to women entrepreneurs: A case of the informal sector,' Available at:

https://www.macrothink.org/journal/index.php/bms/article/view/17911/1399, Accessed 25 May 2022.

Mhlanga, D. & Ndhlovu, E. (2020) 'Socio-economic implications of the Covid-19 pandemic on smallholder livelihoods in Zimbabwe,' Available at: https://www.preprints.org/manuscript/202004.0219/v1, Accessed 27 May 2022.

Mpofu, M. (7 May 2020) 'So sad: Corona virus (Covid-19) lockdown bites Zimbabwean vendors,' Available at: https://www.myzimbabwe.co.zw/news/64056 html, Accessed 27 May 2022.

Mukeredzi, T. (16 June 2020) 'Dying of hunger: Zimbabwe street vendors hit by Corona virus clampdown,' Available at: https://news.trust.org/item/20200616041603-v7z5f/, Accessed 27 May 2022.

Mukeredzi, T. (2020) 'Zimbabwe's triple threat: Corona virus, food shortages and an economy in meltdown,' Available at: https://www.thenewhumanitarian.org/news, Accessed 27 May 2022.

Ndebele, L. & Matimaire, K. (3 April 2020) 'Fruit and vegetables impounded during Zimbabwe lockdown,' Available at: https://www.timeslive.co.za/news/africa/2020-04-03-fruit-and-vegetables-impounded-during-zimbabwe-lockdown/, Accessed 27 May 2022.

OECD (March 2020) 'Interim Economic Assessment Corona virus: The world economy at risk,' Available at: https://www.oecd.org/berlin/publikationen/Interim-Economic-Assessment-2-March-2020.pdf, Accessed 26 May 2022.

Ozili, P. K. (2020) 'Impacts of the Covid-19 pandemic and economic crisis: The Nigerian experience and structural causes,' Available at: https://www.researchgate.net/publication/, Accessed 26 May 2022.

Rafaeli, T. and Hutchinson, G. (2020) 'The secondary impacts of Covid-19 on women and girls in sub-Saharan Africa,' Available at: https://resource-centre-uploads.s3.amazonaws.com/uploads/830, Accessed 27 May 2022.

Shaik, H. (2020) 'Responding to the impacts of Covid-19 on informal workers in South Asia,' Available at: https://www.theigc.org/blog/, Accessed 27 May 2022.

United States Embassy (2020) 'Human Rights Report: Zimbabwe, 2020,' Available at: https://zw.usembassy.gov/2020-human-rights-report-zimbabwe/, Accessed 27 May 2022.

Zimbabwe Human Rights NGO Forum (17 April 2020) 'Illegalities, human rights violations, and inadequacy of measures in response to Covid-19,' Available at: https://kubatana.net/2020/04/23/illegalities-human-rights-violations-and-inadequacy-of-measures-in-response-to-covid-19, Accessed 27 May 2022.

Zimbabwe Ministry of Health and Child Care (2020) 'Zimbabwe preparedness and response plan: Covid-19,' Available at: https://kubatana.net/2020/03/19/, Accessed 27 May 2022.

Zimbabwe Statistics Agency (2012) 'Updated 2012 population census projections report,' Available at: http://www.citypopulation.de/php/zimbabwe, Accessed 12 May 2022.

Zimbabwe Peace Project Report (2021) 'Impact of Covid-19 on socio-economic rights in Zimbabwe,' Available at: https://reliefweb.int/sites/reliefweb.int/files/resources/, Accessed 12 May 2022.

Chapter 10

Covid-19 Mitigation Dynamics in Zimbabwe: A New Battleground for Political Contest and Human Rights Debate?

Benice Farai Nkomo

Introduction

In response to the advent of Covid-19 in Zimbabwe, the government adopted a battery of mitigation measures to manage the impact of the pandemic. The implementation, however, largely assumed political undertones as the ruling Zimbabwe African National Union Patriotic Front (ZANU-PF) party under President Emmerson Mnangagwa sought to gain undue political advantage, dismember and ultimately 'annihilate' political opposition parties and supress civil society movements, muzzle the media, and narrow democratic space under the guise of managing a health emergency. The government prohibited gatherings, suspended electoral and parliamentary programmes, limited court processes and orchestrated the arrest of opposition players for 'disregarding' Covid-19 containment regulations. Opposition political parties and pro-democracy movements criticised the government for its politicised and militarised management of the pandemic and its role in brazenly fomenting opposition intra-party conflicts as well as inhuman and degrading treatment of citizens by the state security forces. A whole spectrum of citizens' rights and liberties, including freedom of political choice and participation, of assembly, of information and of movement, right to peaceful protest and legal or legislative representation were trampled upon as the ruling regime pushed for political survival.

In this chapter, events, regulations and pronouncements related to Covid-19 pandemic will be examined to illustrate that, while considerable restrictions to certain rights and liberties during emergencies is an acceptable global phenomenon, the manner in which mitigation dynamics of the pandemic panned out in the Zimbabwean case points to political weaponisation of a health emergency situation. The pandemic evolved into a new theatre for political contestations that ensued in Mnangagwa's so-called 'New Dispensation' and amplified debates around the highly contested 2018 polls wherein issues of leadership legitimacy and human rights continued to be persistently raised by the opposition.

Covid-19, human rights and politics in Africa

Various nations across the globe implemented an array of interventions with a view to combat the spread of Corona virus infections. The main constituent features of these measures included declarations of lockdowns, deployment of state security personnel to enforce adherence with protocols, closure of borders, restrictions or complete banning of large public gatherings and movements, wearing of masks, physical distancing, closure of recreational facilities and events, establishment of testing, quarantine and treatment facilities as well as vaccination. This presentation leans much on those measures which had implications for politics and enjoyment of rights and liberties from early 2020 to early 2022 with specific reference to Zimbabwe.

Amnesty International (2020) documented cases in about 60 countries which adopted 'punitive and coercive measures' which resulted in a range of human rights violations, divided societies and failed to effectively tackle the pandemic. The human rights watchdog concluded that, while certain rights and norms can justifiably be restricted on account of legal fundamentals and legitimate reasons like public health protection and them being proportionate, there were numerous cases of 'state over-reach' and abuse of power that were wrongly justified in the name of protecting public health. Examples are referenced from the organisation's survey in 2020 and other sources. A Zambian police spokesperson summed up their lockdown policing thrust thus: 'We hammer you, we hit you and then we do detention. If you escape you are lucky'. In Kenya, seven people were killed and 16 left hospitalised during enforcement of curfew while seven men had been arrested by April 2020 for going to buy food. Kenya's President had to apologise for 'overzealous policing' while killings by security officers enforcing lockdowns were reported in Ghana, Nigeria, Kenya and South Africa (Allen & Du Plessis, 2020). In Uganda, human rights violations were reported involving 19 youths at a shelter for lesbian, gay, bisexual and transgender persons in Kampala where they were accused of not observing social distancing rules and other Covid-19 offences. They were questioned, assaulted and detained for 50 days, with some among them being denied access to HIV/AIDS medication (Obasa *et al*, August 2020).

Even though the situation gradually eased, South Africa had arguably one of the world's most restrictive lockdowns, some of whose provisions were declared 'invalid' and 'unconstitutional' (Ibid). A total of up to 73 000 troops were deployed in that country until end of June 2020 to enforce the lockdown. By April 2020, hundreds (including the homeless) had been arrested or assaulted for Covid-19 offences. In some instances, the police fired rubber bullets at supermarket shoppers and in three cases this heavy-handedness turned fatal (Allen & Du Plessis, 2020; Noko, 2020). President Ramaphosa had to comment on police 'over-enthusiasm' as by late May 2020 more people had been arrested in his country than any other for violating Corona virus lockdown measures and at least 11 men had died owing to state security actions (Parker, 2020).

In Togo, a state of emergency and a curfew were declared in April 2020 while 5 000 soldiers were deployed to clear public markets. In Nigeria, police had killed 18 people by April 2020 in a wave of police brutality during the lockdown while Ethiopia, citing anti-Covid-19 precautions, postponed an election scheduled for August 2020 (Aidi, 2020). Uganda's Covid-19 Taskforce was led by the army and a series of misconduct cases, abuses and excesses against civilians by soldiers and local defence units were noted during the lockdown. This resulted in some officers being arrested and convicted, the military chief apologising to victims, and the President directing that the brutalities be investigated (*Conversation*, 12 May 2020).

While it is beyond the scope of this chapter to comprehensively evaluate the effectiveness of various measures implemented against the pandemic, these few examples from 2020 clearly bring to the fore how rights and freedoms were heavily trampled on the back of claims to the objective of fighting the Covid-19 threat. It is the submission of this chapter that Zimbabwe was no exception to the infringement of legally protected rights in that context. The deployment of security officers, in particular, blighted the otherwise well-intentioned mitigation strategies against the pandemic.

Overview of Covid-19 mitigation dynamics and human rights abuses in Zimbabwe

In Zimbabwe, Corona virus cases were first detected in March 2020 (Maulani *et al*, December 2020) and thereafter, the number went on an upward trend. It was reported around 22 July 2020 that confirmed cumulative cases nationally rose by 65.6% in a week from 1 034 to 1 734 while the cumulative statistics for localised cases rose by 204.9% from 286 to 872, with most of the cases reported in Bulawayo and Harare (*Herald*, 22 July 2020). Despite its socio-economic fragilities, Zimbabwe also adopted a raft of Covid-19 curtailment measures in line with recommendations from the World Health Organisation such as lockdowns, closure of ports of entry and educational institutions, banning and/or restriction of gatherings, establishment of testing, isolation and quarantine facilities, wearing of masks and practising social distancing. The lockdown element, with its various facets, became the highly controversial aspect of these measures in relation to its impact on citizens and communities socially, politically, economically, culturally and psychologically. The first 21-day national lockdown was declared and implemented from 30 March 2020 and then extended indefinitely on 16 May 2020 with provision for two-week reviews (Price, 2020). Thus, throughout 2020 until 2022, lockdowns were frequently reviewed.

Although there is no universally accepted definition of lockdown, Haider *et al* (2020) regard it as "a set of measures aimed at reducing transmission of Covid-19 that are mandatory, applied indiscriminately to a general population and involve some restrictions on the established pattern of social and economic life." This definition is quite comprehensive and suffices for this chapter. A National Taskforce was also set-up to coordinate the national response to the pandemic (*Herald*, 28 March 2020) while the majority of measures were promulgated through statutory instruments by the Health Minister and presidential proclamations. Nelson Chamisa, the leader of the then opposition Movement for Democratic Change Alliance (MDC-A) endorsed the adoption of these measures against the pandemic, declaring: "Politics aside, we must unite to save lives", even when President Mnangagwa intimated a total lockdown some of whose measures were going to be drastic and "sure to upset the daily routines of our lives" (*Reuters*, 27 March 2020). Chamisa's party was later to emerge the number one victim of these measures as ZANU-PF sought to dominate the political terrain and maintain power at all costs.

This chapter contends that the implementation of Covid-19 mitigation measures, particularly lockdowns, wearing of masks, physical distancing, prohibition of 'unnecessary' movements, and gatherings by the public resulted in serious breaches of the citizens' rights and freedoms that were enshrined in both the national constitution and many international rights instruments. With reference to various incidents and developments since from early 2020 until 2022, it is further submitted that the implementation of laws and guidelines to combat the pandemic in Zimbabwe was blighted by outright politicisation.

For a long time since independence, political contestations and debates had revolved around the Gukurahundi massacres in the provinces of Matabeleland and the Midlands, Economic Structural Adjustment Programmes (ESAPs), one party state ideology, role of opposition parties, war veterans and status of civil society in post-colonial political transitioning, citizens' rights, the violent land reform programme, electoral (mal-)practices, sanctions, militarisation of politics, and economic malaise among others. The onset of Covid-19 and interventions implemented to mitigate its impact added a new facet to this long list. Discourses around the Covid-19 pandemic intersected with, and reinforced these already existing contentious scenarios and in the process, raised renewed focus on human rights and civil liberties, as well as introducing other dimensions to the political landscape.

In Zimbabwe, the army and the police historically played the role of protecting state power and their harassment of communities appeared motivated by a "desire to instil fear than to protect citizens from the potentially deadly virus" (Rivers & Ndlovu, 2020). Zimbabwe was judged to have had the largest number of arrests of journalists and "most pandemic-related press freedom violations" in Africa (International Press Institute, 17 March 2021). The police denied breaching human rights yet non-governmental organisations documented numerous incidents to the contrary. In addition, social media platforms also circulated video evidence of abuses. It should be noted that around 2 000 people had been arrested during the first week of the lockdown allegedly for defying anti-Covid-19 protocols (*Al-jazeera*, 6 April 2020).

The pandemic set in against the background of a highly charged political environment following the 2018 polls, wherein the main opposition MDC Alliance cited electoral malpractices and refused to endorse the victory of ZANU-PF under President Emmerson Mnangagwa. It is argued here that the resultant leadership legitimacy issues emanating from those elections persisted and largely came to characterise the contest between the major political parties during the pandemic. The government was accused of using the lockdown restrictions on freedoms to dismantle strong opposition from the MDC Alliance and its civil society allies while propping up 'insignificant' political parties. On the other hand, the opposition actively took steps to portray the government in bad light (Raquel, 2020). Nelson Chamisa declared the 'New Dispensation' under Emmerson Mnangagwa 'a rogue regime' where citizens lived in a 'pariah state' (*Reuters*, 20 November 2019)

The Constitution of Zimbabwe (2013) as well as regional and international conventions are key referral documents for this chapter as they outline and elaborate the human rights and liberties which the government should avail for the enjoyment of citizens. Right from the preamble, the constitution emphasises the need to entrench democracy, good, transparent and accountable governance and rule of law and reaffirmation to upholding and defending fundamental human rights and freedoms. It also advocates for multi-party democracy, free, fair and regular elections in addition to adequate representation of the electorate and respect for the rights of all political parties. Chapter 4 of the Constitution, which dwells on the Declaration of Rights, urges the state, every person, every institution and agents of government at every level to "respect, protect, promote and fulfil the rights and freedoms set out in this Chapter". The rights and freedoms captured include right to personal liberty (not to be detained without trial, not to be deprived of liberty arbitrarily or without just cause); rights of arrested and detained persons (to be informed of reason of arrest promptly, to be allowed to inform a person of their choice or a lawyer at the state's expense without delay, allowed to consult a legal or medical practitioner of their choice promptly, be treated humanely and with dignity, to be released unconditionally or on reasonable bail pending a charge or trial); right to human dignity, to personal security, to privacy, to political rights and to a fair hearing. Freedoms include freedom from torture, cruel, inhumane and degrading treatment or punishment, of assembly and association, to demonstrate and petition, of the media and of expression. It will be argued that these rights and freedoms were, to a greater extent, thrown out of the window despite them being guaranteed by the constitution. The state agents and institutions mandated by the constitution to protect and promote rights and freedoms were in fact the biggest violators of the same.

Civil society organisations compiled detailed reports, baseline surveys and sustained debates on Covid-19 mitigation frameworks and these constituted valuable sources for this chapter. Perspectives of political party leaders, activists and reports of civil society organisations were also captured to illustrate how political contestations were amplified on the back of the Corona virus. The alleged sensationalisation, fabrication and politicisation of certain reports by some of these organisations and active political players should be borne in mind. Yet they remain important as government and its agents rarely documented, investigated and publicly reported alleged human rights infringements and political malpractices.

According to the Zimbabwe Peace Project Report for February 2021 captioned 'Smothered, oppressed and crushed', the army and police contributed to 12.12% and 59.6% of human rights violations respectively. That month saw increased police patrols and a resultant surge in arbitrary and random arrests, harassment, rising frequency of rights violations and increased vulnerability of citizens. Of much concern were reports of 10 Covid-19 related killings to be detailed in this chapter. The Zimbabwe Human Rights Commission acknowledged the reports of abuses from non-governmental organisations, and promised to further investigate and monitor the situation (*VOA News*, 29 April 2021). The so-called 'New Dispensation' under President Mnangagwa, which came to power in 2017, largely inherited the legal, administrative and security architecture from the Mugabe regime and stepped up repression to safeguard its authority (UK Home Office, September 2020). The majority of human rights violations in 2020 were attributable to heavy-handed policing of the Covid-19 pandemic by security sector and state proxies, including ZANU-PF, with the median proportion of these committed by the police increasing from 29% in 2019 to 51% by mid-2021. The proportion attributable to ZANU-PF over the same period declined to 19% from 35% and all these trends are accounted for by enforcement of Covid-19 protocols and the role of the enforcing agents (Ibid).

Since 'Covid-19 politics' is a major consideration for this study, it is noteworthy to state that according to Armed Conflict Location & Event Data Project for 2020, 16% of the events which involved interaction between state agents and protestors/civilians had a specific reference to MDC participation. Suspected state security operatives tortured and abducted 70 government critics while a series of arbitrary arrests and violent assaults continued in that year, indicating a deterioration of the human rights situation (Ibid).

Situating the study in academic discourse

This section acknowledges a number of scholarly works which are relevant to the central argument of this contribution. Matthew *et al* (2020) identified hidden variables in the management and mitigation of Covid-19 among which are: civil-security relations, the use of executive orders without input of the affected people leading to resistance, politicisation of measures, lack of education on the pandemic, impact of conspiracy theories and high politicisation of the pandemic, as well as the use of technology. These scholars deploy the term 'Covid-19 politics' to refer to a new political culture where disasters and pandemics become a new political tool and cite the sabotage strategy by the opposition MDC in Zimbabwe which involved undermining government initiatives. They further submit that the Covid-19 pandemic became a highly politicised discourse.

Raquel (2020) briefly considered the contestation for political power in Zimbabwe in the context of the Covid-19 pandemic. In their study of the gendered socio-economic implications of the pandemic, Ndhlovu & Tembo (2020) focused on gender-based violence, implications of the pandemic on livelihoods and, more significantly, noted that rights to social protection, food and health were not fully attended to while the police and army enforced the lockdown in an 'unfriendly' manner thereby denying people access to services.

Nkomo and Mangiza (2021) studied civil disobedience and images of war, anchoring on the role of the military and police. While some issues raised therein bear similarities with this chapter, the difference exists in the latter placing more emphasis on the political dimensions. The work of Moyo and Phulu (2021) titled 'The Weaponisation of the Corona Virus Crisis in Zimbabwe: Legal and Extra-Legal Instruments' is an elaborate contribution which informs the thrust of this chapter which attempts to pursue that debate further. By weaponisation, the authors refer to the repurposing of the fight against the Covid-19 crisis for goals other than public health considerations by the ruling executive-military alliance. They concluded that the government's highly securitised approach sought to use the lockdown measures to clamp down on political opposition, silence critics, and contain a restive population while entrenching its power and control on key accountability institutions such as the judiciary, legislature and media. Mawere (2020) sought to unpack other dangerous pandemics within the lockdown by discussing the case of female MDC supporters allegedly abducted and savagely tortured. Tofa (2020) also highlighted how the authorities used the pandemic to justify disproportionate repression and suspension of fundamental rights and freedoms as well decimate remnants of political pluralism.

Rights, politics and the face mask

In early May 2020, the government extended but relaxed the lockdown to Level 2 which entailed, among other issues, that citizens must wear face masks of any type (including home-made cloth ones) in all public spaces or when they went outside their homes. It was emphasised that failure to wear a mask as gazetted in the statutory instrument was henceforth an offence that people could be arrested for. Police advised against the tendency of putting on a mask on approaching a check-point and removing it afterwards (Zimbabwe Republic Police, 30 June 2021). It was ironic, particularly in the early days, that police officers who arrested mask offenders did not wear them themselves, neither did they practise social distancing (Maulani *et al*, 2020). By early April 2020, however, rising numbers of officers were observed at roadblocks with masks and gloves (*Herald*, 10 April 2020).

The face mask was endorsed by the World Health Organisation as a critical mitigation tool in the fight against the Corona virus and though Zimbabwean authorities adopted a liberal stance as to the types and quality that people could wear, the mask gained notoriety for being one of the major Covid-19 preventive requirements that so many people were arrested, detained, beaten and fined for. More poignantly, this little piece of cloth emerged as a platform on which intolerance of alternative political opinion and politicisation of the Covid-19 pandemic and attendant suppression of rights, liberties and freedoms played out. According to press and police sources, about 800 000 people had been arrested between late March 2020 and July 2021 for violating Covid-19 preventive regulations such as failure to wear a mask, travelling and gathering unnecessarily, operating outside prescribed business hours (*VOA News*, 12 July 2021). Of the 3 236 arrested on 3 February 2021 for contravening Covid-19 curtailment measures, 997 were for not wearing masks (*New Zimbabwe*, 5 February 2021).

It became common for people to wear masks for fear of the police and the military rather than for their safety. Thus, the lockdown was to some extent not well appreciated from a health security perspective by the general public (Matthew *et al*, September 2020). Some spirit mediums, headmen and chiefs declined to wear masks as they regarded the pandemic as punishment from angry gods or ancestors (Ibid). From July 2021, the fines for violating various Covid-19 containment regulations were increased steeply, with failure to put on a mask attracting ZWL$1 000 which was a 100% increment. The responsible minister argued that there was need for deterrent fines to curb the spread of the pandemic (*Zim Metro*, 29 July 2021).

On 13 April 2021, two prominent MDC Alliance members from Masvingo Province, Charles Zaranyika (Secretary for Information, Gutu North Constituency) and Edward Chagonda (Branch Secretary for Information, Gutu Central Constituency) were arrested at Mupandawana Growth Point for allegedly wearing red masks inscribed 'MDC Chamisa *Chete Chete*' (Chamisa the only one) though the police details prevaricated over the real crime committed (*Zimbabwean*, 7 May 2021). Police constables Munyaradzi Mashamba and Rufaro Kufakunesu accused them of criminal nuisance or touting for passengers at a bus terminus while the former had an additional charge of 'not properly wearing a mask'. On the way to the police station, the accused alleged that the constables warned them that the police did not recognize opposition party masks. The two accused MDC officials were locked up in custody for close to a week before a lawyer bailed them. Their attorney expressed outright shock that someone could be incarcerated and lose freedom over minor issues (Ibid). The Presiding Magistrate, Madlenkosi Ndhlovu, later dismissed the duo's case before full trial on account of failure to establish a *prima facie* case and his detailed commentary intimated strongly on the abuse of power and non-observance of people's rights by the police. The Presiding Magistrate argued: "…Police abused their power in the arrest of the two and depended more on mere speculation…This case is like a boxing ring scenario where the law-enforcement agents have an upper hand over their opponents before the match has even begun" (*Mbare Times*, 25 May 2021). He further criticised the police statements for inconsistency, contradictions and for lacking the most crucial evidence to establish a case. On the issue relating to criminal nuisance, the Magistrate added, the police needed members of the public as independent eye-witnesses to testify, yet they had none. The accused argued in court that they were arrested for donning 'MDC masks' (Ibid). The opposition activists alleged being harassed for their right to belong or associate and advance the interests of a political movement of their choice (Ibid).

For the greater part of 2020, the 'Ferret Team', a joint team comprising the police, the military and secret intelligence officers, also terrorised government critics, opposition leaders especially from the MDC Alliance, and activists and their families who were found distributing masks with labels supporting opposition political parties (Amnesty International, 2020). On 7 August 2020, for example, four men abducted Noxolo Maphosa from the streets and sexually assaulted her in a bid to force her to reveal the whereabouts of her uncle, Josphat Ngulube of the MDC Alliance, who was reportedly distributing face masks with anti-ZANU-PF slogans (Ibid). Ngulube had contested the 2018 polls as an independent candidate in the Bulawayo South Parliamentary Constituency but lost. He later joined the MDC Alliance and rose to become the party's Provincial Youth Assembly Secretary for Research and Policy. During the 2019 fuel price protests, Ngulube was accused of burning three cars and property belonging to a ZANU-PF provincial leader in Bulawayo. He was sentenced to six years in prison but served only two months after applying for bail pending appeal (*Chronicle*, 22 April 2020; *Standard*, 3 May 2020; *ZimEye*, 22 April 2020). Throughout 2020, Ngulube was a key character in the battles for political space and appropriation of masks for political advantage during the Covid-19 lockdown. He was a lead figure for a team of people who manufactured and distributed masks all over the country written '#ZANU-PF must go!' Ngulube and Mthulisi Hanana, Director of the Dumiso Dabengwa Foundation, trended on social media after pictures showed them distributing those masks in Bulawayo (*Newsday Zimbabwe*, 30 July 2020). Thus, a pandemic mitigation tool in the form of a face mask came to symbolise freedom of expression and association. It became a platform for relaying political messaging pitting ZANU-PF and opposition parties, especially the MDC-A, with accusations and counter-accusations featuring prominently.

In late July 2020 suspected state security agents, whom Ngulube termed 'ZANU-PF thugs' armed with AK47 rifles, allegedly stormed into his Bulawayo home, stole 22 000 Rands and US$850, looted alcohol and took away documents while they threatened his wife and children (*Mbare Times*, 29 July 2020). He further alleged on Facebook that the intruders demanded that:

> I should stop leading the demonstration but the leader of the demonstration, Ngaruvhume, is in prison. They have just abducted Otillia Sibanda this morning [in] a white Honda Fit and a Toyota Platz…Is this the Second Gukurahundi or what? The 'ZANU-PF must go' was formed by Thandekile Moyo and liking it is not a crime. We should fix the nation, not persecute other people. People are hungry, people want jobs not guns (Ibid).

Ngulube and an accomplice, Noxolo, later fled to South Africa where they sought refuge at a police station. Back home, in Bulawayo during the night of 28 July 2020, masked assailants suspected to be state security agents forcibly broke locks and doors into Hanana's home. Armed with machetes, they demanded to be given the '#ZANU-PF must go' branded masks. They allegedly pointed a gun at a six-week-old baby and a two-year-old toddler. Furthermore, they placed a machete on the neck of Hanana's wife in an effort to force her to disclose his whereabouts (*Nehanda Radio*, 7 August 2020). Writing on Twitter, Ngulube located the intersectionality between Covid-19 and the broader protest movement in the country and rallied citizens to embrace the mask as a symbol of protest. He argued:

> I played my part to introduce the masks to you Zimbabwe to promote silent protest and to make sure democratic space does not close even under lockdown. It is up to you what you will do. I have lost contact with [the masks] distribution teams but I know they are producing and working…A new Zimbabwe is possible…Get a mask and inscribe '#Zanu-PF must go' even [with a] pen. Let the rule knowing [sic] how you feel about them. Revolutionary salutations! (Twitter: Umalume@UncleMthwithi, 28 July 2020).

Another case which illustrates how the long-drawn bruising battle between the country's political protagonists found expression and new traction through Covid-19, and in particular face masks, was that of an MDC Alliance senior official Prince Dubeko Sibanda, the then Matabeleland North Provincial Chairman and Member of Parliament for Binga, who was arrested, interrogated at the Law and Order Section, and remanded on bail to 17 September 2020. He was accused of inciting public violence after distributing #ZANU-PF-must-go-inscribed masks to two employees of TM Pick and Pay Supermarket, Marvellous Ndaba and Brian Maunze, on 2 August 2020 in Bulawayo (*New Zimbabwe*, 24 July 2020; *New Zimbabwe Vision*,

27 August 2020; *Pindula News*, 18 September 2020; *Zim Live*, 24 August 2020). A witness, Matthew Mutavayi, who testified in court, claimed:

> As a citizen who was waiting to get a service [at the supermarket] I felt irritated…They proudly showed me their face masks [they got from Sibanda] and reiterated that indeed '#ZANU-PF must go'. [The workers] infringed on my rights as a citizen who was waiting to get a service at a shopping centre [when they allegedly discarded serving me to go to Sibanda]. Also judging from the political atmosphere in the country at that time, I feared for my life and safety as I felt Sibanda's conduct would incite violence (*Pindula News*, 18 September 2020).

In his defence, Sibanda accused the witness of overzealousness and intolerance towards people with different political beliefs. He also insisted that he was entitled to freedom of expression, right of choice of political affiliation and that, as a member of the opposition, he was allowed to say 'ZANU-PF must go' through peaceful democratic processes (Ibid). He therefore described the charges as spurious and added: "I think it is a continuation of persecution of opposition members and leaders" (*Newsday*, 25 August 2020). Sibanda raised political stakes further when he made sensational claims on Twitter that through his interface with government employees, including during his court appearances, police, prison officers, prosecutors and other civil servants requested the '#ZANU-PF must go' masks from him (*IndaAfrica*, 25 August 2020). While it is difficult to establish the veracity of the claims, such employees were not expected to actively participate in party political activity and had for years been pressurised to pay loyalty to the governing ZANU-PF party.

Despite having opposition cadres arrested and harassed over masks, ZANU-PF made its own masks and distributed them across the length and breadth of the country. These masks, featuring the party President's portrait and ZANU-PF party symbols and images, together with similarly branded hand sanitisers, were integrated into the ruling party's paraphernalia and distributed widely across the nation in an endeavour to attain political mileage (Moyo & Phulu, 2021). In Harare, the ZANU-PF Women's League launched a Covid-19 awareness programme where President Emmerson Mnangagwa donated 1 450 rolls of fabric to make masks (*Sunday Mail*, 13 January 2021). The party's National Youth League donated groceries, sanitary wear and face masks in Hatclife Suburb, Harare, which a member of the public denounced: "Politicising donations from somewhere…Rubbish!!" (Twitter, @ZANU-PF-patriots, 25 June 2020). In the Matabeleland South Province, the ZANU-PF Women's League launched a massive face mask production project (*Herald*, 21 August 2021). At the launch of the project, 13 000 masks were freely distributed to 13 parliamentary constituencies with each constituency receiving 1 000 masks and material to produce more (Ibid). Such incidents clearly show that the ruling party distributed masks and other Covid-19 sundries freely along partisan lines as opposed to MDC Alliance activists who had to contend with a lot of harassment and arrests. Otherwise, in line with their rights, all citizens were expected to have equal access to Corona virus mitigation accessories from a government-led initiative.

While elections remained suspended throughout 2020 into 2021 as a measure against the spread of the Corona virus, ZANU-PF's prospective candidates for vacant parliamentary and local council seats, and some eyeing the 2023 polls, campaigned visibly across the country, using face masks in most cases as bait to lure the electorate. In early September 2021, for example, one candidate donated face masks in the Mberengwa East Constituency's Wards 5, 6 and 8 (*Newsday*, 8 September 2021). In Zvishavane, some losing candidates in ZANU-PF primary polls prior to the 2018 general elections showed renewed interest in future contests by distributing masks inscribed with the party logo across the constituency (Personal Observations: 2020 & 2021). In early June 2020, a delegation of senior ruling party officials in the Midlands Province donated face masks, sanitisers and gloves to Mvuma District Hospital (*Herald*, 8 June 2020). From the ongoing, it became a matter of serious concern for human rights advocates when Covid-19 and materials to control its spread were distributed along partisan lines, especially by ruling party leaders. In this manner, the mask was being weaponised for purposes of political campaigning, and privileging party supporters with protective clothing while leaving out political supporters unprotected and vulnerable to the pandemic.

President Mnangagwa followed suit and donated 50 000 face masks to the Johane Masowe eChishanu Apostolic Church in Bulawayo as part of the fight against Covid-19 (*Herald*, 14 June 2021). During the handover ceremony, the church leader, Bishop Mutumwa, urged congregants to join ZANU-PF which he said was under an effective and pro-development leadership. Mutumwa proceeded to appeal to the government to allocate his denomination a farm, mine and other forms of assistance as part of economic empowerment in line with President Mnangagwa's Vision 2030 (*Bulawayo 24 News*, 14 June 2021). The political dimension of this donation is quite apparent considering that ZANU-PF was mobilising support in the build-up to the upcoming 2023 elections. Apostolic sects, which boast of large followings, were a favourite hunting ground for ruling party support, a trend which continued during the Covid-19 lockdown with the face mask playing a critical part in the dynamics. In such cases, ordinary citizens were being lured to lend support to a particular political party by appropriating masks, thereby comprising their freedom to freely chose parties as well as other decisions in that regard without being shepherded by partisan leaders.

The administration of face masks in the fight against Covid-19 was often accompanied by human rights abuses on civilians by the law-enforcement agents. An example can be drawn from the arrest and detention of a woman, together with her two toddlers who were below the age of four years, at Rhodesville Police Station in Harare because the two kids "were not wearing masks [though she] had a mask herself" (*Herald*, 14 February 2021). In an analysis and opinion piece in a local newspaper, the *Herald*, the editor argued that the incident was sad, most unfortunate, shocking and regrettable, pointing further that among other psychological issues, the children were more exposed to Covid-19 in the cells as they had no masks. The editor further opined that throwing minors into confined and presumably overcrowded cells demonstrated high levels of excitement over common sense by police officers, adding that young children were entitled to protection and care by both the adults and law-enforcement agents (Ibid). This case clearly flew in the face of the Zimbabwean Constitution (2013, Part 3: Section 81) very elaborately provides that every child below the age of 18 years has a right "not to be detained except as measure of last resort and, if detained, to be detained for the shortest appropriate period, to be kept separately from detained persons over the age of eighteen years and to be treated in a manner, and kept in conditions, that take account of the child's age. A child's best interests are paramount in every matter concerning that child". Thus, the police action rode roughshod over the constitutional demands on children's rights and logic in pursuit of compliance concerning the wearing of masks. Worse still, the police force showed no progress and commitment to investigate the case (Zimbabwe Peace Project, February 2021).

In a separate scenario in late August 2020, the police at Murehwa Growth Point reportedly arrested 15 roadside vendors after they had greeted, mobbed, cheered and chanted 'President! President!' to Nelson Chamisa, the opposition party leader, and his convoy as they passed by. Besides being irked by the support that had been shown to Chamisa, the police and ruling party activists were also irritated by the fact that after the opposition leader's departure some ZANU-PF officials distributed their party masks at the growth point which the vendors reportedly rejected. The vendors were then arrested and fined ZWL$500 on trumped up charges of obstructing free movement of traffic and persons, in addition to having their merchandise confiscated (*Zim Daily*, 1 September 2020; *Zim Live*, 1 September 2020). Again, this incident raises human rights and political complexities as the vendors were by law entitled to freedom of political choice, including masks they preferred to put on and the political leader of their preference as guaranteed by the constitution. Chapter 56 of the Zimbabwean Constitution guarantees the right to freedom of conscience, which includes freedom of opinion and that of expressing their thought/opinion even in public together with others. Chapter 57 gives the right to join and freely participate in the peaceful activities of a party of their choice as well as support a political cause while Chapter 58 states that citizens have to freedom of association and the right not to associate with others (Zimbabwe Constitution, 2013).

Years back, following the emergence of the MDC around 1999/2000, the red-coloured scarfs, cards, whistles and overalls became popular symbols of resistance and the struggle of the opposition party's quest to dislodge ZANU-PF from power. During the Covid-19 period, the cloth masks assumed the similar significance of political messaging on the political landscape that pitted the ruling ZANU-PF and opposition parties. While opposition activists, officials and legislators were often arrested, interrogated and tried in court for issuing partisan masks, ZANU-PF freely and widely embarked on a massive mask distribution exercise involving thousands of units, often at large gatherings, without being subjected to restrictions and thus enjoying advantages of incumbency. Thus, among other things, masks present a long narrative of Zimbabwe's political dynamics and amplify unequal opportunities before the law.

'Corona virus court ruling' and implications for political space

During the pandemic, human rights discourses and political contestations were also amplified through the judiciary. The nature and circumstances of judicial decisions seemed to lend credence to the perception that they were propping up the ruling party and trampling on the civil and political rights of opposition parties and their supporters. In this section, focus is given to one particular ruling through which ZANU-PF sought to decimate its opponents and, in the process, compromise their rights.

In the aftermath of the 2018 polls, one Elias Mashavira, mounted a court case which eventually spilled into the Supreme Court, seeking to challenge the appointment of Nelson Chamisa and Elias Mudzuri as Vice Presidents by the then MDC President Morgan Tsvangirai as well as the controversial subsequent rise of the former to become the main opposition party leader (Tofa, 2020). On 30 March 2020, the Supreme Court, in its judgement on the leadership wrangle, made four pronouncements as can be discerned from a summary by Veritas (31 March 2020). Firstly, it confirmed a 2019 High Court ruling that the appointment of Chamisa and Mudzuri in 2016 as additional party Vice Presidents breached the constitution of the MDC and was therefore null and void. Secondly, the appointment of Chamisa as Acting President of the party and his subsequent rise to becoming President was equally null and void and so were the appointments or re-assignments he made in those purported capacities. Thirdly, going by the party Congress of 2014 as well as the constitution, Vice President Thokozani Khupe was supposed to become Acting President following Tsvangirai's demise. Finally, the court directed that the MDC, under the interim stewardship of Khupe, was to hold an extraordinary congress to elect a new leadership for the party or in case she failed, Morgan Komichi was to convene that congress as National Chairperson (Ibid).

It is beyond the scope of this contribution to explore the long-drawn leadership wrangle and the legal nuances over the years, but suffice to highlight that the judgement attracted political, legal and academic scrutiny. What is of interest in this chapter is that this 'judgement' came to be sarcastically labelled the 'Corona Virus Judgement' by citizens, particularly the opposition leaders and supporters (Moyo & Phulu, 2021). The judgement was viewed as a deliberate move by a captured judiciary to enable ZANU-PF to manipulate political space to its advantage and weaken the main opposition party. The court decision was 'convoluted' and 'bizarre' and enabled Khupe to assume the interim leadership of both the MDC Tsvangirai and the MDC Alliance after which she proceeded to orchestrate the recalling of over 30 parliamentarians and many local councillors for continuing to pay allegiance to Chamisa. When Khupe was sworn in as a legislator, ZANU-PF recognised her as Leader of the Opposition in Parliament (Tofa, 2020). Among those recalled from the MDC-T were Prince Sibanda, Erica Murai, Wellington Chikombo, Dorcas Sibanda, Caston Matewu, Lynette Kore, Concillia Chinanzwavana, Susan Matasunga and Unganai Tarusenga. On 23 June 2020 the Speaker announced the expulsion of nine more opposition Members of Parliament (Moyo & Phulu, 2021). In March 2021, six opposition Members of Parliament, including Tendai Biti, were also expelled from the house after being recalled by a faction of their party while 15 members reportedly defected to the MDC Tsvangirai to safeguard their seats (*Reuters*, 18 March 2021; Freedom in the World Country Report, 2021).

While the law stipulated that if a Member of Parliament was recalled or expelled, a by-election should follow within the stipulated time-frame, Zimbabwean authorities suspended these processes citing the Covid-19 pandemic. As such, over 30 legislative seats remained vacant for a prolonged period thereby denying many ordinary Zimbabweans the right to political representation in parliament as stipulated by the constitution. The mainstream MDC faction led by Chamisa accused ZANU- PF of working in cahoots with the Khupe faction to punish them for refusing to recognise President Mnangagwa's 2018 victory as well as "using the cover of the Covid-19 pandemic to stifle the opposition and fan divisions in its ranks" (*Reuters*, 18 March 2021).

The year 2020 will go down in Zimbabwean politics as an historic year for the MDC as it split into two, with one faction, the MDC Alliance, led by Chamisa, and the MDC Tsvangirai led by Khupe and later by Douglas Mwonzora following the December 2020 Congress (UK Home Office, September 2020). Following the 'Corona Virus Judgement', the government also re-directed political funding that was supposed to be allocated to the MDC Alliance under the Political Parties Act to the Khupe/Mwonzora formation. Against the background of the 'Corona Virus Judgement', recalls, and the handing of funding to another party, an argument can be sustained that ZANU-PF, through various state apparatus and institutions, aimed to dismember, suffocate, manipulate and annihilate the MDC

Alliance, the then only viable opposition political party in the country. Alex Magaisa, a political analyst and law expert, argued that ZANU-PF aimed to "crush and fragment" the opposition, destabilise the MDC Alliance, destroy multi-party democracy, and inevitably create a one-party state in the country (UK Home Office, September 2020). Yet the Constitution and subsidiary legal enactments were abundantly clear in guaranteeing a multi-party democracy and an electoral system hinged on universal suffrage and equality of votes, free and fair elections, adequate representation of the electorate and making of political choices freely (Zimbabwe Constitution: Chapters 1, 56 58 and 67). These provisions were not respected as electoral representation came to be shaped by both the Corona Virus Judgement and ZANU-PF-initiated political machinations.

The timing of the 'Corona Virus Judgement' also raised suspicions of a politically conflicted judiciary. The case had been pending for some time but ruling was delivered a day into lockdown and became a shock to many as the Chief Justice had announced two days earlier that courts would be closed on account of the pandemic restrictions except for urgent matters. This case could not be deemed urgent as it had been pending for at least three years and an appeal having been lodged about a year before (*Daily Maverick*, 9 April 2020). The following lengthy citation by Thandekhile Moyo, a media correspondent, illustrates the nexus between Covid-19 and the political terrain and how the pandemic was manipulated contrary to the right of equality before the law:

> The same courts which ruled that the November 2017 coup was constitutional are the ones that ruled…that Chamisa's rise to power in his political party was unconstitutional. The double standards and hypocrisy are breath-taking. But what is truly appalling is the fact that our ZANU-PF government had no qualms in relying on the courts to take advantage of a pandemic that is devastating the world… by using the lockdown to settle political scores. They knew that, because of the lockdown, supporters of Nelson Chamisa and the MDC would be unable to publicly protest the ruling. How are Zimbabweans meant to take the lockdown seriously when those who imposed it abuse it in this manner? (Ibid).

Political temperatures were heated up by two incidents around the day of the judgement. Firstly, before court proceedings were concluded a police contingent had already been deployed to barricade the road leading to Morgan Tsvangirai House (formerly Harvest

House), the headquarters of the MDC, raising suspicions that they knew of the outcome in advance (Ibid). Secondly, Mwonzora and Komichi read what appeared to be a prepared speech in the immediate aftermath of the judgement, again raising accusations of their being privy to the outcome prior to the ruling being publicised. That the fight against what was essentially a health emergency was repurposed to attain political objectives was illustrated by the grabbing of the MDC party headquarters from the Chamisa faction, over and above to it being stripped of its Members of Parliament. Again, all this was on the basis of the 'Corona Virus Judgement'. Khupe's MDC-T supporters seized control of the MDC Alliance head-offices while police watched, yet according to the Chamisa's formation, which building "stood as a symbol of the MDC's fight against Mnangagwa's ruling ZANU-PF party for the past 20 years" (*Aljazeera*, 5 June 2020). Biti, Karenyi-Kore and five other senior MDC Alliance leaders were arrested and bailed after a day when they attempted to reclaim their offices which, according to Biti, "had been taken over by security forces in the name of a fake MDC faction they control" (Ibid). Biti brazenly accused the military, ostensibly on Covid-19 enforcement duties, of physically seizing the party headquarters and handing it over to the MDC Tsvangirai faction basing on a "curious judgement" which culminated in them losing leadership to a separate party they contested against and defeated in the 2018 elections (*Africa Arguments*, June 2020). On the other hand, Chamisa himself claimed the police and soldiers obstructed his officials and staff from re-occupying the building. His party restated its perception that they were being persecuted for refusing to recognise President Mnangagwa's legitimacy and that the government was eroding political rights under the cover of the Corona virus lockdown which included a ban on protests (*Aljazeera*, 5 June 2020).

The charges levelled against Biti and his colleagues in the above-mentioned incident revolved around Covid-19 but were continually altered. In the end, the charges came to be presented differently by various sources. Some stated that they were arrested for breaching lockdown regulations while a disorderly conduct charge was later changed to criminal nuisance. Others stated they were accused of criminal nuisance by disturbing peace (*Africa Arguments*, June 2020; *Kubatana.net*, June 2020). According to the Zimbabwe Human Rights NGO Forum, the charges of breaking lockdown regulations appeared to have been added as an "afterthought, and therefore police [were] using lockdown measures to restrict human rights unjustifiably" (*Kubatana.net*, June 2020). In any case, it is a constitutionally-guaranteed right to be informed of your crime clearly at the time of arrest. Yet ordinary citizens and political critics were harassed, beaten, arrested and detained indefinitely during the lockdown for opaque reasons like unnecessary movement, conduct likely to incite violence or insurrection against an elected government, improper wearing of masks, or photographing security forces abusing citizens.

From the foregoing, it is clear that the political landscape of the country was fundamentally altered as a direct and indirect consequence of the Supreme Court judgement and the politicisation of Covid-19. Political opposition was fractured at various levels, including its dominant representative role in parliament. Its Members of Parliament and leaders at different levels were stripped of their positions, with others even eventually joining the ruling party while tussling ensued over ownership of party assets, finances and rights to the party name. Covid-19 thus became transformed into a piece of the political chessboard as ZANU-PF strategically moved the pieces to its advantage while fostering infighting and factionalism in the mainstream MDC. The twists and turns eventually culminated in Chamisa's MDC formation rebranding to a 'new' party christened Citizens' Coalition for Change (CCC) in January 2022 (Mazingaizo, 22 January 2022). Meanwhile, the rights to choose own legislators and enjoyment of regular elections as and when due, and to be adequately represented, were not honoured during the pandemic.

Covid-19, electoral politics and the democratic dispensation

Following the deaths and numerous recalls of parliamentarians and councillors, parliamentary and electoral management authorities were expected to set in motion legal processes to fill in the vacancies as dictated by the Constitution. This was by way of the Zimbabwe Electoral Commission (ZEC), a body whose members are appointed by the president, organising and administering by-elections. Section 158(3) of the Constitution states that polling in by-elections must take place within 90 days after vacancies have occurred unless the vacancies arose within nine months before a general election is due to be held in which event vacancies remain unfilled until the general election. In this case, ZEC did not proceed as demanded by the Constitution and attendant electoral laws ostensibly owing to restrictions imposed by the Covid-19 lockdown (*Sunday Mail*, 10 April 2021).

On 25 March 2020, ZEC suspended all electoral activities, including the much anticipated by-elections, reportedly in compliance with lockdown regulations, at a time when one such by-election was scheduled for April 2020 in the Chiredzi Rural Council. However, according to a legal think-tank, Veritas (2020), and some researchers, the commission was not permitted by the supreme law of the country to do this on its own accord since the Covid-19 measures largely comprised regulations promulgated by the executive without the law-making institution of parliament (Moyo & Phulu, 2021). Anchoring its argument on the premise of the Constitution stipulating that free, fair and regular elections are one of the principles of good governance, which itself is a founding value of Zimbabwe which binds the state and all government institutions and agencies, Veritas (2020) concluded that there was nothing in the law which said ZEC could proceed the way it did. According to the supreme law of the country, these free, fair and regular elections to public office are availed as fundamental rights to citizens, which can only be limited provided that the limitation is "fair, reasonable, necessary, and justifiable in a democratic society based on openness, justice, human dignity, equality and freedom" (Zimbabwean Constitution, 2013: Section 86, Section 87). Thus, the suspension was "not done in terms of any law; it was merely an administrative decision, apparently not even a written one" (Veritas, 2020).

Further scrutiny of the constitution and legislation governing electoral regimen in Zimbabwe clearly suggests non-compliance and some measure of credibility to sentiments of politicisation of the unfolding electoral scenario. Section 158(3) of the constitution does not provide for the postponement of by-elections beyond the 90 days and there is no other provision in that law that gives a commission power to postpone elections or by-elections. Even the Electoral Act (Sections 39 & 121A) do not give the President or ZEC the powers beyond the 90-day stipulation within which to fill vacancies through by-elections for the National Assembly and local authorities. For the avoidance of doubt, while Section 132 of the Act gives ZEC some leeway to change dates, it "cannot extend polling dates beyond the constitutionally fixed time-limit of 90 days. In any event, if ZEC does change the dates of a by-election…it must give notice of the change in the gazette and in a newspaper", yet in this case the commission did not give that requisite notice and no consultations with all interested political parties were done (Veritas, 2020). Owing to the failure to adhere to the legal procedures, ZEC's action seemed to have exploited the lockdown to tilt the electoral landscape to the advantage of the ruling party (Moyo & Phulu, 2021).

Other considerations and precedencies also cement perceptions of weaponisation of the Covid-19 pandemic for parochial objectives and the manipulation of ZEC by the ruling party in the discharge of its duties. In August 2020, ZEC developed a Covid-19 Policy on Electoral Activities whose import was to set out procedures, mechanisms and guidelines on how it was to conduct electoral processes and activities in compliance with the pandemic protocols, with the ultimate aim of ensuring that the constitutionally-guaranteed right to elections could not continue to be infringed indefinitely (Tofa, 2020). To political parties, the electorate and interested stakeholders, this was a commendable step. However, this forward-looking initiative was thrown out of the window when Vice President Constantino Chiwenga, who doubled as Minister of Health, again indefinitely suspended holding of by-elections through a Statutory Instrument on 2 October 2020, further raising the political temperature and re-igniting the human rights debate. According to the instrument, (Public Health, Covid-19 Prevention, Containment & Treatment Amendment Regulations, 2020: No.4) the holding of any by-election to fill vacancies in parliament or local authority was "for the duration of the period of the declaration of the Covid-19 as a formidable epidemic disease, suspended" (*Kubatana.net*, 4 October 2020)

By late December 2021, there were 133 vacant seats (*Herald*, 27 December 2021). Tofa (2020) argued that ZEC should have objected to the suspension since it was illegal. Tofa (Ibid) also opined that the nation was also primed to proceed with elections in a Covid-19 compliant manner adding that, while it was in the interest of public health and safety to restrict rights and freedoms, it was "vile to use the pandemic as a smokescreen behind which to exterminate political pluralism". He further opined that Chiwenga had ulterior motives as the ruling party feared that the MDC Alliance could reclaim the vacant seats at the expense of its preferred MDC Tsvangirai. In this case, Chiwenga's political decision to suspend by-elections under the guise of Covid-19 was a flagrant violation of freedoms of association, assembly and expression as well as the right to political representation. In conformity with Section 134 of the Constitution, statutory instruments were not supposed to infringe or limit any rights or freedoms provided for in the Declaration of Rights and procedurally, they should have been brought before Parliament and its Legal Committee for scrutiny (Tofa, 2020).

The Zimbabwe Election Support Network (ZESN), an election monitoring organisation, weighed in and complained that the indefinite suspension of by-elections undercuts constitutional principles on freedom of expression, good electoral practice and curtail the independence of ZEC as well as parliamentary oversight. More importantly, the move had the net effect of quarantining democracy as it was not clear when restrictions would be removed or when the pandemic was to end. In view of the reality that during the lockdown, parliament had conducted public hearings on Constitutional Amendment Bill Number 2, people queued for food, other commodities and cash at banks as well as transfer agencies while organisations, government and churches distributed aid, it was, therefore, possible to conduct elections (*Kubatana.net*, 4 October 2020).

Other countries successfully held elections even at the national levels during the ravaging pandemic yet Zimbabwe could not even hold local council elections where numbers of voters involved were far less and therefore manageable in terms of compliance to Covid-19 prevention requirements such as masks, temperature checks and physical distancing. South Korea, Israel, Ireland, Mali, Guinea, Cameroon, Malawi, Tanzania, USA and South Africa held elections in 2020 but had no rise in infections attributable to the exercises (*Kubatana.net*, 4 October 2020; Veritas, 2020). It is without doubt that the suspension of Zimbabwean polls violated the right to participate in elections, yet this right is located at the core of democracy and is also a fundamental value of the Zimbabwean Constitution (Ibid). It was only in early 2022 that President Mnangagwa announced modalities of the by-elections and scheduled them for 26 March 2022 (*Herald*, 27 December 2021.

One can surmise that the restrictions on ZEC were meant to muzzle the opposition since the lockdown itself was eased to lesser stringent levels at different periods in 2020 and 2021, yet the holding of by-elections remained banned until it was only conveniently announced in early 2022 after ZANU-PF had carried out its internal party restructuring exercise, including District Coordinating Committee and Provincial Executive elections. The elements of appropriateness, necessity, time-frame and proportionality demanded by the constitution when it comes limitation of rights were not well considered by ZEC and the executive authorities. In conclusion, it should be restated that the politically-conflicted management of the Covid-19 pandemic compromised enjoyment of citizens' rights and multi-party democracy.

'The MDC trio': Politics and human rights

To further amplify how the intersecting themes of human rights observance and the appropriation of the Covid-19 pandemic for political capital played out, this section selects a particular scenario for detailed review. The incident illuminates how, in the process of enforcing lockdown restrictions, state security agents compromised and disrespected many citizens' rights, violated the constitution and brutally pursued a parochial political agenda to the detriment of the opposition. It is emphasised that the heavy-handed implementation of Covid-19 protocols added another layer to an already existing vicious contest that had unfolded on the political scene since the emergence of the MDC as the most credible challenger to the ruling elite.

In April 2020, some members of the public filed a lawsuit, through the Zimbabwe Lawyers for Human Rights, and the High Court ruled that security forces must respect human rights and barred them from beating up people and subjugating them to inhuman treatment when enforcing the lockdowns (*Herald*, 14 April 2020; United Nations, 2020; *VOA News*, 15 April 2020). The court ruling came on the back of some incidents, among many, where basic human rights were openly violated. The High Court ruling came after a lawsuit had been filed following brutal police action that had resulted in the fracturing of the arm and leg of 28-year-old Tendai Mtombeni as they forced him to stay indoors. As a result of the injury, Mtombeni could not return to South Africa where he worked and was claiming compensation through the lawsuit (*VOA News*, 15 April 2020). The Zimbabwe Lawyers for Human Rights also petitioned the High Court seeking to annul the lockdown for violating the constitution after police set their dog on a 26-year-old Karoi woman, Lucia Masvondo, for violating the curfew. She was found cooking outside her house but within her yard yet the police and soldiers assaulted her. In fact, over 100 cases of abuse of civilians were recorded, including the detention of practising journalists, in the first two weeks of the initial lockdown (*VOA News*, 10 April 2020).

While there were numerous cases of violation of rights and liberties and political manipulation of the Corona virus, this section unpacks in considerable detail an incident involving three MDC activists which attracted attention and scrutiny both within the country and globally. On 13 May 2020, MDC Alliance youths held a demonstration in the Warren Park Suburb of Harare, protesting against the state's failure to provide care and sustenance especially to the vulnerable and disadvantaged citizens during lockdown as well as pervasive hunger, poverty and corruption in the country (Mawere, 2020; Moyo & Phulu, 2021; UK Home Office, September 2020). Following the flash demonstration, three young women leaders from the party, referred herein as the MDC trio: Joanna Mamombe, also Member of Parliament for Harare West; Cecilia Chimbiri, MDC Youth Assembly Deputy Chair; and Netsai Marova, MDC Alliance Deputy Organising Secretary, were arrested at a police roadblock. The police spokesman confirmed that they had been taken into custody at Harare Central Police Station for breaking Covid-19 regulations. As a police spokesperson announced:

> I can confirm that the police arrested the three…in connection with an illegal demonstration…earlier in the day. They are in our custody and we are making further investigations…We want to warn members of the public, or any groups who are engaging in acts which affect efforts by the government to fight Covid-19 that they will be arrested without fear or favour. They will only have themselves to blame (*Herald*, 18 May 2020; Mawere, 2020; *News dzeZimbabwe*, 14 May 2020).

Curiously, and despite Mamombe's car being located at the Harare Central Police Station, the police later professed ignorance about the whereabouts of the trio and denied media reports of them being detained, with speculation rife that they were taken over by abductors. The three women were only found after about two days near the town of Bindura badly injured and traumatised (*Herald*, 15 May 2020; Mawere 2020; MDC Alliance Statement, 3 June 2021). What appeared initially a 'minor' charge of violating Covid-19 lockdown regulations and perhaps warranting a fine quickly degenerated and assumed political connotations characterised by an uproar over human rights abuses, and prolonged court processes. Mawere (2020) distinguished two narratives around this incident. The first centred on the MDC trio's claims, and those of pro-opposition sympathisers and human rights defenders, that they were abducted and subjected to inhumane treatment by alleged state security agents.

Chimbiri's version below elaborates their ordeal after their abduction to a remote wooded area:

> [We] were beaten, stripped naked, sexually assaulted with firearms, and forced to drink each other's urine. They beat me on my back, all over the body using sticks. They used a gun to beat us, then molested me. They pushed [us] out of the truck on the road. They left us there. They said: "We will be watching you! ...What is so special about you that you want to turn against the government?" (*Guardian*, 17 May 2020).

Mamombe alleged being forced to march, sing protest songs, poured water on, beaten for stopping singing, swallowing each other's urine, and fondled (Ibid). The US Embassy in Zimbabwe (2020), as well as Amnesty International (2020), also made conclusions similar to the trio's versions, stating that the women sustained injuries as a result of 36 hours of physical, sexual and psychological torture and being dumped far away from their homes. The MDC called on the United Nations to lead in the investigation of the case (Amnesty International, 2020).

Meanwhile, the second narrative from the government and the pro-government media was that the MDC trio's case was nothing more than stage-managed political theatrics. A statement to that effect issued by the then Minister of Foreign Affairs, Sibusiso Moyo, was rebutted by the MDC Alliance as "cynical, reckless and disingenuous" (Mawere, 2020; MDC Alliance Statement, 3 June 2021). Indeed, they were later charged in court for faking their abduction and tarnishing the country's image while new charges piled up. Re-arrests and warrants of arrest ensued resulting in them being remanded and harassed while seeking medical attention in a hospital (Amnesty International, 2020; *Herald*, 22 March 2021). They also faced other allegations of lockdown violations and were denied bail. In the case of lockdown infringements, their lawyers argued that Statutory Instrument 200 of 2020 required police officers to disperse a gathering if deemed unlawful or order them to observe social distancing and the wearing of masks. If they resisted, the lawyers submitted that they could be arrested and, as such, it was incumbent upon the state to demonstrate that these steps were followed prior to the eventual arrest (*Herald*, 14 April, 2021). While human rights issues of such a magnitude were being raised from many quarters, the then Deputy Minister of Information, Energy Mutodi, even had the audacity to insinuate on Twitter that the trio had gone on a romantic night out with some artisanal miners but the deal went sour when the women demanded payment in foreign currency (Mawere, 2020). In the state-controlled media, a Masimba Mavaza opined that the trio should be locked up in jail and keys thrown away as they were a danger to public order (*Herald*, 22 March 2021).

Another politicised pro-government view was publicised in an opinion piece in the state media. In addition to labelling the demonstration a flagrant disobedience of Covid-19 regulations, it questioned what sudden shift of events had occurred to warrant a sudden demonstration against hunger in the midst of a lockdown; why out of a crowd of more than 50 youths, only three females 'disappeared'; and why, within a short time of their 'disappearance', social media went ablaze while tweets from the US and the European Union embassies ignited an overdrive about their 'abduction' (*Herald*, 18 May 2020). The government sought to consolidate its narrative further to discredit the claims of abductions and violations of rights and liberties of the trio by broadcasting a television production compiled from closed circuit footage, cell-phone tracking and pictures tracing their movements (*Herald*, 11 September 2020).

The trio's case, along with many others, also brought to the fore the gendered dimensions of the Covid-19 pandemic. In Moyo & Phulu's (2021) view, the incident illustrated how women were disproportionately affected by the weaponisation of lockdowns. As the then MDC Alliance Spokesperson, Fadzayi Mahere, lamented: "The horrific abuses that the three women suffered are a violation of the Zimbabwe Constitution which strictly prohibits torture, cruel, inhumane and degrading treatment, and guarantees personal security and dignity of all citizens" (MDC Alliance Statement, 3 June 2021). Medical testimonies in court stated that, as result of the horrifying experiences, Mamombe was hospitalised for anxiety issues and suffered from "racing thoughts" (*Herald*, 15 September 2020; *Herald*, 17 September, 2020). When a magistrate ordered Mamombe's continued detention pending mental examination, the High Court released her declaring that her incarceration was irrational (*Mail & Guardian*, 18 October 2020).

The Zimbabwe Human Rights Commission confirmed the abductions, torture and sexual abuses (MDC Alliance Statement, 3 June 2021). Contrary to the Zimbabwean Constitution, this was a clear case of denial of the right of assembly, right to peaceful protest and unlawful detention. Worse still, the state did not show any eagerness to investigate. Though freedom of assembly, rights to protest and petition are guaranteed by the supreme law of the land, they were rarely upheld during the pandemic. The trio's case also got intertwined with other cases downstream. On 22 May 2020, for example, two journalists, Frank Chikowere and Samuel Takawira, were arrested ostensibly for violating Covid-19 lockdown measures when they attempted to interview the MDC trio following their ordeal, yet the media had been exempted from many lockdown restrictions as an essential service. They were acquitted close to five months later (US Embassy, 2020; Zimbabwe Freedom in the World Country Report, 2021).

From a gender perspective, it may be informative to cite other examples apart from the trio's highly publicised one, as this exhibits a pattern suggesting that women arguably suffered more from the pandemic than their male counterparts during the Zimbabwean lockdown in 2020 and 2021. In the city of Bulawayo on 6 April 2020, two sisters, Nokuthula and Ntombizodzwa, were accused of breaching the lockdown after which they were assaulted, arrested, labelled prostitutes and "tribally-insulted" by police officers when they had gone out to purchase food provisions (Moyo & Phulu, 2021; Martin & Ahlenback, 2020). Another incident involved the spokeswoman of MDC Alliance and six others who were arrested for protesting against the government in Harare and later released on ZWL$5 000 bail each for 'unnecessary movement' in violation of the lockdown (UK Home Office, September 2020). Sitabile Dewa, a gender justice activist, commented that the pandemic made life difficult as the government took advantage of restrictions to clamp down on those women who dared challenge abuses and state excesses (*Mail & Guardian*, 18 October).

While there is need for credible research data, there were reports of sexual abuse by police officers on commercial sex workers after accusing them of breaking lockdown restrictions as well as abuse of female migrants at quarantine centres and points of entry (Martin & Ahlenback, 2020). Nyahunda *et al* (2021) documented the inhumane and diabolical treatment, mainly of vendors, hawkers and cross-border traders in the Nyanga District at the hands of state security officers during the lockdown which included disrespect and harassment of elderly citizens. They further unearthed cases of soldiers soliciting for bribes for women traders to pass through roadblocks or sexual favours to be allowed to sell their goods. Thus, women experienced "grave human rights violations compounded by their low social status and vulnerability which [was] different from men" (Ibid).

The trio's case sparked and amplified discourses on human rights and civil liberties. From the perspective of government critics, it was another example of the deliberate appropriation of Covid-19 to muscle the opposition out of the political race. The ruling party dismissed such claims as the 'usual' opposition antics to discredit the government and enlist external sympathy. In other jurisdictions, what happened to the three could have culminated in an in-depth state-sponsored inquiry rather than simply dismissing it as political theatrics.

The case of the trio was not an isolated one. Police declared that they would ensure that citizens religiously adhered to curfew regulations and deal with unnecessary movements by effecting arrests (Zimbabwe Republic Police, 30 June 2021). From March to September 2020, there were reports of soldiers and police "systematically [using] clubs to beat civilians in the central business district and suburbs for violating curfews, failure to wear masks, or failure to exercise social distancing" (US Embassy in Zimbabwe, 2020). Meanwhile, about 3 400 people were arrested on average daily following enhanced measures around July 2021 (*All Africa*, 4 July 2021). More alarming were reports of the alleged killing of at least 10 people in 2020 as the regime continued to exploit the pandemic to step up abuses (*Mbare Times*, April 2021). According to the Amnesty International Report (2020-2021), those allegedly killed with impunity for breaching Corona virus lockdown regulations, among other reasons, included Bhekhani Moyo from Silobela; Levison Moyo and Paul Munakopa, both from Bulawayo; MDC councillor, Lavender Chiwaya; "and Mazwi Ndlovu, murdered by suspected ZANU-PF supporters in Plumtree for asking why opposition supporters were being denied access to Covid-19 aid." In the case of Levison Moyo, he was beaten by police on allegations of violating Covid-rules and died four days later from brain haemorrhage (Amnesty International, 2020). Mazwi's alleged killer was released without appearing in court or applying for bail (Zimbabwe Human Rights Organisation, 2 September 2021).

It needs to be reemphasised that the case of the MDC trio and other related ones ignited broader issues pertaining to political rights and political pluralism during the Covid-19 pandemic with some analysts suggesting that there was nothing 'new' about Mnangagwa's 'New Dispensation.' Among other issues, debates heated up over the extent to which the pandemic was being used to stifle freedoms and rights to organise and participate in political activities. The right to participate in peaceful protest was also flouted while those who attempted to do so were subjected to various forms of abuses such as abduction and torture. Given these developments, many critics wondered if the government had suspended the constitution owing to the Covid-19 pandemic. Section 59 of the constitution, for example, protects every person's right to demonstrate and present petitions while Section 60(b) provides for freedom of conscience (*Nehanda Radio*, 7 August 2020).

Lockdown, rights and selective application of the law

This section unpacks a couple of rather unrelated scenarios, but fitting into some pattern, which raised further political debate over how the Corona virus-induced restrictions were implemented and how they impacted on the activities and programmes of political parties and civil society. Even when restrictions were relaxed at different times, political space remained constrained and but nevertheless skewed in favour of the ruling establishment.

The police turned down a request for a 2 June 2020 demonstration by ZANU-PF against continued sanctions on the country and the killing of George Floyd in the USA, insisting this would contravene lockdown regulations outlined in Section 5 (i) of Statutory Instrument 83 of 2020 (*Herald*, 4 June 2020). On 21 June 2021, the police in the city of Mutare arrested over 20 ruling party youths and informal traders after an attempted demonstration to force the opening of vegetable and flea markets that had been closed in 2020 as part of the government's efforts to control the spread of Covid-19 (UK Home Office, 2020). Such prohibitions against ruling party sympathisers were, however, very rare and few.

In Bulawayo in late June 2021, MDC youths, Calvin Moyo, Phumzile Moyo and Thandiwe, were arrested and released only after paying ZWL$500 fine each while carrying their party's door to-door voter registration campaign in Pumula Suburb as part of a broad strategy to mobilise six million new voters, including in the rural areas, in the build-up towards the 2023 elections. The MDC viewed this as intimidation and unfairness as its members were harassed over petty issues while their ruling party opponents mobilised for support unhindered. The opposition party also accused the police of aiding ZANU-PF to water down its political predominance in the city (*New Zimbabwe*, 26 June 2021; *Newsday*, 1 July 2021). As was the case with many lockdown arrests, there was prevarication to the charges preferred against the youths, which suggests that 'Covid politics' was at play as suggested by the Bulawayo MDC Provincial Spokesperson, Swithern Chirowodza, who said:

> When it became clear that three people could not constitute a gathering, the police changed the charge to 'unnecessary movement'. The police then changed the charges again to 'improperly wearing of masks.' This is the hazard that MDC Alliance face while doing voter campaign activities (*Newsday*, 1 July 2021).

Even though the government banned political meetings during the lockdown, the ruling party continued with similar activities and programmes despite the prohibition, a development that flouted freedom of assembly and the right to equal treatment before the law for many opposition supporters. In the Matabeleland North Province, for example, the ZANU-PF Member of Parliament for Umguza, who was also the Provincial Affairs Minister, addressed a large gathering during the same period when the three Bulawayo opposition youths mentioned above were detained for breaching lockdown regulations. Many attendees at the ZANU-PF rally had no masks and did not observe social distancing (Ibid). In early February 2021, a media platform used a headline 'ZANU-PF MP gives middle finger to ED's lockdown, holds rally,' referring to the Bindura North Member of Parliament who was also a member of the ruling party's Politburo, Kenneth Musanhi, who had held a rally despite President Mnangagwa's (referred to as ED) directive limiting gatherings (*New Zimbabwe*, 3 February 2021). To make matters worse, video images showed supporters singing songs without masks or donning them improperly and without physical distancing (*All Africa*, 3 February 2021).

Another news headline stated that President Mnangagwa had also violated protocols imposed by himself or his functionaries (*Nehanda Radio*, 23 May 2021). In May 2021 the President addressed thousands of people at a 'cultural' event, just hours after his Health Minister had tightened lockdown restrictions following the detection of the Covid-19 Indian variant. And again, no masks were worn and social distancing was not adhered to by many (*Zimbabwean Mail*, 22 May 2021). The Zimbabwe Democracy Institute argued that the flagrant or outright disregard of mitigation protocols meant that the ruling party's mass gatherings, exceeding the regulated Level Two maximum number of 100 people, could be "super-spreaders" of infections. The ruling party also held a series of meetings to prepare for internal restructuring exercises and eventually conducted elections of the District Coordinating Committees throughout the country while the President addressed numerous events attended by tens of thousands of people (*New Zimbabwe*, 6 December 2021). In August 2021, in the Muzarabani area in Mashonaland Central Province, the police were reportedly denying the MDC Alliance clearance to hold gatherings on account of lockdown laws yet ZANU-PF carried on without hindrances (UK Home Office, September 2020). ZANU-PF fought back at such criticisms, saying they were abiding by protocols as everyone else and rubbished selective application of the law, citing the arrest of over 20 of its youths in Bulawayo for not respecting anti-pandemic guidelines (*Newsday*, 1 July 2021).

There was heightened political activity within ZANU-PF from 2021 in anticipation of the holding of by-elections as well as the 2023 polls as prospective candidates embarked on door to door campaigns and donations, disregarding restrictions and the suspension of electoral activities. In Gokwe Central, Dangamvura-Chikanga, Mberengwa West and East and Masvingo Parliamentary Constituencies, candidates held door-to-door mobilisation exercises, distributed rice and masks, organised sports tournaments, and donated to schools (*Newsday*, 8 September 2021). The Zimbabwe African Peoples Union (ZAPU), an opposition outfit, complained bitterly that the political playground was tilted in favour of ZANU-PF:

> ZANU-PF is abusing Covid-19 restrictions and regulations to fine-tune its rigging apparatus. All gatherings and unnecessary visits are banned under Covid-19 regulations, but [it] is allowed to break those regulations, just as they are doing with every facet of life… as they are a law unto themselves (*Newsday*, 8 September 2021).

In July 2020, the Zimbabwe Association of Doctors for Human Rights also observed that mostly opposition and human rights activists were quickly arrested yet ruling party members, including the First Lady, organised gatherings with people way above the recommended 50 without any hustles (*The World*, 21 July 2020).

Even food relief to ameliorate the plight of the poor during the lockdown was not spared from the political turf battles. The MDC Alliance Member of Parliament for Mutasa South, Regai Tsunga, for example, was harassed, humiliated and arrested, together with the local councillor and some residents, for 'unnecessary movement' when police found him distributing meal-mealie to the needy in his constituency in 2020. Although he pleaded that he was implementing a localised food and nutrition scheme to ameliorate Covid-19-induced suffering, he was bundled into the back of a police truck to the station and secured his release after a paying a ZWL$500 fine under protest (*ZimEye*, 26-7 April 2020).

Another opposition legislator, Jasmine Toffa, was similarly arrested in Bulawayo for delivering meal-mealie in April 2020 (Moyo & Phulu, 2021). Even where government had noble intentions, political interests still set in. According to ZimRights, there were cases of partisan listing of beneficiaries for Covid-19 cushion funds in the informal sector in places like Harare where citizens were required to produce ZANU-PF membership cards to be registered. The ruling party's affiliate structures screened out those deemed pro-opposition (Gukurume & Oosterom, 2020). Yet the ruling party and government distributed aid freely, albeit in a partisan manner. The Minister of Provincial Affairs in Manicaland allegedly distributed meal-mealie to ZANU-PF members only (Samutereko, 2021). In Mashonaland West and East Provinces, ZANU-PF activists forced villagers to attend party meetings or else they would not benefit from food aid (Zimbabwe Peace Project, October 2021). Even in the face of the confirmed figure of 6.8 million Zimbabweans needing urgent humanitarian assistance in 2021 due to Covid-19 and the economic crisis, among others, the ruling party continued to use food aid as "a political weapon to coerce people to gain political support" (Ibid). Some ruling party and government officials, as well as some traditional leaders, denied those perceived to be supporters of the opposition access to government-sponsored food aid and subsidised meal-mealie vouchers, even when they were so desperate for assistance. In other cases, they purchased all the government-subsidised meal-mealie and proceeded to sell only to verified ZANU-PF members (Zimbabwe Peace Project, April 2021).

During 2020, some political players, civil society members and government critics were detained without charges for days while others were ill-treated through physical abuse. On the other hand, officials manning the judiciary unnecessarily delayed or prolonged cases of such activists (UK Home Office, September 2020). The cases of journalist Hopewell Chin'ono, politicians Jacob Ngarivhume and Job Sikhala, the MDC trio, student representatives and many civic players, as discussed earlier in this chapter, are typical examples, yet citizens were entitled to fair and speedy trials.

An apparent 'unholy alliance' between the ruling party/government and security forces also persisted during the lockdown as they pursued an agenda to annihilate the opposition. With the more vicious Delta variant of the disease ravaging in 2021, the opening of schools was delayed and inter-city travel was suspended. To the surprise of many, one of the biggest apostolic sects in the Marange area of Manicaland Province held a big annual gathering despite the banning of gatherings. Police professed ignorance of the gathering despite it being widely publicised. As far as this incident was concerned, the hands of the police were tied most probably because the ruling ZANU-PF party was well known to draw massive support from the church (*The Standard*, 16 July 2021). In Zimbabwe, police who did not tow the ZANU-PF political line were known to have faced consequences. In October 2021, for instance, 15 police details were arrested in the mining town of Bindura and hauled before the court after disrupting a ZANU-PF meeting in the build-up to a party conference. They reportedly assaulted the crowd with batons, set dogs and teargassed them and "by so doing, the accused forcibly, and to a serious extent, disturbed peace, security or order of the public and violated the rights of the complainants" (Zimbabwe Peace Project, October 2021). The Home Affairs Minister, himself a leading politician in that province, reportedly instigated the transfer and suspension of senior police officers and ordered that charges against ZANU-PF members involved in the incident to be dropped (Ibid). Thus, this incident and several others discussed in this section have shown how the ruling ZANU-PF party used the Covid-19 lockdown to remind people of its might and who was in charge (*Daily Maverick*, 9 April 2020).

Conclusion

This chapter has argued that Covid-19 and its mitigation dynamics undoubtedly saw the emergence of a protracted battle to access political power at the expense of many rights and freedoms. As the Covid-19 pandemic raged on, the contest, especially between ZANU-PF and the main opposition MDC Alliance, and later the CCC, revolved around the legitimacy carry-over issues from the 2018 elections as much as it then morphed into a battle for the 2023 polls in the future. The opposition persistently expressed their disquiet over the outcome of the 2018 polls throughout 2020 to early 2022 while ZANU-PF protected its turf and its legitimacy claims.

From the perspective of both sides, groundwork for the forthcoming 2023 general elections also became an integral component of the Covid-19 political chessboard and the human rights debate. The chapter contends that the government used Covid-19 in the political realm as a tool to ratchet up its stranglehold on power, with some opponents arrested, harangued, fined, detained or prosecuted for 'opaque' charges, including unnecessary movement, criminal nuisance, disorderly conduct in a public place, plotting against a democratically-elected government, undermining the President's authority, intention to incite public violence, failure to produce exemption letters, breaking curfew rules, spreading fake news, faking abductions or beatings as well as tarnishing the image of the country (*Daily Maverick*, 9 April 2020). Those who sought to demonstrate peacefully or express opinions regarding how the pandemic was managed were accused of such crimes and also penalised for disregarding measures to combat the spread of the global disease. The enforcement of lockdown measures accorded police officers wide discretionary powers which they used to stifle the enjoyment of rights and liberties. It is not surprising that they could arrest thousands of people in a few days unnecessarily, with critics arguing that most of the arrests targeted opposition and anti-government activists in the build-up towards planned protests such as the one that had been planned for 31 July 2020 (*BBC News*, 19 July 2020). This culminated in the significant muzzling of multi-party democratic space. Despite the restrictive atmosphere, political activity and manoeuvring somewhat fiercely continued and found expression in the design of masks espousing political messages, slogans and symbols, expulsion of legislators and councillors from parliament and local authorities and stifling of guaranteed rights. Even after forming the CCC, Chamisa's party continued to have its planned rallies hindered by strict demands from police to have a limited number of people, which restrictions were not applied to other parties in the build-up to the 26 March 2022 by-elections.

It is beyond doubt that strict implementation of Covid-19 mitigation measures helped in the management of the pandemic. However, it was the manner in which the Covid-19 preventive guidelines and protocols were implemented that the management of an otherwise purely health issue became a politically-charged dynamic in which human rights violations were experienced by ordinary citizens, civic leaders and opposition party members. Many of the accusations of human rights infringements were directed at state security apparatus as well as ruling party members and senior officials in their quest to safeguard and consolidate authoritarian power.

References

Aidi, H. (May 2020) 'Public trust, capacity and Covid-19: Early lessons from Africa- Policy Brief,' Policy Centre for the New South, Available at: www.policycenter.ma, Accessed 12 January 2022.

Aljazeera (5 June 2020) 'Zimbabwe: Top opposition officials held in dispute over party headquarters' Available at: www.aljazeera.com/news/2020/6/5/Zimbabwe-top opposition-officials-held-in-dispute-overparty-hq, Accessed 21 December 2021.

Allen, K. & Du Plessis, A. (3 May 2020) 'Deployment of security forces in Africa to fight Covid-19 must not morph into a crackdown on rights,' Available at: www.dailymaverick.co.za/article/2020-05-03-deployment-of-security-forces-in-africa-to-fight-covid-19-must-not-morph-into-a-crackdown-on-rights, Accessed 15 January 2022.

Amnesty International (2020) 'Covid-19 crackdowns: Police abuse and the global pandemic,' Available at: www.amnesty.org/download/Documents/ACT3034432020, Accessed 14 December 2021

Amnesty International (2020) 'Zimbabwe 2020,' Available at: www.amnesty.org/en/countries/africa/zimbabwe/report-zimbabwe/, Accessed 20 January 2022.

Biti, T. (8 June 2020) 'The story of my arrest in Mnangagwa's tin-pot Zimbabwe', in: *African Arguments*, Available at: www.afriacarguments.org/2020/06, Accessed 10 July 2021.

Bulawayo24 News (14 June 2021) 'Mnangagwa donates 50 000 masks to Apostolic Sect,' Available at: www.bulawayo24.com/news/local/205059, Accessed 13 January 2022.

Comparative Constitutions Project (26 August 2021) 'Zimbabwe's Constitution of 2013,' Available at: www.constituteproject.org, Accessed 5 January 2021.

Dzirutwe, M. (18 March 2021) 'Zim parliament expels six lawmakers as opposition infighting escalates,' Available at:

www.reuters.com/article/us-zimbabwe-politics-idUSKBN2BAOV6, Accessed 6 January 2022.

Dziva, F. (26-27 April 2020) 'MP Tsunga speaks on persecution by police,' Available at: www.zimeye.net/page/4617/?p=10707<amp, Accessed 13 January 2022.

Freedom House (2021) 'Zimbabwe: Freedom in the World 2021 Country Report,' Available at: https://freedomhouse.org/country/zimbabwe/freedom-word/2021, Accessed 20 December 2021.

Guardian (17 May 2020) 'Zimbabwean MDC activists 'abducted' and sexually assaulted,' Available at: https://www.theguardian.com, Accessed 12 December 2021.

Gukurume, S. & Oosterom, M. (20 May 2020) 'The impact of the Covid-19 lockdown on Zimbabwe's informal economy,' Available at: www.ac.uk/about/, Accessed 16 January 2022.

Haider, N. *et al* (2020) 'Lockdown measures in response to Covid-19 in nine sub-Saharan African countries', in: *BMJ Global Health,* Volume 5, Available at: www.e003319.doi:10:1136/bmjgh-2020-003319, Accessed 16 December 2021.

Herald (14 May 2020) Harare: Zimbabwe.

Herald (15 May 2020) Harare: Zimbabwe.

Herald (18 May 2020) Harare: Zimbabwe.

Herald (4 June 2020) Harare: Zimbabwe.

Herald (8 June 2020) Harare: Zimbabwe.

Herald (11 September 2020) Harare: Zimbabwe.

Herald (22 March 2021) Harare: Zimbabwe.

Herald (21 August 2021) Harare: Zimbabwe.

Human Rights Watch (2021) 'World Report 2021,' Available at: www.hrw.org/world-report/2021/country-chapters/Zimbabwe, Accessed 6 January 2022.

Indafrica (25 August 2020)'Police are requesting for #ZANU-PF Must Go Masks: MDC-A Chairman', Available at: www.indafrica.com/2020/08/25/police-are-requesting-for-zanu-pfmustgo-masks-mdc-a-chairman, Accessed 12 December 2021.

International Press Institute (17 March 2021) 'In Zimbabwe, one year of Covid-19 saw surge in harassment of free press,' Available at: https://ipi.>in-zimbabwe-one-year-covid-19-saw-a-surge-in-harrasment-of-free-press, Accessed 13 January 2022.

Moyo, T. (9 April 2020) 'Covid-19 and the suppression of freedom of expression - Part 2,' in: *Daily Maverick*, Available at: https://www.dailymaverick.co.zw, Accessed 12 January 2022,

Mabhiza, L. (29 July 2020) 'State agents armed with AK47s storm activist Ngulube's house', Available at: www.mbaretimes.com/2020/07/report-statubes-house/, Accessed 18 December 2021.

Mabhiza, L. (7 April 2021) 'Amnesty International: At least 10 killed as Mnangagwa dialled up rights abuses in 2020,' Available at: www.mbaretimes.com/2021/04/am2020, Accessed 4 January 2022.

Mabhiza L. (25 May 2021) 'MDC activists acquitted for wearing Chamisa-faced masks', Available at: www.mbaretimes.com/2021/05, Accessed 17 December 2021.

Mabuza, S. (24 August 2020) 'MDC Alliance MP Sibanda in court over #ZanuPF Must Go masks', Available at www.zimlive.com, Accessed 22 December 2021.

Mahere, F. (3 June 2021) 'Statement on MDC-A National Council meeting resolutions,' Available at: www.mdcallianceparty.org/blog-style2-with-sidebar/page/5/, Accessed 3 January 2022.

Mashininga, K. (18 October 2020) 'Women who defy Mnangagwa are jailed, raped, tortured,' in: *Mail & Guardian*, Available at: www.mg.co.za/Africa/2020-10-18-women-who-defy-mnangagwa-are-jailed-raped-tortured/, Accessed 15 December 2021.

Martin, R. & Ahlenback, V. (10 November 2020) 'Evidence synthesis: Secondary impacts of Covid-19 on gender-based violence against women and girls in Zimbabwe,' Available at: www.sddirect.org.uk/media/2136/, Accessed 2 January 2022.

Matthew, M. Chingono, F. Mbazangi, S. Mangezi, S. & Mare, A. (14 September 2020) 'Hidden variables to Covid-19: Zimbabwe: A working paper, Version 1', in: *Cambridge Open Engage*, Available at: www.doi:10.33774/coe-2020-Imqn2, Accessed 15 December 2021.

Maulani, N. Nyaburi, I.N & Wandekha, B. (2020) 'The generals and the war against Covid-19: The case of Zimbabwe', in: *Journal of Global Health*, Volume 10, Number 2.

Mavhunga, C. (10 April 2020) 'Zimbabwean sues government to end lockdown over alleged abuse,' Available at: https://www.voanews.com, Accessed 12 December 2021.

Mavhunga, C. (15 April 2020) 'Rights groups welcome court ban on brutal Zimbabwe Covid-19 lockdown', Available at: https://www.voanews.com, Accessed 12 December 2021.
Mavhunga, C. (29 April 2021) 'Zimbabweans take stock of abuses during Covid-19 lockdowns,' Available at: www.voanews.com/africa, Accessed 3 January 2022.
Mawere, T. (17 August 2020) '(Un)Masking other dangerous pandemics within the Covid-19 lockdown,' Available at: www.csagup.org/tag/zimbabweanlivesmatter/, Accessed 21 December 2021.
Mazingaizo, S. (22 January 2022) 'Zimbabwe opposition leader Nelson Chamisa forms new political party,' Available at: https://www.timeslive.co.za, Accessed 26 May 2022.
Moyo, G. & Phulu, K.I. (March 2021) 'The weaponisation of the Corona virus crisis in Zimbabwe: Legal and extra-legal instruments,' in: *iBusiness*, Volume 13, Number 1, pp.36-66.
Munhende, L. (3 February 2021) 'Zimbabwe: ZANU-PF MP gives middle finger to ED's lockdown, holds rally,' Available at: www.allAfrica.com/stories/202102030163.html, Accessed 16 December 2021.
Nehanda Radio (7 August 2020) 'MDC Alliance Bulawayo Province statement on abductions, torture and violence,' Available at: www.nehandaradio.com/2020/08/07/, Accessed 2 January 2022.
News dzeZimbabwe (14 May 2020) 'MDC MP, two others nabbed after demo,' Available at: www.newsdzezimbabwe.co.uk, Accessed 2 January 2022.
New Zimbabwe (24 July 2020) 'MDC-A MP arrested for distributing #ZANU-PF must go masks,' Available at: www.newzimbabwe.com, Accessed 13 January 2022.
Newsday (25 August 2020) 'MP Arrested over ZANU-PF-Must-Go masks,' Available at: www.newsday.co.zw/2020/08, Accessed 13 January 2022.
Ndhlovu, E. & Tembo, A. (2020) 'Gendered socio-economic implications of the Covid-19 pandemic in rural Zimbabwe', in: *Bizecons Quarterly*, Volume 12, pp.21-40.
Ndlovu, N. (30 July 2020) 'Another MDC Alliance activist "abducted",' Available at: www.pressreader.com, Accessed 13 January 2022.

New Zimbabwe (26 June 2020) 'MDC Alliance youths arrested while conducting voter registration exercise,' Available at: www.newzimbabwe.com, Accessed 15 January 2022.

Nkala, S. (1 July 2021) 'MDC blasts selective application of the law,' Available at: https://www.newsday.co.zw, Accessed 12 January 2022

Nkomo, B.F. & Mangiza, O. (2020) 'Civil disobedience and images of war: The military and police in the face of the Covid-19 pandemic in Zimbabwe,' Unpublished manuscript under advanced review by the *Dyke Journal*, Midlands State University: Zimbabwe.

Noko, K. (2 April 2020) 'The problem with army-enforced lockdowns in the time of Covid-19', Available at: https://www.aljazeera.com, Accessed 12 December 2021.

Nyahunda, L. Chibvura, S. & Tirivangasi, H.M. (May 2021) 'Social work practice: Accounting for double injustices experienced by women under the influence of the Covid-19 pandemic and climate change impacts in Nyanga, Zimbabwe', in: *Journal of Human Rights & Social Work*, Available at: https://doi.ora/01.1007/s41134-021-0017-4, Accessed 15 January 2022.

Nyathi, P. (30 June 2021) 'Enforcement of enhanced Covid-19 national lockdown measures by the Zimbabwe Republic Police,' Available at: www.zrp.org.zw/index.php?option=com-content&view=category&layout=blog&id=45&Itermid=743, Accessed 4 January 2022.

Obasa, A.E. et al (2020) 'Comparative strategic approaches to Covid-19 in Africa: Balancing public interest with civil liberties', in: *South African Medical Journal*, Volume 110, Number 9, pp.858-863.

Parker, M. (2020) 'Public authority and enforcement', in: *Cross-cultural Studies in Health & Illness*, Volume 39, Issue 8.

Pindula News (18 September 2020) 'Prince Dubeko Ssibanda in court for inciting public violence after distributing two masks written ZANU-PF must go,' Available at: www.news.pindula.co.zw/2020/09/18, Accessed 13 January 2022.

Price, R.A. (2020) *Impacts of Covid-19 regulatory measures on small scale and informal trade in Zimbabwe, K4D Helpdesk Report*, Brighton, United Kingdom: Institute of Development Studies.

Raquel, A. (2020) 'Contestation of political power in Zimbabwe under the Covid-19 lockdown', in: *Gender and Behaviour: Supplementary Edition*, Issue 4, pp.16811-16826.

Rashai, P. (2020) 'ZANU-PF Women's League donates 50k face masks,' Available at: www.hararepost.co.zw/en/the-news/4084-zanu-pf-women-s-league-donates-50k-face-masks, Accessed 14 January 2022.

Rivers, M. & Ndlovu, P. (24 June 2020) 'Covid raises the stakes for Zimbabwe's civil society movement,' Available at: https://www.usip.org, Accessed 13 January 2022.

Samutereko, E.Z. (June 2021) 'A critical analysis of social distancing as a policy to combat the spread of Corona virus in Zimbabwe', in: *Technium Social Sciences Journal*, Volume 20, pp.782-790.

Standard (3 May 2020) Harare: Zimbabwe.

Standard (16 July 2021) Harare: Zimbabwe.

Sunday Mail (13 June 2021) Harare: Zimbabwe.

Tofa, M. (2020) 'How Zimbabwe is decimating political pluralism behind the smokescreen of Covid-19', in: *African Leadership Centre Covid-19 Research OP-ED Series,* Volume 6, Issue 1.

United States Embassy in Zimbabwe (2020) '2020 Human Rights in Zimbabwe,' Available at: www.zw.usembassy.gov/2020-human-rights-report-zimbabwe/, Accessed 12 December 2021.

Veritas Zimbabwe (2020a) 'Judgement No: SC56/2020 MDC *et al* vs Mashavira *et al*, Civil Appeal No: SC289/2019,'Available at: www.veritaszim.net/node/4063, Accessed 18 January 2022.

Veritas Zimbabwe (2020b) 'Election Watch: Suspension of Election Activities,' Available at: www.veritaszim.net/node/4168, Accessed 14 January 2022.

Vinga, A. (5 February 2021) '3 236 nabbed in one day for violating Covid-19 regulations,' Available at: www.newzimbabwe.com, Accessed 18 January 2022.

World (21 July 2021) 'Mass arrests in Zimbabwe over Corona virus regulation violations,' Available at: www.peri.org/stories/2020-07-21, Accessed 15 January 2022.

Zimbabwe Human Rights NGO Forum (June 2020) 'Zimbabwe Covid-19 Lockdown Monitoring Report 6, Day 69,' Available at: www.kubatana.net, Accessed 3 January 2022.

Zimbabwean (7 May 2021) 'MDC activists arrested for wearing masks with Chamisa's name,' Available at: https://www.thezimbabwean.co.zw. Accessed 12 January 2022.

ZimDaily (1 September 2021) 'Police arrest vendors for cheering president for Chamisa,' Available at: www.zimdaily.com/police-arrest-vendors-for-cheering-president-for-chamisa/, Accessed 17 December 2021.

Zimbabwe Election Support Network (4 October 2020) 'Statement on the indefinite suspension of by-elections in Zimbabwe,' Available at: www.kubatana.net, Accessed 18 December 2021.

ZimEye (22 April 2020) 'Four MDC officials finally granted bail,' Available at: www.zimeye.net/2020/04/22/four-mdc-officials-finally-granted-bail/, Accessed 18 December 2021.

Zim-Metro (29 July 2021) 'Hefty fines for violating Covid-19 regulations approved,' Available at: www.zimetro.co.zw, Accessed 3 January 2022.

Chapter 11

Covid-19 Protocols and the Shrinking Democratic and Human Rights Space in Zimbabwe

Aaron Rwodzi & Terence Tapiwa Muzorewa

Introduction

The Covid-19 virus that first appeared at the end of 2019 in Wuhan, China, and was declared a global pandemic by the World Health Organisation (WHO) in March 2020 created an unstable political environment around the globe. The period after the declaration was characterised by a proliferation of Covid-19 clinical experiments, vaccines and forced inoculations especially on reluctant and hesitant citizens of the sub-altern who doubted the sincerity of the pharmaceutical companies of the developed countries. In order to satisfy the Covid-19 protocols and stay in the good grace of the WHO, the Zimbabwean government opportunistically weaponised the pandemic and sanitised the 'rule of men' as opposed to the 'rule of law.' All these developments took place as the pandemic took its toll on the unsuspecting public.

This chapter, apart from analysing the enforcement of Covid-19 protocols in Zimbabwe under heightened political tensions, explores how the pandemic indeed became a weapon to stifle democratic processes in Zimbabwe. It interrogates neo-liberal Western values of electoral and democratic 'fair play' and their applicability to the Zimbabwean scenario that was replete with serious contestations around President Mnangagwa's political legitimacy since the harmonised elections of 2018. The chapter argues that given the history of the armed struggle in Zimbabwe, the ruling Zimbabwe African National Union Patriotic Front (ZANU-PF) party could not effectively 'open up' political spaces during the pandemic era, but had to shrink them to circumscribe critical voices from below in contravention of the law of the land.

The chapter further examines the nature of legislation, policies, institutional practices and decision-making processes adopted in Zimbabwe in response to the challenges engendered by the Covid-19 pandemic so as to show how their implementation substantially negated various forms of human rights and human dignity. It also reveals how contrived and shoddy some of the Covid-19 responses initiated from above by the government of Zimbabwe, usually through its Ministry of Health and Child Welfare in collaboration with the Ministry of Information, were and how badly they fared in terms of protecting human rights as enunciated under international, regional and national law.

Background

Zimbabwe was not spared from the devastating effects of the Covid-19 pandemic which was already causing havoc around the world by the beginning of 2020. Covid-19 became known as a contagious disease caused by a novel virus that harms the respiratory system of infected people and may turn deadly to segments of the world population. Zimbabwe's first case of Covid-19 was recorded on 20 March 2020 (Makombe, 2021; Rahardjar, 2020). The case was an adult male resident of the town of Victoria Falls who had travelled from the United Kingdom via South Africa (Ibid).

At first, the majority of infected people recorded were coming from countries with high infection rates such as South Africa, China, Italy and the United Kingdom. Before long, however, local transmissions became prevalent. With only a relatively few confirmed cases as compared to other countries in the world, the Zimbabwean government proactively proceeded to declare Covid-19 a national disaster on 27 March 2020 (Ibid). This was followed by the issuance of Statutory Instrument 83 of 2020 Public Health (Covid-19 Prevention, Containment, and Treatment) (Ibid). The Statutory Instrument was meant to slow down the spread of the pandemic through a national lockdown where all public activities and informal non-essential businesses were suspended. In addition to the lockdown, the government announced that it was mandatory for all people arriving from other countries to go through strict screening procedures, including enforcement of a 21-day self-quarantine (Ibid). The general public was encouraged to remain in their homes, sanitise their hands, and wear face masks. Covid-19 testing and contact tracing became procedural especially in government institutions. However, over time the government would review and amend its response measures through statutory instruments and press briefings (Ibid).

There is extant literature on issues to do with Covid-19 and how the government reacted in an endeavour to curb the spreading of the disease. Makombe (2021), for example, examined the socio-economic impact of Covid-19 in Harare's high density suburbs. He explored the experiences of low-income households during the pandemic and compared them with higher income households as informed by sex-based differences and access to health care and food. For Makombe (2021), while the measures adopted by the government to curb the spread of Covid-19 were laudable on the surface, they disproportionately and adversely affected the poor. He goes on to show how the government, through its ill-conceived Covid-19-related policies such as demolitions of 'illegal' structures and vending stalls in Mbare, Epworth and Chitungwiza, further threatened the survival of the poor during the lockdown period. In his narrative, Makombe deplored police brutality against the poor when enforcing the lockdown regulations. His work is important in highlighting some of the experiences of the poor during the Covid-19-induced lockdown. This chapter builds on this knowledge by looking at the human rights abuses of Zimbabwean citizens and the consequent erosion of democracy, though the poor were the major victims.

It soon became apparent even in the eyes of the ordinary that the Covid-19 regulations were being abused by the government in order to meet its political agendas. Scholars such as Moyo & Phulu (2021) argue that President Mnangagwa's administration in Zimbabwe weaponised Covid-19 in order to achieve some objectives beyond the public health concerns. In particular, the government sought to use the lockdown measures to clamp down on political opposition, silence critics, contain the restive population, and entrench its power and control over some key accountability institutions including the legislature, judiciary, and the media. To achieve its objectives, the government deployed armed security forces to enforce the Covid-19 measures. Moyo & Phulu (2021) noticed that following the imposition of the lockdown measures, parliament suspended its regular sessions on 5 May 2020. This compromised democratic space and respective processes in the country. The scholars argue that in most of the cities in Zimbabwe, armed soldiers and members of the police detained and beat up those who questioned their motives for such actions (Ibid). In general, the government capitalised on the context of the Covid-19 crisis to manage its political and economic problems. Although Moyo & Phulu (2021) touch on some aspects of democracy and human rights abuse in their study, this chapter provides vivid and concrete accounts and examples of such acts.

Human rights abuse is not a new phenomenon in Zimbabwe but was happening well before the advent of Covid-19. Chitimira & Mokone (2017) traced human rights violations involving torture in Zimbabwe from the colonial period, especially in the late 1970s. These torture-related human rights violations were rampant during the liberation struggle when guerrillas and other people who were suspected of being enemies of the ruling minority Rhodesian government were often captured and brutally tortured, especially in the rural areas from 1965 to the 1970s (Ibid). However, some instances of torture continued to be employed by the new independent black government's law-enforcement agencies such as the police, intelligence officers and soldiers against members of the opposition parties, non-governmental organisations and other human rights activists. The scholars also highlighted gross human rights abuses that were perpetrated by the government during the ethnic civil war which resulted in a number of civilians being raped, tortured and killed in the early 1980s. It is also alleged that between 1999 and 2013, many human rights activists and members of the Movement for Democratic Change (MDC) were subjected to various forms of abuse such as rape, torture, beatings and killings (Ibid). This shows that human rights abuses and undemocratic practices in Zimbabwe started way back before the advent of the Covid-19 pandemic.

Most of the human rights abuses in independent Zimbabwe usually occurred during elections thereby compromising democratic processes in the country. The extant literature on elections in Zimbabwe, for example, by Boone & Kriger (2005), Magure (2014) and Raftopoulos (2013), to name a few, provides informative accounts of election-associated gross human rights abuses. In 2000, after the ruling ZANU-PF party was faced with its stiffest political opposition ever and sharp economic decline since the inception of its rule in 1980, the party orchestrated land occupation, confiscation and reallocation of white-operated farms to mobilise and reward loyalists and, to a limited extent, opponents in a process known as the Fast Track Land Reform Programme (Boone & Kriger, 2010). Many human rights abuses against the farmers and farm labourers were committed.

Kriger (2005) also demonstrates how ZANU-PF used organised violence and intimidation as political strategies to ensure victory in every election since 1980. Besides violence, the ruling party engaged strategies that demonised its opponents as reactionary, subversive and stooges of the whites (Ibid). Apart from violence and coercion, Southall & Slabbert (2013) point to various forms of rigging as part of the election-winning formula used by ZANU-PF. They point out that ZANU-PF controlled the electoral machinery such as the Zimbabwe Electoral Commission (ZEC) and the Registrar General's Office. Through these electoral institutions, the ruling party was often accused of wielding the power to temper with the voters' roll and the "counting of what is contained in the ballot boxes" (Ibid: 140). It was also alleged that during election time, ZANU-PF clandestinely bused rural voters to urban areas to cast their ballots in an endeavour to dilute the urban vote. In the worst scenario, it was claimed that the party imported voters from neighbouring Mozambique into areas across the Zimbabwean border where the opposition MDC was popular (Ibid). Accounts from these scholars show that the ZANU-PF government had a long history of undemocratic practices which included human rights abuses before the Covid-19 pandemic. Hence, this chapter analyses how the pandemic gave the ZANU-PF government an opportunity to further its selfish political desires without remorse.

In assessing the extent of democratic space and human rights compliance during the Covid-19 pandemic in Zimbabwe, this chapter utilises both primary and secondary sources to derive research data. Primary data was mainly obtained from documents of various human rights organisations and institutions. Newspapers were a crucial source of information on the experiences of citizens during the lockdown period. Personal interviews based on convenience and snowball sampling were used as one of the data gathering tools. Limitations in face-to-face activities brought by Covid-19 regulations resulted in us using telephones and other online platforms for interviews. Peoples' verifiable accounts of their experiences on social media platforms were critical in complementing other sources of data. Our engagement with secondary sources such as journals, books, articles and newspapers was useful in situating the chapter in the broader studies on Covid-19-related discourses on human rights and democracy in Zimbabwe.

From the shrinking of democratic space towards closure

This section focuses on how the democratic space shrank and finally closed during the Covid-19 pandemic period. The strategies that were deployed by the ZANU-PF government to monopolise political space included restricting civic activities, creating an uneven playing field for elections, undermining the constitutional separation of powers among the Executive, the Legislature and the Judiciary, and manipulating pliant opposition parties in order to scuttle meaningful political change.

Democratic space can be defined as "produced social space" in which there is political contestation and inclusiveness reflected in the extent to which citizens have the opportunity to formulate their preferences, articulate their preferences and have their preferences weighed equally in the conduct of government (Netherlands Institute for Multiparty Democracy, 2017: 10). Taking it from this understanding, the closure of democratic space involves state and non-state actors restraining space and openings for political contestation and participation. When democratic space shrinks, it means there are deliberate obstacles on civic space, the rule of law, separation of government powers, checks and balances and fair and inclusive political participation and contestation (Ibid). Due to political polarisation in Zimbabwe dating back to the harmonised elections of 2018 whose results were disputed by the rival opposition MDC Alliance party, reactive legal frameworks were proposed and assented into law with a view to closing democratic space, hence the catch phrase: "In Zimbabwe there is rule by law instead of rule of law" (European Partnership for Democracy, May 2020: 17). President Mnangagwa's regime quickly quelled hopes of widening space for contestation from opposition and civil society as evidenced by violence in the aftermath of peaceful elections in 2018, as well as a series of extremely violent crackdowns on protestors and internet shutdowns in January 2019 (Ibid).

Using Zimbabwe as an example, the European Partnership for Democracy (2020) identified three broad strategies deployed by the government to close democratic space. The first was to restrict civic space, particularly freedom of expression, assembly and association by making use of various legal, administrative, extra-legal and political measures. In this strategy, the state also sought to constrain the proper functioning of media outlets, political opposition formations and civil society organisations. The second strategy was to change the rules of the game so as to create an uneven playing field for political contestation, a move that encapsulated the abuse of state resources by the incumbent, skewed reforms in political party and electoral legislation, and one-sided private and illicit financing in campaigning. The third strategy was to deliberately undermine the separation of powers as constitutionally enshrined, particularly the independence of the judiciary, and thus, politicising legal processes, and allowing impunity and violence to shape the activities of citizens, media actors and civil society organisations (Ibid). Zimbabwe was not alone in frustrating democracy and human rights during the pandemic era. During the same period, there was, indeed, a growing trend of challenges and threats to democracy in many countries as noted by scholars and research institutions under various terms such as democratic backsliding (Nancy, 2016), democratic rollback (Diamond, 2008), and authoritarian resurgence (Azar, 2007).

It can be argued that the Covid-19 pandemic was also exploited to compromise the independence of the judiciary, among other state institutions in Zimbabwe. Although the judiciary retained a modicum of independence where some judges would still uphold constitutionalism, politically sensitive cases were given to partial judges (European Partnership for Democracy, 2020). The ruling ZANU-PF party opportunistically used the legitimacy of smaller political parties to create the illusion of contestation and inclusiveness, as was the case with the Political Actors Dialogue (POLAD). The ruling party set up its own platform for interparty dialogue which lacked the participation of the main opposition MDC Alliance. POLAD largely became irrelevant as a platform of contestation, but very useful in building the illusion of a multiparty democracy and winning allies. Political parties in Zimbabwe, whether ruling or in opposition, were essentially populist in that they appealed to the potential voters through mass propaganda rallies that theoretically addressed the economic concerns of the voting constituencies. But once in government, experience showed that populists regularly used their democratic mandate to undermine the very institutions that got them into office in the first place (European Political Strategy Centre, 2019).

The other arm of democracy whose functions were crippled during the Covid-19 period in Zimbabwe is parliament. Statutory Instrument 77 of 2020 which provided for Covid-19 prevention, containment and treatment and all its subsequent amendments, did not consider parliamentary business as essential. The parliament was not included among the institutions that were exempted from movement restrictions such as health, finance, mining and agriculture. Hence, parliament suspended its regular sessions on 5 May 2020 after the announcement of lockdown measures (Moyo & Phulu, 2021). This shows that the government did not prioritise democracy as essential to the citizens in time of crisis. While the ZANU-PF-dominated parliament was closed for business on grounds of Covid-19 prevention and containment, it would quickly convene to deal with matters that disadvantaged opposition politics, thus unmasking the ruling party's insincerity. Despite the lockdown restrictions on movement, the parliament presided over the recalling of MDC Alliance Members of Parliament after internal wrangles in opposition politics called for such moves. This shows that the government was just using Covid-19 as an excuse to disable parliament which is one of the major pillars of democracy.

Lockdown measures and the right to freedoms of association, assembly and expression

In simple terms, the word 'lockdown' means limiting or restricting people from travelling from one place to another, from one urban location to another, from one village to another unless an excusable explanation with the support of an exemption letter was officially given by the police or any such state institution or organisation mandated to do so. It was not surprising that the measures put in place to curb the spread of the pandemic eroded people's right to freedom of association, assembly and expression of divergent opinion. In the technological context, digital rights in those closing civic spaces disappeared. The concept 'digital rights' is used to refer to the right to access the internet as a means to ensure freedom of information, expression and association (United Nations, 2011). This section, in essence, explores the impact of lockdown measures on human dignity and rights.

Within the realm of civil and political rights, the freedoms of association, assembly and expression were the most violated in Zimbabwe (Action Aid, 2020). Under normal circumstances, the right to demonstrate should not have been automatically suspended on grounds of the Covid-19 lockdown. Measures adopted by states in using Covid-19 to limit rights were supposed to meet the Emergency Measures and Covid-19 Guidelines issued by the United Nations High Commissioner for Human Rights on 27 April 2020, which advised that restrictions "must meet the requirements of legality, necessity and proportionality, and be non-discriminatory" (Ibid: 10). The rights of freedom of association, assembly and expression faced perhaps their worst attack since independence in Zimbabwe. The Covid-19 pandemic was often manipulated to justify and intensify the crackdown on these rights. This appeared to be part of a broader campaign to shrink the democratic and civic space (Ibid).

The Cyber Security and Data Protection Bill was passed in 2020. Its avowed purpose was to curtail online freedom of speech. In August 2020, the Zimbabwean Lives Matter Campaign caught the attention of the world by exposing human rights abuses perpetrated by the government, with President Mnangagwa threatening to "flush out the dark forces" involved in the campaign (Mashininga, 2020). The Maintenance of Peace and Order Act of 2020 that superseded the defunct Public Order and Security Act (POSA) was equally constraining in the exercise of association and assembly rights. The government introduced the Constitution of Zimbabwe Amendment (No. 2) Bill of 2019 in order to cut back on democratic practices that included checks and balances and oversight, as well as transparency, accountability and openness. The government also successfully took advantage of the Covid-19 lockdown to conduct rushed public consultations across the country in respect of the bill (Action Aid, 2020).

Since the 2018 elections which were won by ZANU-PF amid controversy, the judiciary was often manipulated by the ruling party (*Guardian*, 28 April 2021). The judiciary was captured and weaponised as manifested by the use of pre-trial detentions to punish government critics. It was this weaponisation that saw the journalist Hopewell Chin'ono being charged on the basis of a defunct law, which saw him incarcerated for more than 14 days. There was also the harassment and abuse of lawyers who elected to handle political cases involving members from the opposition political formations. On 18 August 2020, human rights lawyer Beatrice Mtetwa was barred from representing Hopewell Chin'ono at the Harare Magistrate Court. In an unprecedented move, Magistrate Ngoni Nduna ordered that Mtetwa be charged with contempt of court in relation to comments about the case that was posted on a Facebook page. State prosecutors argued that these comments scandalised the state (Civil Society Submission to the APRM in Zimbabwe, 2020/2021).

As the Crisis in Zimbabwe Coalition (2019), a civil rights organisation, reported, the Covid-19 era witnessed a worrying ascendancy of authoritarian tendencies and a clamp down on human rights activists in countries such as Zimbabwe, Swaziland and Zambia. In the same vein, Nganje (2021) noticed the apparent shift away from "using primitive and crude tactics of violence and naked brutality" to a more sophisticated approach of controlling the civic space through the use of draconian laws that monitored and constrained the activities of NGOs and other civil organisations.

The violent clampdown on activists behind the 31 July 2020 protests was a stark revelation of a government that was ready to pounce on its own people, thereby mocking and contradicting its claims of turning Zimbabwe into a democracy after the 2017 coup. Many political activists went into hiding after the police had published a list of human rights defenders and opposition politicians whom they wanted to question in connection with the protests. The police also ransacked the home of prominent journalist, Mduduzi Mathuthu, on the eve of the protests. When they failed to locate Mathuthu, they arrested his sister and cousins. They held them hostage until the journalist, who was instrumental in exposing alleged corruption in the government's procurement of medical supplies to fight Covid-19, presented himself at the Bulawayo Central Police Station (Solidar Foundation, 28 May 2020).

The wave of repression of freedom of association and peaceful assembly affected many Zimbabweans from all walks of life. It is important to note that Zimbabwean human rights defenders, opposition supporters, civil society and trade union activists were the most targeted for critiquing national policies insofar as they related to health and security during the Covid-19 era. The International Trade Union Confederation (ITUC) reported the repression of workers' protests in July 2020 and that of the nurses against poor wages and the lack of adequate personal protective equipment (Ibid). The protesting health personal were violently dispersed by the police. Trade union leaders Peter Mutasa, President of the Zimbabwe Congress of Trade Unions (ZCTU), and Secretary General Japhet Moyo, together with the Amalgamated Rural Teachers Union (ARTUZ) official, Obert Masaraure, were harassed and had their homes broken into by armed people who identified themselves as security officers, in the middle of the night. At a press conference convened by ZANU- PF, trade union leaders were humiliated and the ruling party's Acting Secretary for Information labelled the

ZCTU as a terrorist organisation. This demonisation of the ZCTU explains why its president, Mutasa, appeared on the list of wanted persons compiled by the Zimbabwe Republic Police and published by the Zimbabwe Broadcasting Corporation (ZBC) on the same day (Ibid).

Figure 1: Police chasing a health worker during a demonstration, 2020

Source: *ZW News*, 26 March 2020

In May 2020, Amnesty International criticised Mnangagwa's government for denying humanitarian food aid to those who did not support the ruling party (Gagare, 7 July 2020). This behaviour negated the right to food and exhibited political exclusionary food politics at a time most Zimbabweans suffered widespread hunger and starvation partly because of the Covid-19 pandemic whose subsequent lockdown had resulted in the suspension of many income-generating activities. Civil society groups also criticised bills in Parliament that would amend 30 sections of Zimbabwe's Constitution to give Mnangagwa what the Zimbabwe Human Rights NGO Forum called "medieval monarch-type" powers that weakened democratic checks and balances (Zimbabwe Human Rights NGO Forum, 2020). The government pressed hard for the amendments and held public hearings despite the Covid-19 pandemic and the shutdown of other public activities, thus, exhibiting an inconsistency that the labour unions and citizens' groups protested against (Ibid). As the crackdown on civilians under Covid-19 conditions continued, Zimbabwe became one of the most authoritarian governments worldwide, comparable to countries such as China, Jordan, the Philippines, Poland and Hungary whose ruling parties gained notoriety for using the pandemic to consolidate their power (Rivers & Ndlovu, 2020).

The area of digital technology was instrumental in creating public awareness and familiarisation with Covid-19 protocols such as wearing of masks, social distancing and sanitising, among others. Digital rights are human rights in online spaces and include the right to privacy, freedom of opinion and speech, freedom of information and communication, gender rights, and the right to freedom from violence (APC & Hivos, 2014; Abraham, 2014). This technology also worked equally well in exposing governance deficits across the globe. Roberts & Ali (2021) focused on digital technology and explored how civic space remained open in only two of Africa's 54 countries during the Covid-19 pandemic. There was a significant reduction in safe public spaces where democratic debates could occur and this represented a breach of citizens' digital rights and rendered the achievement of the Sustainable Development Goals virtually impossible (Roberts & Ali, 2011). It is interesting to note how in Zimbabwe, Covid-19-related laws were hurriedly promulgated to elude public scrutiny simply because, in essence, they impinged on the fundamental human rights that the citizens were supposed to exercise and enjoy. Nganje (2021) made an analysis of how governments responded to the Covid-19 pandemic and concluded that there was a strong desire in the southern African region to police the internet as a way of managing the increased scrutiny and criticism of public policy and officials that had come with the growing use of digital technologies. It is beyond the scope of this chapter to identify and compile a list of internet users who were victimised on digital platforms, but the fact of the matter remains that as part of securitisation efforts, Zimbabwean authorities invaded the field of digital technology or social media platforms, raising fears about whether what one communicated would not be construed as subversive.

The autocratic tendencies of the government of President Mnangagwa led to the use of Covid-19 as a pretext to suffocate democracy in what now seemed to be the norm of authoritarian leaders globally. Patrick Chinamasa, a key member of the ZANU-PF Politburo, the executive arm of the party, also framed his response to the allegations of democratic regression as a struggle against neo-imperialism, yet the motive was to demonise and delegitimise the opposition. Brian Nichols, the American ambassador to Zimbabwe at that time, was accused of funding a regime-change agenda and Chinamasa labelled him a gangster and a thug (Zamchiya, 2020).

Panos Institute Southern Africa (PISA) strongly condemned the harassment and intimidation of journalists who were at the forefront of producing in-depth content on the management of public resources, including funds meant for the Covid-19 response. Award-winning investigative journalist Hopewell Chin'ono was arrested on 20 July 2020 on charges of "incitement to participate in public violence as provided for in section 187(1) (a) of the Criminal Law (Codification and Reform) Act, Chapter 9: 23" (*The Standard*, 2-8 August 2020). On 30 July 2020, suspected armed members of the Zimbabwe Republic Police besieged the home of *ZimLive* editor, Mduduzi Mathuthu, in search of subversive material (Ibid). These two journalists, Chin'ono and Mathuthu, had courageously exposed corruption and encouraged citizens to demand accountability in the management of public resources, including those meant for the Covid-19 response (Ibid).

Owing to lockdown measures, the right to freedoms of association, assembly and expression became non-existent during the Covid-19 era in Zimbabwe. Indeed, democratic spaces not only shrank but systematically closed. Reactive legislation was enforced, usually to criminalise activities that were originally carried out within the bounds of the law. The autocratic tendencies of the regime wiped away whatever remnants of democratic tenets that had miraculously survived in former president Robert Mugabe's First Republic. The ordinary poor in rural and urban areas suffered in silence for fear of government reprisals as outspoken critics of the government became the objects of unrelenting harassment, ridicule and persecution in courts that were apparently captured to deliver lopsided justice that favoured ZANU-PF and its government.

Suppression of the opposition and a campaign of terror

Many tactics were devised in several parts of the world to either close or suppress democratic space during the Covid-19 era. In Zimbabwe under the Second Republic led by President Mnangagwa, democratic space was gradually eroded by means of subtle attacks on the opposition and the government's hysterical protection of the political status quo. This involved creating an uneven political playfield, infringing the rule of law by undermining judicial independence, and having the ZANU-PF-dominated legislative bodies rubber-stamping executive decisions. This section assesses the Covid-19-related suppression of the opposition and the campaign of terror that accompanied seemingly legitimate and justifiable attempts to uphold the WHO protocols to mitigate the impact of the pandemic.

In 2020, when the Covid-19 pandemic was at its peak in Zimbabwe, Joana Mamombe, Cecilia Chimbiri and Netsai Marova, all members of the Movement for Democratic Change (MDC) Alliance, took part in a demonstration in the capital, Harare, to draw the government's attention to escalating poverty among vulnerable communities during the Covid-19-induced lockdown (Mangena, 2021). Mamombe, a Member of Parliament for Harare West, Chimbiri and Marova participated in that demonstration organised by the MDC Alliance Youth Assembly. The demonstration also cited the government's failure to provide social protection for the poor during the Covid-19 lockdown given the fact that the urban economy was heavily informalised, with no industrial expansion taking place over many years (Ibid). They were reportedly abducted and tortured by unidentified male state agents before the state accused the women of being instrumental in an illegal demonstration. At law, for a demonstration to be protected, it ought to be peaceful. This explains why the United Nations (UN) High Commissioner for Human Rights in Zimbabwe issued the following statement on 24 July 2020 ahead of a planned demonstration at the end of the month:

> Merely calling for a peaceful protest or participating in a peaceful protest is an exercise of recognised human rights. Demonstration have thus become an acceptable platform of public engagement and a medium of communication on issues of a public nature in open societies based on justice and freedom (Action Aid, 2020: 5).

Besides the physical violence and torture that they were subjected to, Mamombe, Chimbiri and Marova further had to endure symbolic and emotional violence emanating from their being portrayed as criminals, rather than survivors of violence, by the ZANU-PF government (Mangena, 2021). The state also deployed silencing strategies that involved using language through state-controlled media reports to frame and dismiss outright the alleged torture as a false claim (Ibid). The case of the trio, indeed, somehow confirmed the manner in which the Zimbabwean state-controlled media was utilised to sustain and buttress the hegemonic liberation narratives of the ruling ZANU-PF party (Ranger, 2004). Mamombe was systematically denigrated as a rogue legislator and a breaker of the law in a manner that criminalised female agency (Fanghanel, 2019). The three testified in court that some unidentified men took them to a forest where they were thrown into a pit, tortured, beaten, sexually assaulted, and forced to drink each other's urine and eat each other's faeces (Moyo & Kingsley, 2020).

Tsitsi Dangarembga, a renowned novelist and filmmaker with keen interest in women's emancipation, was also arrested during an anti-corruption protest march in Harare on 31 July 2020. The corrupt tendencies in the procurement and prioritisation of Covid-19 vaccines also led to popular outrage leading to demonstrations against the Zimbabwean government's Covid-19 policies. Under these circumstances, Dangarembwa positioned herself as a female activist for which reason she was arrested. She noted:

> My arrest and the arrests of others who protested on July 31, or even in the days leading up to July 31, indicate that the right to peaceful protest is seriously eroded in Zimbabwe. Zimbabwean citizens are expected to keep silent and docilely accept whatever the authorities decide to do, or face arrest for peacefully expressed differences of opinion (Dangarembga, 2020a).

Given the Dangarembwa and the MDC Alliance trio sagas, it can be argued that the government's heavy-handedness, ostensibly in an attempt to implement Covid-19 lockdown measures, systematically restricted the movement of citizens and their right to assembly and expression. Above all, gendered violence and the shrinking of democratic space carried the day. The state's use of institutionalised violence, arrests, abductions and torture as tools of repression of political dissent that was characteristic of Robert Mugabe's era (Sachikonye, 2011), was skilfully carried over by President Mnangagwa's government to silence critics and the opposition. As seen in these developments, lockdown regulations were manipulated and purposed to frustrate opposition members and punish perceived enemies, real or imagined.

During the Covid-19 period, state agents consistently tormented political activists, human rights defenders and critical journalists resulting in many of the fugitives going into hiding and sometimes living in the bush like wild animals. These included Job Sikhala, an MDC Alliance official and Zengeza West Member of Parliament; Ostallos Siziba, MDC Alliance Secretary General; Denford Ngadziore, MDC Alliance Harare Province Organising Secretary;

Makomborero Haruzivishe, MDC Alliance Youth Assembly Chairman; and Mduduzi Mathuthu, a prominent journalist (Zamchiya, 2020). Others like Hopewell Chin'ono, a prominent journalist, and Jacob Ngarivhume, the Transform Zimbabwe president, were locked up and denied bail well ahead of the 31 July 2020 demonstrations on frivolous charges (Ibid). There were many instances where lockdown regulations were selectively applied using reactive pieces of legislation to silence and cow critics. This resulted in the prohibition of political gatherings, arbitrary arrests, labelling and name-calling of the opposition and the West by ZANU-PF officials who were safeguarding their party's waning support resulting from their mismanagement of the pandemic (Vanyoro & Mutekwe, 2021).

Although closing democratic space was a global phenomenon, this practice was arguably more evident in Zimbabwe than elsewhere in southern Africa as many ruling party perpetrators of politically-motivated violence and arbitrary arrests enjoyed unqualified impunity from institutions designed to safeguard the law of the land. Women with voices to represent the poor and the marginalised in rural and urban areas could not withstand gendered politics of the Covid-19 period and, in most cases, could not endure the harsh realities of a patriarchal political dispensation. Indeed, the institutionalisation of fear that the government of Zimbabwe engendered during the Covid-19 era shrunk the available democratic and human rights spaces in Zimbabwe.

Covid-19 policy enforcement, the constitution and human rights abuses

The enforcement of Covid-19 rules and regulations in line with the WHO international guidelines ought to be evaluated against the Zimbabwean Constitution in order to assess the extent to which human rights were observed. Other international conventions on human rights to which Zimbabwe was a signatory were breached as citizens progressively lost their mobility rights as well as rights and freedoms to work. Among other things, the restricted people's movements under the guise of mitigating the spread of Covid-19.

On 9 February 2020, President Mnangagwa signed the African Peer Review Mechanism (APRM) resulting in Zimbabwe becoming the 39th member state of this accord. His predecessor, President Robert Mugabe, had staunchly and consistently resisted joining the

APRM even when he ascended to the African Union's rotating chairmanship in 2015. Incidentally, at that time, Mugabe was described as a "despotic pariah responsible for human rights abuses, rigged elections and turning one of Africa's most promising nations into a basket case" (Blair, 2015). It was important for President Mnangagwa to join APRM on behalf of the Zimbabwean people. By so doing, he had, as Head of State and Government, committed himself to APRM principles insofar as they related to improved governance in the member states. This became particularly important too, given the Covid-19 pandemic that made governments react in different ways especially where there were already signs and symptoms of governance deficit. The APRM, therefore, is Africa's premier watchdog on governance self-assessment and promotion. It was established in 2003 to improve governance on the continent by fostering the adoption of policies, standards and practices that lead to political stability, economic growth, sustainable development and accelerated sub regional and economic integration, through the reinforcement of best practices (New Partnership for Africa's Development, 2002).

As a means of dealing with human rights issues, Section 242 of the 2013 Zimbabwean Constitution created the Zimbabwe Human Rights Commission (ZHRC) whose main functions include the promotion of awareness of and respect for human rights and freedoms at all levels of society; the promotion, protection, development and attainment of human rights and freedoms; monitoring, assessing and ensuring observance of human rights and freedoms; receiving and considering complaints from the public and taking such action in regard to the complaints as it considered appropriate; protecting the public against abuse of power and maladministration by the state and public institutions and by officers of those institutions (Zimbabwe Constitution, 2013). As part of its mandate, the ZHRC released a statement urging the government to respect the constitution and refrain from using various state machinery to instil fear and despondency ahead of demonstrations scheduled for 31 July 2020. It voiced its concerns about the possibility during the Covid-19 era of the state apparatus inflicting constitutionally-proscribed measures such as torture or cruel, inhuman or degrading treatment or punishment on dissenting political voices (Veritas Zimbabwe, 2020). The commission called for an end to escalating politically-motivated abductions and torture of human rights defenders that were on the increase in 2020. Despite the presence of the ZHRC, the Mnangagwa government appeared to trivialise the roles of human right actors, opposition political parties and NGOs in ensuring that the government acted in accordance with the constitution on human rights issues. Conversely, these entities were reduced to addressing the government through press statements that were usually ignored (Human Rights Watch, 2020). This was just as good as not having these entities at all.

The government introduced restrictive measures through Statutory Instrument 83 of 2020 which declared the first 21-day lockdown that began on 30 March 2020. Apart from physical violence, the government routinely deployed legislative instruments to shrink democratic space (Hove & Chenzi, 2020). On 30 September 2020, the government issued Statutory Instrument 225A of 2020, entitled Public Health (Covid-19 Prevention, Containment, and Treatment) (Amendment) Regulations, 2020 (No. 4), which suspended the holding of by-elections due to the Covid-19 pandemic. Despite the easing of lockdown measures in February 2021, the suspension remained in place. The ZEC announced the indefinite suspension of by-elections noting that some lockdown measures of Statutory Instrument 10 of 2021 were still in force (*Bulawayo24 News*, 2021).

According to Maciel (2021), emergency restrictions have impacts, both intended and coincidental, on democratic and legislative processes as well as on civic space. When enacting measures that restrict people's rights, freedoms and liberties, it is important to ensure that they meet the requirements of legality, necessity, proportionality, and non-discrimination (United Nations, 2020b). International instruments regulating measures that restrict human rights in times of crisis include Article 4 of the International Covenant on Civil and Political Rights as well as the accompanying Siracusa Principles on the Limitation and Derogation Provisions (Ibid). When faced with extraordinary circumstances such as the Covid-19 pandemic, governments tend to resort to extreme measures that limit certain freedoms in order to mitigate the crisis (Duri *et al*, 2020). In this context, the parliament plays a central role not only in the enactment of emergency laws (Murphy, 2020), but also to prevent the government from adopting draconian measures that can plunge countries into authoritarianism (Freedom House, 2021).

Emergency measures by the police and the military

Zimbabwe's post-independence history shows that the military and the police largely played the traditional role of protecting state power. Put more succinctly, this usually involved harassing citizens and threatening communities. During the Covid-19 period, both the army and police appeared very motivated as they made patrols in city centres and mounted roadblocks across the country. A feeling of vulnerability and insecurity gripped many citizens because the security institutions seemed to be more determined to instilling fear rather than protecting them from the potentially deadly virus. Primarily, security forces were deployed to physically disperse gatherings. In addition, arrests and detentions were oftentimes unlawful and calculated to discourage and thwart rights to freedom of assembly and free speech (Action Aid, 2020). This was despite the fact that the Defence Act obliged the military to respect the fundamental rights and freedoms of all persons and to execute their duties in a patriotic, professional and non-partisan manner (Chitimira & Mokone, 2017). This also applied to the police who are regulated by the Police Act which outlines their duties in the maintenance of public order and safety in Zimbabwe. The police are constitutionally required to respect the fundamental rights and freedom of all persons and not to engage themselves in the political activities of any political party (Ibid). However, notwithstanding the clear legislation on the conduct of the military and police, these institutions were used by the state to oppress and violate the human rights of the people they were supposed to protect.

The state's enforcement of emergency measures meant to curb the spread of Covid-19 such as the lockdown, were heavy-handed. The police and military personnel tasked with managing lockdown regulations resorted to violence on both real and suspected violators. Numerous arrests and subsequent arbitrary detentions of those who breached lockdown regulations occurred. It was very difficult for those arbitrarily arrested and detained to access legal services because most law firms were closed in line with lockdown regulations. Under these circumstances, non-governmental organisations offering legal support such as the Zimbabwe Lawyers for Human Rights, Zimbabwe Human Rights NGO Forum and the Legal Resources Foundation made efforts to legally represent the victims. Despite this intervention, lawyers still faced challenges to attend to their clients as legal firms were not on the list of essential services that enjoyed government exemption orders from the lockdown (Ibid).

In 2021, a mother and her two minor children were detained in a cell at Harare's Rhodesville Police Station in Zimbabwe on grounds that the toddlers, both below the age of four years, were not putting on face masks. There was an outcry from the public after the picture, shown in Figure 2 below, went viral on the social media. Detaining minors is a form of child abuse which the police were accused of committing on several occasions. The police responded by putting up a press release which promised the public that investigations on the matter were taking place. However, the results of the investigation were not published in the state media as originally promised (*Zimbabwe Daily*, 2021).

The state agencies which enforced Covid-19 regulations were not sincere in their cause to stop the spread of the pandemic but wanted to capitalise on the power they wielded to loot from the poor. The Highfield Paradise vendors' community reported that police officials moved around confiscating their stock, in most cases targeting foodstuffs for forceful seizure (Makombe, 2021). In some instances, vendors bribed the police to secure their release. Pedestrians who witnessed the arrest of vendors in Harare's CBD confessed that they were usually brutal and callous. Vendors were often bundled into open trucks with others whose Covid-19 status was not known thereby exposing them to a greater risk of infection (Ibid).

Another approach used by the government to instil fear in the citizens was deploying the military for intelligence gathering. In order to make the military less identifiable, thereby limiting the overt abuse of the military uniform, soldiers were stripped of their right to wear uniforms in public (*Pindula*, 9 February 2019). This resulted in the formation of an intricate network of military detectives (Ibid). These developments show that the extreme attacks on human dignity in Zimbabwe found expression in the ruthlessness of state security machinery. These were the people responsible for 35 cases of abductions and torture documented by the Zimbabwe Human Rights NGO Forum in 2020 (Zimbabwe Human Rights NGO Forum, 2020). The abduction and torture incidents included that of journalist Tawanda Muchehiwa that went viral because the event was caught on CCTV. Muchehiwa was suspected of taking part in organising demonstrations against the government (*Mail & Guardian*, 2020). It was also four of these security personnel who, on 8 August 2020, abducted, tortured and sexually abused Noxolo Maphosa, whereupon they asked the whereabouts of her activist uncle, Josphat Ngulube (*Zim Live*, 8 August 2020). In addition, according to the Zimbabwe Human Rights NGO Forum (2021), seven attacks on journalists were recorded in the cities of Mutare, Gweru, Harare, Masvingo, and Bulawayo.

Figure 2: Woman in cells with two minors for allegedly violating lockdown regulations

Source: *Zimbabwe Daily*, 11 February 2021

The state-orchestrated human rights abuses during the Covid-19 pandemic raised serious questions about the government's sincerity in upholding various international instruments related to the Bill of Rights that it had ratified. These, though not exhaustive, included the Universal Declaration of Human Rights (UDHR); the International Covenant on Economic, Social and Cultural Rights (ICESCR), the International Covenant on Civil and Political Rights (ICCPR); the Convention on the Rights of the Child (CRC); the Convention on the Elimination and Discrimination Against Women (CEDAW); the African Charter on Human and Peoples' Rights (Banjul Charter); the African Charter on the Rights and Welfare of the Child; and the Protocol to the African Charter on the Rights of Women in Africa (Zimbabwe Human Rights Association, July 2020). Even more importantly, the Constitution of Zimbabwe also has an elaborate Bill of Rights which recognises and protects civil and political rights as well as economic, social and cultural rights (Constitution of Zimbabwe, 2013).

In spite of Zimbabwe being a signatory to all the human rights protocols as stated above, the Zimbabwe Human Rights NGO Forum secretariat recorded at least 676 politically-motivated human rights violations from 1 January to 31 March 2021 (Zimbabwe Human Rights NGO Forum, 2020). This suggests that during the pandemic era when the state declared a state of emergency, the risk of the emergency powers being abused became very high in Zimbabwe. This gave the state extensive powers which could be applied through coercive means using the army and police. The judiciary was also manipulated, resulting in the violation of many rights and freedoms of citizens. An example can be drawn from Practice Direction 2 of 2020 issued by Chief Justice Luke Malaba under which he remanded all the accused persons in absentia by extending the remand dates for those that were to appear in the courts in the next two weeks. This extension of remand dates, though necessitated by the Covid-19 outbreaks, seemed to be in violation of the fair trial rights of accused persons who had to be brought before the courts within 48 hours of their arrest (Zimbabwe Human Rights Association, 2020).

It is without doubt that the Covid-19 pandemic saw the militarisation of critical democratic spaces in Zimbabwe. The military infiltrated key positions in government ministries and departments, commissions, the media and the judiciary. For example, in the 2018 harmonised elections, the Zimbabwe Electoral Commission (ZEC) admitted to having employed serving members of the army, the police and the Central Intelligence Organisation, raising concerns about its impartially in the 2023 elections with the same personnel (*Newsday*, 2 March 2018). Another case worth noting was the post of Minister of Health and Child Welfare, held by the Vice President of the Republic of Zimbabwe, Constantine Chiwenga, a liberation war veteran and a serious critic of the 2020 doctors' and nurses' strike for living wages and adequate safeguards against Covid-19 that paralysed the heath delivery system altogether. This chapter argues that there is no constitutional provision that permits a Vice President to hold another ministerial post, and the fact that he took over the post during the Covid-19 era when many people in the medical profession overtly expressed their disdain over the government's hostile stance against them suggests that the freedoms, dignity and human rights of those in the health profession were not prioritised.

Demolition of illegal structures during the Covid-19 period

Many interviewees considered the move by the government to demolish illegal structures which harboured the poor and their enterprises at the peak of the pandemic as the most sinister act. With unemployment soaring in most of the high-density suburbs in the urban areas after most of the poor lost their livelihoods, the government embarked on a campaign of mass demolitions. According to Makombe (2021), barely two weeks passed into the lockdown before the municipal police started razing down market stalls and illegal cabins in Harare. In Mbare, one of the most densely populated suburbs in Harare, the municipal police and Harare City Council employees destroyed vending stalls and informal shops near Rufaro Stadium, Magaba informal market, and stalls in the open space near Shawasha Grounds. In Glen View Suburb, residents lamented the demolition of grinding mills that had been serving communities during the lockdown when there were acute mealie-meal shortages in the country. In Epworth Suburb, the Epworth Residents Association engaged the Zimbabwe Lawyers for Human Rights to approach the High Court to stop the local authorities from demolishing vending stalls and tuck shops but this was to no avail as the municipal police went on with the demolitions (Chidakwa, 2021). In the town of Chitungwiza, the Jambanja Market was taken down despite vendors' efforts to brandish a 2010 court order that protected the market from demolition (Ibid).

Although a number of demolitions were carried out in all urban districts in the country, some of them had nothing to do with Covid-19 pandemic containment. One such example was the knocking down of vending stalls at Mbudzi roundabout after the government announced that it wanted to upgrade road infrastructure by building an interchange-flyover to replace the continuous clogged roundabout around the area where the vending stalls were located (Ibid). However, five months after the demolitions, there were no signs of any interchange-flyover being built around the area. The timing of the demolitions violated the less privileged in high density suburbs and robbed them of their right to shelter and other forms of livelihoods. This worsened the predicament of the already starving poor.

Conclusion

This chapter has argued that the outbreak of Covid-19 engendered serious human rights abuses in Zimbabwe that were masterminded by the government and its security institutions. This was meant to provide safety props to buttress the regime of President Mnangagwa amidst growing disillusionment against uncontrolled autocracy. Lockdown measures instituted by the government in a bid to curb the spread of the pandemic impacted negatively on the citizens' right to freedom of association, assembly and expression.

At their worst, these restrictive measures, indeed, locked democratic space against people and barred them from exercising their rights of movement and association, among others. As more deaths and infections continued to be recorded and publicised by the national broadcaster, the shrinking democratic space closed further as more Covid-19-related regulations and statutory instruments were promulgated ostensibly to salvage the worsening situation. The chapter has also shown the extent to which the government was prepared to deploy the police and the military to enforce emergency measures. The roadblocks mounted on the major roads leading into the Central Business Districts of all major towns and cities in Zimbabwe constituted scare sites where those without the requisite travel documents to justify their movements were harassed and ordered to go back, or at times extorted. These policy enforcement methodologies overtly violated the national constitution and caused serious human rights abuses of huge proportions.

Furthermore, the suppression of the opposition that was accompanied by a campaign of terror involving the detention of activists resulted in the shrinking of democratic space. The freedom of expression and speech, among many other fundamental human rights as enshrined in the Universal Declaration of Human Rights, were also severely compromised. It is important to note that as Covid-19 continued to wreak havoc in Zimbabwe, the enforcement of the health protocols, of necessity, presented the state with a pretext to circumvent the opening up of political spaces for all citizens and organisations with different development strategies and philosophies from those of the incumbent ruling ZANU-PF party.

References

Abraham, K. (2014) 'Sex, respect and freedom from shame: Zambian women create space for social change through social networking', in: I. Buskens & A. Webb (eds.) *Women and ICT in Africa and the Middle East*, London: Zed Books.

Action Aid (7 July 2020) 'Rights to the freedoms of association, assembly and expression in Zimbabwe', A position paper on the rights to freedoms in Zimbabwe, Women and Law in Southern Africa- Zimbabwe.

APC & Hivos (2014) *Global Information Society Watch: Communications surveillance in the digital age*, Johannesburg and The Hague: Association for Progressive Communications and Humanist Institute for Cooperation with Developing Countries, Available at: https://www.amazon.com/Global-Information-Society-Watch-2014/dp/9295102150, Accessed 15 December 2021.

Asuelime, L.E. & Simura, B. (2014) 'The Movement for Democratic Change and the changing geo-political landscape in Zimbabwe,' in: L.E. Asuelime & B. Simura (eds.) *Selected themes in African political studies*, Springer, Cham, pp. 69-81.

Azar, G. (2007) 'The return of authoritarian great powers', in: *Foreign Affairs*, Volume 86, Number 4, pp.59-69.

Blair, E. (30 January 2015) 'Zimbabwe's Mugabe, 90, becomes African Union Chairman,' Available at: https://www.reuters.com/article/us-africa-mugabe-idUSKBN0L319F20150130, Accessed 21 December 2021.

Boone, C. & Kriger, N. (2010) 'Multiparty elections and land patronage: Zimbabwe and Côte d'Ivoire,' in: *Commonwealth and Comparative Politics*, Volume 48, Number 2, pp.173-202.

Bulawayo24 News (1 April 2021) 'Clarification on further suspension of by-elections', Available at: https://bulawayo24.com/index-id-opinion-sccolumnist-byo-201811.html, Accessed 19 November 2021.

Chidakwa, B. (6 October 2021) 'City demolishes Mbudzi roundabout illegal structures,' in: *The Herald*, Harare: Zimbabwe.

Chitimira, H. & Mokone, P. (2017) 'A general legislative analysis of torture as a human rights violation in Zimbabwe', in: *Pioneer in Peer Reviewed Journal*, Volume 20, pp.2-41.

Dangarembga, T. (2020) 'Tsitsi Dangarembga: Life in an ever-narrowing Zimbabwe', Available at:

https://www.newzimbabwe.com/tsitsi-dangarembga-life-in-an-ever-narrowing-zimbabwe, Accessed 13 December 2021.

Diamond, L. (2008) 'The democratic rollback: The resurgence of the predatory state,' in: *Foreign Affairs*, Volume 8, Number 2, pp.36-48.

Duri, J. Zuniga, N. & Vrushi, J. (2020) 'Civil and political rights', in: M. Chêne & J. Vrushi (eds.) *Getting ahead of the curve: Exploring post-Covid-19 trends and their impact on anti-corruption, governance and development*, Available at: https://knowledgehub.transparency.org/product, Accessed 10 January 2022.

European Partnership for Democracy (2020) 'Thinking democratically: A comprehensive approach to countering and preventing shrinking spaces,' The European Democracy Support Network, Available at: https://epd.eu/wp-content/uploads/2020/05, Accessed 12 December 2021.

European Commission: European Political Strategy Centre (21 November 2019) *Ten trends shaping democracy in a volatile world*, Available at: https://books.google.co.zw/books, Accessed 8 October 2021.

Fanghanel, A. (2019) *Disrupting rape culture: Public space, sexuality and revolt*, Bristol: Bristol University Press.

Csaky, Z. (2021) *Nations in transit: The anti-democratic turn,* Available at https://freedomhouse.org/report/nations-transit/2021/antidemocratic-turn/acknowledgements, Accessed 12 December 2021.

Gagare, O. (24 June 2020) 'Covid-19: Zimbabwe and the rule of law', in: *Good Governance Africa*, Available at: https://gga.org/c-19-zimbabwe-andthe-rule-of-law/, Accessed 11 January 2022.

Government of Zimbabwe (2013) *Zimbabwe Constitution Chapter 12, pt.3, s.243, cl.1(a)-(e)*, Harare: Government of Zimbabwe.

Guardian (28 April 2021) 'Zimbabwe court quashes charges against journalist Hopewell Chin'ono,' Available at: https://www.theguardian.com/world/2021/apr/28, Accessed 15 September 2021.

Hove, M. & Chenzi, V. (2020) 'Social media, civil unrest and government responses: The Zimbabwean experience', in: *Journal of Contemporary African Studies*, Volume 38, Number 1, pp.121-137.

Human Rights Watch (2020) 'Zimbabwe: Events of 2020', Available at: https://www.hrw.org/world-report/2021/country-chapters/zimbabwe, Accessed 16 January 2022.

Kriger, N. (2005) 'ZANU-PF strategies in general elections, 1980-2000: Discourse and coercion,' in: *African Affairs*, Volume 104, Number 414, pp.1-34.

Levitsky, S. & Ziblatt, D. (2018) *How democracies die,* New York: Crown Publishing.

Mabuza, S. (8 August 2020) 'Woman, 23, abducted and sexually abused in Mnangagwa reign of terror,' Available at: https://www.zimlive.com/2020/08/08, Accessed 23 July 2021.

Magure, B. (2014) 'Land indigenisation and empowerment: Narratives that made a difference in Zimbabwe's 2013 elections,' in: *Journal of African Elections*, Volume 13, Number 2, pp.17-48.

Makombe, E.K. (2021) 'Between a rock and a hard place: The Corona virus, livelihoods, and socio-economic upheaval in Harare's high density areas of Zimbabwe,' in: *Journal of Developing Societies,* Volume 37, Number 3, pp.275-301.

Mangena, T. (2021) 'Female bodies, agency, real and symbolic violence during the Corona virus pandemic: The experiences of women politicians and activists in Zimbabwe', Available at: https://doi.org/10.1080/10130950.2021.1996773, Accessed 7 November 2021.

Mashininga, K. (7 August 2020) 'As opposition mounts, Zimbabwe's president lashes out,' in: *The Guardian*, Available at: https://mg.co.za/africa/2020-08-07-as-opposition-mounts-zimbabwes-president-lashes-out/, Accessed 10 September 2021.

Mashininga, K. (13 September 2020) 'The brutal abduction caught on camera in Zimbabwe', in: *Mail & Guardian*, Available at: https://mg.co.za/africa/2020-09-13-the-brutal-abduction-caught-on-camera-in-zimbabwe/, Accessed 10 November 2021.

Mhlanga, B. & Chidza, R. (2 March 2018) 'ZEC in soldiers' storm,' Available at: https://www.newsday.co.zw/2018/03/zec-soldiers-storm/, Accessed 25 January 2022.

Moyo, G. & Phulu, K.I. (2021) 'The weaponisation of the Corona virus crisis in Zimbabwe: Legal and extra-legal instruments,' in: *I-Business*, Volume 13, pp.48-66.

Moyo, J. & Kingsley, P. (31 July 2020) 'Zimbabwe locks down capital, thwarting planned protests,' in: *The New York Times*, Available at:

https://www.nytimes.com/2020/07/31/world/africa/zimbabwe-coronavirus-protest, Accessed 19 February 2021.
Murphy, J. (2020) 'Parliaments and crisis: Challenges and innovations' Available at: https://doi.org/10.31752/idea.2020.22, Accessed 28 February 2021.
My Zimbabwe (20 June 2020) 'Police arrest nurses for protesting over poor salaries in Zimbabwe,' Available at: https://www.myzimbabwe.co.zw/news/66166-police-arrest-nurses-for-protesting-over-poor-salaries-in-zimbabwe.html, Accessed 17 December 2021.
Nancy, B. (2016) 'On democratic backsliding,' in: *Journal of Democracy*, Volume 27, Number 1, pp.5-19.
Ndakaripa, M. (2020) 'Zimbabwe is open for business: Aspects of post-Mugabe economic diplomacy,' in: *South African Journal of International Affairs*, Volume 27, Issue 3, pp.363-389.
Netherlands Institute for Multiparty Democracy (2017) 'Research methodology on closing democratic space: El Salvador case study,' Available at https://epd.eu/wp-content/uploads/2020/05/Closing-democratic-space, Accessed 19 November 2021.
Nganje, F. (2021) 'Building anticipatory governance in SADC: Post-Covid-19 governance outlook,' South African Institute of International Affairs, Occasional Paper 324, Available at: https://www.africaportal.org/publications/building-anticipatory-governance-sadc-post-covid-19-governance-outlook/, Accessed 19 November 2021.
Pindula News (9 February 2019) 'Zimbabwe soldiers banned from wearing uniform outside barracks unless when deployed - Report,' Available at: https://news.pindula.co.zw, Accessed 21 December 2021.
Raftopoulos, B. (2013) 'The 2013 elections in Zimbabwe: The end of an era,' in: *Journal of Southern African Studies,* Volume 39, Number 4, pp.71-98.
Rahardja, D.P. (2020) *Democracy and the Covid-19 pandemic: A reflection of the Bali Civil Society and Media Forum*, Kantor: Friedrich Ebert Stiftung
Ranger, T. (2004) 'Nationalist historiography, patriotic history and the history of the nation: The struggle over the past in Zimbabwe,' in: *Journal of Southern African Studies*, Volume 30, Number 2, pp.215-234.

Rivers, M. & Ndlovu, P. (24 June 2020) 'Covid raises the stakes for Zimbabwe's civil society movement,' Available at: https://www.usip.org/publications/2020/06/covid-raises-stakes-zimbabwes-civil-societymovement, Accessed 13 December 2021.

Roberts, T. & Ali, A.M. (eds.) (2021) *Digital rights in closing civic space: Lessons from ten African countries,* Brighton: Institute of Development Studies.

Sachikonye, L.M. (2011) *When a state turns on its citizens: 60 years of institutionalised violence in Zimbabwe,* Auckland Park: Jacana.

Solidar Foundation (28 May 2020) 'Shrinking space: Worrying crackdown on opposition and unions' leaders in Zimbabwe,' Available at: https://www.solidar.org/en/news/shrinking-space-worrying-crackdown-on-opposition-and-unions-leaders-in-zimbabwe, Accessed 13 December 2021.

Southall, R. & Slabbert, V. (2013) 'How and why ZANU-PF won the 2013 Zimbabwe elections,' in: *Strategic Review for Southern Africa*, Volume 35, Number 2, pp.135-151.

Times Live (16 March 2020) 'Zim minister's bizarre Corona virus claim: 'It's to punish the West for sanctions,' Available at: https://www.timeslive.co.za/news/africa/2020-03-16, Accessed 19 February 2021.

United Nations (2011) 'Report of the special rapporteur on the promotion and protection of the right to freedom of opinion and expression,' Human Rights Council, Seventeenth Session Agenda Item 3, United Nations General Assembly.

United Nations (2020) 'Emergency measures and Covid-19: Human rights at the heart of response, topics in focus,' Available at: https://www.ohchr.org/Documents/Events/EmergencyMeasures_COVID19.pdf, Accessed 11 January 2022.

Vanyoro, K.P. & Mutekwe, P. (2021) 'Politicising Covid-19: An analysis of selected ZANU-PF officials' 2020-2021 media statements on the pandemic in Zimbabwe,' in: *Acta Academica*, Volume 53, Number 2, pp.12-37, Available at: http://dx.doi.org/10.18820/24150479/aa53i2/2, Accessed 15 September 2021.

Veritas Zimbabwe (29 July 2020) 'Commissions Watch 13: Zimbabwe Human Rights Commission (ZHRC) statement on freedom to demonstrate,' Available at: http://www.veritaszim.net/node/4364, Accessed 11 January 2022.

Youngs, R. Fowler, G. Larok, A. Marczewski, P. Vjayan, M. Nodia, G. Shapovalova, N. Sombatpoonsiri, J. Bulow, M.V. & Zihnioglu, O. (2018) 'The mobilisation of conservative civil society: What conservative civic activism portends for global civil society,' Available at: https://carnegieeurope.eu/2018/10/04/mobilization-of-conservative-civil-society-pub-77366, Accessed 7 January 2022.

Zamchiya, P. (2-8 August 2020) 'July 31 exposed Mnangagwa,' in: *The Standard*, Harare: Zimbabwe.

Zimbabwe Human Rights NGO Forum (May 2021) 'Quarterly political violence report,' Available at: https://drive.google.com/file, Accessed 17 October 2021.

Zimbabwe Human Rights NGO Forum (2020) 'Political and human rights violations report, April to September 2020,' Available at: https://kubatana.net/wp-content/uploads/2020/11/PVR-April-to-September-2020.pdf, Accessed 18 October 2021.

ZW News (26 March 2020) 'Pictures and videos,' Available at: www.Zimnews-com/video-pictures-police-striking-harare-hospital-nurses, Accessed 17 October 2021.

Chapter 12

The Impact of Covid-19 Mitigation Protocols on Vulnerable Groups in Sub-Saharan Africa

Mudadirwa Mujuru & Innocent Rupoterera Madenga

Introduction

This chapter examines how vulnerable population groups in sub-Saharan African countries were affected by the Covid-19 pandemic and the watershed mitigation protocols rolled out by various governments in the region. 'Covid-19' is short for 'Corona virus disease' which first appeared in Wuhan, a city in China, in 2019. As Tosh (2022: online) stated: "A new virus called 'Severe Acute Respiratory Syndrome Corona virus (SARS-CoV-2)' was identified as the cause of the disease outbreak that began in China in 2019. The disease came to be called Corona virus disease." The Harvard Medical School (2022), in concurrence, went on to describe Covid-19 as a highly contagious disease resulting from the SARS CoV-2 virus. The outbreak of Covid-19 and its swift spread across the globe negatively impacted on different socio-economic population groups in different ways which included loss of jobs, food insecurity, inability to manage personal medical conditions, and failure to observe social distancing protocols as they could not avoid proximity and physical contact with aides (Waterfield *et al,* 2021).

The pandemic's rapid spread across the globe found most countries unprepared for the devastating havoc it caused, particularly in sub-Saharan Africa. Going by the statistics of a study carried out by the UNESCO Regional Office, vulnerable population groups were disproportionately impacted upon by Covid-19, usually resulting in emotional and psychological stress and at times death (Moyo, 2021). From November 2019 to April 2021, according to estimates by Saalim *et al* (2021), 40 million Covid-19 positive cases and over 3 million deaths were recorded worldwide. The pandemic threatened mostly the socio-economic, physical, psychological, emotional and spiritual stability of vulnerable population groups (Mugadza, 2022; Mujuru, 2022). Vulnerable persons became notable victims of emotional release through being abused in various ways by those who, ironically, were normally supposed to give them support and assistance. Reporting on West African countries, Saalim *et al* (2021) made similar observations and stated that vulnerable population groups experienced a wide variety of direct and indirect negative effects of Covid-19 which included sexual abuse, rape, domestic violence, arbitrary arrests, healthcare inaccessibility and education-related challenges.

The vulnerable population groups looked at in this chapter are persons with disabilities, those aged 65 and over, people living with HIV/AIDS, beggars, and street children, generally known as street kids. The chapter explores how the outbreak of Covid-19 affected such vulnerable population groups physically, emotionally, psychologically, socially and spiritually. The argument being advanced in this chapter is that much of sub-Saharan Africa was ill-prepared for the Covid-19 outbreak resulting in vulnerable population groups whose livelihood options were already compromised being the worst affected. Among other things, these already disadvantaged sections of the population ran the highest risk of being infected and affected by the Corona virus and were also the target of abuse by those in privileged positions. By and large, most sub-Saharan African governments did not do much to safeguard those vulnerable groups. Furthermore, corruption perpetrated mostly by those in positions of authority further aggravated the plight of vulnerable population groups as they were usually denied materials and services which they deserved by right. Oftentimes, in countries like Zimbabwe, relief aid was politicised and distributed on partisan lines in ways that flouted both moral and legal tenets of justice. It is against this background that the chapter closes by presenting a raft of recommendations on how various stakeholders can best prepare for such disasters in future.

Legal frameworks for vulnerable population groups

Many countries in the world signed international treaties in an effort to address issues to do with human rights, health and disability (Cabbasi, 2004). As Mannan *et al* (2012: 159) wrote:

> The Convention on the Rights of Persons with Disabilities (UNCRPD) was adopted by the United Nations General Assembly in 2006 and entered into force on May 3rd 2008. The NCRPD is the first legally binding integrated instrument with comprehensive protection of

the rights of persons with disabilities and sets out the legal obligations on states to promote and protect the right of persons with disabilities.

Zimbabwe launched its National Disability Policy on 9 June 2021 (FODPZ, n.d.). The policy was aligned to the Zimbabwean Constitution of 2013. Article 56.3 of the Constitution of Zimbabwe Amendment (Number 20) Act reads:

> Every person has the right not to be treated in an unfairly, discriminatory manner on such grounds as their nationality, race, colour, tribe, place of birth, ethnic or social origin, language, class, religious beliefs, political affiliation, opinion, custom, culture, sex, gender, marital status, or whether they were born in or out of wedlock (Zimbabwe National Disability Policy, 2021).

Zimbabwe became a signatory to the United Nations (UN) Convention on the Rights of Persons with Disabilities on 23 November 2013 (Ibid). South Africa became a signatory to the United Nations Declaration for Human Rights in 1994 when it gained its political independence. Prior to that, Apartheid South Africa was reluctant to be a signatory of the UN Declaration of Human Rights due to its racially segregatory laws. The other African countries which are discussed in this chapter are all signatories of the UN; hence their terms of reference with regard to the sanctity of human rights are basically the same. Other selected African countries that provide the sample context of the discussion in this chapter are Liberia, Nigeria, Sierra Leone and Guinea. However, like most African countries, they, in one way or another failed to fulfil their obligations in this regard. The failure can largely be explained in terms of financial constraints, lack of commitment, poverty and corruption, or all rolled into one. Though some of the legal frameworks of various sub-Saharan African countries do not specifically itemise categories of vulnerable populations and their inalienable human rights, it is subsumed that by being fully human, the persons constituting vulnerable population groups ought to enjoy full human rights like anyone else.

Covid-19 and the vulnerable population groups in sub-Saharan Africa

Covid-19 is one of the worst pandemics ever witnessed owing to its rapid spread and high death rate. In response to the alarmingly fast pace in the spread of Covid-19 and the very high death rates, various countries across the globe instituted preventive measures guided by the World Health Organisation (WHO) which included lockdowns (Burke, 2021; Kawala *et al*, 2020; Saalim, 2021). Even though the lockdowns achieved their intended goals in many sub-Saharan African countries to a considerable extent, they also had adverse ripple effects that hurt the vulnerable sections of the society. Mubangizi (2021) underscored the disproportionate effect of Covid-19 on vulnerable population groups worldwide, particularly those living in abject poverty. These groups tended to be the most prone to infection and were also the most adversely affected by the ripple effects of the lockdown protocols recommended by WHO (Cilliers & Kwasi, 2021; Saalim *et al*, 2021). The disabled, the aged, people living with HIV/AIDS, beggars and street children were not only already compromised, but they were also marginalised owing to their physical and/or socio-economic condition. Citing disabled people as an example, Moyo (2021) observed that they were usually peripherised during the pandemic with hardly much being done in terms of precautionary measures to safeguard their human rights and welfare. Quoting Mevison Chawota in an interview with *Anadolu Agency*, Moyo (2021), a Zimbabwean living with disability, lamented: "When some of us went to the hospital after catching the virus, we were sent straight back to our homes. Even the visually-challenged were told to return home and quarantine there. By and large, persons belonging to the vulnerable groups tended to be worse affected than their handicap-free and socio-economically stable counterparts."

The disabled and the aged were at greater risk of being infected by the virus as most of them, especially the physically challenged, had to rely on assistance which usually required bodily contact with family members, aides, friends and at times total strangers. Beggars, usually comprising street children, the elderly and persons with disabilities virtually had no one to beg from as everyone was locked down. Put in other words, movement restrictions and shutting down of business worsened the plight of the vulnerable population groups as they mostly relied on spill-over benefits from the more economically viable members of the society. As was to be expected, more often than not, the human rights of such people were infringed upon with impunity. As far as infection and mortality rates were concerned, the elderly people constituted the vulnerable population group that was most severely affected by Covid-19 (Bonanad *et al*, 2020; Levin *et al*, 2020; WHO, 2021). However, WHO (2021: 3) pointed out some challenges regarding the accuracy of the statistics which led to such conclusions, stating: "Data collection on Covid-19 and its impact on vulnerable people across the region has been patchy due to low capacity and disruptions in statistical data collection by ministers of health and national statistical offices as well as Covid-19 testing capacity."

Covid-19 swept across the globe in a relatively very short space of time prompting WHO to declare it a pandemic in March 2020. Describing the gravity of the disaster caused by Covid-19 in Africa, Cilliers & Kwasi (2021: online) noted: "[I]n fact within a year of Africa's reported case in Egypt, Covid-19 had wreaked extraordinary destruction upon Africa's development prospects. The pandemic has rapidly evolved from a health crisis to an all-encompassing economic quagmire with serious international ramifications." In such critical times, the vulnerable population groups were simply side-lined into obscurity, and forgotten. Moyo (2021) summed it up all stating that such vulnerable groups were simply pushed to the periphery and forgotten. Owing to Covid-19's high fatality rate, WHO and many public health groups launched nine monitoring mechanisms and regularly posted updates and recommendations on their websites on how to curb the spread of the pandemic (Tosh 2021).

Despite having poor health facilities, West African countries, like most of those in the sub-Saharan African region, registered relatively lower incidences of Covid-19 infections and related deaths despite their being poorer than the Western world (Cilliers & Kwasi, 2021; Saalim *et al,* 2021). However, Cillier & Kwasi (2021) were quick to caution that it was not yet time for celebration, considering the limited testing and the not-so-efficient reporting systems. These challenges meant that there was a great likelihood of never knowing the actual numbers of those who were infected and those who succumbed to Covid-19. Making particular reference to West African countries, Saalim *et al* (2021: online) noted: "The Covid-19 incidence rate in West Africa is 14 times lower than the global incidence rate and the Covid-19 fatality rate is 1.7 times lower than globally." Be that as it may, the scholars observed that the advent of the Covid-19 pandemic in those countries had devastating socio-economic and political consequences (Ibid). What that meant was that Covid-19 not only caused a lot of despondency by making people very sick with a considerably large number succumbing to the disease, but also brought about considerable emotional and socio-economic stresses. To this end, Saalim *et al* (2021) posited that Covid-19- related illnesses and high death rates brought about psychological trauma on the variously affected community groups. The situation was made worse by some of the World Health Organisation's recommendations of curbing the spread of the Corona virus. For instance, movement restrictions of people coupled with lockdowns, temporal suspension of economic activities, prohibition of social entertainment, closure of formal learning institutions and resorting to in-home virtual learning to enforce social distancing, not only increased anxiety and stress on many people concerned, but also disrupted the livelihoods of many globally (Ozili, 2021; Saalim *et al*, 2021).

If people without underlying conditions, be they physical, mental or psycho-social, were so adversely affected by the Covid-19 pandemic, it stands to reason that those with underlying conditions suffered a lot more. Saalim *et al* (2021) aver that due to socio-economic inequalities, physical and mental disabilities, social discrimination and exclusion, certain populations tended to be more vulnerable to the ravages of the Covid-19 pandemic. That being the case, it follows that vulnerable population groups such as people with disabilities, the elderly, people living with HIV/AIDS, street children and beggars, who are the main focus of this chapter, were among the worst affected from Covid-19 because they were already compromised either physically, mentally or economically well before the advent of the pandemic.

There is a considerable number of studies on the varied negative effects of the Covid-19 pandemic on vulnerable population groups. One such study is by Durizzo *et al* (2021) who looked at the impact of Covid-19 on the urban populations in African countries. Another study by Fawole *et al* (2021) examined intimate partner violence targeting women due to Covid-19-related socio-economic stress. However, very few studies so far have been carried out on the impact of Covid-19 on the wellbeing of vulnerable population groups in Africa. Consequently, there has hardly been any suggestion about possible interventions to mitigate the knock-on effects of pandemics and subsequent lockdowns on vulnerable populations.

Economic and food insecurity

Food insecurity already affected a huge percentage of the African population well before the outbreak of the Covid-19 pandemic. This means that the pandemic aggravated the already compromised situation of vulnerable population groups (Chamunogwa, 2021;

Mohamed *et al*, 2021). The direct and indirect knock-on effects of Covid-19 included "…deaths of food systems, interruption of food supply chains, unemployment, depreciation of currency value, and disruption of social protection networks" (Mohamed *et al*, 2021: 1613). Covid-19 not only posed a serious threat to human life, as was ostensibly evidenced by the very high rate of fatalities, but also negatively impacted on both public life and economic activities Only those considered to offer essential services were allowed to remain operational but their hours of operation were reduced by half the normal time (Saalim *et al.* 2021). In Zimbabwe, the government imposed lockdown regulations that required people who travelled within cities and towns to have exemption letters stamped by their employers and this only applied to those designated as essential workers who included health personnel, security forces, and NGO employees (Chamunogwa, 2021). In addition, manpower complements were also cut and staggered so as to avoid crowding in compliance with the stipulations of social distancing (Ibid).

Teachout & Zipfet (2020) estimated that Covid-19 containment measures adopted by most sub-Saharan African countries "…pushed an additional 9.1% of the population into extreme poverty." Because of lockdown protocols, accessing food became dicey as locking down work places usually meant loss of wages and therefore lack of money to procure food (Saalim *et al*, 2021). In much of sub-Saharan Africa, the informal sector was hardest hit as there was hardly any means of putting food on the table. As a matter of fact, most of the people who belong to vulnerable groups eke their livelihoods in the informal sector and the lockdowns literally constricted their lifelines. Writing on Guinea, Ghana, Liberia and Niger, Saalim *et al* (2021) noted that before the advent of Covid-19, informal sector workers, low income earners, farmers and beggars were categorised as vulnerable. The lockdowns shattered their livelihoods owing to loss of jobs and food insecurity.

Covid-19 and people living with disabilities

Categories of disabled persons include: "…those who have long-term physical, mental, intellectual or sensory impairments which, in interaction with various barriers, may hinder their full participation in society on equal basis with others" (United Nations, 2016: online). The number of persons with disabilities around 2016 was estimated at about one billion, which translated to 15% of the global population

(Ibid). From these figures, it can be noted that disabled people constitute a significant percentage of the global population.

The United Nations stated that disability is but only some kind of human state (Ibid). Thus, all people, including those who are physically or mentally challenged, are fully human and should not be discriminated against on account of their disadvantaged status. Research has also shown that, given the right kind of education and training, the disabled can be competently productive to the extent of even surpassing able-bodied people. This being the case, persons with disabilities ought not be discriminated against or side-lined for whatever reason in socio-economic, socio-cultural and socio-political spheres. According to Article 1 of the Convention of Rights of Persons with Disabilities (CRPD): "Disability is an evolving concept and that disability results from the interactions between persons with impairments and attitudinal and environmental barriers that hinder their full and effective participation in society on an equal basis with others" (United Nations, 2016: online). So, as a concept, disability is not cast in iron but is in a state of flux owing mostly to societal constructs and barriers that persons with physical and mental impairments encounter in their physical and socio-economic, socio-cultural and socio-political spheres.

Before the outbreak of Covid-19, persons with disabilities were already grappling with a multiplicity of barriers owing to significant inequalities with regard to poverty, health, education, social participation and work (UDESA, 2018). The Covid-19 protocols recommended by WHO in a bid to curb the spread of the pandemic impacted negatively on the processes of accessing healthcare services by the physically and mentally handicapped, the elderly aged 60 years old and over, people living with HIV/AIDS, beggars and street children (Mohamed *et al*, 2021; Mugadza, 2022). The disabled, particularly the visually-impaired, paraplegics and quadriplegics, and the mentally-handicapped needed assistance requiring bodily contact to be taken to relevant facilities thus presenting conflict with social distancing regulations. Worse still, more often than not, this tended to increase the risks of members of the vulnerable groups contracting the Corona virus from their chaperons and care-givers or aides (Moyo, 2021; Mugadza, 2022; Mujuru, 2022).

It is noteworthy that the disabled, particularly the blind, paraplegics and quadriplegics, were at great risk of being infected considering that their movement involves touching a lot of surfaces either to support themselves or turning wheels of their mobile chairs

(Moyo, 2021). Helen, a physically disabled and wheelchair-bound Zimbabwean woman, explained: "The disabled use their bare hands turning wheel chairs or move on the ground and times come in touch with infected surfaces. This has put the disabled among the high risk groups" (Ibid). Even though health centres in most countries readily offered critical service, their operational hours were drastically cut resulting in very small numbers of patients being attended to (Mugadza, 2022). To make matters worse, although healthcare givers were issued with personal protective clothing, they feared for their lives and reluctantly attended to patients. The physically and mentally disabled and the elderly who would have struggled to get to such health centres to access medical help were usually turned away and never returned out of frustration. It was not strange then that such vulnerable persons usually did not have much choice but to stay at home.

Covid-19 and the elderly

This section examines the impact of Covid-19 on the elderly people, women and men aged 60 years and over, in the context of social security systems that prevailed in some sub-Saharan African countries. Countries looked at include, but not limited to the following: Ghana, Sierra Leone, Nigeria, Guinea, South Africa, Eswatini, Zambia and Zimbabwe. Science has shown that as people grow older their immunity diminishes progressively making them prone to contract opportunistic diseases. According to Juergens & Galvani (2020), "Covid-19 is most dangerous for older people as risks of serious sickness increase with age." As the pandemic raged on, it disproportionately infected and affected the poor and marginalised populations who had very little resources, if any, to protect themselves. Some of the most wretched sections of many societies were the elderly because their incomes, social security and access to social protection also diminished with age (Ibid). Since the health of elderly people was at great risk during the Covid-19 pandemic, most of them were forced to stay at home to avoid infection and this sometimes made them to avoid going out to access food and routine medical care (Ibid).

Considering their already compromised immunity, elderly persons were at great risk of being infected and dying from Covid-19. Chingono (2021) described the elderly in the Covid-19 environment as "...the pandemic's silent victims." This effectively captures the degree of vulnerability that this key population group was exposed to. Global trends reflected that elderly persons were at grave risk of contracting Covid-19, especially those with comorbidities (Nhapi & Dhemba, 2020; Zhou, 2020). In addition to being at great risk of contracting Corona virus, the elderly also risked both physical and social isolation (Nhapi & Dhemba, 2020). Chingono (2021) gives the example of an old woman, Chibiku, who lamented being lonely and having lost the will to live due to the depression she was experiencing in the old people's home where her children had placed her. Chibiku was quoted saying:

> I do not have grand-children and my children come to see me sometimes. I am always depressed because I don't have anyone to see me. I used to exercise, but now I cannot do that anymore. I just spend my day sitting…My condition depresses me so much that I sometimes lose my mind (Ibid).

Considering the plethora of physical, social, psychological and emotional dangers, it was quite clear that the elderly persons were in dire need of adequate social protection and other supportive services to ensure maintenance of their physical and mental health.

The economies of some sub-Saharan African countries under discussion were weak and unstable and when coupled with endemic corruption, resulted in a conundrum that deprived the elderly person of social protection. The already grim situation was further aggravated by very weak and unstable health delivery systems (Lloyd-Sherlock *et al*, 2020). The conclusion arrived at by Nhapi & Dhemba (2020) that Eswatini and Zimbabwe did not have any effective social and economic safety nets to protect their vulnerable population groups, particularly the elderly, applies to all the sub-Saharan African countries looked at in this chapter. Some of the major challenges faced by the elderly included failure to access information and humanitarian assistance, and being side-lined in decision-making processes regarding resource allocation (Help Age, 2020; Nhapi & Dhemba, 2020). In Zimbabwe, the ZW$200 per month facility set up by the government to cushion the vulnerable was not only inadequate (Nhapi & Dhemba, 2020), but was often diverted and ended up being disbursed on partisan lines to benefit members of the ruling Zimbabwe African National Union Patriotic Front (ZANU-PF) party.

By comparison, Eswatini, though considered to be one of the poorest countries in the world apart from having a very high prevalence rate of HIV/AIDS cases, did a lot better than Zimbabwe in cushioning its elderly population against the vagaries of Covid-19. According to Nhapi & Dhemba (2020), apart from providing other social welfare services to its elderly population groups, Eswatini had the Old Age Grant, a flagship programme which specifically aimed at addressing poverty and vulnerability of those aged 60 years and above. The government of Eswatini, in collaboration with the Eswatini Post and Telecommunication Corporation, MTN Eswatini and Eswatini Mobile, built retiring homes for the elderly (Ibid.).

Covid-19 and people living with HIV/AIDS

In 2002, the Zimbabwean government declared HIV/AIDS a national emergency (National Aids Council, 2006). By 2005, Zimbabwe and the rest of Southern Africa had recorded an estimated 11.4 million cases of HIV-positive people which, at that time, translated to 36% of the infected global population (Ibid). By all standards, the percentage was alarmingly too high. When the government of Zimbabwe declared HIV/AIDS a national emergency, the public and private sectors, together with local and international NGOs and donor organisations, among many others, forged a united front to combat the disease through various programmes targeting prevention and treatment as well as provision of palliative care (Chevo & Bhatasara, 2014).

Pandemics such as HIV/AIDS and Covid-19 impacted more negatively on the socio-economically vulnerable communities such as the poor, street children, persons with disabilities, and those living with HIV/AIDS (RWI Leibniz, 2022). Given that sub-Saharan countries which fall under the category of developing countries were generally poor, the effects of pandemics were more pronounced, particularly in the lives of vulnerable population groups. This was largely because these countries lacked adequate resources and funds to cushion disadvantaged sections of the population. In times of crises, they relied mostly on donor funding.

The outbreak of Covid-19 caused great concern with regard to its impact on the estimated 40 million people living with HIV/AIDS worldwide (Prabhu *et al*, 2020). Among the vulnerable population groups most adversely affected by the outbreak of the fast-spreading Covid-19 pandemic were persons living with HIV/AIDS (Waterfield *et al*, 2021). However, according to a review carried out by Prabhu *et al* (2020), there was no evidence of high prevalence of Covid-19 in people living with HIV/AIDS. All the same, what cannot be disputed is the fact that HIV-positive persons or those prone to being infected with the disease were at higher risk of contracting Covid-19 especially if they had certain comorbidities (Waterfield *et al*, 2021). Also, HIV care-delivery systems were adversely affected in a number of countries worldwide (Prabhu *et al*, 2020). So, to ensure that people on anti-retroviral treatment were not prejudiced and continued with their treatment uninterrupted, care-delivery systems resorted to multi-months anti-retroviral treatment. In other words, to minimise movement to opportunistic infection clinics or hospitals for their monthly supply of anti-retroviral drugs, patients were given a supply of drugs to last several months. This arrangement resonated well with Covid-19 prevention protocols which required people to minimise movement as much as possible.

All having been said, the fact remains that, worldwide, the outbreak and spread of the Corona virus brought about unprecedented challenges to both HIV-positive persons and the health delivery personnel that was supposed to attend to them. As it turned out, it did not come as a surprise that the numbers of healthcare personnel who were prepared to attend to people living with HIV/AIDS decreased drastically (Ibid). As Prabhu *et al* (2020: 4) pointed out: "The reasons for these are unsurprising. People who have faced stigma for decades due to their HIV status and live under the burden of a chronic virus are hesitant to engage in care with another more deadly virus…This fear has even led to some to question the safety of going to pharmacies to collect anti-retroviral treatment."

The impact of the Covid-19 pandemic on street children

This section focuses on children 'living' in the streets. The Consortium for Street Children (2020) describes street-connected children as "all groups of children and youths who have a meaningful relationship with the street; some live on the street; some work on the street, some maintain relationships with their family, whereas others break all contact… All of them have a strong connection on the street." There are three categories of street children. The first category, according to Olanipekun (2020), comprises those children who eke their living on the street but retire home in the evening and re-join their families. The second category constitutes: "…those children who exist in urban spaces and are exposed to the tortures of poverty and mostly engage in social vices as part of the normative culture" (Ibid). The third and last category comprises those children who virtually live on the street throughout. This category lives and works on the street and their only sense of family draws from their social communion with the other children mentioned above (Ibid). There are varied reasons which drive children to end up living on the street but the common ones include death of parents, maltreatment at home, and poverty (Kawala *et al*, 2020). Due to the dire socio-economic situation in Zimbabwe, street children became a common phenomenon in most human settlement centres (Bourdillon, 1994). Beggars and street children can be categorised as persons living in the streets. The Covid-19 pandemic had debilitating effects on the rights and livelihoods of street children in Zimbabwe (Zimbabwe Peace Project, 2021). The Conversation (2020) posited that the imposition of lockdown protocols to contain the spreading of Covid-19 in Zimbabwe seemed to have had no thought of the plight of children living on the street.

While Covid-19 preventive protocols recommended by WHO yielded positive results to some extent, the measures brought more harm than good to most vulnerable population groups. For instance, the mandatory lockdowns and movement restrictions made life very miserable for street children. Some of the requirements which were adopted by most sub-Saharan countries, including Zimbabwe, such as regular hand-washing with soap under running water, strict observation of curfews, staying at home and self-quarantine required a proper home to retreat to (Clark, 2020). For most street children and beggars, the street is their home; they scrounge for food on the street, live and sleep on the street without any place to call home. Many street children and beggars had to move from street to street for fear of being arrested for breaking Covid-19 restrictions such as the curfew. Thus, many of them spent more time evading law-enforcement agents instead of looking for food (Ibid).

A considerable number of people living in the streets eke their living from informal jobs, begging and scavenging for food in bins. The locking down of economic activities meant that this vulnerable population group was deprived of its livelihoods. Some members of this group could not engage in their normal economic activities which deprived most of them of access to food while others were deprived of socialisation and entertainment (Kawala *et al*, 2020). Since a considerable number of persons living in the streets survive mostly through begging, closing down places of business activities meant that they were deprived of their usual source of income. Writing in the context of Nigeria, Olanipekun (2020) posited: "Lockdowns and social distancing have untold effects on street children who cannot afford the economic cost of forced immobility, since their livelihood depends on the benevolence of informal street activities." In other words, Covid-19 containment measures imposed by the Nigerian government, just as most sub-Saharan countries did in compliance with WHO recommendations to curb the spread of Corona virus, exacerbated "...the vulnerability of the already vulnerable street children in Ibadan, Oyo State, Nigeria" (Ibid).

Challenges faced by school-going children

Even before the outbreak of the Covid-19 pandemic, about 550 million children in sub-Saharan Africa already faced a horde of varied challenges (UNICEF, 2020). Among the most critical challenges faced by about 40% of school-going children included inadequate nutrition and failure to access to safe water while approximately two-thirds of them lacked proper toilet facilities. Worst of all, most of them had their hopes of ever completing education and competently marketing themselves on the labour market shattered by the closure of schools as a pandemic-curtailment measure (Ibid). Furthermore, almost two-thirds of the children languished in abject poverty-stricken households while others were displaced and lived as refugees in slums (Ibid). In a nutshell, from its onset, 2020 was generally characterised by critical economic challenges in most sub-Saharan African countries (Ibid). Under Covid-19 lockdown conditions, the hardships that were already being faced by most school-going children became worse. In its 35th Ordinary Session, Human Rights Watch reported on the findings of interviews conducted on the effects of the Covid-19 pandemic on education. From the interviews that were held with education officials, teachers and students from Nigeria, Morocco, Madagascar, Kenya, Burkina Faso, the Democratic Republic of Congo, Zambia, South Africa and Zimbabwe, Human Rights Watch (2020) concluded: "Our research shows that school closures caused by the pandemic exacerbated previously existing inequalities, and that children who were already most at risk of being excluded from a quality education have been most affected."

During the Covid-19 lockdown period, most children, particularly those from low-income families, did not receive any education at all.

A Congolese woman interviewed by Human Rights Watch (2020) stated: "My child is no longer learning; she is only waiting for the reopening of schools to continue with her studies" (Ibid). Another Congolese mother of two pre-school children voiced her concerns, stating: "It does not make me happy that my children are no longer going to school. Years do not wait for them. They have already lost a lot…What will become of our uneducated children?" (Ibid). Even, though in some instances children got printed notes they felt this was not comparable to physical lessons. As a Congolese student stated: "We were just told to regularly re-read our notes while waiting for the new instructions from the authorities… At first I thought school would start again soon so I did not read my notes and when I saw that it was going to go on, I started to read them. I had forgotten them" (Ibid). Natalie, a 15-year-old Zambian girl, said that her headmistress told them to study on their own just before total closure of schools, adding that: "Without the help of teachers…it has been a little bit nerve-racking. Next year, I have my [school-leaving] examination and I think I will have to work harder for that" (Ibid). Such experiences were common among most students in sub-Saharan countries particularly from marginalised socio-economic population groups. Some teachers tried to teach using social media platforms such as WhatsApp (Ibid). Although the idea of online learning was quite noble, it had a number of shortcomings. Most children from disadvantaged families did not have electronic gadgets such as cell phones. Again, not all parents were educated enough for them to competently and effectively mark the work given to their children. Furthermore, continued lockdowns in Zimbabwe, as in other sub-Saharan countries, had a disproportionate negative impact on children from poor economic backgrounds who could not afford the means to access digital education for the two years that the lockdown was in effect (Moyo 2021).

The Zimbabwean government initiated online learning as well as radio and television learning in an attempt to ensure continuation of education programmes at various levels (Ibid). Unfortunately, as it turned out, online learning proved to be a preserve for the elite because they had the financial means to buy the requisite electronic gadgets and data bundles. In an interview with the *Anadolu Agency*, the Secretary General of the Amalgamated Rural Teachers' Union of Zimbabwe, Robson Chere, averred that education had become a preserve of the elite, arguing:

Covid-19 brought alternative ways of learning like online lessons and private lessons. But due to economic hardships faced by many Zimbabweans, this has seen only the elite being able to access education while the poor and those from rural backgrounds remain disadvantaged and without access to education" (Ibid).

To that end, Takavafira Zhou, the President of the Progressive Teachers' Union of Zimbabwe (PTUZ) weighed in: "Sadly, the Ministry of Education preferred radio and television lesions, well aware that 85% of the areas where students reside in (sic) have no radio and television frequencies. The program failed to take off or even to reach 8% of the students" (Ibid). Zhou added: "We certainly have a generation of condemned students who have missed so much and may not function beyond the classroom. Several beginners have not been provided with a foundation for learning and will certainly have challenges in reading, arithmetic (sic), and mastering local languages" (Ibid). His counterpart, Obert Masaraure, President of the Amalgamated Rural Teachers' Union of Zimbabwe, bemoaned the automatic promotion of students to next grades despite the fact that they had not learnt anything (Ibid).

Faced with challenges related to long absence from school owing to the closure of schools, many girl children, mostly those from low-income and rural backgrounds (Pfunye & Ademola-Popoola, 2021), became very vulnerable to abuses that included "… increase in child marriage, teenage or early pregnancy, and gender-based violence" (Ibid). Some girl children were even married off due to Covid-19-induced economic hardships. Pfunye & Ademola-Popoola (2021) gave an example of Cecilia, a 7-year-old girl from Gokwe South District in Zimbabwe who lived with her father and was in Grade 1 when the pandemic broke out. As a result of the pressure of Covid-19, she was married off as a second wife to an elderly man who already had a wife and two children. Apart from being subjected to early marriages, idle girl children who had dropped out of school as a result of Covid-19-related dynamics were sometimes raped, oftentimes by very close family members (Ibid).

Conclusion

This chapter explored the effects of Covid-19 on vulnerable population groups in sub-Saharan Africa. It established that the outbreak of Covid-19 caught everyone off-guard and threw the whole world into disarray as no one was prepared for the devastating havoc it caused wherever it went. Even though Africa was generally not as hard-hit by the pandemic as First World countries, the knock-on effects of Covid-19 were catastrophic mostly with regard to human rights abuse. The already marginalised and vulnerable population groups such as persons with disabilities, the elderly, persons living with HIV/AIDS, street children and school children were disproportionately exposed to the impact of Covid-19 and thus were the hardest hit.

To try and mitigate the various challenges faced by vulnerable population groups, it is recommended that risk reduction legal frameworks be put in place to protect such key groups in the event of a pandemic or disaster outbreak. In setting up such frameworks, there ought to be wide consultations with all stakeholders including the various vulnerable groups. It is also recommended that resources be mobilised and funds pooled in readiness for cushioning the vulnerable groups when catastrophe strikes. When emergency measures such as blanket Level 4 lockdowns are declared, governments have to ensure that vulnerable population groups are well catered for in terms of access to food and health services. In addition, help lines should always open for girl children to report any forms of abuse. Properly planned and resourced online education programmes should be put in place to ensure that meaningful learning continues uninterrupted during times of emergencies. In short, there is need for governments to institute pandemic or disaster preparedness mechanisms to cushion vulnerable population groups when such eventualities strike.

References

African Development Bank (3 March 2021) 'Zambia: The bank cushions the impact of Covid 19 with livestock and agriculture projects,' Available at: https://www..afdb.org/en/success-stories, Accessed 23 December 2021.

BBC News (20 June 2020) 'Corona virus: Zimbabwe health minister in corruption charges,' Available at: https://www.bbc.com/news/world africa-53119989, Accessed 28 December 2021.

Bonanad, C. Garcia-Blas, S. Tarazona-Santabalbina, E. Sanchis, J. Berlomeu, Gonzalez, V. Facila, L. Ariza, A. Nunez, L. & Galdero, A. (25 May 2020) 'The effect of age mortality in patients with Covid-19: A meta-analysis with 611 583 subjects,' Available at: https://doi/org/10.1016/j.jamda,2020.05.045, Accessed 28 December 2021

Bourdillon, M.F.C. (1994) 'Street children in Harare,' in: *Africa: Journal of the International African Institute* Volume 64, Number 4.

Cabbasi, J. (2004) *Reviewing our voice: Code of good practice for NGOs responding to HIV/AIDS*, Geneva: NGOs HIV/AIDS Code of Practice.

Chamunogwa, A. (5 May 2021) 'The impact of Covid-19 on socio-economic rights in Zimbabwe,' Available at: www.zimpeaceproject.com, Accessed 3 February 2022.

Chevo, T. & Bhatasara, S. (26 January 2014) 'HIV/AIDS programmes in Zimbabwe: Implications for health,' Available at: www.doi:10.5402/2012/609128, Accessed 16 February 2022.

Chirisa, I. Mutambisi, T. Chivenge, M. Mabaso, E. Matamanda, A.R. & Ncube, R. (27 August 2020) 'The urban penalty of Covid-19 lockdowns across the globe: Manifestations and lessons for Anglophone sub-Saharan Africa,' Available at: www.DOI:10.1007/s10708-020-10281-6, Accessed 13 January 2022.

Cilliers, J. & Kwasi, S. (2021) 'Strategies for preserving gains in human development in Africa in the time of Covid-19,' in: *Human development: Protecting vulnerable populations*, Available at: www.brookings.edu, Accessed 13 February 2022.

Durizzo, K. Asiedu, E. Van der Merwe, A. Van Nie Kerk, A. & Gunther, I. (5 January 2021) 'Managing the Covid-19 pandemic in poor urban neighbourhoods: The case of Accra and Johannesburg,' Available at: https://www.sciencedirect.com, Accessed 23 January 2022.

Fawole, O.I. Okedere, O.O. & Reed, E. (20 January 2021) 'Home was not a safe haven: Women's experiences of intimate partner violence during the Covid-19 lockdown in Nigeria,' Available at: https://doi.org/10.1186/s1295-021-0117-9, Accessed 19 February 2022.

Featured News (14 June 2021) 'How Covid-19 has affected education in sub-Saharan Africa,' Available at: https://www.ashnaga.org/en/media/general/29238, Accessed 27 January 2022.

Federation of Organisations of Disabled People in Zimbabwe (n.d) 'The national disability policy: A new dawn in disability inclusive development or a farce?' in: *Newsletter: Federation of Organisations of*

Disabled Persons in Zimbabwe, Volume 5, Available at: https://www.facebook.com/Federation-of-Organisations-of-Disabled-People-in-Zimbabwe-FODPZ, Accessed 10 February 2022.

Gil-Llario, B.A. (24 July 2020) 'The virus that changed Spain: Impact of Covid-19 on people living with HIV/AIDS,' Available at: https://doi.org/10.1007/s10461-020-02877-3, Accessed 5 February 2022.

Guardian (9 July 2020) 'Zimbabwe health minister facing Corona virus corruption charged, sacked,' Available at: www.theguardian.com, Accessed 12 February 2022.

Guardian (10 November 2021) 'South Africa issues arrest warrant for ANC's Ace Magashule,' Available at: https://www.theguardian.com/world/2020/nov/10/south-africa-issues-arrest-warrant-for-ancs-ace-magashule, Accessed 3 January 2022.

Harvard Medical School (10 January 2022) 'Corona virus Resource Centre: As Corona virus continues to spread, many questions and answers,' Available at: https://wwwhealth.harvard.edu/diseases-and-conditions/coronavirus-resources-center, Accessed 2 March 2022.

Help Age (15 April 2020) 'UN humanitarian response plan for Covid-19 fails to prioritise elder people,' Available at: https://news.gov.sz/index.php.;latest-neews/2430-partil-lockdown-updatecovid-19-april, Accessed 7 January 2022.

Holtz, L. (4 May 2022) 'Covid-19's impact on overall health care services: Africa in focus,' Available at: https://www.brookings.edu/blog/africa-in-focus-/2021/10/10/covid 19-on-overall-health- care-service-in-Africa, Accessed 5 March 2022.

Juergens, F. & Galvani, F. (17 April 2020) 'Social protection for older people during Covid-19 and beyond,' Available at: www.helpage.org/social protection-for-older-people.juergens, Accessed 26 February 2022.

Kawala, B.A. Kirui, B.K. & Cumber, S.N. (25 June 2020) 'Effects of Covid-19 response in Uganda on street children,' in: *Pan African Medical Journal*, Available at: https://www.panafrican-med-journal.com/content/series/35/2/56/full, Accessed 11 February 2022.

Mannan, H. Maclachlan, M. & McVeigh, J. (2012) 'Core concept of human rights and inclusion of vulnerable groups in the United Nations Convention of the Rights of Persons with Disabilities,' in: *ALTER European Journal of Disability Research*, Volume 6, pp.159-177, Available at: www.sciencedirection.com, Accessed 29 January 2022.

Mapaire, L. & Lumadi, M.W. (22 April 2013) 'HIV/AIDS impact in the Zimbabwean school curriculum,' in: *Mediterranean Journal of Social Sciences*, Available at: www.DOI:10.5901/mjss.2013av13p773, Accessed 19 March 2022.

Moyo, J. (15 May 2021) 'Covid-19: Disabled in Zimbabwe cry for attention,' Available at: https://www.aa..co.tr/en/africacovid-19-disabled-in-zimbabwe-cry-for-attention, Accessed 2 March 2022.

Mohamed, E.M.A. Abdel, A. & Lucero-Prisno, I. (22 May 2021) 'Food security and Covid-19 in Africa: Implications and recommendations,' Available at: www.Doi:10.4268/aimh.20-1590, Accessed 11 January 2022.

Mubangizi, J. (12 September 2021) 'Vulnerable groups with specific reference to poverty and inequality in South Africa,' in: *Journal of African Law*, Available at: https://10.1017/S0021855321000292, Accessed 13 March 2022.

Mugadza, N. (2 February 2022) Interview: Redcliff City Council, Zimbabwe.

Mujuru, N. (3 February 2022) Interview: Island Hospice, Bulawayo, Zimbabwe.

National Aids Council of Zimbabwe (4 June 2006) 'Zimbabwe National HIV and AIDS Strategic Plan (ZNASP) 2006-2010', Harare: National Aids Council.

Nhapi, T.G. & Dhemba, J. (2020) 'The conundrum of old age and Covid-19 perceptions in Eswatini and Zimbabwe,' in: *Journal of Social Work*, Volume 63, Number 6, pp.842-846, Available at: www.surgepub.com/journals, Accessed 1 February 2022.

Olanipen, T. (13 July 2020) 'Don't come close': The plight of street children during Covid-19's forced immobility,' Available at: https://www.routedmagazine.com, Accessed 17 March 2022.

Ozili, P.K. (15 November 2021) 'Covid-19 in Africa: Socio-economic impact, policy, response and opportunities,' Available at: https://papers.ssrn..com/abstract=3574767, Accessed 6 March 2022.

Prabhu, S. Poongalali, S. & Kumarasamy, N. (2020) 'Impact of Covid-19 on people living with HIV: A review,' in: *Journal of Virus Eradication*, Volume 6, Available at: www.viruseradication.com, Accessed 27 January 2022.

Saalim, K., Sakyi, K.S. Fatema-Tuz-Zohra, Morrison, E. Owusu, P. & Dalglish, S.L. (23 April 2021) 'Reported health and social consequences of the Covid-19 pandemic on vulnerable populations and implanted solutions in six Western African countries: A media content analysis,' Available at: https://doi.org/10.1371/journal, Accessed 14 March 2022.

Tosh, M.D. (18 June 2021) 'Corona virus: What is it and how can I protect myself?' Available at: https://www.mmayoclinicorg.disease.conditions/coronavirus/expert answers/novel-coronavirus/faq-20478727, Accessed 14 January 2022.

United Nations (4 November 2016) 'Tool-kit for disability for Africa: Introducing the United Nations Convention for the Human Rights of Persons with Disabilities,' Available at: https://www.un.org/esa/socdev/documents/disability/Toolit/intro-UN-CRPD.pdf, Accessed 10 January 2022.

Waterfield, K.C. Shah, G.H. Etheredge, G.D. & Ikhile, O. (13 September 2021) 'Consequences of the Covid-19 crisis for people with HIV: The impact of social determinants of health,' Available at: https://doi..org/10.1186/s/12889-021-10296-9, Accessed 29 January 2022.

Word Health Organisation (10 November 2021) 'Assessing the impact of Covid-19 on older people in the African region: A study conducted by the World Health Organisation Regional Office for Africa,' Available at: https://reliefweb.int/caters/relifweb-int-.files/resources/9789290234548 eng pdf, Accessed 8 March 2022.

Zeufack, A.G. Calderon, C. Kambou, G. Djiofack, C.Z. Kubota, M. & Korman, V. (19 July 2020) 'Africa's pulse: An analysis of issues shaping Africa's economic future,' Available at: https://openknowledge.worldbank.org/handle/10986/33541, Accessed 26 January 2022.

Zhou, E.T. Yu, R. Du, G. Fan, Y. Liu, J. Xiang, Y. Wang, B. Song, X. Gu, L. Guan, Y. Wei, H. Li, X. Wu, S. Yu, Y. Zhang, H. & Cao, B. (3 November 2020) 'Clinical course and risk factors for mortality and adult inpatients with Covid-19 in Wuhan, China,' in: *Lancet*, Volume 385, Issue 10229, pp.1054-1062.

Chapter 13

Effects of the Covid-19 Pandemic on Labour Rights in Zimbabwe

Takavafira Masarira Zhou & Peter Machenjera

Introduction

The outbreak of the Covid-19 pandemic affected workers in Zimbabwe in various ways. It is the argument of this chapter that the Covid-19 invasion and the mitigation measures put in place by the government to combat it aggravated the poor labour relations and compromised the right to fair labour practices in Zimbabwe. While it is undeniable that before the outbreak of the Corona virus, labour and workers' rights were in bad shape, it should be noted that the pandemic worsened that situation. Before the advent of the pandemic, labour and workers' rights were violated but there was some semblance of respect for workers in both the public and private sectors in terms of statutory meetings. In the public sector, statutory meetings took place under the National Joint Negotiation Council (NJNC) while those in the private sector happened under the Labour Act. There were also attempts to revive the Tripartite Negotiation Forum (TNF) in which private and public workers engaged the government and industry to foster industrial harmony and productivity at a broad national scale. However, with the outbreak of Covid-19, labour and workers' rights were flouted by both the government and the private sector using lockdowns as a *casus belli* for paying starvation wages, let alone unilateralism to determine salaries and conditions of service of workers. Through various statutory instruments and circulars, the government adopted a paternalistic approach to labour issues, and unilaterally took over the role of wage-setting to 'improve' the operational conditions of workers but ultimately ended in gross income inequalities among workers.

The government's promise to restore the purchasing power parity of workers' salaries to the pre-October 2018 level by January 2021 failed to materialise. Mandatory deductions such as Government Employees Mutual Savings (GEMS) were put into effect without the consent of workers, while the meaningless cost-of-living adjustments were randomly given, leaving government workers worse off than before the purported adjustments. The private sector used the Covid-19 pandemic to adopt neo-liberal policies of low productivity to justify flouting of (or failure to reach) collective bargaining agreements with workers, retrenchment of workers and starvation wages thereby resorting to unfair labour practices, and thus treating workers in a degrading and servitude manner. Covid-19 lockdowns inhibited freedom of assembly and the right to organise industrial actions for purposes of advancing workers' interests, thereby exacerbating their plight. While many workers were incapacitated and could not afford to regularly report for work, the government also adopted a policy of no-work-no-pay thereby entrenching poverty and penury. Unions that called for better salaries and conditions of work were accused by the Zimbabwe African National Union Patriotic Front (ZANU-PF) government under President Emmerson Mnangagwa of working in cohorts with foreigners for a regime-change agenda. That said, this chapter seeks to unravel how the outbreak of the Covid-19 pandemic and the subsequent lockdowns and restrictions adversely affected the exercise of labour and workers' rights in Zimbabwe.

Labour and workers' rights in Zimbabwe before the Covid-19 pandemic

Since Zimbabwe, like many other countries, was a signatory to international conventions administered by the International Labour Organisation (ILO), it was obliged to uphold the principles enshrined in the 1998 Declaration on Fundamental Principles and Rights at Work which encouraged member states to abide by its protocols (Mariwo, 2008). These conventions also required governments to respect, fulfil and refrain from violating socio-economic rights when it came to decent and fair working conditions. Mariwo (2008) states that the Zimbabwean government should have domesticated ILO conventions through acts of parliament. However, what must be noted is that although these conventions had a significant influence on Zimbabwe's labour legislation, their implementation always had challenges. In Zimbabwe, as Chikwanha (2009) submits, the history of violations of human rights, workers' rights included, was complicated by the inheritance of a colonial system that did not universally respect and protect basic human entitlements.

It is undeniable that under Mugabe's regime, particularly between 1991 and 2017, political and economic crises led to deindustrialisation and the consequent spread of informalisation that weakened the labour movement (Sachikonye *et al*, 2018). Systematic targeting of the labour movement for giving birth to the opposition Movement for Democratic Change (MDC) led to its fragmentation at both national and sectoral levels. These developments weakened the labour movement's ability to advance the interests of workers and the general populace on one hand, and defend any gains that had been made on the other. By the end of Mugabe's reign in 2017, unions were nowhere near the movements that produced Benjamin Burombo, Joshua Nkomo and Morgan Tsvangirai. Indeed, the roar of the 1948, 1955 and 1997 lions had by 2017 been reduced to a cat's meow by fragmentation, deindustrialisation and de-proletarianisation.

A coup in November 2017 ended Mugabe's long rule but Mugabeism continued with the consequent intensification of repressive laws against the labour movement. The continued use of the Public Order and Security Act (POSA) (2002, Chapter 11: 17) and the Criminal Law (Codification and Reform) Act (2004, Chapter 9: 23) by the 'new dispensation' under President Mnangagwa are cases in point. Therefore, the same apparatus of brutality and force employed by Mugabe were used with vigour to suppress democratic space and undermine workers' rights. Deindustrialisation and de-proletarianisation continued under the new political dispensation despite claims that the country was open for business (Zhou, 2019). The optimism that the workers seemed to have immediately after the coup quickly evaporated.

Inflation and fuel shortages cumulatively eroded the salaries of workers and increased poverty. The rejuvenated Zimbabwe Congress of Trade Unions (ZCTU) under a leadership elected at the 2016 Congress found its voice in January 2019 and called for protests over fuel prices hikes. The demonstrations, which took place in the major urban centres, were crushed by security forces in one of the most brutal crackdowns in Zimbabwe's recent history (Zhou, 2021). Throughout 2019, many trade union leaders were abducted and charged with treason for advancing workers' rights, with the threats going as far as sending wrapped parcels containing bullets to the then ZCTU President, Pater Mutasa, and Secretary-General, Japhet Moyo. Martial law was also used against the labour movement, with the state summarily dismissing nurses and doctors for protesting over low salaries and poor working conditions. Yet, despite government repression, workers in the health and education sectors in particular adopted incapacitation as an industrial model of protest (Ibid).

Despite the aforesaid setbacks, there was some semblance of respect for workers' rights by the government of Zimbabwe. The Labour Act (2006, Chapter 20:01), together with numerous amendments up to 2019, ensured that shop-floor workers engaged with management to discuss matters ranging from productivity, incentive schemes, disciplinary measures to welfare in the private sector. Fundamentally, through the Labour Act, private sector workers could reach binding collective agreements applicable at sectoral level. Amendments to the Labour Act after 2015 were tailor-made to reverse the casualisation of labour following the July 2015 court ruling to the effect that an employer had common law rights to terminate a contract of employment without any reason, provided notice was given. Civil servants had hope to realign Statutory Instrument 141 of 1997 and the Public Service Act with Section 65 of the National Constitution to guarantee binding collective bargaining and social dialogue that could guarantee industrial harmony and productivity.

With the coming into effect of the Tripartite Negotiating Forum Act (TNFA) on 4 June 2019 (Zvobgo, 2019), expectations were high with regards to better salaries and conditions of service for workers in Zimbabwe. This Act, as Zvobgo (2019) adds, institutionalised the tripartite social dialogue process in Zimbabwe. The TNF had its fair share of challenges because its success was hinged on political will on the part of the government, commitment, sound respect of fundamental human rights and labour rights, freedom of association and collective bargaining. Even the adoption of the National Constitution in 2013, especially Section 65 and Section 69, was a giant step towards respecting workers' rights, there was need to align the labour laws to the Constitution. Arguably, by the beginning of 2020, there was growing impatience of workers with the new dispensation. Civil servants were more irked by the government's unilateral reduction of their salaries from US$540 to ZWL$540 which, by January 2020, had been eroded by inflation. The adoption of austerity measures for prosperity was fast becoming a prescription that treats the disease by killing the patient as Zimbabwean workers were fast sinking deeper into malice and poverty (Mhere, Interview: 15 January 2022). The advent of Covid-19 was taken by President Emmerson Mnangagwa's government as an ideal opportunity to control workers' growing militancy, discontent and disillusionment. Thus, the coming of the pandemic in early 2020 severely compromised the respect for workers' rights. In the process, the government emasculated fair labour practice and decent work agenda. Furthermore, the state flouted the fundamental rights of the human person as well as the rights of workers in terms of conditions of work, safety and remuneration.

Outbreak of the Covid-19 pandemic and the Zimbabwe government's reaction

The history of mankind is marked by pandemics that affect people at various times and levels. In the past, as Mashapure *et al* (2021) state, people were affected by pandemics like Influenza (1918-1919), Black Death, Ebola, Severe Acute Respiratory Syndrome (SARS) and others that had disastrous effects on national economies, health and securities. Covid-19 is the name for a new Corona virus that emerged in Wuhan City in the Hubei Province of China in December 2019 and was declared a "public health emergency of international concern" on 30 January 2020 by the World Health Organisation (WHO) (Patel, 2020: 2). A survey by E-Learning Africa and EdTech Hub (2020) shows that Africa's first Covid-19 case was reported on 14 February 2020 in Egypt, although WHO's first case in the African region, which does not include Egypt, was reported on 25 February in Algeria. Zimbabwe was also not spared by this ravaging pandemic. ZCTU (2020) reports that as of 27 March 2020, the Ministry of Health and Child Care announced that out of the 188 tests conducted, seven cases were Covid-19 positive, 181 cases were negative, and one death was recorded. By 25 February 2022, Zimbabwe had recorded 234 967 cases of infections, 5 390 deaths and 225 447 recoveries (Ibid).

It is important to note that the Covid-19 pandemic affected all countries in the world in various ways. According to E-Learning Africa & EdTech Hub (2020), the pandemic arrived in Africa at a time when the continent was optimistic about growth. Many African countries were enjoying moments of growth at rates that were envied by countries in Europe, North America and even in Asia and the Pacific region. Most of the 54 African countries had committed themselves to creating the world's largest Common Free Trade Area (AfCFTA) (Ibid). The African Union (AU) even had a future vision, Agenda 2063, which aimed to provide a blueprint and master plan for transforming Africa into a global powerhouse of the future, entrenching sustainable growth and consigning poverty, conflict and disease to the past (Ibid). The advent of Covid-19 therefore prompted governments to take stringent measures to deal with the viral pandemic that threatened people's lives and derailed the development trajectory.

In Zimbabwe, the Covid-19 pandemic coincided with multiple threats and challenges which had intensified in the years before its outbreak. The epidemic affected Zimbabwe's already distressed economy, health, education, livelihoods, agriculture, and food security. These challenges also generated discontent among workers and the general populace that called for urgent government intervention. The government did not fold its hands when confronted by such a threatening pandemic, let alone growing disgruntlement. On 19 March 2020, the government launched the National Preparedness and Response Plan and went on to declare a state of disaster on 20 March 2020 (Price, 2020). Suspending all democratic standards, a national lockdown was out in place on 30 March 2020 and was extended indefinitely on 16 May 2020, with the undertaking that restrictions were to be reviewed every two weeks, a situation that prevailed until 2022. The government also announced a ZWL$600 million cash transfer programme that targeted one million vulnerable households over the next three months, with each household expected to get ZWL$200, which was later increased to ZWL$300. On 2 April 2020, the government launched a US$2.2 billion domestic and international humanitarian appeal covering the period from April 2020 to April 2021. This was targeted at Covid-19 containment, critical health spending, water, sanitation and hygiene and other urgent needs (Ibid). On 4 April, the government announced a broad Covid-19 economic recovery and stimulus package, including measures to provide liquidity support to several sectors, expand social safety nets and food grants, set up a health sector support fund, and upscale investments in social and economic infrastructure in Cyclone Idai-affected areas. In addition, the authorities restored the multi-currency system and allowed both the Zimbabwe dollar and the United States dollar to be legal tenders (Price, 2020).

Coupled with the above government interventions were lockdowns, restricted hospital visits, bans on entertainment and recreational activities, border controls and others (ZCTU, 2020). However, a closer look at these measures and interventions reveal that they were not necessarily meant to help the general populace, especially the workers. The workers found themselves on the receiving end as the lockdowns, restrictions and declarations affected them in various ways which included loss of jobs, salary cuts, state interventions, oppressive neo-liberal policies and others as discussed below.

Effects of Covid-19 on labour and workers' rights

The Covid-19 pandemic was responsible for a vast array of disturbances in the labour sector that happened either directly or indirectly. The lockdowns and related restrictions affected industrial relations. Indeed, the Southern African Development Community (SADC) acknowledged that the employment and labour sector was one of the components of the economy that was hardest hit by the pandemic and its impacts (SADC Secretariat, 2020). Employment levels dropped across all sectors with increases in underemployment, informality and poverty being experienced. At least 60 million jobs were affected through reduced working hours, lay-offs and general inactivity during the height of the lockdown measures (Ibid). The jobs that were mostly at risk were those dependent on trade, tourism and transport, notably those in the hospitality industry such as hotels, restaurants, wholesale and retail because there was a time when there was a total shut down of the economy in 2020 (Ibid). Sharukayi (2020) posits that the general social life in Zimbabwe during the Covid-19 pandemic was characteristically sad as many people were retrenched, with fear of loss of terminal benefits and other incentives such as education and health facilities. In addition, the chances of reabsorption into the formal employment system were very slim and almost non-existent owing to the high unemployment rates. So, generally, many people in the formal sector lost their jobs because of the pandemic and a significant number were relegated to the informal sector or the rural areas where they embarked on subsistence farming.

The informal sector was not spared either by the Covid-19 pandemic. According to Chamunorwa (2021), the advent of the pandemic in 2020 had a tremendous impact on millions of people who had depended on the informal economy. When the pandemic struck, 60% of Zimbabwe's economy was informal and over 90% of the working-age population worked in the informal economy, with most of the people living from hand to mouth (Ibid). The Covid-19 lockdown restrictions led to the closure of informal economy businesses and marketplaces. In some cities and towns, market stalls or vending sites deemed illegal and/or unsafe were demolished by the local authorities and trading on the street pavements was banned (Ibid). This meant a loss of income for households dependent on the informal economy for their daily survival.

Lockdowns also meant restricted movements, with only essential service providers allowed to move while other people were required to produce exemption letters stamped by their employers for them to pass various checkpoints. The informal sector was not regarded as an essential service provider and many such traders did not have letters of employment because they were not formally employed. The enforcement of lockdowns during which the police descended on vendors, raided vegetable markets and destroyed produce, affected many people (Price, 2020). Border closure and the resultant denial of access to markets was another existential threat posed by the Covid-19 pandemic. This means that the lockdowns that the government of Zimbabwe imposed upon its people as a way of containing the spread of the Corona virus ended up affecting most workers in the informal sector, yet millions of Zimbabweans made a living from vending.

To aggravate the situation, the Covid-19 lockdowns imposed by the government were not supported by meaningful alternatives to help those who had lost business owing to the closure of the informal sector. The ZCTU (2020) complained that a lockdown without alternative sources of income and livelihood support for the informal workers had the potential to push workers into abject poverty as any day's loss of income had ripple effects on their livelihoods. The ban on cross-border and inter-city passenger transportation caused a severe loss of livelihood sources, with some even failing to recover after the pandemic had subsided. When stringent lockdown conditions were eventually relaxed, vendors reported low sales, high rates of produce leftovers and spoilages for those selling perishable goods and a decline in the number of customers visiting vending sites or informal economy markets (Chamunorwa, 2021). As such, workers in the informal sector suffered because their operations were disrupted in many ways.

A survey carried out by the Zimbabwe National Chamber of Commerce (ZNCC) in 2020 on the effects of Covid-19-induced lockdowns revealed that businesses lost production time, resulting in reduced production output as well as revenue losses (Chitongo *et al*, 2020). UN Zimbabwe (2021) observed that the Covid-19 pandemic exacerbated Zimbabwe's social and economic challenges on the back of pre-existing structural problems, climate-induced shocks and a weak social contract. The pandemic increased unemployment and caused a general fall in incomes. In 2020, the economy was initially projected to grow by 3%. However, the government revised the estimate of economic growth to a contraction of about -4.1% due to Covid-19-induced disruptions and impacts of drought (Ibid). The workers were the ones who bore much of the brunt of these changes brought about by the Covid-19 scourge in the economy.

Owing to the Covid-19 pandemic and subsequent lockdowns, as the Employers' Confederation of Zimbabwe (ECZ) reported in June 2020, over one million Zimbabweans were thrown out of formal employment, adding to about five million more who earned a living through menial jobs. Most of those affected were contract workers who were laid off at a time when the cost of living was on the rise (Chamunorwa, 2021). A survey conducted by the Confederation of Zimbabwe Industries (CZI) in July 2020 revealed that many companies reacted to the advent of the Covid-19 pandemic by implementing staff rationalisation measures which included reducing labour costs by non-renewal of fixed-term employment contracts, retrenching permanent and temporary employees, sending staff on forced leave and cutting salaries (Ibid). This was also confirmed by the Zimbabwe Statistical Agency's Rapid Poverty, Income, Consumption and Expenditure Surveys (PICES) during which 44% of workers interviewed reported a reduction or disappearance of wages (Ibid). All these developments tended to go contrary to the ILO conventions which safeguard workers' wages and salaries. Examples of the conventions are: the Labour Clauses (Public Contracts) Convention, 1949 (Number 94); Protection of Wages Convention, 1949 (Number 95); Minimum Wage Fixing Convention, 1970 (Number 131); Protection of Workers' Claims (Employer's Insolvency) Convention, 1992 (Number 173); and the Equal Remuneration Convention, 1951 (Number 100) (Muchichwa, 2016). The safeguards embedded in the Labour Act (2006, Chapter 28: 1), just as ILO conventions, could not guard against the casualisation of labour as companies justified losses on the Corona virus and clamoured for retrenchment of some workers to keep them afloat during the pandemic period. Arguably, the Covid-19 pandemic was weaponised to retrench workers or unilaterally cut salaries. These unfair labour practices critically infringed the rights of workers and condemned many of them to absolute poverty.

The violation of workers' rights under the guise of Covid-19 also impacted on trade unionism. Trade unions could not exercise their rights because of lockdowns and restrictions. Patel (2020) noted that Covid-19 did not only expose the vulnerability of workers around the continent, Zimbabwe included, but also the ability of the trade union movement to represent and organise workers when traditional interactions were not feasible. In Zimbabwe, the government took advantage of the Covid-19 pandemic to unilaterally declare policies that disadvantaged workers with the full knowledge that lockdown restrictions would not allow unions to come together and challenge them. One such move by the government was the unilateral introduction of the GEMS loan fund in 2021 without consulting the workers. The loan facility was allegedly meant to rescue civil servants, most of who had fallen prey to loan sharks and high-interest hire purchase agreements (Mudzviti, 23 February 2021). Yet sound as this appeared, the GEMS fund did not benefit much as many civil servants failed to access it. This raised fears that the fund was either a cash cow for elites or a facility tailor-made to sponsor the ruling ZANU-PF party's campaign for the 2023 local government, parliamentary and presidential elections. Thus, the Progressive Teachers Union of Zimbabwe (PTUZ) (2021) called it "a project only meant to spin money and benefit the government by raking millions of dollars from poor civil servants."

With the rights to organise and participate in lawful activities of unions or collective job action permissible under Section 65, as well as freedoms to assemble and demonstrate guaranteed in Sections 58 and 59 of the Zimbabwean Constitution (2013) curtailed by Corona virus restrictions, the government had an open cheque to undermine fair labour practice. Attempts to challenge the state's labour abuses were often frustrated by the government's use of an opt-out clause which ruled out the possibility of filing urgent court applications. Closely linked to these issues was the failure by non-state employers to respect collective bargaining protocols during the pandemic. It is a fact that the decimation of trade union activities, the reduced hours of work, and casualisation of labour during the Covid-19 period watered down the workers' collective bargaining capacity and empowered the employer to unilaterally determine salaries and conditions of service.

Covid-19 also delayed the implementation of the collective bargaining process, with the employers taking advantage of the prevailing situation. According to ILO Convention 154, collective bargaining refers to all negotiations which take place between an employer, a group of employers or one or more employers' organisations, on one hand, and one or more workers' organisations, on the other, for determining working conditions and terms of employment, regulating relations between employers and workers and/ or regulating relations between employers or their organisations and workers' organisations (ILO: nd). ILO Convention 98 set basic principles for making collective bargaining work for workers, employers and the society. Zvobgo (2019) argues that in practice, priority should be given to collective bargaining to settle disputes arising in connection with the determination of the terms and conditions of service, not only in the private sector but also where it concerns public servants who are not engaged in the administration of the state. A survey carried out by the Southern Africa Coordination Council (SATUCC) in 2020 on the impact of Covid-19 on workers in Southern Africa revealed that many collective bargaining negotiations stalled, with 55 % of the respondents indicating that collective bargaining rights were suspended (Soure, 2021). Therefore, Covid-19 negatively affected the collective bargaining process much to the detriment of the suffering workers. In countries like Zimbabwe, the few steps that were taken towards realising the collective bargaining forum were side-lined with the government dictating the pace of events in the labour sector.

After the outbreak of the Covid-19 pandemic, all physical meetings and attempts at face-to-face collective bargaining processes were suspended and employers and trade unions resorted to virtual platforms such as Zoom, Google, Meet and Skype (Ibid). Attempts to have a virtual meeting in January 2022 failed to take off because of connectivity problems. Whether the connectivity failure was deliberate or not, it is not clear, but the workers found themselves on the receiving end because whatever was supposed to be deliberated on failed. For trade unions, as Soure (2021) posits, their internal technological deficits, including limited smart gadgets and financial resources for online data bundles had a detrimental effect on their effective participation in virtual collective bargaining processes. Indeed, virtual collective bargaining presented its own challenges compared to physical meetings. This is so because the art of collective bargaining incorporates factors such as reading and gauging of emotions, facial expressions and body language by both parties. For trade unions, who are generally on the weaker side, these factors help in communicating, motivating and strategically overcoming conflicts and reaching an agreement, all of which are taken away by virtual collective bargaining. Another challenge is that organising and setting up the virtual collective meeting is a responsibility of the employer, posing a risk of manipulating the whole process. For example, bad employers can decide to mute or unmute speakers as a way of undermining or frustrating the trade union representative(s), especially those who are outspoken (Ibid). So, for Zimbabwe, the workers continued to be side-lined by the employers because during the Covid-19 era, collective bargaining processes or attempts at collective bargaining failed and workers' grievances remained unresolved.

Since the outbreak of the Corona virus in early 2020, only one union in the country, the Zimbabwe Allied and Diamond Workers Union (ZIDAWU), managed to reach a collective bargaining agreement at the national level in their sector (Sunguro, 2022). The government was the chief culprit in weaponising Covid-19 to perpetuate unjust labour relations. Instead of harmonising labour laws and adopting a robust collective bargaining modus operandi outlined under Section 65 of the Constitution (2013), it intransigently clung to Statutory Instrument 141 of 1997 that allowed for mere consultations and collective begging. During the pandemic, the government even abandoned the begging concept and moved to a precarious level of unilateralism where the cabinet decided what to give civil servants with the 'government-controlled' Apex Council often being called to rubber-stamp decisions under the so-called Joint Negotiation Council (NJNC).

Under the Covid-19 conditionalities, the government strategically positioned itself to disarm trade unions through co-optation and defective 'consultation', patronage and resourcing. The state facilitated the registration of the Zimbabwe Confederation of Public Service Trade Unions (ZCPTU) in August 2020 without federations in a clear top-down state paternalism tailor-made to divide civil servants and counteract the growth of the ZCTU as a labour centre (Zhou, 2021). The government also refused to register the Federation of Zimbabwe Educators' Union (FOZEU), initially comprising eight teacher unions, for its undiluted call for the restoration of the purchasing power of teachers' salaries to the October 2018 level of US$540. In practice, the government systematically used Covid-19 to violate the right to fair and safe labour practices and standards and to be paid a fair and reasonable wage; the right to engage in collective bargaining, organise, and form and join federations of unions and organisations; let alone the right to participate in collective job action, including the right to strike, sit in, withdraw labour, and take other similar action guaranteed under Section 65 of the Zimbabwean Constitution (2013). These rights and freedoms were also guaranteed by SADC protocols (2014) and ILO Conventions 87 and 98 both of which were ratified by the Zimbabwean government. Workers who sought to exercise their rights to organise, collectively bargain and strike were frequently met with arbitrary arrests, detentions, violence, torture, intimidation and harassment in desperate efforts by the government to curb union activities. Even nurses and doctors who staged a peaceful demonstration in March 2020 against low salaries and lack of Covid-19 personal protective equipment were beaten up and arrested by state security operatives (Moyo & Phulu, 2021).

The weaponisation of the Covid-19 pandemic was also evidenced by the government's prevention of workers from gathering or organising themselves whilst gatherings of the ruling party were allowed to go on without restrictions and disturbances. Demonstrations by workers were quelled with brutality but at the end of 2021 and the beginning of 2022, the ruling ZANU-PF party had the latitude to conduct its primary district and provincial elections countrywide, respectively, in preparation for the March 2022 by-elections and the harmonised 2023 elections. Unions were compelled to shift towards e-campaigning and e-mobilisation to complement traditional forms of exerting pressure on governments, employers, parliamentarians and opinion leaders to uphold workers' rights (Soure, 2021). As UN Zimbabwe (2021) rightly argued, the measures to contain the spread of the Corona virus limited access to justice and a wide range of democratic and civic rights such as the right to peaceful assembly, free movement and access to information. Unions, like companies, were compelled to close their offices and operate from home. This greatly militated against the execution of duties by the unions and eventually affected the workers.

The attempt to revive the Tripartite Negotiating Forum (TNF) was frustrated both by the Covid-19 restrictions and the government's lack of political will. The TNF Act, which came into effect on 4 June 2019, institutionalised the tripartite social dialogue process between government, business and labour in Zimbabwe (Zvobgo, 2021). However, the powers accorded to the Minister of Labour made the TNF subjective and partisan (Chamunorwa, 2021). According to Zhou (2021), it seemed as if the tripartite forum was tailor-made to reduce worker militancy by shifting emphasis away from workplace struggles to fruitless negotiations. The government was always arrogant and refused to abide by ILO regulations on fair labour practice, thereby setting itself at loggerheads with the labour movement, and some regional, continental and global partners. Given the Covid-19 restrictions on movements and gatherings, TNF meetings died a natural death with the government making unilateral decisions about employment conditions without consultations.

The outbreak of the Covid-19 pandemic in Zimbabwe exposed many workers to the deadly disease. The most affected were frontline workers like doctors, nurses, teachers and miners, among many others. Since Zimbabwe's economy was mainly supported by the informal sector, most of the informal sector workers were also vulnerable. Chamunorwa (2021) claims that challenges at workplaces that exposed the workers to Covid-19 included inadequacy of personal protective equipment; transport problems and crowding in private vehicles; irregular Covid-19 testing for workers; lack of standard procedures to deal with Covid-19 cases; delayed Occupational Safety, Health and Environment (OSHE) inspections by the Ministry of Labour; and delayed sectoral collective bargaining processes. The SADC Secretariat (2020) decried that the employment sector was directly affected by the virus itself in the context of the safety and health of workers in essential services who continued to report for duty, thereby being at high risk of infection or infecting others unknowingly. McClanahan & Barrantes (2021) argue that the pandemic increased the health and safety vulnerability of millions of workers in both formal and informal employment. However, it is important to note that it is the duty of employers to make the work places safe for their workers. Sadly, employers failed to take Covid-19 as an occupational health disease, with mining companies, universities and government using buses to ferry workers to and from work with standing passengers. This posed serious threats to their health given that the Corona virus is easily transmitted under conditions of close distance.

Worse still, many employers used command and control tactics of giving ultimatums to employees for mandatory vaccination instead of explaining the efficacy and giving incentives. Although government claimed to have allocated funds for Covid-19 abatement equipment for schools, much of that money found its way into private pockets with the consequent quantum leap of Corona virus cases in these institutions in 2020, 2021 and 2022 (PTUZ, 2022). The burden of providing abatement equipment ended in up the hands of School

Heads, School Development Committees (SDCs), and parents. Thus, the Covid-19 pandemic threatened the health and safety of workers and many even lost their lives. While the health insurance assistance for illness or death due to Covid-19 was accessible to security forces, it never benefited most civil servants, particularly teachers.

Workers in the tourism and hospitality industry had their fair share of the impact of the Covid-19 pandemic. ZCTU (2020) posits that the lockdowns on weddings, conferences and workshops severely affected companies in the hospitality and tourism sectors. Some operators in this sector recorded cancellations of bookings and trips by international travellers, and by extension, the government also lost revenue. Resultantly, workers, mostly casual and contract, were affected through forced leave and loss of income. As a result, the majority of such workers could barely sustain decent livelihoods due to eroded incomes or termination of employment. Rodriguez-Anton & Alonso-Ameida (2020) argue that the immediate-term impacts on the tourism and hospitality industry were the severe decrease in tourists, occupancy levels and a fall in average daily revenue, and revenue per available room. In the short-term, the impacts included job cuts, changes in operations and reduction in services which threatened the recovery of the hospitality industry. Therefore, the tourism and hospitality industries were not spared from the ravages of the Covid-19 pandemic.

Workers living with disabilities were also negatively affected by the pandemic. The UN High Commissioner for Human Rights (2020) noted that people living with disabilities who were more likely to be employed in the informal sector had less access to social insurance based on employment than others, which decreased their resilience in the Covid-19 context. Those who were formally employed or self-employed could be prevented from working from home due to the absence of equipment and support which were available in the workplace and thus faced the risk of losing their income and jobs. Thus, the lack and loss of income represented a disproportionate burden on persons living with disabilities and their households, which typically faced extra costs and expenditure related to disability such as accessible housing and equipment, assistive devices, specific goods and services. Consequently, many people living with disabilities were rapidly plunged into poverty (Ibid). Workers living with disabilities found it difficult to live under the Covid-19 pandemic because of their special conditions which required special attention. The UNESCO Rapid Assessment Report of November 2020 on the effects of Covid-19 asserted that the majority of people living with disabilities survived from informal sector activities such as vending and begging in the streets. These people faced difficulties to access support from the government, non-governmental organisations and private individuals due to travel restrictions imposed during the lockdown period (Chamunorwa, 2021). The Covid-19 regulations and restrictions did not consider that there were some workers living with disabilities whose removal from sources of income affected them more than other workers.

The Covid-19 pandemic was also responsible for the loss of working hours which directly translated to loss of income. According to the *ILO Monitor* (2021), over the 15 years before the onset of the pandemic, the average working time per person of working age (aged 15 to 64 years) fluctuated between 27 and 28 hours per week. This then dropped sharply by 2.5 hours from 27.2 hours per week in 2019 to 24.7 hours per week in 2020. Given this massive loss of working hours, workers suffered significant reductions in their income. The reduction in labour income was distributed unevenly between workers, meaning that the problem of income loss was combined with that of greater inequality (Ibid). Therefore, the Covid-19 pandemic changed the working patterns of the workers with the reduction in the working hours affecting the workers negatively as shown above. Indeed, the period 2020-2022 witnessed the most precipitous decline of salaries and conditions of service of workers in Zimbabwe.

The pandemic also came at a time when the government was implementing austerity measures as a way of improving the economy. The Transitional Stabilisation Programme, published on 5 October 2018, detailed the reforms that were to be made in future and emphasised private ownership in business (Mhlanga & Ndhlovu, 2020). UN Zimbabwe (2021) advised that austerity measures and severe wage compression amid high inflation had negatively impacted on the welfare of civil servants, resulting in industrial action and adverse repercussions on social service delivery. Covid-19 lockdowns and restrictions exposed the real pathetic value of workers' salaries. In fact, the pandemic exacerbated the socio-economic challenges of workers on the back of pre-existing structural economic problems, climate-induced shocks and a weak social contract. This left workers with little power to challenge the employers, including the government, who had long since forgotten that proper labour engagement enhances industrial harmony and productivity.

Teachers who tried to demonstrate against low salaries were arrested and tortured, resulting in many of them staying at home after declaring incapacitation. An example can be drawn from early February 2022 when 90% of teachers who declared being incapacitated were summarily and unlawfully suspended the government (Minister of Primary and Secondary Education, Press Statement: 10 February 2022) The suspended teachers were later ordered to report for work by 22 February 2022, failure of which they were deemed to have resigned (Public Service Commission, Press Statement: 16 February 2022). These developments clearly showed the weaponisation of the Covid-19 pandemic in which labour rights were emasculated under an *alibi* of preventing the spread of the Corona virus. It is quite apparent that the government of Zimbabwe and other employers grabbed the Covid-19 pandemic as an opportunity to limit the exercise of labour rights and victimise workers and their union leaders. Arguably, as much as the labour movement continued to strive at engagement and the socio-economic development of its clientele, the employers, including the government, largely focused on weaponising Covid-19 to maximise profit-making at the expense of the health, safety and general livelihood of workers.

This section has illustrated how the rights of the workers in Zimbabwe were severely contravened during the Covid-19 period. Among other things, the right to strike, which is of cardinal importance in any labour law regime based on social justice and democracy in the workplace (Gwisai *et al*, 2018), was unilaterally withdrawn by the government for reasons that went beyond health concerns. Consequent upon Covid-19 lockdowns, workers were also deprived of their freedom of association and the right to collectively bargain for better working conditions. Ultimately, poverty on the part of workers was entrenched owing to the violation of many of their rights, freedoms and liberties.

Conclusion

All in all, the outbreak of Covid-19 in Zimbabwe, like in many other countries around the world, caused devastating effects on labour relations, more so because capital weaponised the pandemic against labour. Despite capital and labour being strange bad fellows,

Zimbabwe was walking along a better labour trajectory before the advent of Covid-19 with private sector employers and employees mostly guided by the Labour Act to reach binding collective agreements. Similarly, the government and its workers also showed some semblance of consultation and collective begging prior to the pandemic. The Covid-19 pandemic worsened labour relations in Zimbabwe as it affected various industries, both informal or formal, public or private. The stringent measures that were put in place by the government, especially in the first days of the pandemic, to curb the spread of infections, diluted the workers' rights to participate in lawful activities of unions. Workers were also barred from engaging in collective bargaining, organising themselves, and participating in collective job action, including the right to strike. Attempts at withdrawing labour were treated as acts of sabotage and workers who embarked on such acts were arrested, brutalised and summarily dismissed. Thus, workers were effectively denied the right to fair and safe labour practices. Indeed, the workers' pursuit of a decent work agenda was therefore frustrated.

Furthermore, many workers lost their jobs while some lost incomes as businesses and companies were closed. Therefore, the Covid-19 pandemic did not only affect the general populace in terms of deaths and illness but in many other aspects of life. The pandemic was weaponised by employers to entrench unfair labour practices, unleash callous and monumental injustice against workers, let alone to disarticulate, marginalise and impoverish them. Undoubtedly, the period of the Covid-19 pandemic will go into the annuals of industrial relations as an epoch that caused unmitigated misery to workers and left them more vulnerable to caprices of employers, let alone more penurious than before.

References

Chamunorwa, A. (2021) *The impact of Covid-19 on socio-economic rights in Zimbabwe*, Harare: The Zimbabwe Peace Project.

Chikwanha, A.N. (October 2009) 'The trajectory of human rights violations in Zimbabwe,' in: *Institute for Security Studies,* Available at: www.files.ethz.ch>isn, Accessed 26 December 2021.

Chitongo, L. Chikunya, P. & Marango, T. (July 2020) 'Do economic blueprints work? Evaluating the prospects and challenges of Zimbabwe's transitional stabilisation programme,' in: *African*

Journal of Governance and Development, Volume 9, Number 1, pp.7-20.

E-Learning Africa & EdTech Hub (September 2020) 'The effects of Covid-19 on education in Africa and its implications for the use of technology: A survey of the experience and opinions of educators and technology specialists,' in: *Creative Commons Attribution 4.0 International*, Available at: www.guninetwork.org>files, Accessed 5 December 2021.

Gwisai, M. Mucheche, C. & Matsikidze, R. (2018) 'The right to strike in Zimbabwe in the context of the 2013 Constitution and international law,' in: *University of Zimbabwe Law Journal,* Volume 1, Number 1, pp.35-75.

Government of Zimbabwe (2002) *Public Order and Security Act [Chapter11: 17] 2002*, Harare: Zimbabwe Government.

Government of Zimbabwe (2004) *Criminal Law (Codification and Reform) Act [Chapter 9: 23], No. 23, 2004*, Harare: Zimbabwe Government.

Government of Zimbabwe (2006) *Labour Act [Chapter 28: 01] 2006*, Harare: Zimbabwe Government.

Government of Zimbabwe (2013) *Constitution of Zimbabwe Amendment (No.20) Act 2013*, Harare: Zimbabwe Government.

ILO (not dated) 'ILO Convention No. 98: Right to organise and collective bargaining convention,' Available at: https://www.ilo.org/hanoi, Accessed 6 December 2021.

ILO Monitor (2021) *Covid-19 and the world of work, Seventh Edition: Updated estimates and analysis*, Available at: www.ilo.org>WCMS_767028>lang--en, Accessed 5 December 2021.

International Trade Union Confederation (ITUC) (19 and 21 October) *Internationally-recognised core labour standards in Zimbabwe: Report for the WTO General Council review on the trade policies of Zimbabwe*, Geneva: ITUC.

Mariwo, T. (2008) 'Working conditions and labour relations in the private security industry in Zimbabwe', Research Paper, Issues Paper Number 27, Harare: ILO Sub-Regional Office for Southern Africa.

Mashapure, R. Chikazhe, L. Chavhunduka, D. & Hamunakwadi, P. (2021) 'Socio-economic implications of Covid-19 pandemic to women entrepreneurs: A case of the informal sector in Zimbabwe,' in: *Business Management and Strategy*, Volume 12, Number 1, pp.10-27.

McClanahan, S. & Barrantes, A. (2021) 'Workers' rights and human rights: Resolving historical tensions through multi-tiered social security agenda,' in: *International Journal of Labour Research*, Volume 10, Issue 1-2, pp.13-26.

Mhere, F. (15 January 2022) Interview, Gweru: Zimbabwe

Mhlanga, D. & Ndhlovu, E. (2020) 'Socio-economic implications of the Covid-19 pandemic on smallholder livelihoods in Zimbabwe', Available at: www.researchgate .net/publication/340675720, Accessed 7 December 2021.

Ministry of Primary and Secondary Education (10 February 2022) 'Press statement: Suspension from service,' Harare: Zimbabwe.

Moyo, G. & Phulu, K.I. (2021) 'The weaponisation of the Corona virus crisis in Zimbabwe: Legal and extra-legal instruments,' in: *iBusiness*, Volume 13, pp.48-66.

Muchichwa, N. (2016) 'Working without pay: Wage theft in Zimbabwe', Available at: www.solidaritycenter,org>2016/07, Accessed 31 January 2022.

Mudzviti, K. (23 February 2021) 'Civil servants to register for GEMS loan fund before deductions,' in: *Business Mail*, Available at: https://www.businessmail.co.zw/bus, Accessed 20 January 2022.

Patel, S. (2020) 'Emergency online solutions to the Covid-19 pandemic for African trade unions: A report based on interviews with the five Africa-GUF General Secretaries,' Fredrich Ebert Stiftung and International Federation of Workers' Education Associates, Available at: www.library.fes.de>bueros>festucc, Accessed 2 January 2022.

PTUZ (14 January 2021) 'Case of government primitive looting from poor teachers,' Unpublished Report, Masvingo: Zimbabwe.

PTUZ (12 January 2022) 'Government allocation of $750 million has not filtered to schools,' Unpublished Report, Masvingo: Zimbabwe.

Price, R.A. (2020) *Impacts of Covid-19 regulatory measures on small-scale and informal trade in Zimbabwe,* K4D Helpdesk Report, UK: Institute of Development Studies.

Public Service Commission (16 February 2022) 'Press statement,' Harare: Zimbabwe.

Rodriguez-Anton, J.M. & Alonso-Almeida, M.M. (2020) 'Covid-19 impacts and recovery strategies: The case of the hospitality industry in Spain,' in: *Sustainability 2020*, Volume 12, Number

8599, Available at: www.mdpi.com/journal/sustainability, Accessed 4 January 2022.

Sachikonye, L. Raftopoulous, B. & Kanyeze, G. (eds.) (2018) *Building from the rubble: The labour movement in Zimbabwe since 2000*, Harare: Weaver Press.

SADC (2014) 'Protocol on employment and labour, Signed at Victoria Falls, Republic of Zimbabwe on the 18th day of August 2014,' Available at: www.sadc.int>files>, Accessed 7 January 2022.

SADC Secretariat (2020) 'SADC regional response to Covid-19 pandemic with focus on health system, labour, food security, law enforcement, air travel, transport and trade facilitation in the region', in: *Bulletin Number 9: Situation in African and SADC Region*, SADC: SADC Secretariat.

Sharukayi, O. (2 September 2020) 'Retrenchment,' Available at: www.zenaslegalpractice.com.zw, Accessed 12 January 2022.

Soure, M.K. (2021) 'Covid-19 and recovery: The role of trade unions in building forward better,' in: *International Journal of Labour Research*, Volume 10, Issue 1-2, Geneva: Bureau for Workers' Activities of the ILO, International Labour Office.

Bulawayo24 News (15 January 2021) 'Zimbabwe teachers ridicule government savings facility,' Available at: www.bulawayo24.com/index-id-news-sc-nat, Accessed 20 January 2022.

Sunguro, C. (25 January 2022) Interview, Harare: ZIDAWU Unions' Convergence Meeting.

UN High Commissioner for Human Rights (2020) 'Covid-19 and the rights of persons with disabilities: Guidance-OHCHR,' Available at: https://www.ohchr.org, Accessed 15 February 2022.

UN Zimbabwe (2021) *The United Nations common country analysis: Zimbabwe 2021*, Harare: UN Resident Coordinator's Office.

Zimbabwe Congress of Trade Unions (ZCTU) (2020) 'ZCTU response to the impact of Covid-19 (Corona virus) pandemic on workers and the Zimbabwe economy,' Available at: www.lo.no>intenasjonalt>zctu-response-to-co, Accessed 17 February 2022.

Zhou, T.M. (2019) 'Governance, democratisation and development in post-Mugabe Zimbabwe', in: F. Duri, N. Marongwe & M. Mawere (eds.) *Mugabeism after Mugabe? Rethinking legacies and the new dispensation in Zimbabwe's 'Second Republic,'* Masvingo: Africa Talent Publishers, pp.75-144.

Zhou, T. M. (2021) 'Labour in Zimbabwe, 1980-2020,' in: C. Chidoko & P. Mupa (eds.) *Social policy and development matrix in Zimbabwe: Where is the missing link?* Gweru: Dream Discoveries Publishers, pp.15-46.

Zvobgo, T.M. (2019) 'Collective bargaining and collective agreements in Africa', in: *Turin School of Development Working Paper Number 11*, Turin (Italy): International Training Centre of the ILO.

Chapter 14

Covid-19, Gender-Based Violence and Human Rights Abuses: The Case of Zimbabwe

Lisa Mubaiwa

Introduction

Gender-based violence is the general term used to capture various forms of abuse that occur as a result of the normative role expectations associated with each gender, as well as the unequal power relations between the genders within the context of a specific society (Bloom, 2008). Essentially, gender-based violence is socially sanctioned and by its nature, deep-rooted and pervasive in the lives of girls and women who are often subjugated primarily because of their female gender identity. In Zimbabwe, the advent of the Covid-19 pandemic and the measures announced on 30 March 2020 to curb its spread saw cases of gender-based violence and related human rights abuses on the rise. In particular, various forms of violence were unleashed on girls and women. Reports of domestic violence, child marriage, violence by state officials and armed guards, online abuse and other forms of gender-based violence increased globally and during the pandemic, and Zimbabwe was no exception to this trend (OCHA, 2020a; OCHA, 2020b; SAFE, 2020).

Prior to the Covid-19 pandemic, gender-based violence had proven to be a growing cancer in Zimbabwe. The implementation of measures to curb the spread of the virus brought about a surge in the cases of gender-based violence nationwide. According to a 2019 survey carried out by the Zimbabwe National Statistics Agency (ZimStat), cited by Martin & Ahlenback (2020), of women aged 15 49 years who had experienced violence since the age of 15 years, 11.6% had been victims of sexual violence. In addition, 33.7% of women aged 20-24 years were first married or entered a marital union before they were 18 years old (Ibid). Evidence presented in this chapter will prove that Covid-19 lockdown measures resulted in the skyrocketing of pre-existing cases of gender-based violence. It is the central argument of this chapter that the Covid-19 pandemic exposed and exacerbated existing gender inequalities globally, with increasing reports of gender-based violence, including domestic violence, child marriages, sexual exploitation, and harassment by armed security officers (Fraser, 2020; UN Women, 2020).

It is not possible for this chapter to exhaust all forms and respective details of gender-based violence and related human rights abuses in Zimbabwe during the Covid-19-related lockdown period. It focuses on six themes with the hope that other academics will carry out further research on various other aspects related to gender-based violence during the period of the pandemic. This chapter is organised into six sections. The first section dwells on the physical, emotional and sexual abuses experienced by women within households as a result of the Covid-19 pandemic. The second section focuses on the additional household chores which women had to undertake owing to pandemic pressures which severely compromised their economic rights and other freedoms. The third section concentrates on the manner in which women were made victims of economic violence and deprivation by the Covid-19 pandemic. The fourth section pays attention to violence on women and girls with disability occasioned by the epidemic. In the fifth section, attention shifts to the sexual abuse of girl children while the final part examines the plight of female commercial sex workers, all being related by and large to the advent of the Covid-19 pandemic and the subsequent measures that were imposed by the government to curb its spread.

Physical, emotional and sexual abuse of women within households

One of the most common form of gender-based violence among partners is domestic violence. It often involves physical violence or threats of violence. This kind of violence may also involve battery, coercion and sexual harassment (Sigsworth, 2009; Tshwaranang Legal Centre, 2012). Measures which included restricted movement, quarantines, social distancing and other stay-at-home orders were some of the most identifiable preconditions for the surge in domestic violence cases during the lockdown. The risk of domestic violence was heightened by lockdown measures which promoted forced coexistence and curtailed access to service providers in the event of perpetrated violence.

Intimate partner violence was reported to have increased during the Covid-19 lockdown(s) in Zimbabwe. According to SAFE (2020), intimate partners constituted 69.5% of intimate partner violence perpetrators during the lockdown. Several non-governmental organisations noted with concern that the cases of intimate partner violence during the lockdown were characterised by advanced severity (Martin & Ahlenback, 2020). A UNESCO Covid-19 Disability Assessment Report published in November 2020 stated that even some disabled female partners were caught up in the domestic violence cases during the lockdown period (Chamunogwa, 2021). Physical violence, which includes hitting, slapping, kicking, punching, and pushing, was another notable form of gender-based violence during the lockdown period. Knives and other sharp items were frequently used as weapons during physical conflicts (Sigsworth, 2009; Tshwaranang Legal Centre, 2012).

Within households, many women were sometimes sexually abused by their spouses during prolonged stays indoors owing to the Covid-19 lockdown measures such as travel bans and stay-at-home orders. Sexual abuse may or may not be coupled with physical abuse (Musasa Project, 2008). It can also include pressing or forcing a spouse to perform particular sexual actions against her will (Ibid). Arguably, sexual assault is the most common form of gender-based violence and includes rape, sexual harassment, sexual exploitation, and sexual trafficking (Macheka & Nhongo, 2021; Mathews, 2010; Vetten, 2003). There was a surge in cases of marital rape occasioned by the Covid-19-induced lockdown which forcibly confined many couples at home. With most income-generating activities temporarily banned, and travel prohibitions and stay-at-home orders in place to contain the spread of the pandemic, many women fell prey to marital rape by their frustrated spouses. The explanation why many women fell victim to marital rape is the institution of the *lobola* (bride price) practised by most indigenous people in the country. Under this system, a man formalises marriage to a woman by making payment to her parents or in laws. Consequently, some men treat their wives as commodities with whom they can have sex whenever they want (Chataika, Interview: 9 May 2022).

Closely linked to this patriarchal chauvinism within households was emotional violence which also became common among men during the lockdown period in Zimbabwe. This form of violence often involves verbal abuse, name calling and belittling of the other. It entails acts of embarrassment, humiliation and disrespect. These acts affect one's sense of self, self-esteem and self-confidence (Ludsin & Vetten, 2005). In September 2020, cases of emotional violence, mostly committed by men, reportedly went up by 80%

"…possibly due to heightened household tensions resulting from confined living conditions and increased financial stresses" (Adult Rape Clinic, September 2020). Thus, the lockdowns that were instituted to curb the spread of the Covid-19 pandemic were accompanied by considerable emotional abuse. Among other things, being confined to the home intensified the levels of tensions in the household leading to partners, mostly husbands, venting off their anger or distress on their female spouses through emotional abuse.

Many women failed to report gender-based violence incidences partly because they could not access referral and support systems owing to lockdown travel restrictions (Chamunogwa, 2021). There were also concerns that if female spouses reported violence by their male counterparts, they risked retaliation and retribution in the form of greater violence. Despite the existence of various laws that protect women from gender-based violence, many were hesitant to report such incidents for fear of losing family income or even their homes, as many were unaware of their property rights. Financial constraints, social stigma, and family pressure all had an impact on a woman's ability to seek legal action. Women's economic disparities and perceptions of what constituted a good woman thus made it difficult for them to even protect themselves from gender-based violence (Ibid).

Women and additional household chores occasioned by the Covid-19 pandemic

For many Zimbabwean women, the Covid-19-induced lockdown exacerbated the already existing unequal burden of care in the households. Prior to the lockdown, many women, especially in the country's rural areas, spent more than four times as many hours per day than men on unpaid care and domestic work (Oxfam, 2020). Pandemic dynamics added more burden of caring for the sick on many women who now had to take care of family members and relatives suffering from Covid-19 and other illnesses, including the elderly, as many hospitals were either closed or admitted emergency cases only as a way of curbing the spread of the virus.

In addition, the closure of schools in an effort to curtail the spread of the Covid-19 pandemic meant that additional time was required to care for children and meet their home schooling needs. In 2020, a Zimbabwe Resilience Building Fund (ZRBF) survey found out that 67% of women in rural Zimbabwe and 54% of men reported a significant increase in time that was now being taken to care for children (Rosen *et al*, 2020). In a CARE International Zimbabwe Rapid Assessment Survey conducted in April 2020, women reported being overwhelmed and working long hours to meet the needs of family members during the lockdown (Masomera & Chigwanda, 2020). Women and girls also provided care support for sick family members in the context of deteriorating health institutions and the high cost of health services during the Covid-19 pandemic (Ibid). Indeed, this constituted an additional burden on women and girls.

Added to these issues, women also formed the majority of frontline health workers, for example, nurses, nurse aides and community health/social workers. They were classified as essential service workers who had to report for duty during the lockdown period. Poor and inadequate personal protective equipment and other below-standard health facilities at government medical institutions often exposed the essential service workers, the majority of who were women, to greater risks of contracting Covid-19. The fact that women were also overrepresented in sectors regarded as essential services, such as retail and agriculture, before and during the lockdown, meant that their level of exposure and risk to infection was very high.

The exponential increase of unpaid care and domestic work impacted on the general welfare of persons with disabilities who were usually cared for by the same women whose burden was increased. The UNESCO Report (2020) on Covid-19 and Disabilities noted that female caregivers of people with disabilities carried the extra burden of looking after the rest of the family. Broadly, this affected the well-being of not only the person with disability but that of the caregiver as well. Unpaid care and domestic work increased considerably during the lockdown, as women and girls were confined at home and were expected to take up more responsibilities of maintaining the household, and providing care to the rest of the family. In most households, women tended to be the ones providing learning guidance to children who were doing distance learning and home schooling when educational institutions were closed down during the lockdown. This was in addition to their traditional household chores, thus an added burden on the part of the women engaged in unpaid domestic care and work. This burden severely compromised women's economic rights as it significantly ate into the time they could have devoted to their own income-generating projects.

Women as victims of economic violence and deprivation

Economic violence was also banal during the Covid-19 period in Zimbabwe. This form of gender-based violence included taking control of a partner's assets, money and other economic resources. Some male partners were reluctant to allow their female partners to work while others who allowed them to do so abused the financial and other proceeds from the work done (Ludsin & Vetten, 2005). In this context, economic abuse or economic deprivation is largely characterised by the perpetrator withholding necessary household finance and preventing his or her spouse from earning money. It can also involve confiscating the money that might have been earned, controlling the whole house and spending money to his or her benefit. Most of the gender-based violence cases went unreported for a number of reasons. First and foremost, gender-based violence was often treated as a private family affair to the extent of being ignored by communities and some government policies. Secondly, since the perpetrators were mainly males, the victims were normally economically dependent on their abusers hence they covered up the violence by not reporting the abusers because of fear that they could lose material support.

In addition, the Covid-19 pandemic had wide-ranging implications for women's livelihoods and rights, which were already under threat before the crisis. The pandemic's effects had a disproportionate impact on women's economic and productive lives compared to men, as women had less access to decent employment and dominated the informal sector and unpaid care work (UN Secretary-General, 2020; Womankind, 2020). In Zimbabwe in 2020, women represented 65% of informal sector workers such as vendors and cross-border traders (Masomera & Chigwanda, 2020). Lockdown restrictions had significant impacts on their livelihoods, as their work often required access to public spaces and social interaction. Furthermore, informal sector workers often relied on daily earnings and had few safety nets, making them increasingly vulnerable when work opportunities were lost during times of emergencies such as the Covid-19-induced lockdown. When the lockdown began, many informal trading places were destroyed and informal traders were arrested along the streets (SAFE, 2020). The police earned notoriety for trashing street vendor stalls and products. Women, who made up the majority of Zimbabwe's informal traders, were disproportionately affected by these efforts (Chitando, 2020;

Shumba *et al*, 2020). Women accused of 'defying' lockdown regulations were sometimes physically assaulted by authorities (DIA, 2020). Border closures also jeopardised the livelihoods of cross-border traders, most of who were women, and disrupted the supply chains of key commodities, contributing to rising prices (Nevill, 2020). During an October 2020 ZRBF survey in Zimbabwe's rural areas, 42% of the respondents reported a complete loss of job or income, and 60% reported a partial loss of job or income over the previous fortnight, all these losses being mainly attributed to the Covid-19 lockdown (Rosen *et al*, 2020).

In metropolitan areas, the lockdown resulted in job losses and a drop in informal sector income. Food insecurity increased in rural areas as a result of the return of unemployed migrants from urban areas and the lack of remittances from family members at various workplaces that had scaled down operations or closed down in line with lockdown measures. The Covid-19 pandemic also had secondary effects on Zimbabwe's agriculture, which employed 70% of women by 2020 (World Bank, 2020). In a July 2020 poll, 85% of coffee producers indicated that the Covid-19 pandemic caused them to lose money, and one in eight said they went to bed hungry because of lack of food (Techno Serve, 2020). The Covid-19 lockdown caused financial instability in households. Plan International (2020) revealed that during the lockdown in Zimbabwe, at least 83.4% of interviewees, the bulk of whom were women, said their households were unable to meet their families' basic necessities, hence their rights to food and livelihoods were severely compromised.

Furthermore, basic food prices soared. This put more strain on household economies, with prices in local currency payments rising by an average of 424% in 2020 (OCHA, 2020d). Since the advent of the Covid-19 pandemic, 74% of respondents in Zimbabwe's rural districts said their household expenses had increased, and 90% said food prices had skyrocketed (Rosen *et al*, 2020). Cases of domestic disputes and violence rose significantly, this being largely caused by an increase in financial instability and household confinement. Typically, social standards and inflexible gender roles imposed the burden of financial obligation for the family on males, while women were responsible for care and home tasks. Men's ability to meet this expectation was constrained by Covid-19 restrictions, which also increased the possibility of violence against their female partners and wives. Moreso, due to Covid-19 restrictions, many women were no longer able to play the mediatory role of supplementing family income through informal work (SAFE, 2020).

In most households in Zimbabwe, husbands had always been the breadwinners. Prevalent cases of economic abuse were those when husbands and male partners, as breadwinners, failed to take care of their wives and children (SAFAIDS, 2009). The fact that women were usually not empowered to decide their own destiny meant that many a time they were economically dependent on their male partners some of whom took advantage of their financial position to be abusive. As a result of a broad range of abuses, many women became captives in their homes.

Violence on women and girls with disabilities

Women and girls with disabilities have always been at a higher risk of violence around the world, with an approximately twice higher risk of intimate partner violence than women without disabilities (Dunkle *et al*, 2018). During the Covid-19 pandemic, women with disabilities across the globe became more vulnerable in various ways. Travel restrictions, for example, prevented care workers from reaching women with disabilities. In this way, women and girls with disabilities were at greater risk of neglect and violence by family members during the Covid-19 pandemic (UN Women, 2020b). While there is limited data on the number of women and girls with disabilities in Zimbabwe who fell victims to violence, there are increasing reports and warnings from women's rights, development, and humanitarian organisations that abuses against women and girls with disabilities increased during the Covid-19 pandemic.

A growing number of women with disabilities contacted human rights organisations over various abuses and vulnerabilities they increasingly experienced during the Covid-19-induced lockdown (SAFE, 2020). Sexual violence by family members, relatives, or neighbours, as well as other forms of abuses, were reported by women with disabilities. Indeed, such abuses became inevitable given the increasing reliance of disabled women on caregivers, mostly relatives and family members who were themselves frustrated and increasingly incapacitated by the Covid-19 lockdown measures (Ibid). Deaf Women Included, an organisation that assisted deaf women and girls as well as those with different impairments, noticed an upsurge in incidences of violence against people with disabilities during the Covid-19 lockdown period. Furthermore, the organisation pointed out that people with disabilities encountered considerable challenges in obtaining services such as health care and rehabilitation throughout the lockdown (Ibid).

In late 2020, the Institute of Community Development (IOCD) in Zimbabwe warned that if the lockdown was extended further, more females with disabilities were likely to commit suicide as a result of stress, depression, and abuse (IOCD, 2020). Given that the movement of many girls and women with disabilities was severely limited by stay-at-home orders passed by the government to curb the spread of the pandemic, the IOCD predicted that violence and abuse against them would treble during the Covid-19 period. The UNFPA Zimbabwe also expressed worry about the higher risk of violence faced by disabled women and girls (UNFPA, 2020). In addition to the increased danger of violence in the limited space of the home, girls and women with disabilities were at higher risk of exploitation and abuse by community members and support providers. As dependants, disabled women and girls also had very limited influence on household response decisions which, when combined with alterations in access to social safety nets, information, and restricted mobility, enhanced the risk of gender-based violence (Ibid).

Sexual abuse of girl children

Schools in Zimbabwe were closed on 24 March 2020 as the government sought to contain the spread of the Covid-19 pandemic. The school closure saw the disruption of the education of more than 4.6 million Zimbabwean children (Moshiri *et al,* 2020). A Plan International (2020b) Rapid Assessment Survey carried out in May 2020 found that 98.2% of children in Zimbabwe were not accessing education during the Covid-19 lockdown. The closure of schools in an effort to curb the spread of the pandemic exposed girls of school-going age to a number of sexual abuses. Children are vulnerable to a variety of abuses outside of the safe atmosphere of schools. The implementation of the lockdown, which included school closures, witnessed a significant rise in gender-based violence in the form of sexual violence of young girls and child marriages. As World Vision, a non-governmental organisation, noted, reported cases of gender-based violence against girls in Zimbabwe more than doubled from the time the lockdown was implemented, with increases in early pregnancies and child marriages being most noticeable (World Vision Zimbabwe, 2020). Among other things, these developments violated many rights of the girl child, including their right to protection (Moshiri *et al*, 2020).

According to Plan International's (2020a) Rapid Assessment Report of Covid-19's secondary effects in Africa, adolescent girls were at higher risk of multiple forms of gender-based violence, including domestic abuse, child marriage, and sexual violence, as well as increased transactional sex as a result of the pandemic's negative economic effects. In normal times, adolescent girls and young women are more vulnerable to intimate partner violence, sexual assault and sexual coercion than older women due to intersecting gender and age inequities, which were exacerbated during the Covid-19 crisis. While many children were largely spared from the direct health impacts of Covid-19, there is evidence that the secondary effects of the pandemic had a profound and long-lasting negative impact on them. Mitigation strategies taken by the Zimbabwean government, including lockdowns and school closures, had multiple direct and indirect negative effects on children's lives, including the disruption of their access to education and other essential services. Women's rights organisations saw an increase in such reports and campaigners believed that many more cases went undetected due to movement restrictions (SAFE, 2020). In addition, prior to the advent of the pandemic, schools were able to report girls who were absent and those who were at risk of abuse or early pregnancy to the police or education boards, which was not possible during the lockdown when educational institutions were closed (Masekesa, 2020).

Given the significant rise in early child marriages owing in part to the Covid-19 lockdowns around the world from 2020, the UNFPA projected that 13 million extra child marriages would have occurred before 2030 (UNFPA, 2020b). Evidence from East and Southern Africa also confirmed the rise in child marriages during the Covid-19 period (UN Women, 2020b). The imposition of the Covid-19 lockdown in Zimbabwe from March 2020 also witnessed multiple reports of child weddings in Zimbabwe. These reports were mostly provided by NGO workers, traditional leaders and village health workers. In the Manicaland Province alone, at least 415 girls dropped out of examination classes during the Covid-19 lockdown period mainly due to early marriage and pregnancy (Tapfumaneyi, 2020a). In some parts of the country, girls who were at risk of, or those who had undergone child marriage, were admitted and offered protection at Gender-Based Violence Shelters availed by some child rights watchdogs (Sachiti, 2020; UNCT, 2020). At one of the shelters, five girls in the age range of 15-16 years were admitted after being exposed to underage marriage and sexual violence by their new 'husbands' (SAFE, 2020).

Furthermore, the increase in household poverty owing to the countrywide Covid-19-induced lockdown led some young girls to engage in sex work (Matiashe, 2020b). In particular, there were reports of increasing numbers of young girls engaging in transactional sex in return for cash, food or even sanitary products (Plan International, 2020b). From March to June 2020, for instance, Roots Africa, a human rights organisation, received 350 reports of children having sex in exchange for money or gifts in Zimbabwe's Mazowe District alone, a figure that doubled that of the previous year (Matiashe, 2020a).

The plight of female commercial sex workers

Sex workers faced particular challenges as curfews and bar closures meant a critical loss of business for them. Their livelihood rights were consequently jeopardised as they struggled to make ends meet. These developments led many of them to meet clients in more secluded and less safe places (Salamander Trust, 2020). In these secluded places, many commercial sex workers risked being abused by rowdy clients, some of whom refused to pay them while others actually turned violent (Ibid).

There were many reports of sex workers being harassed by security officials enforcing Covid-19 lockdown measures across the African continent. In April 2020, for instance, the Global Network of Sex Work Projects (NSWP) ran a global study to analyse the effects of the Covid-19 pandemic on sex workers. The organisation received 156 submissions in all, including 22 from 13 African countries. During Covid-19-induced lockdowns, the sex workers alleged, the law-enforcement officers employed a variety of oppressive means against them, including increased raids, arrests and prosecutions (NSWP, 2020). According to SAFE (2020), there were instances of police officers committing sexual violence against commercial sex workers. The incidents occurred after sex workers had reportedly violated lockdown regulations. There were also reports of sex workers being arrested for breaking curfew and then getting raped by the police (Ibid).

Given that commercial sex work desperately needs the support of medical facilities such as condoms and other drugs to prevent and treat Sexually-Transmitted Infections, the health of many sex workers was in severe jeopardy owing to the Covid-19-induced lockdown measures. The travel bans and stay-at-home orders meant that they could not easily travel to health institutions to access contraceptives and treatment. In addition, as some clinics and hospitals either closed or suspended some services in an effort to contain the spread of the Covid-19 pandemic, many commercial sex workers were unable to access free condoms, thereby increasing the risk of unplanned pregnancies and contracting Sexually Transmitted Infections and HIV/AIDs (Ibid).

Conclusion

This chapter has demonstrated that the Covid-19 pandemic perpetuated the longstanding gender inequalities in Zimbabwe in particular and the world in general. These disparities largely disadvantaged ordinary and marginalised women and children, most of who suffered various forms of violence and abuse that were occasioned by the advent of the pandemic. The first section illustrated how frustrations caused by the Covid-19 lockdowns contributed to the rising cases of physical, psychological and sexual abuse of women within households. The second section articulated the way women were overloaded with household chores owing to pandemic pressures resulting in many of them failing to embark on their own income-generating activities. In this way, many women's socio-economic rights and freedoms were severely compromised resulting in them continuing to be dependent on men. The third section examined how women were economically disempowered by, among other things, the closure of small-scale businesses in which they were predominant in an effort by the government to curb the spread of the pandemic. The last three sections focused on particular groups of vulnerable females, namely women and girls with disabilities, girl children, and commercial sex workers, and showed how the pandemic made their lives more vulnerable to gender-based violence.

References

Amnesty International (2020) 'Southern African Development Community: Regional leaders must fix the deteriorating human rights situation across the region,' Available at: https://www.amnesty.org/en/latest/news/2020/08/sadc-regional-leaders-must-fix-the-deteriorating-human-rights-situation-across-the-region/, Accessed 28 April 2022.

Anderton, C.H. (2020) 'The other virus: Covid-19 and violence against civilians,' in: *Peace Economics: Peace Science and Public Policy*, Volume 26, Issue 3, Available at: https://www.degruyter.com/view/journals/peps/ahead-of/print/article-10.1515-peps-2020-0039/article-10.1515-peps-2020-0039.xml, Accessed 3 May 2022.

Bishop, A. (2020) 'Vulnerability amplified: The impact of the Covid-19 pandemic on LGBTIQ people,' Available at: https://outrightinternational.org/sites/default/files, Accessed 12 April 2022.

Burke, J. & Chingono, N. (2020) 'Zimbabwean MDC activists abducted and sexually assaulted', Available at: https://www.theguardian.com/world/2020/may/17/zimbabwean-mdc-activists-abducted-and-sexually-assaulted, Accessed 11 April 2022.

Cassim, J. (7 October 2020) 'Zimbabwe parents face huge burden from school reopening', Available at: https://www.aa.com.tr/en/africa, Accessed 19 April 2022.

Chamunogwa, A. (2021) *The impact of Covid-19 on socio-economic rights in Zimbabwe*, Harare: Zimbabwe Peace Project.

Chitando, M. (2020) 'Narrowing the "physical distance" between public health policies and gender: An analysis of government responses to Covid-19 in Zimbabwe and South Africa,' in: *African Journal of Governance and Development*, Volume 9, Special Issue 1.1, Available at: https://journals.ukzn.ac.za/index.php/jgd/article/view/1773/169, Accessed 3 April 2022.

Democracy in Africa (15 June 2020) 'Abductions, brutality, and demolitions: When the state becomes more harmful than Covid-19,' Available at: http://democracyinafrica.org, Accessed 26 April 2022.

Dunkle, K. van der Heijden, I. Stern, E. & Chirwa, E. (2018) 'Disability and violence against women and girls: Emerging evidence from the What Works to Prevent Violence against Women and Girls Global Programme,' Available at: https://www.whatworks.co.za/documents/publications/195-disability-brief-whatworks-, Accessed 6 April 2022.

Fraser, E. (2020) 'Impact of the Covid-19 pandemic on violence against women and girls,' VAWG Helpdesk Research Report Number 284, Available at: https://www.frontlinedefenders.org/en/campaign/covid-19-attacks-hrds-time-pandemic, Accessed 13 April 2022.

Institute of Community Development (IOCD) Zimbabwe (2020) 'The impact of Covid-19 on women with disabilities in Masvingo urban, Zimbabwe,' Available at: http://kubatana.net/2020/05/12/the-impact-of-covid-19-on-women-with-disabilities-wwds-in-masvingo-urban/, Accessed 17 April 2022.

Jachi, F. (2020) 'Guardians urged to protect children from cyber bullying', Available at: https://www.zbcnews.co.zw/guardians-urged-to-protect-children-from-cyber-bullying, Accessed 3 May 2022.

Macheka, M.T. & Nhongo, K. (2021) 'Women's access to reproductive health services during the Covid-19 pandemic in Zimbabwe,' in: S. Kenis & M. Shivdas (eds.) *Gender and human rights in the context of the Covid-19 pandemic: Findings from four countries*, Raoul Wallenberg Institute of Human Rights and Humanitarian Law, Available at: https://www.google.com/search?q=Macheka%2CM%2CT.%2C+and+Nhongo%2C+K.%2C, Accessed 19 April 2022.

Martin, R. & Ahlenback, V. (2020) 'Evidence synthesis: Secondary impacts of Covid-19 on gender-based violence against women and girls in Zimbabwe,' Funded by Stopping Abuse and Female Exploitation (SAFE), Zimbabwe Technical Assistance Facility, Available at: https://www.google.com/search?q=Martin%2C+R.+%26+Ahlenback%2CV.+%282020%29+ Accessed 20 March 2022.

Masekesa, C. (26 September 2020) 'Shock as Grade 7 pupils fall pregnant during lockdown,' Available at: https://nehandaradio.com/2020/09/26/, Accessed 30 April 2022.

Masomera, A. & Chigwanda, E. (2020) 'CARE rapid gender analysis for Covid-19,' Harare: CARE International Zimbabwe.

Matiashe, F. (2020a) 'Zimbabwe makes it illegal for schools to expel pregnant girls,' Available at: https://www.reuters.com/article/us-zimbabwe-education-women-idUSKBN25L1UW, Accessed 2 May 2022.

Matiashe, F. (2020b) 'Zimbabweans turn to sex work amid economic crisis and Covid-19,' Available at: https://uk.reuters.com/article/us-zimbabwe-women-rights-trfn, Accessed 3 May 2022.

Moshiri, L. Gasasira, A. & Gijzen, H. (2020) 'Children's learning and welfare should be at the centre of decisions around school re-opening, UNICEF Zimbabwe,' Available at: https://www.unicef.org/zimbabwe/stories/childrens-learning-and-welfare-should-be-centre-decisions-around-school-re-opening, Accessed 1 May 2022.

Mukeredzi, T. & Mashininga, K. (22 July 2020) 'Ministry suspends all contact teaching in universities,' in: *University World News: Africa Edition*, Available at: https://www.universityworldnews.com/post.php?story=20200722075158726, Accessed 3 May 2022.

Nevill, C. (11 June 2020) 'We cannot stay indoors or we will die of hunger: Corona virus fears mount for Zimbabwe's urban poor,' Available at: https://insight.wfp.org/we-cant-stay-indoors-or-we-ll-die-of-hunger-coronavirus-fears-mount-for-zimbabwe-s-urban-poor-1a4b40cc4299, Accessed 2 May 2022.

News dzeZimbabwe (9 October 2020b) 'Pupils turn to sex, drugs,' Available at: http://www.newsdzezimbabwe.co.uk/2020/10/pupils-turn-to-sex-drugs.html, Accessed 12 April 2022.

News dzeZimbabwe (14 October 2020a) 'Two Mabvuku women kill robber,' Available at: http://www.newsdzezimbabwe.co.uk/2020/10/two-mabvuku-women-kill-robber.html, Accessed 12 April 2022.

Network for Sex Work Projects (NSWP) (2020) 'Covid-19 impact survey: Africa,' Available at: https://www.nswp.org/sites/nswp.org/files/covid19-impact, Accessed 14 April 2022.

Office of the UN High Commissioner for Human Rights (2020) 'UN rights experts fear Uganda is using Covid-19 emergency powers to target LGBT people,' Available at: https://www.ohchr.org/EN/NewsEvents/Pages/DisplayNews.aspx?NewsID=25832&LangID=E, Accessed 2 May 2022.

Oxfam (2020) *Unlocking sustainable development in Africa by addressing unpaid care and domestic work*, London: Oxfam.

Plan International (2020a) 'Under siege: Impact of Covid-19 on girls in Africa,' Available at: https://www.plan.ie/under-siege-impact-of-covid-19, Accessed 26 April 2022.

Plan International (2020b) 'Impacts of Covid-19 on girls' rights and reproductive health,' Available at: https://plan-international.org/jordan/publications/impacts-of-covid-19-on-girls-rights-and-reproductive-health/, Accessed 11 May 2022.

Rosen, H. Sundsmo, A. Tirivanhu, D. Chevo, T. & Musandu, N. (2020) 'Resilience Knowledge Hub, Covid-19 Risk Communications Campaign: Knowledge Attitude and Practice Assessment,' by The Zimbabwe Resilience Building Fund, Available at: https://www.resilienceknowledgecentre.co.zw/sites/default/files/2020-, Accessed 10 May 2022.

Sachiti, R. (13 April 2020) 'Lockdown with your abuser: Over 700 GBV in 11 days,' Available at: https://www.herald.co.zw/lockdown-with-your-abuser-over-700-gbv-in-11-days/, Accessed 16 April 2022.

Stopping Abuse and Female Exploitation (SAFE) (2020) 'Violence against women and girls during the Covid-19 crisis in Zimbabwe: Analysis of practice-based data from Women's Coalition of Zimbabwe, Stopping Abuse and Female Exploitation (SAFE) Zimbabwe Technical Assistance Facility,' Available at: http://www.adultrapeclinic.org.zw/wp-content/uploads/2020/09/SAFE-Report-on-Gender-Based-Violence-Data-in-Zimbabwe-during-C19-for-publication-with-log, Accessed 2 May 2022.

Salamader Trust (2020) 'Our voices: Impact of Covid-19 on women's and girls' sexual and reproductive health and rights in Eastern and Southern Africa,' Available at: https://salamandertrust.net/wp-content/uploads/2020/09, Accessed 13 May 2022.

Shumba, K. Nyamaruze, P. Nyambuya, V.P. & Meyer-Weitz, A. (2020) 'Politicising the Covid-19 pandemic in Zimbabwe: Implications for public health and governance,' in: *African Journal of Governance and Development*, Volume 9, Special Issue 1.1, Available at: https://journals.ukzn.ac.za/index.php/jgd/article/view/1807/1671, Accessed 4 April 2022.

Smith, J. (2020) 'Violence against women in Africa spikes during Covid-19,' Available at:

http://www.vanguardafrica.com/blog/2020/6/18/violence-against-women-in-africa-spikes-during-covid-19-new-africa-woman-magazine-june-18, Accessed 11 April 2022.

Tapfumaneyi, R. (2020a) 'Over 400 girls drop out of Manicaland schools due to lockdown pregnancies,' Available at: https://www.newzimbabwe.com/over-400-girls-drop-out-of-manicaland-schools-due-to-lockdown-pregnancies/, Accessed 2 May 2022.

Tapfumaneyi, R. (2020b) 'Sex for water in Mabvuku-Tafara,' Available at: https://www.newzimbabwe.com/sex-for-water-in-mabvuku-tafara/, Accessed 2 May 2022.

Techno Serve (2020) 'Coffee farmers and Covid-19 in Zimbabwe: Survey round 1,' Available at: https://www.technoserve.org/wp-content/uploads/2020/11/Survey-Rounds-1-3-Coffee-Farmers-Covid-19-In-Zimbabwe.pdf, Accessed 13 April 2022.

Tshuma, A. (2020) Girls vulnerable as Covid-19 drives child marriages,' Available at: https://genderlinks.org.za/news/girls-future-at-stake-as-covid-19-drought-drive-child-marriages, Accessed 5 May 2022.

United Nations Office for the Coordination of Humanitarian Affairs (OCHA) (2020a) 'Zimbabwe cluster status: Protection (Gender-based violence),' Available at: https://reports.unocha.org/en/country/zimbabwe/card/2XxB9GOV93/, Accessed 28 April 2022.

United Nations Office for the Coordination of Humanitarian Affairs (OCHA) (2020b) 'Zimbabwe Situation Report, July 2020' Available at: https://reliefweb.int/sites/reliefweb.int/files/resources, Accessed 1 May 2022.

United Nations Office for the Coordination of Humanitarian Affairs (OCHA) (2020c) 'Zimbabwe Situation Report, August 2020,' Available at: https://reliefweb.int/sites/reliefweb.int/files/resources, Accessed 1 May 2022.

United Nations Office for the Coordination of Humanitarian Affairs (OCHA) (2020d) 'Zimbabwe Situation Report, September 2020, Available at: https://reliefweb.int/sites/reliefweb.int/files/resources, Accessed 1 May 2022.

United Nations Population Fund (UNFPA) (2020a) 'Lockdown with your abuser: Over 700 GBV in 11 days', Available at:

https://zimbabwe.unfpa.org/en/news/lockdown-your-abuser-over-700-gbv-11-days, Accessed 3 May 2022.
United Nations Population Fund (UNFPA) (2020b) 'Millions more cases of violence, child marriage, female genital mutilation, unintended pregnancy expected due to the Covid-19 pandemic,' Available at: https://www.unfpa.org/news/millions-more-cases-violence-child-marriage-female-genital-mutilation-unintended-pregnancies, Accessed 19 April 2022.
UN Secretary General (2020) 'Policy brief: The impact of Covid-19 on women,' Available at: https://www.un.org/sexualviolenceinconflict/wp-content/uploads/report, Accessed 16 April 2022.
UN Women (2020a) 'The shadow pandemic: Violence against women during Covid-19,' Available at: https://www.unwomen.org/en/news/in-focus/in-focus-gender-equality-in-covid-19-response/violence-against-women-during-covid-19 , Accessed 29 March 2022.
UN Women (2020b) 'Covid-19: Ending violence against women and girls. Key priorities and interventions for effective response and recovery. Policy Brief: UN Women East and Southern Africa,' Available at: https://www2.unwomen.org , Accessed 12 April 2022.
Womankind (2020) 'Womankind response to IDC inquiry on the impact of Corona virus (Covid-19) on developing countries,' Available at: https://committees.parliament.uk/writtenevidence/1931/pdf, Accessed 22 April 2022.
World Vision Zimbabwe (2020) 'Covid-19 aftershocks and their impact on girls' education in Zimbabwe,' Available at: https://www.wvi.org/sites/default/files, Accessed 21 April 2022.

Chapter 15

The Church's Pursuit of Human Rights, Freedoms and Liberties during the Covid-19 Pandemic in Africa

Cuthbert Mavedzenge

Introduction

Responses to the Covid-19 pandemic by various African countries generated tension and challenges between national governments and the church on the approach to reducing the spread of the virus and the need to protect human rights. The social life and interactions of people were greatly disrupted by the banning of gatherings and prohibitions of mobility, both nationally and internationally. Religious congregations were also prohibited and churches turned to the social media for virtual ministry which was not always accessible to all people. Schools were closed, with some institutions turning on to e-learning which again was not accessible to many, especially in Africa where many economies had been underperforming for some time. Many statutory instruments were gazetted by governments with the parliaments of many countries giving their executives extraordinary powers to deal with the pandemic.

Amid this crisis, the church became the voice of the voiceless. Human rights violations became the norm and most people suffered due to the drastic regulations that were imposed to contain the spread of the global pandemic. The church's work in support of human rights was essentially connected to its mission to proclaim the good news. Human rights and the mission of the church are inseparable. The vocation of every church is to promote equal worth for all human persons. The church was the focal point in championing human rights in most African countries during the period of the Covid-19 pandemic. It is against this background that this chapter argues that the church was a critical stakeholder in the pursuit of human rights, freedoms, and liberties during the Covid-19 pandemic in Africa.

Security sector brutalities and criticism from the church

The impacts of the Covid-19 pandemic were multi-faceted and touched every sphere of human life. The pandemic was securitised and weaponised by most African governments, much to the detriment of people's rights, liberties and freedoms. In response to the pandemic, several African governments introduced severe restrictions on many aspects people's lives. The enforcement of pandemic curtailment measures triggered arbitrary arrests, beatings, torture, and extrajudicial killings by government forces in Nigeria, Kenya, Rwanda and South Africa, among other African countries (Egwu, 2020).

According to the National Human Rights Commission of Nigeria (2020), Nigerian security forces killed 18 people in the early weeks of lockdown enforcement. The Commission added that most of the violations witnessed during the period arose as a result of excessive or disproportionate use of force, abuse of power, corruption, and non-adherence to national and international laws. Egwu (2020) observed that the Covid-19 pandemic perpetuated the culture of police brutality and impunity and resulted in gross human rights violations in Nigeria. Police barbarity was also shown in some cases where citizens were arrested, tortured, and killed for the slightest of offenses such as having an expensive phone (Ibid). In the wake of these brutalities during the lockdown, Nigerian religious leaders spoke out against the use of force by the police. Henry Ihuoma, a parishioner at St. Jude's Catholic Church, for example, pointed out: "The police brutality in our country is unacceptable and it is irresponsible for the police to be the ones killing those they are meant to protect" (Ibid).

These sentiments were echoed by Father Aniedi Okure who noted: "In other countries, the police are trained to protect the people and keep law and order, and not to kill them as we have in Nigeria and other African countries. And this was happening even before the Corona virus" (Ibid). Speaking on the growing brutality by security details, Okure said the police in Africa were created along with colonial enterprise and trained to suppress the people. Since independence, he noted, that culture had not been changed. He argued: "The state still uses the police to suppress people while the politicians use the police to suppress the people and their opponents" (Ibid). Sister Eucharia Madueke of the Sisters of Notre Dame de Namur also lamented:

> The police is never for the people but for institutions that created it. I knew it was going to be very brutal because the security agents who are going to be implementing this are not interested in the people…In Nigeria, they say police is your friend, but that is not the case. With the number of people they have killed during the lockdown, how will I trust the police again? When you are not trained in human rights, the chances of violating human rights will be high. I think there is something wrong with the way security agents are trained in the world, including Nigeria (Egwe, 2020).

Commenting on security sector ruthlessness during the Covid-19 pandemic, Obinana Udeh, a parishioner at Thomas More Catholic Chaplaincy, described Nigeria as a nation that created a lot of laws but was not guided by them. He moaned: "Police brutality has always been with us even before [the] Corona virus, and every new regulation by the government is always used as an excuse by the police to brutalise members of the society" (Ibid). For Udeh, the policing system needed to be evaluated and corrected because the police were created for the people and not against the people, and people did not have to continue overlooking the consequences of their actions (Ibid). In the wake of these killings during the lockdown and numerous reports of brutality, Nigerian priests were speaking out and condemning the use of force by the police.

The church also actively supported public demonstrations that were held against police brutality during the enforcement of Covid-19 lockdown provisions in Nigeria in October 2020. The demonstrations began when citizens protested against the bestial conduct of the Special Anti-Robbery Squad (SARS), an elite police unit that had been formed in 1992 to specifically deal with violent crime. As the unit gained notoriety for brutally ill-treating citizens, particularly during the enforcement of Covid-19 alleviation protocols, protests erupted, mostly led by the youths calling for the disbanding of SARS in particular and police reforms in general (Asadu, 29 October 2020). In support of the protesters, the Catholic Church held an outdoor mass on 18 October 2020 at the Lekki Toll Gate, the major site of the demonstrations in Lagos (Ibid). The Catholic Bishops' Conference of Nigeria also put its weight behind the anti-SARS campaign and called on government authorities to "listen to the cry for justice so that peace can reign in our country" (Ibid). Some 48 hours after the outdoor mass, Lagos authorities declared a 24-hour curfew to stop the growing protests. Soldiers went on to storm the Lekki Toll Gate and opened fire on the peaceful protesters, most of whom were sitting down and singing the national anthem. People were badly injured while about 12 demonstrators died. The Catholic Bishops' Conference of Nigeria publicly expressed concern at the sight of soldiers in uniform unleashing live ammunition on defenceless citizens (Ibid).

Commenting on the Lekki Toll Gate massacre, Fr. Emmanuel Bekomson, a Catholic priest from the Archdiocese of Calabar in southern Nigeria's Cross River State, who had consistently condemned police brutality on his social media accounts, said it was the duty of the church "to provide spiritual care and support for her children despite the circumstances" (Ibid). He described the church as a mother filled with sympathy and empathy, adding that it was the responsibility of the mother to provide spiritual care and support for her children in all situations of life (Ibid). Bishop Mattew Kukah of the Sokoto Diocese challenged Nigerian President Muhammadu Buhari to address the nation on many problems the country was facing, including police brutality in the enforcement of Covid-19 lockdown provisions, police reform, corruption and nepotism. President Buhari eventually bowed to pressure and gave a nationwide broadcast following the attack on protesters (Ibid).

From these critical interventions by the clergy in Nigeria, some insights can be drawn on the relations between the church and law-enforcement agents during crisis situations such as the Covid-19 pandemic as far as the upholding of human rights is concerned. From the concerns raised, it appears that the church mandated itself to mediate between the police and the civilians to ensure that human rights, liberties and freedoms were safeguarded. In this regard, the church had the moral capacity to open dialogue involving the police, communities, youths, and families and advocate for cooperation and coexistence for the benefit of lawfulness, peace and stability. Where tension arose after the police had blundered, the church could also play the important role of calming nerves by reaching out to people through its instrument of grass-root orientation. As Egwe (2020: 1) notes, such mediation processes could proceed as follows:

> … [The church] talks to the family of the deceased young man or woman, and so, when the nerves are calm, we can now move to the second stage, which is that of mediation by talking to the government, police, community, and when this happens, you discover that everybody is brought to the table. When it goes into the level of mediation, the police will begin to acknowledge that some of its officers were wrong in the first place and sometimes the officers involved are disciplined.

From the concerns raised against the police in Nigeria during the Covid-19 pandemic, the church also saw itself as duty-bound to challenge and advise the government on issues of compassion in law-enforcement because not every problem is addressed by using force or firing gun shots. This explains why some church officials advised the Nigerian government on the need for the police to be retrained especially in the use of arms to ensure that civilians were not killed extra-judicially. Above all, the church felt that the government needed to retrain the police and make them understand that their mission was to protect the people and ensure that the law was observed.

On the part of South Africa, the South African Council of Churches (SACC), an inter-denominational forum comprising 36 member churches and organisations, and other faith leaders also held protests against police brutality during the enforcement of Covid-19 curtailment regulations. On Sunday 7 June 2020, for example, the SACC and other church officials congregated to condemn the high-handedness of law-enforcement agents that had resulted in the deaths of Collins Khosa in South Africa, George Floyd in the United States, and others. Khosa was reportedly killed by the South African National Defence Force (SANDF) soldiers who were on lockdown duties. The SACC strongly condemned the killing of people by security operatives, saying it was reminiscent of apartheid (Karrim, 7 June 2020). As the SACC General Secretary, Bishop Malusi Mpumlwana, bemoaned: "It feels like we have been here before, yes, in apartheid days; or in George Floyd's Minneapolis! What a week to announce this 'No One to Blame' verdict" (Ibid: 1).

The 7 June 2020 event was organised in such a way that protests took place in Pretoria while prayers were conducted in Cape Town. The protests took place at St Alban's Anglican Cathedral in Pretoria while prayers were conducted by Archbishop Thabo Makgobo at St George's Anglican Cathedral in Cape Town. Moulana Abdul Khaliq Ebrahim Allie of the Muslim Judicial Council also took part along with other faith leaders. Protesters marched into Pretoria, the nation's capital, for what was arguably the city's largest demonstration yet against police brutality. Authorities estimated that up to 200 000 people participated in the protests. During the demonstrations, the names of civilians who had died at the hands of law-enforcement agents on Covid-19 containment duties were announced. In all, 12 people had been killed, including Petrus Miggels, a 55-year-old male who was killed in Ravensmead, Cape

Town, on 27 March 2020; Sibusiso Amos, a 40-year-old male, who was murdered in Valorous, Ekurhuleni, on 29 March 2020; Adane Emmanuel, a male who died in Isipingo, Durban, on 2 April 2020; Robyn Montsumi, a 39-year-old female, killed at Mowbray Police Station on 12 April 2020; and Collins Khosa, a 40-year-old male, who was killed in Alexandra Suburb, Johannesburg, on 10 April 2020 (*News 24*, 7 June 2020).

In Uganda, the clergy was also deeply involved in monitoring human rights infringements committed by security operatives on alleged Covid-19 lockdown violators. An investigation conducted by the Justice and Peace Commissions (JPC) of the Catholic Archdiocese of Gulu and Lira Diocese in Uganda in April 2020 established that the Covid-19 lockdown had come with torture, sexual violence, unfair arrests, and deaths in police custody, among other serious violations of human rights (Aineah, 20 April 2021). In a report shared by the Denis Hurley Peace Institute (DHPI), which commissioned the study across the two regions, there was a call for action against the perpetrators of the crimes (Ibid). The majority of respondents in the study described the human rights situation during the Covid-19 lockdown in both Gulu and Lira as very bad and characterised by torture; cruel, inhuman or degrading treatment; sexual violence; and excessive use of force. The investigation also revealed deaths in custody, and denial of access to information regarding Covid-19, among other things (Ibid). In its recommendations, the JPC proposed the formation of joint advocacy by both civil society organisations and religious leaders to address the human rights violations that were committed. They also proposed that individuals who committed human rights violations should be traced and held accountable for their actions. Furthermore, they called upon the Ugandan government to compensate the victims of alleged human rights abuses. In addition, they encouraged the Ugandan police force to undergo retraining on human rights and the rule of law (Ibid).

This section has illustrated the involvement of church organisations in safeguarding people's rights during the Covid-19 pandemic in Africa. In particular, the church was very vocal against police and army brutalities during the enforcement of Covid-19 containment measures. In most cases, church leaders teamed up to make representations to governments to reign in their security operatives and reorient them to pursue a rights-based approach when enforcing Covid-19 lockdown provisions.

The church's concern at rights to food and health during the Covid-19 pandemic

The rights to good health and food are very critical to human existence. As the Corona virus was wreaking havoc around the world, many ordinary people were in desperate need for protective materials as well as hospital facilities and medication for those who had been infected. Worse still, many people were left severely food insecure owing to the imposition of Covid-19 containment measures such as informal sector closures, stay-at-home orders and travel bans. The church was also very active in reminding African governments not to abrogate their mandate to ensure the rights of citizens to food and good health even during times of emergencies.

During the Covid-19 lockdowns across the African continent, the right to good health for many ordinary people was acutely desecrated by government resource challenges and incompetence as well as corruption on the part of its officials, among other factors. In most African countries, hospital bed capacities were critically limited. Hospitals in Africa are usually understaffed and lack appropriate resources compared with the Global North (*Mail & Guardian*, 11 June 2020). Healthcare workers in Malawi, for instance, experienced discrimination and there were protests over salaries and lack of personal protective equipment (Masina, 23 April 2020). With all these challenges, the church pointed out the need for African countries to improve their healthcare systems beyond the response to Covid-19. Prioritisation of care resources such as Intensive Care Unit (ICU) beds and ventilators for Covid-19 patients also raised significant ethical concerns in countries such as Uganda and Zimbabwe (*Mail & Guardian*, 11 June 2020).

In Uganda, an investigation conducted by the Justice and Peace Commissions (JPC) of the Catholic Archdiocese of Gulu and Lira Diocese in April 2020 bewailed the inadequate access to health and protective health materials like face masks and sanitisers in the country by many citizens (Aineah, 20 April 2021). In addition, Uganda only had one ICU bed per 1 million people at the start of the first wave of Covid-19 infections while Zimbabwe was not much better off with only about 25 ventilators the whole country of more than 15 million people (*Mail & Guardian*, 11 June 2020). The JPC report also regretted the inadequate food supply to the local population among other inequalities that were experienced during the Covid-19 lockdown. Most shops had been closed as well as many informal businesses and this resulted in high unemployment rates and chronic food insecurity (Aineah, 20 April 2022).

In an effort to address issues of food insecurity brought about by the Covid-19 lockdown, some Ugandan church leaders urged the government to give preference to vulnerable sections of the population. Archbishop Stephen Samuel Kaziimba of the Church of Uganda, for example, requested that food distribution by Uganda's National Covid-19 Taskforce prioritise HIV/AIDS patients, many of whom had not been able to access their anti-retroviral treatment due to the lockdown (Mukhaye, 8 May 2020). The Chairperson of the National Forum for People Living with HIV/AIDS Network in Uganda, Dr Stephen Waititi, said the major challenge faced by HIV patients was the failure to access their medication and lack of food, adding:

> Some patients had missed taking their medication because they had nothing to eat. You know HIV/AIDS medicine is strong and cannot be taken on an empty stomach. The church respects the right to life regardless of the status of an individual. It is concerned about the basic needs of the people (Ibid: 1).

South Africa, like most African countries, was also unable to adequately provide its citizens with safety nets such as food aid during the Covid-19 pandemic with corruption being blamed for contributing significantly towards the crisis. President Cyril Ramaphosa warned government officials and business people who were enriching themselves during the Covid-19 crisis through corrupt activities. Ramaphosa fumed: "Corruption during a national disaster is a particularly heinous type of crime, and perpetrators are going to be dealt with decisively and harshly" (Isilow, 5 August 2020: 1). In 2020, South Africa had the highest number of Covid-19 cases in Africa and was the eighth most-affected country globally with 650 749 cases and 15 499 deaths (Ibid). Many company officials in South Africa were interrogated for corruption in Covid-19-related contracts. These companies were probed by the Special Investigations Unit for tender irregularities linked to personal protective equipment contracts for a 500 billion rand (over US$34.4 billion) Covid-19 scheme (Ibid).

Church leaders across South Africa protested against Covid-19-related corruption as several companies and officials were being investigated for alleged fraud. The South African Council of Churches was proactive in the fight against this virus-related corruption. Speaking at an anti-corruption webinar attended by several church leaders, Bishop Malusi Mpumlwana, the Secretary General of the South African Council of Churches, for example, expressed concern at this form of graft, arguing that it jeopardised the safety of people in need (Ibid). He urged citizens to confront corruption at all levels of society. Some of the complaints raised against these companies and individuals included corruption related to the manufacturing of face masks, distribution of food parcels, and siphoning funds fraudulently through fake awareness campaigns. Mpumlwana added: "We the churches of South Africa, together with our congregations, say corruption will not be our heritage or identity" (Ibid).

This section highlighted the role played by the church in ensuring the right to food and good health for marginalised sections of the population during the Covid-19 pandemic in Africa. Many people were food insecure while their health was severely threatened by the pandemic. The incompetence of many governments and corruption on the part of some officials aggravated the situation. During these dire times, churches across the continent did not tire when it came to pressuring governments to put their houses in order and alleviate the plight of downtrodden citizens. Some churches even took matters into their own hands by organising food handouts which they distributed to needy people.

The church and gender-based violence during the Covid-19 period

Before the Covid-19 pandemic, gender-based violence had already become a serious human rights concern in most African countries. The pandemic contributed significantly to the spike in cases of gender-based violence in Kenya, Uganda, Nigeria, South Africa and Zimbabwe, among other African countries. Gender-based violence in these countries, in which women were mostly the victims, was worsened by government restrictions intended to curb the Corona virus. The explanations for the increase in gender-based violence during this period are quite varied: movement restrictions made it impossible for women to leave abusive spouses while increased interpersonal and economic stress resulted in rising intimate partner violence. School closures also drove many adolescent girls and young women into prostitution or temptations to transactional sex with older men in exchange for gifts, money or food. School closures also corresponded with an increase in child marriages, as lockdowns limited access to services on rights as well as sexual and reproductive health issues. Families had not been used to staying together for a long time as was the case during the lockdown periods. In many cases, confinement to the home as decreed by travel bans and stay-at-home orders resulted in the abuse of women and children.

In the Southern African region, church leaders expressed great concern at the rising cases of gender-based violence from the onset of the Covid-19 lockdowns that were declared by governments in an effort to contain the spread of the pandemic. In mid-May 2020, for example, three women were reportedly killed by their spouses in Lusaka, the Zambian capital (Nzwili, 19 May 2020). As women's organisations cried out to the Zambian government for redress, church authorities weighed in and urged their followers to shun violence and use the lockdown period to consolidate family ties. As Bishop George Zumaire Lungu, the President of the Zambian Bishops' Conference, advised: "This is the time when families need to sober up, unite and allow the nation to fight the common enemy, Covid-19" (Ibid).

In neighbouring Zimbabwe, a number of programmes were set in motion by various stakeholders, including the government, the private sector and the churches, to raise public awareness against gender-based violence during the lockdown period. The Zimbabwe Bishops' Justice and Peace Commission, for example, was very active in this regard (Global Fund, 25 November 2021; Nzwili, 1 December 2020). The Roman Catholic Jesuits at Silveira House also used national radio stations to mobilise the general public to shun domestic violence (Nzwili, 1 December 2020).

Similarly, in South Africa, where Covid-19 had infected over 97 000 people and killed 1 930 by mid-June 2020, President Cyril Ramaphosa declared gender-based violence a "second pandemic in the country" (Allen, 23 June 2020: 1). The Southern African Catholic Bishops' Conference (SACBC) Justice and Peace Commission also expressed concern at the surge in gender-based violence in South Africa during the Covid-19 period (Ibid). The bishops emphasised the importance of an inclusive approach to gender-based violence and femicide and urged government departments, the business sector, and civil society to pool their financial resources along with ordinary citizens in fighting this problem which had seen at least 21 women and children being murdered in South Africa during the Level 3 lockdown in June 2020 alone. The bishops pledged to ensure that churches continued to work towards the restoration of a harmonious social fabric by pushing for change in "toxic masculinities" and social norms that propelled gender-based violence (Ibid: 1). They called on all parishes to provide care and preach a clear message that God is against violence inflicted by men on women and children. They also condemned the culture of bystanders that needed to be eradicated and argued that gender-based violence thrived in a climate of silence. The bishops also urged the government to prosecute the perpetrators of gender-based violence (Ibid). The South African Council of Churches (SACC) concurred and noted that cases of domestic abuse in the region had reached frightening levels, with the survivors living in lockdown with their abusers. On 9 May 2020, the SACC released a pastoral letter calling upon all its members, including the Catholic Bishops' Conference, to form ecumenical family support units in all communities (Ibid).

More examples on the church's role in campaigning against gender-based violence occasioned by the Covid-19 pandemic, particularly the lockdowns, can also be drawn from East Africa. In Uganda, for instance, Archbishop Stephen Samuel Kaziimba of the Church of Uganda rallied Ugandans against gender-based violence during the Covid-19 lockdown period. In his message, he articulated the church's concern about the increasing gender-based violence cases. He noted:

> We have witnessed an increase of cases of gender-based violence during the lockdown. As religious leaders, we appeal to and encourage people to work together to prevent it in our homes and communities. We should also provide psycho-social support to the victims during this pandemic (Mukhaye, 8 May 2020: 1).

During the lockdown period in March and April 2020, the Ugandan police registered 328 cases of gender-based violence (Ibid). Archbishop Kaziimba attributed the increase in cases of gender-based violence across the country to a lack of money and food brought about by the Covid-19 lockdown, arguing:

> When there is no food in the house, men tend to get mad and resort to beating their wives. But some women are busy abusing their husbands because their husbands do not have money and this has further intensified anger among the couples. I ask all men to desist from beating their wives, but women should also respect their husbands (Ibid).

Archbishop John Baptist Odama of Gulu in Uganda, who chaired the Bishops' Justice and Peace Department, noted with concern that while it was positive that the national lockdown in Uganda had seen families spending considerable time together, the period had seen a spike in cases of domestic violence. He encouraged people to stop domestic violence and cherish the value of "unity of the family, the unity of the nation, the unity of the continent, and the unity of the world" (Nzwili, 19 May 2020: 1).

Still in East Africa, Mwombeki, a Tanzanian Lutheran pastor, was also very vocal against the rise in gender-based violence during the Covid-19 period in Africa. She voiced this concern at a meeting of African leaders held in Nairobi, the Kenyan capital, on 1 December 2020 to observe 16 days of gender-based violence. Mwombeki deplored that one in three women were victims of physical and sexual violence more than 20 years since the adoption of the United Nations Declaration on the Elimination of Violence against Women. She went on to advocate for the inclusion of men and boys in the campaigns against gender-based violence (Nzwili, 1 December 2020). Other church leaders who attended the meeting acknowledged that the pandemic had caught the African continent by surprise, adding that lockdown confinement had triggered stress among the people and increased tensions in homes thereby creating fertile ground for domestic and sexual violence. They also noted that fears around loss of jobs and financial stress were increasing the likelihood of violent conflicts within homes (Ibid).

On a similar note, in West Africa, Liberia, as was the case with many other countries in the region, experienced a high number of rape cases during the Covid-19 lockdown. According to Jefferson Knight, the Head of the Human Rights Department of the United Methodist Church in Liberia, sexual violence against women increased by 50% within four months of the Covid-19 lockdown period. He noted that before the pandemic, the country witnessed about nine incidents of sexual violence against women, a figure that had since doubled in September 2020 at the height of the lockdown (Chikwanah, 10 September 2020). Knight believed that the increase was largely brought about by the lockdown and the state of emergency which made law-enforcement officers to pay more attention to health protocols than other violations (Ibid). The United Methodist Church in Liberia intensified its public information-sharing process by encouraging family members not to shield perpetrators of gender-based violence from getting their just punishment. The church also engaged the government to prosecute perpetrators, while at the same time offering psychosocial support to victims (Ibid).

In Nigeria, the National Agency for the Prohibition of Trafficking in Persons (NAPTIP) recorded increased cases of gender-based violence against women in the form of rape, incest, and domestic abuse during the country's Covid-19 lockdown period. In explaining some of the factors behind the surge, Julie Okah-Donli, the NAPTIP Director-General, noted: "I think some men are suffering from cabin fever. They are not used to staying at home with their wives. So, the more their wives are in their faces, the more they get angry and beat them up. We recorded over 30 cases in a certain period" (Nzwili, 19 May 2020: 1). In response to this worrying increase in gender-based violence cases, Nigerian church leaders, including the Catholic Bishops' Conference, released a pastoral letter on 9 May 2020 urging all its members to form ecumenical family support units in all communities (Ibid).

In many cases, gender-based violence outside households was perpetrated by governments and their agencies under the guise of enforcing Covid-19 containment measures, sometimes for purposes of political expediency, and many church denominations were always unrelenting and unwavering in their determination to safeguard human rights, liberties and freedoms. On 13 May 2020, for instance, three female political activists and members of the opposition Movement for Democratic Change (MDC) Alliance, Joanna Mamombe, a legislator, Cecilia Chimbiri and Netsai Marova were arrested for demonstrating against the government's poor Covid-19 response, only to be found days later dumped by the roadside north of the capital city, Harare (Dube, 7 April 2021; Mafundikwa, 21 September 2020). This violent incident against the women leaders came a few weeks after two sisters, Ntombizodwa and Nokhuthula Mpofu, were brutally assaulted on 16 April 2020 by police officers in Cowdray Park Suburb in Bulawayo, Zimbabwe's second largest city, reportedly for violating Covid-19 lockdown rules (Catholic Commission for Justice and Peace, 2020; Dube, 7 April 2021; Gukurume, 22 May 2020; Kudzayi, 7 April 2021; Tshili, 8 May 2020).

The abduction and torture of women, including political leaders in Zimbabwe, caught the attention of leaders of various Christian denominations in the country who collectively issued a statement denouncing the gender-based "inhumane treatment" and called for urgent and independent investigations into the matter. The

Zimbabwe Heads of Christian Denominations (ZHOCD), which comprised representatives from the Zimbabwe Catholic Bishops' Conference (ZCBC), Evangelical Fellowship of Zimbabwe (EFZ), Union for the Development of Apostolic Churches in Zimbabwe Africa (UDACIZA), and the Zimbabwe Council of Churches (ZCC), issued a joint statement, part of which read:

> The Zimbabwe Heads of Christian Denominations (ZHOCD) has received with shock and disbelief the news of yet another abduction and inhuman treatment of three young women, including a Member of Parliament. This is against the heart of the Constitution of Zimbabwe and the various international conventions to which Zimbabwe is a signatory and, above all, to our cultural norms and our Christian fundamental beliefs regarding the sanctity and dignity of life. It is deeply disturbing that the country has seen so many cases of abductions in the last few months, most of which have not been conclusively investigated. What is further disturbing are the insinuations, from some state agents, that all these abductions are either stage-managed or carried out by an unrecognisable 'third force' without substantiating such claims with credible and irrefutable evidence. This constitutes the denigration of responsibility of the highest order on the part of government…We have realised that one of the major effects of the Covid-19 lockdown has been the worrying increase in domestic violence, especially against women and children. It is unthinkable that such violence could be replicated in even more severe proportions with state sanction… (Kahiu, 21 May 2020: 1).

In the statement, the church leaders also regretted that "this ill-treatment of women takes place in 2020 when the whole world is celebrating the 25th Anniversary of the Beijing Declaration, which was a global high point in the recognition of the dignity of women after centuries of patriarchal domination and treatment of women as second-class citizens of the world" (Ibid: 1). The church leaders were also appalled to see how "women could suffer in the custody of the state, not only in the case of these three women but also the brutal assault of the two women from Cowdray Park in Bulawayo on 16 April by six police officers" (Ibid).

ZHOCD went on to call for urgent independent investigations into the circumstances around the attack on the two sisters and the three female opposition leaders and recommended that the findings be made public with appropriate and swift disciplinary action being instituted against the perpetrators. The church leaders also urged the

Zimbabwean government to stop undermining the constitutional rights of citizens under the pretext of Covid-19 intervention (Ibid). Furthermore, they called for the immediate restoration of the integrity of parliament so that it could exercise its oversight of the government and urged all security operatives to discharge their duties with honour while upholding the dignity, decency and sanctity of human life. They also urged all institutions of the state, especially the National Peace and Reconciliation Commission, the Zimbabwe Human Rights Commission, the Gender Commission, and the National Prosecution Authority to effectively exercise their constitutional mandates by ensuring that the state, all government agencies and all people at every level respect, promote, protect and fulfil the rights and freedoms set out in the Zimbabwean Constitution (Ibid).

As this section has illustrated, the church was a notable human rights watchdog during the Covid-19 period in Africa. Broadly, the approach employed by church leaders to tackle the scourge of gender-based violence occasioned by the Covid-19 pandemic was multi-pronged. Churches communicated with communities through pastoral letters and other forms of communication such as the social and electronic media, to raise public awareness against gender-based violence. Religious leaders were also unwavering in their attack on societal and customary norms that seemed to spur gender-based violence. They also implored governments to institute firm policies against gender-based violence and ensure that the perpetrators were prosecuted. In cases where the government and its agencies were the villains while enforcing Covid-19 lockdown measures, the churches openly voiced their concerns and demanded that the victims be compensated. Many churches were also pragmatic in their approach as evidenced by the formation of ecumenical family support units in some communities and the counselling services which they rendered to victims of gender-based violence.

Church versus the state on freedom of worship and assembly

A broad range of human freedoms were curtailed in various ways by Covid-19 restrictions. Governments in most African countries imposed restrictions on the public practice of religion as part of an array of responses to the global health crisis. Generally, churches were instructed to completely close their places of worship for a period of time while in some cases, a limited number of congregants was stipulated. Churches that breached the lockdown regulations by holding face-to-face services ran the risk of being prosecuted. Some churches either resumed face-to-face services or never stopped their regular gatherings, in direct violation of national regulations aimed at containing the spread of Covid-19. While most people appreciated the efforts of the governments to reduce the spread of the Covid-19 pandemic, the reopening of restaurants, beer halls, and shops, among other sectors, while religious institutions were ordered to remain closed caused tension between the church and the state in some countries.

Indeed, the banning of gatherings, including religious ones, at the height of the Covid-19 pandemic in many African countries was justified on grounds of saving lives and controlling the spreading of the virus. It should be acknowledged, however, that there were some religious officials and their congregants who defied government orders banning any kind of public gatherings. In a number of cases, the police raided such gatherings and arrested the worshippers. In Kenya, in late March 2020, for example, the Bungoma South Deputy County Commissioner, Michael Yator, reported one such raid as follows: "We arrested two priests, several nuns, and over 40 congregants for defying the law which aims at reducing and preventing the spread of Corona virus. They were arrested at St Paul's Kanduyi Parish and Christ the King Catholic Church" (Wasike, 28 March 2020: 1).

In Zimbabwe, as was the case in other parts of the African continent, some church denominations disregarded the government's lockdown regulations by congregating when gatherings were banned, or holding night vigils despite the curfew. In July 2021, for instance, the police in the city of Chitungwiza arrested two men, Clayton Makavi and Tendai Zhakata, aged 35 and 30 years respectively, for leading a Johane Masowe Apostolic Church service, with approximately 23 members comprising men and women, at an open space in the Zengeza 5 Extension. The congregants were also arrested and fined (*Zimbabwe Herald*, 28 July 2021). Assistant Commissioner Paul Nyathi, the National Police Spokesperson, said it was worrying to note that people were continuing to engage in such practices countrywide and warned the public against breaching Covid-19 regulations by holding church services (Ibid). He was supported by Reverend Edson Tsvakai, the Secretary-General of the Union for the Development of Apostolic Churches and Zionists in Africa, who urged all apostolic sect members to adhere to the national lockdown regulations. He said: "We cannot win the fight against Covid-19 when we still gather to worship. We should obey and follow what our government is saying about this disease which is continuing to threaten the lives of the majority of people in the world" (Ibid).

It is a fact that most church leaders across the African continent understood and appreciated that the ban on religious gatherings, despite interfering with the freedoms of worship and assembly, were necessary in order to contain the spread of the Covid-19 pandemic. Many church denominations devised strategies of reaching out to their congregants without physical contact in compliance with the lockdown measures instituted by governments. These strategies included online media platforms. In many African countries, church congregants met online, using a range of media platforms such as WhatsApp, YouTube, and Twitter. In addition, Small Christian Communities were set up by the Roman Catholic Church in many countries to distribute food parcels in their local areas (Wild-Wood *et al*, 2021).

When lockdown conditions were eventually relaxed, some governments allowed churches to reopen but under strict conditions. The conditions included adhering to stipulated numbers of worshippers per gathering, social distancing, putting on face masks and administering hand sanitisers. Surprisingly, however, there were cases when some over-zealous security officers stormed church gatherings and harassed congregants even when lockdown conditions had been eased. A case of this nature was recorded in Kenya where, despite the relaxation of a ban on religious gatherings, the police raided a place of worship and disrupted proceedings. This was on 4 April 2021 when Kenyan armed officers besieged Jesus Celebration Centre (JCC) Ongata Rongai Church in Kajiado County and interrupted its live proceedings for allegedly contravening the laid-down Covid-19 rules. In a video that went viral on social media, police officers were seen standing against the altar, asking the church leader to vacate. There was a heated exchange between a pastor at the church and the police which triggered fury among a section of worshippers who protested that the police were acting inappropriately. The JCC authorities felt hard done by the fact that their live stream service was interrupted despite fully complying with Covid-19 preventive measures that had been issued by the Interfaith Council. Under the new regulations, churches were allowed a maximum of 15 congregants to conduct an online service to the generality of worshippers. When the raid took place, the church was conducting an online service in line with the Covid-19 curtailment protocols. Many churches came out to condemn the incident which they regarded as a threat to religious freedom, and in particular Christian freedom of worship. The churches were particularly concerned at the deployment of armed officers on peaceful congregants, their aggressive conduct, and harassment at the church altar which was disrespectful of the worshippers, the clergy and even God (Ndungu, 6 April 2021).

Under the umbrella of the Federation of Evangelical and Indigenous Christian Churches of Kenya (FEICCK), the churches condemned the police for invading a religious service whose actors had fully adhered to the newly-stipulated Covid-19 protocols. As Bishop David Munyiri Thagana, the Secretary General of FEICCK, stated: "We may be in denial but we just cannot believe that this could happen in Nairobi's environs 58 years after Kenya's independence" (Ibid: 1). FEICCK demanded that the Inter-Faith Council pronounces itself on the matter to avert confusion among churches that were offering online services, adding: "Unless this pronouncement happens as a matter of urgency, we do not know which Inter-Faith Council guidelines we should follow and which ones will expose us to police brutality" (Ibid).

As the pandemic subsided in many African countries from mid-2021, several church leaders increasingly pressured their governments to further lift lockdown restrictions in order to allow for more people to attend church services. An example can be drawn from South Africa in late July 2021 during Level Four of the lockdown when church leaders from the Gauteng Province who had met in Pretoria called on President Cyril Ramaphosa to allow the resumption of religious gatherings. The church leaders requested for religious gatherings with a limited number of people of up to 50% of the venue capacity to be permitted. The clergy argued that they should not be left out since the government had recently lifted Covid-19 restrictions in other sectors such as schools, restaurants, gyms, agricultural livestock, and game auctions (Maila, 25 July 2021). Apostle Moafrika Wa Maila, the National Convenor for Pastors against Church Closure, urged the government to lift the ban on religious gatherings, arguing that South Africans needed prayer and support from their church leaders:

> It is a fair and reasonable way to open churches in this pandemic. Remember that during Easter, we were told that the third wave will have

after effects. We managed to curb the spread of Covid-19 as the church by being compliant and following regulations. Spiritual support from the church plays a major role in the lives of people when they are going through a difficult time. They need spiritual support so that they do not get to lose more lives (Ibid).

These sentiments were echoed by Pastor Boshoff of the Christian Revival Church who emphasised that South Africa desperately needed the guidance of religious leaders. He argued:

> Do we even see what is happening? 36 000 businesses close down in KwaZulu Natal [Province] because of a week of violence. Hundreds of thousands have lost their jobs on a scale as we have never seen. How many of those young people used to be in a church two years ago? Faithful church members are on fire for God. Now they have lost the plot. Why? Because they no longer have a house. They no longer have a place of safety (Boshoff, 25 July 2021: 1).

Similarly, in Zimbabwe, as the government began to relax some lockdown provisions, church leaders requested for permission to worship in bigger congregations. In early August 2021, for instance, churches in Zimbabwe questioned the government's sincerity in allowing them to hold services for vaccinated worshippers when only about 10% of the country's population had been inoculated against Covid-19 in a country where more than 70% of the total population was Christian (Mavhunga, 13 August 2021). The government pronounced this measure after noting a decline in new Covid-19 cases. Representatives of the Zimbabwe Catholic Bishops Conference, the Evangelical Fellowship of Zimbabwe, and the Union for Development of Apostolic and Zionist Churches in Zimbabwe noted that the order was difficult to implement because theologically and practically, the church was an open and welcoming space for everyone. They therefore argued that there was no need for qualifications or qualifiers to enter churches because they are places of God's grace (Ibid).

In this section, it has been made clear that most religious leaders in Africa appreciated and comprehended that the Covid-19 lockdown measures which banned church gatherings were necessary. Even though the bans on church gatherings imposed by many governments across the African continent infringed the freedoms of assembly and worship, religious leaders, with the exception of a few, complied as they felt that human life had to be safeguarded by such measures against the ravages of the Covid-19 pandemic. It has been noted, however, that church leaders began to raise issues of freedoms of worship and assembly when the rate of pandemic infections declined. It was during these times when governments relaxed lockdown measures on some sectors that church leaders requested to be included. Again, churches were always critical of security officers who abused their powers by harassing worshippers who fully complied with lockdown provisions.

Conclusion

This chapter has demonstrated how, during the Covid-19 pandemic era, the church played a critical role in ensuring that rights, freedoms, and liberties were observed in order to promote human dignity, happiness and security in Africa. In its endeavours, the church proved to be the soul of the society in every sphere of life on the African continent. Since time immemorial, pandemics had always been a challenge to humanity. As several examples from across the African continent showed, the church sought to defend the rights of ordinary citizens during the Covid-19 pandemic. As the chapter illuminated, the church was very consistent in advising governments to guarantee the well-being and lives of individuals and societies during the enforcement of Covid-19 mitigation protocols. It was also unwavering in its call for Covid-19 responses to comply with international standards on emergency legislation and respect human rights and the rule of law. The church was also steadfast in its insistence that Covid-19 lockdown measures needed to be used necessarily and proportionately, and always be aligned with international human rights law. Overall, the chapter proved that churches became the voice of the voiceless where governments and other perpetrators violated human rights, liberties and freedoms during the Covid-19 pandemic.

References

Aineah, A. (20 April 2021) 'Catholic leaders in Uganda reveal chilling human rights violations in Covid-19 report,' Available at: https://www.aciafrica.org/news/3283/catholic-leaders-in-uganda-reveal-chilling-human-rights-violations-in-covid-19-report/, Accessed 21 February 2022.

Allen, J. (23 June 2020) 'South Africa bishops warn against "second pandemic" of gender-based violence,' Available at: https://cruxnow.com/church-in-africa/2020/06/south-africa-bishops-warn-against-second-pandemic-of-gender-based-violence/, Accessed 1 April 2022.

Asadu, C. (29 October 2020) 'Nigeria's Catholic Church on the front line in protests against police brutality,' Available at: https://www.ncronline.org/news/justice/nigerias-catholic-church-front-line-protests-against-police-brutality/, Accessed 28 January 2022.

Catholic Commission for Justice and Peace (2020) 'Two Zimbabwean journalists charged with violating Covid-19 lockdown,' Available at: https://cpj.org/2020/06, Accessed 30 April 2022.

Chikwanah, E. (10 September 2020) 'Violence against women, girls in Africa spikes amid Covid-19', Available at: https://www.umnews.org/en/news/gender-based-violence-in-africa-spikes-amid-covid-19/, Accessed 3 April 2022.

Dube, G. (7 April 2021) 'Amnesty International: Zimbabwe security forces killed 10 people under nation's Covid-19 lockdown,' Available at: https://www.voazimbabwe.com/a/amnesty-international-zimbabwe-report-killed-security-forcces/5844319.html, Accessed 12 February 2022.

Egwu, P. (25 June 2020) 'Nigerian priests condemn police brutality during the lockdown, offer solutions,' Available at: https://www.catholicworldreport.com/2020/06/25/nigerian-priests-condemn-police-brutality-during-lockdown-offer-solutions/, Accessed 27 February 2022.

Global Fund (25 November 2021) 'Fighting violence against women and girls during Covid-19,' Available at: https://www.theglobalfund.org/en/blog/2021-11-25-fighting-violence-against-women-and-girls-during-covid-19/, Accessed 10 April 2022.

Gukurume, S. (22 May 2020) 'Abductions, brutality, and demolitions: When the state becomes more harmful than Covid-19,' Available at: http://democracyinafrica.org, Accessed 30 April 2022.

Human Rights NGO Forum (2020) 'Solidarity statement issued in response to the state's attack on the Zimbabwe Catholic Bishops Conference: The march is not ended,' Available at: https://kubatana.net/2020/08/16/solidarity-statement-issued-in-response-to-the-states-attack-on-the-zimbabwe-catholic-bishops-conference-the-march-is-not-ended/, Accessed 16 April 2022.

Isilow, H. (5 August 2020) 'South Africa to firmly act on Covid-19 corruption cases,' Available at: https://www.aa.com.tr/en/africa/south-africa-to-firmly-act-on-covid-19-corruption-cases/1931823/, Accessed 23 April 2022.

Isilow, H. (15 September 2020) 'South African bishops protest virus-based corruption claims,' Available at: https://www.aa.com.tr/en/africa/safrican-bishops-protest-virus-based-corruption-claims/1974348, Accessed 22 April 2022.

Kahiu, M. (21 May 2020) 'Church leaders in Zimbabwe denounce "inhumane treatment" of women, demand investigations,' Available at: https://www.aciafrica.org/news/1373/, Accessed 19 April 2022.

Karrim, A. (7 June 2020) 'Faith leaders hold silent protests against police brutality,' Available at: https://www.news24.com/news24/SouthAfrica/News/sa-council-of-churches-hold-silent-protests-against-police-brutality-20200607/, Accessed 12 January 2022.

Kudzayi, E. (7 April 2021) 'At least 10 killed as Mnangagwa dialled up rights abuses in 2020: Amnesty,' Available at: https://www.zimlive.com/2021/04/07, Accessed 2 May 2022.

Mafundikwa, T. (21 September 2020) 'Critics: Zimbabwe stepping up arrests and assaults against female protesters,' Available at: https://www.zenger.news/2020/09/21/zimbabwe-steps-up-arrests-and-assaults-against-female-protesters/, Accessed 29 March 2022.

Mail & Guardian (11 June 2020) 'Call in the medics: Beds don't cure people,' Available at: https://mg.co.za/coronavirus-essentials/2020-06-11-call-in-the-medics-beds-dont-cure-people/, Accessed, 10 April 2022.

Maila, M. (25 July 2021) 'Church leaders call for relaxed Covid-19 lockdown regulations,' Available at: https://www.sabcnews.com/church-leaders-call-for-relaxed-covid-19-lockdown-regulations/, Accessed 15 March 2022.

Masina, L. (23 April 2020) 'Malawi health workers face stigma, discrimination over Covid-19,' Available at: https://www.voanews.com/covid-19-pandemic/malawi-health-workers-face-stigma-discrimination-over-covid-19/, Accessed 19 April 2022.

Maulani, N. Nyadera, I.N. & Wandekha, B. (2020) 'The generals and the war against Covid-19: The case of Zimbabwe,' in: *Journal of Global Health*, Volume10, Number 2, Available at: https://www.ncbi.nlm.nih.gov/pmc/articles/PMC7648907/, Accessed 26 April 2022.

Mavhunga, C. (13 August 2021) 'Zimbabwe churches scoff at a government decision to allow vaccinated to attend services,' Available at: https://www.voanews.com/a/covid-19-pandemic_zimbabwe-churches-scoff-government-decision-allow-vaccinated-attend-services/6209529.html/, Accessed 24 April 2021.

Mukhaye, D. (8 May 2020) 'Uganda: Kaziimba rallies Ugandans against violence,' Available at: https://allafrica.com/stories/202005110119.html/, Accessed 11 March 2022.

Ndungu, M. (6 April 2021) 'Churches condemn the police for interrupting JCC's online services,' Available at: https://www.pd.co.ke/news/churches-condemn-police-for-interrupting-jccs-online-services-71017/, Accessed 20 March 2022.

Nzwili, F. (19 May 2020) 'African church leaders work to curb domestic abuse during the lockdown,' Available at: https://www.catholicnews.com/african-church-leaders-work-to-curb-domestic-abuse-during-lockdown/, Accessed 14 March 2022.

Nzwili, F. (1 December 2020) 'African faith leaders urged to redouble efforts against gender-based violence,' Available at: https://www.oikoumene.org/news/african-faith-leaders-urged-to-redouble-efforts-against-gender-based-violence/, Accessed 20 March 2022.

OSV News (19 May 2020) 'African church leaders work to curb domestic abuse during lockdown,' Available at: https://www.osvnews.com/2020/05/19/african-church-leaders-work-to-curb-domestic-abuse-during-lockdown/?print=print/, Accessed 10 April 2022.

Repucci, S. & Slipowitz, A. (2020) 'The impact of Covid-19 on the global struggle for freedom,' Available at: https://freedomhouse.org/report/special-report/2020/democracy-under-lockdown/, Accessed 12 April 2022.

Segun, M. (18 January 2021) 'Human rights abuses escalate in Africa during the pandemic,' Available at: https://www.hrw.org/news/2021/01/18/human-rights-abuses-escalate-africa-during-pandemic/, Accessed 20 April 2022.

Swart, M. (17 May 2020) 'South Africa court issues orders to end police abuse during lockdown,' Available at: https://www.aljazeera.com/news/2020/05/africa-court-issues-orders-police-abuse-lockdown-200516105512595.html/, Accessed 26 April 2022.

Tshili, N. (8 May 2020) 'Police "brutality": Women battered for lockdown defiance,' Available at: https://www.chronicle.co.zw/coronavirus-zimbabwe-records-first-death/, Accessed 9 March 2022.

Wasike, A. (28 March 2020) 'Covid-19: Kenya police raid church, arrest priests, nuns,' Available at: https://www.aa.com.tr/en/africa/covid-19kenya-police-raid-church-arrest-priests-nuns/1783293/, Accessed 22 April 2022.

Wild-Wood, E. Grant, L. Adedibu, B. & Bernard, A.B. (2021) 'The public role of churches in early responses to Covid-19 in Africa: Snapshots from Nigeria, Congo, Kenya and South Africa,' in: *Studies in World Christianity*, Volume 27, Number 1, pp.65-84, Available at: https://www.euppublishing.com/doi/epub/10.3366/swc.2021.0326, Accessed 11 April 2022.

Zimbabwe Herald (28 July 2021) 'Zimbabwe: Defiant churches face prosecution,' Available at: https://allafrica.com/stories/202107280472.html/, Accessed 4 March 2022.

Zimbabwe Catholic Bishops Conference (2020) 'The march is not ended: Pastoral letter of the Zimbabwe Catholic Bishops' Conference (ZCBC) on the current situation in Zimbabwe,' Available at: https://kubatana.net/2020/08/14/the-march-is-not-ended-pastoral-letter-of-the-zimbabwe-catholic-bishops-conference-on-the-current-situation-in-zimbabwe/, Accessed 12 April 2022.

Chapter 16

In Defence of the Weak and the Vulnerable: The Zimbabwe Lawyers for Human Rights and the Fight against Covid-19 Human Rights Infringements

David Tobias

Introduction

This chapter examines the role played by the Zimbabwe Lawyers for Human Rights (ZLHR) in the fight against human rights abuses related to the Covid-19-induced lockdown in Zimbabwe. Following the outbreak of the Covid-19 pandemic in 2020 in Zimbabwe, the government instituted a series of control measures to combat its spreading. Basically, these were restrictive mechanisms which had to be implemented through a myriad of strategies. Chief among them were the lockdown, curfew, travel restrictions, and the closing down of all public places. These measures were mainly enforced by state institutions, especially the army and the police. In the process of enforcing Covid-19 restrictions, excessive and unlawful use of force was often used resulting in gross human rights infringements. It was against this background that some human rights defenders came in to ensure that people's rights, freedoms and liberties were safeguarded at a time when the pandemic was wreaking havoc countrywide. One such human rights defender was the Zimbabwe Lawyers for Human Rights, a non-governmental organisation that played a prominent role in this regard.

The chapter illuminates the important role played by non-governmental organisations in guarding against human rights violations in Zimbabwe at a time when the government and its arms were preoccupied with fighting the Covid-19 pandemic, using heavy-handed and abusive tactics in most cases. The central argument advanced in the chapter is that the fight by the Zimbabwean government against Covid-19 was accompanied by another fight by civil organisations against human rights violations that often took place during the process of containing the pandemic. The study employed various research methods in order to unpack the incidents of human rights violations and the work of the ZLHR during the

Covid-19 era. Oral interviews were conducted with some victims, law-enforcement agents, and representatives of human rights organisations. The interviews were conducted in the Zimbabwean cities of Bulawayo, Masvingo, Harare, and Beitbridge. Sources such as newspapers and the internet were consulted in order to capture specific events and cases involving rights abuses and the role of the ZLHR.

Brief historical background of the Zimbabwe Lawyers for Human Rights

The Zimbabwe Lawyers for Human Rights was formed in 1996 as a non-profit making human rights organisation whose core objective was to foster a culture of human rights in Zimbabwe as well as encourage the growth and strengthening of human rights at all levels of the society through observance of the rule of law (ZLHR, 28 March 2022). Its mission and mandate is to protect and defend human rights through sustainable litigation, education and advocacy which contribute positively to a culture of tolerance and adherence to democratic values and practices. It was formed as a membership organisation of lawyers with Arnold Tsunga, Otto Saki and Irene Petras being the founding members. Arnold Tsunga was its first director who later handed over the mantle to Irene Petras at the end of 2007 to join the International Commission of Jurists in Geneva as the African Director (Ibid).

From 1996 to 2000, the ZLHR operated as a loose association on an *ad hoc* basis, responding to significant rule of law-related human rights violations as and when they took place (ZLHR Annual Report, 2006: 4). The increasing demand for its services, together with a strategic plan workshop held in July 2000, contributed as positive factors towards the organisation's institutional transformation, especially considering the establishment of a full-time secretariat. Furthermore, a board was established to give policy and direction to the organisation (Ibid).

From the time of its formation, the aims and objectives of the ZLHR were quite wide and dynamic. These included the determination to foster a culture of human rights in Zimbabwe and to encourage the growth and strengthening of human dignity at all levels of Zimbabwean society. The organisation also strove to protect, promote, deepen and broaden the human rights provisions in the Constitution of Zimbabwe. It is important to note that the

ZLHR works alongside other Zimbabwean civic groups, organisations, activists and persons who share a broadly similar concern for, and interest in human rights. It also considers the implementation and protection of international human rights norms in Zimbabwe, as contained in important sub-regional and international human rights instruments. Over and above, it works to promote and protect human rights, the rule of law and separation of powers in Zimbabwe and the region (Ibid).

In order to enhance its efficiency and effectiveness, the ZLHR established specific and special units for various operations. The International Litigation Unit, for example, was mandated to consider the state's compliance to international and regional instruments which authorities would have signed and ratified. These include the African Charter, the International Convention on Economic, Social and Cultural Rights, and the Convention on Rights of the Child, among others. The second unit deals with HIV/ AIDS and human rights. The third unit deals with human rights training and public education. Basically, this unit seeks to increase the general awareness on human rights through the training of human rights defenders by providing expertise on their duties and highlighting their risks (Ibid).

Another notable ZLHR organ is the Public Interest Litigation Unit. This unit is responsible for the access to justice as a priority area of the organisation's strategic plan. It is the oldest and most established of ZLHR's units, which carries out various types of litigation in order to contribute to all forms justice and democratic reform in Zimbabwe. The ZLHR Public Litigation Unit is composed of lawyers who work on constitutional litigation, challenging the constitutionality of both laws and state policies in Zimbabwe. The unit seeks to expand the Bill of Rights of the Zimbabwean Constitution by emphasising the importance of anti-impunity litigation (Bhora, Interview: 25 January 2022). In many court cases, ZLHR lawyers have demanded civil claims for damages against named perpetrators in their official capacities. Thus, they work tirelessly to reduce impunity and enhanced the accountability of the state for human rights violations against the public. The ZLHR, through this unit, worked to expose potential perpetrators and tried to prevent intended unlawful conduct by state security agents in Zimbabwe during the Covid-19 lockdown period (Madora, Interview: 22 January 2022).

It is important to note that the ZLHR deals with the entire spectrum of human rights as enshrined in the Zimbabwean

Constitution. Section 52 of the Constitution provides that every person has the right to bodily and psychological integrity (Constitution of Zimbabwe Amendment Act, Number 20 of 2013: 29). This implies freedom from all forms of violence from both public and private sources. Section 56 of the Constitution provides that all persons are equal before the law and have the right to equal protection and treatment, adding that people should not be discriminated on the basis of nationality, race, colour, class and political affiliation. Section 58 of the Constitution provides that every person has the right to freedom of assembly and association, and also the right not to assemble or associate with others. No person may be compelled to belong to an association or to attend a meeting or gathering. Section 59 states that every person has the right to demonstrate and present petitions (Ibid: 30). But these rights must be exercised peacefully. Section 60 states that everyone has the right to freedom of conscience. This implies the right to freedom of thought, opinion or belief. Section 61 states that everyone has the right to freedom of expression, to seek, receive and communicate ideas (Ibid: 31). The same section emphasises academic freedom which normally comes through scientific research and creativity. Section 69 provides that everyone has the right to a fair trial within a reasonable time before an independent and impartial court. Over and above, everyone has the right to administrative justice as stipulated in Section 68 of the Constitution. Most of these rights were violated by state machinery during the Covid-19 lockdown and the ZLHR often found itself battling the authorities in an effort to protect citizens from a broad range of abuses.

Contextualising Covid-19 curtailment measures in the human rights discourse

Just like other countries around the globe, the Covid-19 pandemic plunged Zimbabwe into its biggest health crisis in history. The virus caused a severe humanitarian and economic burden that overwhelmed the health system (Mahmud *et al*, 2021). As a result, there was need for the government to put in place extraordinary measures to curb the spread of the pandemic in order to protect the lives of the generality of the population which were at great risk. Some of these measures included compulsory confinement, quarantines and border closures. Initially, the response was perceived by many as robust and appropriate as the government joined other countries in fighting the global pandemic. The President of Zimbabwe, Emmerson Mnangagwa, using his presidential powers, declared a state of disaster on the 19th of March 2020 (Zimbabwe Human Rights NGO Forum Report, 22 May 2020).

The President's decisions and actions had to be based on the law to avoid conflicts and legal challenges from some sections of the Zimbabwean society who would feel that the highest authority was somehow acting contrary to the national constitution. In Zimbabwe, the statutes which gave the President state power to take action were basically three: (1) the Emergency Powers Act, which conferred power to the President to take action in the event of a national disaster. Accordingly, he was expected to issue out a proclamation declaring a state of public emergency under Section 113 of the Zimbabwean Constitution; (2) the Civil Protection Act, which also conferred power to the Head of State to declare a state of disaster if extraordinary actions were needed to protect the public against any disasters such Covid-19. This was well spelt out if one considered Section 27 of the Civil Protection Act; and (3) the Public Health Act of 2018, which gave powers to the Head of State to deal with formidable health disasters which could emerge and threaten public health and people's lives (Kenneth, Interview: 12 February 2022).

In line with the above three statutes, the President of Zimbabwe declared Covid-19 a national disaster through the issuance of Statutory Instrument I77 of 2020. Available evidence indicates that he worked closely with the Minister of Health and Child Care who, according to Section 68 of the Public Health Act, could institute regulations to combat the pandemic. Against this background, he was authorised to quarantine, isolate and detain patients, close public institutions like churches, schools, liquor outlets, restrict gatherings, and order medical examinations. Throughout the world, the implementation of such regulations was assigned to the army and police, some of whom took the law into their own hands, sometimes killing civilians in countries like Nigeria and Kenya (Odigbo *et al*, 2020). In the Zimbabwean situation, such measures were enforced mainly by the Zimbabwe Republic Police (ZRP) and the Zimbabwe National Army (ZNA). The generality of the population was expected to comply with all Covid-19 containment regulations which included maintaining social distance, washing hands using sanitisers and putting on face masks. Furthermore, people were ordered to remain confined to their homes except those who were regarded as offering essential services to the nation. It was against this backdrop that President Mnangagwa announced the initial lockdown measures to combat the Covid-19 pandemic on 17 March 2020 (Rogers, Interview: 22 February 2022).

From the onset, it should be noted that the struggle waged by the Zimbabwean government against Covid-19 had another dimension as several civic organisations stood against human rights violations that often took place during the process of containing the pandemic. Despite the fact that the Covid-19 lockdown and quarantine restrictions were premised on a legal foundation, they violated many clauses in both the United Nations Universal Declaration of Human Rights and the Zimbabwean Constitution. There is abundant evidence to show that Covid-19 containment measures declared by President Mnangagwa actually became the breeding ground for human rights infringements (Cephas, Interview: 22 February 2022). In fact, the pandemic opened new opportunities for state repression which targeted certain citizens, human rights defenders and some opposition political activists. At times, the army and the police who were deployed became overzealous and used excessive force. It is against this background that the ZLHR came in as a human rights defender in support of the defenceless whose dignity was violated in many ways during the Covid-19 lockdown period (Ibid).

Overview of ZLHR strategies to safeguard human rights during the Covid-19 lockdown

Among other strategies, the ZLHR embarked on constitutional litigation to safeguard people's rights during the Covid-19 period. The organisation focused on the supreme law of the land to assert rights and liberties guaranteed in the Declaration of Rights. As mentioned earlier in this chapter, despite the fact that the constitution protected various civil, political and socio-economic rights, human rights defenders continued to be persecuted through various pieces of legislation, policies and practices throughout Africa in general, and Zimbabwe in particular. Yet it is common knowledge that when a law is inconsistent with the constitution, it becomes invalid (Zamchiya, 2011: 4). The ZLHR sought to litigate before the Constitutional Court to assert enshrined rights. It also challenged the conduct and certain state practices that were not in sync with the Zimbabwean Constitution. In this regard, the Public Interest (Strategic Impact) Litigation Unit of the ZLHR took up cases that were meant to benefit the public and advance the protection and enjoyment of human rights at a broader level (Chiwara, Interview: 28 February 2022). The unit engaged in strategic human rights litigation that had an impact on the larger community and benefited more people beyond the primary litigant in specific cases. Some of the key issues targeted by the unit included revising and reforming bad and draconian pieces of legislation, influencing state policy, promoting equality, and fostering public accountability and access to justice.

The ZLHR also employed the anti-impunity strategy during the lockdown period (Musekiwa, Interview: 14 February 2022). Generally, much of the information gathered for this research indicates that during lockdown, the ZLHR realised that some state security agents violated human rights of the public under the guise of enforcing Covid-19 curtailment measures (*Legal Monitor*, 10 May 2021). Instances of police brutality and heavy-handedness by state security agents continued to be a common occurrence in public life. Yet it was necessary in Africa, and particularly Zimbabwe, to have a truly professional police force that applied the law without fear or favour and one that took prompt action against those that committed violence with impunity (Mavhinga, 2011). In order to deter such human rights violations, the ZLHR employed anti-impunity civil proceedings against perpetrators during the lockdown period. The organisation made numerous claims for damages, most of which were demanded through courts against the defendants. The major reason behind these civil suits was to discourage further acts of human rights violations on the public by state security agents (*Legal Monitor*, 10 May 2021).

The ZLHR also used mobile legal clinics during the lockdown period (Nevanji, Interview: 12 February 2022). Their main function was to ensure access to justice for all. Mobile legal clinics provided human rights literacy, free legal aid and legal counselling for the most marginalised Zimbabwean communities. The idea of mobile legal clinics was to avail justice right at the door-step of the marginalised people, most of who needed it most but did not ordinarily have access to it.

It was through the use of some of these strategies that many Zimbabweans who experienced human rights violations and required legal assistance immensely benefitted from the ZLHR. The organisation also offered legal help to all individuals and institutions who had their rights violated by state institutions such as the police, the army and the Central Intelligence Organisation. Furthermore, it gave legal assistance and advice to state organs which needed institutional reforms. While the ZLHR gave legal assistance to regional and continental bodies like the Southern African Development Community (SADC) and the United Nations (UN), it offered considerable help to local communities in Zimbabwe. Thus, this chapter focuses on the assistance rendered to some youths, men, women and ordinary Zimbabweans by the ZLHR during the lockdown period. Although the ZLHR was perceived by many as a 'lawyers' club', it is important to note that many citizens became part and parcel of the organisation by virtue of them being beneficiaries. The next section focuses on some specific instances in which the ZLHR assisted legally defenceless citizens whose rights had been violated by state security agents and other actors operating under the guise of fighting the Covid-19 pandemic during the lockdown period.

The ZLHR to the defence of the defenceless during the Covid-19 lockdown period

On 1 April 2020, Lydia Chapalapata, a 63-year-old female resident of Nkulumane Suburb in the city of Bulawayo, was assaulted by Assistant Inspector Brighton Machingambi. She was queuing to purchase maize meal at Sekusile Shopping Centre and Machingambi assaulted her over allegations that she had violated national lockdown regulations (Nkala, 12 June 2021). With the help of Prisca Dube, a lawyer from the ZLHR, Chapalapata filed an application to the High Court for damages. The application revealed that the said victim sustained injuries on her head, back, thighs and knees, and suffered from trauma, anxiety and shock as a result of the attack. Consequently, she was hospitalised at Mpilo Central Hospital and was referred for special medical attention due to the severity of the attack. In the court application which was done by the ZLHR, Police Commissioner General Godwin Matanga and Home Affairs Minister Kazembe Kazembe were cited as first and second respondents respectively. They were asked to pay damages amounting to ZWL$3 million, broken down as ZWL$2.5 million being damages for pain and suffering, trauma and nervous shock, while ZWL$500 000 was to cater for future medical expenses (Ibid).

The case of Edmund Zengeya and Benson Tavenga also indicates the blatant violation of human rights by security agents on lockdown duties and how the ZLHR subsequently stepped in to provide legal support. The above-mentioned citizens were severely mauled by a police dog on 1 August 2020 at a fuel station in the border town of Beitbridge (Chikandiwa, 26 November 2021). They were arrested and fined for breaking Covid-19 regulations. It was against this background that Patrick Tererai, representing the ZLHR, came in and challenged the conviction that had been made and sought a court order for a refund of the fine. Home Affairs Minister Kazembe and ZRP Commissioner General Godwin Matanga were blamed for the police-dog attack on the Beitbridge residents. The ZLHR filed summons on 4 December 2020 at the Beitbridge Magistrate's Court demanding refund and compensation. The police agreed and paid ZWL$425 000 to Zengeya and ZWL$85 000 to Tavengwa as damages (Ibid). This incident shows how justice was restored through the efforts of the ZLHR.

In another case, Lucia Masvondo, a 26-year-old woman from the town of Karoi in Mashonaland West Province, was assaulted by ZNA soldiers on 3 April 2020 as she was cooking on an open fire outside her home (Tapfumanei, 10 April 2020). The security officers set their patrol dogs on her after accusing her of violating national lockdown regulations. They took the law into their own hands and punished her through beating. They also created an opportunity and possibility of bringing the Corona virus into her home since they came in numbers and beat her up without even maintaining the Covid-19 prescribed social distancing. Against this background, lawyers from the ZLHR quickly filed an urgent chamber application at the High Court in Harare and asked the court to issue an order to protect the Karoi woman against the conduct of the ZRP and ZNA officers. Senior government officials were sued and cited as respondents. These included the Minister of Defence, Oppah Muchinguri; Minister of Local Government, July Moyo; Minister of Health, Obadiah Moyo; Minister of Home Affairs, Kazembe Kazembe; and Police Commissioner General, Godwin Matanga (Ibid). Although the outcome could not be established with certainty in this case, the ZLHR assisted with advocacy and asked the victim to demand compensation from the government. They further asked the court to consider issuing out a court order which deterred security agents from assaulting citizens while enforcing the country's Corona virus lockdown. The court order was issued out (Ibid).

Another case involved the 28-year-old Tendai Mthombeni, a returning resident from South Africa, who had his arm and leg broken by state security agents (Mavhunga, 16 April 2020). This happened on 10 April 2020 when the security agents forced him to stay indoors. As a result of this development, Mthombeni could not go back to South Africa where he worked. He was expected to report back for duty in South Africa but was now stuck in Zimbabwe. The ZLHR came to his rescue and advised him to demand compensation from the government for his broken arm and leg. The ZLHR assisted and offered advocacy and forced the court to issue out an order emphasising that the state security agents should not assault citizens while enforcing the country's Corona virus lockdown. Kumbirai Mafunda, the spokesman for the ZLHR, had already taken other similar cases to the High Court on 7 April 2020 through an urgent petition and the High Court made it clear that it had already received numerous rights abuse cases by the army and the police (Ibid). The police and the army were forced through the High Court order to comply with the idea of respecting people's fundamental rights as demanded by the national constitution. While the idea of fighting Covid-19 was generally accepted and perceived as necessary and noble, many other rights were violated, especially the right to movement, right from assault, right to food and the right to fend for the family as the government forced the generality of the Zimbabwean population to stay in-doors.

As lockdown restrictions continued to be implemented in the year 2021, the authorities increasingly abused citizens and violated their rights. This was evidenced by the case of a Harare Polytechnic College student, Yolanda Musithu, who was suspended from her studies for hugging a colleague, Blessing Pasipanodya, inside the campus premises on 22 March 2021 (*Legal Monitor*, 10 May 2021). A letter of suspension was served to Musithu on 22 March 2021 by the Harare Polytechnic authorities who accused her of violating Covid-19 preventive regulations set by the World Health Organisation and adopted by the Zimbabwean government. The ZLHR, being represented by Godfrey Mupanga, came in with haste and filed an urgent chamber application at the Harare High Court seeking an order to compel Harare Polytechnic to allow Musithu access to the college so that she could be allowed to attend classes and be granted all rights and privileges enjoyed by all students for the National Diploma in Office Management. As a result of this legal representation, the suspension was lifted (Ibid).

Tafadzwa Mudondo, the Harare Polytechnic College Principal, eventually wrote a letter stating that the institution had resolved to lift Musithu's suspension after consultation with the Ministry of Higher and Tertiary Education. The move by Mudondo resulted in lawyers representing Musithu and Harare Polytechnic College agreeing to withdraw the urgent chamber application (*Legal Monitor*,

17 December 2021). In the process, it was learnt that Yolanda Musithu was actually one of the several human rights defenders who, in recent months, had challenged Zimbabwean authorities on their flagrant use of Covid-19 regulations to suppress citizens' fundamental rights and freedoms (Ibid).

In some cases, the ZLHR intervened and tried to restore justice with regard to the selective application of Covid-19 restrictions. In late July 2021, for example, Clyton Makavi and Tendai Zhakata, two men aged 35 and 30 years respectively, were arrested by the ZRP for leading a Johanne Masowe Apostolic Church service at an open space in Zengeza 5 Extension in the city of Chitungwiza (Murwira, 27 July 2021). The church service was attended by 23 members including men and women. This was in direct violation of the set Covid-19 restrictions which had, among other things, suspended indefinitely all church gatherings (*Herald*, 19 March 2020). It should be noted, however, that the ZRP had recently allowed 1 000 of Johanne Marange Apostolic Church followers to hold their annual pilgrimage at Mafararikwa Village in the Bocha area of Manicaland Province. This was perceived to be a selective application of the Covid-19 regulations by many. ZLHR lawyers were quick to come in and petitioned the police to enforce Covid-19 restrictions without fear or favour (Ibid). In this case, the ZLHR played an important role as it fought against some instances of corruption, favouritism and selective application of the set Covid-19 restrictions.

Through the effort and work of the ZLHR, three acquaintances of Zengeza West legislator, Job Sikhala, were acquitted after being accused of breaching Covid-19 lockdown regulations (*Voice of America*, 5 June 2021). The three were Terrence Manjengwa, Blessed Changara and Barnabas Gura, all residents of Harare. They were arrested on 3 September 2020 outside the Harare Magistrate's Court while legal proceedings for Sikhala, who had been arrested and detained for inciting public violence by urging people to participate in the 31 July 2020 anti-corruption protest, were taking place (Ibid). The three citizens mentioned above were charged with unnecessary movement during the national lockdown as defined in Section 4 (a) of the Public Health Covid-19 Prevention, Containment and Treatment Act. The prosecutors claimed that the three unlawfully and unnecessarily moved from their residence during the national lockdown by gathering at the Harare Magistrate's Court without exemption letters. Fighting for their defence, Kossam Ncube, a lawyer working under the ZLHR, objected to the charges of unnecessary movement on the basis that this did not exist in the national constitution. The three were acquitted and set free (Ibid).

In another success story, the ZLHR, represented by Moses Chikomo, managed to have twin sisters, Precious and Privilege Gwatidzo, acquitted by a Mutare magistrate after they had been arrested by police officers on 12 April 2020 in Mutare's Dangamvura Suburb. They were accused of violating national lockdown regulations of confining themselves to their place of residence when they were found outside their home (Tapfumaneyi, 8 April 2021). The police forced them to pay ZWL$500 each as fine for unnecessary movement during the national lockdown. Through the work and advocacy provided by the ZLHR lawyer, Moses Chikomo, a defence was built. It was discovered that while the two were detained in police cells, they were harassed and denied access to sanitary wear by the police. The lawyer argued that it was essential for them to move around because they were sourcing some prescribed medication at a pharmacy for their grandmother who was chronically ill (Ibid). Chikomo successfully challenged the decision by the police who had ordered them to pay RTGS$500 each as fine for unnecessary movement saying this was illegal. As a result of these efforts, the magistrate, Audrey Muzhingi, ordered for refunds of the fine and the girls were subsequently acquitted (Ibid).

In some cases, the ZLHR challenged some aspects pertaining to legalities of certain statutory instruments which brought confusion among citizens during the Covid-19 lockdown period. For example, they challenged the relevance of Statutory Instrument 174 of 2020 which compelled business to close by 3pm (Munyoro, 17 August 2020). Another issue involved business and curfew hours and the operations of the courts of law. During the initial phase of the lockdown, security forces were instructed to enforce a curfew between 6:00 pm and 6:00 am while all non-working people were required to stay at home, except when they wanted to buy groceries and seek medical attention. Only those providing what was termed 'essential services' were allowed to work outside the stipulated hours. Following the arrest of Hopewell Chin'ono, an investigative journalist, and Jacob Ngarivhume, an opposition politician, Beatrice Mtetwa and Moses Nkomo, lawyers representing the two and both instructed by the ZLHR, could not persuade a Harare magistrate to continue hearing court applications beyond 3:00 pm. The court officials could not continue with the proceedings saying they were adhering to business hours stipulated by lockdown regulations. This prompted the ZLHR to rush to the High Court to challenge the regulations, arguing that this unconstitutionally disadvantaged arrested people. In this regard, the ZLHR was striving to protect the right to administrative justice as required by the Zimbabwean Constitution during the Covid-19 lockdown period (Ibid).

In its lawsuit, the ZLHR listed the Judicial Services Commission (JSC), the National Prosecution Authority (NPA), Minister of Justice, Legal and Parliamentary Affairs and the Minister of Health and Child Care as respondents. The lawyers insisted that Statutory Instrument 174 of 2020 should not limit the sitting of the Magistrate's Court when dealing with initial bail applications. Roselyn Hanzi, the ZLHR Director, insisted that once a bail application or challenge to placement on remand had commenced, it was supposed to be heard to finality before the court adjourned for the day. Normally bail matters had previously been granted or refused well after hours and sometimes well into the evening. So, such approaches were unconstitutionally disadvantaging arrested persons like Hope Chin'ono, an investigative journalist who had used a Twitter account to expose alleged government corruption. He was detained at Chikurubi Maximum Security Prison for nearly six weeks before being granted bail on charges of inciting violence by twitting his supporters for an anti-government protest. Tsitsi Dangarembwa was also arrested on 22 July 2020 and spent a night in jail for a placard that demanded the release of Hopewell Chin'ono. It was against this background that the ZLHR provide advocacy and legal advice to many such people who were arrested during the Covid-19 lockdown period. The ZLHR exposed many cases of abductions, torture, and alleged corruption. It went further to show that the government of Zimbabwe was using the Covid-19 lockdown restrictions to suppress political criticism. (Tarisai, Interview: 25 February, 2022).

Similar cases included the trials of the Zimbabwe National Students Union (ZINASU) leaders. In February 2021, the police arrested several student leaders in Harare in a crackdown on human rights defenders. First to be arrested on 26 February 2021 were three students namely Richard Paradza, Paidamoyo Masaraure and Lean Kanengoni. They were apprehended at the Harare Magistrate's Court on allegations of unnecessary movement (*Legal Monitor*, December 2021). Paradzayi, Masaraure and Kanengoni, who were represented by Tinashe Chinopfukutwa of the ZLHR, were detained at Harare Central Police Station. The ZRP also arrested ZINASU leaders who included Takudzwa Ngadziore, Nancy Njenge and Tapiwa Chiriga.

Tinashe Chinopfukutwa and Jeremiah Bamu, both lawyers of the ZLHR, teamed up to represent the arrested students who were charged with contravening Section 4 (1) (a) of the Public Health (Covid-19 Prevention, Containment and Treatment) (National Lockdown) Order Statutory Instrument 200/2020 as read with Statutory Instrument 42/2021. Basically, these were controversial accusations centred on unnecessary movements as they were being blamed for failing to confine themselves at home during the lockdown. Tapiwa Chiriga was also accused together with Takudzwa Ngadziori of convening a public gathering (*Legal Monitor Newsletter*, 17 December 2021). Furthermore, prosecutors claimed that Takudzwa Ngadziore and Tapiwa Chiriga, together with other accomplices who included Harare West Constituency Legislator, Joanna Mamombe, and opposition MDC Alliance Party youth leader, Cecilia Chimbiri, had convened a media briefing denouncing the arrest and detention of pro-democracy campaigner Makomborero Haruziveishe, castigated police brutality and called for the resignation of ZRP Commissioner General Godwin Matanga (Ibid).

Another case involved Belvedere Technical Teachers' College students. In September 2021, ZRP officers detained 10 student teachers at the college after arresting them for allegedly staging protests in the capital city against a steep hike in tuition fees (*Legal Monitor Newsletter*, 17 December 2021). ZRP officers swooped on the students as they were gathered and arrested them. The students were due to write examinations in October 2021. The 10 students, namely: Lavender Makoni, Stephen Mariwo, Julia Munyanyi, Tariro Chineganda, Talent Madzivanyika, Nqobizitha Masuku, Blessing Nyamarowa, Nokhuthula Zengeni, Walter Muzami and Tracy Ngomambi were first detained at Milton Park Police Station (Ibid). They were accused of breaking lockdown regulations. They were later transferred to Harare Central Police Station where they were charged with disorderly conduct in a public place as defined in Section 41 of the Criminal Law (Codification and Reform) Act (Ibid). The ZLHR gave free legal assistance during the trials of the 10 students. They were represented by Tinashe Chinopfukutwa and Paidamoyo Saurombe until they were eventually acquitted (Ibid).

The lockdown restrictions categorised the generality of the population into essential service providers and non-essential persons. The essential service providers included health workers, company workers, as well as commercial A2 farmers and A1 farmers, communal farmers. These were required to carry with them exemption letters written by their chief executive officers stating the place, date and time of reporting on and off duty. The contact details of the issuing authority had to be indicated on the letter. For A1 and A2 farmers, an offer letter/ lease agreement and an exemption certificate from a local ZRP Officer-in-Charge was required. For communal farmers, a supporting letter from the headman or village head stating the business to be done, the date, time, place and an exemption letter from the Officer-in-Charge was also required. The contact details of the headman or village head had to be indicated. When attending a funeral, concerned relatives were to produce a copy of a burial order at road blocks. Police officers commanding both districts and provinces were to issue exemption letters showing the destination and dates of movement for those who intended to bury relatives in other towns and rural areas. Many people were arrested for travelling without such documents. There was widespread corruption as many ZRP officers demanded bribes to allow passage to some citizens (Mahachi, Interview: 12 February 2022). The ZLHR was quick to come in together with other organisations challenging the legality of exemption letters. They clearly showed that nowhere in the principal order nor in any other lockdown statutory instrument was it stated that exempted persons must be in possession of the so-called movement exemption letters. They argued that although the ZRP had been issuing movement exemption letters, these documents were not backed by the law since their issuance was declared through a press statement, thus media statements are only regarded as awareness tools. Due to the pressure from the ZLHR and outcry from the public, the government finally relaxed the lockdown regulations, including the need for people to produce exemption letters at check points (Benjamin, Interview: 13 February 2022).

Conclusion

This chapter has demonstrated that being a law-based non-governmental organisation established in 1996, the ZLHR worked tirelessly to protect human rights during the Covid-19 lockdown period in Zimbabwe. It sought to foster a culture of respect for human rights at all levels of society. It tremendously assisted the public in issues of litigation, backed human rights defenders, and increased public knowledge on constitutional rights. It issued media statements against unlawful arrests, unwarranted fines, abductions and torture of some lawyers, journalists, nurses, doctors, political opposition members, some human rights defenders and ordinary citizens for allegedly violating Covid-19 rules. The ZLHR also forged links with other rights groups such as Women of Zimbabwe Arise (WOZA), Zimbabwe Women Lawyers Association, and Zimbabwe National Association for Non-Governmental Organisations (NANGO), Crisis in Zimbabwe Coalition, Law Society of Zimbabwe, and ZINASU. Furthermore, the ZLHR often worked in unison with lawyers from other organisations and individual lawyers when human rights were violated during the Covid-19 period. They provided advocacy and put pressure on the government to desist from violating citizens' rights under the pretext of enforcing Covid-19 restrictions. They used newspapers and the electronic media, among other things, to challenge some controversial lockdown regulations and practices. They mainly criticised the government for using Covid-19 restrictions to suppress political criticism and abuse citizens' rights beyond public health concerns.

References

Chikandiwa, H. (6 November 2021) 'Court orders $500k compensation for police brutality,' in: *Newsday*, Harare: Zimbabwe.

Community Perceptions and Tracker (June 2021) 'Understanding perceptions, rumours and question of Zimbabwean communities,' in: *Community Perceptions and Tracker*, Bulletin 5.

Legal Monitor (10 May 2021) 'Student suspended for hugging: ZLHR to rescue,' in: *Legal Monitor*, Harare: ZLHR.

Legal Monitor (December 2021) 'Spectacular collapse to trial of ZINASU leaders,' in: *Legal Monitor*, Harare: ZLHR.

Mavhinga, D. (2011) 'Gender representations in Zambian elections: Lessons for Zimbabwe,' in: *Journal of Alternatives for Democratic Zimbabwe,* Volume 1, Number 16, pp.3-14.

Mavhunga, C. (16 April 2020) 'Zimbabwe: Rights groups welcome court ban on brutal Covid-19 lockdown,' Available at: www.voa.com, Accessed 10 September 2021.

Mohamed, N.A. Solehan, H.M. Rani, M.D. Ithnin, M. & Isahak, C.I. (2021) 'Knowledge, acceptance and perception on Covid-19 vaccine among Malaysians: A web-based survey,' in: *PLOSE One Journal,* Volume 16, Number 8, pp.1-17.

Munyoro, F. (17 August 2020) 'Covid-19 restrictions legal: High Court,' in: *The Herald*, Harare: Zimbabwe.

Murwira, S. (27 July 2020) 'Johane Masowe leaders arrested for breaching Covid-19 regulations,' Available at: www.263Chat.com, Accessed 10 November 2021.

Nkala, S. (12 June 2021) 'Bulawayo resident sues police, minister over lockdown brutality,' in: *Newsday*, Harare: Zimbabwe.

Odigbo, B. Eze, F. & Odigbo, R. (2020) 'Covid-19 lockdown controls and human rights abuses: The social marketing implications,' in: *Journal of Emerald Open Research*, Volume 2, Number 45, pp.1-18.

Tapfumanei, R. (8 April 2021) 'Court acquits twin sisters charged for unnecessary movement,' Available at: www.newzimbabwe.com, Accessed 16 June 2021.

Tapfumaneyi, R. (10 April 2020) 'Karoi woman seeks compensation,' Available at: www.newzimbabwe.com, Accessed 3 June 2021.

Voice of America (5 June 2021) 'Job Sikhala's acquaintances acquitted for breaching Covid-19 lockdown regulations,' Available at: www.voa.com, Accessed 12 September 2022.

Zamchiya, P. (2011) 'No need for presidential run-off: Zambian election lessons for Zimbabwe,' in: *Journal of Alternatives for Democratic Zimbabwe*, Volume 1, Number 16, pp.4-5.

Zimbabwe Government (2013) *Constitution of Zimbabwe*, Harare: Government Printer.

Zimbabwe Human Rights NGO Forum (22-23 May 2020) 'Report on Zimbabwe Covid-19 lockdown monitoring,' Harare: Zimbabwe Human Rights NGO Forum.

Zimbabwe Lawyers for Human Rights (2006) 'Annual Report,' Harare: ZLHR.

Chapter 17

Informal Human Rights Struggles amid the Covid-19 Pandemic: Insights into Subaltern Initiatives in Africa

Trust Makwinja Asima & Fidelis Peter Thomas Duri

Introduction

This chapter explores the agency of marginalised populations in defending and reclaiming their rights, liberties and freedoms in the wake of a host of vulnerabilities occasioned by the Covid-19 pandemic and subsequent mitigation measures across the African continent. Upon the advent of the Covid-19 pandemic in Africa in early 2020, many countries introduced curtailment regulations that included national lockdowns during the months of March and April. The national lockdowns and the manner in which they were enforced compromised the rights, freedoms and civil liberties of many people, particularly the subaltern sections of the population, who employed a surfeit of strategies to address their plight.

It is without doubt that human rights campaigns in defence of the downtrodden populations in post-independence Africa in general and during the Covid-19 period in particular have largely been waged by civil organisations, churches and government commissions and their efforts are well documented. In their accounts detailing the infringements of human rights, freedoms and liberties during the Covid-19 period, these organisations roundly portrayed subaltern populations as victims of abuse at the hands of governments and other institutions such as the police and the army. While literature on the victimhood of vulnerable people is quite substantial in human rights discourses, the same cannot be said as far as the initiatives of the victims themselves are concerned.

There is also a dearth of scholarly literature on the agency of the victims of human rights abuses themselves to defend and reclaim their rights, liberties and freedoms that were increasingly being violated in the wake of the Covid-19 pandemic. It is the central argument of this chapter that the ordinary people are not always passive victims of manipulation, marginalisation and subordination who sit idly while their rights, freedoms and liberties are being trampled upon by those with privileges. Rather, they have the potential to rise in defence of their entitlements as human beings in ways that are mostly informal owing to their resource limitations and inability to command significant influence beyond their immediate communities. This chapter therefore explores the grit of marginalised and downtrodden people in determining and shaping their own destinies. By doing so, the chapter departs from elitist (top-bottom) analyses and takes a social history approach or bottom-up anatomy to human rights discourses.

While Covid-19 lockdown orders largely curtailed the occurrence of public protests through the banning of large gatherings (Green & Kirk, 2020), they sometimes triggered fairly widespread demonstrations against the inconsiderate manner in which such measures were implemented and enforced. In countries such as Algeria, Egypt, Guinea, South Africa and Somalia, for example, demonstrations became common (ACCORD, 8 July 2020). In many cases, the demonstrations were violently suppressed under the guise of enforcing Covid-19 lockdown measures. In early July 2020, for example, Malian security forces killed 11 civilians who were protesting against the government (Gargard, 15 September 2020). The fact that security sector brutality often characterised the enforcement of lockdown protocols and the handling of related protests in most African countries meant that many disgruntled sections of the population mostly resorted to informal means of defending and reclaiming their rights, freedoms and liberties that were compromised during the Covid-19 period. As Malematja & Busisiwe (5 May 2020: 2) also noted in South Africa:

> The national lockdown has resulted in a number of limitations to the right to protest. Gatherings continue to be entirely prohibited…This means that traditional forms of protests such as marching on public roads, sit-ins, unauthorised occupation of public spaces and other mass-based disruptive protest repertoires are outlawed. The lockdown does not negate the fact that mass protests are an important component for holding government accountable. The essence of protests is the ability of a group of people to speak in one voice, with the same objective in mind…Fortunately, there are other ways in which people can protest without necessarily gathering and risking their health. Therefore, the limitation imposed on the right to protest does not imply that people cannot stand as one and fight for their fundamental human rights.

Given this background, the chapter explores the largely informal ways employed by subaltern populations in Africa to defend their rights, liberties and freedoms in the wake of the Covid-19 pandemic and subsequent lockdown measures that were put in place to curtail its spread. Subaltern responses were largely tacit. In the case of demonstrations, they were informal and easily identifiable, among other things, by their organisational nature of being "protest[s] without leadership" (Iroulo, 2021: 1). In other words, protest action was either individualised or people-driven. Put in another way, such protests were usually "spontaneous citizen action" (Green & Kirk, October 2020: 3), and without elaborate organisational and administrative hierarchies. In terms of scale and extent, informal protests spread though snowballing without evidence of being driven by formal organisational and mobilisation structures.

Overview of human rights abuses occasioned by the Covid-19 pandemic in Africa

In many African countries, the enforcement of Covid-19 curtailment regulations exposed the majority of citizens to gross human rights abuses. To start with, most Covid-19 containment provisions decreed by African governments imposed stay-at-home orders, travel bans and curfews for all citizens except for essential service workers and providers. Lamentably, most informal businesses and workers were condemned to poverty as they were not classified as essential service providers. When the lockdowns were gradually eased across the continent, many informal workers, mostly food and vegetable vendors, were allowed to operate at central markets, most of which were far away from their usual customers. The restrictions imposed on the informal economy were grievously impoverishing given that the sector accounted for the livelihoods of the majority of people across the African continent. In Zimbabwe, for example, the employment survey of 2019 reported that the informal economy contributed 84% of the country's labour force (Chigudu, 2021). In Ghana, as of 1 February 2022, about 80% of the country's workforce worked in the informal sector (Boateng, 2 February 2022). These examples clearly show that the Covid-19 lockdown orders across the African continent severely compromised the socio-economic rights of many ordinary people to the extent of jeopardising their right to livelihood, and ultimately life!

In addition to further impoverishing many ordinary people owing to the closure of informal income-generating businesses, security officers on lockdown assignments often aggravated the situation by handling civilians in ways that were often brutal and humiliating. In actual fact, the enforcement of Covid-19 curtailment measures by most African governments was largely "over-securitised" and reinforced by "narratives associated with masculinity, and by referring to the pandemic response as a fight" (Safer World, 2020: 3). Consequently, many Covid-19 lockdown taskforces were generally heavy-handed and bestial. Such approaches often caused bodily harm on many people and sometimes led to fatalities. Thus, many innocent civilians came to live in fear with their rights to dignity and security critically transgressed and without guarantees to their right to life.

Violence often characterised the enforcement of Covid-19 containment measures across Africa. By May 2020, 50% of all violent incidents in West African countries that were not at war were occasioned by the Covid-19 pandemic, either as state security officers ruthlessly enforced lockdown measures or as civilians retaliated and demonstrated against the heavy-handedness (Safer World, 2020). In Nigeria, widespread complaints against security officials enforcing Covid-19 mitigation measures included shootings, torture, inhumane and degrading treatment, unlawful arrests and detentions, seizure/confiscation of properties, sexual molestations, and bribery (Odigbo *et al*, 2021). In South Africa, most of the concerns against law-enforcement agents on lockdown assignments cited shootings, beatings, teargassing and water bombing people, and sexual harassment (Ibid). In Kenya, there were similar misgivings about police use of excessive and brute force, extortions, unlawful arrests and detentions, and teargassing people (Ibid). In Mozambique, it was common practice for street vendors, young men drinking alcohol in public domains, those gathering in groups, and others who were not putting on face masks to be rounded up and force-marched to police stations where they were severely clobbered (Kyed, 29 June 2020). These few examples illustrate the high-handed approach employed by security operatives to ensure compliance to Covid-19 amelioration provisions across the African continent.

Police brutality against citizens during Covid-19 lockdown enforcements resulted in many individuals losing their lives. An example can be drawn from Nigeria by 13 April 2020 when the security forces on lockdown assignments in various parts of the country had killed more people than the Corona virus itself. At this time, when the lockdown was just a fortnight old, 18 people had been killed by security operatives while 12 had lost their lives as a result of the virus (Khalid, 16 April 2020; Mugabi, 20 April 2020; Ohajuruka, 16 November 2020). In South Africa, by the end of May 2020, 11 people had been killed by the police on lockdown duties (Kyed, 29 June 2020). In Kenya, it was reported that six people lost their lives as a result of police brutality during the first 10 days of the Covid-19 dusk-to-dawn curfew in that country (Odigbo *et al*, 2021). By early June 2020, Kenya's security personnel on lockdown engagements had killed at least 15 people (*British Broadcasting Corporation News*, 26 June 2020). In Uganda, "not a single Covid-19 death was registered until 23 July 2020. By that date, a half dozen Ugandans had been killed by police using pandemic conditions as an excuse for brutality" (Wilmot, 25 January 2021: 1).

It is not possible to document all brutalities and human rights abuses associated with the Covid-19 pandemic and the subsequent containment measures instituted by various governments across the African continent. Such a task would require dozens of thick books, if not more. What this section has done is to provide a few insights into some human rights issues related to the pandemic. Such insights constitute a valuable background or context against which subaltern informal struggles for human rights, liberties and freedoms during the Covid-19 pandemic were premised.

Circumventing lockdown orders by informal sector workers

The circumvention of stay-at-home orders by the ordinary people in pursuit of livelihoods was very noticeable across the African continent. While the stay-at-home orders and travel bans imposed by most African governments in an effort to curb the spread of the Covid-19 pandemic directly infringed the right to freedom of movement, justifiably though, they also had telling implications on livelihood rights. In many African urban areas, the livelihoods of most informal sector workers were acutely jeopardised owing to lockdown measures that did not classify them as essential service providers and therefore obliged them to stay at home. Faced with this predicament, they devised an array of strategies to bypass these orders and avoid being arrested by security operatives on lockdown assignments. Even though it is a fact that people from all walks of life employed such strategies at one time or the other, this section focuses on informal sector workers because they were the most predominant section of the population when it came to the circumvention of lockdown restrictions since they were the worst affected.

The dodging of Covid-19 stay-at-home orders and travel bans by informal workers and traders was rampant in many African countries. In their desperate bid to secure livelihoods, many informal workers devised a number of strategies to pass through police checkpoints or to avoid them altogether. Examples can be derived from Accra and Kumasi, Ghana's capital and second largest city respectively, where Boateng (2 February 2022: 1) shed light on some of the strategies as follows:

> Some commuters tried to outwit law-enforcement officials by faking identity cards designed for people exempted from the restrictions. Others tried to avoid security officials at checkpoints by trekking long distances or boarding *okadas* (motorbikes) that used narrow walkways and bushes to beat the police and transport people to various destinations.

Despite breathing sighs of relief after circumventing or successfully passing through police checkpoints, the struggle was far from over as more hurdles lay ahead. Upon reaching their destinations, which could be in central business districts, informal traders and workers had to contend with law-enforcement agents on lockdown patrols. In an effort to decongest the central business districts of urban centres, authorities in countries such as Zimbabwe designated areas in outlying residential areas as vending markets. Vending stalls at undesignated sites were often destroyed as part of precautionary measures to prevent the spread of the Covid-19 pandemic. All these moves did not go down well with the generality of informal workers as they constituted "human rights violation against people trying to make ends meet" (Chigudu, 2021: 1).

In an effort to salvage livelihoods under very difficult circumstances, informal traders were often engaged in cat-and-mouse games with security operatives. Many informal traders such as street vendors chose to risk being apprehended by security officers than suspend their businesses, in line with Covid-19 lockdown measures, and starve to death. As Moses Muhumuza, a 25-year-old Ugandan roadside shoe vendor, insisted in mid-May 2020: "Corona virus or hunger, which one kills you faster? I think it is hunger! How many Ugandans have died of this disease? Zero! Maybe I will also get it and not die. Anyway, I am ready to find out for myself' (Anguyo, 19 June 2020: 1).

Similarly, at the Mimias Market in Kenya's Kakamega County on 30 March 2020, defiant market vendors were doing business as usual in defiance of a government ban on open-air markets when the police arrived. The raid saw the traders fleeing the scene with the police in hot pursuit. During the confusion, the police shot Grace Muhati, a 24-year-old trader, with live ammunition. Fellow traders whisked her to hospital where doctors removed two bullets from her body (Human Rights Watch, 22 April 2020). On the next day, 1 April 2020, the police again besieged the very same market. The drama that unfolded saw the police chasing the traders while beating and kicking them. During the melee, shots were fired by the police while Idris Mukolwe, a 45-year-old tomato vendor, died after being struck with a teargas canister thrown at him (Ibid). Such scenes were also witnessed in many other countries. In the Ugandan capital of Kampala during the period 1 May-1 June 2020, for example, the police regularly tormented street vendors during which the "public flogging of female street vendors by security forces" became common sight (Anguyo, 19 June 2020: 1).

In addition to such harsh treatment, street vendors often had their wares confiscated by marauding security operatives without hope of ever getting them back. This was indeed a quadruple tragedy involving the Corona virus health hazard, lockdown restrictions, security sector brutality, and loss of livelihood-earning commodities. In late June 2020, for instance, a 30-year-old street vendor in the Mozambican town of Tete, expressed similar sentiments. He lamented:

> My job is to sell bags and stuff on the street, but now the situation is difficult because the police are prohibiting it. But to sustain my family I have to continue to risk circulating in the streets to sell, trying to avoid the police, because if they catch you, the police will take all your goods. It is very risky, but I have no choice. I do not have a lot of money because the money I have comes from the daily sales and if I stay at home, we will not die of the virus but of hunger (Kyed, 29 June 2020: 1).

It was indeed distressing for some ruthless and corrupt security officials enforcing Covid-19 lockdown measures to raid market stalls and make off with seized products for their own personal use. This was very cruel considering that market vendors are usually impoverished people desperately seeking livelihoods. In most cases, those who had their wares seized could not physically fight the police out of fear of being arrested or being banned from trading again. It was in the context of this predicament that in mid-June 2020, some food vendors at a market in the Mozambican town of Chimoio devised a plan to punish unscrupulous security details who had developed the practice of pouncing on their products. Kyed (29 June 2020: 1) provides details of the plan and what transpired thereafter as follows:

> In Chimoio…information has spread that four police officers died and three others hospitalised because market vendors had poisoned some of their food products. The police officers had previously come to the market stalls and taken the vendors' products in exchange for allowing them to go on selling during the lockdown. Poisoning the products that the police had 'stolen' from them was the market vendors' way of getting their revenge on the police and protesting against their conduct. This form of self-justice and popular counter-violence reflects a strong belief that the police and the government will not do anything against those officers who misuse their power and exceed their mandate. It also signals the deeper mistrust of the Frelimo government and the widespread erosion of justice and the rule of law in the country that people have been familiar with since long before the Corona virus crisis.

Informal sector workers sometimes turned violent to the authorities after their livelihood rights were gravely threatened by Covid-19 lockdown restrictions. This was the case in the coastal settlement of Tumbu in the Western Area Rural District of Sierra Leone on 6 May 2020 when the local fishermen were angered by the government's restrictions on their operations in an effort to curtail the spread of the Covid-19 pandemic. The authorities had, without previous notice, reduced the number of vessels going out to the sea to 15. Many fishermen were stranded as they waited to get into the sea to conduct business. With their livelihoods on the margin, the local fishermen stormed a health centre and a police station in Tumbu. They also attacked the house of a local community chief. In all the attacks, no injuries were reported (*Crisis 24*, 7 May 2020).

Similarly, there were violent disturbances in some poor urban localities in the Democratic Republic of Congo where citizens who solely depended on the informal sector for a living openly thumbed their noses at the stay-at-home orders that had been decreed by the government to curtail the spread of the Covid-19 pandemic. In the

Ibanda Commune of the city of Bukavu, for example, many people complied with the three days of total confinement declared by the government in early June 2020 with the exception of residents in the neighbourhood of Essence who remained defiant. Most Essence residents were poverty-stricken with the majority being either unemployed or salvaging livelihoods from the informal sector in various parts of the city. Since the livelihoods of such sections of the population largely depended on mobility, the stay-at-home orders potentially threatened their existence (Green & Kirk, 2020). Consequently, many Essence residents "chased out the police and threatened them with death should they try to enforce the lockdown… The population refused, and the police had no option but to flee the neighbourhood and enforce Covid-19 measures elsewhere" (Ibid: 11-12).

This section illuminated how adversity bred resilience among some of the most brow-beaten sections of the African population during the Covid-19 period. The adversity comprised the Covid-19 health crisis, lockdown restrictions, and security sector brutality. These tribulations markedly watered down the rights, liberties and freedoms of many already impoverished populations as their livelihoods were critically jeopardised while their lives hung precariously by the thread. Despite the Covid-19-impelled trepidations, the underprivileged populations devised a surfeit of initiatives to salvage sustenance. They had little option as they had to survive against the odds. As this section has amplified, some of the strategies they improvised included circumventing lockdown orders, outwitting law-enforcement officers, engaging in cat-and-mouse encounters with security operatives, and fighting back in direct and indirect ways.

Looting of Covid-19 aid by hungry people

In times of national and global emergencies such as the Covid-19 pandemic, national governments have an obligation to safeguard the livelihoods of their citizens through the provision of safety nets, among other things. The right of people, particularly the vulnerable, to social security was extremely compromised by the advent of the Covid-19 pandemic and the subsequent orders to curtail its spread, especially lockdowns, which either curtailed or suspended many critical income-generating activities that sustained livelihoods for many down-pressed citizens, most of who were plunged into a sea of poverty.

African governments struggled to cushion their citizens with social support and had to rely on international donor aid. The citizenry across the continent increasingly became restive, accusing their respective governments of failing to provide effective welfare safeguards and guarantees. These concerns were further reinforced by reports of various abuses of Covid-19 relief aid by government officials in many African countries. In a number of cases, the ordinary people, most of them famished, took matters into their own hands and looted government warehouses and vehicles with Covid-19 relief food.

In Uganda, for example, there was widespread disgruntlement over the government's failure to distribute food to needy people despite a loan of about US$500 million from the International Monetary Fund to manage the Covid-19 pandemic (Wilmot, 25 January 2021). In Ghana, as was the case across the African continent, "there were heart-rending footages of people forcing their way through thick crowds for a chance at [government] food supplies to feed their families. Aside from opening up the beneficiaries to potential infections, the mode of distribution also effectively denied access to vulnerable people like women, children, the elderly and persons with disability who, for obvious reasons, cannot shove their competitors and pick some of the food" (Boateng *et al*, 2022: 11).

Similarly, in Mozambique, as one woman from the town of Chimoio lamented in late June 2020, the government was unable to adequately support and assist people whose livelihoods had been seriously eroded by the pandemic. She complained: "To be fed by the government, this is impossible. All they [government officials] can do is to order people to stay home, and then they spread out the police to all corners so they can punish the people" (Kyed, 29 June 2020: 1). In the Democratic Republic of Congo, "accusations abound that money earmarked for responses to the pandemic has been embezzled by various state and provincial authorities. This has led to widespread resentment, as dismayed populations long familiar with the resources that the region's Ebola epidemic generated now view Covid-19 as the latest 'business' for local public authorities and internationals" (Green & Kirk, October 2020: 6). As can be noted, these concerns centred on the right to livelihood in general and food in particular. In some African countries, as will be noted in this section, there were widespread allegations of the uneven and unfair distribution of aid and protests sometimes arose as disadvantaged people asserted their right to equal treatment.

In some cases, governments with limited resources had to prioritise some individuals, groups and communities over others in the distribution of Covid-19 relief food. The prioritisation of certain sections of the society sometimes sparked protests from non-recipients in demand of the rights to food and equal treatment. On 14 April 2020, for instance, residents of a community in Cape Town, South Africa, "violently protested government's failure to provide them with food aid, following an alleged handover of food parcels at an adjacent community. Police fired tear gas and rubber bullets to disperse protesters" (Davids, 6 May 2020: 1). Similar incidents took place in various parts of South Africa. In one such incident in Cape Town, protesters "attacked and looted three trucks, barricaded roads and threw stones at the trucks, forcing them to stop" (Davids, 6 May 2020: 1). In late April 2020, disgruntled community members from the Booysens squatter camp, an informal settlement in Johannesburg, South Africa, blocked several roads with burning tyres and rocks. They complained that the government had not given them any food handouts to cushion them from the hardships they were facing during the lockdown. The residents went on to loot many stores (Pijoos, 28 April 2020; Thomas, 2021). By 6 May 2020, more than 20 incidents of looting had been recorded by the South African media (Ibid). It should be noted that there is no evidence to suggest that the incidents of looting of Covid-19 aid in various parts of South Africa were pre-planned and coordinated. Rather, they appeared "opportunistic and [were] usually carried out by fringe participants within protesting groups" (Davids, 6 May 2020: 1).

In Uganda, the month of May 2020 witnessed sporadic upheavals by groups of poor urbanites demanding adequate government safety nets to alleviate the suffering brought about by the Covid-19-induced lockdown measures. In Kampala's Namungoona Suburb, for instance, "dozens of youths took to the streets, blocking roads with debris and lighting fires, protesting against slow food distribution" (Anguyo, 19 June 2020: 1). In the town of Iganga, women twice stormed the district offices demanding food. A few days later, the youths from the town looted food aid donated to the Iganga Covid-19 Taskforce by the local Member of Parliament (Ibid).

In Nigeria, there was widespread outcry from vulnerable sections of the population that the government was not doing enough to cushion them from the vagaries of the Covid-19 pandemic which included closure of businesses, income cuts and food insecurity. More worrying were reports that some of the Covid-19 food relief had been found in the homes of some authorities such as politicians (Orjinmo, 26 October 2020). On 26 October 2020, groups of hungry people looted government warehouses storing Covid-19 aid at Gwagwalada on the outskirts of Abuja and made off with bags of rice, noodles and sugar, among other food items. The Nigerian authorities denied hoarding the items in order to share them with families and friends. Many state governors argued that the items were being reserved for the vulnerable members of the society in anticipation of the second wave of the Corona virus infections (Ibid).

By late October 2020, about a third of Nigeria's 36 states and the capital Abuja had had their warehouses looted. In many states, governors declared curfews in an attempt to monitor the raids on warehouses. In the city of Lagos, more than 400 people had been arrested for looting during the same period. In the city of Calabar, the state government directed security officers to conduct house-to-house searches and apprehend those found with looted goods (Ibid). The pillagers were mostly young people who had the energy to "climb the high stacks of bags of rice and other items and hoist them in one swing" (Ibid: 1). There were some cases, however, when the looters were joined by poor old people and those who lived in the vicinity of the warehouses (Ibid). In assessing the criminal blameworthiness of such acts of despoilment, many commentators viewed them as "a moral issue" in which people were "collecting what rightfully belongs to them…And the actions of some of the looters has been described in terms of Robin Hood, that is, taking from the rich to give to the poor" (Ibid: 1).

Given the social negligence on the part of many African governments during the Covid-19 lockdown periods, this section showed how vulnerable people across the African continent took matters into their own hands to assert their right to food. The fact that hunger knows no bounds becomes quite apparent. Thus, the section illustrated how "the burden of providing civic protection…shifted from the hands of the state and…landed at the feet of the people" (Mxesibe, 27 August 2020: 1).

Overt interventions and backlashes at security sector abuses

Human rights infringements that emanated from inconsiderate government policies and security sector brutalities in the enforcement of Covid-19 containment measures sometimes prompted individual interventions and collective backlashes, both informal and often serendipitous, from the marginalised sections of the population. This section begins by looking at fortuitous voluntary interventions by individuals to rescue victims from police assault. The greater part of the section devotes considerable attention to collective backlashes from groups of vulnerable people against brutalities perpetrated by law-enforcement agents on lockdown duties.

Some ordinary people, who can be likened to the biblical Good Samaritans, sometimes voluntarily intervened to rescue victims from the brutalities of security details enforcing lockdown measures. Such people, in their individual capacities, displayed a great sense of altruism by sacrificing self for the benefit of the other in the face of horrendous abuses by law-enforcement operatives. In Nigeria, on 5 April 2020, for example, Stanley Azu, a police officer on lockdown assignments, shot dead Chibuisi Okameme, a 29-year-old Greenmac Energy Limited Service Station fuel attendant, in the Obingwa Local Government Area, Abia State (Adiele, 29 April 2020; Busari, 8 March 2021). Okameme was shot as he intervened to rescue one of their regular male customers who was being flogged by rowdy policemen for flouting Covid-19 stay-at-home orders. The manager of the filling station, who happened to be at the scene, stated that the shooting of Okameme was unprovoked as he was actually begging the police to stop assaulting their customer (Busari, 8 March 2021). After the shooting incident, the police officers fled the scene. A group of well-wishers, with the help of an off-duty soldier who had witnessed the incident, managed to catch up with the fugitives whom they forced to take the victim to hospital. Unfortunately, Okameme died before being admitted (Ibid).

Another incident that took place in late June 2020 on the outskirts of Kenya's western city of Lessos also illustrates how some people sometimes committed themselves to the philanthropic role of safeguarding the rights of victims of police brutality during the Covid-19 lockdowns, sometimes sacrificing their lives in the process. On the day in question, Lazarus Kirop, a 40-year-old cobbler, was pained after witnessing a motorbike taxi driver being harassed by policemen for not putting on a face mask. The security operatives went on to demand a bribe of 50 Kenyan shillings (US0.50) from the man but he refused resulting in further harassment. The cobbler intervened and urged the policemen to exercise restraint. The police then shot Kirop dead for his attempt to rescue the motorbike driver (*British Broadcasting Corporation News*, 26 June 2020).

There are many cases across the African continent where the ordinary people openly denounced the abuses of law-enforcement agents on lockdown duties. In the majority of cases, "the resistance was spontaneous, people in anger supporting one another against police abuse" (Green & Kirk, 2020: 12). This was the case on 2 April 2020, in the city of Warri in Nigeria's Delta State, when Joseph Pessu was shot dead by a soldier on lockdown duties for disregarding Covid-19 stay-at-home orders and the curfew. The shooting incident immediately triggered protests by angry youths across the city. During the nightlong protests, irate demonstrators lit fires along the streets and denounced the police for their trigger-happiness (*Associated Press*, 3 April 2020).

Another incident that fuelled protests in Nigeria on 15 April 2020 was the fatal shooting of Amobi Igwe, a commercial truck driver, by Eke Richard, a Nigeria Security and Civil Defence Corps officer, near a tollgate along the Umuahia-Aba Expressway in the Abia State (Ezeigwe, 2021). Igwe had been ferrying food provisions to Aba when the police stopped him and demanded bribes to allow him passage since travel was prohibited by lockdown orders. When Igwe refused, the police officer fatally shot him (Sanction, 29 April 2020). The callous incident incensed youths in Ebem who went on to burn down a local police station after setting detainees free (African Centre for Media and Information Literacy *et al*, 1 May 2020).

Again, in Nigeria on 21 May 2020, protests broke out in the Waterside Local Government Area of Ogun State as a result of abuses committed by heartless security operatives enforcing Covid-19 curtailment regulations. On this day, Waidat Adedeji, a pregnant woman who was in labour, died after she was allegedly delayed by security agents at the Sore River roadblock for violating stay-at-home orders and failure to put on a face mask (Kabir, 22 May 2020; Sylvester, 21 May 2020). The pregnant woman was delayed for hours while she bled profusely and later died (Sylvester, 21 May 2020). The woman's death at the hands of unsympathetic security operatives brewed furore among surrounding communities. A group of livid youths from Ibiade, for instance, blamed the police for causing the woman's death and allegedly retaliated by taking her corpse to the Abigi Divisional Police Headquarters where they dumped it (Oludare, 21 May 2020; Sylvester, 21 May 2020). One of the youths explained the event as follows: "When we got to the police station, we dropped the remains of the woman on their counter and some of the officers ran away" (Kabir, 22 May 2020: 1). As the youths besieged the local police station threatening violence, community leaders intervened to pacify them after which the corpse was taken away for burial by family members and relatives (Ibid; Oludare, 21 May 2020; Sylvester, 21 May 2020).

Informal demonstrations against police brutality during the enforcement of Covid-19 alleviation measures in Nigeria reached a climax in October 2020. Typical of informal upheavals, the *#End-SARS* struggle was a decentralised movement (Wilmot, 25 January 2021). Many Nigerians had long been aggrieved by the barbarous conduct of the Special Anti-Robbery Squad (SARS) since its formation in 1992 as an elite police unit to specifically deal with violent crimes. Protest action against SARS in particular and the whole Nigerian police organisation in general resurged on 6 October 2020 after a video went viral on social media showing its officers "shoot a man at point blank range and drive away in his car," allegedly for Covid-19 lockdown infractions (Olurounbi, 5 October 2020). The incident allegedly took place in the Ughelli Delta (Law Care Nigeria, 26 October 2020).

The demonstrations were largely organic, leaderless, without formalised administrative and organisational structures, and galvanised mostly by the youths (Olurounbi, 5 October 2020). The youths, in the age group of 18-35 years, most of who were the main victims of police brutality, were the major driver of the protests (Ibid). In actual fact, the protests marked "one of the most unprecedented youth movements in the history of the country" (Law Care Nigeria, 26 October 2020: 1). The anonymity or absence of a leadership structure for the protests had some considerable advantages. The fact that the movement had no known leaders or organisers made it difficult for the government to suppress it. The young participants within the movement also saw it convenient to be leaderless for fear of being infiltrated or having their movement hijacked by older generations (Olurounbi, 5 October 2020). As Law Care Nigeria (26 October 2020: 1) observed:

> This movement was doubtlessly spontaneous. There was neither prior organisation nor a plan. It was an upsurge of popular anger and frustration that seemed to emerge from nowhere. The protesters even declared that theirs was a leaderless movement. This is not accidental, but the result of a lesson drawn from the consistent sell-outs and betrayals on the part of the labour leadership over the years.

By mid-October 2020, the protest had spread to about a third of Nigeria's 36 states (Olurounbi, 5 October 2020), particularly those in the northern and southern parts of the country (Law Care Nigeria, 26 October 2020), including Lagos, the commercial capital, and Abuja, the country's capital city (Olurounbi, 5 October 2020). The protests forced the Nigerian government to disband SARS and institute police reforms (Ibid).

Outside Nigeria, similar incidents in which agitated citizens, mostly the ordinary people, openly condemned security sector human rights abuses during the enforcement of Covid-19 curtailment orders were also taking place across the African continent. On 25 April 2020, hundreds of enraged people thronged the streets of Mogadishu, the Somali capital, to protest against police brutality while enforcing Covid-19 preventive regulations. What sparked off the protest was the fatal shooting of two Somali citizens by the police in the Bondhere neighbourhood, south of the city, during the night of 24 April 2020 for violating the overnight curfew that had been imposed by the government to contain the spread of the Covid-19 pandemic (Hassan, 25 April 2020). The disgruntled protesters shouted anti-government slogans, burnt rubber tyres and put to flame the photographs of President Mohamed Abdullahi Mohamed. The protests subsided after the Mayor of Mogadishu, Omar Mohamud Mohamed, addressed the demonstrators and assured them that the policeman who had fired the lethal shots had been arrested and was awaiting prosecution. The country's Police Chief also conceded to some of the demands of the protestors by dismissing the Commissioner-in-Charge of Security in the Binhere District and pushing back the starting time of the night curfew by one hour for it to run between 8pm and 5am (Ibid).

In the town of Toamasina in eastern Madagascar on 3 June 2020, a scuffle broke out between protesters and the police as citizens rioted in the streets to denounce the heavy-handedness of security operatives in the enforcement of Covid-19 containment measures. The disturbances started when a police officer reportedly beat up a street vendor for contravening an afternoon ban on commercial activities (*Africa News*, June 2020). The tension was evidently expressed by one eye witness who said: "People must respect the measures taken by the state and things will work out. But the police are severe and they scare people. That is why people are extremely angry with them, and that is why the situation…is tense" (Ibid: 1). A vendor also weighed in, arguing that police brutality was provoking a backlash from agitated citizens: "I am very afraid of the police but faced with the lack of money, we act as if we are not afraid" (Ibid).

On 16 June 2020, in the city of Bukavu, the capital of the South Kivu Province in the eastern Democratic Republic of Congo, there were spontaneous protests in the Bagira Commune after the police had shot dead a young taxi driver the previous day (*Crisis 24*, 17 June 2020; Green & Kirk, 2020). Word had gone round in the local community that the young man, who was popular among the youths in the neighbourhood (Green & Kirk, 2020), had been killed by the police for violating lockdown orders but there were two versions on the particular measure that had been breached. One version stated that the taxi driver had been killed for breaching the curfew that had been decreed by the government to curb the spread of Covid-19 (*Crisis 24*, 17 June 2020). The other version was that he had been fatally shot for not putting on a face mask (Green & Kirk, 2020). The incident provoked angry responses from residents, particularly the youths, many of whom burnt tyres and barricaded the main roads in the Bagira Commune (Ibid). The enraged protesters went on to vandalise the Bwindi Covid-19 Isolation Centre in Bukavu which was under police guard (*Crisis 24*, 17 June 2020; Green & Kirk, 2020). The patients at the isolation facility allegedly fled to unknown destinations after the attack (Green & Kirk, 2020), understandably so given that many people, for example, immigrants and returning residents, were quarantined against their wish. The centre was damaged, with some windows shattered (Ibid), but there were no reported injuries to staff members and patients (*Crisis 24*, 17 June 2020; Green & Kirk, 2020).

On 25 June 2020, in city of Lessos, in the Rift Valley in western Kenya, police brutality triggered protests from passers-by and residents. It all began when some policemen were harassing a motorbike taxi driver for not putting on a face mask in line with Covid-19 curtailment regulations declared by the government. Lazarus Kirop, a 40 year old a cobbler who sought to intervene to save the taxi driver from being harassed, was shot dead by the police. On the instant, passers-by who witnessed the incident gathered on the scene and verbally attacked the police for their barbarity and failure to respect the right to life (*British Broadcasting Corporation News*, 26 June 2020; *Voice of America News*, 26 June 2020). As one protester shouted: "The police are killing us, not Corona virus!" (*British Broadcasting Corporation News*, 26 June 2020). Upon noticing that the number of protesters had swelled into the hundreds, the police panicked and opened fire into the crowd, killing two people before fleeing the scene (Ibid). Witnesses reported that at least five shots were fired into the crowd (*Voice of America News*, 26 June 2020). Hundreds of protesters "followed the police back to their police station and set alight a police officer's house" (*British Broadcasting Corporation News*, 26 June 2020: 1). They also attacked the local police station with stones (*Voice of America News*, 26 June 2020). Indeed, the exasperated protesters were vindicated when the government promised to conduct investigations into the shootings and prosecute the policemen who would have been found to be responsible for the fatalities (Ibid).

In this incident, the determination of the ordinary people to defend and reassert their rights to dignity, security and life is very evident. It is a fact that while the subaltern do not have the capacity, in terms of resources, to effectively subdue repressive state apparatus, they should not be taken for granted as they have the potential to openly challenge abusive institutions. Indeed, Al-Amin Kimathi, a Kenyan human rights activist, commended the public for their boldness in condemning police bestiality and failure to respect people's rights despite the loss of life: "It is heartening that this time, after the cops killed the first man, the people did not sit back but went for the police in protest. [This] serves notice that any other time will not be the usual resignation" (Ibid).

Some citizens resisted being arbitrarily arrested by police officers who themselves did not lead by example. Examples can be drawn from cases where errand law-enforcement agents openly flouted some Covid-19 mitigation measures but went on to apprehend civilians for committing the very same offences. In addition, there were concerns in some cities in the eastern Democratic Republic of Congo about "police chasing residents without face masks as opposed to robbers" (Green & Kirk, 2020: 11). As Patrycja Stys & Papy Muzuri, quoted by Green & Kirk (2020: 11), observed in the Democratic Republic of Congo in 2020:

> In response, residents rose up against such abuse, particularly in terms of mandatory face masks. The ridiculousness of police officers stopping and harassing residents for not having face masks, or wearing them as chin straps, bracelets, or headbands, when they themselves were doing the same, did not go unnoticed.

There were reports from Goma, the capital of the North Kivu Province in the eastern Democratic Republic of Congo, of citizen arrests being effected on police details who attempted to arrest civilians for not putting on face masks when they themselves were not putting them on. From these incidents, it becomes quite apparent that there is "a negotiated limit to what people will tolerate in terms of police abuse of their Covid-19-augmented power…There comes a point where people rise up…and support one another, taking on the police's role through civilian arrests" (Ibid: 11).

This section has articulated the antagonistic relationship that developed between the authorities and the ordinary people during the Covid-19 pandemic in Africa. In the case of the security sector, it has been noted that their belligerent conduct largely accounted for the tension that arose in many African countries as many downtrodden people sought to defend their rights, liberties and freedoms that were being eroded on the pretext of enforcing Covid-19 mitigation initiatives. In early September 2020, Andrew Natumanya, a photographer in Kampala, Uganda's capital, for example, stated that the general impression of the public towards the law-enforcement agents was characterised by hatred and bitterness: "Whenever people see the police here in Uganda, what comes to their mind is impunity, torture and arbitrary arrests" (Sakpa, 7 September 2020: 1). Chineye, a banker in Lagos, Nigeria's commercial capital, weighed in: "It is bad, really bad. Most people avoid the police intentionally. It is sad that one has to avoid the very people who should provide security" (Ibid).

The social media as a weapon of informal protest

In the words of Iroulo (2021: 1), the social media increasingly became "a weapon of the weak" during the Covid-19 period in Africa. This development should be understood in the context of the ravaging pandemic during which the brutality of security operatives in many African countries became more pronounced in the name of curtailing its spread. Worse still for many ordinary people, their avenue to raise concerns pertaining to security sector brutality and the infringement of their rights, freedoms and liberties owing to the Covid-19 lockdown measures was blocked as public gatherings were banned, which meant an indirect prohibition of demonstrations. Furthermore, stay-at-home orders and travel restrictions imposed by many African governments to contain the spread of the pandemic made it difficult to organise and coordinate demonstrations beyond localities. Inevitably, the social media became one of the most popular means of expressing grievances related to Covid-19 lockdown abuses. In addition, this facility became convenient in coordinating protests at a time when the army and the police often brutally dispersed meetings and any other gatherings.

In South Africa, for example, the social media increasingly became an important platform used by many sections of the society to discuss the Covid-19 lockdown and related security sector brutalities. As Malematja & Busisiwe (5 May 2020: 4) observed:

> Internet activism has become an important form of protest that informs protests on the ground and has helped bring attention to issues that South Africans face…During the lockdown, the use of social media to document force used by police and the military in communities has been a very important source of activism.

Similarly, the social media played a significant role in publicising police brutalities in the enforcement of Covid-19 preventive measures in Madagascar. On 3 June 2020, in the town of Toamasina in eastern Madagascar, for instance, a police officer officer allegedly whipped a street vendor for doing business during the afternoon in violation of lockdown measures imposed by the government (*Africa News*, 4 June 2020). The video of the incident went viral on social media and helped to mobilise people to protest against police brutality in the streets. The protesters reportedly "burned tyres, blocked roads and pelted security officers with stones, who in-turn responded with rubber bullets" (Ibid: 1).

Nigeria also presents a good example of a country where the social media was fully utilised by disgruntled people across classes, ethnic groups, and religions to protest against police excesses and abuses during the Covid-19 lockdown period. In particular, the disbandment of Nigeria's notorious SARS proved that "the social media can make the voices of the weak heard" (Iroulo, 2021: 1). As mentioned earlier in this chapter, the SARS had been formed in 1992 as an elite police unit to specifically deal with issues of armed robbery, carjacking and other violent criminal activities. The unit soon abrogated its mandate as a protector of the people and became a violent tormentor that committed a broad range of human rights abuses such as unlawful arrests and incarcerations, harassment, torture, sexual violence, bribery, extortion and extra-judicial killings (Human Rights Watch, 19 October 2021; Iroulo, 2021; Oyebanji, 30 October 2020). On 3 October 2020, a video was circulated widely on social media showing a SARS operative on lockdown duties opening fire on a young Nigerian at a hotel in Ughelli in the Delta State. The incident ignited non-violent demonstrations in the major urban areas across the country such as Lagos, Abuja, Port-Harcourt and Kano. During the period 7-20 October, these protests broadened in scope to call for wider police reforms and spread to many other parts of the country (Human Rights Watch, 19 October 2021; Iroulo, 2021; Oyebanji, 30 October 2020).

The End-SARS protest on Twitter, Facebook and Instagram was "a milestone people-led movement. It is the first time Nigerians from different classes, ethnic groups, and religions have united behind a cause" (Iroulo, 2021: 1). In addition to calling for the disbanding of the SARS, the movement pushed for the release of people who had been arrested for violating the Covid-19 lockdown by demonstrating. Among other things, the social media also pressed for the prosecution of security operatives who brutalised civilians during the enforcement of Covid-19 containment measures (Ibid). By 16 October 2020, the hashtag #EndSARS had garnered 3.3 million tweets (Okunola, 2020).

The social media outrage against police savagery amid a pandemic got support from Nigerian public figures and celebrities such as Falz and DJ Switch in the Lagos State, Flavour in the Anambra State, Kiss Daniel in the Ogun State, and Davido in Abuja. People from various walks of life, locally and abroad, contributed to raise funds to provide medical attention, legal assistance, security, food, and water to protestors (Iroulo, 2021). Despite its national and international reach, the *#EndSARS* protest was largely informal in terms of organisation. As Iroulo (2021: 1) notes:

> For a protest without leadership and occurring amidst government suppression, EndSARS succeeded in systematically organising funds, welfare packages, lawyers, doctors, and ambulances at protest sites, including cleaning up themselves at the end of each protest. However, one might wonder: How was a leaderless movement even able to emerge and sustain itself? A number of individuals and groups were responsible for mobilising the necessary resources for sustaining the protest. Nigerian celebrities were active in using their social media platforms to mobilise and organise protests across the country.

It was largely through the pressure from the social media and the subsequent demonstrations that the Nigerian government disbanded SARS on 11 October 2020 (Human Rights Watch, 19 October 2021; Iroulo, 2021). Given these achievements, Iroulo (2021: 1) highlights the importance of the social media during protest movements in the contemporary world:

> Although traditional forms of social movement have remained, protests have since gone beyond the previous mass gatherings, strikes, picketing, and sit-ins in form - partly due to the rise of social media. Therefore, it is difficult to ignore the role the latter has played in the evolution of social movements. Since the arrival of social media, there is no doubt that the success rate of social movements has increased. Social media has made group mobilisation a lot more seamless. Without formal organisation, social media has made it possible for consistent and sustained participation even beyond borders - this was not possible before the Internet. Also, social media has fostered creativity and innovation regarding social movements. For instance, hashtags and memes have proven to be valuable tools in capturing audiences' attention and directing it towards specific movements.

In the Democratic Republic of Congo, as Patrycja Stys and Papy Muzuri, cited by Green & Kirk (2020) observed during the Covid-19 lockdown period in 2020, the social media was very proactive in publicising police abuses. The details and videos of many citizen arrests made on abusive police officers on lockdown duties in the eastern part of the country were also widely circulated on the social media (Ibid).

This section has demonstrated how online-organised protests became "a new weapon of the weak" (Iroulo, 2021: 1), particularly during the Covid-19 period in Africa. Among other things, the social media gave impetus to informal protests by publicising through print, picture and video, security sector brutalities during the enforcement of Covid-19 mitigation regulations. In addition to alerting and mobilising the general public over the bestiality of security details, the social media also drew the attention of the authorities on the need for redress. While most informal protests were localised, the social media managed to broaden them in terms of space as messages and images were communicated far and beyond. Social media platforms also avoided direct confrontations with the law-enforcement operatives as protesters communicated electronically at a time when gatherings and demonstrations had been prohibited under Covid-19 curtailment protocols in many African countries. Overall, the section has shown beyond reasonable doubt that even the marginalised populations can exploit technological advancements within their reach and use them as arsenal in their quest for recognition.

Conclusion

This chapter has discussed an array of informal strategies devised by the ordinary people to defend, safeguard and reclaim their human rights, freedoms and civil liberties that were increasingly being compromised by Covid-19 mitigation protocols in many African countries. The lockdown orders that were imposed to contain the spread of the pandemic infringed many rights and freedoms of the ordinary people. The stay-at-home orders and the curfew, for example, limited the freedom of movement and infringed the socio-economic rights and the entitlement to life of those people whose livelihoods largely depended on mobility. People's rights, freedoms and liberties were further trampled upon by the various forms of abuses perpetrated by security officers while enforcing Covid-19 curtailment orders.

Above all, the chapter has illustrated that the ordinary people are not passive victims of abuse as they have the potential, ability and capability to devise a surfeit of initiatives to reassert their rights, freedoms and liberties when they are grossly violated. As Green & Kirk (October 2020: 12) rightly noted: "Power is negotiated. People can handle just so much of its abuse, and they will refuse and rise up when it is illogical and threatens their very existence."

References

ACCORD (8 July 2020) 'Social and political protests exacerbated by the Covid-19 pandemic on the increase in Africa,' Available at: https://www.accord.org.za/analysis/social-and-political-protests-exacerbated-by-the-covid-19-pandemic-on-the-increase-in-africa/, Accessed 29 April 2022.

Adiele, P. (29 April 2020) 'Covid-19. Police and military brutality,' Available at: https://www.sunnewsonline.com/covid-19-police-and-military-brutality, Accessed 3 March 2022.

Africa News (4 June 2020) 'Anti-lockdown protest in Madagascar over alleged police brutality,' Available at: https://www.africanews.com/2020/06/01/anti-lockdown-protest-in-madagascar-over-alleged-police-brutality//, Accessed 28 April 2022.

African Centre for Media and Information Literacy (AFRICMIL), Rule of Law and Accountability Advocacy Centre (RULAAC) &

Human Environment Development Agenda Resource Centre (HEDA) (1 May 2020) 'Nigeria: Covid-19 response should not be used to violate the right to life and intimidate journalists,' Available at: https://www.article19.org/resources/nigeria-covid-19-response-should-not-be-used-to-violate-the-right-to-life-and-intimidate-journalists/, Accessed 21 April 2022.

Anguyo, I. (19 June 2020) 'What strategies do traders in Kampala use to survive Covid-19 under lockdown?' Available at: https://blogs.lse.ac.uk/africaatlse/2020/06/19/what-strategies-do-traders-use-food-survive-covid19-lockdown-kampala/, Accessed 3 May 2022.

Associated Press (3 April 2020) 'African man shot dead for breaking virus curfew,' Available at: https://www.courthousenews.com/african-man-shot-dead-for-breaking-virus-curfew/, Accessed 24 April 2022.

Boateng, F.G. (2 February 2022) 'Ghana's Covid lockdown - Why it triggered a toxic mix of mass defiance and police violence,' Available at: https://allafrica.com/stories/202202030120.html, Accessed 26 April 2022.

Boateng, F.G. Kusi, S. & Ametepey, S. (2021) 'Covid-19 lockdown defiance, public "indiscipline", and criminalisation of vulnerable populations in Ghana,' in: *African Review of Economics and Finance*, pp.1-30.

British Broadcasting Corporation News (26 June 2020) 'Corona virus in Kenya: Police kill three in motorcycle taxi protest,' Available at: https://www.bbc.com/news/world-africa-53191358, Accessed 25 April 2022.

Busari, K. (8 March 2021) 'Blood on uniforms: In Nigeria's south-east, no justice for people killed during Covid-19 lockdown,' Available at: https://www.premiumtimesng.com/news/headlines/447496-blood-on-uniforms-3-in-nigerias-south-east-no-justice-for-people-killed-during-covid-19-lockdown.html, Accessed 24 April 2022.

Chigudu, D. (2021) 'Street entrepreneurship in the wake of Covid-19: The dilemma of street vending and strategies for endurance,' in: *International Journal of Economics and Business Administration*, Volume IX, Issue 1, pp. 257-273.

Crisis 24 (17 June 2020) 'DRC: Protesters attack Covid-19 treatment centre in South Kivu on June 16,' Available at: https://crisis24.garda.com/alerts/2020/06/drc-protesters-attack-covid-19-treatment-center-in-south-kivu-on-june-16-update-16, Accessed 30 April 2022.

Davids, D. (6 May 2020) 'Demonstrations under lockdown: The threat of increased violent protests in South Africa,' Available at: https://insights.s-rminform.com/lockdown-protests-in-south-africa, Accessed 1 May 2022.

Ezeigwe, A.C. (2021) 'Addressing the human rights abuses occasioned by the Corona virus lockdown,' in: *Nnamdi Azikiwe University Journal of International Law and Jurisprudence*, Volume 12, Number 2, pp.160-176.

Gargard, G. (15 September 2020) 'African regimes are using Covid-19 to stifle the third wave of protests,' Available at: https://theglobepost.com/2020/09/11/covid-19-protests-africa/, Accessed 26 April 2022.

Green, D. & Kirk, T. (eds.) (October 2020) 'Observing Covid-19 in Africa through a public authorities lens,' London: London: Firoz Lalji Centre for Africa, London School of Economics and Political Science. Working paper funded by the Centre for Public Authority and International Development.

Hassan, M.O. (25 April 2020) 'Covid-19 pandemic: Police killings spark street protests in Somali capital,' Available at: https://www.voanews.com/a/covid-19-pandemic_police-killings-spark-street-protests-somali-capital/6188196.html,' Accessed 30 April 2022.

Human Rights Watch (22 April 2020) 'Kenya: Police brutality during curfew,' Available at: https://www.hrw.org/news/2020/04/22/kenya-police-brutality-during-curfew, Accessed 25 April 2022.

Human Rights Watch (19 October 2021) 'Nigeria: A year on, no justice for #EndSARS crackdown - Prosecute those responsible for abusing protesters,' Available at: https://www.hrw.org/news/2021/10/19/nigeria-year-no-justice-endsars-crackdown, Accessed 16 February 2022.

Iroulo, L (2021) 'A weapon of the weak: Fighting police brutality through social media,' Available at: https://www.giga-hamburg.de/en/publications/giga-focus/a-weapon-of-the-weak-fighting-police-brutality-through-social-media, Accessed 26 April 2022.

Kabir, A. (22 May 2020) 'Covid-19: Pregnant woman dies in Ogun after police check-point delay,' Available at:

www.premiumtimesng.com/regional/ssouth-west/394053, Accessed 22 April 2022.

Khalid, I. (16 April 2020) 'Corona virus: Security forces kill more Nigerians than Covid-19,' Available at: https://www.bbc.com/news/world-africa-52317196, Accessed 26 February 2022.

Kyed, A.M. (29 June 2020) 'Covid-19 in Mozambique: Police violence, mistrust of government and the fear of hunger,' Available at: https://www.diis.dk/en/research/covid-19-in-mozambique, Accessed 26 April 2022.

Law Care Nigeria (26 October 2020) 'Lessons of Nigeria's October 2020 youth protest,' Available at: https://lawcarenigeria.com/lessons-of-nigerias-october-2020-youth-protest/, Accessed 2 May 2022.

Malematja, S. & Busisiwe, Z. (5 May 2020) 'The impact of the national lockdown on the right to protest,' Available at: https://www.wits.ac.za/news/sources/cals-news/2020/op-ed-the-impact-of-the-national-lockdown-on-the-right-to-protest.html, Accessed 29 April 2022.

Mugabi, I. (20 April 2020) 'Covid-19: Security forces in Africa brutalising civilians under lockdown,' Available at: https://www.dw.com/en/covid-19-security-forces-in-africa-brutalizing-civilians-under-lockdown/a-53192163, Accessed 21 February 2022.

Mxesibe, L. (27 August 2020) 'Reports from the coalface: Informal traders share their lockdown stories of survival and making do,' Available at: https://www.southernafricafoodlab.org/reports-from-the-coalface-informal-traders-share-their-lockdown-stories-of-survival-and-making-do/, Accessed 28 April 2022.

Odigbo, B. Eze, F. & Odigbo, R. (2021) 'Covid-19 lockdown controls and human rights abuses: The social marketing implications,' in: *Emerald Open Research*, pp1-18, Available at: https://doi.org/10.35241/emeraldopenres.13810.2, Accessed 11 May 2022.

Ohajuruka, U. (16 November 2020) 'Police brutality and the girl child,' Available at: https://globalgirlsglow.org/police-brutality-and-the-girl-child/, Accessed 12 January 2022.

Okunola, A. (2020) 'Four ways you can support Nigeria's #EndSARS protests,' Available at: www.globalcitizen.org/en/content/ways-to-support-endsars-nigeria-around-the-world/, Accessed 2 May 2022.

Oludare, I. (21 May 2020) 'Covid-19 lockdown: Crisis in Ogun as pregnant woman allegedly dies at police check-point,' Available at: https://dailypost.ng/2020/05/21/covid-19-lockdown-crisis-in-ogun-as-pregnant-woman-allegedly-dies-at-police-checkpoint/, Accessed 22 April 2022.

Olurounbi, R. (15 October 2020) 'Nigeria: #EndSARS movement avoids pitfalls of leadership,' Available at: https://www.theafricareport.com/46106/nigeria-leaderless-movement-endsars-may-be-missing-ingredient-to-end-police-brutality/, Accessed 1 May 2022.

Orjinmo, N. (26 October 2020) 'Why Nigerian looters are targeting Covid-19 aid,' Available at: https://www.bbc.com/news/world-africa-54695568, Accessed 26 April 2022.

Oyebanji, O. (30 October 2020) 'Two cases of SARS: Fighting police brutality and Covid-19 in Nigeria,' Available at: https://blogs.bmj.com/bmjgh/2020/10/30/two-cases-of-sars-fighting-police-brutality-and-covid-19-in-nigeria/, Accessed 11 January 2022.

Pijoos, I. (28 April 2020) 'Protesters break lockdown rules, block roads over food parcels in Johannesburg,' in: *Sowetan Live*, Available at: at: https://www.sowetanlive.co.za/news/south-africa/2020-04-28-protesters-break-lockdown-rules-block-roads-over-food-parcels-in-joburg/, Accessed 1 May 2022.

Safer World (2020) *Briefing: The role of the security sector in Covid-19 response: An opportunity to 'build back better'?* London: Safer World.

Sakpa, D. (7 September 2020) 'In Africa, concerns over rising police brutality,' Available at: https://www.dw.com/en/in-africa-concerns-over-rising-police-brutality/a-54845922, Accessed 30 April 2022.

Sanction (29 April 2020) 'Human rights violations during the Covid-19 lockdown in Nigeria,' Available at: https://saction.org/human-rights-violations-during-covid-19-lockdown-in-nigeria/, Accessed 2 March 2022.

Sylvester, T. (21 May 2020) 'Covid-19: Pregnant woman in labour dies while being delayed at police check-point in Ogun State,' Available at: https://www.kanyidaily.com/2020/05/covid-19-pregnant-woman-in-labour-dies-while-being-delayed-at-police-checkpoint-in-ogun-state.html, Accessed 22 April 2022.

Thomas, M.T. (2021) 'Protests during the 2020 Covid-19 lockdown in South Africa,' Available at: https://www.eth.mpg.de/molabinventory/securitizing-mobilities/protests-during-the-2020-covid19-lockdown-in-south-africa, Accessed 21 April 2022.

Voice of America News (26 June 2020) 'Kenya: Three people killed in clash with police over face masks,' Available at: https://www.voanews.com/a/covid-19-pandemic_kenya-3-people-killed-clash-police-over-face-masks/6191788.html, Accessed 26 April 2022.

Wilmot, P. (25 January 2021) 'Resisting police brutality in Africa: Highlights from 2020,' Available at: https://www.nonviolent-conflict.org/blog_post/4-resisting-police-brutality-in-africa-highlights-from-2020/, Accessed 30 April 2022.

Chapter 18

"The End Justified the Means": Laxity of Zimbabweans during the Covid-19 Pandemic and the Government's Hobbesian Intervention

James Hlongwana

Introduction

The advent of the Covid-19 pandemic, which developed in the Chinese province of Wuhan, produced far-reaching ramifications. While diseases have been part of human history, Covid-19 profoundly affected humanity owing to its mutability, transmissibility, incurability and fatality. Owing to its transmissibility, the disease defied international boundaries and continued unabated in its killing spree of humans and destruction of economies. Contrary to observing precautions as advised by the World Health Organisation (WHO) and the Zimbabwean government to prevent the spread of the disease, the majority of Zimbabweans displayed laxity and distrust of scientific practices to contain the virus. Consequently, when the Corona virus got into the country, it found an environment that favoured its existence. It was in the above context that the government of Zimbabwe introduced a cocktail of measures which included, among other things, force to compel the population to observe the imposed restrictions.

A corpus of literature exists on the Covid-19 pandemic. Researchers such as Dube (2020), Mutekewete & Vanyoro (2021), Chakanya (2021), Cassim (2021), and several others made significant contributions to the Corona virus pandemic discourse. Their studies focused primarily on human rights infringements by Zimbabwe's state agents during the pandemic. While building on the aforementioned studies, this chapter makes a slight departure by drawing attention to the desirability of the deployment of 'force' by the Zimbabwean government to contain the pandemic.

In terms of structure, the chapter firstly focuses on the background information relating to the history of the virus. Secondly, the chapter draws attention to the people's care-free attitude to the pandemic. Thirdly, the chapter discusses government's response to the people's misconduct in the midst of the menacing Corona virus. While, it has been postulated that the government of Zimbabwe went beyond the enforcement of discipline among citizens, this chapter argues that the government deployed 'force' to save life as people had demonstrated sloppiness in the face of the dangerous viral disease.

The chapter predominantly utilised qualitative research methods, namely document interrogation, field observations and interviews to collect, collate and synthesise data. Document interrogation for this study entailed analysing written documents such as newspapers, theses, books, journal articles and electronic media sources. To complement insights derived from textual analysis, data was also solicited from interviewees. In keeping with the ethos of qualitative research, semi-structured interviews were conducted with respondents. This presented an opportunity to gather ground-based responses from the participants.

Origins of the Covid-19 pandemic

Beginning December 2019, Chinese health authorities in the city of Wuhan recorded several unexplainable cases whose symptoms matched those of pneumonia (Wu *et al*, 2020). It was later on confirmed to be an acute respiratory disease caused by a new type of Corona virus. Alarm bells rang when it became evident that the disease was highly infectious as it had spread from Wuhan to other Chinese places and other countries in the world within a short space of time (Ibid). Preliminary studies on the origins of the disease pointed to a market centre where water and farmed wild animal products were sold to be the source of the epidemic (Nishiura *et al*, 2020). Here, researchers were quick to conclude that wild animals were the probable vectors because previous studies on other Corona pandemics had correctly identified them as hosts of viruses. Wild animals such as chimpanzees and bats, for example, are historically known to have transmitted viral diseases such as Nipah, Ebola, Corona viruses and others to humans (Cui & Shi, 2019). On the basis of the law of association, civets such as pangolins were initially suspected to be the vectors and transmitters of the disease. However, epidemiological and epizootic studies that were carried out to establish the real vector excluded pangolins in the outbreak of the Corona virus (Joint WHO Report, 2021).

It can be asserted that the failure to identify the real vector has left room for speculation with people subscribing to 'biological warfare' as the possible cause of the pandemic. The causative virus of the Covid-19 was at first isolated from people suffering from the Corona attack and sequenced with findings from China (Wu *et al*, 2020). The findings indicated that it was a positive-type RNA virus belonging to the larger Corona virus group and was attacking humans for the first time (Joint WHO Report, 2021). Studies further established that the main source of infection were people who had contracted the virus from the primary vector (Jin *et al,* 2020). What also emerged from clinical tests was that the Covid-19 virus tended to have adverse effects on elderly members of the society because of the group's declining immunity due to old age. On the contrary, the majority of young people who contracted the virus exhibited mild symptoms of the disease (Wu *et al*, 2020).

Worth making reference to in this study is the name which the disease had to be identified with. According to the World Health Organisation, naming a virus after geographical places or some people was morally indefensible as it could create negative implications such as stigmatisation for the people of Chinese origin. It was feared that the Chinese would become the bodily personification of the disease and be consequently viewed with suspicion and segregation. Rightly so, in Zimbabwe during early days of the pandemic, people of Chinese origin were suspected of 'carrying' the virus with some people avoiding them in public places (Moyana, 2022). Luckily, state officials remained friendly to the Chinese and it helped to eradicate misgivings towards them (Ibid).

While WHO was opposed to associating the disease with particular groups, the then President of the United States (US) of America, Donald Trump, who had scores to settle with the Chinese leadership deliberately called it a Chinese disease. It can be commented that Trump felt challenged by China's sudden rise as an economic and military power (Kurilla, 2021). There was also an ideological dynamic at work which contributed to the US/Chinese estrangement of relations. China's rise as an economic giant inevitably questioned the US global narrative on politics which depicted democracy and a free market model as basic conditions for the realisation of prosperity. The US argument was slowly losing its global appeal as the Chinese, guided by a one party system and having a state-directed economy, were registering astronomical success without following the US path of development (Ibid). Indeed, the Chinese success put them on collision course with the Americans whose global unilateralism had not been significantly rivalled since the end of the bi-polar World in 1990 (Vukovich, 2019). Trump defended his unsavoury remarks, arguing that he was fighting back as the Chinese had alleged that the virus was manufactured by US soldiers (Kurilla, 2021). As mudslinging continued, Trump insisted that China was to blame for the failure to alert the world immediately after the outbreak of the disease (Ibid). Here, it can be opined that Trump was not far from the truth as Chinese authorities in Wuhan summoned Dr Li Wenliang, the first person to suspect the outbreak of the pandemic, to the Public Security Bureau in Wuhan where he was forced to sign a statement in which he was accused of spreading false rumours and disturbing the public (Nie & Elliot 2020). However, accusations and counter accusations by global powers continued unabated. Russia also presented information before the United Nations Security Council which placed the blame for the outbreak of Covid-19 on the shoulders of the US. Here, Russia alleged that the pandemic was part of the US biological warfare against its perceived enemies (Rankin & Farrer, 2022). Without shooting down the Russian claims, the US complicity in the alleged warfare looked questionable as the virus also ravaged the American society. In spite of the global powers' accusations over the pandemic, the World Health Organisation eventually named the 2019 Corona virus 'Covid-19'.

Covid-19 is highly contagious, spreading with astonishing rapidity and within a short period of time, it had affected the entire globe (Lone & Ahmad, 2020). The most affected countries were the United States of America, Spain, Italy, Germany, France, Britain, China, Russia, France and several others in the Global North (Ibid). A cursory look at the aforementioned countries shows that they were characterised by high population densities which constituted a favourable environment for mass infections. The first case of Covid-19 infection in Africa was reported in Egypt in early 2020 and in sub-Saharan Africa it was registered in Nigeria in early 2020 (NCD, 2020). In the southern African region, South Africa recorded its first Corona virus case on 5 March 2020 (Moonasa & Pillary, 2020) and within a short period of time, it had become the continental epicentre of the pandemic, recording alarming levels of infection and fatalities comparable to those that were occurring outside Africa. South Africa could not escape the virus owing to its big urban population and interactions with the outside world. Consequently, an infected South Africa became an additional source of the virus to its neighbours, Zimbabwe included (Moyana, 21 April 2022).

Undeniably, the situation in South Africa posed danger to Zimbabwe. This was because South Africa was host to millions of Zimbabwean legal and illegal economic refugees who would certainly return home at any given time (Ibid). To make matters worse, Zimbabwe had no capacity to test its returning citizens from South Africa since many crossed into the country via informal entry points. With the alarming surge in infections within South Africa and the repatriation of Zimbabwean citizens from abroad, it was inevitable that Zimbabwe would soon register its first case. Soon, Zimbabwe received an avalanche of returnees and quarantine centres that were established to handle them were poorly managed and did not receive meaningful support from the government. This compromised the health of returning residents as well as that of the communities that were going to host them (Mutendi, 2022). There were complaints of poor conditions at the isolation facilities, including inadequate water and sanitation while precautions such as social distancing were not fully enforced and in some cases there were food challenges (*African News Agency*, 2020). This resulted in some quarantined returnees escaping from the centres (Chakanga, 2021).

Predictably, Zimbabwe recorded its first fatal Covid-19 case in 2020 with Zororo Makamba being the victim (Matenga, 2020). While Makamba's untimely death signalled that the country was not safe from the Corona pandemic, many thought that it would remain an isolated case as he was believed to have contracted it from abroad (Band, 2020). Moreover, people found solace in medical reports that Makamba had underlying conditions which could have contributed to his failure to recover from the disease (Matenga, 2020). Consequently, people threw caution to the wind thereby exposing themselves to Covid-19. The next two sections look at the conduct of untoward Zimbabweans that exposed their rights to life to the Corona virus. The argument advanced here is that many Zimbabweans diced with death owing to their failure to exercise diligence to keep the Corona virus at bay.

Daring the Corona virus: Attitudinal problems

During the early days of the pandemic, some sections of the Zimbabwean population subscribed to the then popular, but yet unfounded, belief that Covid-19 did not pose a serious threat to Africans. The myth, which widely circulated in the social media circles during the initial outbreak of Covid-19, opined that Africans were immune to the virus. It can be postulated that these Zimbabweans and other Africans subscribed to the myth because Covid-19 originated outside Africa and the continent took time to get infected (Africa Centre for Strategic Studies, 2021). However, African immunologists rejected the claims arguing that people of African origin were dying alongside whites in North America and Europe (Ibid). Equally disturbing was the rumour that the virus did not pose a serious threat to climatically warm and hot areas like Zimbabwe (Gwenzi, 2022). The misinformation was probably a result of the fact that Covid-19 initially adversely affected cold regions of the world, especially Europe.

Perhaps what was nearer to reality about the myth was that exposure to light would assist a person to get Vitamin D that boosts immunity against the Corona virus' severity. However, a closer scrutiny reveals that hot countries elsewhere in the world were equally affected by the virus, for example, the Republic of Iran which is found in a hot region (Ndhlovuyavo, 2022). Closely related to the above analysis were astonishing remarks that were made by Oppah Muchinguri, Zimbabwe's Minister of Defence and War Veterans, in relation to the prevalence of Covid-19 in the Western countries. She insinuated that the catastrophic impact of the virus was God's revenge on Western countries because they had caused suffering in Zimbabwe owing to their imposition of economic sanctions on the country (*News 24*, 15 March 2020). However, the Zimbabwean government, which had abandoned combative diplomacy to promote engagement with the international community, distanced itself from Muchinguri's comments. A closer evaluation of Muchinguri's comments points to a misconception among Zimbabweans that Covid-19 would not get to Africa. However, as shall be highlighted later in this chapter, time proved Minister Muchinguri and her compatriots wrong when Zimbabweans, regardless of class or any other categorisation, also died of Covid-19.

In spite of the government's consented efforts to educate the people about the danger posed by the Corona virus, some did not take heed of the warning (Zinyuke, 2022). Related to this, some bars and night clubs were opened behind closed doors to the public in some parts of the country (Maposa, 2022). A visit by the *Herald* news crew to the Showground and Mverechena areas in the northern outskirts of Harare presented shocking news. It was reported that people were behaving as if the national lockdown had never been ordered with commercial sex workers and other imbibers enjoying their drinks in broad day light in bars dotted at the centres (*Herald*, 30 May 2020).

Some individuals devised strategies to deceive police intelligence. Instead of opening their beer outlets to the public, they sold beer at home during the night when police had retired to their stations. In the Mbizo Suburbs of Kwekwe Town in Zimbabwe, several houses were turned into beer-selling points especially during the night and continued to do so even after the lockdowns were eased (Banda, 2022). While Mbizo Suburbs had several municipal council beerhalls which were established as formal places for selling alcohol to the public, the informal retailers gained popularity from local imbibers because they lowered prices to undercut their competitors. Also, apart from operating within the area where imbibers were found, and also serving during odd times, they sometimes sold beer on credit to reliable patrons (Maposa, 2022). It is important to comment that while the informal suppliers of alcohol contravened lockdown rules, some individuals became successful entrepreneurs from these illegal transactions during the Covid-19 pandemic (Ibid).

Worth mentioning also was the flagrant breach of the Covid-19 regulations by some religious groups. In spite of the call by the Union for the Development of Apostolic Churches and Zionists in Africa (UDACZA) to adhere to the national lockdown regulations (*Herald*, 14 July 2021), reports indicated that members of the apostolic sects were holding services as usual in some parts of the country with no social distancing in place in spite of a government ban on public gatherings (Ibid). Thousands of Johane Marange Apostolic Church followers, for example, held their annual pilgrimage at Mafararikwa Shrine in the Bocha Communal Lands, Manicaland Province, at a time when all public gatherings were banned as a Covid-19 containment measure (Ibid). While members of this sect were not cleared by the police to gather at their shrine, this chapter argues that the group could have gained confidence to violate the law because of the sect's good relations with the ruling Zimbabwe African National Union Patriotic Front (ZANU-PF) party. The church's leadership was known to have attended highly politicised national events such as Independence Day celebrations, as well as burials of prominent ZANU-PF officials at the National Heroes Acres in Harare (Gwenzi, 2022). In a show of reciprocity, ZANU-PF and government officials attended the funeral of the Bishop of the Johane Marange Church which was held at the shrine in late April 2022 (*New Zimbabwe*, 21 April 2022). It can be argued that this religious group dared both the

Covid-19 virus and the country's law out of confidence that it was safe from prosecution and indeed nothing was done to it, a clear testimony that justice was selectively instituted among Zimbabwe's citizenry during the Covid-19 era.

Also, interesting to note was the collusion of individuals and government officials in breaching lockdown regulations. New Year celebrations which involved large crowds were held in Zimbabwe especially in towns. Worth mentioning here was the New Year celebration that was held at Matapi Hostels in Harare's Mbare Suburb (Zimoyo & Maphosa, 2021). The occasion attracted thousands of revellers with little social distancing or mask wearing (Chingono, 2021). The Mbare event, which attracted top musical artists, was held less than a kilometre from Matapi Police Station. Indeed, it appears members of the public were taking the Covid-19 pandemic for granted and were not taking precautionary measures seriously. However, owing to people's outrage over police failure to enforce lockdown regulations, the organiser of the Matapi celebration party was arrested and prosecuted (Ibid).

There was also selective application of Covid-19 regulations in favour of ZANU-PF officials. When Covid-19 killed prominent ZANU-PF leaders such as Presence Shiri, Sibusiso Moyo and others, the government allowed a high number of people to attend the funerals (Mutekwe & Vanyoro, 2021). Zimbabwe's Minister of Information, Publicity and Broadcasting Services, Monica Mutsvangwa, publicly celebrated her 60th birthday with other senior government officials during a government-imposed lockdown to prevent the spread of Covid-19 (Moyo, 2021). Similarly, Kudakwashe Tagwireyi, a businessman and ruling party apologist, threw a lavish Christmas party in December 2020 which was attended by several high profile ZANU-PF members. These parties were described as super spreaders of the Corona virus in the country (Ibid).

It is interesting to note that contrary to what was happening in Zimbabwe, wrong-doers were prosecuted elsewhere regardless of their positions in the society. In South Africa, for example, President Cyril Ramaphosa put the Communications Minister, Stella Ndabeni-Abrahams, on 'special' leave for two months from early April 2020 and deprived her of a month's salary for breaking Covid-19 regulations (Winning & Heiberg, 2020). Similarly, the British Prime Minister, Boris Johnson, was reportedly fined for attending rule-breaking gatherings during the lockdown in one of the most damaging developments in his tenure, a scandal that came to be dubbed 'party-gate' by the media (Mayes & Morales, 2022). In view of the preceding analysis, it can be argued that Zimbabwe's Constitution was evidently subject to manipulation as none of the powerful transgressors was prosecuted.

Worth mentioning in this regard was the role of funerals in spreading the virus. While the government, as shall be detailed below, did what it could to draw attention to the dangers posed by funerals, some people did not take heed of the advice (*Aljazeera*, 11 January 2021). In many cases, attendance exceeded the recommended numbers of not more than 30 people at a funeral (Ibid). Respondents argued that while people were aware of the danger posed by large congregations, no one was there to enforce the rule (Muchato, 3 April 2022). Also, compliance with policy was compromised by a sense of longing which forced people to attend funerals. It was argued that absence from a funeral without acceptable excuse made one an outcast and people would demonstrate their bitterness by ignoring the concerned member of the community when faced with situations that required collective participation (Ibid). Consequently, the customary need to show empathy and togetherness with community members forced many people to overlook the government's decree on funeral matters.

Underestimating the potency of the virus: Vaccine hesitancy and the anti-vaccine rhetoric

The rollout of the Covid-19 vaccines was supposed to be light at the end of the pandemic tunnel. Yet just as the supply of vaccines was increasing in Africa, so too was misinformation about their safety (Africa Centre for Strategic Studies, 2021). Rumours went round suggesting that China, Russia and the United States were competing with one another in the production of lethal vaccines to kill Africans in order to control and exploit the continent's resources (Muchato, 2022). The argument that was advanced in this context was that Covid 19 was a fake disease created by China and Russia to ruin African economies because they saw how close the continent was getting to them. The myth was an extension of the narratives that had circulated in the social media on vaccine safety. China had mocked the United States Covid-19 response and portrayed itself as a more competent world power (Timisit, 2020). Equally, in 2020, public health officials in the United States expressed scepticism over Chinese and Russian claims to have developed vaccines prior to testing. In fact, the United States of America, China and Russia used identical vaccines that became available in Africa which were: Astrazeneca, Moderna, Pfizer, Johnson & Johnson Sinopharm and Sputnik V, all of which had been approved by WHO (Ibid).

The competing narratives on vaccine safety reached Zimbabweans and many doubted the efficacy of the Chinese and Russian-made vaccines (Mungwiro, 2022). The people's suspicion was not wholly unfounded as some Chinese products available in Zimbabwe rarely lasted (Ibid). Further, some sections of the society suspected 'sinister' motives when the government of Zimbabwe chose Russian and Chinese vaccines ahead of Western-manufactured ones such as Astrazeneca, Moderna, Pfizer and Johnson & Johnson. Many government critics argued that the choice of the vaccines was a consequence of political and economic considerations as Zimbabwe, since 2000, had begun relying on the East, particularly China, when it was slapped with economic sanctions by the West. Moreover, Zimbabwe had forged sound diplomatic ties with Russia and China (Machivenyika, 2020). Relations between China and Zimbabwe dated back to Zimbabwe's anti-colonial struggle when the Chinese government supported the liberation war. After the outbreak of the Covid-19 pandemic in Zimbabwe, the Chinese government donated large quantities of Sinovac and Sinopharm vaccines (Chingwere, 2021).

In spite of repeated efforts by government officials to allay fear, scepticism remained high with some people driven by falsehoods from the social media that the uptake of such vaccines would cause death, sterility and other physiological damages (Mutendi, 2022). The President of Zimbabwe, Emmerson Mnangagwa, and his Vice President, Constantine Chiwenga, together with leading individuals such as politicians, church leaders, chiefs, and captains of industries were publicly vaccinated to inspire confidence in the population (*Reuters*, 24 March 2021). Despite these strides to encourage Zimbabweans to be inoculated, scepticism also arose in the public domain as to whether the country's president and his deputy had really been vaccinated with Chinese Sinovak and Sinopharm doses (Mugwizo, 2022). Some even suggested that nothing was injected into the two leaders. As divisive opinions attracted significant following, few could deny that the public vaccination programme was a gimmick to drive the population into taking unsafe vaccines from the East (Muchato, 2022).

Similarly, while most liturgical churches embraced vaccination early in the national campaign as evidenced by the Catholic Church Archbishop for Harare Diocese, Robert Ndhlovu, leading scores of priests, nuns and lay workers from his diocese to be vaccinated, resistance was seen in some evangelical churches (*Herald*, 14 April 2022). The United Family International Church leader, Emmanuel Makandiwa, for example, concurred with the anti-vaccine rhetoric, arguing that he was prepared to go to prison in defiance of the vaccination programme (*Zim Live*, 26 July2021). However, Makandiwa later revisited his position on vaccine safety and endorsed vaccination against Covid-19, urging his followers to get vaccinated and saying there were no theological grounds to forgo the protection (*Herald*, 14 April 2022). He argued that the vaccine was not a mark of the beast and that there was no chip in the jab (Ibid). However, the change of mind could have been motivated by the need to mend relations with state actors whom he had antagonised by his opposition to the vaccine rollout and also that he had seen that the vaccines had saved lives from the Covid-19 pandemic.

It is important to note that vaccine hesitancy was an act of self-preservation as people had no answers on the origins of the Corona virus and vaccine efficacy. While it was asserted that the world was able to develop vaccines faster than anticipated because scientists and governments collaborated in a manner that had never been witnessed before (*Herald*, 17 March 2021), the speed with which the vaccines were produced raised doubts about their safety. Closely related to the pervasive suspicion on vaccine safety were some negative aftermaths of the vaccination, for example, mild illness in some people and an isolated case of death which occurred after inoculation that involved a health officer who was stationed at Mutema Health Centre in the Gutu District of Zimbabwe (Chagonda, 2021). Even though it was later reported that the deceased suffered from high blood pressure (Ibid), some people snubbed the call to get vaccinated (Gwenzi, 2022).

Contextualising the government's intervention in the human rights discourse

The discussion in this section is largely shaped by Thomas Hobbes' insights on the role of the sovereign or leader in using force to promote an ideal environment for humanity. According to Hobbes' Social Contract Theory, every person consents to lay down his or her inherent rights in exchange for safety under the law (Cahn, 2010). His argument was that force is needed to command people's obedience in the interest of public good to create an ideal living environment. Thomas Hobbes opined: "Covenants without the sword are but words and have no strength to secure a man at all, it can equally be argued that covenants made at the point of the sword are nevertheless binding and therefore a source of genuine obligations" (Ibid: 341). Here, Hobbes insinuated that the lack of a political society engenders a state of anarchy in which people are at war with one another (Hamilton, 2020). His answer to the predicament of chaos lay in relinquishing liberty and power of judgement to the ruler. In relinquishing the natural right to freedom, Hobbes argued that people place themselves under the command of the ruler who, depending on circumstances, uses the bestowed power to goad the nation to promote safety for the citizens. Drawing from the same line of reasoning the President of the Republic of Zimbabwe, Emmerson Mnangagwa, made a proclamation to utilise additional powers in the administration of the country during the Covid-19 era (Mutendi, 2022). The government claimed that in issuing the proclamation, it was acting in accordance with the dictates of the constitution because it gave the Head of State power in emergencies to make regulations for the safety of the citizens (Constitution of Zimbabwe, 2013). However, it is instructive to note that few people understood such constitutional provisions as government intervention to save life was generally seen in bad light.

At the time of the Covid-19 pandemic, the Constitution of Zimbabwe guaranteed various socio-economic rights as part of the expanded Bill of Rights and laid the foundation of the legal, policy and institutional frameworks that supported the progressive delivery and realisation of the rights. Broadly, these included the right to food and water, and the right to health care (Chakanga, 2021). The aforementioned rights served the purpose of ensuring that the downtrodden had access to minimum critical materials and services which were fundamental to their survival (Ibid). For a considerable proportion of urban-based school children, learning was mainly done via mobile applications and parental assignments for those having literate and numerate parents and guardians but this also meant that learners from underprivileged sections of the community had to wait for the resumption of conventional learning when lockdowns had been lifted (Moyo, 2021). Further, the closure of schools owing to nationwide lockdowns took away the safe environment rendered to learners, resulting in them facing abuses at home and in the streets (Ibid). Also, the Covid-19 lockdowns affected millions of Zimbabweans who relied on informal pursuits for survival (Dzawada *et al*, 2021). Unlike the formally employed people such as teachers, police officers and soldiers, to mention a few who continued to receive salaries during the lockdowns, the closure of informal businesses made the lives of many people insecure and even precarious (Banda, 2022).

After President Mnangagwa had imposed lockdowns, something akin to a state of emergency, in an effort to contain the spread of the Corona virus, there was a mass deployment of police operatives and soldiers to monitor the urban residential areas (Chakanga, 2021). Mutekwe & Vanyoro (2021) argued that the manner in which Zimbabwean lockdowns were administered was not to save life but to control political gatherings and manage citizen protests. In concurrence with these scholars, Dube (2020) postulated that it was not a secret that in Zimbabwe, the Covid-19 pandemic took place in the context of a pre-existing despotic political climate. Similarly, the Zimbabwe Lawyers for Human Rights (2020), quoted by Mutekwe & Vanyoro (2021), noted that police officers in Zimbabwe took advantage of Covid-19 restrictions to persecute the ZANU-PF government's political rivals.

In light of the preceding submissions, it can be argued that lockdowns gave the ruling elites some opportunities and advantages to silence their critics, especially opposition politicians (Ibid). It was alleged that the arrest of the three Movement for Democratic Alliance (MDC-A) female activists, Cecilia Chimbiri, Jooana Mamombe and Netsai Marova for holding a demonstration in breach of Covid-19 regulations was a classic example of the weaponisation of the Covid-19 decree against members of the opposition (*BBC News*, 11 June 2020; Mutekwe & Vanyoro, 2021). The MDC-A activists claimed that they were abducted, beaten up and forced to drink each other's urine besides being sexually assaulted by suspected state security agents (Ibid). The government denied any involvement and the three female political activists were charged with making false accusations (Moyo & Kingsley, 2020). Without condoning the abuse of state power, it can be argued that the MDC Alliance activists deliberately crossed the red line. Among other things, the presidential decree outlawed gatherings and on that basis it can be argued that they were indeed guilty of breaching the lockdown regulations. Since the activists knew what the decree entailed, it can be opined that their outing was a political antic to provoke the police in order to win international attention.

The freedom of the press was also infringed during the lockdown. According to the International Press Institute (2020), Zimbabwe was one of countries which gained notoriety for press freedom violations in Africa. Among other violations of press freedom, the police reportedly arrested Kudzanai Musengi, a journalist, for covering the impact of the lockdown regulations in the city of Gweru (Ibid). Reacting to reports on the arrest of Musengi, the police argued that the journalist was operating illegally since he had not been accredited (Ibid). However, it was argued that the arrest was an indication of the Zimbabwean government's desperate endeavours to deal with what it regarded as irresponsible journalism. In view of increasing police high-handedness against people covering news in the country, the High Court of Zimbabwe ordered that they stop interfering with the operations of journalists (*News 24*, 20 April 2020).

Closely related to this was the arrest of residents in the town of Gwanda who had moved a stone's throw away from their homes to answer to the call of nature at nearby community toilets as theirs were lacking running water at the time (Cassim, 2021). This was certainly a classic example of the blind application of the law as no attention was given by law enforcement agents to the circumstances necessitating the movement of the residents (Ibid). Given these circumstances, any police officers with some rudimentary appreciation of the law should have exercised their power in a way that did not frustrate citizens, for example, arresting people for visiting the toilet.

The apparatus of control used by the Zimbabwean government during the Covid-19 era can be seen as an example of bio-political power, that is, interaction of the ruler and the regulatory authority (Mutekwe & Vanyoro, 2021). According to Foucault (1998: 44), bio-power is the term under which the regulation of biological processes such as propagation, births and mortality, life expectancy and longevity with all the conditions that can cause these to vary. The above bodily regulatory controls inform the bio-politics of the country's population. Bio-power is defined here as a state's exercise of regulating citizens via an "explosion of numerous and diverse techniques for achieving the subjugation of bodies and the control of population" (Mutekwe & Vanyoro, 2021: 1). In this regard, pandemic lockdowns were part and parcel of biological approaches meant to save life while at the same time preserving the essence of the state.

Even though lockdowns infringed basic human rights and freedoms, this chapter argues that they were allowable for the safety of the nation and lifesaving in this matter could not be effectively implemented without undermining some fundamental human rights. It is the contention of this chapter that the infringed rights were inevitably caught in the cross-fire during a constitutional commitment to save life.

Critical reflection

Owing to the non-availability of drugs to treat Covid-19 patients, restrictive measures were instituted to minimise the infection rate in the country. The Zimbabwean population became very vulnerable to the Corona virus scourge due to a comatose economy and weak health care system that were already overwhelmed by a considerable proportion of an immuno-compromised citizenry occasioned by HIV/AIDS and a host other diseases. Under these ominous circumstances, the pandemic indeed posed danger to many Zimbabweans. Consequently, the government of Zimbabwe resorted to restrictive measures such as social distancing, isolation, community containment, national lockdowns and travel restrictions to contain the virus. It is worth noting that command administration of the country remarkably reconfigured people's conduct in the context of survival tactics in a Covid-19 endangered environment. While the state of 'terror' regrettably rattled the citizenry, it implicitly reminded them that the outdoor environment had to be dreaded (Mutendendi, 2022). Not only were the people made to fear their surroundings, but they were also coerced to view their colleagues as potential carriers of the virus. Consequently, gregariousness was replaced with isolation which greatly minimised the spread of the virus. Further, threats by President Mnangagwa that in future, access to services such as public transport would depend on one's vaccination status made some people to abandon their anti-vaccine stance (Banda, 2022). This was confirmed by one respondent who argued that such pronouncements, though undermining freedom of conscience to make informed decisions, forced many people to get vaccinated (Interview with Moyana, 2022).

It should be noted, however, that the decision by the majority to get vaccinated was a result of the Covid-19-induced deaths. Many people were left with no choice but to embrace vaccination as the second best option for the protection of life against Covid-19. The result was that although head immunity was not achieved, a significant fraction of Zimbabwe's population was vaccinated. Consequently, it was not mere coincidence that the infection rate, hospitalisations and fatalities went down largely because of the determination of the Zimbabwean government to minimise the spread of the virus (Maposa, 2022). While the Covid-19-induced decree undermined people's rights, the pandemic's potential to cause havoc in Zimbabwe was greatly averted.

Conclusion

The chapter drew attention to the deployment of force by the Zimbabwean government to contain the Covid-19 pandemic. Background information relating to the origins of the virus was discussed. The discussion in the chapter centred on the care-free attitude of Zimbabweans in the face of the devastating Corona virus. It was in this context that the Zimbabwean government made decisive interventions to save lives. Accordingly, both subtle and overt tactics of public control were employed ostensibly to limit human contact which had been identified as the principal cause of infections. However, it was reported that security operatives inflicted more harm than the perceived danger of Covid-19 on the population. Indeed, police brutality left people petrified especially considering the fact that the country was not in a war situation which would necessitate their pacification to prevent them rendering support to rebellious elements in the society.

In spite of the suffering that was inflicted on the society by law-enforcement agents, the draconian measures posted remarkable achievements. Broadly, compliance with lockdown measures deprived the virus of a climate that favoured its existence. Consequently, the spread of the virus and the fatalities it caused were severely constrained. However, it is important to note that the implementation of the restrictive lockdown regulations required the suspension and violation of some fundamental human rights. Overall, the chapter argued that the deployment of 'force', though violating human rights, saved many lives from the danger posed by the Covid-19 pandemic.

References

Africa Centre for Strategic Studies (2021) 'Dispelling Covid-19 vaccine myths in Africa,' Available at: https://africacenter.org/spotlight/dispelling-covid-vaccine-myths-in-africa/, Accessed 10 January 2022.

African News Agency (10 July 2020) '209 people escape from Covid-19 quarantine centres in Zimbabwe,' Available at: https://www.iol.co.za/news/africa/209-people-escape-from-covid-19-quarantine-centres-in-zimbabwe-50802504, Accessed 16 January 2022.

Aljazeera (11 January 2021) 'Zimbabwe bans traditional funerals after spike in Covid-19 cases,' Available at: https://www.aljazeera.com/news/2021/1/11/zimbabwe-bans-traditional-funerals-after-spike-in-covid-19-cases, Accessed 26 January 2022.

Banda, G. (2 April 2022) Interview: Mbizo 8, Kwekwe, Zimbabwe.

BBC News (11 June 2020) 'Zimbabwe's MDC's abductees arrested for lying about torture,' Available at: https://www.bbc.com/news/world-africa-53005447, Accessed 17 January 2022.

Benjamin, E. (2021) 'Trump, the Corona virus pandemic,' in: *Asian American Xenophobia and Humanistic Psychology*, Volume 61, Number 2, pp.244-259.

Cahn, S.M. (2010) *Political philosophy: The essential texts,* New York: Oxford University Press.

Cassim, J. (3 February 2021) 'Zimbabwe: Arrests for using public toilets after curfew,' Available at: https://www.aa.com.tr/en/africa/zimbabwe-arrests-for-using-public-toilets-after-curfew/2132547, Accessed 14 January 2022.

Chagonda, C. (5 March 2021) 'Gutu man dies after taking Covid-19 vaccination,' in: *Masvingo Mirror*, Masvingo: Zimbabwe.

Chakanya, N. (2021) 'The impact of Covid-19 on socio-economic rights in Zimbabwe,' Available at: https://reliefweb.int/sites/reliefweb.int/files/resources, Accessed 11 January 2022.

Chingono, N. (5 January 2021) 'Zimbabwe enters Covid-19 lockdown amid fears over crowded new year parties,' Available at: https://www.theguardian.com/global-development/2021/jan/05/zimbabwe-enters-covid-lockdown-amid-fears-over-crowded-new-year-parties, Accessed 3 February 2022.

Chingwere, M. (18 May 2021) 'China commends Zimbabwe's Covid-19 response,' in *Herald*, Harare, Zimbabwe.

Cui, J. & Shi, Z. (2019) 'Origin and evolution of pathogenic Corona virus,' in: *Nature Reviews Microbiology*, Volume 1, pp.181-192.

Dube, B. (2020) 'Covid-19 and Zimbabwe-lives-matter: Respect for human rights in Zimbabwe,' in: *Gender and Behaviour*, Volume 18, Number 4, pp.16827-16838.

Dzawada, R. Matsa, M. & Nicolau, M. (2021) 'Poverty on the rise: The impact of Covid-19 lockdown on the informal sector of Gweru in Zimbabwe,' in: *International Social Science Journal*, Volume 5, pp.1-12.

Foucault, M. (1998) 'Right of death and power over life: The history of sexuality, Volume 1: An Introduction,' in: P. Rainow (ed.) *The Foucult Reader*, New York: Pantheon.

Government of the Republic of Zimbabwe (2013) *Zimbabwe Constitution, 2013*, Harare: Zimbabwe Government.

Gwenzi, F. (2 December 2021) Interview: Gwenzi Village, Chipinge, Zimbabwe.

Hamilton, J.J. (2020) 'The origins of state of nature,' in: *Hobbes Studies*, Volume 26, Number 2, pp.152-170.

Herald (30 May 2020) 'Bars defy lockdown,' Harare: Zimbabwe.

Herald (28 July 2020) 'Defiant churches face prosecution,' Harare: Zimbabwe.

Herald (17 March 2021) 'Myths and facts about Covid -19 vaccines,' Harare: Zimbabwe.

Herald (14 July 2021) 'Sects urged to observe lockdown,' Harare: Zimbabwe.

Herald (14 April 2022) 'Makandiwa endorses vaccination,' Harare: Zimbabwe.

Holcombe, H. (2020) 'Long term social distancing may be traumatic: Here is what to expect and what to do,' Available at: https://www.cna.com/2020/04/09/health/coronavirus-mental health-longterm.wellness/index.htm/, Accessed 20 January 2022.

Hussin, A. & Siddappa, N.B. (2020) 'The epidemiology and pathogenesis of Corona virus disease (Covid-19 outbreak)' in: *Journal of Autoimmunity*, Volume XXX, Available at: https://do.org/1016/ji.JQut.2020.102433, Accessed 2 July 2021.

International Press Institute (17 March 2020) 'Zimbabwe: One year of covering Covid-19 saw surge in harassment of free press,' Available at: https://ipi.media/in-zimbabwe-one-year-of-covid-19-saw-surge-in-harassment-of-free-press/, Accessed 19 February 2022.

Jin, Y.H. Cai, L. & Cheng, Z.S. (2020) 'A rapid advice guideline for the diagnosis and treatment of 2019 novel Corona virus (2019-n cv) infected pneumonia: Standard version,' in: *Military Medical Research Journal*, Volume 7, Number 4, pp.21-29.

Karombo, T. (26 July 2021) 'Makandiwa rows back from vaccine conspiracy, urges followers to get jabbed,' Available at: https://www.zimlive.com/2021/07/26/makandiwa-rows-back-from-vaccine-conspiracy-urges-followers-to-get-jabbed/, Accessed 19 February 2022.

Lone, S.A. & Ahmad, A. (2020) 'Covid-19 pandemic: An African perspective,' in: *Emerging Microbes and infections*, Volume 9, pp.1300-1308.

Machivenyika, F. (16 October 2020) 'Zimbabwe: All-weather friend China stands by Zimbabwe,' in: *Herald*, Harare: Zimbabwe.

Maposa, T. (2 April 2022) Interview: Mbizo 8, Kwekwe, Zimbabwe.

Matenga, M. (24 March 2020) 'Zimbabwe closes border after Covid-19 death,' in: *Newsday*, Harare: Zimbabwe.

Mayers, J. & Morales, A. (12 April 2022) 'UK Prime Minister Boris Johnson fined for breaking Covid-19 lockdown rules,' Available at: https://time.com/6166099/boris-johnson-fined-covid-lockdown-partygate/, Accessed 12 May 2022.

Moonasa, D. & Pillary, A. (2020) 'Lessons and experiences from South Africa's first surge,' in: *British Medical Journal*, Volume 6, Number 2, pp.23-29.

Moyana, K. (21 April 2022) Interview: Mbizo 8, Kwekwe, Zimbabwe.

Moyo, J. (7 July 2021) 'Continuous lockdowns to hit literacy rate in Zimbabwe,' Available at: https://www.aa.com.tr/en/africa/-continuous-lockdowns to-hit-literacy-rate in-zimbabwe-/2357594, Accessed 28 January 2022.

Moyo, J. & Kingley, P. (31 July 2020) 'Zimbabwe lockdown capital thwarting planned protests,' in: *The New York Times*, Available at: https://www.nytimes.com/2020/07/31/world/africa/zimbabwe-coronavirus-protest.html, Accessed 19 January 2022.

Muchato, D. (3 April 2022) Interview: Mbizo 6, Kwekwe, Zimbabwe.

Mungwiro, S. (3 April 2022) Interview: Mbizo 5, Kwekwe, Zimbabwe.

Mutedendi, C. (3 April 2022) Interview: Mbizo 7, Kwekwe, Zimbabwe.

Mutekwe, P. & Vanyoro, K.P. (2021) 'Practising Covid-19: An analysis of selected ZANU officials, 2020-2021 media statements on the pandemic,' in: *Acta acad. Bloemfontein Online*, Volume 5, Number 2, pp.1-7.

Ndhlovuyavo, T. (30 December 2021) Interview: Muzite Township, Muzite, Chipinge, Zimbabwe.

News 24 (15 March 2020) 'Corona virus, God's punishment of the West: Zimbabwe Defence Minister,' Available at: https://www.news24.com/news24/Africa/News/coronavirus-gods-punishment-of-west-zimbabwe-defence-minister-20200315, Accessed 12 January 2022.

News 24 (20 April 2020) 'Covid-19: Zimbabwe court orders police to stop harassing journalists,' Available at: https://www.news24.com/news24/africa/news/covid-19-zimbabwe-court-orders-police-to-stop-harassing-journalists-20200420, Accessed 4 January 2022.

Nie, J. & Elliot, C. (2020) 'Humiliating whistle blowers: L. Wenliang, the response to Covid-19 and the call for a decent society,' Available at: https://www.ncbi.nlm.nih.gov/pmc/articles/PMC7445730/, Accessed 7 February 2022.

Nishiura, H. Linton, N.M. & Akhmetzhanov, A.R. (2020) 'Initial cluster of novel Corona virus (2019-ncv) infections in Wuhan China is consistent with substantial human to human transmission,' in: *Journal of Clinical Medicine*, Volume 9, Number 2, pp.488-499.

Rankin, J. & Farrer. S. (11 March 2022) 'Russia makes claims of US-backed biological weapon plot at UN,' in: *The Guardian*, Available at: https://www.theguardian.com/world/2022/mar/11, Accessed 9 May 2022.

Reuters (24 March 2021) 'Zimbabwe's President gets Covid-19 dose, urges citizens not to hesitate,' Available at: https://www.reuters.com/article/health-coronavirus-zimbabwe-vaccine-idUSL8N2LM5M6, Accessed 11 February 2022.

Sachiti, R. (22 July 2021) 'Covid-19 community death defiance,' in: *Herald,* Harare: Zimbabwe.

Timisit, A. (2 May 2020) 'A Chinese propaganda video mocks America's response to Covid-19 crisis,' in: *Geopolitics Report*, Available at: https://qz.com/1850097/chinese-propaganda-video-mocks-us-response-to-coronavirus-crisis/, Accessed 6 February 2022.

Vukovich, D.F. (2019) *Liberal China: The ideological challenge of the People's Republic of China*, Singapore: Palgrave.

Winning, A. & Heiberg, T. (8 April 2020) 'South Africa Minister disciplined for lockdown lunch,' Available at: https://www.reuters.com/article/us-health-coronavirus-safrica-idUSKBN21Q1D8, Accessed 11 February 2022.

Wu, D. Wu, T. Liu, Q. & Yangu, Z. (2020) 'The SARSCvo-2 outbreak: What we know,' in: *International Journal of Infectious Diseases*, Volume 94, pp.44-48.

Wu, F. Zhao, S. & Yu, B. (2020) 'A new Corona virus associated with human respiratory disease in China,' in: *Nature*, Volume 579, Issue 7798, pp.265-269.

Zhu, H. Wei, L. & Niu, P. (2020) 'The novel Corona virus outbreak in Wuhan, China,' in: *Global Health Research and Policy*, Volume 5, Number 6, pp.1-5.

Zimoyo T. & Maposa, V. (5 January 2021) 'Cops suspended over illegal show,' in: *Herald*, Harare: Zimbabwe.

Zinyuke, R. (8 March 2022) 'Experts warn of surge in cases as laxity creeps,' in: *The Sunday Mail*, Harare: Zimbabwe.